Introduction to Mediation, Moderation, and Conditional Process Analysis

Methodology in the Social Sciences

David A. Kenny, Founding Editor
Todd D. Little, Series Editor

www.guilford.com/MSS

This series provides applied researchers and students with analysis and research design books that emphasize the use of methods to answer research questions. Rather than emphasizing statistical theory, each volume in the series illustrates when a technique should (and should not) be used and how the output from available software programs should (and should not) be interpreted. Common pitfalls as well as areas of further development are clearly articulated.

RECENT VOLUMES

THEORY CONSTRUCTION AND MODEL-BUILDING SKILLS:
A PRACTICAL GUIDE FOR SOCIAL SCIENTISTS
James Jaccard and Jacob Jacoby

DIAGNOSTIC MEASUREMENT: THEORY, METHODS, AND APPLICATIONS
André A. Rupp, Jonathan Templin, and Robert A. Henson

ADVANCES IN CONFIGURAL FREQUENCY ANALYSIS
Alexander von Eye, Patrick Mair, and Eun-Young Mun

APPLIED MISSING DATA ANALYSIS
Craig K. Enders

PRINCIPLES AND PRACTICE OF STRUCTURAL EQUATION MODELING, THIRD EDITION
Rex B. Kline

APPLIED META-ANALYSIS FOR SOCIAL SCIENCE RESEARCH
Noel A. Card

DATA ANALYSIS WITH Mplus
Christian Geiser

INTENSIVE LONGITUDINAL METHODS: AN INTRODUCTION
TO DIARY AND EXPERIENCE SAMPLING RESEARCH
Niall Bolger and Jean-Philippe Laurenceau

DOING STATISTICAL MEDIATION AND MODERATION
Paul E. Jose

LONGITUDINAL STRUCTURAL EQUATION MODELING
Todd D. Little

INTRODUCTION TO MEDIATION, MODERATION, AND CONDITIONAL
PROCESS ANALYSIS: A REGRESSION-BASED APPROACH
Andrew F. Hayes

Introduction to
Mediation, Moderation, and Conditional Process Analysis

A Regression-Based Approach

Andrew F. Hayes

Series Editor's Note by Todd D. Little

THE GUILFORD PRESS
New York   London

© 2013 The Guilford Press
A Division of Guilford Publications, Inc.
72 Spring Street, New York, NY 10012
www.guilford.com

Printed in the United States of America

This book is printed on acid-free paper.

Last digit is print number: 9   8   7   6   5   4   3   2

Library of Congress Cataloging-in-Publication Data

Hayes, Andrew F.
  Introduction to mediation, moderation, and conditional process
  analysis : a regression-based approach / Andrew F. Hayes.
      pages cm. — (Methodology in the social sciences)
  Includes bibliographical references and index.
  ISBN 978-1-60918-230-4 (hardcover)
  1. Social sciences—Statistical methods. 2. Mediation (Statistics)
3. Regression analysis. I. Title.
HA31.3.H39 2013
001.4'33—dc23
                                                    2013008807

Series Editor's Note

It's a good thing that research questions have become more complex. Researchers are no longer satisfied with demonstrating simple associations or unqualified multivariate associations. Fortunately, most areas of research have identified and established the important connections among distinguishable constructs. Now, researchers' questions are peering into the realm of process, mechanism, and the conditional features that impact how a process or mechanism might unfold: "How?," "In what way?," "By which pathway?," and "Under what circumstances?" exemplify the burning questions that we now can answer. These kinds of questions now squarely rely on accurate applications of mediation and moderation analysis principles. Enter Andrew F. Hayes. Andy has devoted much of his academic acumen to understanding the causal foundations of mediation and moderation and to effectively applying the statistical tools that will implicate the causal elements of human behavior. He has even gone so far as to develop PROCESS, his free user-friendly tool for SPSS and SAS that simplifies many of the tasks in testing for mediation and moderation.

Readers of the Guilford Methodology in the Social Sciences series may notice now that we have recruited outstanding contributions that are often pitched at different levels of the learning journey. Paul Jose's book on mediation and moderation, for example, is a perfect first course on these topics. The second course, however, is this book by Andrew Hayes. Andy's treatment of these topics provides you with a definitive statement of where both theory and practice with these topics has evolved and where we are headed. Andy's presentation of the cutting edge on these topics is easy to follow and grasp. Beginning with a review of ordinary least squares regression, the book covers the estimation and computation of direct and indirect effects in mediation analysis, modern methods of inference about indirect effects, models with multiple mediators, estimating and probing of interactions in moderation analysis, conditional direct and indirect effects, testing moderated mediation, and other topics pertaining to exploring, quantifying, and answering questions about the mechanisms and contingencies of process-related effects. Andy details each step of analysis using real data examples along with tips on writing up and reporting mediation analyses, moderation analyses, and conditional process models. Applied researchers will enjoy this work as a go-to resource for how to test and report on their tests of mediation and moderation. Andy gifts us with an easy-to-follow guide to the techniques that allow us to navigate the tangled web of today's refined research questions.

Andy is a great communicator. He's taught scores of workshops and short courses on mediation and moderation, and Andy makes a regular appearance with Kris Preacher, such as in the annual summer institute on statistics that we offer at the University of Kansas. The course on mediation and moderation that Andy and Kris co-teach is one of our most popular offerings. The popularity of this course is a testament to the well-honed didactic devices that they have developed. As you will discover, no topic or issue that is essential to accurately applying a mediation or moderation analysis is given slight treatment. Andy presents it all and covers it thoroughly, clearly, and satisfyingly. The dessert to this intellectual meal comes in the form of the sweet elements Andy provides throughout his book. His wit and wisdom permeate this resource. It's a work that is both essential and easy to enjoy.

As you read and begin to fully appreciate the nuance in using these procedures, you will also list Andrew Hayes as an MVM (most valuable methodologist). As an MVM, Andy has crafted a resource that will be a staple in the personal library of every serious researcher. It will be your personal guide to asking and answering the new wave of complex research questions. With better answers to better questions, we all will be better for it.

TODD D. LITTLE
The Short Branch Saloon
Lakeside, Montana

Preface

When research in an area is in its earliest phases, attention is typically focused on establishing evidence of a relationship between two variables, X and Y, and ascertaining whether the association is causal or merely an artifact of design, measurement, or otherwise unaccounted-for influences. But as a research area develops and matures, focus eventually shifts away from demonstrating the existence of an effect toward understanding the mechanism or mechanisms by which the effect operates, as well as establishing its boundary conditions or contingencies. Answering such questions of *how* and *when* results in a deeper understanding of the phenomenon or process under investigation, and gives insights into how that understanding can be applied.

Analytically, questions of *how* are typically approached using *process* or *mediation analysis*, whereas questions of *when* are most often answered through *moderation analysis*. The goal of mediation analysis is to establish the extent to which some putative causal variable, X, influences some outcome, Y, through one or more *mediator* variables. For example, there is evidence that violent video game play can enhance the likelihood of aggression outside of the gaming context. Perhaps violent video game players come to believe through their interaction with violent game content that others are likely to aggress, that doing so is normative, or that it is an effective solution to problems, or perhaps it desensitizes them to the pain others feel, thereby leading them to choose aggression as a course of action when the opportunity presents itself. In contrast, an investigator conducting a moderation analysis seeks to determine whether the size or sign of the effect of X on Y depends in one way or another on (i.e., "interacts with") a moderator variable or variables. In the realm of video game effects, one might ask whether the effect of violent video game play on later aggression depends on the player's sex, age, ethnicity, or personality factors such as trait aggressiveness, or whether the game is played competitively or cooperatively.

Both substantive researchers and methodologists have recently come to appreciate that an analysis focused on answering only *how* or *when* questions is going to be incomplete. A more fine-grained understanding of a phenomenon comes from uncovering and describing the contingencies of mechanisms—the "when of the how." The analytical integration of moderation and mediation analysis was highlighted in some of the earliest work on mediation analysis, but it is only in the last 10 years or so that methodologists have begun to talk more extensively about how to do so. Described using easily confused terms such as *moderated mediation* and *mediated moderation*, the goal is to empirically quantify and test hypotheses about the contingent nature of the mechanisms by which X exerts its influence on Y. For example, such an analysis could be used to establish the extent to which the influence of violent video game play on aggressive behavior through the mechanism of expectations about the aggressive behavior of others depends on age, sex, the kind of game (e.g., first-person shooter games relative to other forms of violent games), or the player's ability to manage anger. This can be accomplished by piecing together parameter estimates from a mediation analysis with parameter estimates from a moderation analysis and combining these estimates in ways that quantify the conditionality of various paths of influence from X to Y.

Mediation and moderation analysis are two of the more widely used statistical methods in the social, behavioral, and health sciences, as well as in business, medicine, and other areas. Some of the most highly cited papers in social science methodology this century are about mediation or moderation analysis. Indeed, it is nearly imperative these days that readers and producers of research understand the distinction between these concepts and know how to implement moderation and mediation analysis in their own work. The volume you are now holding is one of the few book-length treatments covering the statistical analysis of both mechanisms and contingencies. The contents of this book, classroom-tested in university courses and workshops I have conducted throughout the world over the last few years, cover the fundamentals of mediation and moderation analysis as well as their integration in the form of *conditional process analysis*, a term I am introducing in these pages. By the time you finish this text, you will be well prepared to conduct analyses of the sort you see here and describe those analyses in your own research.

This is an introductory book, in that I cover only basic principles here, primarily using data from simple experimental or cross-sectional studies of the sort covered in most elementary statistics and research design courses. I do not cover longitudinal research, multilevel analysis, latent variables, repeated measures, or the analysis of categorical outcomes, for instance. I presume no special background in statistics or knowledge of matrix algebra or advanced statistical methods such as structural equation modeling. All the methods described are based entirely on principles of ordinary least squares regression (and two chapters in the beginning introduce and review regression analysis). Most students in the social and behavioral sciences who have taken a first course in statistical methods and research design will be able to understand and apply the methods described here, as will students of public health, business, and various other disciplines.

The examples I use throughout these pages are based on data from published studies that are publicly available on the book's web page at *www.afhayes.com*, so that the reader can replicate and extend the analyses reported. To facilitate the implementation of the methods introduced and discussed, a computational aide in the form of a freely available macro for SPSS and SAS (named PROCESS) that I wrote specifically for this book is introduced beginning in Chapter 4. PROCESS combines many of the functions of computational tools about which I have written and published over the years (tools that go by such names as INDIRECT, SOBEL, MODPROBE, and MODMED) into a single integrated command. PROCESS takes the computational burden off the shoulders of the researcher by estimating the models, calculating various effects of interest, and implementing modern and computer-intensive methods of inference, such as bootstrap confidence intervals for indirect effects and the Johnson–Neyman technique in moderation analysis. Example PROCESS commands are provided throughout the book, and SPSS users not interested in using the syntax version of PROCESS can install a dialog box into SPSS, which makes the use of PROCESS literally as simple as pointing and clicking. This can greatly facilitate the teaching of the methods described here to students who are just getting started in the use of computers for data analysis.

This book is suitable as either a primary text for a specialized course on moderation or mediation analysis or a supplementary text for courses in regression analysis. It can be used by educators, researchers, and graduate students in any disciplines that use social science methodologies, including psychology, sociology, political science, business, and public health. It will benefit the reader as a handy reference to modern approaches to mediation and moderation analysis, and Appendix A is critical to users of PROCESS, as it is the only official source of documentation for this powerful add-on for SPSS and SAS. This book will be useful to anyone interested in identifying the contingencies of effects and associations, understanding and testing hypotheses about the mechanisms behind causal effects, and describing and exploring the conditional nature of the mechanisms by which causal effects operate.

You will find 12 chapters between the front and back covers defining four broad parts of the book. The first part, containing Chapters 1 through 3, introduces the concepts in moderation and mediation analysis and provides an example of their integration in the form of a conditional process model. I also cover a bit about my philosophy on the link between statistics and causality and describe how we should not let the limitations of our data dictate the mathematical tools we bring to the task of trying to understand what our data may be telling us. In this section I also overview ordinary least squares regression analysis, first with a single predictor (Chapter 2) and then with multiple predictors (Chapter 3). I assume that most readers of this book have been exposed to least squares regression analysis in some form already, but for those who have not or for whom much time has passed since their last regression analysis, these two chapters will be useful while also introducing the reader to my way of thinking and talking about linear modeling.

The second part focuses exclusively on mediation analysis and how linear regression can be used to conduct a simple path analysis of a three-variable $X \rightarrow M \rightarrow Y$ causal system. The estimation and interpretation of direct and indirect effect is the first focus of this chapter, both with a dichotomous causal agent X and then with a continuous X. After an introduction to PROCESS, I cover inference about direct and indirect effects, with an emphasis on newer statistical methods such as bootstrap confidence intervals that have become the new standard in the 21st century for testing hypotheses about mechanisms in a mediation analysis. Chapter 5 extends these ideas to models with multiple mediators, including the parallel and serial multiple mediator model. Chapter 6 covers miscellaneous additional topics in mediation analysis, such as dealing with confounds, estimation and interpretation of models with multiple X or Y variables, and quantifying effect size. In this chapter I also provide the rationale for why the historically significant *causal steps* procedure is no longer recommended by people who think about mediation analysis for a living.

Part III temporarily puts aside mediation analysis and shifts the discussion to moderation analysis. In Chapter 7, I show how a multiple regression model can be made more flexible by allowing one variable's effect to depend linearly on another variable in the model. The resulting *moderated multiple regression model* allows an investigator to ascertain the extent to which X's influence on outcome variable Y is contingent on or interacts with a so-called *moderator* variable M. Interpretation of a moderated multiple regression model is facilitated by visualizing and probing the moderation, and techniques for doing so are introduced, along with a discussion of how PROCESS can be used to make the test a lot easier than it has been in the past. Whereas Chapter 7 focuses exclusively on the case where X is a dichotomous variable and M is a continuum, Chapter 8 continues this line of analysis to models where X is quantitative rather than dichotomous and shows how the principles from Chapter 7 generalize and can be extended to models with more than one moderator, whose moderating influences on X's effect are either additive (the *multiple moderator* model) or multiplicative (the *moderated moderation* model). Chapter 9 addresses various additional topics in moderation analysis, such as equivalence between the 2×2 factorial analysis of variance and moderated multiple regression, and the reasons not to test moderation questions using subgroups analysis. I also address a widespread myth regarding the need to mean-center or standardize predictor variables prior to conducting a moderated regression analysis.

The last part of the book, Chapters 10 through 12, integrates the concepts and lessons described in the prior two parts by introducing *conditional process analysis*. A model that includes both a mediation and a moderation component is a conditional process model—a model in which either the direct and/or indirect effect of X on Y through M is moderated by or conditioned on one or more variables. Chapter 10 offers an overview of the history of this form of modeling—sometimes referred to as *moderated mediation analysis*—and provides examples in the literature of such conditional processes hypothesized or tested. An introduction to the concepts of conditional direct and indirect effects is provided, along with their mathematical bases, and an example of conditional process analysis is provided, including estimation and inference using regression analysis or, more conveniently, using PROCESS. Chapter 11 provides a further example of a conditional process model with moderation of both the direct and indirect effects simultaneously, and shows the equivalence between this one specific model form and something known as *mediated moderation*. But I take a stand in this chapter and argue that unlike moderated mediation, mediated moderation is not a particularly interesting concept or phenomenon and probably not worth hypothesizing or testing. I end the book in Chapter 12 by suggesting a step-by-step framework for conducting a conditional process analysis and introduce a formal test of moderated mediation.

I have taken care to maintain a light and conversational tone throughout the book while discussing the concepts and analyses, and avoid getting heavily into the mathematics behind them. I believe that maintaining a reader's interest is one of the more important facets of scientific writing, for if one's audience becomes bored or uninterested and attention begins to wander, the power and influence of the message is reduced. Indeed, it is this philosophy about writing that guides the advice I give at the end of Chapters 6, 9, and 12, where I talk about how to report a mediation, moderation, or conditional process analysis. Most importantly, the advice I offer in these parts of the book is intended to empower you as the one best positioned to determine how you tell the story your data are telling you.

Acknowledgments

I began writing this book well before the first word of it was typed. Several years ago I started receiving invitations from former strangers, many of whom are now colleagues and friends, to come and speak on the topic of papers I have published. These invitations allowed me to interact with people I otherwise would not likely have ever had the opportunity to get to know. Speaking to audiences diverse in background and interests has provided a means to fine-tune and hone my message as my own ideas and philosophy about the contents of this book evolved. Without those invitations, the hospitality of my hosts, and the time sacrifices they made orchestrating and coordinating my visits, this book would not be anything like what it is. So I offer my thanks to Jonathan Cohen, Grete Dyb, Truls Erikson, Shira Dvir Gvirsman, Tilo Hartmann, Jörg Matthes, Osvaldo Morera, Peter Neijens, Toon Taris, Annika Tovote, Jens Vogelgesang, Claes de Vreese, Etty Wielenga-Meijer, Anna Woodcock, Gülden Ülkümen, H. Onur Bodur, and everyone else who has spent time with me during my travels talking about their research interests and their lives.

As much as I enjoy speaking and teaching abroad, I do most of my teaching a mere 3 miles from my house. I have had the pleasure of teaching graduate students, both beginning and advanced, in my home departments of Psychology and Communication and elsewhere at my university. Their questions over the years have helped me sharpen my language when it comes to describing abstract concepts in terms that are concrete without being too imprecise or oversimplified. I appreciate their tolerance for numerous typos on PowerPoint slides, patience with my occasional need to repeat myself when I botch an explanation, and now and again waiting attentively as I retype SPSS or SAS code that generates a string of errors when using macros and other tools I invented but can't always remember how to use.

Heartfelt thanks also go to numerous people who have been generously willing to donate their data for use in my classes, workshops, journal articles, and in this book. These include Daniel Ames, George Bonanno, Nyla Branscombe, Heike Bruch, Jonathan Cohen, Michael S. Cole, Carsten K. W. De Dreu, Ryan Duffy, Naomi Ellemers, Chip Eveland, Francis Flynn, Donna Garcia, Friedrike X. R. Gerstenberg, Al Gunther, Sri Kalyanaraman, Anthony Mancini, Jörg Matthes, Erik Nisbet, Kirsi Peltonen, Jeffrey Pollack, Raija-Leena Punamäki, Michael Schmitt, Michael Slater, Nurit Tal-Or, S. Shyam Sundar, Yariv Tsfati, Eric Van Epps, and Frank Walter. Writing and reading about methodology is much more interesting when examples are based on real data from existing and published studies rather than hypothetical studies made up for the purpose of illustration. For the record, I should point out that all analyses conducted in this book and claims I make based on others' data are my own and are not necessarily endorsed by those who collected the data in the first place.

I also want to acknowledge the contributions and friendship of Kris Preacher, with whom I first starting thinking about much of the material in this book. We recently celebrated the 10-year anniversary of our collaborative intellectual bromance that started when he was a PhD student at The Ohio State University. I wonder how rare it is that two people can complete each other's sentences when discussing some topic of mutual academic interest. We have our disagreements to be sure—no doubt he disagrees with at least some of the advice I offer in this book—but those disagreements often turn into new ideas that keep us thinking forward, resulting in new collaborations we pursue together or with someone else. We get the occasional opportunity to teach together, and I am always looking forward to our next meeting and our next paper.

C. Deborah Laughton at The Guilford Press was very supportive and enthusiastic about this project. I appreciate her contributions both before the writing began and during the production process. No doubt she will continue to influence its course well after this book is printed. Matthew Fritz offered a review of the manuscript prior to production and I appreciate his insights and recommendations.

The support of my wife, Carole, and kids, Conor and Julia, has been critical. As anyone who has been a part of a research team knows, a study is much more than just the journal article that describes it. There is much that happens behind the scenes of a study that is invisible to outsiders but without which the study just doesn't get done. My family is similar to members of a research lab in that sense. Fortunately, they understand the time commitment that a project like this entails. This is the second time in 10 years they have had to put up with the divided attention that comes with writing a book, especially as the due date approaches, and I appreciate their tolerance.

Finally, I would also like to tell the world in writing about the gratitude I feel toward my father for buying me my first computer in high school, and my mother for allowing me to lock myself away in my room as I taught myself BASIC. I imagine my father didn't think long or deeply about his decision to spend $300 on a Commodore VIC-20 back in the early 1980s, but it is the machine I learned to program on, and it turned out this decision had a big influence on where I ended up in my professional life. Without this early introduction to computer science, I probably wouldn't have chosen this career, I probably wouldn't have written PROCESS, and, as a consequence, this book simply would not exist.

Contents

Data files for the examples used in the book and files
containing the SPSS and SAS versions of PROCESS are
available on the companion web page at *www.afhayes.com.*

Part I
FUNDAMENTAL CONCEPTS

1

Introduction

Research that establishes the mechanism or mechanisms by which effects operate or the conditions that facilitate and inhibit such effects deepens our understanding of the phenomena scientists study. Mediation analysis and moderation analysis are used to establish evidence or test hypotheses about such mechanisms and boundary conditions. Conditional process modeling is used when one's research goal is to describe the boundary conditions of the mechanism or mechanisms by which a variable transmits its effect on another. Using a regression-based path-analytic framework, this book introduces the principles of mediation analysis, moderation analysis, and their unification as conditional process analysis. In this initial chapter, I provide a conceptual overview of moderation and mediation and describe an example of a conditional process analysis that combines elements of both mediation and moderation analysis. After articulating my perspective on the use of statistical methods when testing causal processes, I end with a synopsis of the chapters that follow.

1.1   A Scientist in Training

As an undergraduate student studying psychology at San Jose State University back in the 1980s, one of the first empirical research projects I undertook was a study on the relationship between students' attitudes about college and their selection of seat in the classroom. I developed an instrument that purportedly (although in hindsight, not really) measured whether a person felt getting a college education was generally a good and important thing to do or not. After the participants in the study completed the instrument, I presented each of them with a diagram of a generic college classroom, with seats arranged in a 6 (row) by 5 (column) matrix, and I asked them to mark which seat they would choose to sit in if they could choose any seat in the classroom. Based on which row he or she selected, I scored how close to the front of the room that participant preferred (6 = front row, 5 = second row, 4 = third row, and so forth).

With these two measurements collected from over 200 students attending San Jose State, I could test my prediction that students with a more positive attitude about college (i.e., who scored higher on my attitude scale) would prefer sitting closer to the front of the classroom. Indeed, when I calculated Pearson's coefficient of correlation between the two measurements, I found the relationship was positive as expected, $r = 0.27$. Furthermore, a hypothesis test revealed that the probability of obtaining a correlation this extreme or more extreme from zero (positive or negative, as I tested the hypothesis two-tailed even though my prediction was directional) was too small ($p < .001$) to consider it just a fluke or "chance." Naturally, I was excited, not realizing as I do now that *any* result is exciting whether consistent with a prediction or not. Unfortunately, three anonymous reviewers did not share my enthusiasm, and the then-editor of the *Journal of Nonverbal Behavior* let me know in no uncertain terms that this finding was neither of sufficient interest nor derived with sufficient rigor to warrant publication. Rather than rewriting the paper and resubmitting elsewhere, I filed the paper away and moved to upstate New York to pursue a PhD in social psychology.

After more than 20 years, I still have this paper, and now and then I take it out of my file drawer when reflecting on where I have been in my professional life and where I am going. Looking at it now, it is clear to me that the reviewers were correct and the editor's decision sound and justified. Even if the study had been conducted with the kind of rigor I now ask of myself and my own students, in the paper I offered nothing but speculation as to why this association existed. Furthermore, I could not establish the direction of cause, if any. Although I argued that variations in attitudes caused variation in seat choice, it is just as plausible that where one sits influences one's attitude about college. For example, perhaps students who sit closer to the front receive more attention and feedback from the instructor, can hear and see better and therefore learn more, and this in turn leads them to feel better about the college experience in general. Even if I was able to ascertain why the association exists or the direction of cause, I was in no position to be able to describe its boundary conditions, such as the type of people in whom this relationship would be expected to be larger or smaller. For instance, no doubt there are many bright students who love the college experience but for one reason or another choose to sit in the back, just as there are students who sit in the front even though they would much rather be somewhere else—anywhere else—than in that classroom.

I have learned many lessons about research over the years—lessons that began with that first early and unsuccessful attempt at academic publishing.

I have learned that research is tough, that it takes patience, and that our egos often get too involved when we interpret feedback from others. Although this particular study never was published, I have learned that resilence to rejection combined with persistence following failure often does lead to success. But I think one of the more important lessons I've learned being both a producer and a consumer of research is how much more impressive a study is when it can speak to more than just whether an effect exists, whether a relationship is different from zero, or whether two groups differ from each other. Instead, some of the best research I have done and the best research I have read goes further by answering not only "whether" or "if," but also "how" and "when." Approaches to analyzing one's data with the goal of answering these latter two questions is the topic of this book.

1.2 Questions of Whether, If, How, and When

Questions of "whether" or "if" focus primarily on whether two variables are related, causally or otherwise, or if something is more or less likely to happen in one set of circumstances or conditions than another. Such questions are often the first ones a scientist-in-training asks, sometimes merely by observing the social world around him or her and wondering about it. For example, I occasionally teach a large undergraduate course on research methods to students in the social sciences. In this course, I require the students to conceive a study, collect some data, and write up the results. By far the most popular research topic proposed by students in this class is the effects of exposure to the thin ideal on self-esteem and body dissatisfaction. Term after term several groups of students want to design a study to see if women who are exposed to images of women depicted in beauty magazines, the Internet, popular television, and music videos—as thin and beautiful—suffer in some way from this exposure. I believe this is such a popular topic because it is nearly impossible to avoid the daily bombardment by the media of depictions of what the ideal woman should look like and, by extension, what society seems to value. Naturally, many wonder whether this is bad for women and society—if women's sense of worth, image of their bodies, and likelihood of disordered eating are affected by this exposure.

Questions of the whether or if variety also serve as a starting point in our quest to understand the effects of something that has happened in society, when a new technology is developed, when a new problem confronts the people of a community or nation, and so forth. After the twin towers of the World Trade Center in New York City were brought down by terrorists on September 11, 2001, researchers started asking whether and what kind of physical and psychological health effects it had on those who experienced it (e.g., Cukor et al., 2011; DiGrande et al., 2008), those who only observed it from a distance (e.g., Mijanovich & Weitzman, 2010), or how people's behavior changed after the event (e.g., Richman, Shannon, Rospenda, Flaherty, & Fendrich, 2009). And a relatively new genre of television known as *political entertainment* has spawned much research about its viewers and whether shows like *The Daily Show* or *The Colbert Report* serve to politically educate, mobilize, or demotivate those who view them (e.g., Baumgartner & Morris, 2006; Xenos & Becker, 2009).

The empirical literature in most every scientific discipline is replete with research that provides answers to questions of whether or if, and for good reason. Many theoretical and applied questions in the sciences focus on whether there is evidence of association between some presumed causal antecedent X and some putative consequent or outcome Y. Is a particular therapeutic method effective at reducing depression (e.g., Hofmann & Smits, 2008)? Does combining drugs with psychotherapy work better than therapy alone (e.g., Cuijpers, van Straten, Warmeredam, & Andersson, 2009)? Does playing violent video games or watching violent television make people aggressive (e.g., Anderson & Bushman, 2001; Anderson et al., 2010)? Does exposure to negative political advertisements turn people off from participating in the political process (e.g., Lau, Silegman, Heldman, & Babbit, 1999)? Are the children of divorced parents more prone to behavioral or psychological problems than children of married parents (e.g., Amato, 2001; Amato & Keith, 1991)? Does rewarding performance at work increase employee satisfaction and reduce turnover (e.g., Judge, Piccolo, Podsakoff, Shaw, & Rich, 2010)? What sets science apart from armchair speculation is that we can answer such questions by collecting data. Being able to establish that two variables are associated—that an effect or relationship of some kind exists—is in part what science is about, and research that does so is worth undertaking. Indeed, the drive to answer questions of this sort is one of the things that motivates scientists to get up in the morning.

But establishing association does not translate into deep understanding even when a causal association can be established. We know that we better understand some phenomenon when we can answer not only whether X affects Y, but also *how* X exerts its effect on Y, and *when* X affects Y and when it does not. The "how" question relates to the underlying psychological, cognitive, or biological process that causally links X to Y, whereas the "when" question pertains to the boundary conditions of the causal association—under what circumstances, or for which types of people, does

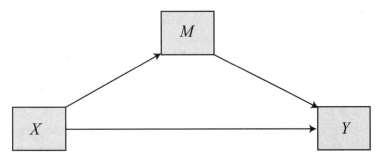

FIGURE 1.1. A simple mediation model with a single mediator variable *M* causally located between *X* and *Y*.

X exert an effect on *Y* and under what circumstances, or for which type of people, does *X* not exert an effect?

Mediation

A researcher whose goal is to establish or test how *X* exerts its effect on *Y* frequently postulates a model in which one or more intervening variables *M* is located causally between *X* and *Y*. One of the simplest forms of such a model is depicted in Figure 1.1. These intervening variables, often called *mediators*, are conceptualized as the mechanism through which *X* influences *Y*. That is, variation in *X* causes variation in one or more mediators *M*, which in turn causes variation in *Y*. For example, there is clear evidence that exposure to the thin ideal through the mass media is a risk factor if not an actual cause of body dissatisfaction in women (e.g., Grabe, Ward, & Hyde, 2008; Levine & Murnen, 2009). But how does this occur? Research suggests that internalization of the norm functions as a mediator of this relationship (Lopez-Guimera, Levine, Sanchez-Cerracedo, & Fauquet, 2010). Women who report greater exposure (or who are given greater exposure experimentally) to the thin-as-ideal image of women are more likely to internalize this image and seek thinness as a personal goal than those with less exposure. Such internalization, in turn, leads to greater body dissatisfaction (Cafri, Yamamiya, Brannick, & Thompson, 2005). So internalization of the standard portrayed by the media is one mechanism that links such exposure to body dissatisfaction. Of course, other mechanisms may be at work too, and Lopez-Guimera et al. (2010) discuss some of the other potential mediators of the effect of such exposure on women's beliefs, attitudes, and behavior.

Investigators interested in examining questions about mechanism resort to *process modeling* to empirically estimate and test hypotheses about the two pathways of influence through which *X* carries its effect on *Y* depicted in Figure 1.1, one *direct* from X to Y and the other *indirect* through M. More popularly known as *mediation analysis*, this type of analysis is extremely common in virtually all disciplines. Some of the most highly cited journal articles in methodology both historically (e.g., Baron & Kenny, 1986) and more recently (e.g., MacKinnon, Lockwood, Hoffman, & West, 2002; Preacher & Hayes, 2004, 2008a) discuss mediation analysis and various statistical approaches to quantifying and testing hypotheses about direct and indirect effects of X on Y. I describe the fundamentals of mediation analysis in Chapters 4 through 6.

Moderation

When the goal is to uncover the boundary conditions for an association between two variables, moderation analysis is used. An association between two variables X and Y is said to be moderated when its size or sign depends on a third variable or set of variables M. Conceptually, moderation is depicted as in Figure 1.2, which depicts moderator variable M influencing the magnitude of the causal effect of X on Y. Moderation is also known as *interaction*. For example, experimental studies of exposure to the thin-as-ideal standard reveal that such exposure tends to have a larger effect on body dissatisfaction and affect among women who have already internalized the thin-as-ideal standard (see, e.g., Groetz, Levine, & Murnen, 2002). In other words, relative to women who strive for thinness as a personal goal, women who buy in less to the social norm that thinner is better are less likely to show evidence of body dissatisfaction after exposure to thin models through media images. So internalization of the norm (M) functions as moderator of the effect of exposure to images reflecting the thin-as-ideal norm (X) on body dissatisfaction (Y).

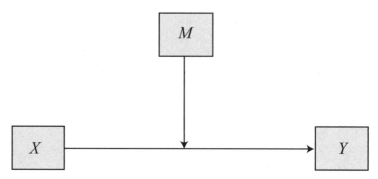

FIGURE 1.2. A simple moderation model with a single moderator variable M influencing the size of X's effect on Y.

Statistically, moderation analysis is typically conducted by testing for *interaction* between M and X in a model of Y. With evidence that X's effect on Y is moderated by M, the investigator typically will then quantify and describe the contingent nature of the association or effect by estimating X's effect on Y at various values of the moderator, an exercise known as *probing an interaction*. The basic principles of moderation analysis are introduced in Chapters 7 to 9.

This example illustrates that the answers to how and when questions can be intertwined. A variable could function as either a mediator or a moderator, depending on how the phenomenon under investigation is being conceptualized and tested. And in principle, the same variable could serve both roles simultaneously for certain processes that evolve and operate over long periods of time. For instance, early exposure to media images that portray the thin-as-ideal norm can persuade adolescents that thin is indeed better, which results in body dissatisfaction given that few women can live up to this unrealistic and even unhealthy standard. Of course, not all young women will buy into this message. Among those who do, once this norm has been internalized and adopted as a personal goal, it is more likely to influence how such women perceive themselves following later exposure to this norm relative to those who don't believe thinner is better.

1.3 Conditional Process Analysis

It is not difficult to find examples of mediation and moderation analysis in the empirical literature, and there have been numerous papers and book chapters emphasizing the value of moderation and mediation analysis to further understanding processes of interest to researchers in specific disciplines, many of which also provide methodological tutorials (e.g., Baron & Kenny, 1986; Breitborde, Srihari, Pollard, Addington, & Woods, 2010; Bryan, Schmiege, & Broaddus, 2007; Dearing & Hamilton, 2006; Eveland, 1997; Fairchild & McQuillin, 2010; Frazier, Tix, & Barron, 2004; Gogineni, Alsup, & Gillespie, 1995; Holbert & Stephenson, 2003; James & Brett, 1984; Kraemer, Wilson, Fairburn, & Agras, 2002; Krause, Serlin, Ward, & Rony, 2010; Lockhart, MacKinnon, & Ohlrich, 2011; MacKinnon, Fairchild, & Fritz, 2007; Magill, 2011; Maric, Wiers, & Prins, 2012; Preacher & Hayes, 2008b; Ro, 2012; Whisman & McClelland, 2005). However, rather infrequently is the combination of the two discussed in the same article. Researchers are advised to estimate indirect effects and look for interactions, but rarely both in an integrated analytical model. This lack of attention to the integration of moderation and mediation analysis may be due in part to the fact that analytical procedures that combine moderation and mediation were introduced in a systematic fashion to the research community only in the last 10 years or so. For instance, Muller, Judd, and Yzerbyt (2005) write about the mediation of a moderated effect and the moderation of a mediated effect, Edwards and Lambert (2007) provide a framework for testing hypotheses that combine moderation and mediation using path analysis, and Preacher, Rucker, and Hayes (2007) introduce the concept of the "conditional indirect effect" as a quantification of the contingent nature of a process or mechanism and provide techniques for estimation and inference (additional articles include Morgan-Lopez & MacKinnon, 2006; Fairchild & MacKinnon, 2009).

In part as a result of these articles, researchers are now throwing around terms such as "mediated moderation," "moderated mediation," and "conditional indirect effects" relatively frequently, but often are only somewhat awkwardly implementing the corresponding analytical methods because of a lack of clear guidance from methodologists for how to properly do so and write about it. To be sure, the few methodology articles that do exist attempt to speak to the user, and some provide statistical software code or tools to ease the implementation of the methods discussed, but only so much can be accomplished in a single journal article. Furthermore, the advice that does exist is fragmented and spread across multiple articles in different journals. Part IV of this book is dedicated to the analytical integration of mediation and moderation using a data-analytical strategy I have termed *conditional process modeling* or *conditional process analysis*.

Conditional process analysis is used when one's research goal is to describe the conditional nature of the mechanism or mechanisms by which a variable transmits its effect on another and testing hypotheses about such contingent effects. As discussed earlier, mediation analysis is used to quantify and examine the direct and indirect pathways through which an antecedent variable X transmits its effect on a consequent variable Y through one or more intermediary or mediator variables.[1] Moderation analysis is used to examine how the effect of antecedent variable X on a consequent Y depends on a third variable or set of variables. Conditional process analysis is both of these in combination and focuses on the estimation and interpretation of the conditional nature (the moderation component) of the indirect and/or direct effects (the mediation component) of X on Y in a causal system. Although not known by this name, the methodology articles mentioned earlier have prompted an increasingly widespread adoption of this analytical method. It is not difficult to find examples of conditional process modeling in the empirical literature of many disciplines, including social psychology (Popan, Kenworthy, Frame, Lyons, & Snuggs,

---

[1] *Antecedent* and *consequent* variables will be formally defined in Chapter 3.

2010; van Dijke & De Cremer, 2010), health psychology (Luszczynska et al., 2010), biological psychology (Oei, Tollenaar, Elzinga, & Spinhoven, 2010), developmental psychology (Parade, Leerkes, & Blankson, 2010), clinical psychology and psychiatry (Goodin, McGuire, Stapleton, et al., 2009; Rees & Freeman, 2009), cognitive psychology (Naumann, Richter, Christmann, & Groeben, 2008), public health (Blashill & Wal, 2010), sociology (Li, Patel, Balliet, Tov, & Scollon, 2011), women's studies (Sibley & Perry, 2010), neuroscience (Goodin, McGuire, Allshouse, et al., 2009), business and management (Cole, Bedeian, & Bruch, 2011; Cole, Walter, & Bruch, 2008), and communication (Antheunis, Valkenburg, & Peter, 2010; Jensen, 2008, 2011; Palomares, 2008), among others.

A concrete example will help to clarify just what conditional process analysis is all about. Just prior to writing this chapter, the U.S. Congress held the American and world economies hostage over largely politically motivated disagreements and fighting over the conditions under which the amount of money the government is allowed to borrow can be raised—the so-called *debt ceiling*. In part as a result of this political bickering and a failure of Congress to adequately address spending and revenue problems, Standard & Poor's lowered the credit rating of the U.S. government for the first time in history, from AAA to AA+. U.S. unemployment is currently at a recent high at over 9%, housing prices are falling, and so too is the value of people's retirement portfolios. The Greek economy was recently bailed out by the International Monetary Fund, the European Union is facing economic instability, and a few months ago a major earthquake followed by a tsunami and near-nuclear meltdown at a power plant in Japan roiled the Japanese people and its economy. Not to downplay the significance of a bad economy for the public at large, but imagine owning a business in this kind of environment, where your economic livelihood and your ability to pay your workforce and your creditors depends on a public that is reluctant to let go of its money. Personally, I'd seriously think about finding another profession. Perhaps that is why I chose the relatively recession-proof profession of university professor.

It is in this context that Pollack, VanEpps, and Hayes (2012) conducted a study examining the affective and cognitive effects of economic stress on entrepreneurs. Of primary interest was whether economic stress prompts business owners to contemplate pursuing other careers, giving up their entrepreneurial roles, and just doing something else instead. But they went further than asking just whether economic stress is related to such "withdrawal intentions." They proposed that such economic stress leads to depressed affect, which in turn enhances their intention to leave entrepreneurship and pursue another vocation. This is a question about not whether but *how*. On top of this, they proposed that entrepreneurs who are more socially connected to others in their field would be less susceptible to the deleterious effects of economic stress. Having the support of other entrepreneurs in your business community could help to buffer the effects of that stress on depression and, in turn, the desire to leave the business. This proposed explanation addresses a question of *when*. Under what circumstances, or for which type of people, is the effect of stress on depression and business withdrawal intentions large versus small or even zero?

To conduct this study, Pollack et al. (2012) sent a survey to members of Business Networking International, a social networking group for small business owners. The 262 respondents were asked a series of questions used to score the economic stress they felt related to their business (higher score = more stress), whether and how much they thought about withdrawing from entrepreneurship (higher score = greater intentions to leave), the extent to which they felt various emotions (e.g., discouraged, hopeless, inadequate) related to their business over the last year (higher score = more depressed affect), and how many people they spoke to, e-mailed, or met with face-to-face about their business on a daily basis from this networking group (higher score = more social ties).

Somewhat surprisingly perhaps, there was no evidence of an association between economic stress and withdrawal intentions. Entrepreneurs who reported feeling more economic stress were no more or less likely to report greater intentions to withdraw from their business than those who felt less stress ($r = 0.06, p > .05$). But that is not the whole story, for this finding belies what is a more interesting, nuanced, and, ultimately, conditional process. A moderation analysis revealed that those who reported relatively higher stress did report relatively higher withdrawal intentions compared to those with lower stress (i.e., the relationship was positive), but this was true only among those with relatively few social ties with network members. Among those who reported relatively more social ties, there was little or even a *negative* association between economic stress and withdrawal intentions. So social ties seemed to buffer the effects of stress on desire to withdraw from their business enterprise. This is *moderation*; social ties moderates the effect of economic stress on withdrawal intentions.

Pollack et al. (2012) proposed that the effect of economic stress on entrepreneurial withdrawal intentions operated through negative affect. That is, economic uncertainty and the resulting stress it produces bums business owners out, makes them feel inadequate and helpless, and leads them to choose to pursue other careers. This is *mediation*. In fact, participants who reported more economic stress did report more depressed affect ($r = 0.34, p < .01$), and those who reported more depressed affect

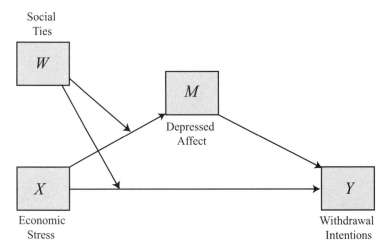

FIGURE 1.3. A conceptual diagram of a conditional process model corresponding to the Pollack et al. (2012) study.

reported greater intentions to withdraw ($r = 0.42, p < .01$). But this process, according to Pollack et al. (2012), can be "interrupted" by strong social ties. Having people you can lean on, talk to, or bounce ideas off to manage the business-related stress can reduce the effects of such stress on how you feel and therefore how you think about your future as a business owner. The evidence was consistent with the interpretation that economic stress affects how business owners feel, depending on their social ties. Entrepreneurs under relatively more economic stress who also had relatively few social ties reported relatively more business-related depressed affect. But among those with relatively more social ties, economic stress was unrelated or even negatively related to negative affect. So social ties moderated the effect of stress on negative affect as well as on withdrawal intentions.

A conceptual diagram of a conditional process model corresponding to this example can be found in Figure 1.3. This diagram depicts what some have called *moderated mediation* and others have called *mediated moderation*. In fact, it depicts both. It has been given other labels as well, such as a *direct effect and first stage moderation model* (Edwards & Lambert, 2007) or simply "model 2" (Preacher et al., 2007). Regardless, observe that this diagram depicts two moderated relationships, one from economic stress to depressed affect ($X \rightarrow M$), and the other from economic stress to withdrawal intentions ($X \rightarrow Y$), both of which are diagrammed as moderated by social ties (W). In addition, there is an indirect effect of economic stress on withdrawal intentions through depressed affect depicted ($X \rightarrow M \rightarrow Y$), but because this indirect effect includes a component that is proposed as moderated (the $X \rightarrow M$ association), the indirect effect is also moderated

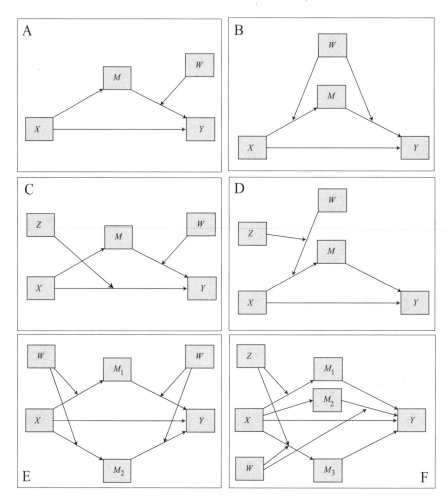

FIGURE 1.4. Some variants of a conditional process model, from quite simple (A) to fairly complex (F).

or *conditional*. The direct effect of economic stress on withdrawal intentions ($X \rightarrow Y$) is also depicted as moderated. According to this diagram, it too is conditional, for it depends on social ties. Thus, the process linking economic stress to withdrawal intentions through depressed affect is moderated or conditional, hence the term *conditional process model*. Throughout this book I describe how to piece the components of this model together and estimate and interpret direct and indirect effects, moderated as well as unmoderated.[2]

[2]It turns out in this case that there was no evidence that the direct effect of economic stress on withdrawal intentions was moderated by social ties, even though the so-called *total effect* was moderated. The moderation of the total effect of economic stress on withdrawal

The example depicted in Figure 1.3 is only one of the forms that a conditional process model can take. A few additional possibilities can be found in Figure 1.4, but these still represent only some of the many, many ways that moderation and mediation can be combined into a single integrated model. Panel A depicts a model in which the $M \rightarrow Y$ effect is moderated by W, called a *second stage moderation model* in terms introduced by Edwards and Lambert (2007). For examples of this model in published research, see Cole et al. (2008) and Antheunis et al. (2010). The model in panel B adds moderation of the $X \rightarrow M$ effect to the model in panel A, yielding a *first and second stage moderation model* (Edwards & Lambert, 2007). Parade et al. (2010) provide an example of this model. Panel C is like the model in panel A but adds moderation of the direct effect of X ($X \rightarrow Y$) by Z. Panel D depicts moderation of the $X \rightarrow M$ effect by W, which itself is moderated by Z. See Chang (2010) for an example. Panels E and F show models with two mediators. The model in panel E is similar to panel B but includes moderation by W of all effects to and from M_1 and M_2 (see, e.g., Takeuchi, Yun, & Wong, 2011). Panel F depicts a complex model (see Andreeva et al., 2010) with three mediators and two moderators. In this model, the $X \rightarrow M_3$ effect is moderated by both W and Z, the $X \rightarrow M_1$ effect is moderated by Z, and the $M_2 \rightarrow Y$ effect is moderated by W.

1.4 Correlation, Causality, and Statistical Modeling

The study of economic stress in entrepreneurs just described illustrates what conditional process modeling is all about, but it also illustrates what some construe as a weakness of mediation analysis in general, as well as how liberally people often attribute causality as the mechanism producing the associations observed in any kind of study. These findings come from a cross-sectional survey. This study is what is often called called *observational* rather than experimental. All measurements of these entrepreneurs were taken at the same time, there is no experimental manipulation or other forms of experimental control, and there is no way of establishing the causal ordering of the relationships observed. For example, people who are feeling down about their business might be more likely to contemplate withdrawing, and as a result they work less, network less often with other business leaders, and feel more stress from the economic pressures that build up as a result. The nature of the data collection makes it impossible to establish what is causing what. In terms of the three criteria often described as necessary conditions for establishing causation (covariation,

---

intentions is not depicted in Figure 1.3. The distinction between a total effect and a direct effect will be introduced in Chapter 4.

temporal ordering, and the elimination of competing explanations), this study establishes, at best, only covariation between variables in the causal system.

Experimentation and, to a lesser extent, longitudinal research offer some advantages over cross-sectional research when establishing causal association. For example, suppose economic stress was experimentally manipulated in some way, but otherwise the same results were found. In that case, we would be in a much better position to argue direction of cause, at least in part. Random assignment to levels of economic stress would ensure that neither social ties, depressed affect, nor withdrawal intentions could be affecting the stress the study participants felt. It also guarantees that economic stress and depressed affect are not spuriously associated, meaning they share a common cause. But random assignment would not help establish the correct temporal ordering of depressed affect and withdrawal intentions. Although it could be that economic stress influences depressed affect which, in turn, influences withdrawal intentions ($X \rightarrow M \rightarrow Y$), it remains possible that economic stress influences withdrawal intentions, which then influences depressed affect ($X \rightarrow Y \rightarrow M$).

To deal with this limitation of one-shot experimental studies, a sequence of experimental studies can help to some extent (see Stone-Romero & Raposa, 2010). First, one attempts to establish that X causes M and Y in one experimental study. Success at doing so can then be followed with a second experimental study to establish that M causes Y rather than Y causing M. The estimates from such analyses (perhaps including a moderation component as well) could then be pieced together to establish the nature (conditional or not) of the indirect effects of X on Y through M. But as Spencer, Zanna, and Fong (2005) note, it is not always easy or even possible to establish convincingly that the M measured in the first study is the same as the M that is manipulated in the second study. Absent such equivalence, the ability of a sequence of experiments to establish a causal chain of events is compromised.

Collecting data on the same variables over time is an alternative approach to studying causal processes, and doing so offers some advantages. For instance, rather than measuring entrepreneurs only once, it would be informative to measure their experience of economic stress on multiple occasions, as well as their depressed affect and intentions to withdraw from entrepreneurial activity. If economic stress influences withdrawal intentions through its effect on depressed affect, then you'd expect that people who are under more stress *than they were before* would express stronger intentions to withdraw *than they expressed earlier* as a result of feeling more depressed affect *than they were feeling earlier*. But covariation over time does not imply cause, just as covariation at a single time fails to establish a causal association. There are statistical procedures that attempt to disentangle contemporaneous from time-lagged association (e.g., Finkel, 1995), and there is a growing literature on moderation and mediation analysis, as well as their combination, in longitudinal studies (e.g., Bauer, Preacher, & Gil, 2006; Cole & Maxwell, 2003; Cheong, MacKinnon, & Khoo, 2003; Selig & Preacher, 2009). However, I do not address this literature or corresponding methods in this book.

One could advance the argument that scientists really should not attempt to model purportedly causal processes with data that do not afford causal interpretation. However, I could not make that argument convincingly because I don't believe this. We don't use statistical methods to make causal inferences. Establishing cause and effect is more a problem in research design than it is in data analysis. Statistical methods are just mathematical tools that allow us to discern order in apparent chaos, or signals of processes that may be at work amid random background noise or other processes we haven't incorporated into our models. The inferences that we make about cause are not products of the mathematics underneath the modeling process. Rather, the inferences we make are products of our minds—how we interpret the associations we have observed, the signal we believe we have extracted from the noise. To be sure, we can and should hold ourselves to a high standard. We should strive to design rigorous studies that allow us to make causal inferences with clarity when possible. But we won't always be able to do so given constraints on resources, time, the availability of data, the generosity of research participants, and research ethics. We should not let the limitations of our data collection efforts constrain the tools we bring to the task of trying to understand what our data might be telling us about the processes we are studying. But we absolutely should recognize the limitations of our data and couch our interpretations with the appropriate caveats and cautions.

Causality is the cinnamon bun of social science. It is a sticky concept, and establishing that a sequence of events is a causal one can be a messy undertaking. As you pick the concept apart, it unravels in what seems like an endless philosophical spiral of reductionism. Even if we can meet the criteria of causality when testing a simple $X \rightarrow M \rightarrow Y$ model, what is the mechanism that links X and M, and M to Y? Certainly, those causal processes must themselves come into being through some kind of mechanism. What are the mediators of the individual components of the causal chain? And what mediates the components of those components? And if those mediators can be established as such, what mediates those effects?

In other words, we have never really explained an association entirely, no matter how many intervening variables we propose and account for linking X and Y. This does not mean that it is not worth thinking deeply about what cause means or discussing and debating what kinds of standards we must hold ourselves to as scientists in order to accept causal interpretations. But that isn't going to happen in this book. There are other books and journal articles on the topic of causality if you want to explore the concept on your own (e.g., Davis, 1985; Holland, 1986; Morgan & Winship, 2007; Pearl, 2009), and there is a growing chorus of quantitative social scientists who reject the regression-based orientation I outline here on the grounds that linear modeling and statistical adjustment simply don't do the job many people claim it does. That said, this book is about statistically modeling relationships—relationships that may but may not be causal in the end—and I think you will find the techniques and tools described here useful in your quest to understand your data and test some of your theoretical propositions and hypotheses. Just how large an inferential chasm between data and claim you attempt to leap is your decision to make, as is how you go about justifying your inference to potential critics. I will not, nor should I or anyone else, forbid you to use the methods described here just because your data are *only* correlational in nature.

1.5 Statistical Software

I believe that the widespread adoption of modern methods of analysis is greatly facilitated when these methods are described using software with which people are already familiar. Most likely, you already have access to the statistical software I will emphasize in this book, primarily SAS and IBM SPSS Statistics (the latter of which I refer to henceforth simply as SPSS). Although other software could be used (such as Mplus, LISREL, AMOS, or other structural equation modeling programs), most of these don't implement at least some of the procedures I emphasize in this book. And by eliminating the need to learn a new software language, I believe you more quickly develop an understanding and appreciation of the methods described herein.

Throughout the pages that follow I will emphasize estimation of model parameters using ordinary least squares (OLS) regression. Although any program that can conduct OLS regression analysis can estimate the parameters of most of the models I describe, such programs can only get you so far when taken off the shelf. For instance, no program I am aware of implements the Johnson–Neyman technique for probing interactions, and neither SPSS nor SAS can generate bootstrap confidence intervals for products of parameters, a method I advocate for inference in mediation analysis and conditional process analysis. Over the last several years, I have been publishing on moderation and mediation analysis and providing various tools for SPSS and SAS in the form of "macros" that simplify the analyses I describe in this book. These go by such names as INDIRECT (Preacher & Hayes, 2008a), MODMED (Preacher et al., 2007), SOBEL (Preacher & Hayes, 2004), MODPROBE (Hayes & Matthes, 2009), and MED3/C (Hayes, Preacher, & Myers, 2011). But each of these tools was designed for a specific task and not others, and keeping track of which tool should be used for which analysis can be difficult. So rather than confuse you by describing the ins-and-outs of each of these tools, I have designed a new macro for this book called PROCESS that integrates most of the functions of my earlier macros into one handy command or dialog box, and with additional features not available in my other macros. My prediction is that you will come to love PROCESS and will find yourself turning to it again and again in your professional life. The PROCESS procedure is freely available and can be downloaded from my home page at *www.afhayes.com*, and documentation describing its use and features can be found in Appendix A.

The advent the the graphic user interface (GUI) in the 1980s made data analysis a point-and-click enterprise for some and turned what is a distasteful task for many into something that is actually quite fun. Yet I still believe there is value to understanding how to instruct your preferred software package to perform using syntax or "code." In addition to providing a set of instructions that you can easily save for use later or give to collaborators and colleagues, syntax is easier to describe in books of this sort than is a set of instructions about what to click, drag, point, click, and so forth, and in what sequence. Users of SAS have no choice but to write in code, and although SPSS is highly popular in part because of its easy-to-navigate user interface, and I do provide a GUI-based version of PROCESS, I nevertheless will describe all SPSS instructions using syntax. In this book, all code for whatever program I am using or describing at that moment will be denoted with **courier** typeface in a shaded box, as below.

```
process vars=attitude exposure social intent/y=intent/x=exposure/m=attitude
    /w=social/model=8/wmodval=1.25/boot=5000/save=1.
```

Some commands will not fit in a single line in this book and must be carried below to the next line. When this occurs, it will be denoted by indentation of the continuing text, as above. A command has ended when you see a *command terminator*. In SPSS, the command terminator is a period ("."), whereas in SAS it is the semicolon (";"). A failure to include a command terminator at the end of your command is likely to confuse your software, and a string of errors is inevitable.

1.6 Overview of This Book

This book is divided into four broad parts. The first part, which you are reading now, consists of the introductory material in this chapter as well as an overview of the basic principles of linear models using OLS regression in Chapters 2 and 3. These chapters should be considered important prerequisite reading. If you are not familiar with the fundamentals of linear modeling, almost nothing else in this book will make any sense to you. So although the temptation to skip the material in this section may be strong, do so at your own risk.

Chapters 4 through 6 define the second part, which is devoted to mediation analysis. Chapter 4 illustrates the basic principles of elementary path analysis, with a focus on the partitioning of the total effect of antecedent variable X on consequent variable Y into direct and indirect effects, as well as means of making statistical inference about direct and indirect effects. Chapter 5 extends the principles and methods introduced in Chapter 4 into the realm of multiple mediator models—models of causal influence that are transmitted by two or more intervening variables operating in parallel or in sequence. Chapter 6 discusses miscellaneous issues in mediation analysis such as measures of effect size, confounding and causal order, and models with multiple causal antecedent or consequent variables.

The third part is Chapters 7 through 9, and the topic is moderation analysis. In Chapter 7 I define the concept of a conditional effect and show how to set up a linear model that allows the effect of one variable on another to depend linearly on a third variable. I illustrate how a hypothesis of moderation is tested and the parameter estimates of the corresponding model interpreted. I also introduce a few methods of dissecting the conditional nature of association and show how to construct a visual representation of moderation. Chapter 8 illustrates the generality of the procedure introduced in Chapter 7, including interaction between quantitative variables or between dichotomous moderators and focal predictors. Chapter 9 ends the section on moderation with discussions of miscellaneous issues in the estimation of models that allow one variable's effect to depend on another, such as models with multiple interactions, and a debunking of myths and misunderstandings about centering and standardization in moderation analysis.

Chapters 10 through 12 end the book with an introduction to conditional process analysis, the fourth and final part. Chapter 10 provides numerous examples of conditional process models proposed and estimated in the literature, introduces the important concepts of conditional and unconditional direct and indirect effects, describes how they are defined mathematically, and shows how they are estimated. Chapter 11 provides a slightly more complex analytical example of conditional process analysis while also illustrating the distinction between moderated mediation and mediated moderation. Chapter 12 addresses various miscellaneous issues and questions about the analysis of the contingencies of mechanisms.

This is an introductory book, and so there are many important, interesting, and some could say critical points and controversies that I gloss over or completely ignore. For example, the majority of the analyses I illustrate will be done using OLS regression-based path analysis, which assumes fixed effects, continuous outcomes, and the absence of random measurement error. Of course, we generally don't measure without error, and it is well known that a failure to account for random measurement error in the variables in a linear model can produce bias and misleading results. And often our outcomes of interest are not continuous. Rather, they may take one of two values or perhaps are measured on a course ordinal scale. In such cases OLS regression is not appropriate. I also neglect multilevel models, modeling change over time, or even the most basic of repeated measures designs. These are interesting and important topics, to be sure, and there is a developing literature in the application of mediation and moderation analysis, as well as their combination, to such problems. But assuming you don't plan on abandoning OLS regression any time soon as a result of some of its weaknesses and limitations, I believe you will be no worse for the wear and, I predict, even a bit better off once you turn the last page and have developed an understanding of how to use OLS regression to model complicated, contingent processes.

1.7 Chapter Summary

The outcome of an empirical study is more impressive, more influential, and more helpful to our understanding of an area of scientific inquiry if it establishes not only *whether* or *if* X affects Y but also *how* and *when* that relationship holds or is strong versus weak. If all effects exist through some kind of mechanism, and all effects have some kind of boundary conditions, then the most complete analysis answers both the how and when question simultaneously. In this chapter I have introduced the concepts of mediation (how X influences Y) and moderation (when X influences Y) and their combination in the form of a conditional process model. Although data analysis cannot be used to demonstrate or prove causal claims, it can be used to determine whether the data are consistent with a proposed causal process. Thus, the methods described in this book are useful for testing causal processes even absent data that lend themselves to unequivocal causal interpretation. My emphasis throughout this book is on the use of regression-based path analysis as a means of estimating various effects of interest (direct and indirect, conditional and unconditional). In order to grasp the material throughout this book, the basic principles of linear modeling using regression analysis must be well understood. Thus, the next two chapters provide on overview of the fundamentals of OLS regression.

2
Simple Linear Regression

Ordinary least squares (OLS) regression analysis serves as the foundation for much of what is discussed in this book. In this chapter, I provide an overview of the principles of OLS regression, including the estimation process, measuring the fit of a model, interpretation of information a linear regression yields, and the fundamentals of statistical inference.

During the U.S. Presidential election campaign of 2000 between Texas governor George W. Bush and Vice President Al Gore, the Bush campaign released a television advertisement in which he described the world as one of "terror, madmen, and missiles." He argued the need for a "sharpened sword" in a dangerous world and promised that if elected, he would rebuild a military suffering from aging equipment and low morale, help to protect the United States and its allies from blackmail by other countries by constructing a missile defense system, and that his foreign policy would be one "with a touch of iron" motivated by U.S. interests. The not-so-subtle message the viewer is to take away from this ad is that this is a scary world full of people who want to harm the United States, and by electing Bush as President rather than Gore, we will all be safer.

Politicians are not the only ones to use emotions in their attempt to influence the public. Consider a public service announcement produced by the Environmental Defense Fund in which a man appearing to be in his 40s stands on a railroad track as a locomotive, whistle blaring, screams toward him. As the screen transitions back and forth between his face and various shots of the train from different angles, he states matter of factly, "Global warming. Some say irreversible consequences are 30 years away." Another shot of the train is shown, and the camera then focuses on his face as he states in a smug tone, "Thirty years? That won't affect me," at which point he steps aside to reveal a young girl standing behind him on the tracks. The camera zooms in on her worried face just before the train hits her.[1]

Such advertisements attempt to appeal to the base nature of humanity by tugging at our hearts rather than engaging our heads. The assumption is that people's actions are guided by how they feel. If you want to stimulate people to act (e.g., vote for a particular politician, donate to a cause, or otherwise mobilize to affect change) appeal to their emotions while giving them a course of action to deal with the emotion that results from the message. Emotional appeals have been used as a persuasive device for as long as people have been able to communicate, and no doubt they will be around as long as we are.

In this chapter, I introduce some principles of linear regression analysis using data from a study examining the extent to which people's beliefs about whether and how government should enact new laws to reduce the impact of an environmental crisis is related to their emotional responses to that potential crisis. Linear regression is the foundation of most of the methods I describe in this book, so a solid understanding of the fundamentals of linear regression is essential. I assume that most readers have been exposed to linear regression in some form before discovering this book, and so some of the material will be review. Even so, I encourage everyone to read this chapter as well as the next. Not only will it help to refresh your understanding of linear regression, but you will also find it easier to understand the material in chapters that follow with familiarity of my way of talking about linear regression. Furthermore, I introduce some notation in these two chapters that will be used throughout the book.

2.1 Correlation and Prediction

To what extent are people's beliefs about the role government should play in mitigating the potential effects of global crisis related to their emotional reactions to such a crisis? To answer this question, I rely on data donated to this book by Erik Nisbet, a colleague of mine who conducts research on the role of communication and the media in the politics of scientific controversy and environmental problems. In this study, 815 residents of the United States (417 female, 398 male) who expressed a willingness to participate in online surveys in exchange for various incentives were invited to complete a survey posted on the Internet. The sampling procedure was designed such that the respondents roughly represent the U.S. population. The dataset

---

[1]As of the date of the publication of this book, these advertisements were available to be viewed at www.livingroomcandidate.org/commercials/2000/dangerous-world and www.youtube.com/watch?v=s-_LBXWMCAM, respectively.

(named GLBWARM) can be downloaded from the web page for this book located on my home page at *www.afhayes.com*.

The dataset contains a variable constructed from how each participant responded to five questions about the extent to which he or she would or does support various policies or actions by the U.S. government to mitigate the threat of global climate change. Examples include "How much do you support or oppose increasing government investment for developing alternative energy like biofuels, wind, or solar by 25%?" and "How much do you support or oppose creating a 'Cap and Trade' policy that limits greenhouse gases said to cause global warming?" Response options were scaled from "Strongly opposed" (coded 1) or "Strongly support" (7), with intermediate labels to denote intermediate levels of support. An index of support for government action to reduce climate change was constructed for each person by averaging responses to the five questions (GOVACT in the data file).

The dataset also contains a variable quantifying participants' negative emotional responses to the prospect of climate change. This variable was constructed using participants' responses to a question that asked them to indicate how frequently they feel each of three emotions when thinking about global warming: "worried," "alarmed," and "concerned." Response options included "not at all," "slightly," "a little bit," "some," "a fair amount," and "a great deal." These responses were numerically coded 1 to 6, respectively, and each participant's responses were averaged across all three emotions to produce a measure of *negative emotions about climate change* (NEGEMOT in the data file). This variable is scaled such that higher scores reflect feeling stronger negative emotions.

Do people who feel stronger negative emotions about the prospect of climate change report greater support for government action than those who feel such negative emotions to a lesser extent? A handy visual tool for depicting the relationship between two variables is the *scatterplot*, as in Figure 2.1. A scatterplot depicts association between two variables in two-dimensional space using the scattering of points in the plot, each of which denotes a pair of measurements on the variables which define the two axes of the plot. Figure 2.1 was generated and edited in SPSS using the command

```
graph/scatterplot=negemot with govact.
```

A comparable command in SAS is

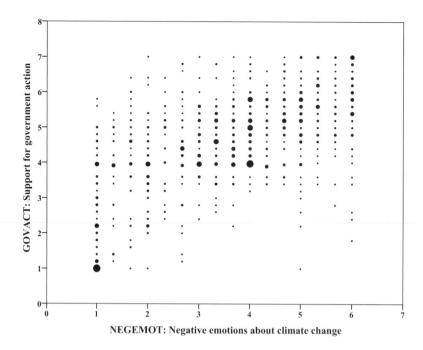

FIGURE 2.1. A scatterplot of the association between negative emotions about climate change and support for government action to mitigate climate change. (Note: The size of the dot reflects the number of cases at that point on the plot.)

```
proc sgscatter data=glbwarm;plot govact*negemot;run;
```

It doesn't take a highly trained eye to detect the pattern here. It appears that there is a tendency for those who report relatively stronger negative emotions about climate change to also be relatively more supportive of government action to help mitigate climate change. To be sure, the association isn't perfect by any means, but the trend is clear.

Our eyes can deceive us, so it is always a good idea to quantify association rather than relying only on a visual depiction such as a scatterplot. There are many ways of numerically quantifying association between two variables X and Y, but by far the most popular is *Pearson's product moment correlation*, more simply known as Pearson's r. It can be used to quantify linear association between two quantitative variables, a quantitative and a dichotomous variable, as well as between two dichotomous variables. Mathematically,

$$r \approx \frac{\sum_{j=1}^{n} Z_{X_j} Z_{Y_j}}{n}$$

where Z_{X_j} and Z_{Y_j} are case j's measurements on variables X and Y expressed as deviation from their sample means in standard deviation units:

$$Z_{X_j} = \frac{X_j - \overline{X}}{SD_X} \qquad Z_{Y_j} = \frac{Y_j - \overline{Y}}{SD_Y}$$

where SD_X and SD_Y are the standard deviations of X and Y, respectively, $\overline{X}$ and $\overline{Y}$ are their sample means, and the summation is over all n cases in the data. Pearson's r can range between -1 and 1, although values of 1 and -1 would rarely be observed in real data. The closer r is to 1, ignoring sign, the stronger the *linear* association. The sign of r corresponds to the direction of the linear association between X and Y. Pearson's r is positive if relatively high values of X tend to be paired with relatively high values of Y, and relatively low values of X tend to be paired with relatively low values of Y. Pearson's r is negative if relatively high values on X tend to be paired with relatively low values on Y, and relatively low values on X tend to be paired with relatively high values of Y. Pearson's r will be close to zero when there is no apparent order to the pairing of values of X and Y, or when the association is better characterized as nonlinear (as Pearson's r is a measure of linear association, not just any kind of association).

There are many procedures in SPSS and SAS that can be used to generate Pearson's r. In SPSS, the command

```
correlations variables = negemot govact/statistics descriptives.
```

calculates Pearson's r as well as the means and standard deviations for both variables. In SAS, try

```
proc corr data=glbwarm;vars negemot govact;run;
```

The SPSS output generated by this command can be found in Figure 2.2. As can be seen, Pearson's $r = 0.578$. The positive sign for r confirms what is seen in the scatterplot. Respondents to this survey who reported relatively stronger negative emotions about climate change were also relatively more supportive of government action.

If Pearson's r is squared, the result is the *coefficient of determination*, which indexes the proportion of the variance in one variable *explained by* or *shared* with the other. In this case, $r^2 = 0.334$. Expressed in percentage terms, we can say that about 33.4% of the variance in people's support for government action to mitigate climate change can be explained by variation

Descriptive Statistics

	Mean	Std. Deviation	N
NEGEMOT: Negative emotions about climate change	3.5580	1.52843	815
GOVACT: Support for government action	4.5870	1.36044	815

Correlations

		NEGEMOT: Negative emotions about climate change	GOVACT: Support for government action
NEGEMOT: Negative emotions about climate change	Pearson Correlation	1	.578
	Sig. (2-tailed)		.000
	N	815	815
GOVACT: Support for government action	Pearson Correlation	.578	1
	Sig. (2-tailed)	.000	
	N	815	815

FIGURE 2.2. SPSS output showing Pearson's correlation between negative emotional responses to climate change (NEGEMOT) and support for government action (GOVACT).

in the negative emotions that people feel about climate change. Most would characterize this association as somewhere between moderate and large.

If two variables X and Y are correlated, this implies that if one were to use knowledge of case j's measurement on X to estimate case j's measurement on Y, doing this for all j cases should produce estimates that are more accurate than if one were to merely estimate $Y_j = \overline{Y}$ for every case in the data. Indeed, one interpretation of Pearson's correlation between two variables X and Y is that it provides an estimate as to how many standard deviations from the sample mean on Y a case is given how many standard deviations from the sample mean the case is on X. More formally,

$$\hat{Z}_{Y_j} = r_{XY} Z_{X_j}$$

where $\hat{Z}_{Y_j}$ is the estimated value of Z_{Y_j}. For instance, a person who is one-half of a standard deviation above the mean ($Z_X = 0.5$) in negative emotions is estimated to be $\hat{Z}_Y = 0.578(0.5) = 0.289$ standard deviations from the mean in his or her support for government action. The sign of $\hat{Z}_Y$ is positive, meaning that this person is estimated to be above the sample mean (i.e., more supportive than average). Similarly, someone who is two standard deviations below the mean ($Z_X = -2$) in negative emotions is estimated to be $\hat{Z}_Y = 0.578(-2) = -1.156$ standard deviations from the mean in support for government action. In this case, $\hat{Z}_Y$ is negative, meaning that such a person is estimated to be below the sample mean in support for government action (i.e., less supportive than average).

Of course, these are just estimates of Y from X. Rarely would they be exactly correct for any particular case in a data file. Rather, they are *expectations* extracted from what is known about the association between X and Y. In statistics, as in life, rarely are our expectations perfectly met. But we hope those expectations come close to reality. Unlike in life, in statistics, we have a numerical means of gauging how close our expectations derived from the association between X and Y are to reality. That gauge is the size of Pearson's r. The closer it is to one (ignoring sign), the more consistent those expectations are with the reality of our data.

So correlation and prediction are closely connected concepts. If two variables are correlated with each other, then you should be able to use information about values on one variable in the X,Y pairs to estimate with at least some degree of accuracy the values on the other variable in the pair. Although there are some circumstances in which you might literally want to make such estimations, in social science research we tend to talk about this process of estimation more as a means of describing and making inferences about the processes that we are studying and how such processes, if at work as we believe, would induce association between our measurements of the variables.

2.2   The Simple Linear Regression Equation

A linear regression model is nothing more than an equation that links one or more input variables to an output variable by exploiting information contained in the association between inputs and output. The input variables are often called *predictor*, *independent*, or *explanatory variables*, whereas the output variable is called the *criterion*, *outcome*, or *dependent variable*. Many of the statistical procedures that scientists use can be represented in the form of a regression model, such as the independent groups *t*-test and analysis of variance, although this is not always apparent the way statistical methods are often taught at the introductory level and described in elementary textbooks.

The goal when conducting a linear regression analysis is to estimate various *parameters* of the regression model such that the resulting equation yields estimations of the output from the inputs that are as good as can be given how one defines "good" and various assumptions one makes about the association between the variables, such as linearity. The information that comes from a regression model can be used to test hypotheses about the processes that link the inputs to the output, which inputs should be used and which should be ignored when attempting to explain variation in the output variable, and various other things that scientists are interested in.

A *simple* linear regression model is one of the more rudimentary forms a regression model takes, in that it contains only a single input variable. Expressed mathematically, the simple linear regression model is

$$Y_j = i_1 + bX_j + e_j \qquad (2.1)$$

where Y_j and X_j refer to case j's measurement on an outcome and predictor variable, respectively, b is the *regression coefficient* or *regression weight* for predictor variable X, i_1 is the *regression intercept* or *regression constant*, and e_j is the error in estimation of case j's value of Y from case j's value of X, also known as a *residual*. The process of estimating the parameters of such a model is referred to as *regressing Y on X*. When analyzing data using a linear regression model, we know X_j and Y_j, as these are the data. Our goal is to find what we don't know, i_1 and b, and then interpret information the regression model yields once those are derived.

Suppose we did know i_1 and b. In that case, we could generate an estimate of Y from X with a variant of this model:

$$\hat{Y}_j = i_1 + bX_j \qquad (2.2)$$

where $\hat{Y}_j$ is case j's *estimated, fitted*, or *predicted* value of Y given case j's X value. Substituting equation 2.2 into equation 2.1 yields

$$Y_j = \hat{Y}_j + e_j$$

and isolating e_j yields

$$e_j = Y_j - \hat{Y}_j$$

Thus, the residual e_j in equation 2.1 is the difference between case j's estimated value for Y from equation 2.2 and case j's actual value of Y.

Putting all this together, if we knew i_1 and b, we could generate an estimate of case j's Y value from case j's X value. This estimate likely will not be exactly equal to Y_j, however. The difference between Y_j and $\hat{Y}_j$ is case j's residual, which represents the difference between case j's actual value on Y and what Y is estimated to be given j's value of X.

For example, suppose $i_1 = 1.000$ and $b = 0.500$. Now imagine a case in a data file with $Y = 4.000$ and $X = 3.000$. Using equation 2.2 as a means of estimating Y from X, we would estimate that case's Y value to be $\hat{Y} = 1.000 + (0.500)3.000 = 2.500$. Therefore, this case's residual would be $e = Y - \hat{Y} = 4.000 - 2.500 = 1.500$. So the model $\hat{Y}_j = 1.000 + 0.500X_j$ underestimates this case's Y value, because the residual is positive. Or consider a case with $Y = 2.500$ and $X = 5.000$. We would estimate that case's Y to be $\hat{Y} = 1.000 + 0.500(5.000) = 3.500$ and therefore this case's residual would be $e = 2.500 - 3.500 = -1.000$. For this case, the model overestimates Y, because the residual is negative.

There is an infinitely large number of pairs of values of i_1 and b that could be used to generate estimates of Y from X from equation 2.2. But when you estimate a simple linear regression model using the *ordinary least squares criterion*, you will get only one of the many possible pairs. The pair of values for the intercept and the regression coefficient that an ordinary least squares (OLS) regression procedure yields is special in that it minimizes the *residual sum of squares* ($SS_{residual}$), defined as

$$SS_{residual} = \sum_{j=1}^{n} \left(Y_j - \hat{Y}_j\right)^2 = \sum_{j=1}^{n} e_j^2 \qquad (2.3)$$

Observe from equation 2.3 that $SS_{residual}$ cannot be negative (as the sum of a bunch of squared values must be positive) and that if $\hat{Y}_j = Y_j$ for all n cases in the data, then $SS_{residual} = 0$. As the discrepancy between the estimated and actual values of Y increases, so too does $SS_{residual}$. In any dataset, the largest that $SS_{residual}$ could possibly be is the *total sum of squares*, defined as

$$SS_{total} = \sum_{j=1}^{n} \left(Y_j - \bar{Y}_j\right)^2$$

So OLS regression derives the values of i_1 and b in equations 2.1 and 2.2 that produce the best fitting model of the data as defined by the least squares criterion—meaning that they make $SS_{residual}$ as small as it can possibly be, and certainly somewhere between 0 and SS_{total}.

Most popular statistical packages include a routine for estimating an OLS regression model. For instance, in SPSS, a simple regression model estimating support for government action to mitigate climate change (Y) from negative emotions regarding climate change (X) would be generated using the command

```
regression/statistics defaults ci/dep=govact/method=enter negemot.
```

In SAS, the command is

```
proc reg data=glbwarm;model govact=negemot/stb clb;run;
```

The resulting SPSS output can be found in Figure 2.3. The regression intercept and regression coefficient can be found under the heading "Un-

Model Summary

Model	R	R Square	Adjusted R Square	Std. Error of the Estimate
1	.578[a]	.334	.333	1.11109

a. Predictors: (Constant), NEGEMOT: Negative emotions about climate change

ANOVA[b]

Model		Sum of Squares	df	Mean Square	F	Sig.
1	Regression	502.869	1	502.869	407.336	.000[a]
	Residual	1003.673	813	1.235		
	Total	1506.542	814			

a. Predictors: (Constant), NEGEMOT: Negative emotions about climate change
b. Dependent Variable: GOVACT: Support for government action

Coefficients[a]

Model		Unstandardized Coefficients		Standardized Coefficients	t	Sig.	95.0% Confidence Interval for B	
		B	Std. Error	Beta			Lower Bound	Upper Bound
1	(Constant)	2.757	.099		27.948	.000	2.564	2.951
	NEGEMOT: Negative emotions about climate change	.514	.025	.578	20.183	.000	.464	.564

a. Dependent Variable: GOVACT: Support for government action

FIGURE 2.3. SPSS output from a simple regression analysis estimating support for government action to mitigate climate change from negative emotions about climate change.

standardized Coefficients: B" in the model coefficients table. As can be seen, $i_1 = 2.757$ and $b = 0.514$; thus, the best fitting OLS regression model is

$$\hat{Y}_j = 2.757 + 0.514X_j \qquad (2.4)$$

As discussed earlier, these two values of i_1 and b are not chosen willy-nilly but, rather, are the pair of values that make $SS_{residual}$ as small as it can possibly be. Observe in Figure 2.3 that $SS_{residual} = 1003.673$. No two values of i_1 and b would produce a smaller residual sum of squares; thus, no model of the form in equation 2.1 would fit the data better than this one, at least not using the least squares criterion as the measure of best fit.

Using equation 2.4, an estimate for each person's support for government action ($\hat{Y}$) can be generated given information about that person's negative emotions about climate change (X). Table 2.1 provides estimates for the first five and last five cases in the data file. For instance, the model generates $\hat{Y} = 2.757 + 0.514(4.670) = 5.159$ (the fourth column in Table 2.1) as the estimate for the first case's support for government action given her measurement of 4.67 on the negative emotions variable (the second column of the table). Her actual support for government action, Y, is 3.600 (the third column). Therefore, this case's residual is $e = 3.600 - 5.159 = -1.559$ (the fifth column). The model *overestimates* her support by 1.559 units.

The simple regression equation can be represented visually in the form of a line on a two-dimensional X, Y plane. In Figure 2.4, the regression line has been superimposed on a scatterplot of the data. Using this visual

TABLE 2.1. Generating Estimated Y and Other Components from the Regression Model

j	X_j	Y_j	$\hat{Y}_j$	$Y_j - \hat{Y}_j$	$(Y_j - \hat{Y}_j)^2$	$(\hat{Y}_j - \bar{Y})^2$	$(Y_j - \bar{Y})^2$
1	4.670	3.600	5.159	−1.559	2.430	0.327	0.974
2	2.330	5.000	3.956	1.044	1.091	0.399	0.171
3	3.670	6.600	4.645	1.955	3.824	0.003	4.052
4	5.000	1.000	5.329	−4.329	18.736	0.550	12.867
5	1.670	4.000	3.616	0.384	0.147	0.943	0.345
.	.	.	.	.	.	.	.
.	.	.	.	.	.	.	.
.	.	.	.	.	.	.	.
811	5.000	3.200	5.329	−2.129	4.531	0.550	1.924
812	1.000	3.400	3.272	0.128	0.016	1.730	1.409
813	1.670	1.600	3.616	−2.016	4.065	0.943	8.922
814	3.330	5.400	4.470	0.930	0.865	0.014	0.661
815	6.000	5.400	5.843	−0.443	0.196	1.577	0.661

$$SS_{residual} = \sum_{j=1}^{n} \left(Y_j - \hat{Y}_j\right)^2 = 1003.673$$
$$SS_{regression} = \sum_{j=1}^{n} \left(\hat{Y}_j - \bar{Y}_j\right)^2 = 502.869$$
$$SS_{total} = \sum_{j=1}^{n} \left(Y_j - \bar{Y}_j\right)^2 = 1506.542$$

representation, an approximation of $\hat{Y}$ can be obtained by choosing a value on the X-axis, projecting up vertically until you intersect the line, and then projecting horizontally to the Y-axis. The point at which the horizontal projection touches the Y-axis is $\hat{Y}$ from the regression model. For example, as can be seen in Figure 2.4, when $X = 3.000$, the model yields $\hat{Y}$ somewhere between 4.000 and 4.500. From the model in its precise mathematical form (equation 2.4), the estimate for $X = 3.000$ is $\hat{Y} = 4.299$.

Figure 2.4 also provides a visual representation of residuals. A case's residual is the vertical distance between its point on the scatterplot and the regression line. So cases that are above the regression line have positive residuals. For these cases, their actual values of Y are higher than what the regression model estimates. That is, the model underestimates their values of Y. In contrast, cases below the regression line have negative residuals. These cases are overestimated by the regression model. Their actual Y values are less than what the regression model estimates.

Interpretation of the Constant and Regression Coefficient

The simple linear regression model links X to Y mathematically by expressing the association between X and Y in the form of an equation for a line.

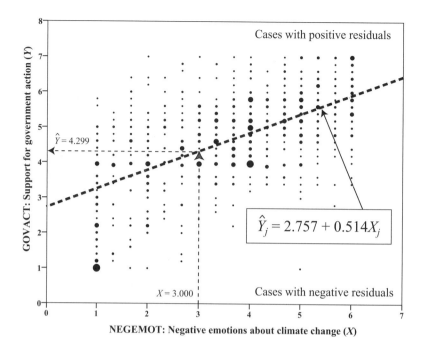

FIGURE 2.4. A visual representation of the least squares regression equation (the dotted line) estimating support for government action (Y) from negative emotions about climate change (X)

Thinking back to secondary school, recall that the equation for a line has two components: the *slope*, and the *Y-intercept*. In the linear regression equation, the regression coefficient corresponds to the slope of the line, and for this reason, the regression coefficient is sometimes called the *regression slope*. It quantifies how much two cases that differ by one unit on X are estimated to differ on Y. More formally, for any value x,

$$b = [\hat{Y}|(X = x)] - [\hat{Y}|(X = x - 1)] \tag{2.5}$$

where the vertical line "|" means "conditioned on," "given," or "when." Thus, equation 2.5 can be read "b equals the estimated value of Y when $X = x$ minus the estimated value of Y when $X = x$ minus one." So applied to the climate change example, two cases that differ by one unit in their negative emotions about climate change are estimated to differ by $b = 0.514$ units in their support for government action.

The sign of b conveys information about the relative difference in Y. If b is positive, the case one unit higher on X is estimated to be b units higher on Y, whereas if b is negative, the case one unit higher on X is estimated to be b units lower on Y. Here, b is positive, meaning the person one unit higher in negative emotions is estimated to be 0.514 units *more* supportive of government action to mitigate global climate change.

The regression constant is conceptually equivalent to the Y-intercept in the equation for a line. It quantifies the estimated value of Y when $X = 0$. In Figure 2.4, the regression constant corresponds to the point at which the regression line crosses the Y-axis. However, this will not be generally true, for where the line crosses the Y-axis will depend on how such a figure is constructed. If the Y-axis is drawn vertically up from the point $X = 0$, then the constant is indeed the Y-intercept, but if the Y-axis begins at some other point on the X scale, the regression line will cross the Y-axis at a location different from the regression constant.

In the climate change model, $i_1 = 2.757$. This is the estimated support for government action for someone who measures zero on the negative emotions scale. Although this has clear mathematical meaning, substantively it makes no sense because the negative emotions scale is bounded between 1 and 6. Often the regression constant has no substantive interpretation, but sometimes it does. It depends on how X is scaled and whether $X = 0$ has any substantive meaning.

It is possible to make i_1 more meaningful by *mean-centering* X prior to estimating the regression model. To mean-center a variable, the sample mean is subtracted from all measurements of that variable in the data:

$$X'_j = X_j - \overline{X} \qquad\qquad (2.6)$$

where X'_j is mean-centered X_j. Estimating Y from not X but, instead, X' produces a model with exactly the same fit as defined by $SS_{residual}$ and other measures discussed below. Furthermore, b will be exactly the same as when X is used as the predictor of Y. However, the regression constant will change to reflect the rescaling of X. The constant is still interpreted as the estimated value of Y when $X' = 0$, but note from equation 2.6 that $X'_j = 0$ when $X_j = \overline{X}$. So i_1 is the estimated value of Y_j when $X_j = \overline{X}$. It is also $\overline{Y}$, for in a simple regression model, the model will always estimate $Y = \overline{Y}$ for a case at the sample mean on X.

Applied to the climate change example, when negative emotions about climate change is mean-centered prior to estimation of equation 2.1, the resulting regression model is $\hat{Y}_j = 4.587 + 0.514X'_j$. As promised, b is unaffected by mean centering of X. The intercept tells us that the estimated support for government action is $i_1 = \overline{Y} = 4.587$, for someone who is average in his or her negative emotional reactions to climate change.

Measures of Model Fit

The least squares regression equation minimizes $SS_{residual}$ and is therefore the best fitting model by the least squares criterion. The size of $SS_{residual}$ can be thought of as a measure of *lack* of fit, for larger values are associated with a greater discrepancy betweeen Y and $\hat{Y}$. However, its absolute size has no meaning, for it is determined by sample size as well as the scale of measurement of Y. All else being equal, as n increases, so too does $SS_{residual}$. And $SS_{residual}$ is not comparable across models of different outcome variables even if the predictor variable is the same.

There are three measures of fit based on $SS_{residual}$ that deal with one or both of these problems with $SS_{residual}$ to at least some degree. The first is the *mean squared residual* ($MS_{residual}$), defined most generally for any linear regression model as

$$MS_{residual} = \frac{SS_{residual}}{n - k - 1} \tag{2.7}$$

where k is the number of predictor variables in the regression model. In a simple regression model, $k = 1$. The quantity $n - k - 1$ in the denominator of equation 2.7 is also called the *residual degrees of freedom* or $df_{residual}$. The mean squared residual can be thought of as a sample-size corrected residual sum of squares. It is approximately the average squared residual. A value closer to zero represents better fit. As can be seen in Figure 2.3, in the climate change example, $MS_{residual} = 1.235$. Because the least squared criterion results in a minimization of $SS_{residual}$, it follows that least squares also minimizes $MS_{residual}$.

Like $SS_{residual}$, $MS_{residual}$ is a scale-bound measure of fit, in that it depends on the metric of measurement of Y. Furthermore, it lacks interpretability, primarily because it is based on a squared metric (i.e., the squared residuals). An alternative measure of fit is the square root of the mean squared residual, known as the *standard error of estimate*, defined as

$$\text{Standard error of estimate} = \sqrt{MS_{residual}} = \sqrt{\frac{SS_{residual}}{n - k - 1}}$$

The standard error of estimate eliminates the problem of noninterpretability inherent in $MS_{residual}$. It can be interpreted as approximately the average amount by which Y differs from $\hat{Y}$ ignoring sign. It is also approximately equal to the standard deviation of the residuals. In the climate change example, the standard error of estimate is 1.111 (see Figure 2.3). In other words, ignoring sign of the error in estimation, the model's estimate of each person's support for government action ($\hat{Y}$) is, on average, in error by 1.111 units from his or her actual support for government action. Clearly, the smaller the average error, the better the fit of the model to the data. Because the standard error of estimate is just a transformation of $SS_{residual}$, it too is minimized by the least squares criterion.

All of the measures of fit introduced thus far are scale bound. Different metrics of Y will produce different values of $SS_{residual}$, $MS_{residual}$, and the standard error of estimate. A measure of fit which eliminates this problem is R^2. To understand R^2, imagine your goal is to drive your car from Chicago, Illinois to New Orleans, Louisiana, a distance of about 930 miles (1,497 kilometers), in as little time as possible without breaking too many speed laws. Most people would find this to be a long distance to drive, and most people couldn't do it in a day without risk of falling asleep at the wheel and hurting someone. If you could make it to, say, Memphis, that would be a pretty good day of driving. It is about 530 miles (853 kilometers) from Chicago to Memphis. If you drove that far in one day, you would have traveled about 56.9% of the distance from Chicago to New Orleans. In proportion terms, the proportion of the 930 miles you would have driven in that one day is 530/930 = 0.569.

R^2 can be thought of as a measure of the proportion of a desired distance traveled, much like your trip from Chicago to New Orleans cut short with a stop in Memphis, but the distance is measured not between points on a map but between the fit of a particular reference model and a perfectly fitting model. Recall that $SS_{residual}$ is bound between 0 and SS_{total}, where SS_{total} is the sum of the squared differences between Y and $\overline{Y}$. SS_{total} can be thought of as the fit of a simple and very "naive" model in which Y is estimated to be $\overline{Y}$ for every case in the data, as if one entirely ignored the information contained in X that could be used to estimate Y with greater precision than the use of this naive strategy. Whenever there is some linear association between X and Y, however small that association is, $SS_{residual}$ will be smaller than SS_{total}. It has to be, but it won't be smaller than zero.

Considering the naive model as the reference model, R^2 quantifies the distance the best fitting linear regression model has traveled between this naive reference model and a perfectly fitting model. Mathematically,

$$R^2 = \frac{SS_{total} - SS_{residual}}{SS_{total}} = 1 - \frac{SS_{residual}}{SS_{total}} = \frac{SS_{regression}}{SS_{total}} \qquad (2.8)$$

where $SS_{regression}$ is the *regression sum of squares*, defined as $SS_{total} - SS_{residual}$. In the climate change example, $SS_{total} = 1506.542$ and $SS_{residual} = 1003.673$, and so $R^2 = (1506.542 - 1003.673)/(1506.542) = 0.334$, and can be found in Figure 2.3. That is, this model has "traveled" 33.4% of the distance between the fit of the naive model and a perfectly fitting model. Because the least squares regression equation minimizes $SS_{residual}$, and $0 \leq SS_{residual} \leq$

SS_{total}, an examination of equation 2.8 reveals that the least squares criterion therefore maximizes R^2.

R^2 has two other interpretations. Most commonly, it is interpreted as the proportion of the variance in Y explained by the model. In a regression model with a single predictor, R^2 is just the square of Pearson's correlation between X and Y (recall from earlier that $r = 0.578$, meaning $r^2 = 0.334$), which has the same interpretation.[2]

In addition, R^2 can be interpreted as the squared correlation between Y and $\hat{Y}$, something you can easily verify yourself by generating $\hat{Y}$ from the climate change model and then correlating it with Y. This interpretation makes it most clear how R^2 can be construed as a measure of model fit. A good-fitting model should produce a strong correlation between what the model estimates for Y and the actual values of Y across the n cases in the data. If this correlation were small, it would be hard to argue that this model does a good job in accounting for or explaining individual differences in Y.

R^2 is not a scale-bound metric, meaning the fit of two models can be compared using the relative sizes of their R^2 values even when they are models of different outcome variables. In addition, R^2 is mostly independent of sample size. All other things being equal, R^2 will tend to be somewhat larger in smaller samples, but the association between sample size and R^2 rapidly levels off as sample size increases. For all practical purposes, the R^2 for two models based on different sample sizes can be directly compared so long as one sample size is not very small.

The Standardized Regression Model

Thus far, the interpretation of parameters (i_1 and b) of the simple regression model has been couched in *unstandardized* or *raw metric* form. Many regression routines will also produce a version of the model in *standardized* form. The standardized regression model is what results when all variables are first standardized prior to estimation of the model by expressing each measurement in units of standard deviations from the sample mean. When this is done, the resulting model takes the form

$$\hat{Z}_{Y_j} = \tilde{b}Z_{X_j} \qquad (2.9)$$

where Z_Y and Z_X are standardized versions of Y and X, and $\tilde{b}$ is the *standardized regression coefficient* for X. Notice that the standardized regression

---

[2]Because R is constrained to be between 0 and 1, so too is R^2, as a legitimate proportion, constrained to between 0 and 1. It would not be appropriate to report, for example, that $R^2 = 33.4\%$. I recommend avoiding the reporting of R^2 in percentage terms. It is better scientific communication to state that a model explains a certain percentage of the variance in the outcome variable while reporting R^2 as a corresponding proportion.

model appears not to contain a constant. In fact, it does, although the constant in a standardized regression model is always zero, so there is no need to formally include it in equation 2.9.

Although one could formally standardize X and Y prior to estimating the regression model, this typically isn't necessary. Most statistical packages that conduct OLS regression will provide the standardized regression model in a section of output. In the SPSS output in Figure 2.3, for instance, the standardized regression coefficient can be found under a column labeled "Standardized coefficients." Thus, in the climate change model, the standardized regression equation is $\hat{Z}_{Y_j} = 0.578Z_{X_j}$, where Z_Y and Z_X are standardized support for government action and standardized negative emotions, respectively.

The standardized regression model will fit just as well as the unstandardized model as measured by R^2, but it will have a different $SS_{residual}$, $MS_{residual}$, and standard error of estimate because, as discussed earlier, these measures are scale bound, and standardization changes the scale of measurement of Y. The standardized regression coefficient will also be different than the unstandardized regression coefficient as a result of the change in the metric.

The standardized regression coefficient is interpreted as the expected difference in Y, *in standard deviations*, between two cases that differ by *one standard deviation* on X. Thus, two people who differ by one standard deviation in their negative emotions about climate change are estimated to differ by $\tilde{b} = 0.578$ standard deviations in their support for government action. The positive coefficient means that the person with more negative emotions is estimated to have stronger support for government action to mitigate climate change.

In a simple regression model, the standardized regression coefficient is exactly equal to Pearson's correlation between X and Y. It can also be derived from the unstandardized regression coefficient with information about the standard deviations of X and Y:

$$\tilde{b} = b\left(\frac{SD_X}{SD_Y}\right)$$

A brief digression is in order at this point. It is important when reporting the results of an analysis to define the symbols you use unless there is a strong convention, for a failure to do so can invite confusion. Different uses of b and β in regression analysis are an important case in point. There is much inconsistency in the substantive and methodology literature as to how regression coefficients are symbolized in unstandardized versus standardized form. Some use b or B to refer to the unstandardized regression coefficient and β to refer to the standardized regression coefficient.

Others, rather than using β, spell it out by referencing "beta weights" or just talk about the "betas." Some use β to refer to a population regression coefficient, to distinguish it from a sample estimate, others use β as the unstandardized regression weight, and there are still others who use $\hat{\beta}$ to refer to a sample unstandardized regression coefficient and leave the hat off for its corresponding population or "true" value. In this book, I use $\tilde{b}$ for the standardized regression weight.

Ultimately, the symbols we use are for the most part arbitrary. We can use any symbols we want. My point is that you should not assume others will know what symbols you use mean, for your familiar symbols to represent certain concepts may not be understood as representing those concepts by all. The same applies to terms such as "beta coefficient" or other verbalizations of symbols. Best to define your symbols in advance, or otherwise let your reader know what your symbols mean when used in text and tables. This will help others better understand and interpret your work.

Simple Regression with a Dichotomous Predictor

In linear regression analysis, a predictor variable can be either a quantitative dimension (e.g., as in the example thus far) or a dichotomous variable. An example of a dichotomous variable would be whether a person is male or female, or which of two conditions a participant was assigned to in an experiment or clinical trial, such as whether a person in a drug study received the experimental drug or a placebo. No modifications are necessary to the mathematics when using a dichotomous variable as a predictor.

To illustrate, I will use a linear regression analysis to estimate differences between men and women (X) in their support for government action to mitigate climate change (Y). The GLBWARM data file contains a variable (SEX) coding whether the participant is male (coded 1, 51.2% of the participants) or female (coded 0, 48.8%). Calculating the mean support for government action in each sex reveals men are slightly less supportive of government action on average ($\overline{Y}_{male} = 4.450, SD = 1.528$) than are women ($\overline{Y}_{female} = 4.718, SD = 1.165$). Regressing Y on X yields

$$\hat{Y}_j = 4.718 - 0.268X_j$$

as can be seen in the SAS output in Figure 2.5. The regression constant i_1 is still the estimated value of Y when $X = 0$. In this case, females are coded $X = 0$, so $\hat{Y} = 4.718$. This is the estimated support for government action among females, and it corresponds to the sample mean for females: $i_1 = \overline{Y}_{female} = 4.718$. The regression coefficient retains its mathematical

```
                          The REG Procedure
                            Model: MODEL1
                      Dependent Variable: govact

                          Analysis of Variance

                                  Sum of          Mean
   Source              DF        Squares        Square     F Value    Pr > F

   Model                1       14.65205       14.65205       7.98    0.0048
   Error              813     1491.89008        1.83504
   Corrected Total    814     1506.54213


            Root MSE               1.35464     R-Square     0.0097
            Dependent Mean         4.58699     Adj R-Sq     0.0085
            Coeff Var             29.53214


                          Parameter Estimates

                     Parameter      Standard                        Standardized
   Variable    DF     Estimate         Error    t Value   Pr > |t|     Estimate

   Intercept    1      4.71799       0.06634      71.12     <.0001            0
   sex          1     -0.26824       0.09493      -2.83     0.0048     -0.09862

                          Parameter Estimates

            Variable    DF        95% Confidence Limits

            Intercept    1         4.58777        4.84820
            sex          1        -0.45457       -0.08190
```

FIGURE 2.5. SAS output from a simple regression analysis estimating support for government action to mitigate global climate change (Y) from participant sex (X).

interpretation as the estimated difference in Y between two cases that differ by one unit on X, with the negative sign telling us that the case higher on X is estimated to be lower on Y. This is consistent with the means reported earlier. Males, who are coded one unit higher on X relative to females, are lower on average in the support for government action. Furthermore, observe that the difference between the means is exactly 0.268 units on the scale (i.e., $\overline{Y}_{male} - \overline{Y}_{female} = 4.450 - 4.718 = -0.268$). So the regression coefficient quantifies the difference between the group means.

In simple regression with a dichotomous predictor, the model will generate estimates for Y that correspond to the means of the two groups. It was demonstrated earlier that for females, $X = 0$ and so the model generates $\hat{Y} = 4.718 - 0.268(0) = 4.718 = \overline{Y}_{female}$. For males, $X = 1$ and the model generates $\hat{Y} = 4.718 - 0.268(1) = 4.450 = \overline{Y}_{male}$.

Although the model will always generate the group means, the regression coefficient and regression intercept will depend on how the two groups are coded. For instance, suppose females were coded $X = -1$ and males were coded $X = 1$. In that case, the regression model would be $\hat{Y} = 4.584 - 0.134X$. Now $b = -0.134$ is one-half of the difference between those means and i_1 is the unweighted mean of the means: $(\overline{Y}_{male} + \overline{Y}_{female})/2$. But the model still reproduces the group means. For females, $\hat{Y} = 4.584 - 0.134(-1) = 4.718$, and for males, $\hat{Y} = 4.584 - 0.134(1) = 4.450$.

When X is a dichotomous variable, the regression coefficient will always be some function of the difference between the values of the codes used to code groups. Specifically, if the larger numerical code is X_L and the smaller numerical code is X_S,

$$b = \frac{\overline{Y}_{X_L} - \overline{Y}_{X_S}}{X_L - X_S}$$

where $\overline{Y}_{X_L}$ and $\overline{Y}_{X_S}$ are the group means for the two groups coded $X = X_L$ and $X = X_S$, respectively. For instance, if the two groups differ by two units on X, then b is one-half of the difference between the group means. If they differ by three units on X, then b is one-third of the mean difference, and so forth. I recommend getting in the habit of always coding a dichotomous variable such that the two groups differ by only one unit, so that b can be interpreted as the difference between the group means.

The choice as to how to code the two groups has no consequence for model fit, however. The fit of the model as measured by any of the measures described earlier will be the same. For any coding made in this example, as well as choices not illustrated, $R^2 = 0.010$, $SS_{residual} = 1491.890$, $MS_{residual} = 1.835$, and the standard error of estimate is 1.355.

A Caution about the Standardized Regression Model. The standardized regression model estimating support for government action from sex is

$$\hat{Z}_{Y_j} = -0.099 Z_{X_j}$$

Thus, $i_1 = 0$ and $\tilde{b} = -0.099$. Although $\tilde{b}$ can be interpreted in mathematical terms as the estimated difference in Y, in standard deviations, between two cases that differ by one standard deviation on X, this is not meaningful substantively. In the original metric of X, males and females differ by one unit. They do *not* differ by one standard deviation. In fact, the number of standard deviations by which two groups differ on a dichotomous variable coding groups will depend on the distribution of the cases across the two groups. In these data, 48.8% of the sample is female ($X = 0$) and 51.2% is male ($X = 1$). The standard deviation of X is 0.499. So females and males differ by just over two standard deviations on X. That means that $\tilde{b}$ is just about one-half of the mean difference between males and females in standard deviation units of Y.

If this were always the case, it would be easy enough to remember that we should just multiply $\tilde{b}$ by about two in order to interpret it as a mean difference in standard deviations of Y. However, the number of standard deviations the groups differ on X is a function of the distribution of the cases across the two groups. In this example, it is just about a 50:50 male–female split, in which case the groups differ by about 2 standard deviations on X, and so $\tilde{b}$ is about half of the mean difference in Y in standard deviations. If the groups were split, say, 40:60, they would differ by about 2.04 standard deviations on X, and $\tilde{b}$ would be less than half of the mean difference in standardized Y. If they were split 30:70, they would differ by about 2.17 standard deviations, and $\tilde{b}$ would be even smaller. At a 20:80 split, the groups differ by 2.5 standard deviations on X, and $\tilde{b}$ smaller still. The more X favors one group, the more standard deviations the groups differ on X, and the smaller $\tilde{b}$ will be.

My point is that when a predictor variable is dichotomous, our substantive interest naturally focuses on differences between the groups on Y. If groups are coded such that they differ by one unit on X, then b is always the mean difference between the groups on Y. Not so for $\tilde{b}$. The standardized regression coefficient is a function of both the mean difference and the distribution of the cases across the groups. This is an undesirable property of $\tilde{b}$ when X is dichotomous. *I recommend that the standardized regression coefficient for a dichotomous predictor variable not be interpreted or reported.*

If you desire an index of mean difference in standard deviation units, I recommend standardizing Y but not X and then interpreting the *unstandardized* regression coefficient in a model estimating Z_Y from X. In such a model, b is a *partially* standardized regression coefficient. In this example, doing so yields

$$\hat{Z}_{Y_j} = 0.096 - 0.197X_j$$

The constant i_1 is the mean standardized Y for females, and b is the mean difference between males and females in standard deviations of Y. The negative sign for b means males are lower than females, on average, in their support for government action. The partially standardized regression coefficient will not depend on the distribution of the cases into the two groups defined by X.

2.3 Statistical Inference

Whether expressed in the form of Pearson's $r = 0.578$ (equivalent to the standardized regression coefficient $\tilde{b}$) or the unstandardized regression coefficient $b = 0.514$, there is a positive association between negative emotions people reported feeling about climate change and their support for government action. And females expressed greater support for government action on average than did males ($b = -0.268$ when females are coded

$X = 0$, males $X = 1$). But both of these claims are just *descriptions* of the association between X and Y based on the data available and so are sample specific. If this study were repeated using a different set of 815 study participants obtained through the same sampling procedure, most certainly the simple regression coefficient for negative emotions would not be $b = 0.514$. It might be $b = 0.412$, or $b = 0.644$, or even $b = -0.143$. Nor would the difference in support for government action between men and women be exactly 0.268 units if the study were based on a different sample. Each sample will yield a different estimate of the association between X and Y. In technical terms, we say that any estimator of the association between two variables has *sampling variance*. There is variation from sample to sample in most any measure of association between two variables one can conceive.

Consider the following thought experiment and illustration. Imagine that the 815 people in the climate change data represent a census of the population of planet Earth. There are no other people on the planet, so to conceive of a different sample of 815 people that could have been in this study is just pointless. In that case, any measure of association we use to describe the relationship between two variables X and Y has no sampling variance. Let's call that measure of association its "true value." We don't have to estimate the true value, because it would be known but of course, it would depend on the index of association chosen and how the variables are measured. In the case of the unstandardized regression weight estimating support for government action from negative emotions about climate change, we could say $_T b = 0.514$, where the T prescript represents "true value." Alternatively, in the case of Pearson's r, we could say $_T r = 0.578$ or, equivalently in terms of the standardized regression coefficient, $_T \tilde{b} = 0.578$. For the difference between men and women in their support for government action, we could say $_T b = -0.268$.

Now suppose that this was your study, but rather than a census, you had only 50 people from the 815, and you obtained these 50 by randomly sampling from the population of 815 inhabitants of Earth. This sampling process wouldn't change the true values of the association, but it would certainly change your estimates of the association. To illustrate this, try running the code below in SPSS with the GLBWARM data file open.

```
compute u=rv.uniform(0,1).
sort cases by u.
temporary.
select if ($casenum < 51).
regression/dep=govact/method=enter negemot.
```

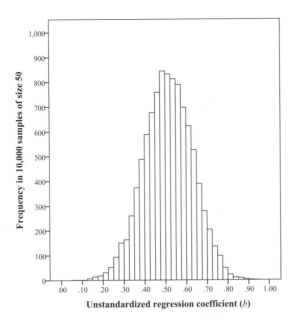

FIGURE 2.6. A histogram of 10,000 estimates of $_T b$.

If you prefer SAS, try

```
data glbwarm;set glbwarm;u=uniform(0);run;
proc sort data=glbwarm;by u;run;
proc reg data = glbwarm (OBS = 50);model govact = negemot;run;
```

This code randomly selects 50 people from the 815 in the data and generates estimates of the association between negative emotions and support for government action using OLS regression (with government support as the outcome variable). When I did this in SPSS, I got $b = 0.559, r = \tilde{b} = 0.568$. When I did it again, I got $b = 0.608, r = \tilde{b} = 0.603$. And yet again, $b = 0.403, r = \tilde{b} = 0.465$.

Figure 2.6 depicts a histogram of values of b from 10,000 repetitions of this procedure. Notice that the estimates vary considerably, from a low of about 0.10 to a high of 0.95, with most of the estimates somewhere between 0.20 and 0.80. This is sampling variance. We can even quantify that sample variance using some kind of statistic, such as the standard deviation of the 10,000 estimates, which is about 0.117 in this example. In statistical theory, this estimate of the sampling variance of b is called the *standard error* of b, although it would be estimated differently in practice.

The original data collection effort can be thought of as the result of a single trial from a similar sampling process but undertaken on a larger scale.

The 815 people who participated in this study represent a single subset of people—a *sample*—from a much larger collection of people who could have been in the study but, in part by the luck of the draw, simply were not. That is, these 815 are analogous to the 50 selected from the 815 in the thought experiment described earlier. This "larger collection" is sometimes called the *population*, although it is not always clear just what this population is defined as in a particular study, because investigators often don't precisely spell out or even know what population they are sampling. In the previous example, the 815 sole inhabitants of Earth were the population. But in the actual study, the population is much, much larger, presumably. That population might be all people living in the United States, all people willing to participate in online surveys, or something of the sort. Regardless, if this entire population provided data in this study (whatever that population is), then $_Tb$, $_Tr$, $_T\tilde{b}$, or any other conceivable measure of association could be known exactly. No estimation would be needed. But given that data analysis is generally undertaken only on a subset of the population, all that can be done is to estimate the true value for a specific measure of association using the data available. We hope that the estimate is close to the true value, but we can never know for certain how close it is because we have observed only a single sample-specific estimate of the true value based on the data available. In any case, a different random sample of 815 would have produced a different estimate of $_Tb$, because b is subject to sampling variance whenever the sample size is smaller than the population size.

Statistical inference in regression analysis focuses on either testing a hypothesis about $_Tb$ or generating an interval estimate that demarcates the lower and upper boundaries between which $_Tb$ is likely to reside with a certain degree of confidence—a *confidence interval*. We have an arsenal of statistical theory and method that can be brought into service to help with the inference.

Testing a Null Hypothesis for Inference

When testing a null hypothesis, an assumption is made about the true value of the measure of association and then an inference is made about the plausibility of that assumption given the data available. The assumption is called the *null hypothesis* and it is statistically pitted against the *alternative hypothesis*, which is the logical complement of the null hypothesis. In regression, the null hypothesis most typically tested when estimating Y from X using linear regression is that X and Y are linearly uncorrelated in the population. In other words, if X is unrelated to Y, then X should be given no weight in the derivation of the estimate of Y. For the unstandardized regression weight, for instance, this corresponds to a null hypothesis that $_Tb = 0$ and an alternative hypothesis that $_Tb \neq 0$. Symbolically,

$$H_0: \quad _Tb = 0$$
$$H_a: \quad _Tb \neq 0$$

To decide between the null hypothesis (or what some call a *nil hypothesis* when the null equals zero) and the alternative hypothesis, it is necessary to derive the probability of the obtained association between X and Y or something more extreme from the null hypothesis in either direction (for a *two-tailed* or *nondirectional* test) assuming the null hypothesis is true. This probability is the *p-value* for the obtained result. If the *p*-value is no larger than the level of significance used for the test (typically, the level of significance or *α-level* used is 0.05), then the null hypothesis is rejected in favor of the alternative hypothesis. Rejection of the null implies that there is some association between X and Y in the population, with the direction of the association in the population implied by the direction of the obtained estimate of the association in the sample.

The *p*-value is derived by converting the obtained association to deviation from the null hypothesis in standard error units and then calculating the probability of such a departure from the null using the $t(df_{residual})$ distribution, where $df_{residual}$ is the residual degrees of freedom for the regression model. The standard error, calculated by any OLS regression program, quantifies how much estimates of the association between X and Y tend to deviate from the true value. Along with the standard error for the measure of association, most all regression programs also calculate the ratio of the estimate to its standard error and a *p*-value for testing the null hypothesis of no association.

The SPSS output in Figure 2.3 provides a test of the null hypothesis that $_Tb = 0$. In this sample of 815 participants, $b = 0.514$, with an estimated standard error (se_b) of 0.025 (provided under the column heading "Std Error" in the SPSS output). Dividing b by its standard error yields

$$t(813) = \frac{b}{se_b} = \frac{0.514}{0.025} = 20.560$$

where 813 is the $df_{residual}$ for the model. SPSS provides the t statistic more precisely as $t = 20.183$. This result has a *p*-value that is so tiny it appears to be zero in the output (under the heading "Sig").[3] Of course, the *p*-value is

[3]Throughout this book, there will be small discrepancies between the computations done in the text by hand, which are completed to only the third decimal place, with output found in various computer outputs or tables based on computer outputs. Computer-generated outputs are based on computations done to much greater precision—at least the eighth decimal place and typically more.

not zero, and it should not be interpreted or reported as such. With three decimals of resolution in the output, we know $p < .0005$, which is less than $\alpha = 0.05$ (or most any other α-level one could imagine actually using). The null hypothesis can be rejected in favor of the alternative, meaning we can conclude that $_Tb \neq 0$. The obtained result of $b = 0.514$ is too discrepant from zero to attribute it to the vagaries of random sampling error or "chance." More specifically, having ruled out zero and with b in the positive direction, we can conclude $_Tb > 0$. In substantive terms, there is evidence that in the population, there is a positive association between negative emotions about climate change and support for government action. People who feel negative emotions to a greater extent are relatively more supportive of such actions.

This null hypothesis testing procedure can also be applied to test the null hypothesis that $_Tr$ or $_T\tilde{b}$ is equal to zero. However, doing so is not necessary. Rejection of the null hypothesis that $_Tb = 0$ also implies that $_Tr$ and $_T\tilde{b}$ are also zero, because the mathematics of the tests are identical. They will produce the same decision as to whether the population association is zero or not.

It is possible to test a null hypothesis that the association between X and Y is some value other than zero, but rarely is this done in practice. Typically our theories and beliefs about the phenomena under investigation are not so sophisticated that they give rise to sensible predictions about the absolute size of an association. Instead, they usually are only precise enough to be able to predict the direction of the association. Thus, ruling out zero is important, using a null hypothesis test or some other procedure, because doing so allows an investigator to make a claim about the direction of the association in the population (see, e.g., Cortina & Dunlap, 1997; O'Keefe, 2011).

Interval Estimation for Inference

A null hypothesis test allows one to determine whether the population association between X and Y is equal to the null hypothesized value. Rejection of the null leads to the conclusion that it is either larger or smaller (depending on the direction of the obtained association) than the null hypothesized value. An alternative approach that accomplishes this same objective while providing a bit more information is *interval estimation*, also known as the construction of a *confidence interval* for the population association. There is much debate in the literature as to the relative merits and disadvantages of null hypothesis testing and confidence intervals. I will not take a stand on this debate in this book and instead refer you to Cortina and Dunlap (1997) for a good discussion.

As illustrated earlier, there is sample-to-sample variation in b (or r, or $\tilde{b}$). In any single sample, b is our best guess as to the value of $_Tb$ and is called a *point estimate* of $_Tb$. If the sample is large enough and the sampling process mimics something akin to random sampling from the population, we can be pretty confident that b will be near $_Tb$. The standard error for b gives us information as to just how close point estimates are likely to deviate from $_Tb$ on average given the sample size used. Yet b almost certainly is not equal to $_Tb$. A confidence interval acknowledges this uncertainty as a range in which $_Tb$ is likely to reside with a specified degree of confidence, while also providing more information about $_Tb$ than a hypothesis test yields.

Construction of a confidence interval for $_Tb$ requires only one additional bit of information not provided by an OLS regression routine, although a good OLS program will provide a confidence interval for b if requested, so hand computation is rarely required. What is needed is $t_{c\%}$, the value of t that cuts off the upper $(100 - c)/2\%$ of the $t(df_{residual})$ distribution from the rest of the distribution, where c is the confidence level desired. For instance, for a 95% confidence interval, we need the value of t that cuts off the upper 2.5% of the $t(df_{residual})$ distribution from the rest. These values are available in any table of critical values of t found in most all introductory statistics books (as well as more advanced ones). Typically, people report 95% confidence intervals, and unless the sample size is fairly small, $t_{c\%}$ is always close to 2, so many people just use 2 for $t_{c\%}$. With $t_{c\%}$ derived, a $c\%$ confidence interval for $_Tb$ is calculated as

$$b - t_{c\%}se_b \leq {}_Tb \leq b + t_{c\%}se_b \qquad (2.10)$$

In the climate change example, $t_{c\%}$ for $df_{residual} = 815$ is 1.962, and so

$$0.514 - 1.962(0.025) \leq {}_Tb \leq 0.514 + 1.962(0.025)$$

That is, we can be 95% confident that $_Tb$ is somewhere between 0.465 and 0.563. The SPSS output in Figure 2.3 provides the confidence interval with slightly higher accuracy than these hand computations: $0.464 \leq {}_Tb \leq 0.564$. In other words, we can be pretty sure that the association between negative emotions about climate change and support for government action is positive, just as we learned from the null hypothesis test. A confidence interval can be constructed for $_Tr$ (and, by extension, $_T\tilde{b}$), but the procedure for doing so is a bit more complicated. See Cohen, Cohen, West, and Aiken (2003) or Hayes (2005) for guidance.

Process Inference

The previous discussion couches the inferential goal of data analysis in terms of populations. That is, sampling variation, typically described in statistical methods books as the result of the random sampling process, adds a discrepancy between the association between two variables observed in a sample and the true association in the population. This "true" association is conceptualized as the association that would have been observed if all members of the population to which an inference is desired provided data to the investigator. Equivalently, it is conceptualized as the association that would have been observed if the sample was infinite in size, or at least as large as the population itself. Regardless, sample-to-sample variation that results when using sample sizes smaller than the size of the population is conceptualized as being due to the random sampling process.

Given that the vast majority of researchers do not randomly sample from specified populations when recruiting research participants, some have questioned the value of the population model of inference and advocated alternative conceptualizations and statistical techniques. This is not the place to go into this large and interesting literature (see, e.g., Bear, 1995; Berger, 2000; Edgington, 1964, 1978, 1995; Frick, 1998; Kennedy, 1995; Ludbrook & Dudley, 1998; Lunneborg, 2000; May, Masson, & Hunter, 1989; May & Hunter, 1993; Mook, 1987; Oja, 1987; Still & White, 1981; ter Braak, 1992). Suffice it to say that in my experience, most researchers appreciate that rarely is population inference the goal, although it is sometimes. Rather, most frequently researchers are interested in making inferences about the *processes at work generating the pattern of association observed* rather than what the association would be if all members of some vague and ill-defined population participated in the study.

These processes at work can be expressed in terms of true values or parameters, such as $_Tb$ or $_T\tilde{b}$, but these symbols mean something different under a process model of inference. The true regression coefficient in process inference terms can be thought of as a representation of the mathematical weight given to the input X in the process that generates the output Y. In the same way that a quality control expert observes only some of the product coming off a production line, a researcher is privy to only a subset of the outputs the process generates (i.e., outputs from the process at work among those participants who were included in the study and measured on the input and output variables). That process can be represented in mathematical form as the "true" model

$$Y_j = {}_Ti_1 + {}_TbX_j + \epsilon_j$$

where $_\tau b$ is the weight for X_j in the process and ϵ_j is a weighted sum of all other unmeasured inputs to the process for case j that yields output Y_j. An OLS regression model estimating a set of outputs Y from a set of inputs X results in estimates of $_\tau i_1$, $_\tau b$, and ϵ_j in the form of i_1, b, and e_j, respectively. Importantly, b departs from $_\tau b$ because only a small subset of possible outputs from the process has been observed. We try to infer $_\tau b$ from what is available to us as researchers. We don't need to assume what is available represents a random sample from some population of outputs. Indeed, if you think of the process as a production line, there is no defined population to make an inference about, as the process will generate outputs as long as there are inputs given to it. Instead, the inference is about the process at work linking inputs to outputs—the gears of a *data generating machine*.

Consider the null hypothesis that $_\tau b = 0$. Such a hypothesis, if true, is akin to saying that the psychological, biological, or cognitive process that gives rise to individual beliefs about what government should do about climate change (output Y) does not use negative emotional responses to the crisis (X) as an input. Alternatively, the null stipulates that these emotional reactions receive no weight (hence, $_\tau b = 0$) in the mental calculus generating responses to questions about beliefs about government action. If this were true, then we'd expect to see an association between X and Y in the sample, using b as the measure of association, that is no larger than what a *random* process would tend to generate, such as randomly assigning values of Y_j to values of X_j. But if the obtained value of b is larger than what a random process would tend to produce, this leads to the conclusion that there is some systematic process linking X to Y (i.e., negative emotions or something confounded with such emotions is being used as an input to the mental calculus). In other words, $_\tau b \neq 0$.

Note that these process inferences do not allow the kind of population generalizations that random sampling affords. Rather, such inferences are specific to the process generating the observed data and thus are sample-specific. But this is perfectly acceptable to most scientists, for population inference is not often the objective. Being able to establish that a random process is not at work producing the association opens the door to other more interesting explanations that probably motivated the study in the first place. In this specific example, however, if one is willing to accept that the sampling method used to recruit participants to fill out the online survey yielded a fairly representative sample of the target population (residents of the United States), generalization can be made about both process and population.

2.4 Assumptions for Interpretation and Statistical Inference

We make assumptions all the time when we conduct research, ranging from the epistemological (e.g., "There is order in the world that can be discerned through the methods of science") to the practical (e.g., "The people who respond to my surveys are not lying to me") to the existential (e.g., "This research I am spending so much time doing is worth the effort and people actually care about what I find"). OLS regression is a very handy tool to have in your statistical toolbox. Its utility as a "general data analytic system," as Cohen (1968) described it, will be apparent in the next chapter and throughout this book. But it is a human invention that isn't perfect, it can lead you astray if used indiscriminately, and it is founded on some assumptions that aren't always realistic or likely to be met in the circumstances in which the method is applied. This is true of any statistical procedure you have ever employed or will employ in the future. These assumptions are worth understanding, but they are abstract and can be confusing at first, and they are hard to do justice to in just a few paragraphs. A more thorough discussion of the assumptions of OLS regression than I provide here can be found in a short and easy-to-read monograph by Berry (1993).

With the exception of the assumption of linearity described first, the assumptions of OLS regression primarily pertain to the errors in estimation that result when the least squares regression equation is used to produce estimates of Y. Whether these assumptions are satisfied can influence the *validity* or *power* of hypothesis tests for measures of association and the width of confidence intervals and their likelihood of including the true value. A test is *valid* in a particular circumstance if, under that circumstance, the probability of rejecting a null hypothesis is no higher than the level of significance chosen for the test. Invalid tests reject true null hypotheses more frequently than desired, and this is not good. The *power* of a test refers to the probability of it correctly rejecting a false null hypothesis. We want power to be high, and an assumption violation that reduces power is not desirable either.

Before introducing these assumptions, I will make my perspective clear. Because assumption violations can have some adverse effects on inference sometimes, we should be mindful of the assumptions OLS regression makes. At the same time, I do not believe you should lose too much sleep over the potential that you have violated one or more of those assumptions. Most likely you have, even if statistical tests of the assumptions you might employ say otherwise. Statistical models are tools we use to help us understand our data, and they can give us insights that are only approximations of reality. The question is not whether we have violated an assumption, but how much doing so is likely to lead us astray when we interpret our results and the inferences we make from them. OLS regression is widely used by researchers because it is fairly easy to understand and describe, widely implemented in software that is readily available, and tends to do a good job approximating reality much of the time when used thoughtfully. Those advantages of OLS regression far outweigh some of the costs of abandoning it for other, perhaps better but much more complicated and less well-understood methods. To be sure, be respectful of the complexities and properties of your data and do your best to analyze them with methods best suited, but don't obsess over every minor assumption violation.

Linearity

When using OLS regression to model some outcome variable of interest Y from some predictor variable X, you must be willing to assume that the relationship between X and Y is *linear* in nature, or at least approximately so. After all, linear regression is based closely on a measure of linear association—Pearson's r. To understand what is meant by linear association, consider the interpretation of the regression coefficient. The regression coefficient for X generated by optimizing the fit of the model using the least squares criterion quantifies how much two cases that differ by one unit on X are estimated to differ on Y. This interpretation is not conditioned on a specific value of X. In other words, regardless of which value of X you choose, a case with $X = x + 1$ is estimated to differ by b units on Y relative to a case with $X = x$. This assumption would be violated if, *in reality*, the difference in Y between two cases that differ by a unit on X depends on X. For example, perhaps cases with $X = 2$ are, on average, 3 units higher on Y than cases with $X = 1$, whereas cases with $X = 3$ are 2 units higher on average than cases with $X = 2$. This would be a violation of the assumption of linearity. There are many nonlinear relationships, such as exponential, quadratic, logarithmic, and so forth. Nonlinear relationships typically appear as curves when Y is plotted as a function of X, although other forms of nonlinearity are possible.

The linearity assumption is important because if it is violated, this jeopardizes the meaningfulness of the interpretation of the regression coefficient (e.g., Darlington, 1990). If in reality, the difference in Y between cases differing by a unit on X depends on X, then b isn't an inadequate description across the range of X of how differences in X map onto differences in Y. Of course, we do not know reality. If we did, we wouldn't need to build a model and make inferences using such a model. All we can do is use our data to try to model what that reality looks like. Fortunately, we can also use our data to test whether the assumption of linearity is plausible given the data available. In addition, it is possible to model nonlinear relationships using OLS regression. For details on testing and modeling nonlinear relationships with OLS regression, see Cohen et al. (2003), Darlington (1990), Fox (1991), and various other books on linear regression analysis.

Normality

The assumption of *normality* states that the errors in estimation of outcome variable Y, conditioned on $\hat{Y}$, are normally distributed.[4] Properties of the normal distribution are described in any good introductory statistics book so I will not discuss them here. Suffice it to say that this assumption is one of the least important in linear regression analysis. Simulation research suggests that only the most severe violations of the normality assumption substantially affect the validity of statistical inferences from a regression analysis unless the sample size is quite small (e.g., Duncan & Layard, 1973; Edgell & Noon, 1984; Havlicek & Peterson, 1977; Hayes, 1996). However, non-normality can influence sampling variance in some circumstances in such a way that power of hypothesis tests is reduced.

In practice, this assumption is rarely met, strictly speaking, primarily because of the measurement procedures researchers typically use. Often, measurement scales are bounded by zero, such as when a variable is a count of things (e.g., how many good friends a person has, how many phone calls a person made today, etc.). Measurement scales also sometimes produce discrete data, meaning only five or 10 unique values are observed on the measurement scale. An example would be the use of a 7-point scale asking someone to evaluate how much he or she likes a television program, or how shy he or she is. Technically speaking, the normal distribution is a continuous distribution, so no model of such a variable using OLS regression would generate normally distributed errors in estimation. Finally, many if not most things that researchers study and measure are not normally distributed, in spite of claims made in many statistics books about the ubiquity of the normal distribution (cf. Micceri, 1989). When modeling non-normal outcome variables using OLS regression, the errors in estimation also tend not to be normal.

Violations of normality are certain when using OLS regression to analyze outcome variables that are discrete or bounded on the lower or upper end of the measurement scale. For example, OLS regression should not be

[4]Contrary to the beliefs of some, the assumption of normality does not pertain to the distribution of Y itself or to the predictors of Y in the regression model. Regression analysis makes no assumption about the shape of these distributions.

used to model dichotomous outcome variables. Logistic or probit regression is more appropriate. For coarse ordinal scales with only a few measurement categories, some kind of ordinal regression model (e.g., probit or ordinal logit regression) would be preferred to OLS regression, although there is some debate in the literature over just how much damage can be done when modeling coarsely measured but still quantitative outcomes with OLS. Count outcomes are better analyzed with Poisson or negative binomial regression, but again, use of OLS is not uncommon or entirely inappropriate if certain precautions are taken. Long (1997) provides a nice introduction to all of these methods. *Throughout this book, I assume you have contemplated the appropriateness of OLS regression for your problem and have decided you are comfortable and want to forge ahead.*

Homoscedasticity

The assumption of *homoscedasticity* states that the errors in estimation are equally variable conditioned on $\hat{Y}$. When this condition is not met, the errors in estimation are said to be *heteroscedastic*. Heteroscedasticity can not only affect the validity of inference, but it can also reduce statistical power of hypothesis tests and influence the accuracy of confidence intervals for regression coefficients, depending on the form of the heteroscedasticity. Simulation research suggests that mild violations of the homoscedasticity assumption are not too much of a concern (e.g., Hayes, 1996), but the assumption is still worth taking seriously. There are some informal tests of homoscedasticity, such as eyeballing a scatterplot of the residuals as a function of $\hat{Y}$, as well as some formal tests of the null hypothesis that the errors in estimation are homoscedastic. See Breusch and Pagan (1979), Berry (1993), Cohen et al. (2003), Cook and Weisberg (1983), Darlington (1990), Downs and Rocke (1979), Goldfeld and Quandt (1965), and White (1980) for a discussion of some of the conditions that can produce heteroscedasticity and various tests of this assumption.

Heteroscedasticity primarily exerts its effect on inference through its effect on the standard error of regression coefficients. The standard error estimator programmed into most OLS regression routines is based on this assumption. If you have reason to believe the homoscedasticity assumption has been violated, increasing the sample size will not help like it does when the normality assumption is violated (Hayes, 1996; Long & Ervin, 2000). Rather, better to use a heteroscedasticity-consistent standard error estimator. The PROCESS procedure for SPSS and SAS described throughout this book provides an option for the use of one of the estimators known in the literature at HC3. Various alternative standard error estimators are available in SAS and STATA, and Hayes and Cai (2007) provide an SPSS and

SAS tool for OLS regression that implements a variety of them as well. For a concise introduction to and discussion of these standard error estimators, see Hayes and Cai (2007) or Long and Ervin (2000).

Independence

We also assume that the errors in estimation are statistically independent. In the most basic sense, two things are independent if information about one gives no information about the other. If the errors in estimation are independent, this means that for all (i, j) pairs of observations, there is no information contained in the error in estimation for case i that could be used to estimate the error in estimation for case j.

Many processes can result in a violation of independence. For example, subsets of cases may share something that is related to Y, and a failure to account for that thing in the model can result in estimation errors that are nonindependent. Often studies are explicitly and intentionally designed in such a way that subsets of cases do share something that at least might be related to Y. An example would be studies that are based on some kind of cluster sampling procedure. In studies of school-age children, for instance, children are often selected for inclusion in a study based on a random sampling of classrooms in a school or in a district. Ten of the children in the study may be students of Mr. Jones at Tremont Elementary, 10 may be from Mrs. Peterson's class at Barrington Elementary, another 20 may come from Mrs. Stewart's room at Hastings Elementary, and so forth. Suppose the goal is to estimate performance on a statewide achievement test from how many days of school a child has missed. The problem is that achievement of students in a particular class is certainly determined in part by how good the teacher is at his or her job, or how kids are assigned to teachers. If Mr. Jones is an exceptionally gifted teacher relative to other teachers, or teaches the exceptionally gifted children in the school, the model will probably tend to underestimate the performance of relatively more of his students. In other words, the errors in estimation would tend to be positive for students in Mr. Jones's class in greater relative frequency than they would for students from other classes. This would be a violation of the independence assumption.

Another example would be ignoring familial relationships when using participants from the same family. Suppose, for instance, you wanted to examine the relationship between income and marital satisfaction by asking 50 husband–wife dyads to each report how satisfied they are in their marriage and how much money they each make. If you regressed the 100 satisfaction measurements on the 100 income measurements to test the hypothesis that income and satisfaction are positively related, the result would almost certainly be contaminated by violation of the independence assumption. The satisfaction of one person in a marriage is almost certainly predictable from how satisfied his or her partner is. As a result, the signs of the errors in estimation for husband and wife pairs are more likely to be the same than different.

As does heteroscedasticity, nonindependence affects the accuracy of the estimation of the standard error of regression coefficients, as the OLS standard error estimator assumes independence of errors in estimation. Whether the standard error is over- or underestimated will depend on the form of nonindependence, but typically the result is underestimation. If the standard error is underestimated, this means that hypothesis tests will be invalid, and confidence intervals too narrow relative to what they should be when the independence assumption is met.

Criticism regarding the likely existence of at least weak nonindependence can be lodged at virtually any analysis. In the example used throughout this chapter, for instance, one could argue that respondents in the same state or from the same city may be nonindependent due to state- or city-level differences in political ideology, religious culture, or other factors that may influence their beliefs about the role of government in social life. And it is common for researchers to collect data in small batches at a time, such as when sets of participants are brought to a computer lab to respond to some stimuli presented on screens in front of them. Anything about that room that differs over time could influence respondents in the room at a given time the same way, such as distractions in the hallway, temperature of the room, and so forth. Nonindependence can be minimized by design and careful consideration of the factors that influence the variables being measured, but it probably can't be completely eliminated. Additional discussion of some of the causes and consequences of nonindependence, as well as how to properly handle it analytically when it is not ignorable, can be found in such places as Griffin and Gonzales (1995), Grawitch and Munz (2004), Hayes (1996), Kenny and Judd (1986), Kenny, Mannetti, Pierro, Livi, and Kashy (2002), Luke (2004), O'Connor (2004), and Raudenbush and Bryk (2002).

2.5   Chapter Summary

A simple linear regression model is a mathematical representation of the linear association between two variables. Using the OLS criterion, a linear regression routine derives the regression constant and regression coefficient defining the best fitting line linking predictor variable X to outcome variable Y. OLS regression is one of the more useful analytical tools a researcher has available, and it is the foundation of many of the statistical methods that researchers use. Understanding how to estimate and interpret a regression model is important, for regression analysis is the method I will emphasize in my discussion of mediation, moderation, and conditional process analysis in this book. But simple regression is too simple for what we will do in this book. Learning and understanding these methods will require modeling an outcome variable from more than one predictor, and an appreciation of the concepts of partial association and statistical control. These are the topics of the next chapter on multiple linear regression.

3

Multiple Linear Regression

This chapter extends the principles of OLS regression introduced in Chapter 2 to models with more than one predictor variable. When a regression model includes multiple predictors, it is known as a *multiple regression* model. Multiple regression is a convenient statistical approach to examining the plausibility of various alternative explanations for association between two variables such as *spuriousness* and *epiphenomenality*. Using multiple regression, measures of partial association can be calculated that quantify association between two variables while "holding constant," "statistically controlling for," or "partialing out" a third variable or set of variables. Regression models can be represented in visual form with a statistical diagram. This chapter also introduces the *statistical diagram* and compares it with an alternative visual representation of a process called a *conceptual diagram*.

In Chapter 2 I introduced the principles of OLS regression in the context of the simple regression model—a model containing only a single predictor variable. In this chapter, I advance this discussion by describing the extension of these principles to models with multiple predictor variables—the *multiple regression model*. Including more than one predictor in a regression model allows the researcher to simultaneously investigate the role of multiple influences on an outcome variable. An additional and important benefit of the multiple regression model is that it provides various measures of *partial association* that quantify the component of the association between a predictor and an outcome that is unique to that predictor relative to other variables in the model. In so doing, multiple regression allows the investigator to examine the plausibility of various explanations for an association between two variables, such as spuriousness or epiphenomenality. This is useful because such alternative explanations reduce the confidence an investigator can muster as to whether an association can plausibly be interpreted as causal—something an investigator often wishes to claim. Although ruling out certain alternative explanations for an association statistically through multiple regression analysis does not itself justify causal claims, it can help as an investigator builds an argument that the association very well may be causal.

3.1 The Multiple Linear Regression Equation

The simple linear regression model is easily extended to the estimation of an outcome variable using more than one predictor variable. In its most general form, a multiple linear regression model with k predictor variables takes the form

$$Y_j = i_1 + b_1 X_{1j} + b_2 X_{2j} + \ldots + b_k X_{kj} + e_j \qquad (3.1)$$

or, more compactly,

$$Y_j = i_1 + \sum_{i=1}^{k} b_i X_{ij} + e_j \qquad (3.2)$$

where X_{ij} is case j's measurement on predictor variable i, b_i is the regression coefficient for predictor variable X_i, and all other terms are defined as before. Simple regression is a special case of equations 3.1 and 3.2 with $k = 1$. The model can also be expressed in terms of fitted values of Y by eliminating the residual, as such

$$\hat{Y}_j = i_1 + \sum_{i=1}^{k} b_i X_{ij}$$

No modifications are otherwise needed to the mathematics of linear regression analysis to accommodate multiple predictors. Using the ordinary least squares criterion, an OLS regression routine will derive a multiple regression model containing a constant i_1 and k regression coefficients, one for each of the k predictor variables, that minimize $SS_{residual}$, $MS_{residual}$, and the standard error of estimate. It will also maximize R^2, the squared correlation between Y and $\hat{Y}$, which in multiple regression analysis is known as the *squared multiple correlation*. However, there are some important differences between simple and multiple regression in terms of both interpretation of the regression weights and questions the model can be used to answer.

In Chapter 2, individual differences in support for government actions to mitigate climate change were estimated from individual differences in negative emotional responses to climate change. Recall that negative emotions about climate change was operationalized from participants' responses as to how frequently they reported feeling concerned, worried, and alarmed when thinking about climate change. At the same time, participants were asked how frequently they felt "hopeful," "encouraged," and "optimistic" about global climate change using the same 1- to 6-point scale. A measure of *positive emotions about climate change* was constructed as the average response a participant provided to these three items (POSEMOT in the data). Like negative emotions, positive emotions is scaled such that higher scores reflect feeling more positive emotion about the prospect of climate change.[1]

Participants were also asked to rate their political ideology (IDEOLOGY in the data file) on a 1 (very liberal) to 7 (very conservative) scale in response to the question "How would you describe your views on most political matters?" Respondents, as a collective, represented the entire spectrum of political ideology, with 39% responding moderate or middle of the road (a rating of 4) and the remaining participants distributing themselves in about equal number on both sides of this middle point.

To illustrate the estimation and interpretation of a multiple regression model, I simultaneously regress support for government action on negative emotions about climate change, positive emotions about climate change, political ideology, sex, and age in years. With these five variables denoted X_1, X_2, X_3, X_4, and X_5, respectively, the model is

$$Y_j = i_1 + b_1X_{1j} + b_2X_{2j} + b_3X_{3j} + b_4X_{4j} + b_5X_{5j} + e_j \qquad (3.3)$$

In SPSS, this is accomplished using the command

```
regression/statistics defaults ci zpp/dep=govact/method=enter negemot
    posemot ideology sex age.
```

whereas in SAS, the command is

```
proc reg data=glbwarm corr;model govact=negemot posemot ideology sex age
    /stb clb pcorr2 scorr2;run;
```

Output generated by the SPSS command can be found in Figure 3.1. The intercept and regression coefficients are found in the section of the output labeled "Parameter Estimates." The regression constant (in the row labeled "Constant") is 4.064, and the five regression coefficients for negative emotions, positive emotions, ideology, sex, and age are, respectively, $b_1 = 0.441$, $b_2 = -0.027$, $b_3 = -0.218$, $b_4 = -0.010$, and $b_5 = -0.001$. In the form

---

[1]A factor analysis of responses to these six emotions using maximum likelihood factor extraction and an oblique rotation method revealed two distinct factors, with one containing the positive emotion items and the other containing the negative emotion items.

of an equation and expressing the model in terms of the estimated value of Y, the model is

$$\hat{Y}_j = 4.064 + 0.441X_{1j} - 0.027X_{2j} - 0.218X_{3j} - 0.010X_{4j} - 0.001X_{5j} \quad (3.4)$$

Expressed not in unstandardized form as in equation 3.4 but instead in standardized form (by standardizing all variables prior to estimation or by looking at the standardized coefficients in the column of output labeled "Standardized Coefficients"), the model is

$$\hat{Z}_{Y_j} = 0.495Z_{X_{1j}} - 0.027Z_{X_{2j}} - 0.243Z_{X_{3j}} - 0.004Z_{X_{4j}} - 0.016Z_{X_{5j}}$$

By all measures of fit discussed on page 36, this is a better fitting model than the one that included only negative emotions as a predictor. The residual sum of squares is smaller (921.523 versus 1003.673) and therefore so too is both the mean squared error (1.138 versus 1.235) and the standard error of estimate (1.067 versus 1.111).[2] Furthermore, the squared correlation between Y and $\hat{Y}$ has increased from $R^2 = 0.334$ to $R^2 = 0.388$. Whereas the model that included only negative emotions explained 33.4% of the variance in support for government action, considering negative emotions as well as positive emotions, ideology, sex, and age results in 38.8% of the variance explained.

This improvement in fit is neither surprising nor unexpected. Except in only the most unusual circumstance that pretty much never occurs in real research, adding predictor variables to an OLS regression model will increase model fit by these measures. The reason has to do with how OLS regression works. OLS regression exploits information contained in the associations between predictor variables and outcome when it derives the regression coefficients. Any linear association *whatsoever* between outcome and a given predictor variable that is *unique* to that predictor variable (more on this below) will be harvested and used, and that will take the form of a regression weight for that predictor variable that is different from zero. It will do this regardless of how large that association is. So unless the unique association between a predictor and an outcome is exactly zero in the data, which generally does not happen, the result will be a regression coefficient for that predictor variable that departs from zero, and a model that fits slightly better than one that doesn't include it.

Another way of thinking about this is to recognize that all these measures of fit are based in one way or another on $SS_{residual}$. When selecting

---

[2]SAS displays the residual sum of squares and mean squared error in a row labeled "error," and the standard error of estimate is denoted "Root MSE."

Model Summary

Model	R	R Square	Adjusted R Square	Std. Error of the Estimate
1	.623	.388	.385	1.06728

ANOVA

Model		Sum of Squares	df	Mean Square	F	Sig.
1	Regression	585.019	5	117.004	102.717	.000
	Residual	921.523	809	1.139		
	Total	1506.542	814			

Coefficients[a]

Model		Unstandardized Coefficients B	Unstandardized Coefficients Std. Error	Standardized Coefficients Beta	t	Sig.	95.0% Confidence Interval for B Lower Bound	95.0% Confidence Interval for B Upper Bound	Correlations Zero-order	Correlations Partial	Correlations Part
1	(Constant)	4.064	.205		19.791	.000	3.661	4.467			
	NEGEMOT: Negative emotions about climate change.	.441	.026	.495	16.676	.000	.389	.493	.578	.506	.459
	POSEMOT: Positive emotions about climate change	-.027	.028	-.027	-.951	.342	-.082	.028	.043	-.033	-.026
	IDEOLOGY: Political ideology (conservatism)	-.218	.027	-.243	-8.071	.000	-.271	-.165	-.418	-.273	-.222
	SEX: female(0) or male(1)	-.010	.077	-.004	-.131	.896	-.161	.141	-.099	-.005	-.004
	AGE: Respondent age at last birthday	-.001	.002	-.016	-.552	.581	-.006	.003	-.097	-.019	-.015

a. Dependent Variable: GOVACT: Support for government action

FIGURE 3.1. SPSS output from a multiple regression analysis estimating support for government action to mitigate global climate change (Y) from negative (X_1) and positive (X_2) emotions about climate change, political ideology (X_3), sex (X_4), and age (X_5).

63

regression weights, an OLS regression routine will never choose a regression weight for a variable that increases $SS_{residual}$ relative to when that variable is ignored entirely and given a weight of zero in the model. Because $SS_{residual}$ can never go down, adding a variable to a model will improve its fit relative to when it is absent. The exception would be if the unique association between a predictor and the outcome is exactly zero, in which case it will be given a weight of zero and $SS_{residual}$ will be the same whether the variable is in the model or not.

Does this mean that one can make a model fit as well as one wants merely by adding predictor variables until fit is perfect? Indeed, it does. At its extreme, a model that contains one fewer predictor variables than observations will exactly reproduce Y. In such a model, $SS_{residual} = 0$, $MS_{residual} = 0$, $R^2 = 1$, and the standard error of estimate is zero. But maximizing these measures of fit is not usually the goal when we construct a regression model. Instead, we include predictor variables in a model for a reason—because they serve an analytical purpose. We do not just put everything in a model so as to maximize fit. Rather, we let OLS regression derive the best model that maximizes fit using the predictors we include in the model for a reason, and we then interpret the model. Maximizing the fit of that model is merely a means to an end—a means of deriving the best combination of regression coefficients—for it is the regression coefficients or derivatives thereof that we typically care most about when doing the kinds of analyses described in this book.

Interpretation of the Constant and Regression Coefficients

The regression constant in a multiple regression model is $\hat{Y}$ for a case with measurements of 0 on all predictors in the model. In the unstandardized model, $i_1 = 4.064$, but this estimate is rather nonsensical substantively given that 0 is outside the bounds of the scale of measurement of emotions (both positive and negative emotions have a lower bound of one) as well as ideology (which is a 1 to 7 scale) and age. In the standardized model, $i_1 = 0$, meaning that $\hat{Z}_Y = 0$ when all other predictors are set to zero. But when a variable is standardized, zero corresponds to the sample mean, so "when all predictors are set to zero" means when all variables are set to their sample means. Here, the constant does have a sensible interpretation. For someone who is average on all predictor variables, the model estimates that person is average on Y.

Interpretative focus in multiple regression is typically directed squarely toward the regression coefficients in a multiple regression model rather than the constant. To understand their interpretation, consider what the regression model estimates for someone with measurements of three on negative emotions ($X_1 = 3$), four on positive emotions ($X_2 = 4$), two on ideology ($X_3 = 2$), and who is male ($X_4 = 1$) and 30 years old ($X_5 = 30$). According to equation 3.4,

$$\hat{Y} = 4.064 + 0.441(3) - 0.027(4) - 0.218(2) - 0.010(1) - 0.001(30) = 4.803$$

Now consider another male who has the same positive emotions, ideology, and age, yet measures one point higher on the negative emotions scale ($X_1 = 4$). For that person, the model estimates

$$\hat{Y} = 4.064 + 0.441(4) - 0.027(4) - 0.218(2) - 0.010(1) - 0.001(30) = 5.244$$

So these two cases that differ by one unit on X_1 but are the same on X_2, X_3, X_4, and X_5 are estimated to differ by $5.244 - 4.803 = 0.441$ units on Y. But this is b_1. It makes no difference what values X_2, X_3, X_4, and X_5 are set to. If they are held constant, two cases that differ by one unit on X_1 are estimated to differ by b_1 units on Y. This interpretation applies to all partial regression coefficients in a multiple regression model such as this. Most generally, if we let **X** refer to a set of values on all variables except variable X_i, then

$$b_i = [\hat{Y} \mid (X_{is} = x; \mathbf{X})] - [\hat{Y} \mid (X_{it} = x - 1; \mathbf{X})]$$

That is, b_i is the estimated difference in Y between two cases s and t that are the same on all predictor variables except X_i but that differ by one unit on X_i. As in simple regression, the sign of the regression coefficient tells whether the case one unit higher on X_i is estimated to be higher on Y (when b_i is positive) or lower on Y (when b_i is negative).

This interpretation applies to the standardized regression coefficients, but the meaning of "one unit" is different following standardization. If X_i and Y are both standardized (regardless of whether or not the other predictor variables are standardized), $\tilde{b}_i$ is the estimated difference in standard deviations of Y between two cases that differ by one standard deviation on X_i but are equal on all other predictor variables in the model. However, unlike in simple regression, the standardized regression coefficient $\tilde{b}_i$ in a multiple regression model is usually not equivalent to the Pearson correlation between X_i and Y.

The standardized regression coefficients generated automatically by an OLS regression program will be based on a model in which all X_i and Y variables are standardized. However, one can standardize only some of the predictor variables rather than all of them if one chooses. This would have to be done before estimating the model. Once this is done and the model generated, the unstandardized regression coefficients rather than the standardized regression coefficients are interpreted. The unstandardized coefficients will be in standardized form for those predictor variables that were first standardized manually. That is, for standardized X_i, $b_i = \tilde{b}_i$. The coefficients for variables that were not standardized will be in *partially standardized* form (not to be confused with the *partial* regression coefficient, a term I introduce later) because Y but not X is in a standardized metric. For such variables, $b_i \neq \tilde{b}_i$. If Y is standardized but X_i is not, b_i is interpreted as the number of standard deviations by which two cases that differ by one unit on X_i are estimated to differ on Y.

For reasons discussed on page 42, if standardization is going to be employed and a standardized model interpreted or reported, I recommend not standardizing the dichotomous predictors in such a model. Almost never would two groups differ by one standard deviation on the variable coding groups, meaning that the standardized coefficient for a dichotomous predictor will have no meaningful interpretation. By keeping dichotomous variables in the original form and getting in the habit of coding groups so they differ by a single unit, the partially standardized coefficient for a dichotomous predictor can be interpreted as the average difference in Y, in *standard deviations*, between the two groups when all other predictor variables are held constant. This is meaningful and easy to understand, unlike a standardized coefficient for a dichotomous predictor.

3.2 Partial Association and Statistical Control

Etched into the brains of all scientists is the dictum that "correlation does not imply causation." We learn early on in our training that just because two variables X and Y are correlated, that doesn't mean that X causes Y or that Y causes X. The ability to infer cause–effect is hardly even a statistical matter in the end. Rather, it is the design of one's study, the data collection procedures one employs, and theoretical plausibility that most directly influence whether a cause–effect claim can be made and with what degree of confidence, not the size or sign of a statistical index of association. Absent certain design features, numerous processes both systematic and haphazard can induce association between two variables. These processes function as alternative explanations for an association, and they interfere with a researcher's ability to make causal claims. The greater the number of such alternative explanations, the less comfortable we must be making cause–effect claims from nothing other than association between variables.

Recall from Chapter 2 that negative emotions about climate change and support for government action to mitigate climate change are positively correlated. In these data, the association is moderate to strong and cannot be attributed to just chance. Does this mean that if we could just make people more anxious and scared about climate change, they would be more supportive of government action? Perhaps, but of course mere association between these two variables is not sufficient to warrant such a causal inference. Alternative explanations abound.

Consider some plausible alternative explanations. Perhaps this association reflects only a difference between men and women in how emotional they are about just about *anything* and in their beliefs about the ability of government to effectively solve social problems. That is, something about how men and women are socialized leads them to differ on both of these dimensions. Indeed, males report less strong negative emotions ($r = -0.117$) as well as less support for government action ($r = -0.099$) than females. So it may be that emotional responses to climate change and support for government action are related not through some cause–effect mechanism but, rather, are *spuriously associated*. Two variables are spuriously associated if their association is induced as a result of a shared cause—in this case, biological sex.

Alternatively, we know that in the United States, people who identify as politically conservative tend to believe that government should play a limited role in the lives of its citizens. Conservatives tend to favor low taxes, minimal regulation of business by government, and are less supportive of government-provided social services such as welfare. By contrast, people who identify as politically liberal favor a greater role of government and tend to favor social safety net programs, such as economic assistance for the disadvantaged and unemployed, strict regulation of business, and higher taxes so that government can provide services for its people. That is, individual differences between people in their support for government policies are attributable in part to differences between them in their political ideology. Not surprisingly, the evidence from this study is consistent with this proposition, as those who self-reported as relatively more politically conservative reported relatively less support for government action to mitigate climate change ($r = -0.418$).

Importantly, there is some existing research suggesting that conservatives and liberals have different emotional lives and experiences (see, e.g., Leone & Chirumbolo, 2008; Napier & Jost, 2008; Vigil, 2010). If so, then the association between emotional reactions to climate change and support for government action may merely be an *epiphenomenon* of the effect of political ideology on support for government action. An association between X and

Y is epiphenomenal if X is correlated with a cause of Y but does not itself causally influence Y. In other words, many things correlated with the cause of Y will also tend to be correlated with Y. But that doesn't make all those things causes of Y as well. Indeed, in these data, political ideology is correlated with negative emotional responses to climate change ($r = -0.349$), with conservatives reporting less negative emotion than liberals. So it is possible the association observed between negative emotional responses to climate change and support for government action is simply epiphenomenal. We don't need to assume that ideology causally influences emotions felt in order to invoke epiphenomenality as an alternative explanation for this association.

Or perhaps it is not negative emotions specifically, but general emotionality that leads to greater support for government action. In these data, there is a positive albeit weak association between positive and negative emotions felt about climate change. Given that people who report relatively more anxiety and concern about climate change also report feeling relatively more optimistic and excited, for example, the unique role of negative relative to positive emotions in this process is obscured. Is it that anxiety and worry lead people to feel that action must be taken by government, or is just the tendency to get worked up and be emotional about things that prompts such people to seek out solutions to problems from a variety of different sources, including the government?

Such is the problem facing the interpretation of association between two variables. Typically there are many processes that can explain association, some causal, others not. Some alternative explanations can be ruled out logically or theoretically. Others can be dealt with prior to data collection by using a design that rules them out a priori, such as experimentation. If negative emotions were experimentally manipulated in some fashion and people were randomly assigned to feel negative emotions or not about climate change, then differences between these experimentally constructed groups in their support for government action following the manipulation has a clearer causal interpretation. Random assignment tends to equate groups, on average, on all variables other than the manipulated variable at the start of the study. If nothing other than the variable the researcher intends to vary differentiates the groups at the beginning of the study, differences observed on an outcome variable of interest can be interpreted as resulting causally from differences between them on the manipulated variable.

When experimental manipulation is not possible, not desired, or simply didn't happen during data collection, multiple regression can be used as a fallback option for dealing with at least some alternative explanations for an association. What makes the association between two variables X and Y ambiguous is that people who differ on X and Y also likely differ on many other things, and it may be those things that are responsible for the association. Multiple regression gives a researcher a means of engaging in a kind of mathematically aided counterfactual reasoning by estimating what the association between X and Y would be among a group of people who do not differ on the other variables in the regression model. It does this by "mathematically equating" people who differ on X on those variables. This equating process is also called *partialing out* those other variables from the association between X and Y, or *statistically controlling* for those variables. These "other variables" are sometimes called covariates in the lingo of linear models, but in practice they are just predictor variables in the regression model of Y, just as X is.

Residuals as "Purified" Measures

An understanding of the process of statistical control is facilitated by introducing an important property of residuals not mentioned in Chapter 2. In any regression model estimating some outcome variable Y from k predictor variables X_i, the residuals will be linearly uncorrelated with $\hat{Y}$ and all k predictors X_i. More formally, defining e_j as

$$e_j = Y_j - \left(i_1 + \sum_{i=1}^{k} b_i X_{ij} \right) = Y_j - \hat{Y}_j$$

it will always be true that $r_{e_j \hat{Y}_j} = 0$ and $r_{e_j X_{ij}} = 0$ for all k X_i variables. Thus, a residual can be thought of as a measure of Y that has been "purified" or "statistically cleansed" of its association with all k predictor variables in isolation, as well as the weighted linear combination of those predictor variables that is $\hat{Y}$. This is useful because it means that we can purify individual differences in any variable in a regression model, whether predictor or outcome, from what is shared mathematically—its covariance—with other variables. This property of residuals is important, and it helps to understand just what measures of partial association quantify.

As described earlier, the positive association between negative emotions about climate change and support for government action has many noncausal interpretations, all of them due to the fact that people who differ on both probably differ on lots of other things as well, among them being positive emotions, political ideology, sex, and age. But we can construct new measures of both negative emotions and support for government action that are uncorrelated with these four variables without any difficulty.

For negative emotions, estimate an OLS regression model predicting negative emotions (X_1) from positive emotions (X_2), political ideology (X_3), sex (X_4), and age (X_5):

$$\hat{X}_{1j} = i_1 + b_2 X_{2j} + b_3 X_{3j} + b_4 X_{4j} + b_5 X_{5j}$$

and then calculate the residuals as

$$e_{X_{1j}} = X_{1j} - \hat{X}_{1j} = X_{1j} - \left(i_1 + b_2 X_{2j} + b_3 X_{3j} + b_4 X_{4j} + b_5 X_{5j}\right) \tag{3.5}$$

Repeating this process for support for government action (Y), estimate

$$\hat{Y}_j = i_1 + b_2 X_{2j} + b_3 X_{3j} + b_4 X_{4j} + b_5 X_{5j}$$

and then calculate the residuals as

$$e_{Y_j} = Y_j - \hat{Y}_j = Y_j - \left(i_1 + b_2 X_{2j} + b_3 X_{3j} + b_4 X_{4j} + b_5 X_{5j}\right) \tag{3.6}$$

Here is the important part. According to the property of residuals described here, both e_{X_1} and e_Y will be linearly uncorrelated with X_2, X_3, X_4, and X_5. Thus, these residuals can be thought of as measures of negative emotions and support for government action that have been statistically cleansed of their shared association with positive emotions, ideology, sex, and age. e_{X_1} and e_Y can be interpreted as *deviations from expectation* given their linear association with these four variables. That is, someone with a positive value of e_{X_1} expresses more negative emotion about climate change than would be expected from his or her sex, political ideology, age, and how much positive emotions he or she feels, and someone with a negative value of e_{X_1} feels less negative emotion than would be expected. A similar interpretation applies to e_Y. Someone with a positive value of e_Y expresses more support than expected given the association between support and sex, political ideology, age, and positive emotion, and someone with a negative value expresses less support than expected.

Partial Association

Before controlling for positive emotions, political ideology, sex, and age, the regression coefficient for negative emotions in a simple regression model predicting support for government action was 0.514 and statistically different from zero. This index of association contains a component that is influenced by their shared association with other variables, and this *in part* is what makes it difficult to interpret 0.514 in causal terms. But by partialing out variables that might be inducing association between negative emotions and support for government action spuriously or epiphenomenally, we can assess their association independent of what they have in common with these four variables statistically. It was established earlier that by regressing both support for government action and negative emotions on positive emotions, ideology, sex, and age, the residuals from these regressions will be uncorrelated with all four of these variables. e_Y and e_{X_1} will share nothing statistically at this point, at least as measured by covariation, with these four variables. They will both be linearly independent of X_2, X_3, X_4, and X_5.

With these residuals generated, it is possible to determine whether people who are relatively more (or less) supportive of government action than would be expected from their positive emotions, ideology, sex, and age also tend to feel relatively more (or less) negative emotions than would be expected from their positive emotions, ideology, sex, and age. This is accomplished by correlating these residuals, or simply regressing e_Y on e_{X_1}. If there is evidence of association between these residuals, then the association observed without controlling for positive emotions, ideology, sex, and age cannot be attributed entirely to shared association with these four variables, and a causal association between them remains a viable explanation. But if the association goes away after this partialing process, this favors a noncausal interpretation—that the association observed without statistical control is spurious or epiphenomenal and driven by one or more of the variables being statistically partialed out.

As will be seen, this process of generating residuals and then regressing residuals on residuals actually is not necessary, but I do it here to illustrate what is happening in the inner workings of multiple regression analysis. The SPSS code below will estimate the models in equations 3.5 and 3.6 and then regress e_Y on e_{X_1}. In this code, e_Y and e_{X_1} are given the variable names govresid and negresid, respectively.

```
regression/dep=negemot/method=enter posemot ideology sex age/save resid.
rename variables res_1=negresid.
regression/dep=govact/method=enter posemot ideology sex age/save resid.
rename variables res_1=govresid.
regression/dep=govresid/method=enter negresid.
```

In SAS, the corresponding set of command is

```
proc reg data=glbwarm;model negemot=posemot ideology sex age;output out=x1
    residual=negresid;run;
proc reg data=glbwarm;model govact=posemot ideology sex age;output out=y
    residual=govresid;run;
```

```
data resid (keep=govresid negresid);merge y x1;run;
proc reg data=resid;model govresid=negresid;run;
```

The resulting output from the SAS commands can be found in Figure 3.2. As can be seen, the regression equation estimating residual support from government action from residual negative emotions is

$$\hat{e}_{Y_j} = 0.000 + 0.441 e_{X_{1j}}$$

The regression coefficient for e_{X_1} is a called a *partial regression coefficient*. It is no coincidence that its value of 0.441 is exactly the same as the value of the regression coefficient for X_1 in the model regressing Y on X_1 as well as X_2, X_3, X_4, and X_5 (see equation 3.4 and the SPSS output in Figure 3.1). That too is called a partial regression coefficient. They are the same value, and they have the same interpretation, because they quantify the same thing. Two people who are equal in positive emotions, ideology, sex, and age but differ by one unit in their negative emotions are estimated to differ by 0.441 units in their support for government action.

The notion of equating on a set of variables introduced earlier has been demonstrated here to be equivalent to the notion of "removing their shared association" with that set of variables statistically. That is what statistical control is about. But obviously, it is not necessary to go through this laborious process of calculating residuals. All that is necessary if one wants to remove the association between an outcome variable and some predictor variable that is shared with a set of additional variables is to put them all of them in a regression model of the outcome variable simultaneously. An OLS regression program does the rest automatically. The result is a set of partial regression coefficients for each predictor variable, each of which measures partial association between Y and a given predictor variable after statistically controlling for all other predictor variables in the model.

The result of this partialing process, automated with multiple regression, shows that the partial association between negative emotions and support for government action holding positive emotions, ideology, sex, and age constant is not much different than the simple association. This suggests that the association observed cannot be attributed to spuriousness or epiphenomenality with respect to these four variables. But this does not mean that the association is not spurious or epiphenomenal. Perhaps the true source of what is a spurious or epiphenomenal association simply has not been accounted for yet. This is an inherent problem with making causal inferences from correlational data. One can never know whether the association is causal or can be attributed to some other variable that simply hasn't

```
                        The REG Procedure
                         Model: MODEL1
                Dependent Variable: govresid Residual

            Number of Observations Read          815
            Number of Observations Used          815


                       Analysis of Variance

                             Sum of         Mean
   Source              DF    Squares        Square    F Value    Pr > F

   Model                1   316.75559    316.75559     279.45    <.0001
   Error              813   921.52330      1.13348
   Corrected Total    814  1238.27889


                Root MSE              1.06465   R-Square    0.2558
                Dependent Mean    -2.4983E-16   Adj R-Sq    0.2549
                Coeff Var         -4.26144E17


                        Parameter Estimates

                              Parameter     Standard
   Variable   Label      DF    Estimate        Error    t Value    Pr > |t|

   Intercept  Intercept   1  2.36048E-16      0.03729     0.0000      1.0000
   negresid   Residual    1      0.44078      0.02637    16.7168     <.0001
```

FIGURE 3.2. SAS PROC REG output from a regression estimating residual support for government action (e_Y) from residual negative emotions about climate change (e_{X_1}).

been statistically controlled for in the model one has estimated. Ultimately, the best one can do absent data that afford more unequivocal causal interpretation is attempt to control for potential confounders that critics might argue are responsible for the association, in the hope that those critics will be satisfied if the association of interest stands up to the statistical control process.

Partial Correlation. Like the simple regression coefficient, the partial regression coefficients in a multiple regression model are in an unstandardized or raw measurement metric. The value of b_i will depend on the scale of measurement of Y as well as X_i, meaning that if all measurements for Y or X_i are multiplied or divided by a constant, the partial regression coefficient for X_i will change. Pearson's r, however, is a scale-free metric. Multiplying or dividing X_i or Y by a constant will not change the correlation between them. There is a comparable scale-free measure of partial association known as the *partial correlation coefficient*, or simply *partial correlation*. The partial correlation between Y and X controlling for a set of covariates is the Pearson correlation between the residuals from a model estimating Y

from the covariates, and the residuals from a model estimating X from the covariates.

What is the partial correlation between support for government action and negative emotional responses to climate change, controlling for positive emotions, ideology, sex, and age? Denoting these four covariates as set W (i.e., $W = X_2, X_3, X_4$, and X_5) this correlation can be expressed symbolically as $pr_{YX_1.W}$, read "the partial correlation between Y and X_1 controlling for W." In these data, $pr_{YX_1.W}$ is the Pearson correlation between e_{X_1} and e_Y from equations 3.5 and 3.6, respectively. Here,

$$pr_{YX_1.W} = r_{e_Y e_{X_1}} = 0.506$$

This can be interpreted as an estimate of the correlation between support for government action and negative emotions after accounting for their shared association with positive emotions, ideology, sex, and age. Alternatively, it can be thought of as an estimate of the association between support for government action and negative emotions among a hypothetical group of people of the same ideology, sex, and age who experience positive emotions about climate change to the same degree.

The partial correlation between Y and X controlling for W can also be squared before interpretation. When it is squared, it is interpreted as the proportion of the variance in Y that is not explained by covariate(s) W that can be uniquely explained by X. In this example, of the variance in support for government action that is not explained by positive emotions, ideology, sex, and age, $100(0.506^2)\% = 25.6\%$ of it is explained by negative emotions.

Semipartial Correlation. An alternative measure of partial association is the *semipartial correlation*, also known as the *part correlation*. The semipartial correlation between Y and X_i controlling for the covariates is estimated with the correlation between Y and the residuals from a regression model estimating X_i from the covariates. In this example, the semipartial correlation between support for government action and negative emotions while controlling for positive emotions, ideology, sex, and age (covariate set W) is

$$sr_{YX_1.W} = r_{Y e_{X_1}} = 0.459$$

The semipartial correlation is typically interpreted after squaring it. The squared semipartial correlation between Y and X_i controlling for covariates W is the proportion of the total variance in Y that is uniquely attributable to X_i. It is equivalent to how much R^2 increases when X_1 is added to a regression model already containing the variables in covariate set W. So we can say that the proportion of the total variance in support for government action that is uniquely explained by negative emotions is $0.459^2 = 0.211$, or 21.1% in a percentage of variance explained metric.

Most good OLS regression routines have a means of producing the partial and semipartial correlations for all predictor variables in a multiple regression model. As can be seen in Figure 3.1, SPSS provides the partial and semipartial correlations, and these agree with the computations completed above using residuals.

3.3   Statistical Inference in Multiple Regression

Inference in multiple regression can focus on either individual partial regression coefficients or subsets of them. For individual coefficients, inference proceeds just as in simple regression by either the testing of a null hypothesis about $_Tb_i$ or the construction of a confidence interval for $_Tb_i$. Rejection of the null hypothesis that $_Tb_i = 0$ (or a confidence interval that does not include zero) leads to the inference that statistically controlling for all other variables in the model (i.e., holding all those variables constant), there is an association between X_i and Y.

As in simple regression, to test the null hypothesis that $_Tb_i = 0$, the obtained b_i is divided by an estimate of its standard error, and a p-value is derived from the $t(df_{residual})$ distribution. Or equation 2.10 can be applied to generate an interval estimate. The SPSS output in Figure 3.1 provides everything that is needed. Indeed, all the computations are already completed for every predictor variable in the model. For example, holding positive emotions about climate change, political ideology, sex, and age constant, there is a statistically significant and positive partial association between negative emotions about climate change and support for government action, $b_1 = 0.441, se_{b_1} = 0.026, t(809) = 16.676, p < 0.001$, with a 95% confidence interval from 0.389 to 0.493. But controlling for emotions, ideology, and age, men and women do not differ on average in their support for government action, $b_4 = -0.010, se_{b_4} = 0.077, t(809) = -0.131, p = .896$, with a 95% confidence interval from −0.161 to 0.141.

Inferences in this example are framed in terms of unstandardized partial regression coefficients. A hypothesis could also be articulated and tested in terms of the partial or semipartial correlations. However, no special test is necessary, for rejection of the null hypothesis that $_Tb_i = 0$ implies rejection of the null hypothesis that the true partial and semipartial correlations are equal to zero. If you can claim that the partial association is different from zero, it makes no difference which measure of partial association you tested. If one is not zero, the others are not as well.

The assumptions for interpretation and inference of partial association are the same as the assumptions outlined in section 2.4 for simple regression analysis, but applied to a regression involving residuals following statistical control. Recall from section 3.2 that the partial regression coefficient for X_1 in the multiple regression analysis can be interpreted as the regression coefficient for X_1 in a model estimating the residuals constructed from equation 3.6 from the residuals constructed from equation 3.5. In order for the partial regression coefficient or partial correlation for X_1 in the multiple regression model to be interpreted meaningfully as described earlier, we must assume that the relationship between these residuals is linear or at least approximately so. In addition, the validity and power of the statistical test for partial association for X_1 will be influenced by the extent to which the errors in estimation (i.e., the residuals from equation 3.6) are normal, homoscedastic with respect to X_1, and independent. Testing these assumptions can be quite an undertaking. For a discussion of various approaches to testing these assumptions, see Berry (1993), Darlington (1990), and Cohen et al. (2003).

Testing a Hypothesis about a Set of Predictors

Multiple regression can also be used to test a hypothesis about a set of predictors in the model. For instance, considering emotions as a set (i.e., both positive and negative emotions), is there evidence that emotional reactions to climate change are related to support for government action while holding constant ideology, sex, and age? This question can be framed in terms of null and alternative hypotheses as

$$H_0: \quad _Tb_1 \text{ and } _Tb_2 = 0$$
$$H_a: \quad _Tb_1 \text{ or } _Tb_2 \text{ or both} \neq 0$$

Conducting this test requires the estimation of R^2 for two regression models. Model 1 has only sex, age, and political ideology as predictors. This model yields $R_1^2 = 0.177$. Model 2 contains all the predictors in model 1 as well as the two emotion variables. This model yields $R_2^2 = 0.388$. A p-value is then constructed by converting the difference between the squared multiple correlations to an F-ratio and finding the p-value corresponding to this F.

Most generally, to test a null hypothesis that all partial regression coefficients for a set of m predictors in a regression model are equal to zero, the F-ratio is calculated as

$$F\left(m, df_{residual_2}\right) = \frac{df_{residual_2}\left(R_2^2 - R_1^2\right)}{m\left(1 - R_2^2\right)} \tag{3.7}$$

where R_1^2 and R_2^2 are the squared multiple correlations for models 1 and 2, respectively, and $df_{residual_2}$ is the residual degrees of freedom for model 2.

The p-value for F is derived from the $F(m, df_{residual_2})$ distribution. Applied to this example, $R_1^2 = 0.177$, $R_2^2 = 0.388$, $m = 2$, and $df_{residual_2} = 809$, and so

$$F(2, 809) = \frac{810\,(0.388 - 0.177)}{2\,(1 - 0.388)} = 139.632, p < .001$$

The null hypothesis can be rejected. There is evidence that emotional reactions to climate change are related to support for government action after accounting for political ideology, sex, and age.

These computations are laborious if done by hand, but not complicated. Fortunately, most good OLS regression routines have a means of implementing this test. In SPSS, the command is

```
regression/statistics defaults change/dep=govact/method=enter ideology
    sex age/method=enter negemot posemot.
```

whereas in SAS, the command is

```
proc reg data=glbwarm;model govact=negemot posemot ideology sex age;
    test negemot=0,posemot=0;run;
```

This test can also be interpreted as a test as to whether the model with the m additional variables in model 2 fits better than the one that excludes them (model 1). In this example, we can conclude that the model that includes positive and negative emotions fits better (i.e., estimates Y with greater accuracy) than the one that does not include these two variables.

It is not uncommon for researchers to use this approach to assess whether including a single specific variable in the model improves its fit relative to when it is absent. Although there is no harm in doing this, it is not necessary, for the test of the null hypothesis that $_Tb_i = 0$ is mathematically equivalent to this approach when $m = 1$. So rejection of the null that $_Tb_i = 0$ leads to the conclusion that including predictor variable X_i in the model improves its fit relative to when it is excluded. The change in the fit of the model resulting from including X_i, indexed by the difference in R^2, is equivalent to the squared semipartial correlation for X_i as defined in section 3.2. Furthermore, the F-ratio generated by equation 3.7 is the square of the t statistic for predictor variable X_i, and their p-values will be the same.

3.4 Statistical and Conceptual Diagrams

Figure 3.3 is a visual representation of the multiple regression model in equation 3.3 using symbolic representations that are common in the path analysis and structural equation modeling literature. In this diagram, which I call a *statistical diagram* in this book, boxes represent explicitly measured or *observed* variables (i.e., variables that actually exist in one's dataset), and the solid unidirectional arrows represent *predictor of* or *predicted from*, depending on whether the arrow points to or from the variable. A statistical diagram is also called a "path diagram" in the structural equation modeling literature. However, path diagrams are typically used in this literature to depict sets of hypothesized or established relations that are presumed to be causal. Resist the temptation to interpret solid unidirectional arrows in a statistical diagram as necessarily implying something about causality. That is not what they are intended to convey, although they may. No distinction is made in a statistical diagram between "cause of" and "predictor of."

Throughout this book, any variable in a statistical diagram that has an arrow pointing at it I will call a *consequent variable*, and any variable that has an arrow pointing away from it I will call an *antecedent variable*. I will also use these terms when referring to variables in a model expressed in equation form. *Antecedent* is synonymous with *predictor* or *independent* variable, and *consequent* is synonymous with *dependent* or *outcome* variable. If a variable has an arrow pointing at it, it is a consequent variable by definition, and it is being predicted by all antecedents that send an arrow to it. The number of consequent variables in a statistical diagram corresponds to the number of equations the diagram represents.

A consequent variable may or may not be an antecedent variable, depending on whether it sends an arrow to another variable. A variable can be both antecedent and consequent in some models discussed later in the book, meaning that the same variable can be an outcome or dependent variable in one equation but a predictor or independent variable in another equation. Antecedent and consequent variables are similar to but not the same as *exogeneous* and *endogeneous* variables in the language of structural equation modeling. An endogeneous variable in structural equation modeling is a consequent variable by definition, but an endogeneous variable can't also be an exogeneous variable in structural equation modeling terms, whereas a consequent variable can also be an antecedent variable if it sends an arrow to another variable.

Looking at Figure 3.3, it is apparent that there are six observed variables in this model, five of which are antecedent and one of which is consequent.

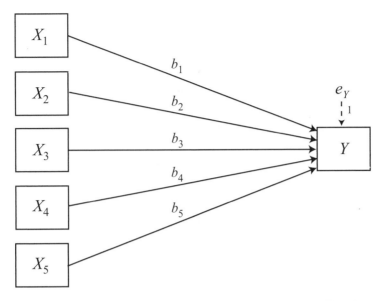

FIGURE 3.3. A multiple regression model in statistical diagram form. This diagram represents equation 3.3.

Because there is only one consequent variable in this diagram, it represents a single equation. The consequent variable Y is being predicted by five antecedent variables, X_1, X_2, X_3, X_4, and X_5, because Y receives an arrow from each of these antecedents. That is, these five antecedents are predictors of the consequent Y because they point an arrow at Y.

Any variable functioning as a consequent in a statistical model is assumed to be predicted from its antecedent variables with some degree of error. The error in estimation of a consequent variable is represented in a statistical diagram with the letter e and a dashed line pointing at its corresponding consequent variable. The subscript for an error will be the same as the label given to the consequent variable it is attached to. I use a dashed line rather than a solid line because we don't usually think of the error in estimation as a predictor of the consequent (which would be denoted by a solid arrow), although it could be construed in that way.

Observe in Figure 3.3 that each arrow in the statistical diagram has a label attached to it. Labels attached to arrows between variables represent the regression coefficients for each antecedent variable in the statistical model of the consequent. Depending on whether the diagram depicts a model prior to estimation of the coefficients or conveys the results after model estimation, these labels will either be numbers or some other symbol, such as a Roman or Greek letter. For instance, without information about the values of b_1, b_2, b_3, b_4, and b_5, it makes sense to label them symbolically and generically in this way, because their values are not known. However if a diagram is being used to depict the results *after* estimation of the model, one might instead use the actual regression weights calculated using the data available. In this case, b_1, b_2, b_3, b_4, and b_5 could be replaced with 0.441, −0.027, −0.218, −0.010, and −0.001, respectively. Alternatively, one might use the labels in the diagram but place their estimated values in a table corresponding to the diagram. The label attached to an arrow leading from a consequent's error in estimation will typically be one, as errors in estimation are almost always given a weight of one in a linear model.[3]

In linear models such as multiple regression, we generally assume that the antecedents of a common consequent either are or might be correlated with each other. Such assumed covariation between antecedent variables is often depicted in path diagrams using curved bidirectional arrows. However, I will not depict such covariation in a statistical diagram, because doing so can very quickly make a compact visual representation of a set of equations very complex and cluttered, and its meaning harder to discern. As a general rule, all antecedent variables not connected with a unidirectional arrow are assumed to be correlated. There may be occasions when it is necessary to include certain covariances in a statistical diagram in order to convey important estimation information, such as in models that combine moderation and mediation. I will do so when needed.

Linear regression models such as those represented by equation 3.3 typically contain a constant or intercept. It may be that this constant is fixed to zero as a result of certain transformations of the data, such as mean centering or standardization, but that doesn't mean it doesn't exist when it isn't formally specified in the equation. I will not visually depict the constant in a statistical diagram corresponding to that model because, like covariation between antecedents, doing so adds unnecessary visual clutter while providing no information that is particularly relevant to interpretation. But its absence from the diagram should not be interpreted as its absence from the model.

A statistical diagram is an information-rich visual representation of a linear model. After a little experience and practice, one can easily discern the equation or equations that a statistical diagram depicts. The problem with statistical diagrams is that they can quickly grow unwieldy as a model becomes more complex. This is partly because they require the explicit representation of all the variables in a model even when only one or two of those variables are of primary focus in the analysis. In addition, a statistical

---

[3]Equation 3.3 could be written as $Y_j = i_1 + b_1 X_{1j} + b_2 X_{2j} + b_3 X_{3j} + b_4 X_{4j} + b_5 X_{5j} + 1e_j$. The weight of one given to e_j in equation 3.3 is implied by its absence.

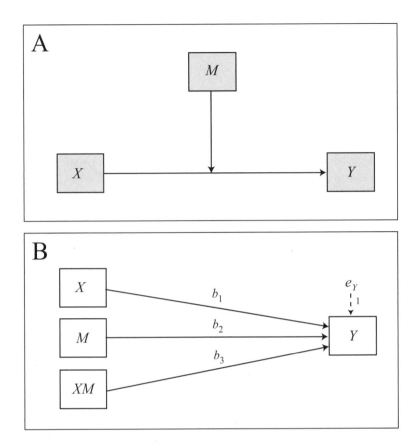

FIGURE 3.4. A simple moderation model depicted as a conceptual diagram (panel A) and a statistical diagram (panel B).

diagram isn't a visually friendly way of representing *moderation*, a concept introduced in Chapter 1 and described in more detail starting in Chapter 7.

A conceptual diagram is an alternative means of representing an analytical model in visual form that is particularly useful for depicting models that include a moderation component, although such a diagram can also be used to represent mediation. Most important, a conceptual model *may but does not necessarily* depict the corresponding equation or set of equations the way a statistical diagram does. Consider, for example, the simple moderation model depicted in Figure 1.2 and replicated in Figure 3.4, panel A. This conceptual model depicts an antecedent variable X's effect on consequent variable Y as moderated by M. If one were to interpret this as a representation of the equation used to estimate moderation of X's effect on Y, it appears that this equation does not include M as an antecedent variable in the equation of consequent Y, because there is no arrow linking M to Y. Doing so would violate a basic principle of moderation analysis.

But this is not a statistical diagram, it is a conceptual diagram. A simple moderation model depicted as a statistical diagram can be found in Figure 3.4, panel B. This translates into the equation $\hat{Y} = i_1 + b_1 X + b_2 M + b_3 XM + e_Y$, as discussed in Chapter 7.

To reduce the potential for confusing a conceptual diagram and a statistical diagram, I make clear in the figure captions whether a diagram corresponds to a model in statistical or conceptual form. In addition, because a conceptual diagram is not intended to be a representation of an equation or set of equations, a conceptual model will not depict the errors in estimation, whereas a statistical model will. Finally, all variables in a conceptual model will be denoted by gray boxes, as opposed to the white boxes used in a statistical diagram.

3.5   Chapter Summary

Two variables X and Y may be correlated as a result of a number of different processes. Investigators often want to interpret association in causal terms, but when there are alternative explanations, causal language must be worded carefully with the appropriate caveats and cautions. Differences between people on both X and Y may be due to some kind of causal effect of X on Y, but it could be because people who differ on X and Y also differ on other variables that influence both X and Y, thereby inducing spurious association between X and Y. Or X may be correlated with a cause of Y and therefore also be correlated with Y even though it itself is not a cause of Y, a phenomenon known as epiphenomenal association. Multiple regression can be used to rule out some alternative explanations for an association between X and Y by including variables representing those alternative explanations as covariates in a linear regression model estimating Y from X. When this is done, a multiple regression model generates various measures of partial association, interpreted as the association between X and Y when holding all other predictor variables in the model constant. Understanding this statistical control process, as well as how to interpret a regression model with multiple predictors, is important because most of the models estimated in the rest of this book, starting with Chapter 4 on mediation analysis, will include more than one predictor variable.

Part II

MEDIATION ANALYSIS

4

The Simple Mediation Model

In this chapter, I introduce the elements of mediation analysis, with a focus on the most basic mediation model possible consisting of a causal antecedent variable linked to a single consequent variable through a single intermediary variable or *mediator*. This very popular and widely estimated *simple mediation model* is used to introduce the mechanics of path analysis and to demonstrate how a variable's effect on an outcome can be partitioned into direct and indirect effects which are easily quantified using OLS regression. Inferential tests for direct and indirect effects are presented, with an emphasis on approaches that do not make excessive or unnecessary assumptions.

There is a body of research in the persuasion and attitude change literature on the differential effects of gain versus loss framing in influencing behavior (e.g., O'Keefe & Jensen, 1997). A gain frame message is one that emphasizes all the things you will acquire or gain if you engage in the behavior advocated by the message. For example, if you wanted to persuade your friend to stop smoking, you could make the argument to him that if he stops smoking, he will feel physically better each day, he will live to an older age, and more people will like him. By contrast, a message framed in terms of losses emphasizes all the things he will lose if he fails to engage in the behavior advocated. For example, you could tell your friend how his health will deteriorate, he will die younger, and his friends will eventually abandon him if he doesn't stop smoking.

The literature suggests that in some circumstances, gain frame messages are more effective, whereas in other circumstances, loss frames work better. In other words, the effect of message framing is *moderated* because it depends on the circumstance. As discussed in Chapter 1, establishing the boundary conditions of an effect and those factors that influence the size of an effect are important scientific goals.

But just as important to scientific understanding and the application of that understanding is figuring out *how* effects occur in the first place. For instance, if a study shows that a gain frame message works better than a loss frame message at influencing smokers to quit, what is it about gain framing that results in greater behavior change? What is the *mechanism* at work that leads to a greater likelihood of smoking cessation after being told about all the potential gains that can occur if one quits smoking rather than all the losses one will experience by continuing to smoke? Is it that messages framed in terms of gains empower people more than loss framed messages, which in turn enhances the likelihood of taking action? Or perhaps loss frame messages are more likely to prompt lots of counterarguing, which reduces the persuasiveness of the message relative to gain frame messages.

Whereas answering questions about *when* or *for whom* are the domain of moderation analysis, questions that ask about *how* pertain to *mediation*, the focus of this and the next two chapters. In this chapter, I introduce the *simple mediation model* and illustrate using OLS regression-based path analysis how the effect of an antecedent variable X on some final consequent Y can be partitioned neatly into two paths of influence, *direct* and *indirect*. I show that the procedure one follows to derive these paths of influence does not depend on whether X is dichotomous (as, say, in an experimental study) or continuous. I also discuss various approaches to making inferences about direct and indirect effects in this most simple of mediation models.

4.1 The Simple Mediation Model

Mediation analysis is a statistical method used to help answer the question as to how some causal agent X transmits its effect on Y. What is the mechanism, be it emotional, cognitive, biological, or otherwise, by which X influences Y? Does framing an anti-smoking message in gain as opposed to loss terms (X) influence the likelihood of smoking cessation (Y) because the type of frame influences how much people counterargue, which in turn influences behavior? Or maybe loss framing leads to certain negative emotional reactions, such as anxiety, which disrupt systematic message processing and elaboration, which in turn reduces the effectiveness of the message.

The most basic of mediation models—the simple mediation model—is represented in conceptual diagram form in Figure 4.1. As can be seen, this model contains two consequent variables (M) and (Y) and two antecedent variables (X) and (M), with X causally influencing Y and M, and M causally influencing Y. A simple mediation model is any causal system in which at least one causal antecedent X variable is proposed as influencing an outcome Y through a single intervening variable M. In such a model, there are two distinct pathways by which a specific X variable is proposed as

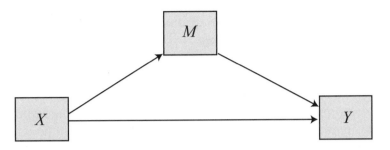

FIGURE 4.1. A conceptual diagram of a simple mediation model.

influencing Y. These pathways are found by tracing every way one can get from X to Y while never tracing in a direction opposite to the direction an arrow points. One pathway leads from X to Y without passing through M and is called the *direct effect* of X on Y. The second pathway from X to Y is the *indirect effect* of X on Y through M. It first passes from antecedent X to consequent M and then from antecedent M to consequent Y. The indirect effect represents how Y is influenced by X through a causal sequence in which X influences M, which in turn influences Y.

In a mediation model, M is typically called a *mediator variable*, although the term *intermediary variable* has been used, and different fields use different terms, such as a *surrogate variable* or an *intermediate endpoint*. I will stick with the term mediator because it is probably the most widely-used and recognized term. In the example used thus far, counterarguing and anxiety are conceptualized as potential mediators of the effect of framing on likelihood of smoking cessation. They represent a possible or proposed mechanism—the contents of the "black box"—by which message framing influences behavior. Once X exerts its effect on M, then M's causal influence on Y produces variation in Y.

Historically, questions of "how" have been thought of as sensible to ask only after one first has established evidence of association between X and Y. As a result, mediation analysis would be undertaken only when one has successfully demonstrated that X and Y are associated. This rationale is based on one of the three popular criteria one must meet to establish cause: correlation between X and Y (the other two criteria being establishing that X precedes Y, and ruling out competing explanations). Thus, suppose one finds no average difference in the likelihood of smoking cessation (Y) between two groups of smokers in an experiment exposed to differently framed anti-smoking messages (X) designed to change behavior. What point would there be in trying to explain how message framing affects behavior when one has no evidence of a difference in behavior following exposure to differently framed messages? If one has no actual evidence that X is related to Y, then, so the argument goes, X does not affect Y, so there is no "how" question to answer.

This conceptualization of mediation analysis as a statistical means of "accounting for an effect" may in part be due to the popularization of a particular approach to mediation analysis I describe in Chapter 6 but which is no longer recommended. This approach has dominated mediation analysis until fairly recently and has become deeply ingrained in how scientists think. On the surface, it seems that the existence of an association between X and Y would be a reasonable precondition of trying to explain the underlying effect of X on Y. But there has been a growing recognition over the last few years that such thinking is misguided. As Bollen (1989) stated some years ago in a couple of sentences tucked away on page 52 of his popular book *Structural Equations with Latent Variables*, "lack of correlation does not disprove causation" and "correlation is neither a necessary nor a sufficient condition of causality." This seems contrary to conventional wisdom and what is taught in graduate school or printed in research methods books. Yet it is true, and most scholars of mediation analysis have now adopted the perspective Bollen articulated (see, e.g., Cerin & MacKinnon, 2009; Hayes, 2009; MacKinnon, 2008; Rucker, Preacher, Tormala, & Petty, 2011; Shrout & Bolger, 2002; Zhao, Lynch, & Chen, 2010). Mediation analysis as practiced in the 21st century no longer imposes evidence of simple association between X and Y as a precondition.

The simple mediation model is the most rudimentary mediation model one can estimate, and no doubt it greatly oversimplifies the complex dynamics through which X influences Y in real processes that scientists study. Later in Chapter 5, more complex mediation models will be described that are more realistic, such as models in which X transmits its effect on Y through multiple mechanisms represented with different mediators. Nevertheless, a thorough understanding of this model is important. Simple mediation models are routinely estimated and their components interpreted in the empirical social psychological (e.g., Alter & Balcetis, 2011; Righetti & Finkenauer, 2011), cognitive (e.g., Debeer, Hermans, & Raes, 2009), clinical (e.g., Costa & Pinto-Gouveia, 2011; Gaudiano, Herbert, & Hayes, 2010), health (e.g., Leonard & Rasmussen, 2011; Ruby, Perrino, Gillis, & Viel, 2011), political (e.g., Duncan & Stewart, 2007; Wohl & Branscombe, 2009), medical (e.g., Meade, Conn, Skalski, & Safren, 2011; Wagner, Tennen, & Osborn, 2010), educational (e.g., Hughes & Coplan, 2010), communication (e.g., Goodall & Slater, 2010; Shrum, Lee, Burroughs, & Rindfleisch, 2011), and business literatures (e.g., Brown & Baer, 2011; Patrick & Hagtvedt, 2011), among many other disciplines. Indeed, by some estimates, it would be tough to read the literature in many fields without encountering models of this sort being advanced and tested empirically. For instance, a content analysis of empirical articles published in the leading journals in social psychology (Rucker et al., 2011) revealed that over one-half of the articles described a mediation analysis, many of which take this simple form. The popularity of mediation analysis has been observed in other fields as well (e.g., Miller, del Carmen, Reutzel, & Certo, 2007; Preacher & Hayes, 2008b).

A second reason for understanding this rather rudimentary three-variable causal model is that the principles described in this chapter will be applied later in this book to more complex models that also are very popular and commonly estimated in many empirical disciplines. So an understanding of the concepts discussed in this chapter is necessary to progress further in this book and to understand at least some of the research published in your chosen area.

When thinking about whether a phenomenon or theory you are studying could be conceptualized as a mediation process, it is important to keep in mind that mediation is ultimately a causal explanation. It is assumed that the relationships in the system are causal, and, importantly, that M is causally located *between* X and Y. It must be assumed, if not also empirically substantiated, that X causes M, which in turn causes Y. M cannot possibly carry X's effect on Y if M is not located causally between X and Y.

Some argue that absent data that allow one to confidently infer cause–effect, a mediation model cannot and should not be estimated or interpreted. I have already articulated my perspective on the relationship between statistics, research design, and cause in Chapter 1, but my position is worth repeating here. I strongly believe that one can conduct a mediation analysis even if one cannot unequivocally establish causality given the limitations of one's data collection and research design. It is often the case that the data available for analysis do not lend themselves to causal claims, perhaps because the data are purely correlational, collected at a single time point, and with no experimental manipulation or random assignment. Sometimes theory or solid argument is the only foundation upon which a causal claim can be built given limitations of our data. But I see no problem in conducting the kind of analysis I describe in the following few chapters even when causal claims rest on shaky ground. It is our brains that interpret and place meaning on the mathematical procedures used, not the procedures themselves. So long as we couch our causal claims with the required cautions and caveats given the nature of the data available, we can apply any mathematical method we want to understand and model relationships between variables.

4.2   Estimation of the Direct, Indirect, and Total Effects of *X*

When empirically testing a causal process that involves a mediation component, of primary interest is the estimation and interpretation of the direct and indirect effects along with inferential tests thereof. To derive these effects, one must also estimate the constituent components of the indirect effect, meaning the effect of X on M as well as the effect of M on Y, although the constituent components of the indirect effect are not of primary interest in modern mediation analysis. Many researchers often estimate the total effect of X on Y as well, although doing so is not required for the purpose of interpretation. The total effect will be defined later.

The simple mediation model represented in the form of a statistical diagram[1] can be found in Figure 4.2. Notice that in comparing Figures 4.1 and 4.2, there is little difference between the conceptual and statistical diagrams representing a simple mediation model. As there are two consequent variables in this diagram, two linear models are required, one for each consequent. This statistical diagram represents two equations:

$$M = i_1 + aX + e_M \tag{4.1}$$

$$Y = i_2 + c'X + bM + e_Y \tag{4.2}$$

where i_1 and i_2 are regression intercepts, e_M and e_Y are errors in the estimation of M and Y, respectively, and a, b, and c' are the regression coefficients given to the antecedent variables in the model in the estimation of the consequents.[2] The coefficients of the model are treated as estimates of the putative causal influences of each variable in the system on others, and the analytical goal is to estimate these coefficients, piece them together, and interpret. These coefficients can be estimated by conducting two OLS regression analyses using the procedures that come with SPSS, SAS, and other statistical packages, using a structural equation modeling program such as LISREL, AMOS, Mplus, or EQS, or through the use of PROCESS, mentioned first in Chapter 1 and illustrated in the next section. In a simple mediation model, it generally makes no difference, although without additional computational aids, OLS regression procedures that come with most statistical packages will not get you all the information you need to conduct some of the more preferred inferential tests described later in this chapter. For now, we can talk about the coefficients and effects in the model with-

---

[1]If you skipped Chapter 3, I recommend you at least take a look at section 3.4, where I introduce the distinction between a conceptual and a statistical diagram.

[2]To simplify mathematical expressions, from this point forward I drop the j subscript indexing case number for measured variables, estimated values of variables, and residuals.

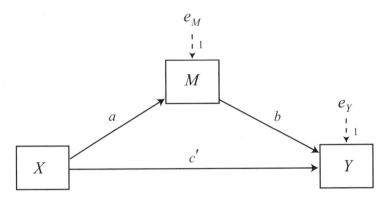

FIGURE 4.2. A statistical diagram of the simple mediation model.

out concerning ourselves with the specifics of the method used to estimate them.

The Direct Effect of X on Y

In equation 4.2, c' estimates the direct effect of X on Y. A generic interpretation of the direct effect is that two cases that differ by one unit on X but are are equal on M are estimated to differ by c' units on Y. More formally,

$$c' = [\hat{Y} \mid (X = x, M = m)] - [\hat{Y} \mid (X = x - 1, M = m)] \qquad (4.3)$$

where m is any value of M, | means *conditioned on* or *given*, and the hat over Y means *estimated* or *expected* from the model. In other words, for two cases with $M = m$ but that differ by one unit on X, c' is the estimated value of Y for the case with $X = x$ minus the estimated value of Y for the case with $X = x - 1$. As can be determined looking at equation 4.3, the sign of c' tells whether the case one unit higher on X is estimated to be higher ($c' = +$) or lower ($c' = -$) on Y. So a positive direct effect means that the case higher on X is estimated to be higher on Y, whereas a negative direct effect means that the case higher on X is estimated to be lower on Y. In the special case where X is dichotomous, with the two values of X differing by a single unit (e.g., $X = 1$ and $X = 0$), $\hat{Y}$ can be interpreted as a group mean, so $c' = [\overline{Y} \mid (X = x, M = m)] - [\overline{Y} \mid (X = x - 1, M = m)]$, meaning c' estimates the difference between the two group means holding M constant. This is equivalent to what in analysis of covariance terms is called an *adjusted mean difference*.

The Indirect Effect of X on Y

Before defining the indirect effect, it is first necessary to discuss what a and b estimate. In this model, a quantifies how much two cases that differ by one unit on X are estimated to differ on M, with the sign determining whether the case higher on X is estimated to be higher (+) or lower (−) on M. That is,

$$a = [\hat{M} \mid (X = x)] - [\hat{M} \mid (X = x - 1)]$$

When X is a dichotomous variable coded by a unit difference, a in equation 4.1 represents the difference between the two group means on M: $a = [\overline{M} \mid (X = x)] - [\overline{M} \mid (X = x - 1)]$.

The b coefficient from equation 4.2 has an interpretation analogous to c', except with M as the antecedent. Two cases that differ by one unit on M but that are equal on X are estimated to differ by b units on Y. As with a and c', the sign of b determines whether the case higher on M is estimated as higher (+) or lower (−) on Y:

$$b = [\hat{Y} \mid (M = m, X = x)] - [\hat{Y} \mid (M = m - 1, X = x)]$$

The indirect effect of X on Y through M is the product of a and b. For instance, if $a = 0.500$ and $b = 1.300$, then the indirect effect of X on Y through M is $ab = 0.650$. The indirect effect tells us that two cases that differ by one unit on X are estimated to differ by ab units on Y as a result of the effect of X on M which, in turn, affects Y. The indirect effect will be positive (meaning the case higher on X is estimated to be higher on Y) if a and b are both positive or both negative, whereas it will be negative (meaning the case higher on X is estimated to be lower on Y) if either a or b, but not both, is negative.

Although one can interpret the indirect effect without considering the signs of a and b, doing so can be dangerous, because the sign of ab is determined by two different configurations of the signs of a and b. A certain theory you are testing might predict ab to be positive because, according to the process the theory explains, a and b should both be positive. But what if, after estimation, a and b turned out to be negative? This would yield a positive indirect effect as predicted, yet this pattern of results for a and b is exactly opposite to what the theory predicts, and this should cast some doubt on whether the theory is adequately describing the process generating your data.

The Total Effect of X on Y

The direct and indirect effects perfectly partition how differences in X map on to differences in Y, the so-called *total effect* of X, denoted here as c. The total effect c quantifies how much two cases that differ by one unit on X are estimated to differ on Y. That is,

$$c = [\hat{Y} \mid (X = x)] - [\hat{Y} \mid (X = x - 1)]$$

In a simple mediation model, c can be derived by estimating Y from X alone:

$$Y = i_3 + cX + e_Y \tag{4.4}$$

When X is a dichotomous variable coded by a single unit difference, c is the difference between the group means on Y: $c = [\overline{Y} \mid (X = x)] - [\overline{Y} \mid (X = x-1)]$. Regardless of whether X is dichotomous, the total effect of X on Y is equal to the sum of the direct and indirect effects of X:

$$c = c' + ab$$

This relationship can be rewritten as $ab = c - c'$, which provides another definition of the indirect effect. The indirect effect is the difference between the total effect of X on Y and the effect of X on Y controlling for M, the direct effect.

That the total effect of X is the sum of the direct and indirect effects can be illustrated by substituting equation 4.1 into equation 4.2, thereby expressing Y as a function of only X:

$$Y = i_2 + b(i_1 + aX + e_M) + c'X + e_Y$$

which can be equivalently written as

$$Y = (i_2 + bi_1) + (ab + c')X + (e_Y + be_M) \tag{4.5}$$

Although it may not look obvious, equation 4.5 is a simple linear function of X, just as is equation 4.4. In fact, equations 4.4 and 4.5 are identical if you make the following substitutions: $c = ab + c'$, $i_3 = i_2 + bi_1$, and e_Y from equation 4.4 $= (e_Y + be_M)$ from equation 4.5. So $ab + c'$ has the same interpretation as c. The sum of the direct and indirect effects quantifies how much two cases that differ by a unit on X are estimated to differ on Y.

4.3 Example with Dichotomous *X*: The Influence of Presumed Media Influence

To illustrate the estimation of direct and indirect effects in a simple mediation model, I use data from a study conducted in Israel by Tal-Or, Cohen, Tsfati, and Gunther (2010). The data file is named PMI and can be downloaded from *www.afhayes.com*. The participants in this study (43 male and

TABLE 4.1. Descriptive Statistics for Presumed Media Influence Study

		Y REACTION	M PMI	Y adjusted
Front page ($X = 1$)	Mean	3.746	5.853	3.616
	SD	1.452	1.267	
Interior page ($X = 0$)	Mean	3.250	5.377	3.362
	SD	1.608	1.338	
	Mean	3.484	5.602	
	SD	1.550	1.321	

80 female students studying political science or communication at a large university in Israel) read one of two newspaper articles describing an economic crisis that purportedly may affect the price and supply of sugar in Israel. Approximately half of the participants ($n = 58$) were given an article they were told would be appearing on the front page of a major Israeli newspaper (henceforth referred to as the *front page* condition). The remaining participants ($n = 65$) were given the same article but were told it would appear in the middle of an economic supplement of this newspaper (referred to here as the *internal page* condition). Which of the two articles any participant read was determined by random assignment. In all other respects, the participants in the study were treated equivalently, the instructions they were given were the same, and all measurement procedures were identical in both experimental conditions.

After the participants read the article, they were asked a number of questions about their reactions to the story. Some questions asked participants how soon they planned on buying sugar and how much they intended to buy. Their responses were aggregated to form an *intention to buy sugar* measure (REACTION in the data file), such that higher scores reflected greater intention to buy sugar (soon and in larger quantities). They were also asked questions used to quantify how much they believed that others in the community would be prompted to buy sugar as a result of exposure to the article, a measure referred to as *presumed media influence* (PMI in the data file).

Tal-Or et al. (2010) reasoned that relative to an article buried in the interior of a newspaper, an article published on the front page of a major newspaper would prompt a belief that others are likely to be influenced by the possibility of a shortage and so would go out and buy sugar. This belief that others were going to respond in this way would, in turn, prompt the participant to believe he or she should also go out and buy sugar. That is, people would use their beliefs about how others would respond to the article anticipating a price increase and supply shortage as a guide to determining their own behavior (i.e.,"Others are going to buy up all the sugar, so I should act while I still can, before prices skyrocket and supplies disappear").

The statistical model is diagrammed in Figure 4.3, and the descriptive statistics for each variable in the two conditions can be found in Table 4.1. To estimate the effects of the manipulation (X in Figure 4.3, COND in the data file, with the front page condition coded 1 and the interior page condition coded 0) on likelihood of buying sugar (Y in Figure 4.3), directly as well as indirectly through presumed media influence (M in Figure 4.3), the coefficients of two linear models defined by equations 4.1 and 4.2 can be generated using any OLS regression program. There are many statistical programs available that can estimate the coefficients of a model such as this with ease. For example, using the PMI data file, in SPSS the commands below estimate a, b, and c':

```
regression/dep=pmi/method=enter cond.
regression/dep=reaction/method=enter cond pmi.
```

The total effect (c) can be calculated as the sum of the direct and indirect effects from the resulting models, or with a third regression analysis:

```
regression/dep=reaction/method=enter cond.
```

In SAS, PROC REG implements ordinary least squares regression, and the commands below estimate the coefficients:

```
proc reg data=pmi;
model pmi=cond;
model reaction=cond pmi;
model reaction=cond;
run;
```

The regression analysis is summarized in Table 4.2, and the regression coefficients are superimposed on the statistical diagram of the model in Figure 4.3. As can be seen, $a = 0.477$, $b = 0.506$, $c' = 0.254$. In terms

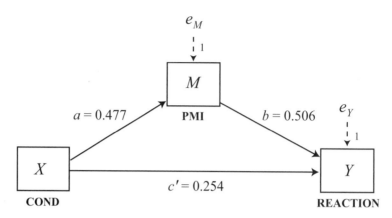

FIGURE 4.3. Simple mediation model for presumed media influence study in the form of a statistical diagram.

of regression equations 4.1 and 4.2, but eliminating the error term and expressing in terms of estimated M and Y,

$$\hat{M} = 5.377 + 0.477X$$

$$\hat{Y} = 0.527 + 0.254X + 0.506M$$

The a coefficient tells us that two cases that differ by one unit on X are estimated to differ by $a = 0.477$ units on M. So those assigned to the front page condition ($X = 1$) are, on average, 0.477 units higher (because a is positive) in their presumed media influence than those assigned to the interior page condition ($X = 0$). As discussed earlier, because the groups are coded on X using a single unit difference, a is the difference between the group means on M: $a = [\overline{M} \mid (X = 1)] - [\overline{M} \mid (X = 0)]$. That is, $a = \overline{M}_{front} - \overline{M}_{interior} = 5.853 - 5.377 \approx 0.477$ (the difference between 0.477 and 0.476 is simply the result of rounding error producing by doing these computations by hand to only the third decimal place).

The regression coefficient for presumed media influence, $b = 0.506$, means that two people assigned to the same experimental condition (i.e., equal on X) but that differ by one unit in their presumed media influence (M) are estimated to differ by 0.506 units in intention to buy sugar (Y). That is, $b = [\hat{Y} \mid (M = m, X = x)] - [\hat{Y} \mid (M = m - 1, X = x)]$. The sign of b is positive, meaning that those relatively higher in presumed media influence are estimated to be higher in their intentions to buy sugar.

The indirect effect is quantified as the product of the effect of the manipulation of article location on presumed media influence (a) and the coefficient for presumed media influence in the model of intention to buy sugar, controlling for article location (b). Doing the math by multiplying

TABLE 4.2. Model Coefficients for the Presumed Media Influence Study

		\multicolumn{3}{c}{Consequent}					
		\multicolumn{3}{c}{M (PMI)}		\multicolumn{3}{c}{Y (REACTION)}	
Antecedent		Coeff.	SE	p		Coeff.	SE	p
X (COND)	a	0.477	0.236	.045	c'	0.254	0.256	.322
M (PMI)		—	—	—	b	0.506	0.097	$< .001$
Constant	i_1	5.377	0.162	$< .001$	i_2	0.527	0.550	.340
		\multicolumn{3}{c}{$R^2 = 0.033$}		\multicolumn{3}{c}{$R^2 = 0.206$}	
		\multicolumn{3}{c}{$F(1, 121) = 4.088, p = .045$}		\multicolumn{3}{c}{$F(2, 120) = 15.557, p < .001$}	

these two coefficients yields the indirect effect of the manipulation of article location on intentions to buy sugar through presumed media influence: $ab = 0.477(0.506) = 0.241$. So relative to those assigned to the interior page condition, those who read an article they were told was to be published in the front page of the newspaper were, on average, 0.241 units higher in their likelihood of buying sugar as a result of the effect of the location of the article on presumed media influence which, in turn, putatively affected people's intentions to buy sugar.

The direct effect of the location of the article on likelihood of buying sugar is estimated as $c' = 0.254$. That is, two cases that differ by one unit on X but are equal on M are estimated to differ by 0.254 units on Y. Because the two groups were coded such that they differ by a single unit on X, substantively, we can say that independent of the effect of presumed media influence on likelihood of buying sugar (because M is being held constant in the derivation of c'), participants assigned to the front page condition ($X = 1$) are estimated to be 0.254 units higher on average in their likelihood of buying sugar than those assigned to the interior page condition ($X = 0$). That is, $[\overline{Y} \mid (X = 1, M = m)] - [\overline{Y} \mid (X = 0, M = m)] = 0.254$.

We could put specific values on these two means by selecting a value of M at which to condition Y and then estimate Y from X and M using equation 4.2. A sensible choice is to condition on being average on the mediator, which produces the *adjusted means* for Y (see Table 4.1), denoted here as $\overline{Y}^*$:

$$\overline{Y}^* = i_2 + b\overline{M} + c'X \tag{4.6}$$

For instance, those assigned to the front page condition ($X = 1$) but who are average ($\overline{M} = 5.602$) in their presumed media influence are estimated to have a score of

$$\overline{Y}^* = 0.527 + 0.506(5.602) + 0.254(1) = 3.616$$

on average, on the intentions measure. In contrast, those assigned to the interior page condition ($X = 0$) who are average in presumed media influence are estimated to have a score of

$$\overline{Y}^* = 0.527 + 0.506(5.602) + 0.254(0) = 3.362$$

on average in their intentions. This difference between these two adjusted means is, of course, 0.254 and is independent of the choice of M at which the estimations of Y are derived.

The total effect of the manipulation on intentions to buy sugar can be derived by summing the direct and indirect effects. In this case, the total effect is $c' + ab = 0.254 + 0.241 = 0.495$, meaning those who read the article they were told was to be published on the front page were, on average, 0.495 units higher in their intention to buy sugar than those told it would be published in the interior of the newspaper. In a simple mediation model such as this, the total effect of X can be estimated merely by regressing Y on X alone, without M in the model. The coefficient for X is the total effect, and it corresponds to the difference between the means of the two groups (i.e., $\overline{Y}_{front} - \overline{Y}_{interior} = 3.746 - 3.250 = 0.496$), which is c (within expected rounding error produced by hand computation).

When X is a dichotomous variable coded by a one-unit difference, and assuming in the equation below that X is coded 0 and 1 for the two groups, the relationship between the total, direct, and indirect effects can be expressed in terms of differences between the means of the two groups along with the effect of M on Y controlling for X:

$$\underbrace{(\overline{Y}_{X=1} - \overline{Y}_{X=0})}_{\text{Total effect } (c)} = \underbrace{(\overline{Y}^*_{X=1} - \overline{Y}^*_{X=0})}_{\text{Direct effect } (c')} + \underbrace{(\overline{M}_{X=1} - \overline{M}_{X=0})\, b}_{\text{Indirect effect } (ab)}$$

Substituting statistics from the previous analysis,

$$\underbrace{(3.746 - 3.250)}_{\text{Total effect } (c)} = \underbrace{(3.616 - 3.362)}_{\text{Direct effect } (c')} + \underbrace{(5.835 - 5.377)\, 0.506}_{\text{Indirect effect } (ab)}$$

Estimation of the Model in PROCESS

Throughout this book I will rely on a tool I created for SPSS and SAS called PROCESS, instructions on the use of which can be found in Appendix A and

```
process vars=pmi cond reaction/y=reaction/x=cond/m=pmi/total=1/normal=1
   /boot=10000/percent=1/model=4.

Model = 4
   Y = reaction
   X = cond
   M = pmi

Sample size
      123

*************************************************************************
Outcome: pmi

Model Summary
         R        R-sq        F         df1        df2          p
      .1808      .0327     4.0878     1.0000   121.0000      .0454

Model
              coeff        se         t          p        LLCI      ULCI
constant    5.3769      .1618    33.2222      .0000     5.0565    5.6973
cond         .4765      .2357     2.0218      .0454      .0099     .9431

*************************************************************************
Outcome: reaction

Model Summary
         R        R-sq        F         df1        df2          p
      .4538      .2059    15.5571     2.0000   120.0000      .0000

Model
              coeff        se         t          p        LLCI      ULCI
constant     .5269      .5497      .9585      .3397     -.5615    1.6152
pmi          .5064      .0970     5.2185      .0000      .3143     .6986
cond         .2544      .2558      .9943      .3221     -.2522     .7609

************************** TOTAL EFFECT MODEL **************************
Outcome: reaction

Model Summary
         R        R-sq        F         df1        df2          p
      .1603      .0257     3.1897     1.0000   121.0000      .0766

Model
              coeff        se         t          p        LLCI      ULCI
constant    3.2500      .1906    17.0525      .0000     2.8727    3.6273
cond         .4957      .2775     1.7860      .0766     -.0538    1.0452
```

Total effect x→y

```
**************** TOTAL, DIRECT, AND INDIRECT EFFECTS ****************

Total effect of X on Y
     Effect        SE         t          p        LLCI      ULCI
      .4957      .2775     1.7860      .0766     -.0538    1.0452

Direct effect of X on Y
     Effect        SE         t          p        LLCI      ULCI
      .2544      .2558      .9943      .3221     -.2522     .7609

Indirect effect of X on Y
       Effect    Boot SE   BootLLCI   BootULCI
pmi      .2413     .1316      .0040      .5239

  Normal theory tests for indirect effect
     Effect        se         Z          p
      .2413      .1300     1.8559      .0635

******************** ANALYSIS NOTES AND WARNINGS ********************

Number of bootstrap samples for percentile bootstrap confidence intervals: 10000
Level of confidence for all confidence intervals in output: 95.00
```

FIGURE 4.4. Output from the PROCESS procedure for SPSS for the presumed media influence simple mediation analysis.

in various places in this book when appropriate. One of the nice features of PROCESS is that it can estimate the coefficients in a simple mediation model such as this, as well as more complex models involving multiple mediators, while providing an estimate of the indirect effect, various inferential tests, and additional output to be discussed later. Furthermore, it can be used for moderation analysis and modeling that combines moderation and mediation. The SPSS version of the PROCESS command for the analysis just conducted is

```
process vars=pmi cond reaction/y=reaction/x=cond/m=pmi/total=1/normal=1
    /boot=10000/percent=1/model=4.
```

In SAS, the equivalent command is

```
%process (data=pmi,vars=pmi cond reaction,y=reaction,x=cond,m=pmi,total=1,
    normal=1,boot=10000,percent=1,model=4);
```

Output from the SPSS version of PROCESS can be found in Figure 4.4. Using OLS regression, PROCESS estimates the models in equations 4.1 and 4.2 and thereby provides a, b, c, and c' along with standard regression statistics such as R^2. It also creates a section of output containing the direct, indirect, and total effects. Several options specified in the command above are not necessary but are present in order to override certain defaults or to produce additional optional output. For example, the **total=1** option produces output for the total effect, and **normal=1**, **boot=10000**, and **percent=1** are pertinent to various inferential tests of the indirect effect to be described below. Additional features of PROCESS will be revealed as necessary throughout this book and are also described in the documentation in Appendix A.

4.4 Statistical Inference

The previous section was dedicated to describing how the effect of X on Y in a simple mediation model can be partitioned into direct and indirect components. When these effects are estimated using OLS regression, it will always be true in any data set you can find, collect, or imagine that $c = c' + ab$. But these effects as represented by c, c', and ab are sample-specific instantiations of their true values $_Tc$, $_Tc'$, and $_Ta_Tb$. They describe the association between variables in the data available, but they say nothing about generalizability. Typically, investigators are interested in generalizability, either by seeing whether "chance" can be discounted as a plausible explanation for the obtained effect by conducting a hypothesis test, or by acknowledging the sampling variance inherent in any estimate through the construction of an interval estimate for these effects. Inference about the direct, indirect, and total effects of X is the topic of this section.

Inference about the Direct Effect of X on Y

The direct effect quantifies the estimated difference in Y between two cases that differ by one unit on X independent of M's influence on Y. Inference for the direct effect of X on Y in a mediation analysis is typically undertaken using the standard method used for inference for any regression coefficient in a regression model. This involves testing a null hypothesis about $_Tc'$ against an alternative hypothesis or the construction of a confidence interval for $_Tc'$. Except in unusual circumstances, researchers focus on ascertaining whether a claim that $_Tc'$ is different from zero is justified based on the data available. If so, this supports the argument that X is related to Y independent of the mechanism represented by M. If not, one can claim that there is no evidence of association between X and Y when the mechanism through M is accounted for. In other words, X does not affect Y independent of M's effect on Y.

In terms of a null hypothesis, this means testing $H_0 : {}_Tc' = 0$ against the alternative $H_a : {}_Tc' \neq 0$. Framed in terms of a confidence interval, this involves determining whether an interval estimate for $_Tc'$ includes zero. The mechanics of both procedures are described in sections 2.3 and 3.3. Any OLS regression program provides the output necessary to implement both approaches, as does the PROCESS procedure.

In the presumed media influence study, is there evidence of a direct effect of the placement of the sugar shortage article on intentions to buy sugar? The answer to this question can be found in two locations in the PROCESS output in Figure 4.4. In the section labeled "TOTAL, DIRECT, and INDIRECT EFFECTS" is the direct effect along with its standard error, t-value, p-value, and 95% confidence interval. This information is also found in the section labeled "Outcome: reaction" in the row labeled "cond," which is the variable name for the experimental manipulation. As can be seen, the direct effect is not statistically different from zero, $c' = 0.254, t(120) = 0.994, p = .322$. The null hypothesis that $_Tc' = 0$ cannot be rejected. The interval estimate for $_Tc'$ is -0.252 to 0.761 with 95% confidence. This confidence interval does include zero, so zero cannot be confidently ruled out as a plausible value for the direct effect. Of course, the hypothesis test and confidence interval lead to the same inference, as they are just different ways of packaging the same information.

Inference about the Indirect Effect of X on Y through M

The indirect effect quantifies how much two cases that differ by a unit on X are estimated to differ on Y as a result of X's influence on M, which in turn influences Y. The indirect effect is relevant as to whether X's effect on Y can be said to be transmitted through the mechanism represented by the $X \rightarrow M \rightarrow Y$ causal chain of events. As with the direct effect, investigators typically want to know whether the data allow for the claim that this estimated difference in Y attributable to this mechanism can be said to be different from zero. If so, one can claim M serves as a mediator of the effect of X on Y. As with inference about the direct effect, this inference can be formulated in terms of a null hypothesis test about $_Ta_Tb$ or by constructing an interval estimate.

In this section I describe only a few of the many approaches to statistical inference for the indirect effect that have been proposed. There are more than a dozen available, and new ones are still being introduced. The ones on which I focus here have been used widely in the past or have become popular recently, and so they are worth emphasizing. For a discussion of some of the approaches I neglect here, see MacKinnon et al. (2002), MacKinnon (2008), Preacher and Hayes (2008b), and Preacher and Selig (2012).

The Normal Theory Approach. Also called the *product of coefficients* approach to inference, the *delta method,* or the *Sobel test,* the normal theory approach is based on the same theory of inference used for inference about the direct effect, as well as other inferential tests widely used in the social sciences and described in elementary statistics books. The indirect effect ab is a sample-specific instantiation of $_Ta_Tb$, which is subject to sampling variance. With an estimate of the standard error of ab and assuming the sampling distribution of ab is normal, a p-value for ab can be derived given a specific null hypothesized value of $_Ta_Tb$, or an interval estimate can be generated.

Before the normal theory approach can be implemented, an estimate of the standard error of ab is needed. There are a few such estimators circulating in the literature that have been used in mediation analysis (see e.g., Aroian, 1947; Baron & Kenny, 1986; Sobel, 1982; Goodman, 1960; MacKinnon, Warsi, & Dwyer, 1995). The simplest is a function of a and b and their standard errors:

$$se_{ab} = \sqrt{a^2 se_b^2 + b^2 se_a^2} \qquad (4.7)$$

where se_a^2 and se_b^2 are the squared standard errors of a and b, respectively. A slightly more complex estimator includes an additional term:

$$se_{ab} = \sqrt{a^2 se_b^2 + b^2 se_a^2 + se_a^2 se_b^2} \qquad (4.8)$$

In practice, it typically makes little difference which estimator is used (Hayes & Scharkow, 2013; MacKinnon et al., 1995). Equation 4.7 is sometimes called the "first-order" delta estimator of the standard error and equation 4.8 the "second-order" estimator. All the information needed to calculate se_{ab} is available in whatever program you might use to estimate a and b. No special software is otherwise needed. For instance, from Table 4.2, $a = 0.477$, $b = 0.506$, $se_a = 0.236$, and $se_b = 0.097$. Plugging this information into equation 4.8 yields the second-order delta estimate of the standard error of the indirect effect in the presumed media influence analysis:

$$se_{ab} = \sqrt{0.477^2 0.097^2 + 0.506^2 0.236^2 + 0.236^2 0.097^2} = 0.130$$

With an estimate of the standard error of the indirect effect, the null hypothesis that $_T a_T b = 0$ can be tested against the alternative that $_T a_T b \neq 0$ by taking the ratio of ab to its standard error:

$$Z = \frac{ab}{se_{ab}}$$

and deriving the proportion of the standard normal distribution more extreme than $\pm Z$. For the indirect effect in the presumed media influence study, $Z = 0.241/0.130 = 1.854$. A table of two-tailed normal probabilities for $Z = 1.854$ yields $p = .064$. This test results in a failure to reject the null hypothesis of no indirect effect using an $\alpha = 0.05$ decision criterion, although some might be comfortable talking about this as "marginally significant" evidence of a positive indirect effect.

If you prefer confidence intervals over null hypothesis testing, the standard error of ab can be used to generate an interval estimate for $_T a_T b$ by assuming normality of the sampling distribution of ab and applying equation 4.9:

$$ab - Z_{ci\%} se_{ab} \leq {}_T a_T b \leq ab + Z_{ci\%} se_{ab} \qquad (4.9)$$

where ci is the confidence desired (e.g., 95) and $Z_{ci\%}$ is the value of the standard normal distribution above which $(100 - ci)/2\%$ percent of the distribution resides. For a 95% confidence interval, $Z = 1.96$. Thus,

$$0.241 - 1.96(0.130) \leq {}_T a_T b \leq 0.241 + 1.96(0.130)$$

So we can be 95% confident that $_Ta_Tb$ is somewhere between −0.014 and 0.496. As with the null hypothesis test, zero cannot be ruled out as a plausible value for $_Ta_Tb$, meaning there is no evidence of an indirect effect of the location of the article on intentions to buy sugar through presumed media influence. In other words, presumed media influence is not functioning as a mediator of the effect of X on Y according to the Sobel test or "normal theory approach" to inference about the indirect effect.

The normal theory approach is simple enough to conduct, and it can be conducted by hand fairly easily if one is careful using the output from any statistical software that estimates a, b, and their standard errors. Even so, unless those computations are done to a high degree of precision, rounding error can easily creep into the calculations and the result can be an inaccurate estimate of the standard error; enough to swing the result of the test in one direction or another. Fortunately, most good structural equation modeling (SEM) programs conduct this test in some form automatically when estimating a simple mediation model. Outside of an SEM program, most statistical software packages require special add-ons or macros to conduct this test, such as the SOBEL (Preacher & Hayes, 2004) or INDIRECT (Preacher & Hayes, 2008a) procedures for SPSS or SAS. PROCESS also conducts this test with the use of the **normal=1** option. The relevant section of output from PROCESS can be found in Figure 4.4 under the section labeled "Normal theory tests for indirect effect."

An additional benefit of the normal theory approach is that it can be conducted even if one does not have the data used to estimate a, b, and their standard errors. Although most researchers would have the original data from their own studies, there could be some circumstances in which it is not available (time has passed; the data were destroyed, lost, or stored on an obsolete storage medium; etc.). In addition, one could apply this approach using the regression coefficients and standard errors provided in the tables or text of published studies conducted by someone else that include a mediation analysis but not a formal test of the indirect effect.

These benefits aside (ease of computation, not requiring the data), the normal theory approach suffers from two flaws that make it difficult to recommend. First, whether inference is based on a hypothesis test or the construction of a confidence interval, this method assumes that the sampling distribution of ab is normal. But it has been shown analytically and through simulation that the distribution is quite irregular in sample sizes that characterize most empirical studies (Bollen & Stine, 1990; Craig, 1936; Stone & Sobel, 1990). Because it is never possible to know for certain whether the sampling distribution is close enough to normal given the characteristics of one's problem to safely apply a method that assumes normality, it is desirable to use a test that does not require this assumption, if one is available. Fortunately, there are several inferential tests available (including one implemented in PROCESS) that do not require this assumption and that better respect the irregularity of the sampling distribution of *ab* than does the normal theory approach.

Second, as discussed at the end of this section, simulation research that has compared this approach to various competing inferential methods has shown that it is one of the lowest in power and generates confidence intervals that tend to be less accurate than some other methods described next (MacKinnon, Lockwood, & Williams, 2004). If X does influence Y indirectly through M, the normal theory approach is relatively less likely to detect it than competing alternatives. So its relatively low power combined with the unrealistic normality assumption leads me to recommend you avoid the Sobel test when possible. For the simple mediation model, and in fact all models discussed in this book, it is always possible to employ a better alternative. I describe a few of those alternatives next.

Bootstrap Confidence Intervals. The downfall of the normal theory approach is the assumption it makes about the shape of the sampling distribution of the indirect effect over repeated sampling from the population. We can assume anything we want, but assuming something doesn't make it so. The evolution of statistics is filled with assumptions people have made in order to make computations tractable, especially in the days before computers were around to make life easier. Often the assumptions made are worth it, as what might be impossible computationally otherwise becomes possible when assumptions are made. Not infrequently, violation of those assumptions has little consequence. But if an alternative method is available that doesn't make a problematic assumption and produces a better inferential test, why not use it instead? Bootstrapping is one of those methods.

As a member of a class of procedures known as *resampling methods*, bootstrapping has been around for at least a few decades. It was made possible by the advent of high-speed computing, and as computer power has increased while the expense of that power has declined, bootstrapping is being implemented in modern statistical software with increasing frequency. Bootstrapping is a versatile method that can be applied to many inferential problems a researcher might confront. It is especially useful when the behavior of a statistic over repeated sampling is either not known, too complicated to derive, or highly context dependent. I will not go into all the subtle details about bootstrapping, as there are good articles and entire books devoted to this topic and variations. For very readable overviews, see Good (2001), Lunneborg (2000), Mooney and Duval (1993), Rodgers (1999) and Wood (2005).

Regardless of the inferential problem, the essence of bootstrapping remains constant across applications. The original sample of size n is treated as a miniature representation of the population originally sampled. Observations in this sample are then "resampled" *with replacement*, and some statistic of interest is calculated in the new sample of size n constructed through this resampling process. Repeated over and over—thousands of times ideally—a representation of the sampling distribution of the statistic is constructed empirically, and this empirical representation is used for the inferential task at hand.

In mediation analysis, bootstrapping is used to generate an empirically derived representation of the sampling distribution of the indirect effect, and this empirical representation is used for the construction of a confidence interval for $_T a_T b$. Unlike the normal theory approach, no assumption is made about the shape of the sampling distribution of ab. Bootstrap confidence intervals better respect the irregularity of the sampling distribution of ab and, as a result, yield inferences that are more likely to be accurate than when the normal theory approach is used. When used to test a hypothesis, the result is a test with higher power.

There are six steps involved in the construction of a bootstrap confidence interval for $_T a_T b$:

1. Take a random sample of n cases from the original sample, sampling those cases *with replacement*, where n is the size of the original sample. This is called a *bootstrap sample*.

2. Estimate the indirect effect ab^* in the bootstrap sample, where ab^* is the product of a and b from equations 4.1 and 4.2.

3. Repeat (1) and (2) above a total of k times, where k is some large number, saving the value of ab^* each time. Generally, k of at least a few thousand is preferred. More than 10,000 typically is not necessary, but in principle, the more the better. I use 10,000 in all examples in this book.

4. Sort the k indirect effects ab^* estimated from steps (1), (2), and (3) from low to high.

5. For a $ci\%$ confidence interval, find the value of ab^* in this distribution of k estimates that defines the $0.5(100 - ci)$th percentile of the distribution. This is the lower bound of a $ci\%$ confidence interval. It will be the value of ab^* in ordinal position $0.005k(100 - ci)$ of the sorted distribution.

6. Find the value of ab^* in this distribution of k estimates that defines the $[100 - 0.5(100 - ci)]$th percentile of the distribution. This is the upper bound

TABLE 4.3. Bootstrap Estimates of *a*, *b*, and the Indirect Effect *ab* When Taking Two Bootstrap Samples from an Original Sample of Size *n* = 10

Original sample				Bootstrap sample 1				Bootstrap sample 2			
Case	X	M	Y	Case	X	M	Y	Case	X	M	Y
1	0	1.500	3.000	4	0	2.500	4.500	10	1	5.000	5.000
2	0	2.000	2.750	8	1	3.000	3.750	3	0	1.000	3.500
3	0	1.000	3.500	2	0	2.000	2.750	7	1	2.500	2.250
4	0	2.500	4.500	3	0	1.000	3.500	5	0	4.500	4.750
5	0	4.000	4.750	1	0	1.500	3.000	6	1	4.500	4.500
6	1	4.500	4.500	2	0	2.000	2.750	8	1	3.000	3.750
7	1	2.500	2.250	6	1	4.500	4.500	8	1	3.000	3.750
8	1	3.000	3.750	8	1	3.000	3.750	4	0	2.500	4.500
9	1	1.500	2.500	5	0	4.000	4.750	10	1	5.000	5.000
10	1	5.000	5.000	9	1	1.500	2.500	2	0	2.000	2.750
a		1.100		*a*		0.833		*a*		1.458	
b		0.700		*b*		0.631		*b*		0.713	
ab		0.770		*ab**		0.526		*ab**		1.039	

of a ci% confidence interval. It will be the value of ab^* in ordinal position $k[1 - 0.005(100 - ci)] + 1$ of the sorted distribution.

To illustrate steps (1), (2), and (3) of this bootstrap sampling and estimation process, Table 4.3 provides a small-scale example. Suppose you have a sample of $n = 10$ cases in a study measured on variables X, M, and Y, and you want to generate a bootstrap sampling distribution of the indirect effect of X on Y through M. Using the original data in the leftmost columns of the table, the obtained indirect effect is $ab = 0.770$. This is a point estimate of $_Ta_Tb$. A bootstrap confidence interval for $_Ta_Tb$ is constructed by repeatedly taking a random sample of size n from the original sample, with replacement, and estimating the indirect effect in each resample. The middle columns of Table 4.3 contain one such bootstrap sample, which yields an indirect effect of $ab^* = 0.526$. The rightmost columns contain a second bootstrap sample with an indirect effect of $ab^* = 1.039$. As this process is repeated over and over, a distribution of ab^* is built which functions as an empirical proxy for the unknown sampling distribution of ab when taking a random sample of size n from the original population.

This table also illustrates the meaning of random resampling with re-placement. Notice in bootstrap sample 1 that cases 2 and 8 from the original sample both appear twice, but by the luck of the draw, cases 7 and 10 do not appear at all. Similarly, bootstrap sample 2 has cases 8 and 10 from the original sample appearing twice, but cases 1 and 9 never appear. That is the nature of random resampling with replacement. This process allows a case to appear multiple times in a bootstrap sample and is necessary in order to mimic the original sampling process, which is the ultimate goal of bootstrap sampling. Suppose case 1 in the original sample is "Joe." Joe happened to be contacted for participation in the study and provided data to the effort. In the resampling process, Joe functions as a stand-in for himself and *anyone else like him* in the pool of potential research partici-pants, as defined by Joe's measurements on the variables in the model. The original sampling could have sampled several Joes or none, depending in part on the luck of the draw. The random resampling process is thus akin to repeating the study over and over again but using the data from those who originally provided data to the study in those replications rather than collecting data on a new set of people. Although it may seem like it on the surface, this is not cheating or creating fake data or falsely inflating one's sample size. It is merely a clever means of ascertaining how ab varies from sample to sample without having to actually sample repeatedly from the original population but, instead, replicating the sampling process by treating the original sample as a representation of the population.

Steps (5) and (6) are generic ways of describing how the endpoints of a confidence interval are constructed given k bootstrap estimates of the indirect effect. A specific example will help. If a $ci = 95\%$ confidence interval is desired, the lower and upper bounds of the interval are defined as the bootstrap values of ab^* that define the 2.5th and 97.5th percentiles in the distribution of k values of ab^*. Suppose $k = 10,000$. In that case, after sorting the 10,000 values of ab^* obtained from repeated bootstrap sampling from low to high, the 2.5th and 97.5th percentiles of the distribution will be in ordinal positions $0.005(10,000)(100 - 95) = 250$ and $(10,000)[1 - 0.005(100 - 95)] + 1 = 9,751$ in the sorted list, respectively. These are the lower and upper bounds of the 95% confidence interval for $_Ta_Tb$.

Obviously, this is a computationally intensive process that requires a computer. Fortunately, it is not difficult to do, as bootstrapping is either hardwired into some data analysis programs (e.g., Mplus) or special code can be written to implement this approach in many popularly used pro-grams, SPSS and SAS among them. Using the presumed media influence study, and with the help of PROCESS, I constructed a 95% bootstrap con-fidence interval for the indirect effect of article placement on intentions to

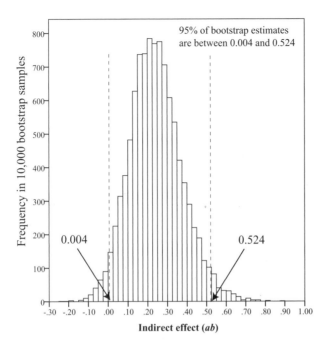

FIGURE 4.5. A histogram of 10,000 bootstrap estimates of the indirect effect in the presumed media influence study.

buy sugar through presumed media influence. A histogram of the indirect effect estimated in 10,000 bootstrap samples can be found in Figure 4.5. Although it may not be apparent at first glance, the distribution is not normal. It has a slight skew and also is more peaked than a normal distribution. Indeed, a hypothesis test leads to a rejection of the null hypothesis of normality, with evidence of positive skew and kurtosis.

As can be seen in Figure 4.5, in the 10,000 bootstrap estimates of the indirect effect, 2.5% were 0.004 or smaller and 2.5% were 0.524 or larger, resulting in a 95% interval estimate for $_Ta_Tb$ of 0.004 to 0.524. As this confidence interval does not contain and is entirely above zero, this supports the conclusion that the indirect effect is positive. Although it is not technically correct to say that one can reject the null hypothesis that $_Ta_Tb = 0$ with a p-value of no greater than .05, in practice the interpretation of the confidence interval leads to essentially the same substantive claim. There is clear evidence that the indirect effect is positive to a "statistically significant" degree.[3]

[3]A p-value from a null hypothesis test is calculated conditioned on the assumption that the null hypothesis is true. Because a bootstrap confidence interval is not derived based on any assumption about the size of $_Ta_Tb$, it would not be strictly correct to say that $p < .05$ if a 95% confidence interval does not include zero.

As noted earlier, PROCESS can be used to generate a bootstrap confidence interval for the indirect effect in a mediation model. In fact, by default it does so with 1,000 bootstrap samples, but the number of bootstrap samples can be changed. In the PROCESS command on page 100, 10,000 bootstrap samples is requested using the option **boot=10000**. The output that results can be found in Figure 4.4 in the section labeled "Indirect effect of X on Y". The lower limit of the bootstrap confidence interval ("BootLLCI") is listed as 0.0040 and the upper limit ("BootULCI") is listed as 0.5239. PROCESS also provides the point estimate using the original data (under "Effect") as well as a bootstrap standard error (under "Boot SE"), defined as the standard deviation of the 10,000 bootstrap estimates of the indirect effect.

Although the bootstrap confidence interval is the inferential approach I emphasize in this book, it is not without its pitfalls and criticisms, and these are worth acknowledging. First, in order to have much confidence in bootstrap-based inference, it is clearly important that one is able to muster some faith in the quality of one's sample as a reasonable representation of the population with respect to the distribution of the measured variables. Bootstrapping is founded on the notion that resampling with replacement from one's sample mimics the original sampling process. But if the sample does not adequately represent the population from which the sample was derived, then bootstrapping will produce results that are hard to trust. It is not required that the original sample be obtained randomly from the population, but merely that the distribution of the measured variables roughly mirrors the population distributions. Random sampling facilitates this representativeness, of course, but it isn't required.

Second, bootstrapping is particularly useful relative to the normal theory approach in smaller samples, because it is in smaller samples that the non-normality of the sampling distribution of *ab* is likely to be most severe, the large sample asymptotics of the normal theory approach are harder to trust, and the power advantages of bootstrapping are more pronounced. But if the original sample is *very* small, in principle, there is a strong potential for one or two cases to distort a bootstrap analysis even more than they do a more traditional inferential procedure. If the original sample is very small, an unusual case or two are highly likely to appear in a bootstrap sample multiple times, and this can distort a bootstrap analysis. I say "in principle" because there is no research on just how much an outlier or two in the sample can nudge bootstrap inferences in the wrong direction. Research on this is needed.

Third, because bootstrap confidence intervals are based on random resampling of the data, the endpoints of the confidence interval are not fixed quantities. Rather, each time a bootstrap confidence interval is produced from the same data, a slightly different confidence interval will result. This is bothersome to some people, for ideally two people analyzing the same data using the same method should get exactly the same results. It also could lead to wrongdoing by unscrupulous investigators who simply repeat a bootstrap analysis until a desired result is obtained.

This latter criticism, while legitimate, can easily be discounted on the grounds that the sampling variation from analysis to analysis can be made arbitrarily small simply by setting the number of bootstrap samples to an arbitrarily large number.[4] This raises the question as to how many bootstrap samples is enough. It can be shown that the variation in the estimation of the limits of a confidence interval shrinks remarkably quickly as the number of bootstrap samples increases. Generally speaking, 5,000 to 10,000 bootstrap samples is sufficient in most applications. There is relatively little added value to increasing it above 10,000, as the gain in precision is fairly marginal beyond that. That said, given the speed of today's desktop computing technology, it is not difficult to use a much larger number to keep the variation due to the random resampling process to an absolute minimum. Do 100,000 bootstrap samples, or even 1,000,000 if you want. Let your computer work on the problem while you sleep.

A bootstrap confidence interval calculated using the approach just described is called a *percentile* bootstrap confidence interval, because it is based entirely on values of ab^* that demarcate the upper and lower $(100 - ci)/2\%$ of the distribution of k bootstrap estimates of the indirect effect. Percentile bootstrap confidence intervals are not produced by default in PROCESS but, rather, must be requested using the **percent=1** option. Absent the use of this option, PROCESS generates a *bias-corrected* bootstrap confidence interval. Bias-corrected bootstrap confidence intervals are like percentile confidence intervals but the endpoints are adjusted as a function of the proportion of k values of ab^* that are less than ab, the point estimate of the indirect effect calculated in the original data. The endpoints will be adjusted upward or downward to varying degrees depending on that proportion. A variation on this variation, known as the *bias-corrected and accelerated* bootstrap confidence interval, makes an additional adjustment based on the skew of the distribution of k bootstrap estimates.

To generate a bias-corrected bootstrap confidence interval for the indirect effect, use the steps below (also see Efron, 1987; Efron & Tibshirani, 1993; Lunneborg, 2000; Preacher & Selig, 2012):

---

[4] A set of bootstrap samples can also be replicated by setting the seed of the random number generator prior to bootstrap sampling. This can be done in PROCESS by using the **seed** option. See the documentation in Appendix A.

1. Follow steps (1) through (4) on page 106 to generate k bootstrap estimates of the indirect effect, ab^*.

2. Calculate $Z(\tilde{p})$, the Z-score that cuts off the lower $100\tilde{p}\%$ of the standard normal distribution from the rest of the distribution, and $\tilde{p}$ is the proportion of the k values of ab^* that are less than ab calculated using the original data.

3. Calculate $Z_{low} = Z_{ci} + 2Z(\tilde{p})$ and $Z_{high} = -Z_{ci} + 2Z(\tilde{p})$, where Z_{ci} is the Z-score that cuts off the lower $(100 - ci\%)/2$ percent of the standard normal distribution from the rest of the distribution. For instance, for a 95% confidence interval, $Z_{95} = -1.96$.

4. Calculate p_{low} and p_{high}, the proportion of the standard normal distribution the left of Z_{low} and Z_{high}, respectively.

5. Find the value of ab^* in the distribution of k estimates that defines the $100p_{low}$ percentile of the distribution. This is the lower bound of a $ci\%$ bias-corrected bootstrap confidence interval, and will be the value of ab^* in ordinal position $(p_{low})k$ of the sorted distribution. If $(p_{low})k$ is not an integer, round it down to the lowest integer.

6. Find the value of ab^* in the distribution of k estimates that defines the $100p_{high}$ percentile of the distribution. This is the upper bound of a $ci\%$ bias-corrected bootstrap confidence interval, and will be the value of ab^* in ordinal position $(p_{high})k$ of the sorted distribution. If $(p_{high})k$ is not an integer, round it up to the next highest integer.

For example, we seek a 95% bias-corrected bootstrap confidence interval for the indirect effect of article location on reactions through presumed media influence. In the data, $ab = 0.241$, and in the 10,000 bootstrap estimates, 5,160 of the estimates were less than 0.241, so $\tilde{p} = .516$ and therefore $Z(\tilde{p}) = 0.040$. For a 95% confidence interval, $Z_{95} = -1.96$. Thus, $Z_{low} = -1.960 + 2(0.040) = -1.880$ and $Z_{high} = 1.960 + 2(0.04) = 2.040$. These convert to $p_{low} = .031$ and $p_{high} = .979$, respectively. So the lower bound of a 95% confidence interval is the value in the distribution of the 10,000 estimates corresponding to the $100(0.031)=3.1$th percentile, which is the 310th value in the sorted distribution. In this case, that value is 0.017. The upper bound of a 95% confidence interval is the value in the distribution of the 10,000 estimates corresponding to the $100(0.979) = 97.9$th percentile, which is the 9,790th value in the sorted distribution, or 0.528. Thus, a 95% bias-corrected bootstrap confidence interval for $_Ta_Tb$ is 0.014 to 0.528. This does not straddle zero, so we can claim with 95% confidence that the indirect effect is positive. For additional computations required to construct a bias-corrected and accelerated bootstrap confidence interval, see Efron (1987) and Efron and Tibshirani (1993).[5]

Alternative "Asymmetric" Confidence Interval Approaches. Observe that the upper and lower bounds of the 95% bootstrap confidence intervals calculated earlier are not equidistant from the point estimate of 0.241. For instance, in the percentile bootstrap confidence interval for the indirect effect, the lower bound is $0.241 - 0.004 = 0.237$ units away from point estimate, and the upper bound is $0.594 - 0.241 = 0.283$ units away. This is not due to the random resampling process but instead reflects the actual asymmetry of the sampling distribution of ab. Confidence intervals based on the normal theory approach to inference, by contrast, impose a symmetry constraint on this distance. The endpoints of a 95% confidence interval using equation 4.9 are necessarily 1.96 standard errors from the point estimate. The endpoints are symmetrical around the point estimate. Thus, percentile-based and BC bootstrap confidence intervals are called "asymmetric," whereas normal theory confidence intervals are "symmetric." Asymmetric approaches to interval estimation are preferred when the sampling distribution of the estimator is asymmetric and non-normal, as is the case for the sampling distribution of ab.

Bootstrapping is not the only approach to the construction of asymmetric confidence intervals. Although I recommend bootstrapping, it does have a few weaknesses, among them that it requires the original data (not usually a real problem typically), the endpoints of the confidence interval will vary from run to run (but not if you seed the random number generator yourself), and it isn't implemented in all software one might choose to use. Two alternatives get around these problems to varying degrees: *Monte Carlo confidence intervals*, and the *distribution of the product* approach.

Monte Carlo confidence intervals are simulation-based. This approach relies on the fact that though the distribution of ab is not normal, the sampling distributions of a and b tend to be nearly so. Furthermore, in simple mediation analysis using OLS regression, a and b are independent across repeated sampling (i.e., their covariance is zero). Thus, an empirical approximation of the sampling distribution of ab can be generated by randomly sampling values of a and b from normally distributed populations with $\mu = a$, $\sigma = se_a$ and $\mu = b$, $\sigma = se_b$, respectively, where a, b, se_a, and se_b are the OLS regression coefficients and standard errors from the mediation analysis. The sampled values of a and b are then multiplied together to produce ab^*, and this process is repeated k times. Over the k replications, the upper and lower bounds of the confidence interval for ab can be gener-

---

[5]The bias-corrected confidence interval is a special case of the bias-corrected and accelerated confidence interval with the acceleration constant set to zero.

ated using the procedure described in steps (4) through (6) on page 106. A generic discussion of the Monte Carlo approach to interval estimation can be found in Buckland (1984). MacKinnon et al. (2004) and Preacher and Selig (2012) further describe the application of this approach to mediation analysis. PROCESS implements the Monte Carlo approach through the **mc** option, as described in Appendix A. Appendix B describes another tool in the form of a macro for SPSS and SAS that could be used to generate a Monte Carlo confidence interval even when you don't have the original data, as PROCESS requires.

The distribution of the product approach relies on a mathematical approximation of the sampling distribution of the product. This complex method defies nonmathematical description. Suffice it to say that it requires a transformation of ab to a standardized metric, finding the values of the standardized metric that define the upper and lower bounds of the confidence interval for the indirect effect in the standardized metric, and then converting these endpoints back into the original metric of ab. Like the Monte Carlo method, all that it needed to implement this approach is a, b, se_a, and se_b from the mediation analysis. For a discussion of this method, see MacKinnon, Fritz, Williams, and Lockwood (2007).

Simulation research shows that both of these methods tend to work pretty well by the standards of relative validity and power, but they are largely exchangeable in that they rarely produce different inferences (Hayes & Scharkow, 2013). They are almost as good as bootstrapping and better than the normal theory approach. Neither approach requires the original data like bootstrapping does. Furthermore, the product of coefficients approach yields endpoints that are fixed rather than varying randomly as a result of the bootstrapping or the Monte Carlo simulation process.

Both of these methods do require special software or some computer programming skill to implement. Fortunately, this work has already been done by others. Tofighi and MacKinnon (2011) provide R code that implements both approaches, the distribution of the product approach is implemented in the PRODCLIN macro for SPSS and SAS (as well as R) described in MacKinnon, Fritz, et al. (2007), and I provide code for SPSS and SAS in Appendix B which constructs Monte Carlo confidence intervals for indirect effects. If you have the original data, PROCESS can also produce Monte Carlo confidence intervals. For example, to generate a Monte Carlo confidence interval for the indirect effect of article location on reactions through presumed media influence based on 10,000 samples, replace the **boot=10000** option in the PROCESS code in section 4.3 with **mc=10000**. The distribution of the product approach is not implemented in PROCESS.

TABLE 4.4. 95% Confidence Intervals for the Indirect Effect in the Presumed Media Influence Study

Method	Lower Limit	Upper Limit
Normal theory	−0.014	0.496
Percentile bootstrap	0.004	0.524
Bias-corrected bootstrap	0.017	0.528
Monte Carlo	0.005	0.523
Distribution of the product	0.011	0.514

To compare confidence intervals using these two methods to bootstrap and normal theory approaches, I generated confidence intervals for the indirect effect in the presumed media influence study, plugging $a = 0.477$, $se_a = 0.236$, $b = 0.506$, and $se_b = 0.097$ into PRODCLIN for SAS (MacKinnon, Fritz, et al., 2007) as well as using the **mc** option in PROCESS. Table 4.4 summarizes the confidence intervals using all the approaches discussed thus far (the percentile and bias-corrected confidence intervals from PROCESS, with 10,000 replications). As can be seen, all four asymmetric confidence intervals are similar, but they differ in an important way from the normal theory confidence interval, in that the normal theory interval is the only one that includes zero. I would trust any of the asymmetric approaches more, as they all honor the irregularity of the sampling distribution of ab. The normal theory "Sobel test" completely disregards and disrespects it.

Does Method Really Matter? In this section I have described several inferential tests for indirect effects in mediation analysis. If you were to apply all of these methods to the same data, you will typically find that it makes no difference which method you use, as they tend to produce the same substantive inference about the indirect effect. But sometimes they will disagree, as demonstrated in Table 4.4. This raises the question as to whether there is one better test among them or one that you should trust more than others, especially when they disagree. There is much research comparing the relative performance of these tests (e.g., Biesanz, Falk, & Savalei, 2010; Fritz & MacKinnon, 2007; Fritz, Taylor, & MacKinnon, 2012; Hayes & Scharkow, 2013; MacKinnon et al., 2004; Preacher & Selig, 2012; Williams & MacKinnon, 2008), and that research says that the answer to this question depends on your relative concern about Type I (claiming an indirect effect exists when it does not) and Type II (failing to detect an indirect effect that is real) errors.

Although the Sobel test is quite conservative, if you are very concerned about Type I errors, it can be a good choice. But the power cost of this conservativeness is likely to be too high for most to tolerate. You are much more likely to miss an indirect effect that is real using the Sobel test. So as noted earlier, I recommend avoiding it. The bootstrap confidence interval tends to have higher power than the Sobel test. In principle, bias-corrected and bias-corrected and accelerated bootstrap confidence intervals should be better than those generated with the simpler percentile method. However, there is evidence that the bias correction (with or without the acceleration component) can slightly inflate the likelihood of a Type I error when either $_Ta$ or $_Tb$ is zero (see, e.g., Fritz et al., 2012). Unfortunately, you can never know whether $_Ta$ or $_Tb$ is zero, so it is difficult to use these findings to guide your decision about which test to use in a particular situation. Regardless, if this elevated risk of Type I error rate concerns you, use a percentile bootstrap confidence interval or a Monte Carlo confidence interval instead. The distribution of the product approach also works quite well, but it almost never disagrees with a Monte Carlo confidence interval.

The bias-corrected bootstrap confidence interval has become the more widely recommended method for inference about the indirect effect in mediation analysis. The simulation research summarized above shows it to be among the better methods for making inferences about an indirect effect balancing validity and power considerations, but this could change as new data come in and new tests are invented. Its popularity has also been enhanced by the existence of freely available tools that make it easy to implement using software scientists are already using, such as INDIRECT for SPSS and SAS (Preacher & Hayes, 2008a), MBESS for R (Kelley, 2007), and now PROCESS. For this reason, I emphasize it throughout this book, and it is the default method used by PROCESS when your model contains a mediation component.

Inference about the Total Effect of *X* on *Y*

In a simple mediation model, the total effect of X on Y is the sum of the direct effect of X on Y and indirect effect of X on Y through M. Whereas there are many choices available for inferences about the indirect effect, inference for the total effect is simple and straightforward. Although the total effect is the sum of two pathways of influence, it can be estimated simply by regressing Y on X. The regression coefficient for X in that model, c in equation 4.4, is the total effect of X. Inference can be framed in terms of a null hypothesis test ($H_0 : _Tc = 0$ versus the alternative $H_a : _Tc \neq 0$) or whether an interval estimate for $_Tc$ includes zero.

The mechanics of both procedures are described in section 2.3. Any OLS regression program provides the output necessary to implement both approaches, as does the PROCESS procedure with the use of the **total=1** option. As can be seen in the PROCESS output in Figure 4.4 under the section labeled "Total effect of X on Y" or in the model information under "TOTAL EFFECTS MODEL," the total effect is $c = 0.496$ but just misses statistical significance using an $\alpha = 0.05$ decision criterion, $t(121) = 1.786, p = 0.077$. With 95% confidence, $_Tc$ resides somewhere between -0.054 and 1.045.

4.5   An Example with Continuous X: Economic Stress among Small-Business Owners

The prior example illustrated the computation of and inference about direct, indirect, and total effects in a study with a dichotomous X. In experiments, X frequently takes only one of two values, such as whether a person is randomly assigned to a treatment or a control condition. X could be dichotomous in a mediation model even if not experimentally manipulated, such as whether a child is diagnosed with attention-deficit hyperactivity disorder (ADHD) or not (Huang-Pollock, Mikami, Pfiffner, & McBurnette, 2009), maltreated by a parent or not (Shenk, Noll, & Cassarly, 2010), or whether or not a soldier killed someone during combat (Maguen et al., 2011), or simply whether a person is male rather than female (Kimki, Eshel, Zysberg, & Hantman, 2009; Webster & Saucier, 2011) or Caucasian rather than Asian (Woo, Brotto, & Gorzalka, 2011). Even in nonexperimental studies such as these, the total, direct, and indirect effects of X can be expressed in terms of differences in $\overline{Y}$ between the two groups, so long as a coding of X is used that affords such an interpretation.

Of course, not all putative causal agents in a mediation model take the form of a dichotomy. For instance, Gong, Shenkar, Luo, and Nyaw (2007) examined the effect of the number of partners in a joint business venture on venture performance both directly and indirectly through partner cooperation. Landreville, Holbert, and LaMarre (2010) studied the effect of individual differences in frequency of viewing of late-night comedy on frequency of political talk during a political campaign. They asked whether more frequent viewing increases political talk in part by increasing interest in viewing political debates, which in turn prompts greater talk. And in an investigation of men with prostate cancer, Orom et al. (2009) reported that men who are relatively more optimistic in their personality find it easier to make decisions about their treatment, because such optimism translates into greater confidence about their decision-making ability, which makes it easier to decide. In these studies, the number of joint venture partners,

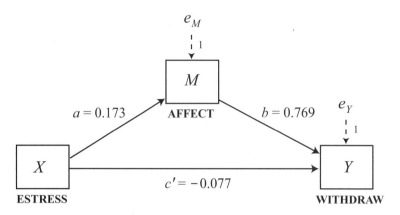

FIGURE 4.6. Simple mediation model for economic stress study in the form of a statistical diagram.

a person's optimism, and how frequently a person reported watching late-night comedy were measured quantitatively—as matters of degree—rather than strictly in binary terms.

When X is a continuum rather than a dichotomy, the total, direct, and indirect effects cannot be expressed literally in terms of mean differences between discrete groups in the study. Indeed, often there are no two people in the study with exactly the same measurement on X. Nevertheless, no modifications are necessary to the mathematics or procedures described in sections 4.2 through 4.4 to estimate these effects, and the general interpretation of these effects otherwise remains unchanged. The total effect of a continuous X on some outcome Y still partitions cleanly into the direct effect and the indirect effect through a mediator M, and these effects can be estimated using the same analytical procedure described thus far.

To illustrate, I use data from the study of economic stress in entrepreneurs by Pollack et al. (2012) introduced in Chapter 1. The data file corresponding to this study is ESTRESS and can be downloaded from *www.afhayes.com*. Participants in this study were 262 entrepreneurs who were members of Business Networking International, a networking group for small-business owners, who responded to an online survey about recent performance of their business, and their emotional and cognitive reactions to the economic climate. As diagrammed in Figure 4.6, Pollack et al. (2012) proposed that economic stress (X) leads to a desire to disengage from entrepreneurial activities (Y) as a result of the depressed affect (M) such stress produces, which in turns leads to a desire to disengage from entrepreneurship. More specifically, the experience of stress results in feelings of despondency and hopelessness, and the more such feelings of depressed affect result, the greater the desire to withdraw from one's role as a small-business owner to pursue other vocational activities. So depressed affect was hypothesized as a mediator of the effect of economic stress on withdrawal intentions.

The participants in this study (162 male, 100 female, with a mean age of 43.8 years) were asked a series of questions about how they felt their business was doing. Their responses were used to construct an index of economic stress (ESTRESS in the data file, with high scores reflecting greater economic stress). They were also asked the extent to which they had various feelings related to their business, such as "discouraged," "hopeless," "worthless," and the like, an aggregation of which was used to quantify business-related depressed affect (AFFECT in the data, with higher scores reflecting more depressed affect). They were also asked a set of questions to quantify their intentions to withdraw from entrepreneurship in the next year (WITHDRAW in the data, with higher scores indicative of greater withdrawal intentions).

The direct and indirect effects of economic stress on withdrawal intentions are estimated just as in the prior example with a dichotomous X. The proposed mediator, depressed affect, is regressed on economic stress (X) to produce a, and withdrawal intentions is regressed on both depressed affect and economic stress, which yields b and c', respectively. In PROCESS for SPSS, the command to estimate the model is

```
process vars=estress affect withdraw/y=withdraw/x=estress/m=affect/total=1
    /boot=10000/normal=1/model=4.
```

and in SAS, use

```
%process (data=estress,vars=estress affect withdraw,y=withdraw,x=estress,
    m=affect,total=1,boot=10000,normal=1,model=4);
```

Output from SAS can be found in Figure 4.7 and is summarized in Table 4.5. As can be seen, $a = 0.173$, $b = 0.769$, and $c' = -0.077$. In the form of two OLS regression models,

$$\hat{M} = 0.799 + 0.173X$$
$$\hat{Y} = 1.447 - 0.077X + 0.769M$$

Multiplying a and b yields the indirect effect, $ab = 0.173(0.769) = 0.133$. This indirect effect of 0.133 means that two entrepreneurs who differ by one unit

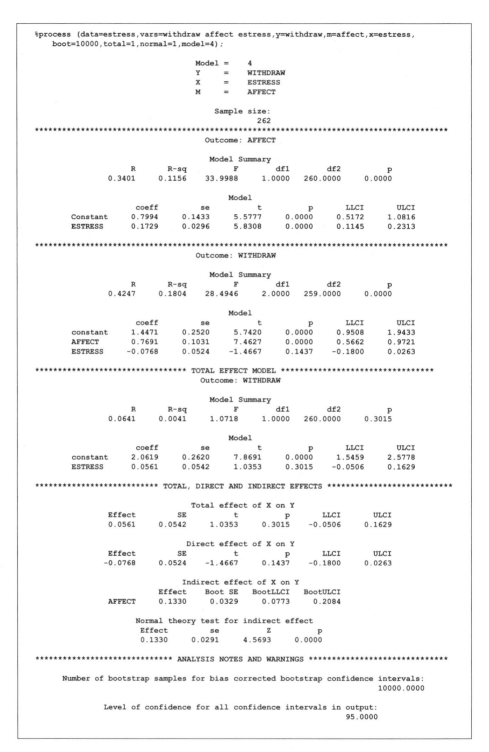

FIGURE 4.7. Output from the PROCESS procedure for SAS for the economic stress simple mediation analysis.

TABLE 4.5. Model Coefficients for the Economic Stress Study

| | | \multicolumn{3}{c}{Consequent} | | | | |
| | | \multicolumn{3}{c}{M (AFFECT)} | \multicolumn{3}{c}{Y (WITHDRAW)} |
Antecedent		Coeff.	SE	p	Coeff.	SE	p
X (ESTRESS)	a	0.173	0.030	$< .001$	c'	-0.077	0.052	.146
M (AFFECT)		—	—	—	b	0.769	0.103	$< .001$
constant	i_1	0.802	0.143	$< .001$	i_2	1.447	0.252	$< .001$
		\multicolumn{3}{c}{$R^2 = 0.116$}	\multicolumn{3}{c}{$R^2 = 0.180$}
		\multicolumn{3}{c}{$F(1, 260) = 33.999, p < .001$}	\multicolumn{3}{c}{$F(2, 259) = 28.495, p < .001$}

in their reported economic stress are estimated to differ by 0.133 units in their reported intentions to withdraw from their business as a result of the tendency for those under relatively more economic stress to feel more depressed affect (because a is positive), which in turn translates into greater withdrawal intentions (because b is positive). This indirect effect is statistically different from zero, as revealed by a 95% BC bootstrap confidence interval that is entirely above zero (0.077 to 0.208 in the PROCESS output under the headings "BootLLCI" and "BootULCI," respectively). In this example, the normal theory-based Sobel test ($Z = 4.569, p < .001$) agrees with the inference made using a bias-corrected bootstrap confidence interval.

The direct effect of economic stress, $c' = -0.077$, is the estimated difference in withdrawal intentions between two business owners experiencing the same level of depressed affect but who differ by one unit in their reported economic stress. The coefficient is negative, meaning that the person feeling more stress but who is equally depressed is estimated to be 0.077 units lower in his or her reported intentions to withdraw from entrepreneurial endeavors. However, as can be seen in the PROCESS output, this direct effect is not statistically different from zero, $t(259) = -1.467, p = .144$, with a 95% confidence interval from -0.180 to 0.026.

The total effect of economic stress on withdrawal intentions is derived by summing the direct and indirect effects, or by regressing withdrawal intentions on economic stress by itself: $c = c' + ab = -0.077 + 0.133 = 0.056$. Two people who differ by one unit in economic stress are estimated to differ by 0.056 units in their reported withdrawal intentions. The positive sign means the person under greater stress reports higher intentions to withdraw from entrepreneurship. However, this effect is not statistically different from zero, $t(260) = 1.035, p = .302$, or between -0.051 and 0.163 with 95% confidence.

4.6 Chapter Summary

Mediator variables function as the conduits through which causal effects operate. When some causal variable X transmits an effect on Y through a mediator M, it is said that X affects Y *indirectly* through M. Indirect effects can be quantified easily using OLS regression and some simple rules of path analysis. X can also affect Y *directly*, meaning independent of its effect on M. These two pathways of influence sum to yield the total effect of X on Y. Relatively recent innovations in computer-intensive methods have made it possible to conduct inferential tests of an indirect effect without making unnecessary assumptions about the shape of its sampling distribution. These basic principles and methods were highlighted here in the context of the simple mediation model—a causal model with only a single mediator variable. A solid understanding of these principles and methods is important, because they serve as the foundation for the discussion in the next two chapters, where they are extended to models with more than one mediator—the *multiple mediator model*.

5
Multiple Mediator Models

This chapter extends the principles of mediation analysis introduced in Chapter 4 to models with more than one mediator. Such models allow a variable's effect to be transmitted to another through multiple mechanisms simultaneously. Two forms of multiple mediator models are introduced here that differ from each other by whether mediators operate in parallel, without affecting one another, or in serial, with mediators linked together in a causal chain. By including more than one mediator in a model simultaneously, it is possible to pit theories against each other by statistically comparing indirect effects that represent different theoretical mechanisms.

Chapter 4 introduced the fundamentals of statistical mediation analysis. In the context of a simple mediation model, I illustrated how the total effect of some causal antecedent X on consequent Y can be partitioned into direct and indirect components, and I described various means of statistically testing hypotheses about direct and indirect effects. As noted at the beginning of that chapter, the simple mediation model is frequently estimated by researchers, but it often represents an oversimplification of the kind of processes that researchers typically study. Specifically, because it is based on only a single mediator variable, it doesn't allow the investigator to model multiple mechanisms simultaneously in a single integrated model.

This limitation of the simple mediation model is important for at least four reasons (see, e.g., Preacher & Hayes, 2008a; MacKinnon, 2000, 2008). First, most effects and phenomena that scientists study probably operate through multiple mechanisms at once. Of course, all models are wrong to some extent, and no model will completely and accurately account for all influences on some outcome of interest (cf. MacCallum, 2003). But some models are more wrong than others. If you have reason to believe that some antecedent variable's effect on a consequent may or does operate through multiple mechanisms, a better approach is to estimate a model that allows for multiple processes at work simultaneously.

Related to this first limitation, it is frequently possible to propose, if not also theoretically likely, that a specific causal influence in a simple mediation model is itself mediated. For instance, the direct effect in a simple mediation model estimates the effect of X on Y independent of M. But there may be identifiable mechanisms responsible for the transmission of this effect. In other words, a direct effect could be interpreted as an estimate of the influence of one or more unmodeled mechanisms that link X to Y other than the M already included in the model. Similarly, in a simple mediation model, the a path estimates the total effect of X on M and the b path estimates the total effect of M on Y controlling for X. Each of these total effects could, in principle, be partitioned into direct and indirect components through one or more mediators, just as can the total effect of X on Y. Doing so requires the addition of at least one mediator to the simple mediation model.

Third, a proposed mediator could be related to an outcome not because it causes the outcome but because it is correlated with another variable that is causally influencing the outcome. This is the noncausal alternative explanation for an association I referred to in Chapter 3 as *epiphenomenality*. For example, recall the simple mediation analysis of the economic stress study presented in Chapter 4. This model proposed that economic stress influences withdrawal intentions through business-related depressed affect, with depressed affect increased through the experience of economic stress, which in turn enhances desire to withdraw from entrepreneurship. But suppose that in fact it is not depressed business-related affect that is the mediator but role conflict. Perhaps economic stress leads entrepreneurs to have to spend more time at work, away from family and friends, in order to keep their business afloat. This conflict between roles (e.g., role as business leader, provider for the family, and husband–wife or father–mother) may enhance the desire to change occupations as a means of bringing the demands of competing roles into better balance. If business-related depressed affect were correlated with feelings of role conflict, then a failure to include role conflict in the model as a mediator could result in the mistaken claim that depressed affect is the mediator transmitting the effect of stress on withdrawal intentions.

Finally, the inclusion of multiple mediators between an antecedent and a consequent allows one to pit competing theories of mechanisms against each other. For instance, theory A may postulate that the effect of X on Y is transmitted primarily through mediator A, whereas theory B perhaps stipulates that a different mediator B is the conduit through which X affects Y. Inclusion of mediators A and B in an integrated model allows for a formal comparison of the size of the indirect effects of X through them.

When the indirect effects are of the same sign, this allows the investigator to determine which indirect effect is the stronger of the two (or three, or four, depending on the complexity of the model).

In this chapter, I extend the principles of path analysis and inference described in Chapter 4 to models with more than one mediator. I focus exclusively on two forms of the multiple mediator model defined by whether the mediators are linked together in a causal chain (the *serial* multiple mediator model) or are merely allowed to correlate but not causally influence another mediator in the model (the *parallel* multiple mediator model).

5.1   The Parallel Multiple Mediator Model

In a parallel multiple mediator model, antecedent variable X is modeled as influencing consequent Y directly as well as indirectly through two or more mediators, with the condition that no mediator causally influences another. For example, Teixeira et al. (2010) simultaneously examined three potential mediators of the effectiveness of a 30-session, 1-year experimental weight loss intervention among middle-aged women. These mediators included emotional eating (e.g., eating to placate a negative mood), restrained eating (e.g., not eating after feeling full), and perceived barriers to exercise. Figure 5.1 depicts this model in conceptual form. They found that relative to women randomly assigned to a control weight-loss program, those who experienced the experimental method did lose more weight over the year. The mediation analysis suggested that the intervention reduced frequency of emotional eating and increased restraint while eating, which in turn resulted in greater weight loss. But independent of these two mechanisms, there was no evidence that the intervention influenced weight loss by changing perceived barriers to exercise.

A statistical diagram of a parallel multiple mediator model with k mediators is depicted in Figure 5.2. Observe that the parallel multiple mediator model looks much like a simple mediation model except that it includes more than one mediator. There are other forms that a multiple mediator model can take, however. A defining feature of the parallel multiple mediator model that distinguishes it from an alternative multiple mediator model—the serial multiple mediator model described in section 5.4—is the constraint that no mediator is modeled as influencing another mediator in the model. This constraint is apparent in Figure 5.2 by the absence of any unidirectional arrows linking any mediator to any other mediator. This is not to say that the mediators are assumed to be independent. In fact, in most circumstances, the mediators are likely to be correlated. Even if they are not, there still may be some advantage to estimating a parallel multiple

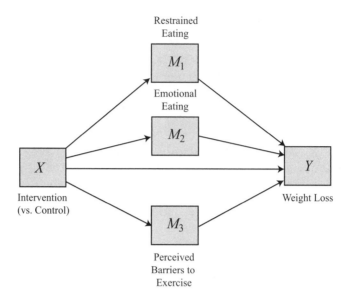

FIGURE 5.1. A conceptual diagram of a parallel multiple mediator model.

mediator model with k mediators rather than k simple mediation models. Doing so could result in a power boost for tests of indirect effects if each mediator is correlated with Y, and doing so affords the ability to compare the sizes of the indirect effects through different mediators.

In principle, the number of mediators one can include in a parallel multiple mediator model is limited only by the number of cases in one's data file and the number of variables one has the foresight to measure as possible mediators. In practice, models with two mediators are most commonly estimated (e.g., Calogero & Jot, 2011; Jackson, 2011; Mesango, Harvey, & Janelle, 2012; Wiedemann, Lippke, Reuter, Ziegelmann, & Ralf, 2011). But parallel multiple mediator models can be found with three (e.g., Bamberger & Belogolovsky, 2011; Duffy, Allen, & Dik, 2011; Jensen, King, & Guntzviller, 2010; Kley, Tuschen-Caffier, & Heinrichs, 2012), four (e.g., Alvarez & Juang, 2010; Chang, 2008; Lecheler, de Vreese, & Slouthuus, 2011; Peréz, Abrams, López-Martínez, & Asmundson, 2012), five (e.g., Brandt & Reyna, 2010; Kalyanaraman & Sundar, 2006; Zadeh, Farnia, & Ungerleider, 2010), six (e.g., Barnhofer & Chittka, 2010; Fonner & Roloff, 2010; Gonzales, Reynolds, & Skewes, 2011), and even as many as seven (e.g., Anagnostopoulos, Slater, & Fitzsimmons, 2010; Hsu et al., 2012) mediators in a model simultaneously.

As can be seen in Figure 5.2, a parallel multiple mediator model with k

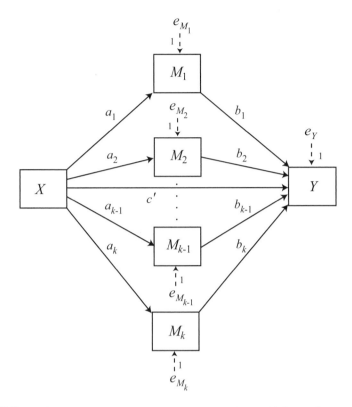

FIGURE 5.2. A statistical diagram representing a parallel multiple mediator model with k mediators.

mediators has $k + 1$ consequent variables (one for each of the k mediators M and one for the outcome variable Y) and so requires $k + 1$ equations to estimate all the effects of X on Y. These equations are

$$M_i = i_{M_i} + a_i X + e_{M_i} \quad \text{for all } i = 1 \text{ to } k \tag{5.1}$$

$$Y = i_Y + c'X + \sum_{i=1}^{k} b_i M_i + e_Y \tag{5.2}$$

In this set of equations, a_i estimates the effect of X on M_i, b_i estimates the effect of M_i on Y controlling for X and the other $k - 1$ M variables, and c' estimates the effect of X on Y holding all k M variables constant.

Consider a parallel multiple mediator with three proposed mediators, like the weight loss example introduced earlier. With $k = 3$ mediators, four equations are needed:

$$M_1 = i_{M_1} + a_1 X + e_{M_1} \tag{5.3}$$

$$M_2 = i_{M_2} + a_2 X + e_{M_2} \tag{5.4}$$

$$M_3 = i_{M_3} + a_3 X + e_{M_3} \tag{5.5}$$

$$Y = i_Y + c'X + b_1 M_1 + b_2 M_2 + b_3 M_3 + e_Y \tag{5.6}$$

In equations 5.3, 5.4, and 5.5, a_1, a_2, and a_3 quantify the amount by which two cases that differ by one unit on X are estimated to differ on M_1, M_2, and M_3, respectively. In equation 5.6, b_1 estimates the amount by which two cases that differ by a unit on M_1 differ on Y holding M_2, M_3, and X constant. Similarly, b_2 estimates the amount by which two cases that differ by a unit on M_2 differ on Y holding M_1, M_3, and X constant, and b_3 estimates the amount by which two cases that differ by a unit on M_3 differ on Y holding M_1, M_2, and M_3 constant. Finally, c' estimates the amount by which two cases that differ by one unit on X differ on Y holding M_1, M_2, and M_3 constant.

The interpretations of a_i and c' are not dependent on the scale of measurement of X. Whether X is a dichotomous variable or a continuum, the interpretation is the same. However, when X is a dichotomous variable with the two groups coded by a one unit difference, these can be interpreted as estimated mean differences. For instance, suppose the two groups are coded with $X = 0$ or $X = 1$. In that case, $a_i = [\overline{M}_i \mid (X = 1)] - [\overline{M}_i \mid (X = 0)]$, and $c' = [\overline{Y}^* \mid (X = 1)] - [\overline{Y}^* \mid (X = 0)]$, where $\overline{Y}^*$ is an adjusted mean, as defined on page 97 with all mediators set to their sample means: $\overline{Y}^* = i_Y + c'X + \sum_{i=1}^{k} b_i \overline{M}_i$.

Direct and Indirect Effects in a Parallel Multiple Mediator Model

In a parallel multiple mediator as in Figure 5.2, X is modeled to exert its effect on Y through $k + 1$ pathways. One pathway is direct, from X to Y without passing through any of the proposed mediators, and the other k pathways are indirect, each through a single mediator. In a multiple mediator model, the indirect effects are referred to as *specific indirect effects*. Thus, a model with k mediators has k specific indirect effects, one through M_1 ($X \rightarrow M_1 \rightarrow Y$), one through M_2 ($X \rightarrow M_2 \rightarrow Y$), and so forth, up through M_k ($X \rightarrow M_k \rightarrow Y$). For instance, in the weight loss study model depicted in Figure 5.1, the experimental intervention (X) is modeled to exert its effect on weight loss (Y) indirectly through three mediators: restrained eating (M_1), emotional eating (M_2), and perceived barriers to exercise (M_3).

As in a simple mediation model, the indirect effect of X on Y through a given mediator M_i is quantified as the product of paths linking X to Y through M_i. In a parallel multiple mediator model, only two paths link X to Y through M_i. The first of these paths is the effect of X to M_i, and the second is the path from M_i to Y. The regression coefficients corresponding to these paths, when multiplied together, yield the specific indirect effect of X on Y through M_i. So consider the three-mediator parallel multiple mediator model estimated with equations 5.3 through 5.6. In this model, the specific indirect of X on Y through M_1 is $a_1 b_1$, the specific indirect effect through M_2 is $a_2 b_2$, and the specific indirect effect of X through M_3 is $a_3 b_3$. Most generally, regardless of the number of mediators, the specific indirect effect of X on Y through M_i is estimated as $a_i b_i$ from equations 5.1 and 5.2.

A specific indirect effect is interpreted just as in the simple mediation model, except with the addition of "controlling for all other mediators in the model." Thus, the specific indirect effect of X on Y through M_i is the estimated amount by which two cases that differ by a unit on X are estimated to differ on Y as a result of the effect of X on M_i, which in turn affects Y, holding all other mediators constant.

When added together, the specific indirect effects yield the *total indirect effect* of X on Y through all mediators in the model. In a model with k mediators:

$$\text{Total indirect effect of } X \text{ on } Y = \sum_{i=1}^{k} a_i b_i$$

For example, in a parallel multiple mediator model with three mediators represented by equations 5.3 through 5.6, the total indirect effect of X on Y is $a_1 b_1 + a_2 b_2 + a_3 b_3$.

The direct effect of X quantifies how much two cases that differ by a unit on X are estimated to differ on Y independent of all mediators. As discussed earlier, this is c' in the model of Y from X and all mediators (e.g., equation 5.6 for the three-mediator model, or equation 5.2 more generally).

As in the simple mediation model, the sum of the direct and indirect effects is the total effect of X. In a model with k mediators, from the coefficients in equations 5.1 and 5.2,

$$c = c' + \sum_{i=1}^{k} a_i b_i \tag{5.7}$$

where c is the total effect of X. The total effect can also be estimated by regressing Y on X alone (as in equation 4.4). For instance, in the three-mediator model, $c = c' + a_1 b_1 + a_2 b_2 + a_3 b_3$. Isolation of the total indirect effect in equation 5.7 shows that the total indirect effect is equal to the difference between the total and the direct effects of X:

$$c - c' = \sum_{i=1}^{k} a_i b_i$$

5.2 Example Using the Presumed Media Influence Study

In Chapter 4, simple mediation analysis was illustrated using the data from a study conducted in Israel in which participants' reactions to a newspaper article about a likely sugar shortage were assessed (Tal-Or et al., 2010). Recall that half of the participants read an article they were told would be published on the front page of Israel's largest daily newspaper, whereas the other half were told it would appear in an internal economic supplement. After reading the article, their beliefs about how others would be influenced were measured (i.e., the extent to which the general public would be prompted to go buy sugar as a result of the article). The model in that chapter placed these beliefs, presumed media influence (PMI in the data file), as the mechanism or mediator intervening between the experimental manipulation of article location (COND in the data file: 1 for those assigned to the front page condition, 0 to the interior page condition) and intentions to buy sugar (REACTION in the data file). That is, people who thought the article was about to be published on the front page would be more inclined to believe that the public would be influenced relative to those told the article would appear in an economic supplement, so they themselves should go out and buy more sugar before it was all gone.

As described at the beginning of this chapter, establishing an indirect effect of X on Y through M through a simple mediation analysis does not imply that M is the only mechanism at work linking X to Y (cf. Rucker et al., 2011). Furthermore, the indirect effect could be due to an epiphenomenal association between the M in a simple mediation model and the "true" mediator or mediators causally between X and Y. Any variable correlated with presumed media influence and also affected by the experimental manipulation of article location could be the actual mediator transmitting the effect of location on intentions to buy sugar.

Fortunately, Tal-Or et al. (2010) recognized this and so had the foresight to measure a variable related to another conceivable mechanism—perceived issue importance. Perhaps people infer from where an article is published the extent to which the issue is something worthy of attention, of local or national significance, and thereby potentially something

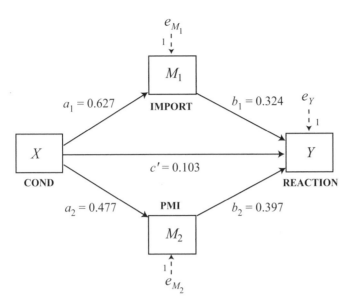

FIGURE 5.3. A statistical diagram of the parallel multiple mediator model for the presumed media influence study.

one should think about and perhaps act upon. So they measured people's beliefs about how important the potential sugar shortage was using two questions that were aggregated to form a perceived importance measure (IMPORT in the data file). Significant to the point made earlier, issue importance is correlated with presumed media influence ($r = 0.282, p < .01$). Those relatively more likely to believe others would be influenced to buy sugar as a result of reading the article also perceived the sugar shortage as relatively more important. Thus, it is conceivable that presumed media influence only appears to be functioning as a mediator of the effect of article location on peoples' reactions and it is perceptions of importance that is the real mediator.

   Estimation of indirect effects in a parallel multiple mediator model with both presumed media influence and perceived importance as potential mediators would allow for a simultaneous test of each mechanism while accounting for the shared association between them. Figure 5.3 provides a statistical diagram of the model. As can be seen, it contains three consequent variables, so it requires three equations to estimate all the effects, one for each of the mediators (M_1 and M_2), and one for the outcome Y. The equations for the mediators contain article location (X) as the only predictor, whereas the equation for intentions to buy sugar (Y) includes both article location and the two mediators.

In SPSS, the coefficients of this model are estimated with three regression commands:

```
regression/dep=import/method=enter cond.
regression/dep=pmi/method=enter cond.
regression/dep=reaction/method=enter import cond pmi.
```

The corresponding commands in SAS are

```
proc reg data=pmi;
model import=cond;
model pmi=cond;
model reaction=cond import pmi;
run;
```

The regression coefficients, standard errors, and other statistics pertinent to the model are summarized in Table 5.1, and the path coefficients are superimposed on the statistical diagram in Figure 5.3.

PROCESS greatly simplifies the estimation process by conducting all these regressions in one command, while also generating various additional statistics and inferential tests discussed in section 5.3 but not available in the OLS regression routines built into SPSS and SAS. In SPSS, the PROCESS command below estimates the model and provides output pertinent to statistical inference:

```
process vars=cond pmi import reaction/y=reaction/x=cond/m=import pmi
   /boot=10000/total=1/normal=1/contrast=1/model=4.
```

In SAS, use

```
%process (data=pmi,vars=cond pmi import reaction,y=withdraw,x=cond,
   m=import pmi,boot=10000,total=1,normal=1,contrast=1,model=4);
```

This PROCESS command looks almost identical to the command for the simple mediation model in Chapter 4, with two exceptions. First, the addition of issue importance (IMPORT) to the model requires it be listed in the **vars=** list, and because it is modeled as a mediator, it also must be listed in the **m=** list. Notice that the inclusion of an additional mediator does not require a different model number; **model=4** is used for both simple mediation

TABLE 5.1. Regression Coefficients, Standard Errors, and Model Summary Information for the Presumed Media Influence Parallel Multiple Mediator Model Depicted in Figure 5.3

		Consequent										
		M_1 (IMPORT)				M_2 (PMI)				Y (REACTION)		
Antecedent		Coeff.	SE	p		Coeff.	SE	p		Coeff.	SE	p
X (COND)	a_1	0.627	0.310	.045	a_2	0.477	0.236	.045	c'	0.103	0.239	.666
M_1 (IMPORT)		—	—	—		—	—	—	b_1	0.324	0.071	<.001
M_2 (PMI)		—	—	—		—	—	—	b_2	0.397	0.093	<.001
Constant	i_{M_1}	3.908	0.213	<.001	i_{M_2}	5.377	0.162	<.001	i_Y	-0.150	0.530	.778
		$R^2 = 0.033$				$R^2 = 0.033$				$R^2 = 0.325$		
		$F(1, 121) = 4.094, p = .045$				$F(1, 121) = 4.088, p = .045$				$F(3, 119) = 19.112, p < .001$		

133

models and parallel multiple mediator models. PROCESS automatically detects the number of variables listed in the **m=** list and estimates a parallel multiple mediator model if it sees more than one variable in the list. The order the variables in this list is not consequential in model 4 for estimation purposes, although it does influence the order in which information about the models and effects is displayed in the output. The second difference is the addition of the **contrast=1** command, which requests PROCESS to conduct a test of differences between specific indirect effects. This test is described in section 5.3.

From Table 5.1 or Figure 5.4, the three best fitting OLS regression models that define this parallel multiple mediator model are

$$\hat{M}_1 = 3.908 + 0.627X$$
$$\hat{M}_2 = 5.377 + 0.477X$$
$$\hat{Y} = -0.150 + 0.103X + 0.324M_1 + 0.397M_2$$

Thus, $a_1 = 0.627, a_2 = 0.477, b_1 = 0.324, b_2 = 0.397, c' = 0.103$. The use of the **total=1** option in PROCESS also generates the total effect, $c = 0.496$, from estimating Y from X alone. Very little of the variance in perceived media influence or issue importance is explained by the manipulation of article location (both $R^2 = 0.033$), but about a third of the variance in intentions to buy sugar is accounted for by both proposed mediators and article location, $R^2 = 0.325$.

The most relevant information pertinent to the process being modeled is the direct and indirect effects of article location on participants' reactions to the article. Starting first with the indirect effect through issue importance, this indirect effect is estimated as $a_1b_1 = 0.627(0.324) = 0.203$. PROCESS does the multiplication automatically and displays the indirect effect in the section of output on page 136 labeled "Indirect effect of X on Y" in the row labeled "import." Two cases that differ by one unit on X (i.e., COND, the front versus the interior page condition in this data set) are estimated to differ by 0.203 units in their intention to buy sugar through perceived importance, with those assigned to the front page condition having higher intentions (because the indirect effect is positive). This positive indirect effect results from two positive constituent effects. Those assigned to the front page condition have stronger intentions to buy sugar as a result of the tendency for those told the article was to be published on the front page to perceive the sugar shortage as more important than those told it would be published in an interior supplement (because a_1 is positive), which in turn was positively related to their own intentions to purchase sugar (because b_1 is positive). Because the two experimental groups are coded by a one-unit difference on X, this indirect effect is equal to the mean difference in

```
process vars = cond pmi import reaction/y=reaction/x=cond/m=import pmi
  /boot=10000/total=1/normal=1/contrast=1/model=4.

Model = 4
    Y = reaction
    X = cond
    M1 = import
    M2 = pmi

Sample size
       123

*************************************************************************
Outcome: import

Model Summary
          R       R-sq         F        df1        df2          p
       .1809      .0327     4.0942     1.0000   121.0000      .0452

Model
              coeff        se          t          p       LLCI       ULCI
constant     3.9077      .2127    18.3704      .0000     3.4866     4.3288
cond          .6268      .3098     2.0234      .0452      .0135     1.2401

*************************************************************************
Outcome: pmi

Model Summary
          R       R-sq         F        df1        df2          p
       .1808      .0327     4.0878     1.0000   121.0000      .0454

Model
              coeff        se          t          p       LLCI       ULCI
constant     5.3769      .1618    33.2222      .0000     5.0565     5.6973
cond          .4765      .2357     2.0218      .0454      .0099      .9431

*************************************************************************
Outcome: reaction

Model Summary
          R       R-sq         F        df1        df2          p
       .5702      .3251    19.1118     3.0000   119.0000      .0000

Model
              coeff        se          t          p       LLCI       ULCI
constant     -.1498      .5298     -.2828      .7778    -1.1989      .8993
import        .3244      .0707     4.5857      .0000      .1843      .4645
pmi           .3965      .0930     4.2645      .0000      .2124      .5806
cond          .1034      .2391      .4324      .6662     -.3701      .5768

************************* TOTAL EFFECT MODEL ***************************
Outcome: reaction

Model Summary
          R       R-sq         F        df1        df2          p
       .1603      .0257     3.1897     1.0000   121.0000      .0766

Model
              coeff        se          t          p       LLCI       ULCI
constant     3.2500      .1906    17.0525      .0000     2.8727     3.6273
cond          .4957      .2775     1.7860      .0766     -.0538     1.0452
```

(continued)

FIGURE 5.4. Output from the PROCESS procedure for SPSS for a parallel multiple mediator model of the presumed media influence data.

```
****************** TOTAL, DIRECT, AND INDIRECT EFFECTS ********************

Total effect of X on Y
       Effect          SE          t          p        LLCI        ULCI
        .4957       .2775     1.7860      .0766      -.0538      1.0452

Direct effect of X on Y
       Effect          SE          t          p        LLCI        ULCI
        .1034       .2391      .4324      .6662      -.3701       .5768

Indirect effect of X on Y
               Effect    Boot SE    BootLLCI    BootULCI
TOTAL           .3923      .1638       .0942       .7408
import          .2033      .1138       .0225       .4814
pmi             .1890      .1054       .0129       .4318
(C1)            .0144      .1458      -.2669       .3069

Normal theory tests for specific indirect effects
               Effect         se          z          p
import          .2033      .1120     1.8154      .0695
pmi             .1890      .1057     1.7872      .0739

Specific indirect effect contrast definitions
(C1)      import     minus       pmi

******************** ANALYSIS NOTES AND WARNINGS *************************

Number of bootstrap samples for bias corrected bootstrap confidence intervals:
   10000

Level of confidence for all confidence intervals in output:
   95.00
```

FIGURE 5.4 continued.

perceived importance times the partial effect of perceived importance on reactions: $a_1b_1 = ([\overline{M}_1 \mid (X = 1)] - [\overline{M}_1 \mid (X = 0)])b_1 = (4.535 - 3.908)0.324 = 0.203$.

A second indirect effect of article location on intention to buy sugar is modeled through presumed media influence, estimated as $a_2b_2 = 0.477(0.397) = 0.189$ and provided in the PROCESS output. Those assigned to the front page condition have stronger intentions to buy sugar (by 0.189 units) as a result of the tendency for those told the article was to be published on the front page to perceive others would be influenced by the story more so than those told it would be published in an interior supplement (because a_2 is positive), which in turn was positively related to their own intentions to purchase sugar (because b_2 is positive). This is equivalent to the mean difference in perceived media influence multiplied by the partial effect of presumed media influence on reactions: $a_2b_2 = ([\overline{M}_2 \mid (X = 1)] - [\overline{M}_2 \mid (X = 0)])b_2 = (5.853 - 5.377)0.397 = 0.189$.

In a parallel multiple mediator model, it is possible to talk about the indirect effect of X on Y summed across all mediators. This is the total indirect effect introduced earlier, defined here as $a_1b_1 + a_2b_2 = 0.627(0.324) + 0.477(0.397) = 0.392$. The total indirect effect is positive, meaning that those assigned to the front page condition were, on average, 0.392 units higher in their intention to buy sugar than those assigned to the interior page condition as a result of the effect of article location on the mediators, which in turn influence intentions. The total indirect effect often is not of much interest in a multiple mediator model, and sometimes it will be small even when the specific indirect effects are relatively large, which seems paradoxical. More on this in section 5.5.

The direct effect, $c' = 0.103$, quantifies the effect of the manipulation of article location on intentions to buy sugar independent of the effect of the proposed mediators on those intentions. Irrespective of differences between the groups in their perceived media influence and issue importance and how those mediators relate to intentions to buy sugar, those told the article was to be published on the front page expressed stronger intentions to buy sugar (because c' is positive) than those told it would be published in the interior supplement. Due to the coding of groups by a difference of one unit, c' is equivalent to the difference between adjusted means, as defined and described on page 97. In this case, $c' = [\overline{Y}^* \mid (X = 1)] - [\overline{Y}^* \mid (X = 0)] = 3.538 - 3.435 = 0.103$, where $\overline{Y}^* = -0.150 + 0.103X + 0.324(4.203) + 0.397(5.603)$ from the model of Y.

The total effect of article location on intentions to buy sugar is not determined at all by the mediators proposed as intervening between X and Y. As it was in the simple mediation model, $c = 0.496$. As promised, this total effect partitions cleanly into the direct effect plus the sum of the specific indirect effects:

$$c = c' + a_1 b_1 + a_2 b_2 = 0.103 + 0.203 + 0.189 = 0.496$$

meaning that the total indirect effect of X (i.e., the sum of the specific indirect effects) is difference between the total and direct effects of X:

$$c - c' = a_1 b_1 + a_2 b_2 = 0.496 - 0.103 = 0.203 + 0.189 = 0.392$$

5.3 Statistical Inference

The prior section illustrated the estimation of the equations defining a multiple mediator model using the OLS regression procedures built into SPSS or SAS as well as using the PROCESS procedure. The discussion thus far has been purely descriptive in nature. Statistical inference allows for generalization to the process generating the data or the population from which the sample was derived. The inferential procedures available for effects in the parallel multiple mediator model are similar to those in the simple mediation model. The inclusion of multiple mediators also allows for a formal test of the difference between specific indirect effects. Such a test is described in this section.

Inference about the Direct Effect

As in the simple mediation model, inference about the direct effect of X on Y is straightforward. A test of the null hypothesis that $_Tc' = 0$ is available in the output from any statistical package that can estimate equation 5.2 using OLS regression. This test is available in two locations on the PROCESS output in Figure 5.4. As can be seen, $c' = 0.103, t(119) = 0.432, p = .666$. The null hypothesis cannot be rejected. Alternatively, a confidence interval can be constructed using equation 2.10, implemented automatically by PROCESS. Note that $-0.370 \leq _Tc' \leq 0.577$. Regardless of which method is used, there is no evidence that participants' reactions to the article differ as a function of article location when presumed media influence and perceived importance are statistically controlled.

Inference about Specific Indirect Effects

Although I don't recommend it, the normal theory approach for the indirect effect in a simple mediation model described in section 4.4 can be used for statistical inference about specific indirect effects in a parallel multiple mediator model without modification. For the specific indirect effect of X on Y through M_i, the first-order standard error estimator is

$$se_{a_ib_i} = \sqrt{a_i^2 se_{b_i}^2 + b_i^2 se_{a_i}^2}$$

where $se_{a_i}^2$ and $se_{b_i}^2$ are the squared standard errors of a_i and b_i. The second-order estimator is

$$se_{a_ib_i} = \sqrt{a_i^2 se_{b_i}^2 + b_i^2 se_{a_i}^2 + se_{a_i}^2 se_{b_i}^2}$$

A test of the null hypothesis that $_Ta_{iT}b_i = 0$ is constructed by dividing a_ib_i by the estimated standard error and deriving a p-value from the standard normal distribution. Alternatively, a $ci\%$ confidence interval can be constructed as

$$a_ib_i - Z_{ci\%}se_{a_ib_i} \leq _Ta_{iT}b_i \leq a_ib_i + Z_{ci\%}se_{a_ib_i}$$

where ci is the confidence desired (e.g., 95) and $Z_{ci\%}$ is the value under the normal distribution that cuts off the upper $(100 - ci)/2\%$ of the distribution from the rest.

Rounding errors and other inaccuracies are nearly inevitable if these computations are done by hand. PROCESS provides normal theory hypothesis tests for specific indirect effects in a parallel multiple mediator model through the use of the **normal=1** option. As can be seen in the output toward the bottom of Figure 5.4 under the label "Normal theory tests for indirect effects," the specific indirect effect of article location on reactions is not statistically significant from zero through either perceived importance ($Z = 1.815, p = .070$) or perceived media influence ($Z = 1.787, p = .074$). But for reasons described in section 4.4, this approach is hard to trust. It makes the unrealistic assumption of normality of the sampling distribution of the specific indirect effect, and it is one of the more conservative tests available. I recommend staying away from this test.

Bootstrap confidence intervals are the better approach to inference when the original data are available for analysis. No assumptions about the shape of the sampling distribution of $a_i b_i$ are made, and bootstrap confidence intervals tend to be more powerful than competing methods such as the normal theory approach (see Williams & MacKinnon, 2008, for simulation results specific to the multiple mediator model). Using the same procedure described on page 106, a bootstrap confidence interval for a specific indirect effect is constructed by taking a random sample with replacement of size n from the sample, estimating each specific indirect effect $a_i b_i^*$ in the resulting data, and repeating this resampling and estimation many times. With several thousand bootstrap estimates of each specific indirect effect, endpoints of the confidence interval are calculated using either the percentile or bias-corrected method. If zero is outside of a $ci\%$ confidence interval, then $_T a_{iT} b_i$ is declared different from zero with $ci\%$ confidence, whereas if the confidence interval straddles zero, the conclusion is that there is insufficient evidence that X affects Y through M_i.

Bias-corrected bootstrap confidence intervals for the specific indirect effects generated by PROCESS can be found in Figure 5.4 under the section of the output that reads "Indirect effect of X on Y." Notice that contrary to the conclusion reached using the normal theory approach, the bootstrap confidence intervals support the claim, with 95% confidence, that article location influences reactions indirectly through both perceived importance (0.023 to 0.481) and presumed media influence (0.013 to 0.432), as both confidence intervals are entirely above zero. I trust this conclusion more, as bootstrap confidence intervals respect the irregularity of the sampling distribution of the indirect effect and provide an inference that is higher in power than the normal theory approach.

Bootstrap confidence intervals require the original data. Although this is not usually a problem for researchers, there are occasions when the data may not be available. Monte Carlo confidence intervals are a good substitute for bootstrapping in such a circumstance. The estimation of a Monte Carlo confidence interval for a specific indirect effect proceeds similarly to the estimation procedure in the simple mediation model. The major difference in the procedure relates to the fact that there are multiple a and b distributions to simulate in a multiple mediator model. For a multiple mediator model with k mediators, one could simply use the Monte Carlo method described in section 4.4 k times, once for each specific indirect effect, plugging the values of a_i, b_i, se_{a_i}, and se_{b_i} into the Monte Carlo sampling procedure (or the code in Appendix B). An alternative approach would acknowledge that the regression coefficients in a multiple mediator model are not necessarily independent, and so the Monte Carlo sampling procedure should accommodate this. Preacher and Selig (2012) describe the construction of Monte Carlo confidence intervals in a multiple mediator model and provide R code which does the computation.

Pairwise Comparisons between Specific Indirect Effects

In a multiple mediator model, it is sometimes of interest to test whether one indirect effect is statistically different from another. For instance, is the specific indirect effect of article location on reactions through perceived importance different from the specific indirect effect through presumed media influence? If the indirect effect of X through mediator i (i.e., $a_i b_i$) is pertinent to the mechanism postulated by one theory and the indirect effect of X through mediator j (i.e., $a_j b_j$) quantifies the mechanism relevant to a second theory, an inference about whether $_T a_{iT} b_i = _T a_{jT} b_j$ affords a claim as to whether one mechanism accounts for more of the effect of X on Y than the other mechanism, with an important caveat described below. For examples of such questions in the literature about difference between indirect effects, answered using the approach described here, see Hart (2011), Peréz et al. (2012), and Zeller, Reiter-Purtill, and Ramey (2008).

Although it might seem that such a comparison between specific indirect effects would be impossible if the mediators are measured on different metrics, it turns out this is not a problem at all. Remember that the specific indirect effect is interpreted as the amount by which two cases differing by a unit on X are estimated to differ on Y through the intervening variable independent of the other intervening variables. Notice that this interpretation does not include the metric of the intervening variable. Specific indirect effects are scaled entirely in terms of the metrics of X and Y (see MacKinnon, 2000, 2008; Preacher & Hayes, 2008a), so two specific indirect effects of the same antecedent on the same consequent can be meaningfully compared even if the mediator variables are measured on entirely different scales.

Thus, standardization or other forms of arithmetic gymnastics applied to the measurement scales is not necessary to conduct an inferential test of the equality of specific indirect effects from X to Y in a multiple mediator model.

Two inferential approaches have been most widely discussed and disseminated in the literature. A normal theory approach is described by Preacher and Hayes (2008a) and MacKinnon (2000) based on dividing $a_ib_i - a_jb_j$ by an estimate of its standard error. One estimator of the standard error of the difference is

$$se_{a_ib_i - a_jb_j} = \sqrt{\begin{array}{c} b_i^2 se_{a_i}^2 - 2b_ib_jCOV_{a_ia_j} + b_j^2 se_{a_j}^2 + \\ a_j^2 se_{b_j}^2 - 2a_ia_jCOV_{b_ib_j} + a_i^2 se_{b_i}^2 \end{array}}$$

where $COV_{a_ia_j}$ is the covariance between a_i and a_j, and $COV_{b_ib_j}$ is the covariance between b_i and b_j. MacKinnon (2000) offers a different standard error estimator that does not require the covariance between a_i and a_j by assuming it is zero, which is equivalent to constraining the correlation between the residuals in the models of M_i and M_j to be zero:

$$se_{a_ib_i - a_jb_j} = \sqrt{b_i^2 se_{a_i}^2 + b_j^2 se_{a_j}^2 + a_j^2 se_{b_j}^2 - 2a_ia_jCOV_{b_ib_j} + a_i^2 se_{b_i}^2}$$

The ratio of the difference to its standard error is then calculated and a p-value for a test of the null hypothesis that $_Ta_{iT}b_i = {}_Ta_{jT}b_j$ can be derived using the standard normal distribution. Alternatively, a 95% confidence interval for the difference can be computed as

$$(a_ib_i - a_jb_j) \pm 1.96se_{a_ib_i - a_jb_j} \tag{5.8}$$

In this expression, 1.96 can be replaced with an appropriate critical Z from a table of normal probabilities for different confidence levels (e.g., 1.645 for 90% or 2.57 for 99% confidence).

A good SEM program such as Mplus can conduct the normal theory approach using the MODEL CONSTRAINT command, and this method is also implemented in the INDIRECT procedure for SPSS and SAS (Preacher & Hayes, 2008a) for parallel multiple mediator models. As of the publication of this book, PROCESS does not offer this test.

Like all normal theory approaches discussed thus far, this method requires the assumption that the sampling distribution of the difference between specific indirect effects is normal. It turns out that this is a fairly reasonable assumption, but since an assumption can never be proven true, bootstrapping offers an alternative test without requiring this assumption. A bootstrap confidence interval is derived by estimating the difference between specific indirect effects over repeated bootstrap sampling and model estimation. Using the resulting empirical approximation of the sampling distribution of the difference between specific indirect effects, a confidence interval for the difference can be constructed using either the percentile method described earlier or through bias correction.

PROCESS does offer bootstrap confidence intervals for pairwise comparisons between specific indirect effects with the addition of **contrast=1** to the PROCESS command. In a model with k mediators, PROCESS will conduct $k(k-1)/2$ pairwise comparisons, one for each possible difference between specific indirect effects. A confidence interval that does not contain zero provides evidence that the two indirect effects are statistically different from each other, whereas a confidence interval that straddles zero supports the claim of no difference between the specific indirect effects.

The output this option generates for the parallel multiple mediator model of the presumed media influence study can be found in Figure 5.4 in the indirect effects section in the row labeled "(C1)." There is only one such comparison listed because in a parallel multiple mediator model with two mediators, there are only two specific indirect effects and so only one pairwise comparison is possible. The PROCESS output provides a key for the meaning of (C1) at the bottom of Figure 5.4, which in this case is the specific indirect effect through importance minus the specific indirect effect through presumed media influence (i.e., $a_1b_1 - a_2b_2$). The point estimate of the difference between specific indirect effects is $0.203 - 0.189 = 0.014$, but a 95% confidence interval straddles zero (-0.267 to 0.307). So we can say with 95% confidence that these indirect effects are not statistically different from each other. The indirect effect of article location on reactions through perceived importance is no different than the indirect effect through presumed media influence.

It is tempting to treat this as a test of the difference in *strength* of the mechanisms at work linking X to Y, or that one indirect effect is larger than another in an absolute sense. However, such an interpretation is justified only if the point estimates for the two specific indirect effects being compared are of the same sign. Consider, for instance, the case where $a_ib_i = -0.30$ and $a_jb_j = 0.30$. A test of the difference between these specific indirect effects may lead to the claim that their difference is not zero, but this does not imply the mechanisms are of different strength or that one indirect effect is bigger. The point estimates suggest one mechanism results in a positive difference in Y, whereas the other yields a negative difference of equal magnitude. In an absolute sense, they are equal in size by the point estimates, yet statistically different by an inferential test which considers their sign. But one indirect effect is not *stronger* than the other. Nor can we say that X exerts a larger effect on Y through one of the mediators relative to the other.

Inference about the Total Indirect Effect

A multiple mediator model also contains a *total indirect effect*, defined as the sum of all specific indirect effects. It is possible to conduct an inferential test of the total indirect effect using either the normal theory approach, a bootstrap confidence interval, or a Monte Carlo confidence interval. The normal theory approach requires an estimate of the standard error of the total indirect effect, but the formula for constructing it is quite complicated even in multiple mediator models with only two mediators. Given such complicated expressions and the fact that I do not recommend the normal theory approach to inference about indirect effects, I don't present the details here. They can be found in Preacher and Hayes (2008a) or MacKinnon (2008). Good SEM programs can conduct a normal theory test of the total indirect effect, as can the INDIRECT procedure for SPSS and SAS (Preacher & Hayes, 2008a). PROCESS does not provide this test.

The Monte Carlo approach is available for the total indirect effect in a multiple mediator model using code provided by Preacher and Selig (2012), and PROCESS provides a bootstrap confidence interval. As I discuss in section 5.5, the total indirect effect is often not of much interest, and I generally deemphasize it when interpreting a multiple mediator model. As can be seen in the PROCESS output in Figure 5.4, we can be 95% confident that the total indirect effect of article location through both mediators simultaneously is somewhere between 0.094 and 0.741. This supports the claim that perceived importance and presumed media influence collectively mediate the effect of article location on intentions to buy sugar.

5.4   The Serial Multiple Mediator Model

Examples of the parallel multiple mediator model like that described in the prior section are in abundance in the literature. A distinguishing feature of this model is the assumption that no mediator causally influences another. In practice, mediators will be correlated, but this model specifies that they are not causally so. Typically, two or more mediators that investigators locate as causally between X and Y will be correlated, if for no other reason than that they share a common cause—X, the causal agent of interest in the model itself. If they are correlated only because they are all affected by X, then they should be uncorrelated after accounting for this shared cause. Thus, estimating the partial correlation (see Chapter 3 for a definition) between two mediators after controlling for X is one way of examining whether all of their association is accounted for by this common cause.

If two or more mediators in a multiple mediator model remain correlated even after adjusting for X, this suggests that either they share an additional common cause other than X, the remaining association is epiphenomenal, or one mediator affects another. It is the latter explanation that is the focus of this section on the *serial multiple mediator model*.[1] In the serial multiple mediator model, the assumption of no causal association between two or more mediators is not only relaxed—it is rejected outright a priori. The goal when an investigator estimates a serial multiple mediator model is to investigate the direct and indirect effects of X on Y while modeling a process in which X causes M_1, which in turn causes M_2, and so forth, concluding with Y as the final consequent.

Though less common than the parallel multiple mediator model, it is not hard to find exemplars of such models in the literature. For instance, Casciano and Massey (2012) compared the anxiety of residents living in a low-income housing development located in a middle-class neighborhood to a matched group who applied to live in the housing development but remained on the waiting list. They argued that life in a middle-class housing development would reduce exposure to neighborhood disorder (e.g., crime, homeless people, drugs and drug use, violence) relative to those living elsewhere, which would in turn reduce the number of stressful life experiences, which in turn would translate into fewer anxiety symptoms. Their analysis supported the environment → disorder exposure → stressful experiences → anxiety symptoms causal sequence. Other examples in the literature in which a causal process is modeled as operating with mediators linked in serial include Bizer, Hart, and Jekogian (2012), Feldman (2011), Knobloch-Westerwick and Hoplamazian (2012), Krieger and Sarge (2013), Lachman and Agrigoroaei (2012), Liu and Gal (2011), Ostrander and Herman (2006), Schumann and Ross (2011), and Van Jaarsveld, Walker, and Skarlicki (2010).

Serial multiple mediator models can grow in complexity quite rapidly as the number of mediators increases, as increasing the number of mediators increases the number of paths that one can draw between causes and effects. In this section, I restrict discussion to a form of serial mediation in which variables presumed as causally prior are modeled as affecting all variables later in the causal sequence. In a sense, this is the most complex serial mediator model possible because it maximizes the number of paths that need to be estimated. In principle, one could make assumptions that

---

[1]In Chapter 6 I discuss the use of controls in a mediation model to account for epiphenomenal or spurious association due to models outside of the causal system as modeled.

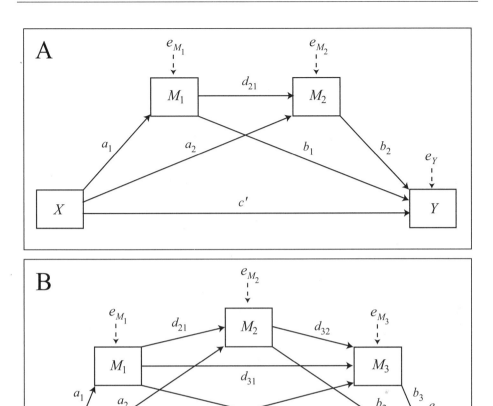

FIGURE 5.5. Two serial multiple mediator models in statistical diagram form with two (panel A) and three (panel B) mediators.

certain variables don't affect others later in the causal sequence, but the estimation of such a model and proper inferential tests for indirect effects require a structural equation modeling program, and there are advantages to estimating a potential causal influence even if you have no basis for believing it exists. If it does not, the data will tell you so, but if it does, you have learned something you might not have otherwise learned.

Two serial multiple mediator models can be found in Figure 5.5 in the form of statistical diagrams. The diagram in panel A depicts a two-mediator model in which X is modeled as affecting Y through four pathways. One pathway is indirect and runs from X to Y through M_1 only, a second indirect path runs through M_2 only, and a third indirect influence passes through both M_1 and M_2 sequentially, with M_1 affecting M_2. The remaining effect of X is direct from X to Y without passing through either M_1 or M_2. This statistical model translates into three equations, because the model contains three consequent variables:

$$
\begin{aligned}
M_1 &= i_{M_1} + a_1 X + e_{M_1} & (5.9) \\
M_2 &= i_{M_2} + a_2 X + d_{21} M_1 + e_{M_2} & (5.10) \\
Y &= i_Y + c' X + b_1 M_1 + b_2 M_2 + e_Y & (5.11)
\end{aligned}
$$

Figure 5.5 panel B is a serial multiple mediator model with three mediators representing eight distinct effects of X on Y, seven indirect and one direct. The seven indirect paths are found by tracing every possible way of getting from X to Y through at least one M. The possibilities include three passing through only a single mediator ($X \to M_1 \to Y$; $X \to M_2 \to Y$; $X \to M_3 \to Y$), three passing through two mediators in serial ($X \to M_1 \to M_2 \to Y$; $X \to M_1 \to M_3 \to Y$; $X \to M_2 \to M_3 \to Y$), and one through all three mediators in serial ($X \to M_1 \to M_2 \to M_3 \to Y$). As always, the direct effect does not pass through any mediators. The four equations (one for each of the four consequent variables) representing the three-mediator serial multiple mediator model are

$$
\begin{aligned}
M_1 &= i_{M_1} + a_1 X + e_{M_1} \\
M_2 &= i_{M_2} + a_2 X + d_{21} M_1 + e_{M_2} \\
M_3 &= i_{M_3} + a_3 X + d_{31} M_1 + d_{32} M_2 + e_{M_3} \\
Y &= i_Y + c' X + b_1 M_1 + b_2 M_2 + b_3 M_3 + e_Y
\end{aligned}
$$

Most generally, a serial multiple mediator model with k mediators requires $k+1$ equations to estimate because there are $k+1$ consequent variables (one for each of the k mediators, plus one for Y):

$$
\begin{aligned}
M_1 &= i_{M_1} + a_1 X + e_{M_1} \\
M_i &= i_{M_i} + a_i X + \textstyle\sum_{j=1}^{i-1} d_{ij} M_j + e_{M_i} \quad \text{for all } i = 2 \text{ to } k \\
Y &= i_Y + c' X + \textstyle\sum_{i=1}^{k} b_i M_i + e_Y
\end{aligned}
$$

Direct and Indirect Effects in a Serial Multiple Mediator Model

In a serial multiple mediator model, the total effect of X on Y partitions into direct and indirect components, just as it does in the simple and parallel multiple mediator models. Regardless of the number of mediators in the model, the direct effect is c' and interpreted as always—the estimated difference in Y between two cases that differ by one unit on X but who are equal on all mediators in the model. The indirect effects, of which there may be many depending on the number of mediators in the model, are all constructed by multiplying the regression weights corresponding to each step in an indirect pathway. And they are all interpreted as the estimated difference in Y between two cases that differ by one unit on X through the causal sequence from X to mediator(s) to Y. Regardless of the number of mediators, the sum of all the specific indirect effects is the total indirect effect of X, and the direct and indirect effects sum to the total effect of X. I illustrate below for two serial multiple mediator models with either two or three mediators, but the procedure generalizes to serial mediator models with any number of mediators.

Two Mediators in Serial. Consider the serial multiple mediator model with two mediators. This model has three specific indirect effects and one direct effect. The three indirect effects are estimated as the product of the regression weights linking X to Y through at least one M. From Figure 5.5 panel A, the specific indirect effect of X on Y through only M_1 is a_1b_1, the specific indirect effect through M_2 only is a_2b_2, and the specific indirect effect through both M_1 and M_2 in serial is $a_1d_{21}b_2$. Combined, these three indirect effects sum to the total indirect effect of X: $a_1b_1 + a_2b_2 + a_1d_{21}b_2$. When the total indirect effect of X is added to the direct effect of X, the result is c, the total effect of X, which as always can be estimated from a regression estimating Y from X only, as in equation 4.4. That is,

$$c = c' + a_1b_1 + a_2b_2 + a_1d_{11}b_2$$

As in the simple and parallel multiple mediator models, the total indirect effect of X on Y in the serial multiple mediator model is the difference between the total effect of X on Y and direct effect of X on Y:

$$c - c' = a_1b_1 + a_2b_2 + a_1d_{11}b_2$$

Three Mediators in Serial. These same definitions, rules, and relationships apply to the multiple mediator model with three mediators. Considering the three-mediator model in Figure 5.5, there are seven indirect effects estimated as products of regression coefficients. For example, the specific indirect effect of X on Y through M_2 only is a_2b_2. Through M_1 and M_3 in serial, the specific indirect effect is $a_1d_{31}b_3$. And the specific indirect effect through M_1, M_2, and M_3 in serial is $a_1d_{21}d_{32}b_3$. Using this same procedure, following all pathways and multiplying coefficients as you go, all seven specific indirect effects can be derived. These sum to the total indirect effect of X on Y through all three mediators: $a_1b_1 + a_2b_2 + a_3b_3 + a_1d_{21}b_2 + a_1d_{31}b_3 + a_2d_{32}b_3 + a_1d_{21}d_{32}b_3$. When the total indirect effect is added to the direct effect, the result is c, the total effect of X on Y

$$c = c' + a_1b_1 + a_2b_2 + a_3b_3 + a_1d_{21}b_2 + a_1d_{31}b_3 + a_2d_{32}b_3 + a_1d_{21}d_{32}b_3$$

which means the total indirect effect of X on Y is the difference between the total effect of X on Y and the direct effect of X on Y:

$$c - c' = a_1 b_1 + a_2 b_2 + a_3 b_3 + a_1 d_{21} b_2 + a_1 d_{31} b_3 + a_2 d_{32} b_3 + a_1 d_{21} d_{32} b_3$$

Statistical Inference

Inferential tests of direct and indirect effects are analogous to methods described already for the simple and parallel multiple mediator model. A test of the null hypothesis that the direct effect $_T c'$ is equal to zero is available in the output of any OLS regression routine, and an interval estimate is constructed as described in section 5.3.

A comparable normal theory approach for inference about the indirect effects in a serial multiple mediator model proceeds as usual by dividing the indirect effect by an estimate of the standard error and then deriving the p-value in reference to the standard normal distribution in order to test the null hypothesis that the indirect effect is zero in the population. The same formulas for the standard errors for indirect effects through a single mediator provided in section 5.3 can be used in the serial multiple mediator model for the $a_i b_i$ indirect effects. With two mediators linked in serial, Taylor, MacKinnon, and Tein (2008) provide the standard error of the indirect effect of $a_1 d_{21} b_2$ as

$$se_{a_1 d_{21} b_2} = \sqrt{a_1^2 d_{21}^2 se_{b_2}^2 + a_1^2 b_2^2 se_{d_{21}}^2 + d_{21}^2 b_2^2 se_{a_1}^2}$$

where $se_{a_1}^2$, $se_{d_{21}}^2$, and $se_{b_2}^2$ are the squared standard errors of a_1, d_{21}, and b_2, respectively. The formula for the standard error of the indirect effect involving two or more mediators in serial is complicated and described in Sobel (1982). Computation of these standard errors by hand is certain to produce inaccuracies, so let a computer do the work for you. Most good SEM programs can generate standard errors for complex indirect effects.

Whether computed by hand or by computer, I don't recommend the normal theory approach for the same reasons I don't recommend it in simple mediation models. It assumes normality of the sampling distribution of the indirect effect—an unrealistic assumption and not necessary to make these days, because simulation research (Taylor et al., 2008) shows that bootstrap confidence intervals generally perform better without making this assumption.

No modifications to the logic or method of bootstrapping is required to apply this method to the indirect effects in a serial multiple mediator model. Bootstrap confidence intervals for indirect effects (specific, total, or pairwise comparisons between) are calculated by repeatedly resampling from the data with replacement, estimating the model in each bootstrap sample, calculating the indirect effects, and deriving the endpoints of a confidence interval for each as described already. An indirect effect (or a difference between two indirect effects) can be deemed different from zero with $ci\%$ confidence if zero is outside of a $ci\%$ confidence interval. If the confidence interval straddles 0, this supports the claim that the indirect effect (or difference between) is not statistically different from zero.

In principle, Monte Carlo confidence intervals can be constructed for all indirect effects in a serial multiple mediator model. As noted earlier, Preacher and Selig (2012) describe Monte Carlo confidence interval construction for specific indirect effects through a single mediator in a parallel multiple mediator model as well as for the total indirect effect. The method and code they illustrate could be adapted without too much difficulty to indirect effects through multiple mediators chained in serial as well.

Example from the Presumed Media Influence Study

The parallel multiple mediator model of the presumed media influence study estimated and interpreted in sections 5.2 and 5.3 assumes no causal association between the mediators. Although plausible, it is perhaps more plausible that people's beliefs about how others are going to be influenced by the media are determined at least in part by perceived issue importance. That is, perhaps those who perceive a particular article pertains to an issue of local, national, or international importance are more likely to believe that others will be affected by what they read about that important topic, then go out and act based on this information. The psychological logic would go something like this: "This article will be published on the front page, so it must be important, and people will take notice of such an important matter and act by buying sugar to stock up. Therefore, I should go out and buy sugar before supplies are all gone."

This process predicts that even after accounting for the effect of article location on both perceived media influence and perceived importance, there should be some association remaining between these mediators. In a parallel multiple mediator model, the partial correlation (see Chapter 3) between M_1 and M_2 controlling for X is an index of association between mediators remaining after accounting for the effect of X on both. In these data, $pr_{M_1 M_2 \cdot X} = 0.258, p < .01$. That is, after statistically adjusting for the effect of the experimental manipulation of article location on both perceived importance and presumed media influence, those who perceive the sugar shortage as relatively more important also presume relatively more media influence. Of course, this correlation remaining after accounting for X could be due to other causes outside of the system being modeled, but it may

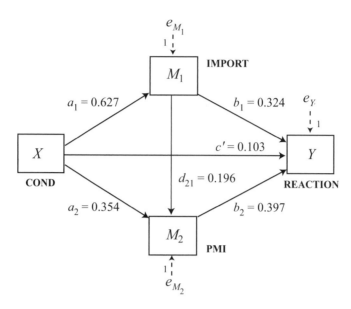

FIGURE 5.6. A statistical diagram of the serial multiple mediator model for the presumed media influence data.

reflect a misspecification resulting from assuming no causal association between M_1 and M_2.

A statistical diagram of a serial multiple mediator model consistent with this proposed process can be found in Figure 5.6. This model contains one direct and three indirect effects of article location on intentions to buy sugar, pieced together by estimating the regression coefficients in equations 5.9, 5.10, and 5.11. In SPSS, the commands are

```
regression/dep=import/method=enter cond.
regression/dep=pmi/method=enter cond import.
regression/dep=reaction/method=enter cond import pmi.
```

In SAS, use

```
proc reg data=pmi;
model import=cond;
model pmi=cond import;
model reaction=cond import pmi;
run;
```

However, the OLS routine built into SPSS and SAS will not calculate any of the indirect effects for you, nor will it provide any inferential tests of the indirect effects such as bootstrap confidence intervals. Better to use PROCESS, which estimates the coefficients and provides additional information needed for inference all in one fell swoop. In SPSS, try the command below.

```
process vars=cond pmi import reaction/y=reaction/x=cond/m=import pmi
   /boot=10000/total=1/contrast=1/model=6.
```

The equivalent PROCESS command in SAS is

```
%process (data=pmi,vars=cond pmi import reaction,y=reaction,x=cond,
   m=import pmi,boot=10000,total=1,contrast=1,model=6);
```

Notice that this PROCESS command looks very similar to the PROCESS command for the parallel multiple mediator model. The major difference is the specification of **model=6**, which tells PROCESS this is a serial multiple mediator model. When model 6 is specified, the order of the variables listed in the **m=** list matters, unlike in model 4 where order is ignored. The order of the variables in the list of mediators is taken literally as the causal sequence, with the first mediator variable in the list causally prior to the second in the list, and so forth. This PROCESS command will also generate bias-corrected bootstrap confidence intervals for all indirect effects as well as all possible pairwise comparisons between indirect effects using $10,000$ bootstrap samples. PROCESS does not provide normal theory tests for indirect effects in a serial multiple mediator model.

Output generated from the SAS command can be found in Figure 5.7, and the various model coefficients and other assorted statistics summarized in Table 5.2. The model coefficients have also been superimposed on the statistical diagram for this model in Figure 5.6. Whether extracted from the summary table, the SAS output, or the statistical diagram, the model expressed in equation form is

$$\hat{M}_1 = 3.908 + 0.627X$$
$$\hat{M}_2 = 4.610 + 0.354X + 0.196M_1$$
$$\hat{Y} = -0.150 + 0.103X + 0.324M_1 + 0.397M_2$$

The direct effect of the manipulation in this serial multiple mediator model is exactly the same as in the parallel multiple mediator model because whether the mediators are modeled as causally influencing each other or not does not change the model of Y. That is, the equation for Y is the same

TABLE 5.2. Regression Coefficients, Standard Errors, and Model Summary Information for the Presumed Media Influence Serial Multiple Mediator Model Depicted in Figure 5.6

			Consequent								
			M_1 (IMPORT)				M_2 (PMI)				
Antecedent			Coeff.	SE	p		Coeff.	SE	p		
X (COND)	a_1		0.627	0.310	.045	a_2	0.354	0.233	.131		
M_1 (IMPORT)			—	—	—	d_{21}	0.196	0.067	.004		
M_2 (PMI)			—	—	—		—	—	—		
Constant	i_{M_1}		3.908	0.213	<.001	i_{M_2}	4.610	0.306	<.001		
			$R^2 = 0.033$				$R^2 = 0.097$				
			$F(1, 121) = 4.094, p = .045$				$F(2, 120) = 6.443, p = .002$				

Antecedent		Y (REACTION)		
		Coeff.	SE	p
X (COND)	c'	0.103	0.239	.666
M_1 (IMPORT)	b_1	0.324	0.071	<.001
M_2 (PMI)	b_2	0.397	0.093	<.001
Constant	i_Y	−0.150	0.530	.778
		$R^2 = 0.325$		
		$F(3, 119) = 19.112, p < .001$		

```
%process (data=pmi,vars=pmi reaction cond import,y=reaction,x=cond,m=import pmi,model=6,
   contrast=1,boot=10000);

                              Model =    6
                              Y     =    REACTION
                              X     =    COND
                              M1    =    IMPORT
                              M2    =    PMI

                              Sample size:
                                   123

*****************************************************************************

                              Outcome: IMPORT

                              Model Summary
                 R         R-sq       F        df1        df2         p
              0.1809     0.0327    4.0942     1.0000   121.0000    0.0452

                                 Model
                 coeff       se        t         p        LLCI       ULCI
Constant        3.9077    0.2127   18.3704    0.0000     3.4866     4.3288
COND            0.6268    0.3098    2.0234    0.0452     0.0135     1.2401

*****************************************************************************

                              Outcome: PMI

                              Model Summary
                 R         R-sq       F        df1        df2         p
              0.3114     0.0970    6.4428     2.0000   120.0000    0.0022

                                 Model
                 coeff       se        t         p        LLCI       ULCI
Constant        4.6104    0.3057   15.0836    0.0000     4.0053     5.2156
IMPORT          0.1961    0.0671    2.9228    0.0041     0.0633     0.3290
COND            0.3536    0.2325    1.5207    0.1310    -0.1068     0.8139

*****************************************************************************

                              Outcome: REACTION

                              Model Summary
                 R         R-sq       F        df1        df2         p
              0.5702     0.3251   19.1118     3.0000   119.0000    0.0000

                                 Model
                 coeff       se        t         p        LLCI       ULCI
constant       -0.1498    0.5298   -0.2828    0.7778    -1.1989     0.8993
IMPORT          0.3244    0.0707    4.5857    0.0000     0.1843     0.4645
PMI             0.3965    0.0930    4.2645    0.0000     0.2124     0.5806
COND            0.1034    0.2391    0.4324    0.6662    -0.3701     0.5768

******************************* TOTAL EFFECT MODEL **************************

                              Outcome: REACTION

                              Model Summary
                 R         R-sq       F        df1        df2         p
              0.1603     0.0257    3.1897     1.0000   121.0000    0.0766

                                 Model
                 coeff       se        t         p        LLCI       ULCI
constant        3.2500    0.1906   17.0525    0.0000     2.8727     3.6273
COND            0.4957    0.2775    1.7860    0.0766    -0.0538     1.0452
```

(continued)

FIGURE 5.7. Output from the PROCESS procedure for SAS for a serial multiple mediator model of the presumed media influence data.

```
*************************** TOTAL, DIRECT AND INDIRECT EFFECTS ***************************

                            Total effect of X on Y

            Effect          SE           t           p          LLCI         ULCI
            0.4957       0.2775      1.7860      0.0766      -0.0538       1.0452


                            Direct effect of X on Y
            Effect          SE           t           p          LLCI         ULCI
            0.1034       0.2391      0.4324      0.6662      -0.3701       0.5768


                        Indirect effect(s) of X on Y

                    Effect       Boot SE     BootLLCI     BootULCI
        Total       0.3923       0.1668       0.0873       0.7398
        Ind1:       0.2033       0.1163       0.0140       0.4808
        Ind2:       0.0488       0.0363       0.0034       0.1554
        Ind3:       0.1402       0.1003      -0.0308       0.3733
        (C1)        0.1546       0.0998       0.0107       0.4214
        (C2)        0.0631       0.1583      -0.2368       0.3885
        (C3)       -0.0915       0.1092      -0.3232       0.1121


                            Indirect effect key

    Ind1:    COND      ->      IMPORT    ->      REACTION
    Ind2:    COND      ->      IMPORT    ->      PMI       ->      REACTION
    Ind3:    COND      ->      PMI       ->      REACTION


                Specific indirect effect contrast definitions

        (C1)          Ind1          minus         Ind2
        (C2)          Ind1          minus         Ind3
        (C3)          Ind2          minus         Ind3

*************************** ANALYSIS NOTES AND WARNINGS ***************************


    Number of bootstrap samples for bias corrected bootstrap confidence intervals:
                                                            10000.0000

            Level of confidence for all confidence intervals in output:
                                                            95.0000
```

FIGURE 5.7 continued.

in both models, as they each contain only X, M_1, and M_2 as predictors of Y. This direct effect is positive but not statistically significant, $c' = 0.103, t(119) = 0.432, p = 0.666$. As we learned from the parallel multiple mediator model, location of the article in the newspaper is unrelated to intentions to buy sugar independent of the effect of perceived importance and presumed media influence.

This serial multiple mediator model contains four indirect effects estimated as products of regression coefficients linking X to Y. These indirect effects can be found in the PROCESS output along with 95% bias-corrected bootstrap confidence intervals based on 10,000 bootstrap samples (as requested with the use of the **boot=10000** option). Because an indirect effect in a serial mediation model may pass through several mediators, a complete label can be quite lengthy, so PROCESS uses a shorthand notation to label them along with a key with a lengthier and more descriptive label.

The first indirect effect is the specific indirect effect of article location on reactions through perceived importance of the sugar shortage ($X \rightarrow M_1 \rightarrow Y$), estimated as $a_1b_1 = 0.627(0.324) = 0.203$ and found in the output in the row labeled "Ind1." This indirect effect can be interpreted as significantly positive because the bootstrap confidence interval is entirely above zero (0.014 to 0.481). Those told the article would appear on the front page of the newspaper perceived the sugar shortage as more important (because a_1 is positive), and this increased importance was associated with an increased intention to buy sugar (because b_1 is positive) independent of presumed media influence.

The second indirect effect is found in the output labeled "Ind2." This is the specific indirect effect of article location on reactions through perceived importance and presumed media influence in serial, with importance modeled as affecting presumed media influence, which in turn influences intentions to buy sugar (i.e., $X \rightarrow M_1 \rightarrow M_2 \rightarrow Y$). Estimated as $a_1d_{21}b_2 = 0.627(0.196)0.397 = 0.049$, this specific indirect effect is significantly positive because the bootstrap confidence interval is above zero (0.003 to 0.155). Relative to those assigned to the interior page condition, those told the article would appear in the front page perceived the sugar shortage as more important (as a_1 is positive), which in turn was associated with a greater perception that others would be influenced by the article (because d_{21} is positive) and this greater perception of influence on others translated into a greater intention to buy sugar (because b_2 is positive).

The third specific indirect effect, labeled "Ind3," is the indirect effect of article location on reactions through only presumed media influence ($X \rightarrow M_2 \rightarrow Y$). Estimated as the product of the effect of article location on presumed media influence (a_2) and the effect of presumed media influence on reactions (b_2), this indirect effect is $0.354(0.397) = 0.140$. However, this path of influence cannot be claimed as different from zero because the bootstrap confidence interval straddles zero (−0.031 to 0.377).

A serial multiple mediator model also contains a total indirect effect, estimated as the sum of all the specific indirect effects. As can be seen in the PROCESS output in the row labeled "Total," the total indirect effect is 0.392 and different from zero as determined by a bootstrap confidence interval that does not contain zero (0.087 to 0.734).

The contrast option of PROCESS, specified by adding **contrast=1** to the command line, calculates all possible pairwise comparisons between specific indirect effects. These comparisons are found in the PROCESS output in the rows labeled "(C1)," "(C2)," and so forth, along with a corresponding key toward the bottom. From the PROCESS output, the three differences are

$$
\begin{aligned}
C1 &= a_1b_1 - a_1d_{21}b_2 = 0.203 - 0.049 = 0.155 \\
C2 &= a_1b_1 - a_2b_2 = 0.203 - 0.140 = 0.063 \\
C3 &= a_1d_{21}b_2 - a_2b_2 = 0.049 - 0.140 = -0.092
\end{aligned}
$$

When used in conjunction with the bootstrapping option in PROCESS, confidence intervals for the comparison are also provided for inference about the difference between specific indirect effects. As can be seen, the indirect effect of X on Y through M_1 is statistically different from the indirect effect of X on Y through both M_1 and M_2 in serial, as the 95% bias-corrected bootstrap confidence interval for this contrast is entirely above zero (0.011 to 0.421). Because these indirect effects have the same sign, the interpretation is that the placement of the article in the paper has a larger effect on sugar purchase intentions through perceived importance in isolation than it does through its effect on perceived importance, which influences presumed media influence, which in turn influences intentions to purchase sugar. The confidence intervals for the other two contrasts (C2 and C3) include zero, meaning those specific indirect effects are not statistically different from each other.

5.5 Complementarity and Competition among Mediators

This chapter has been dedicated to mediation models containing more than one mediator. At this point, the benefits of estimating multiple mechanisms of influence in a single model are no doubt apparent. But the inclusion of more than one mediator in a model does entail certain risks as well, and at times the results of multiple mediator model appear to contradict the results obtained when estimating a simpler model with a single mediator. Some of the risks, paradoxes, and contradictions that sometimes can occur are worth some acknowledgement and discussion.

First, as discussed earlier, a specific indirect effect quantifies the influence of X on Y through a particular mediator while holding constant other mediators. This means that it is possible that a simple mediation analysis reveals evidence of an indirect effect of X on Y through M_1 when M_1 is the sole mediator in the model, but no such indirect effect when M_1 is included in a model along with M_2, M_3, and so forth. This will occur more so or with greater likelihood when the mediators are correlated, which is precisely the circumstance in which a multiple mediator model is most useful.

But when the intercorrelation between mediators becomes too large, the usual problems with multicollinearity in regression models begin to take hold and muddle the results, as the paths from each mediator to the outcome are estimated controlling for all other mediators. Multicollinearity between predictors increases sampling variance in estimates of their partial relationships with an outcome (Cohen et al., 2003; Darlington, 1990; Fox, 1991), and such sampling variance will propagate throughout the estimates of indirect effects and increase the width of confidence intervals for both asymmetric and symmetric confidence intervals or increase p-values from normal theory tests for specific indirect effects.

With evidence of an indirect effect when a mediator is considered in isolation but not when considered in a model with multiple mediators, it is reasonable to ask which result is correct. But there is no good answer to this question. In fact, they could both be correct because the specific indirect effect in a multiple mediator model estimates something different than the indirect effect in a simple mediation model. The indirect effect in a model with a single mediator confounds influence through that sole mediator and other mediators it may be correlated with but that are excluded from the model. Including correlated mediators in the model allow you to disentangle spurious and epiphenomenal association from potential causal association, but this comes at the cost of greater sampling variance and reduced power.

Second, remember that the total indirect effect of X quantifies how differences in X relate to differences in Y through all mediators at once. Evidence that the total indirect effect is different from zero supports the claim that, taken together, X influences Y indirectly in some fashion through one or more of these mechanisms these mediators represent. However, because the indirect effect is a sum over all specific indirect effects, some seemingly paradoxical results are possible.

One possibility is when the total indirect effect is not different from zero according to the outcome of an inferential test, even though one or more of the specific indirect effects is. Two scenarios can produce such an apparent paradox. Because the total indirect effect is a sum of all specific indirect effects, if those indirect effects differ in sign but are of similar magnitude, their sum very well may be zero or nearly so (see, e.g., MacKinnon, 2008; Hayes, 2009). For instance, people who attend more highly or frequently to political campaign advertisements may be more likely to vote because such exposure leads people to believe that the outcome of the election is consequential to the future, which in turn facilitates turnout. On the other hand, such advertisements often are highly negative in tone, which may reduce trust in government and politicians, which could suppress the likelihood of showing up at the ballot box. Such push-and-pull processes could be at work simultaneously, but because the specific indirect effects are opposite in sign (i.e., a positive effect through perceptions of consequence, but a negative effect through trust in government), they may sum to zero.

Such a paradox can also result in models with several specific indirect effects that differ in size, even if those specific indirect effects are the same sign. For instance, an investigator might fit a parallel multiple mediator model with four mediators, only one of which is actually transmitting X's effect on Y. The inclusion of a bunch of potential mediators in the model that actually do nothing to carry X's effect on Y can increase the sampling variance of the estimate of the total indirect effect, rendering it not statistically different from zero when subjected to an inferential test.

The opposite is also possible—evidence of a total indirect effect in spite of absence of compelling evidence from inferential tests that any of the specific indirect effects are different from zero. Consider a variation on the example just presented in which *all* of the specific indirect effects are small in size but are of the same sign. If the sample size is relatively small or the mediators highly correlated, sampling variance will rule the day, making it hard to detect a weak signal (i.e., a small specific indirect effect) amid all the sampling noise. But a few weak signals, when added up (i.e., the total indirect effect), may be strong enough to detect with an inferential test because all other things being equal, power is higher when the effect size is larger.

Such apparently paradoxical inconsistencies between inferential tests for total and specific indirect effects result not so much from the statistics but, rather, from our minds by thinking of these effects in binary terms, as either zero or something else. One escape, which is admittedly difficult given how deeply ingrained the logic of hypothesis testing is in the consciousness of scientists, is to acknowledge the uncertainty inherent in our estimates as communicated through confidence intervals. The fact that a confidence interval for an effect contains zero does not mean the effect is zero. It merely means that zero is in the realm of possibility, or that one cannot say with certainty what the direction of the effect is.

A second, easier escape from such apparent paradoxes is to simply discount the relevance of the total indirect effect when interpreting the results. Although this may not be possible, in some situations, the total indirect effect will have little substantive or theoretical value. The total indirect effect and the outcome of an inferential test thereof are similar to the squared multiple correlation in a regression model or an omnibus test of the equality of several means in analysis of variance. Rejection of the null hypothesis that a regression model fits no better than chance or that all group means are equal in analysis of variance says nothing about the size or statistical significance of the individual predictors in the model or the outcome of various pairwise comparisons between means. One could have a statistically significant R^2 or F-ratio with no significant predictors or pairwise mean comparisons. Conversely, one could find one or more statistically significant predictor variables in a regression model, or two or more statistically significant pairwise comparisons between means even if one is not able to reject the null hypothesis that a model fits no better than chance or that a set of group means are the same using an omnibus test. The total indirect effect is a sum of all specific indirect effects some of which may be large, others small, some positive, some negative. Investigators often estimate multiple mediator models because they are interested in specific mechanisms at work, not the aggregate of all mechanisms. With a few exceptions, such as small specific indirect effects that are too small to detect with the data available but sum to a large total indirect effect, or in a serial multiple mediator model with data collected over time on the same mediator (see, e.g., Cole & Maxwell, 2003, pp. 571–572), inference and interpretation of a multiple mediator model would usually focus more on the direct and specific indirect effects, not the total indirect effect.

5.6   OLS Regression versus Structural Equation Modeling

The use of OLS regression when estimating a simple mediation model is commonplace. But as more boxes and arrows are added to a mediation model, there is the widespread belief that a move to a maximum likelihood-based SEM program such as LISREL, AMOS, or Mplus is required for model estimation or that doing so is in some sense better. Although there are some advantages to the use of SEM, for the estimation of the parallel or serial multiple mediation models described in this chapter, doing so is neither necessary nor better.

To illustrate, I estimated the same serial mediation model for the presumed media influence analysis described beginning on page 149, but using Mplus and LISREL, two popular SEM programs. Using the PMI data, the corresponding Mplus MODEL command is

```
MODEL:
reaction ON import pmi cond;
import ON cond;
pmi ON import cond;
```

In LISREL, the code below[2] estimates the same model:

```
TI pmi example
DA NO=123 NI=4 MA=CM ME=ML
CM
0.25123284
0.15747035 3.01572704
0.11971878 0.64720778 1.74573504
0.12453352 1.25128282 0.91457584 2.40342196
LA
cond import pmi reaction
MO NY=4 NE=4 BE=FU,FI LY=ID PS=DI,FR TE=ZE
LE
xcond ximport xpmi xreaction
FR BE 2 1 BE 3 1 BE 3 2 BE 4 1 BE 4 2 BE 4 3
PD
OU SC ND=3
```

Excerpts of the resulting Mplus and LISREL output containing the coefficients for each of the paths as well as their standard errors can be found in Figure 5.8. Compare these to the OLS regression coefficients and standard errors from the PROCESS output in Figure 5.7 and you will find them to be extremely similar. In fact, notice that the OLS regression coefficients are the same as the maximum likelihood (ML) estimates from Mplus and LISREL to three decimal places. There are tiny differences between the standard errors, as would be expected given differences between OLS and ML in how these are calculated. Indeed, observe that the standard errors from Mplus and LISREL are even different from each other.

The claim that some have made (e.g., Iacobucci, Saldanha, & Deng, 2007, Study 1) that SEM is better or more appropriate than a set of OLS regressions for estimating an observed variable mediation model is, in my opinion, simply not justified. In general, it makes no difference that should be of any concern. Any difference you observe between OLS regression and SEM will be specific to the SEM program you are using, the algorithms for estimation and iteration used by your favored SEM program, convergence criteria set as defaults, how the covariance matrix is calculated, the number of decimal places of accuracy used when inputting data as a covariance matrix rather than using individual data, and so forth. Indeed, it could even be argued that inferential tests for the path coefficients from an SEM program are more likely to be slightly in error in smaller samples, as *p*-values from an

---

[2]I am not a LISREL user. I thank Kristopher Preacher for writing this LISREL code for me.

A

	Estimate	S.E.	Est./S.E.	Two-Tailed P-Value
REACTION ON				
IMPORT	0.324	0.070	4.662	0.000
PMI	0.397	0.091	4.336	0.000
COND	0.103	0.235	0.440	0.660
IMPORT ON				
COND	0.627	0.307	2.040	0.041
PMI ON				
IMPORT	0.196	0.066	2.959	0.003
COND	0.354	0.230	1.540	0.124

B

BETA

	xcond	ximport	xpmi	xreactio
xcond	- -	- -	- -	- -
ximport	0.627 (0.306) 2.048	- -	- -	- -
xpmi	0.354 (0.229) 1.546	0.196 (0.066) 2.971	- -	- -
xreactio	0.103 (0.234) 0.441	0.324 (0.069) 4.681	0.397 (0.091) 4.353	- -

FIGURE 5.8. Mplus (panel A) and LISREL (panel B) output corresponding to the serial multiple mediator model of the presumed media influence data.

SEM program are usually derived from the normal distribution rather than the t distribution. In large samples this won't matter, but in small samples, the t distribution used by an OLS regression procedure is more appropriate for the derivation of p-values for regression coefficients.

I am not saying that there are not advantages to the use of a SEM program when conducting a mediation analysis. An SEM program gives the user considerable control over the estimation method and how variables are configured in the model. Although a computational tool like PROCESS is valuable, it forces the user to estimate a model it is programmed to estimate rather than the exact model the user might want to estimate. For example, PROCESS will estimate all direct effects in a serial mediation model and there is no way around this. In contrast, an SEM program would allow you to estimate a model that constrains certain direct effects to zero if desired, or even fix certain paths to be equal to each other. Although I generally discourage the estimation of mediation models with a priori constraints on direct effects, not all would agree with this perspective.

SEM programs also provide measures of fit for models that are not saturated, thereby allowing for model comparisons. The serial mediation model in this example is saturated, so fit is perfect and not relevant. In complex models which involve constraints of some kind, it is possible to measure the fit of a model using various measures built into SEM programs and compare fit of nested models that differ by constraints imposed by the analyst.

But perhaps the biggest advantage to the use of SEM over OLS regression is the ability of an SEM program to estimate latent variable models, or models that combine observed and latent variables. Random measurement error in the variables in observed variable mediation models such as those described in this book can bias estimates or lower power, depending on the reliability of the observed variables and whether variables measured with error are predictors or outcomes. Combining a structural model with a properly specified latent variable measurement model using SEM can reduce the deleterious effects of random measurement error. I do not cover latent variable models in this book. Discussions of mediation analysis with latent variables can be found in Cheung and Lau (2008), Lau and Cheung (2012), or MacKinnon (2008).

5.7   Chapter Summary

The simple mediation model remains the most frequently estimated model of processes in observational, survey, and experimental research. In this chapter, I extended the principles of simple mediation analysis introduced in Chapter 4 to models with more than one mediator. Acknowledging and explicitly modeling the multiple mechanisms or pathways of influence between X and Y opens the door to more interesting analytical opportunities and tests. Specific indirect effects estimated in models with mediators operating either in parallel or serial estimate causal influences independent of other processes in the model. Tests that compare specific indirect effects provide an analytical means for an investigator to pit competing mechanisms or theories against each other in a single integrated process model.

A solid understanding of the concepts and methods described here and in Chapter 4 is a strong foundation upon which to build as we move toward more complex models that integrate mediation with moderation in the latter chapters of this book. Before launching into the topic of moderation, the next chapter covers some important miscellaneous issues in mediation analysis, including dealing with confounds, quantifying effect size, entertaining questions of causal order, and the estimation of models with more than one causal agent or outcome of interest.

6

Miscellaneous Topics in Mediation Analysis

In this chapter, the historically significant and popular *causal steps approach* to mediation analysis is discussed, and I provide some explanation as to why most experts in mediation analysis don't recommend its use anymore. I then tackle various threats to the validity of the conclusions one might reach using mediation analysis as described in the prior chapters, including confounding, epiphenomenality, and alternative causal orderings of *X*, *M*, and *Y*. After discussion of various measures of effect size in mediation analysis, I take on the estimation of direct and indirect effects in models with multiple causal antecedents and outcome variables. I end with some advice on how to describe the results of a mediation analysis in a scientific article.

The essential elements of modern statistical mediation analysis were the focus of Chapters 4 and 5, and are prerequisite material to understanding the integration of mediation and moderation analysis beginning in Chapter 10. Comfort with these principles allows anyone to conduct mediation analysis and use it to shed light on one's research questions and hypotheses about causal processes.

In this chapter, I take up a variety of miscellaneous issues in statistical mediation analysis, including testing and ruling out various alternative explanations for associations observed in a mediation analysis, effect size, and models with multiple causal agents and outcomes. I begin this chapter with a discussion of an approach to mediation analysis popularized in the last century but that few recommend now. I did not discuss this approach in the prior chapters because I see this approach as more of historical interest now, but an understanding of this approach is important because you will still see it used and you should be familiar with its weaknesses relative to approaches described in Chapters 4 and 5 and why it is no longer recommended.

6.1   What about Baron and Kenny?

Anyone reading this book who has even a remote familiarity with mediation analysis as predominantly practiced until recently will recognize I have given no attention to what has been a very popular approach to mediation analysis: the *causal steps approach*. Although the method can be traced in some form back to the 1950s, it was made popular in the 1980s by a very influential article by Reuben Baron and David Kenny published in the *Journal of Personality and Social Psychology*. For this reason, the causal steps approach has come to be known as the *Baron and Kenny* method.

Historically, the vast majority of published mediation analyses are based on the logic of the causal steps approach, and it remains widely used today. However, its popularity is fading in part because quantitative methodologists who think and write about mediation analysis have argued convincingly against its use while offering better alternatives, such as described in Chapters 4 and 5. I do not recommend this method for reasons I document below, but only after first describing how a mediation analysis is conducted and interpreted using the causal steps approach.

The causal steps strategy is a simple-to-implement procedure used in an attempt to answer the question as to whether or not a certain variable M functions as a mediator of the relationship between X and Y. In terms of the modeling process, the causal steps approach is pretty much the same as the method already discussed at length. But it differs in one important way by focusing entirely on the outcome of a set of tests of significance for each path in the causal system.

Using the causal steps approach, in order for M to be considered a mediator of the effect of X on Y, one must first establish that there is an effect to be mediated, meaning evidence that X and Y are associated. The litmus test as to whether there is an effect of X on Y is the rejection of the null hypothesis that the total effect equals zero, estimated in the sample by regressing Y on X:

$$Y = i_1 + cX + e_Y \qquad (6.1)$$

If c is statistically significant in equation 6.1, then this criterion is met, and the investigator proceeds to the second step. If it is not, all testing stops.

Assuming this first criterion is met, in this second step, the effect of X on M is then estimated by regressing M on X:

$$M = i_2 + aX + e_M \qquad (6.2)$$

If a is statistically significant in equation 6.2, this meets the second criterion of the causal steps strategy, which requires that X affects M. A failure to reject the null hypothesis that $_Ta = 0$ stops this process in its tracks, and the claim is that M is not a mediator of the effect of X on Y.

If this second criterion is met, then a test of the third criterion is undertaken: that M affects Y controlling for X. To establish this criterion, the investigator regresses Y on both X and M

$$Y = i_3 + c'X + bM + e_Y \qquad (6.3)$$

and the null hypothesis that $_Tb = 0$ is tested. If this null hypothesis cannot be rejected, the procedure stops with the claim that M is not functioning as a mediator of X's effect on Y. But if this third criterion is met, then the direct effect of X (c' in equation 6.3) is compared to the total effect c from equation 6.1. If c' is closer to zero than c and c' is not statistically significant, then it is claimed that M *completely* mediates X's effect on Y. That is, M entirely accounts for the effect of X on Y. By contrast, if c' is closer to zero than c but c' is statistically different from zero, then it is said that M *partially* mediates X's effect on Y. Only part of the effect of X on Y is carried through M.

This procedure remains popular in spite of its problems. This popularity is no doubt due to the fact that it is quite simple to understand, it is easy to describe and teach to one's academic offspring, it is still being taught and recommended by researchers who don't follow the methodology literature, it can be summarized in a few sentences in a scientific report, it does not require specialized software, and it doesn't take a strong background in statistics or data analysis to implement. But times are changing quickly, recognition is growing that this approach is not ideal both statistically and philosophically, and soon it will be difficult to get away with the use of the causal steps strategy. Before long, you won't be able to publish your research if you rely on the causal steps method.

Why is this method being abandoned? There are at least four reasons. First, notice that the causal steps procedure neither formally quantifies the indirect effect nor requires any kind of inferential test about it. Rather, according to the causal steps approach, the existence of an indirect effect is inferred logically from the outcome of a set of null hypothesis tests about a quantification of something other than the indirect effect. This is contrary to the way that scientists usually collect evidence and make an argument. When we want to know whether one therapy is more effective than another, we quantify differences between those who do and do not experience that therapy on the outcomes of interest and determine whether there is evidence of a difference with some kind of hypothesis test or a confidence interval. When we want to know whether people who play violent video games frequently are more aggressive than those who play less, we estimate the correlation between violent video game play and aggression, and then conduct some kind of an inferential test about that correlation. When we want to know whether people who listen to conservative political talk radio have more prejudice against immigrants than those who don't after accounting for political ideology, we estimate the partial association between prejudice and conservative talk radio use, controlling for ideology, and determine whether the partial association is different from zero. Why should inference about indirect effects be any different? Our inferences about indirect effects should be based on an estimate of the indirect effect and whether an inferential procedure justifies the claim that $_{T}a_{T}b$ is not zero, not on the outcome of a set of hypothesis tests about $_{T}a$ and $_{T}b$.

A rebuttal to this criticism of the causal steps approach goes something like this:

> "If $_{T}a \neq 0$ and $_{T}b \neq 0$, then if follows that $_{T}a_{T}b \neq 0$. And if $_{T}a = 0$ or $_{T}b = 0$, then $_{T}a_{T}b = 0$. So why do we need to conduct an inferential test about the indirect effect? We know what we need to know using the causal steps procedure."

Although this sounds sensible, the problem is that it is wrong. Although somewhat rare, one can find that a formal inferential test of $_{T}a_{T}b$ leads to the conclusion that there is no indirect effect even when both a and b are statistically different from zero. But even more important, it is possible to conclude $_{T}a_{T}b \neq 0$ using a good inferential test described in Chapters 4 and 5 even if either a or b (or both) are not statistically significant. Because ab is the proper estimate of the indirect effect, inference should be based on ab, not on individual hypothesis tests of $_{T}a$ and $_{T}b$. The indirect effect is not estimated as a and b. It is estimated as the *product* of a and b.

Second, the ability to claim M is a mediator is contingent on the successful rejection of three null hypotheses (about $_{T}c$, $_{T}a$, and $_{T}b$). If even one hypothesis test results in a failure to reject its null, *game over*. In that case, M is not a mediator. But hypotheses tests are human inventions that are fallible. They are based on assumptions that may not be met and which can affect their performance. Even when those assumptions are met, we know the possibility remains that a hypothesis test will fail to reject a false null hypothesis, or it will incorrectly reject a true one. The more hypothesis tests one conducts in order to make or support a claim, the more likely one is to make a mistake. As a result of its reliance on so many hypothesis tests, the causal steps approach is one of the least powerful approaches to testing mediation. This has been demonstrated time and again in simulation studies (e.g., Fritz & MacKinnon, 2007; Hayes & Scharkow, 2013; MacKinnon et al., 2002, 2004; Preacher & Selig, 2012; Williams & MacKinnon, 2008). It is better to minimize the number of inferential procedures one must employ in order to support a claim. A single inferential test of the indirect effect is all that is needed.

Third, investigators routinely begin the causal steps procedure by first testing whether X affects Y by conducting a hypothesis test for $_T c$, the total effect of X. A failure to reject the null hypothesis that $_T c = 0$ means that the remaining criteria to establish M as a mediator are irrelevant, so the causal steps procedure stops in its tracks. This logic is predicated on the belief that an effect that doesn't exist can't be mediated, so there is no point in trying to explain the mechanism generating such a noneffect.

The basis for this logic is flawed, however, for it is possible for X to exert an effect on Y indirectly through M even if one cannot establish through a hypothesis test that the total effect is different from zero. Although this seems paradoxical, that doesn't make it not true. Indeed, two examples of this phenomenon can be found in Chapter 4. Recall that there was clear evidence of an indirect effect of article location on intentions to purchase sugar through presumed media influence even though the total effect of article location on intentions was not statistically different from zero. Similarly, there was no statistically significant evidence of a total effect of economic stress on withdrawal intentions, even though the indirect effect of economic stress through depressed affect was statistically different from zero using a bootstrap confidence interval. This happens much more than people probably recognize, and there is a growing consensus among quantitative methodologists (e.g., Cerin & MacKinnon, 2009; Hayes, 2009; LeBreton, Wu, & Bing, 2009; MacKinnon, 2008; Rucker et al., 2011; Shrout & Bolger, 2002; Zhao et al., 2010) that a total effect of X on Y should not be a prerequisite to searching for evidence of indirect effects.

The discomfort this might induce in some who can't fathom the logic of an indirect effect absent evidence of a total effect can be resolved quite easily merely by acknowledging that the total effect simply is not a good estimator of X's effect on Y at least some of the time. Recall that the total effect is equal to the direct effect plus the sum of all indirect effects. For many if not most phenomena that scientists study, X exerts its effect on Y through multiple pathways. Imagine X actually affects Y indirectly through two mechanisms, and these two mechanisms are the only process at work that links X to Y. What if the indirect effect through M_1 is positive, but the indirect effect through M_2 is negative but of equal magnitude? In that case, the two indirect effects sum to zero, and if there is no other process at work linking X to Y, then the total effect will be zero. So multiple indirect effects, some of which are positive and some of which are negative, may sum to something near zero. If the indirect effects estimated in one's model account for most of the effect of X on Y, the total effect as estimated by regressing Y on X is likely to be zero or nearly so, even though X does affect Y. For additional discussion and examples, see Hayes (2009), MacKinnon (2008), and Rucker et al. (2011).

Another situation that can produce a total effect near zero is the existence of subpopulations in which X exerts opposite effects on Y. For instance, perhaps X positively affects Y among males but negatively among females, and something must account for this differential effect. If the effects are similar in magnitude and the sample is evenly split between the sexes, a regression of Y on X that does not account for the differential effect of X on Y between men and women may lead you to the mistaken conclusion that X is unrelated to and therefore does not affect Y. Alternatively, it could be that X is unrelated to Y among some people but positively related to Y among others. If there are enough people in the sample in the first group, the association between X and Y will be diluted to the point that it is difficult to detect without a large sample.

The point is that it is a mistake to condition the hunt for indirect effects on evidence of a total effect of X. Researchers who use the causal steps strategy and insist on a statistically significant total effect of X before estimating and testing indirect effects will end up underanalyzing their data. They will fail to detect indirect effects when they are there and the result will be false statements about the process generating the data. Fewer mistakes of inference will be made in the long run if this strategy is abandoned.

Finally, because the causal steps strategy is not based on a quantification of the indirect effect, it encourages investigators to think about indirect effects and mediation in purely qualitative terms. M either completely or partially mediates X's effect or it does not mediate its effect at all. If you think in these terms, it becomes difficult to entertain and test more refined questions about processes, such as whether the indirect effect through one mediator is different in size than the indirect effect through another (as discussed in section 5.3). Such qualitative thinking also makes it impossible to conceptualize processes as moderated, which is the focus of the latter few chapters of this book. In order to apply many of the methods covered later, it is necessary to get in the habit of thinking about mediation in quantitative rather than purely qualitative terms.

A Critique of Complete and Partial Mediation

The causal steps approach to mediation analysis results in one of three claims. Either M does not mediate the effect of X on Y, it partially mediates that effect, or it completely mediates it. Partial mediation implies that the mechanism through M does not entirely account for the association observed between X and Y, whereas complete mediation means that the association between X and Y is entirely accounted for by the indirect mechanism. Although these terms are used in abundance in the scientific literature and frequently are the subject of hypotheses being tested, I argue below that they are empty concepts and should be abandoned.

First, notice that complete and partial mediation are defined only when an investigator has ruled that the total effect is different from zero. But we've seen that one can find evidence of an indirect effect absent evidence of a total effect. Thus, in at least some circumstances that do occur in real research, these concepts simply don't apply. This itself is not a criticism of the concepts, but it is important because it means that it is fruitless to try to label a pattern of findings in terms of complete and partial mediation if the pattern of findings is not consistent with the concepts as defined.

Second, there is a sense in which complete mediation seems like a better, more desirable claim, and I think scientists celebrate complete mediation with a bit more excitement and champagne than they do claims of partial mediation. If you propose that M mediates the effect of X on Y and can go away at the end of the study with the claim that M functions as a complete mediator of the effect, this somehow seems like a happier conclusion than the claim that M only partially mediates X's effect. The implication is that if M completely accounts for X's effect, one now knows all one needs to know about the process being studied. No one needs to propose other mechanisms that might be at work because the one you've identified entirely accounts for the effect of X. You deserve a prize because you've found the answer. Being able to claim only partial mediation means you haven't finished the job. It is almost a disappointment. Scientists should keep working on the problem, because there is more to understand about the mechanism by which X's effect operates.

As Rucker et al. (2011) nicely illustrated, the problem with this reasoning is that establishing that some variable M completely mediates the effect of X on Y says nothing whatsoever about the existence or absence of other possible mediators of X's effect. Even if you can say you've completely accounted for the effect of X on Y with your favored mediator, this does not preclude another investigator from being able to make the same claim as you, but using an entirely different mediator. If there are multiple mediators that completely mediate X's effect when considered in isolation, then what value is there to claiming that your favored mediator does? It is an empty claim, with no real value or meaning and nothing especially worthy of celebration much less even hypothesizing in the first place.

Third, a claim of partial mediation is in effect a celebration of a misspecified model. On a philosophical level, all effects are mediated by something. When you claim that M partially mediates X's effect, you are acknowledging that part of X's effect on Y has not been accounted for by M. So what is accounting for X's remaining effect as evidenced by a statistically significant direct effect? Something must be, but whatever it is, it isn't in your model. To be sure, all models are wrong at some level. All our models are misspecified to some degree. I think most researchers recognize this even if they are inclined to believe it is less true for their own models relative to someone else's. But why hypothesize it, and why celebrate when you support a hypothesis of partial mediation? You are hypothesizing and celebrating a misspecified model.

Fourth, consider two investigators who are studying exactly the same process using exactly the same method and exactly the same measurement procedures. Furthermore, imagine that descriptively their results are the same, but that investigator A's study is based on a smaller sample than investigator B's study. If in reality, M only partially accounts for the effect of X on Y, investigator B is more likely than investigator A to claim that M partially mediates X's effect, because investigator B's test of the direct effect (c') will be conducted with more power. So investigator A's findings seem more impressive because the effect of X on Y has been completely accounted for by the indirect mechanism, even though he or she has less data than investigator B. But if complete mediation is a better, more desirable claim than partial mediation, this means that it would be better to limit your sample size such that you have just enough power to be able to claim that M is a mediator, but not enough to detect the direct effect. In other words, if your goal is to establish complete mediation, it is best to use a smaller sample size. Obviously, this is crazy, and it runs absolutely counter to what we generally believe about data collection—that more is better.

Complete and partial mediation are concepts that are deeply ingrained in the thinking of social and behavioral scientists. But I just don't see what they offer our understanding of a phenomenon. They are too sample-size-dependent and the distinction between them has no substantive or theoretical meaning or value of any consequence. They should be abandoned.

6.2   Confounding and Causal Order

One of the beautiful features of experiments is the causal interpretations they afford about differences between groups. Good experimentation is tough and requires lots of careful planning and strict control over experimental procedures, construction of stimuli, treatment of participants, and so forth. But when done well, no research design gives a researcher more confidence in the claim that differences between groups defined by X on some variable of interest is due to X rather than something else. Given that a mediation model is a causal model, the ability to make unequivocal causal claims about the effect of X on M and the direct and total effects of X on Y gives experiments tremendous appeal.

However, mediation models are about more than establishing that X affects M and Y. One must also be comfortable claiming M causes Y. Unfortunately, random assignment to values of X does not establish that M causes Y. Alternative possibilities exist. For example, M may be correlated with some other variable that X is actually affecting, and if that other variable causes Y rather than M, one will go away with the mistaken conclusion that X affects Y indirectly through M when in fact the other variable is the mechanism variable through which X exerts its effect indirectly. This is the phenomenon referred to in earlier chapters as *epiphenomenal association*. That is, the association between M and Y may be an epiphenomenon of the fact that X affects some other variable not in the model, and that other variable affects Y, but because M is correlated with that other variable, it appears that M is the variable through with X's effect on Y is carried. Epiphenomenal association is a serious threat to the validity of the causal inference one makes from a mediation analysis.

Confounding or spurious association also presents a serious validity threat. A causal claim about association is threatened by confounding if the association between the variables can be attributed to a third variable that causally affects both. For example, the fact that children who watch relatively more television are more likely to be overweight (e.g., Brown, Nicholson, Broom, & Bittman, 2011; Jordan, 2010) does not imply with certainty that excessive television viewing causes weight problems. Perhaps parents who don't encourage a healthy lifestyle are more likely to purchase and feed their children less healthy food that is high in fat and calories and are also less likely to encourage their children to play sports, exercise, or engage in other behaviors that are better for their bodies than just watching television. So it isn't necessarily the excessive television viewing causing the weight problems. Perhaps it is the behavior of the parents that causes both excessive television viewing and weight gain in their kids. So differences between the kids' parents in terms of how much they encourage a healthy lifestyle is a potential confound, making it difficult to claim convincingly that watching more TV causes weight gain.

When X is not experimentally manipulated, then things get even worse. Absent random assignment to values of X, *all* of the associations in a mediation model are susceptible to confounding and epiphenomenal association, not just the association between M and Y. Whether one's design includes manipulation and random assignment of X or not, it behooves the

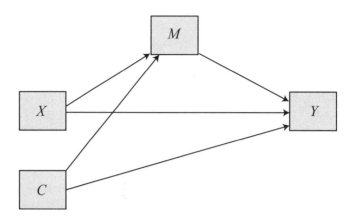

FIGURE 6.1. A conceptual diagram of a simple mediation model with statistical controls.

researcher to seriously ponder these potential threats to causal inference and, if possible, do something to reduce their plausibility as alternative explanations for associations observed.

Accounting for Confounding and Epiphenomenal Association

Fortunately, epiphenomenal association and confounding as threats to the validity of a causal claim can be managed at least in part through statistical control. If two variables M and Y are epiphemenonally associated or confounded due to their association with some variable C, then the association between M and Y should not exist among people who are equal on C. So, for instance, suppose we studied a bunch of kids with parents who are equivalent to each other in how much they encourage a healthy lifestyle in their children. If we found that among such kids, those who watch relatively more television (M) also are more likely to be overweight (Y), it couldn't possibly be variations between kids in how much their parents encourage healthy lifestyles (C) that accounts for the association because we've held that potential confounding variable constant.

Often we can't literally hold C constant through research design in this fashion. However, if we have measured C, we can remove C's influence on the quantification of the putative causal associations in a mediation model mathematically, as described in section 3.2. In a simple mediation model, for instance, confounding and epiphenomenal association due to C can be ruled out simply by including C as a predictor in the models of M and Y, represented conceptually in Figure 6.1. Conveniently, adding C to the models of M and Y will also remove C as an epiphenomenal or confounding threat to a causal claim about the association between X and M and X and Y as well as between M and Y.

Of course, controlling for C does not eliminate other potential sources of confounding or epiphenomenal association. Maybe some variable other than C is confounding the associations in the mediation model, or perhaps both C and some other variable are. The possibility of multiple confounds is not a problem, so long as those other variables are measured. They can just be added as additional predictors to the models of M and Y in the mediation analysis.

In practice, researchers frequently have more than one potential confounding variable in mind that they want to statistically partial out of the association between the variables in a simple mediation model. Denoting C as the set of q variables ($q \geq 1$, frequently called *covariates* in this context) that may threaten a claim of causality due to confounding or epiphenomenal association, their effects on the paths in a mediation model (i.e., a, b, and c') can be statistically removed by estimating the coefficients in the following models of M and Y:

$$M = i_1 + aX + \sum_{i=1}^{q} f_i C_i + e_M$$

$$Y = i_2 + c'X + bM + \sum_{i=1}^{q} g_i C_i + e_Y$$

As can be seen, the only change relative to equations 4.1 and 4.2 from Chapter 4 is the addition of the q covariates to the models of M and Y. The resulting estimates for a, b, and c' now can be said to be "purified" of the influence of the covariates on their value absent the inclusion of C in the model. The covariates are being held constant mathematically or statistically controlled in the estimation of the other effects in the model.

In this model, c' is still the direct effect of X on Y, ab remains the indirect effect of X on Y through M, and the total effect of X on Y is the sum of the direct and indirect effects, $c' + ab$. The total effect will be equal to c in a model of Y without M but including the q covariates:

$$Y = i_3 + cX + \sum_{i=1}^{q} h_i C_i + e_Y$$

The interpretation of the direct, indirect, and total effects remains the same, but with the inclusion of "equal on C," "holding C constant," or "statistically controlling for C" (terms that have the same meaning and can be used interchangeably). So c' quantifies how much two cases that differ by a unit on X are estimated to differ on Y holding M and C constant. The indirect effect, ab, quantifies how much two cases that differ by one unit on X but are equal on covariates C are estimated to differ on Y as a result of the effect of X on M, which in turn affects Y. And the total effect of X, c, estimates how much two cases that differ by a unit on X are estimated to differ on Y, statistically controlling for C.

To illustrate, we shall revisit the economic stress study described in section 4.5. Recall that Pollack et al. (2012) assessed the economic stress and business-related depressed affect that 262 entrepreneurs reported experiencing during an economic downturn, as well as their intentions to withdraw from entrepreneurship. The simple mediation analysis was consistent with the claim that economic stress can prompt a desire to withdraw from the business world indirectly through its effect on depressed affect. That is, those who reported experiencing more economic stress felt stronger business-related depressed affect ($a = 0.173$), and those who were experiencing more depressed affect reported a greater intention to withdraw from entrepreneurship even after accounting for economic stress ($b = 0.769$). The indirect effect was statistically different from zero ($ab = 0.133$, with a 95% bootstrap confidence interval from 0.077 to 0.208). There was no evidence of a direct effect of economic stress on withdrawal intentions ($c' = -0.077, p = .302$).

The indirect effect may reflect a bona fide causal sequence of events in which elevated stress leads to depressed affect, which leads to a desire to withdraw from entrepreneurship. But remember that these data come from a one-shot observational study. Nothing was manipulated, nothing was measured over time, and potential confounds abound. For example, the indirect effect may be a manifestation of nothing other than individual differences such as perceptions of one's own confidence and skill in managing a business. People who feel relatively more confident in their abilities may tend to feel relatively less stress in general, perhaps are less prone to feel negative and down about their business under any circumstances, and enjoy their jobs relatively more than people who are less confident. If so, then statistically controlling for such an individual difference when assessing the indirect effect of economic stress should weaken or eliminate it. That is, among people equal in their confidence, there should be no evidence of an indirect effect of economic stress on withdrawal intentions through depressed affect, because this variable has been taken out of the process that, by this reason, induces spurious association between X and M and between M and Y. But if the indirect effect persists even when holding confidence constant, a causal claim remains viable.

This alternative explanation can be put to the test only if something akin to confidence has been measured. Fortunately, Pollack et al. (2012) included a measure of "entrepreneurial self-efficacy" (Chen, Green, & Crick,

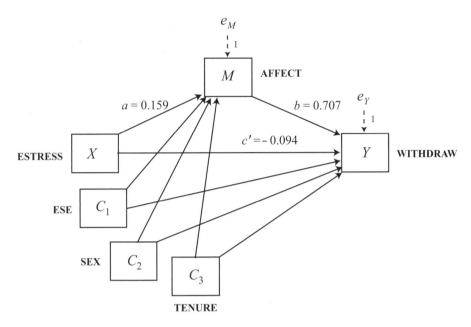

FIGURE 6.2. A statistical diagram of a simple mediation model for the economic stress study with three covariates.

1998). This measure indexes a person's confidence in his or her ability to successfully engage in various entrepreneurship-related tasks such as setting and meeting goals, creating new products, managing risk, and making decisions (ESE in the ESTRESS data file). Indeed, compared to participants relatively low in entrepreneurial self-efficacy, those relatively high in entrepreneurial self-efficacy did report feeling relatively less economic stress ($r = -0.158, p = .010$), relatively less business-related depressed affect ($r = -0.246, p < .001$), and reported relatively weaker intentions to withdraw from entrepreneurship ($r = -0.243, p < .001$). So spurious or epiphenomenal association are plausible alternative explanations for at least some of the relationship observed between economic stress, depressed affect, and withdrawal intentions.

To account for the shared association between entrepreneurial self-efficacy and the key variables in the causal model being estimated, entrepreneurial self-efficacy (C_1) is included in the linear equations for both depressed affect (M) and intentions to withdraw (Y). To illustrate that more than a single variable can be used as a statistical control, I also include sex of the participant (C_2; SEX in the data, 0 = female, 1 = male) and length of time in the business, in years (C_3; TENURE in the data) as predictors. Thus, the linear equations estimated to quantify the direct and indirect effects of economic stress are

$$M = i_1 + aX + f_1C_1 + f_2C_2 + f_3C_3 + e_M \qquad (6.4)$$

$$Y = i_2 + c'X + bM + g_1C_1 + g_2C_2 + g_3C_3 + e_Y \qquad (6.5)$$

Figure 6.2 depicts the complete model corresponding to these equations in the form of a statistical diagram. As always, the coefficients in equations 6.4 and 6.5 could be estimated using any OLS regression routine, but PROCESS makes it easier while providing the inferential tests for the indirect effect that a set of separate regression analyses will not provide. In SPSS, the PROCESS command is

```
process vars=estress affect withdraw ese sex tenure/y=withdraw/x=estress
   /m=affect/total=1/boot=10000/model=4.
```

In SAS, use

```
%process (data=estress,vars=estress affect withdraw ese sex tenure,
   y=withdraw,x=estress,m=affect,total=1,boot=10000,model=4);
```

The only difference between the PROCESS command for this model and the model in Chapter 4 is the addition of the three covariates to the **vars=** list. Any variable included in this list but not given a role anywhere else in the PROCESS command will automatically be treated as a covariate and included in the models of both M and Y.

The resulting PROCESS output can be found in Figure 6.3, and the model coefficients are summarized in Table 6.1 and superimposed on the statistical diagram in Figure 6.2. Comparing the PROCESS output for the model controlling for sex, tenure, and entrepreneurial self-efficacy to the output excluding these controls (see Figure 4.7), it can be seen that substantively, nothing has really changed. Even after adjusting for the possibility of spurious or epiphenomenal association resulting from these three covariates, the indirect effect of economic stress on withdrawal intentions through depressed affect is positive and statistically different from zero (point estimate = 0.113, with a 95% bias-corrected bootstrap confidence interval of 0.067 to 0.184). The direct effect is slightly stronger than it was prior to these controls in the negative direction, but still not statistically significant by commonly used standards, $c' = -0.094, p = .077$.

Use of the **total=1** option in PROCESS generates the total effect of X on Y while controlling for entrepreneurial self-efficacy, sex, and tenure.

```
process vars=estress affect withdraw ese sex tenure/y=withdraw/m=affect/x=estress
    /boot=10000/total=1/model=4.

Model = 4
    Y = withdraw
    X = estress
    M = affect

Statistical Controls:
CONTROL= sex      tenure    ese

Sample size
      262

*************************************************************************
Outcome: affect

Model Summary
        R        R-sq         F        df1         df2          p
     .4039       .1631    12.5231    4.0000    257.0000      .0000

Model
               coeff        se          t          p        LLCI       ULCI
constant      1.7855      .3077     5.8033      .0000     1.1796     2.3914
estress        .1593      .0297     5.3612      .0000      .1008      .2179
ese           -.1549      .0444    -3.4892      .0006     -.2423     -.0675
sex            .0148      .0857      .1726      .8631     -.1540      .1836
tenure        -.0108      .0063    -1.7227      .0861     -.0232      .0016

*************************************************************************
Outcome: withdraw

Model Summary
        R        R-sq         F        df1         df2          p
     .4539       .2060    13.2824    5.0000    256.0000      .0000

Model
               coeff        se          t          p        LLCI       ULCI
constant      2.7461      .5502     4.9913      .0000     1.6626     3.8295
affect         .7071      .1049     6.7420      .0000      .5006      .9137
estress       -.0935      .0527    -1.7751      .0771     -.1973      .0102
ese           -.2121      .0764    -2.7769      .0059     -.3625     -.0617
sex            .1274      .1441      .8838      .3776     -.1565      .4112
tenure        -.0021      .0106     -.1940      .8463     -.0230      .0189

************************* TOTAL EFFECT MODEL ***************************
Outcome: withdraw

Model Summary
        R        R-sq         F        df1         df2          p
     .2550       .0650     4.4667    4.0000    257.0000      .0017

Model
               coeff        se          t          p        LLCI       ULCI
constant      4.0087      .5603     7.1548      .0000     2.9053     5.1120
estress        .0191      .0541      .3535      .7240     -.0874      .1257
ese           -.3216      .0808    -3.9789      .0001     -.4808     -.1624
sex            .1379      .1561      .8831      .3780     -.1695      .4453
tenure        -.0097      .0115     -.8491      .3966     -.0323      .0128

***************** TOTAL, DIRECT, AND INDIRECT EFFECTS *****************

Total effect of X on Y
    Effect        SE          t          p        LLCI       ULCI
     .0191      .0541      .3535      .7240     -.0874      .1257

Direct effect of X on Y
    Effect        SE          t          p        LLCI       ULCI
    -.0935      .0527    -1.7751      .0771     -.1973      .0102

Indirect effect of X on Y
            Effect    Boot SE   BootLLCI   BootULCI
affect       .1127      .0291      .0668      .1837

******************* ANALYSIS NOTES AND WARNINGS ***********************

Number of bootstrap samples for bias corrected bootstrap confidence intervals:
    10000

Level of confidence for all confidence intervals in output:
    95.00
```

FIGURE 6.3. Output from the PROCESS procedure for SPSS for the economic stress simple mediation analysis with three covariates.

TABLE 6.1. Model Coefficients for the Economic Stress Simple Mediation Analysis with Three Covariates

		Consequent						
		M (AFFECT)				Y (WITHDRAW)		
Antecedent		Coeff.	SE	p		Coeff.	SE	p
X (ESTRESS)	a	0.159	0.030	< .001	c'	−0.094	0.053	.077
M (AFFECT)		—	—	—	b	0.707	0.105	< .001
C_1 (ESE)	f_1	−0.155	0.044	.001	g_1	−0.212	0.076	.006
C_2 (SEX)	f_2	0.015	0.086	.863	g_2	0.127	0.144	.378
C_3 (TENURE)	f_3	−0.011	0.006	.086	g_3	−0.002	0.011	.846
Constant	i_1	1.786	0.308	< .001	i_2	2.746	0.550	< .001
		$R^2 = 0.163$				$R^2 = 0.206$		
		$F_{(4, 257)} = 12.523, p < .001$				$F_{(5, 256)} = 13.282, p < .001$		

Observe that the total effect is $c = 0.019$. As promised, the total effect is equal to the sum of the direct and indirect effects of X: $c = c' + ab = 0.019 = 0.113 - 0.094$. This relationship between the total, direct, and indirect effect of X applies to models with covariates so long as the covariates are included in the equations for both Y and M. It is worth emphasizing that this relationship also applies to multiple mediator models, both in parallel and serial form. You can demonstrate this for yourself without difficulty using PROCESS.[1]

This kind of analysis may be done in order to see how sensitive or susceptible the results from a comparable analysis without such controls is to alternative explanations involving those variables being controlled, or it may be done because it is known a priori or based on preliminary analyses that certain variables may be producing spurious association between key variables in the causal system. Ruling out epiphenomenality or spurious association as alternative explanations is an important part of any causal argument that includes associations that are only correlational in nature. This is not to say, however, that we can now interpret these effects unequivocally as causal. Of course, there could be other confounding variables

---

[1]PROCESS does offer the option of including the covariates in the model of M only, or Y only. See the documentation in Appendix A. When this option is used, it will no longer be true that $c = c' + ab$. I don't recommend doing this, although there are some circumstances in which it could be appropriate to do so.

that are producing the associations observed between X, M, and Y that haven't been accounted for in this analysis. This is one of the problems of this approach. One can only account for potential confounds that have been measured, and one can never know whether the correct potential confounds, if they exist, have been statistically controlled. The best one can do when such alternative interpretations may exist for an association is to anticipate those confounding threats, measure them during the study, and hope that no critic is able to conceive a plausible alternative confounding variable that you can't mathematically account for in your analysis.

Causal Order

Even if it were possible to anticipate every possible confound and eliminate its influence on the associations in a mediation model, this does nothing to establish direction of causal order. Mediation is a causal process, and among the criteria for claiming that an association is cause–effect is establishing that the cause precedes the effect in time. Experimental manipulation and random assignment to X all but guarantee that X precedes M and Y in a mediation model. This is because random assignment ensures that the groups which define X are equal on M and Y on average at the beginning of the study. Any differences observed between M and Y following random assignment must have occurred after the assignment of cases to groups (assuming no failure of random assignment to equate groups). But random assignment does not ensure that M precedes Y in time. Who is to say that the direction of causal flow runs from X to M to Y? Perhaps the true causal sequence is X to Y to M. For example, in the presumed media influence study, it could be argued that if people believe they should take action in response to the article about a possible sugar shortage in the country, they then project that decision onto the public at large as a form of rationalization for their own beliefs and chosen course of action. That is, beliefs about how one's self is influenced by the media may function as a mediator of the effect of article location on beliefs about how others are likely to be influenced by the media.

If X is not determined through manipulation and random assignment, then any sequence of causal ordering of X, M, and Y must be entertained as a potential candidate for the direction of causal flow. Even in a simple three-variable mediation model absent random assignment to values of X, six possible directions of causal flow are in the running ($X \rightarrow M \rightarrow Y$; $X \rightarrow Y \rightarrow M$; $M \rightarrow X \rightarrow Y$; $M \rightarrow Y \rightarrow X$; $Y \rightarrow X \rightarrow M$; $Y \rightarrow M \rightarrow X$). Hopefully, strong theory or logical impossibility precludes some of these, but it is likely that someone could piece together a sensible argument supporting at least one direction of causal flow other than your preferred interpretation. Consider an alternative proposal to the process modeled in the economic stress study, where depressed affect was construed as a mediator of the effect of economic stress on withdrawal intentions. It may be just as plausible that people who begin to ponder giving up on a business start putting less time into the enterprise, which in time hurts the profit margin, economic stresses mount, and the owner begins to start getting depressed about having to abandon his or her business, laying off employees, and so forth.

Fortunately, sometimes certain alternative directions of causal flow are so implausible that they can be discounted without difficulty. For instance, suppose X is the highest level of education attained by a person prior to age 25, and M is the grade point average of that person's child at the time of graduation from high school. It is impossible that M could cause X in this case. How could the academic performance of a person's child at graduation from high school influence how much education that person receives prior to age 25? If X and M are causally associated, the direction of causal flow must be X to M rather than the reverse.

Good theory may also help to discount some of the possible causal directions. It may be that a certain theory linking X causally to M has already been tested and accepted by the bulk of researchers and theorists in a particular area, and so few would argue that M is likely to affect X. Or perhaps in principle M *could* cause X, but the theory that gives rise to such a possibility is much weaker and less parsimonious than theory that predicts X causes M. In either of these cases, one might be fairly comfortable with the likelihood that X causes M rather than the reverse and feel no need to have to justify that likelihood empirically other than by establishing association between X and M.

In an attempt to entertain alternative direction of causal flow, one procedure some investigators employ is to estimate a mediation model corresponding to the alternative explanation to see whether the direct and indirect effects are consistent with what that alternative order predicts. For example, Shrum et al. (2011) proposed that people who engage in heavy television viewing tend to be less satisfied with life than less frequent viewers, because excessive consumption of television prompts material values, and such materialism tends to reduce satisfaction with life as one is not able to obtain the goods one desires. The results of a simple mediation analysis based on data from a survey of over 300 residents of the United States were consistent with this process. They found a negative indirect effect of television viewing frequency on life satisfaction just as predicted, but no direct effect. That is, people who reported watching relatively more television tended to be more materialistic, and this materialism was associated with reduced satisfaction with life. Using the same data, they also entertained an alternative model in which materialism influenced life satisfaction indirectly through television viewing frequency. They found no evidence of an indirect effect when the model was respecified with this alternative direction of causal flow.

When this procedure was applied to the presumed media influence study by treating presumed media influence as the final outcome and intentions to buy sugar as the mediator, the results were not consistent with this alternative direction of causal flow. Though the indirect effect of article location on presumed media influence through intentions to buy sugar was indeed positive (ab = 0.181), a 95% bias-corrected bootstrap confidence interval (based on 10,000 bootstrap samples) straddled zero (−0.009 to 0.432), unlike when presumed media influence was specified as the mediator. Similarly, when economic stress was specified as the mediator of the effect of withdrawal intentions on depressed affect, there was no evidence of such a process at work, as a bias-corrected bootstrap confidence interval for the indirect effect (ab = 0.012) contained zero (−0.013 to 0.042). For additional examples of this strategy in use, see Bizer et al. (2012), Coyle, Pillow, Snyder, and Kochunov (2011), Druckman and Albin (2011), Greitemeyer and McLatchie (2011), Guendelman, Cheryan, and Monin (2011), Huang, Sedlovskaya, Ackerman, and Bargh (2011), Oishi, Seol, Koo, and Miao (2011), Usborne and Taylor (2010), and de Zavala and Cichocka (2011).

The results from the analyses just described by no means establish with certainty that the direction of causal flow is as proposed by Pollack et al. (2012), Shrum et al. (2011), or Tal-Or et al. (2010). However, they do help establish an argument against those competing causal orders as plausible accounts of the process at work generating the data, and this is an important part of scientific discovery—ruling out alternative explanations. But sometimes estimation after a reordering of the causal sequence in this fashion does yield evidence consistent with the alternative causal order (see, e.g., Davydov, Shapiro, & Goldstein, 2010; Luksyte & Avery, 2010; Morano, Colella, Robazza, Bortoli, & Capranica, 2011). When this happens, which it no doubt does quite frequently, the data are simply uninformative about causal order, and additional study is required using a design that better affords causal claims and establishes causal direction. Alternatively, some have used such a predicament as supportive of the possibility of reciprocal causation (e.g., Cole et al., 2008; Morano et al., 2011).

6.3 Effect Size

Throughout the previous two chapters, interpretations of the direct and indirect effect have been couched in quantitative terms in the metrics of X and Y. Two cases that differ by one unit on X are estimated to differ by c' and ab units through the direct and indirect processes, respectively. As these effects are scaled in terms of the metrics of X and Y, they are scale bound and so will be determined by decisions about measurement. So the absolute size of the direct and indirect effects say nothing about whether the effects are large or small in a practical or theoretical sense. They can be made arbitrarily large or small by, for instance, multiplying or dividing X or Y by a constant.

This is not to say that c' and ab are necessarily substantively unmeaningful. On the contrary, they may be quite meaningful. Suppose Y is the number of pounds a person loses in a 2-month period, X is a dichotomous variable coding whether a person attended a half-day weight loss seminar two months prior (1) or only made the waiting list to attend some day in the future (0), and M is a measure of confidence in the ability to lose weight at the close of the seminar. Imagine a simple mediation analysis modeling weight loss reveals a direct effect of attendance at the seminar of $c' = 2$ and indirect effect of $ab = 5$ through confidence. So those who attended the weight loss seminar lost 7 pounds more on average than those who did not, with 5 of those pounds coming off through the effect of the seminar on confidence which in turn influenced weight loss, and the remaining 2 pounds due to some other process or mechanism not included in the model. A 7-pound weight loss resulting from attending a brief seminar seems like a meaningful effect. One could also say that the indirect effect is (descriptively at least) bigger than the direct effect because they are both measured on the same metric—the metrics of X and Y. As discussed in section 5.3, the metric of the mediator is not a part of the metric of the indirect or direct effects.

Meaningful effect sizes resulting from meaningful metrics such as this are probably not the norm, however, as measurement decisions often result in quantifications of constructs that are on arbitrary scales. In that case, there isn't much that can be done about the ambiguity in interpretation of the size of direct and indirect effects. In addition, "practical" or "theoretical" significance are subjective terms that defy precise quantification. Finally, what might be considered a small effect in one context or by one investigator might be considered relatively large in a different context or by a different investigator. Although there are many rules of thumbs circulating in the literature for labeling an effect as "small," "medium," or "large," these ultimately are just rough guidelines and cannot be applied indiscriminately to any study regardless of content area and regardless of how variables are measured.

The quantification of effect size in mediation analysis is an evolving area of research, and the literature has generally not developed much beyond the description and study of various measures in simple mediation analysis without statistical controls. Below I describe six measures of effect size, some that apply to both the direct and indirect effect (as well as the total effect) and others that apply only to the indirect effect. These are by no means the only measures available, but they are implemented in PROCESS, so I restrict my discussion to these six. For an excellent discussion of measures of effect size in mediation analysis, see Preacher and Kelley (2011). I use their notation below.

The Partially Standardized Effect

Consider the simple mediation analysis examining the effect of economic stress and intentions to withdraw from entrepreneurial activities. Recall from that analysis (described in section 4.5) that two entrepreneurs who differ by one unit in their economic stress were estimated to differ by $ab = 0.133$ units in their withdrawal intentions indirectly through depressed affect, and $c' = -0.077$ units directly, independent of depressed affect. But are these large effects or small ones? Given the arbitrary nature of the measurement scales used (responses to rating scales aggregated over multiple questions), it is hard to say, because the measurement metric is not inherently meaningful. This can be resolved in part by indexing these effects relative to variability between entrepreneurs in their intentions to withdraw from business-related activity. These effects could be considered quite large if there is very little variation in withdrawal intentions, but it could be quite small if there is lots of variation.

The partially standardized effect size (see, e.g., MacKinnon, 2008) is a transformation of an effect that expresses it relative to the standard deviation of Y rather than in the original metric of Y, thereby giving it context relative to variability in the outcome. The formulas for the partially standardized direct and indirect effects are simple:

$$c'_{ps} = \frac{c'}{SD_Y}$$

$$ab_{ps} = \frac{ab}{SD_Y}$$

In the economic stress analysis, $SD_Y = 1.248$, so the direct and indirect effects expressed in partially standardized form are $c'_{ps} = -0.077/1.248 =$

−0.062 and $ab_{ps} = 0.133/1.248 = 0.107$. This means that two entrepreneurs who differ by one unit in their economic stress differ by about one-tenth of a standard deviation in their intentions to withdraw from entrepreneurship as a result of the effect of stress on depressed affect, which in turn affects withdrawal intentions. Independent of this indirect mechanism, the entrepreneur one unit higher in economic stress is estimated to be 0.062 standard deviations lower in withdrawal intentions (lower because c'_{ps} is negative). These seem like fairly small effects when conceptualized in terms of variation in withdrawal intentions. But who is to say really, as someone's small effect might be someone else's large effect.

As already discussed many times, the direct and indirect effects sum to yield the total effect of X. So too do the partially standardized direct and indirect effects add to yield the partially standardized total effect. That is,

$$c_{ps} = \frac{c}{SD_Y} = c'_{ps} + ab_{ps}$$

So given two entrepreneurs who differ by one unit in their economic stress, the entrepreneur experiencing more stress is estimated to be $-0.062 + 0.107 = 0.045$ standard deviations higher in intentions to withdraw from entepreneurship as a result of the combined direct and indirect pathways by which stress influences withdrawal intentions.

When X is a dichotomous variable and the two groups are coded such that they differ by one unit on the coding scheme (0 and 1, −0.5 and 0.5, etc.), then c'_{ps} and ab_{ps} can be interpreted as the number of standard deviations in Y that the groups differ on average as a result of the direct and indirect mechanisms. In the presumed media influence simple mediation analysis in section 4.3, $c' = 0.254$, $ab = 0.241$, $SD_Y = 1.550$, and so $c'_{ps} = 0.245/1.550 = 0.158$ and $ab_{ps} = 0.241/1.550 = 0.156$. Those told the story was to be published on the front page of the newspaper were, on average, 0.156 standard deviations higher in their intention to buy sugar as a result of the indirect effect through presumed media influence than were those told the story was to be buried inside the paper. Independent of this mechanism, on average, those told the story was to be on the front page were 0.158 standard deviations higher, on average, in their intentions. These direct and indirect influences sum to give the total estimated mean difference in intention to buy sugar between the two conditions: $0.158 + 0.156 = 0.314$ standard deviations (or, more precisely from Figure 4.4, 0.319 standard deviations).

The Completely Standardized Effect

The partially standardized effect rescales c' and ab to the standard deviation of Y but keeps X in its original metric. Therefore, partially standardized effects are in a scale-bound metric, for their size will depend on the scaling of X. Oftentimes, a difference of one unit on X has little substantive meaning. Removing the scaling of X from the partially standardized effect expresses the direct and indirect effects in terms of the difference in standard deviations in Y between two cases that differ by *one standard deviation* in X. This yields the *completely standardized effect*:

$$c'_{cs} = \frac{SD_X(c')}{SD_Y} = SD_X(c'_{ps})$$

$$ab_{cs} = \frac{SD_X(ab)}{SD_Y} = SD_X(ab_{ps})$$

These two measures are identical to the direct and indirect effects when those effects are calculated using standardized regression coefficients (or standardized X, M, and Y are used in the model rather than X, M, and Y in their original metric). That is, $c'_{cs} = \tilde{c}$ and $ab_{cs} = \tilde{a}\tilde{b}$ (see, e.g., Cheung, 2009; Preacher & Hayes, 2008b).

In the economic stress study, $SD_X = 1.424$, $SD_Y = 1.248$, $c' = -0.077$, $ab = 0.133$, and so $c'_{cs} = 1.424(-0.077)/1.248 = -0.088$ and $ab_{cs} = 1.424(0.133)/1.248 = 0.152$. These are larger than the partially standardized effects because they reference differences in standard deviations of Y between two people that differ by 1.424 units on X (i.e., one standard deviation) rather than only one unit. So if entrepreneur i is one standard deviation higher in economic stress than entrepreneur j, entrepreneur i is estimated to be 0.152 standard deviations higher in withdrawal intentions as a result of the effect of stress on affect which in turn influences withdrawal intentions. But the direct effect pulls that difference back toward zero, as independent of depressed affect, the more stressed entrepreneur is estimated to be 0.088 standard deviations lower in withdrawal intentions.

As was true with the partially standardized effect, the completely standardized direct and indirect effects add to yield the completely standardized total effect:

$$c_{cs} = \frac{SD_X(c)}{SD_Y} = c'_{cs} + ab_{cs}$$

So the opposing direct and indirect effect results translate into an estimated difference of $0.152 + (-0.088) = 0.064$ standard deviations in withdrawal intentions between two entrepreneurs that differ by one standard deviation in economic stress. The completely standardized total effect is also equivalent to $\tilde{c}$, the standardized regression coefficient for X in a simple regression model estimating Y from X alone.

The completely standardized effect is generally not meaningful if X is a dichotomous variable. The problem with its use with a dichotomous X is that SD_X is affected by the distribution of the cases into the two groups coded in X (see section 3.1). For example, if the n cases in the sample are equally distributed between the two groups, and assuming the groups are coded with a one-unit difference on X, then $SD_X = 0.50$ (in large samples), and so c'_{cs} and ab_{cs} will be half the size of their corresponding partially standardized values. But if the n cases are distributed unevenly between the two groups, SD_X will be smaller than 0.50, and therefore so too will be c'_{cs} and ab_{cs}, and they will be even more discrepant from c'_{ps} and ab_{ps}.

The discrepancy between the completely and partially standardized effects is itself not a problem. What is a problem is that exactly the same mean difference in Y in standard deviation units resulting from the direct and indirect mechanism (which is what c'_{ps} and ab_{ps} measure) depends on how the cases are distributed into the two groups when the completely standardized effect size measure is used. A measure of effect size for a dichotomous X should not be influenced in this way by something not directly associated with the size of the mean difference. Thus, I cannot recommend the use of the completely standardized effect size when X is a dichotomous variable. It therefore follows that when X is dichotomous, *you should not interpret or report the total, direct, or indirect effects calculated using standardized regression coefficients*.

Ratio of the Indirect Effect to the Total Effect

Historically, mediation analysis has been undertaken when the goal is to establish the process by which an effect operates. Given evidence of an effect of X on Y (the total effect c), mediation analysis can be used to break that effect into its constituent components direct and indirect. A natural question given evidence of an effect of X on Y is to ask is how much of the effect of X on Y operates indirectly through M. Alwin and Hauser (1975) and MacKinnon et al. (1995) discuss an effect size measure often interpreted as the proportion of the total effect that is mediated:

$$P_M = \frac{ab}{c} = \frac{ab}{c' + ab}$$

The closer P_M is to one, the more of the effect of X on Y can be said to operate through M, and the closer P_M is to zero, the less of the effect of X on Y is due to the indirect process through M. For instance, in the presumed media influence simple mediation analysis, $ab = 0.241$ and $c = 0.496$, so $P_M =$

0.241/0.496 = 0.486. So 48.6% of the effect of article location on intentions to buy sugar occurs indirectly through presumed media influence.

Although simple enough to understand, P_M has some serious problems. First, a proportion is by definition between 0 and 1, yet P_M is not so constrained. If either ab or c is negative but not both, then $P_M < 0$, and if c is closer to zero than ab, then $|P_M| > 1$. For instance, in the economic stress simple mediation analysis, $ab = 0.133$ and $c = 0.056$, so $P_M = 2.375$. Is it sensible to say that 237.5% of the effect of economic stress on withdrawal intentions is accounted for by the indirect effect through depressed affect? Clearly, it is not. Indeed, as c approaches zero, P_M explodes toward positive or negative infinity, depending on the signs of ab and c.

In addition, P_M is highly unstable from sample to sample (see MacKinnon et al., 1995). It has large sampling variance, and it is not uncommon for a confidence interval for P_M to include zero even when most other measures of effect size for the indirect effect clearly show evidence that the effect is different from zero. Ignoring the problems described earlier, one must have a fairly large sample (at least 500, according to MacKinnon et al., 1995) before one can have much faith in P_M as a description of the magnitude of an indirect effect.

Given these limitations, I find P_M hard to recommend. If it is to be used at all, I recommend its use be limited to studies based on large samples and when the total effect is larger than the indirect effect and of the same sign, a situation sometimes called "consistent mediation" (MacKinnon, Krull, & Lockwood, 2000). On the balance, I'd stay away from this measure.

Ratio of the Indirect Effect to the Direct Effect

The ratio of the indirect to the total effect is often mistakenly interpreted as the proportion of the effect of X on Y that is mediated. A variation on this measure, the ratio of the indirect to the direct effect, references the size of the indirect effect to the direct effect:

$$R_M = \frac{ab}{c'}$$

R_M is simply a transformation of P_M. A little algebra shows that R_M can be expressed in terms of P_M as

$$R_M = \frac{P_M}{1 - P_M}.$$

(see Preacher & Kelley, 2011). If $|R_M| > 1$, then the indirect effect is larger than the direct effect, whereas if $|R_M| < 1$, the indirect effect is smaller than the direct effect. In the special case where the indirect and direct effects are of the same sign, then $R_M > 1$ means that more of the total effect of X on Y is carried indirectly through M, whereas $R_M < 1$ implies that more of the total effect is determined by the direct rather than the indirect effect.

In the presumed media influence simple mediation analysis, $ab = 0.241$ and $c' = 0.254$, and so $R_M = 0.241/0.254 = 0.949$. The indirect effect is 94.9% of the size of the direct effect. Because ab and c' have the same sign, we can say that more of the total effect of article location on intentions to buy sugar is determined directly rather than indirectly through presumed media influence. In the economic stress analysis, $ab = 0.133$ and $c' = -0.077$. Therefore, $R_M = 0.133/(-0.077) = -1.727$. The indirect effect of economic stress on withdrawal intentions through depressed affect is 172.7% of size of (or 72.7% larger than) the direct effect. The negative sign of R_M in this example doesn't carry information that is substantively interpretable.

I can't recommend this measure of the size of the indirect effect. Notice that as c' approaches zero, even tiny indirect effects will explode in size relative to the direct effect, as R_M quickly becomes massive with shrinking c'. And as Preacher and Kelley (2011) note, minor sample-to-sample fluctuations in estimates of c' can really sway R_M in one direction or another. Simulation research has verified that like P_M, R_M is unstable as an estimator except in large samples. It simply can't be trusted as a description of the size of the indirect effect unless the sample size is at least 2,000 or so (MacKinnon et al., 1995).

Proportion of Variance in Y Explained by the Indirect Effect

Fairchild, MacKinnon, Toborga, and Taylor (2009) derived a measure of effect size for the indirect effect in simple mediation analysis that is an attempt to quantify the proportion of the variance in Y attributable to the indirect effect of X on Y through M. Their measure, which they label R^2_{med}, is calculated as

$$R^2_{med} = r^2_{MY} - (R^2_{Y.MX} - r^2_{XY})$$

where r^2_{MY} and r^2_{XY} are the squared correlations between M and Y and X and Y, respectively, and $R^2_{Y.MX}$ is the squared multiple correlation estimating Y from both X and M. In the presumed media influence simple mediation analysis, $r^2_{MY} = 0.199$, $r^2_{XY} = 0.026$, and $R^2_{Y.MX} = 0.454$, and so $R^2_{med} = 0.199 - (0.206 - 0.026) = 0.019$. In the economic stress simple mediation analysis, $r^2_{MY} = 0.173$, $r^2_{XY} = 0.004$, and $R^2_{Y.MX} = 0.180$, and so $R^2_{med} = 0.173 - (0.180 - 0.004) = -0.003$.

The meaningfulness of R^2_{med} is predicated on the assumption that there is an association between X and Y, meaning that X explains some of the variation in Y. When this occurs, presumably some fraction of that explained variation is attributable to the indirect mechanism. But as we have seen, it is possible for an indirect effect to exist absent evidence of detectable association between X and Y. Rephrased, it is possible for ab to be larger in absolute value than c. In such situations, R^2_{med} can be negative, as in the economic stress example, and this violates its interpretation as a proportion which must by definition be between 0 and 1. Like the ratio of the indirect to the total effect, I recommend R^2_{med} be used if and only only if the c and ab are the same sign and c is larger than ab. And even then, given that it isn't constrained to be a proportion, its meaning is suspect.

Preacher and Kelley's Kappa-Squared

With the exception of ab/c' all indices of the size of the indirect effect discussed thus far typically are interpreted relative to zero. Thus, an effect size that is close to zero is generally seen as small, and the further the index gets from zero, the larger the effect is perceived to be. However, the size of an effect can always be interpreted relative to some other reference, and depending on the choice of reference, any effect can be perceived as large or small. For instance, although a partially standardized indirect effect of 0.50 is certainly larger than zero, it is only half as large as one. So is 0.50 large or small? It depends on what you compare it to.

The newest entrant to the growing list of effect size measures in simple mediation analysis, introduced by Preacher and Kelley (2011), acknowledges that the variances and correlations between the variables observed in the data constrain just how large the indirect effect can be. Given this, it is sensible to gauge the size of an indirect effect relative to how large it could possibly be given these constraints. They call their index "kappa-squared" (κ^2) and define it as the ratio of the indirect effect relative to its maximum possible value in the data:

$$\kappa^2 = \frac{ab}{MAX(ab)}$$

where $MAX(ab)$ is the largest that ab could be given the observed variability of X, Y, and M and their intercorrelations in the data. The computation of $MAX(ab)$ is somewhat tedious—something best left to PROCESS (see below), so I will not describe how it is calculated. See Preacher and Kelley (2011) for details if you are interested.

Unlike all other effect size measures discussed thus far, κ^2 is bound between 0 and 1, with a value closer to 1 representing a bigger indirect effect. In the economic stress analysis, $\kappa^2 = 0.153$, meaning that the observed indirect effect of $ab = 0.133$ is about 15% as large as its maximum possible

```
                    Indirect effect of X on Y
                            Effect     Boot SE    BootLLCI    BootULCI
                    affect      .1330       .0329      .0773        .2084

                    Partially standardized indirect effect of X on Y
                            Effect     Boot SE    BootLLCI    BootULCI
                    affect      .1066       .0266      .0619        .1662

                    Completely standardized indirect effect of X on Y
                            Effect     Boot SE    BootLLCI    BootULCI
                    affect      .1518       .0376      .0884        .2365

                    Ratio of indirect to total effect of X on Y
                            Effect     Boot SE    BootLLCI    BootULCI
                    affect     2.3694   487.4688    -1.0712     230.5781

                    Ratio of indirect to direct effect of X on Y
                            Effect     Boot SE    BootLLCI    BootULCI
                    affect    -1.7302   383.6704   -38.4984       3.4935

                    R-squared mediation effect size (R-sq_med)
                            Effect     Boot SE    BootLLCI    BootULCI
                    affect     -.0027      .0183     -.0338        .0381

                    Preacher and Kelley (2011) Kappa-squared
                            Effect     Boot SE    BootLLCI    BootULCI
                    affect      .1532       .0350      .0939        .2319
```

FIGURE 6.4. Effect sizes with bootstrap confidence intervals generated by PROCESS for the economic stress simple mediation analysis.

value given the association between the variables observed in the sample. In the presumed media influence simple mediation analysis, $\kappa^2 = 0.081$. The indirect effect of article location on intentions to buy sugar through presumed media influence is around 8% of its maximum possible value.

Effect Size Estimation and Inference in PROCESS

PROCESS estimates all of the effect sizes described earlier for *indirect effects only* and only in simple mediation models with no covariates. For multiple mediator models (without covariates), the completely and partially standardized measures are available, along with the ratio of the indirect to total effect and the ratio of the indirect to the direct effect. To obtain these measures in the output, add **effsize=1** to the PROCESS command line. When used in conjunction with the bootstrapping option, PROCESS also generates bootstrap confidence intervals for these effects. Output generated by this option for the economic stress study can be found in Figure 6.4.

   If the confidence interval for $_T a_T b$ does not contain zero, an analogous confidence interval for the indirect effect after conversion to a sensible effect size metric also should not contain zero. Yet observe in Figure 6.4 that this is not true for three of the effect size measures previously described. I do not believe this reflects new uncertainty about whether one can really claim an indirect effect in this analysis after conversion of ab to an alternative effect size measure. Rather, I believe this reflects the problems with ab/c, ab/c', and R^2_{med} and why you should be hesitant to use them uncritically. Indeed, observe the massive sampling variance in ab/c and ab/c' as evidenced by the large standard deviation of the bootstrap estimates ("Boot SE" in the output) and limits for the upper (for ab/c) and lower bound (for ab/c') of confidence intervals that are so distant from zero. This is consistent with simulation research that shows sample sizes must be quite large before one can have any faith in these measures of effect size. Personally, I would stay away from ab/c, ab/c' as well as R^2_{med}, but if you want to use one of these, do so only if the total effect is larger than the indirect effect and of the same sign.

6.4 Multiple Xs or Ys: Analyze Separately or Simultaneously?

Researchers sometimes propose that several causal agents (X variables) simultaneously transmit their effects on the same outcome through the same mediator(s). For instance, Von Hippel, Issa, Ma, and Stokes (2011) examined the direct and indirect effects of social comparisons with the opportunities of men and of women in their place of work on their perceived likelihood of career advancement through a sense of "stereotype threat." And Simpson et al. (2011) examined how posttherapeutic severity of obsessive-compulsive disorder symptoms is affected by pretreatment severity, pretreatment hoarding, and perceptions of a "working alliance" with the therapist, both directly and indirectly through a patient's adherence to the procedures and strategies taught during cognitive-behavioral therapy.

Multiple X Variables

The computation of the direct and indirect effects in models with multiple X variables requires no modification to the procedure discussed thus far. Each consequent is regressed on the variables in the model that putatively cause it, and the resulting coefficients are pieced together or directly interpreted. But the estimation and interpretation of the effects in such models have some special considerations worth discussing. Primarily, the considerations revolve around the question as to whether the inclusion of multiple Xs in a single model will have any effect on the results one would obtain if one instead estimates several models, each one focusing on a single X variable at a time.

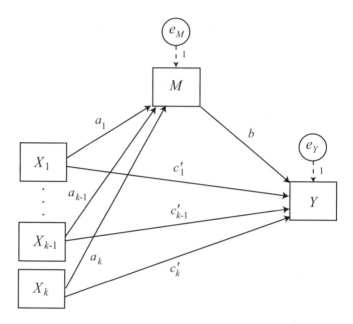

FIGURE 6.5. A simple mediation model with k antecedent X variables.

Figure 6.5 represents a simple mediation model with k X variables passing their effects directly to a single Y, and indirectly through a single M. In such a model, there are k direct and indirect effects, one of each for each X. There are two consequent variables in this model, so two linear models are required to estimate the effects. These two models are

$$M = i_1 + a_1 X_1 + a_2 X_2 + \ldots + a_k X_x + e_M$$

$$Y = i_2 + c_1' X_1 + c_2' X_2 + \ldots + c_k' X_k + bM + e_Y$$

and they can be estimated as a set of separate OLS regressions. The indirect effect of X_i on Y through M is $a_i b$, and the direct effect is c_i'. The total effect of X_i is the sum of its direct and indirect effects: $c_i = c_i' + a_i b$. The total effect of X_i on Y could also be estimated by predicting Y from all k Xs but not M:

$$Y = i_3 + c_1 X_1 + c_2 X_2 + \ldots + c_k X_k + e_Y$$

When all k Xs are in the model simultaneously, the direct and indirect effects of X_i are interpreted as the estimated difference in Y between two cases differing by a unit on X_i but that are equal on the other $k - 1$ X_i variables (or, rephrased, holding the remaining $k - 1$ X variables constant, or controlling for those variables). In other words, these represent the direct and indirect effects of X_i on Y that are unique to X_i. As such, these effects are interpreted just as they are when the remaining $k - 1$ X variables are conceptualized as statistical controls rather than variables whose effects are substantively interesting.

In a model with k X variables, the total, direct, and indirect effects of X_i may or may not be the same as the corresponding effects in a simple mediation model that excludes all other $k - 1$ X variables (as in Figure 4.2). Any differences will depend on the size of the correlations between X_i and the other $k - 1$ Xs, as well as the correlation between other Xs and M and Y.

It is sensible to ask which approach is "better" or "more correct," in terms of the estimates they yield and their substantive meaning. With k causal Xs, should one include all X's in a single model (as did Von Hippel et al., 2011) or estimate k models each with a single X (as did, e.g., Gibbs, Ellison, & Lai, 2011). The answer is that either approach can be legitimate, and sometimes one can learn from doing it both ways, but it is important to recognize that the direct and indirect effects estimate different things and so interpretation of the results must be undertaken with due care. The former approach, including all Xs in a model, yields an estimate of the part of one X's effect on Y (directly and indirectly through M) that is unique to that X relative to the other Xs in the model. The latter approach, estimating several models each with a single X, yields an estimate of X's direct and indirect effects on Y and, potentially, the effect of other Xs excluded from the model.

The danger in including multiple Xs in a mediation model, as when including statistical controls, is the possibility that highly correlated Xs will cancel out each others' effects. This is a standard concern in linear models involving correlated predictors. Two X variables (or an X variable and a control variable) highly correlated with each other may also both be correlated with M or Y, so when they are both included as predictors of M or Y in a mediation model, they compete against each other in their attempt to explain variation in M and Y. Their regression coefficients quantify their unique association with the model's mediator and outcome variable(s). At the extreme, the two variables end up performing like two boxers in the ring simultaneously throwing a winning blow at the other at precisely the same time. Both get knocked out and neither goes away appearing worthy of a prize. The stronger the associations between the variables in the model, the greater the potential of such a problem. As a result, one could find that when included as the sole X, each variable exerts a direct and/or indirect effect on Y through M, but when considered together, neither appears to have any effect at all.

Estimation of a Model with Multiple X Variables in PROCESS

One of the constraints programmed into PROCESS is that only a single X variable can be listed in the **x=** part of the command line. However, compare Figure 6.5 to Figure 6.3. Mathematically, these are the same model. The only difference is in the construal of the additional variables sending arrows to M and Y—as either covariates and not of substantive interest or as additional causal influences whose effects are very much of interest. As discussed in section 6.2, PROCESS can estimate a mediation model with statistical controls as in Figure 6.3, so it follows that it can also estimate a model with multiple X variables. However, in order to estimate the direct and indirect effects of all k X variables in Figure 6.5, PROCESS must be executed k times, each time putting one X_i in the model as X and the remaining k − 1 X variables as covariates. Each time PROCESS is run, the direct and indirect effects of the variable listed as X will be generated. Repeating k − 1 times generates the indirect effects for all k X variables. Mathematically, all resulting paths, direct, and indirect effects will be the same as if they had all been estimated simultaneously (as in a structural equation modeling program).

For instance, consider a mediator model with one mediator (MED1), one outcome (Y1), and three X variables (IV1, IV2, and IV3). The set of SPSS PROCESS commands below would estimate the effects of IV1, IV2, and IV3 on Y1 directly and indirectly through MED1:

```
process vars=y1 iv1 iv2 iv3 med1/y=y1/x=iv1/m=med1/boot=10000/model=4
    /seed=5235.
process vars=y1 iv1 iv2 iv3 med1/y=y1/x=iv2/m=med1/boot=10000/model=4
    /seed=5235.
process vars=y1 iv1 iv2 iv3 med1/y=y1/x=iv3/m=med1/boot=10000/model=4
    /seed=5235.
```

In SAS, the corresponding set of commands is

```
%process (data=datafile,vars=y1 iv1 iv2 iv3 med1,y=y1,x=iv1,m=med1,boot=
    10000,model=4,seed=5235);
%process (data=datafile,vars=y1 iv1 iv2 iv3 med1,y=y1,x=iv2,m=med1,boot=
    10000,model=4,seed=5235);
%process (data=datafile,vars=y1 iv1 iv2 iv3 med1,y=y1,x=iv3,m=med1,boot=
    10000,model=4,seed=5235);
```

In the preceding code, the random number generator is seeded with a common (and arbitrary) seed using the **seed=** option so that at each run,

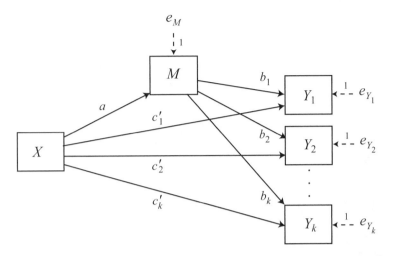

FIGURE 6.6. A simple mediation model with k consequent Y variables.

the bootstrap confidence intervals will be based on the same set of 10,000 resamples from the data. It makes no difference what seed is used—pick it randomly if you choose as I did in the code above—so long as it is a positive integer. This trick is easily extended to parallel and serial multiple mediator models as well as models with statistical controls merely by including the additional mediators and covariates in the **vars=** list and the additional mediator(s) in the **m=** list.

Multiple Y Variables

Sometimes investigators are interested in the direct and indirect effects of some putative causal antecedent on several different outcome variables. For example, Broeren, Muris, Bouwmeester, van der Heijden, and Abee (2011) estimated the direct and indirect effects of neuroticism (X) on anxiety symptoms (Y_1), depression symptoms (Y_2), and sleep difficulties (Y_3) in 158 Dutch children, with worry (M_1) and rumination (M_2) specified as mediators of neuroticism's effect. And Webster and Saucier (2011) found evidence that following a mortality salience manipulation, gender (X) differences between men and women in homonegativity (Y_1), acceptance of restrictions on the employment opportunities for gay men (Y_2), and affective prejudice toward gay men (Y_3) were mediated by acceptance of traditional gender roles (M_1) but not by empathy (M_2).

A mediation model with k Y variables is displayed in the form of a statistical diagram in Figure 6.6. A close examination shows that this model really is just three simple mediation models with a common X and

M. Because Y_i is determined only by X and M, the direct and indirect effects of X on Y_i will be the same regardless of whether they are estimated simultaneously with the other $k - 1$ variables in the model analytically (which would require a structural equation modeling program) or using k separate analyses, one for each Y variable. PROCESS can be used to estimate the paths in a model such as in Figure 6.6 by running k PROCESS commands, substituting one Y variable for another at each run and seeding the random number generator with a common seed for bootstrap sampling at each run.

6.5 Reporting a Mediation Analysis

I am always somewhat reluctant to provide strict advice or spell out explicit rules about how to write about data analysis. I believe writing the results section of a scientific article is not much different than writing about anything else, whether it is a biography, science fiction, or a trashy romance. There are as many ways to write a good scientific article as there are ways to write a good novel. There is no specific formula that will produce good scientific prose, for so much of what makes writing good is what you bring to the task that is unique to you—your style, your background, writing models who have inspired you, and so forth. Most important is that you be interesting and engaging, focus on the human dimensions that make your research matter, minimize your use of jargon as much as possible, and deemphasize things that the reader won't care about. If you do that, almost anything else goes. You should have fun when you write, and if you have passion for and interest in your subject matter, that will come across in your writing if you let it. That said, I recognize that writing about data analysis can be a challenge until you get used to it and develop your own style, and it can be difficult to know what is and is not important. So I offer a few guidelines below.

First, it is easy to bore the reader with excessive discussion of regression coefficients, tests of significance, and statements of hypotheses supported or not. Try to pack as much of the pallid statistical information as you can into a table or figure summarizing the analysis (such as in Figures 4.3 or 5.3 or Tables 4.2 or 5.1). Let the reader scan this information as he or she chooses while you walk the reader through the analytical procedure and the substantive interpretation of the results in the text. Use statistics in the text as support for substantive claims being made, but as punctuation for those claims rather than as the subject and focus of the results. Unless necessary when using them in formulas, try to avoid the use of symbolic representations for variables in the text itself (with variable names in the dataset such as COND, PMI, ESTRESS, etc.).

For instance, consider the following description of a simple mediation analysis:

> A mediation analysis was conducted by estimating perceived media influence (PMI) from article location (COND) as well as reactions to the story (REACTION) from both article location and perceived media influence. Supporting hypothesis 1, COND was positively related to PMI ($a = 0.477, p = .045$). Supporting hypothesis 2, PMI positively predicted REACTION while controlling for COND ($b = 0.506, p < .001$). A bootstrap confidence interval for the indirect effect of COND (ab) using 10,000 bootstrap samples was 0.004 to 0.524, meaning that there was evidence of an indirect effect of COND on REACTION through PMI. Contrary to hypothesis 3, the direct effect of COND on REACTION of $c' = 0.254$ was not statistically significant ($p = .322$).

Now compare this to the one below:

> From a simple mediation analysis conducted using ordinary least squares path analysis, article location indirectly influenced intentions to buy sugar through its effect on beliefs about how others would be influenced. As can be seen in Figure 4.3 and Table 4.2, participants told that the article would be published on the front page believed others would be more influenced to buy sugar than those told that the article would appear in an economic supplement ($a = 0.477$), and participants who believed others would be more influenced by the story expressed a stronger intention to go buy sugar themselves ($b = 0.506$). A bias-corrected bootstrap confidence interval for the indirect effect ($ab = 0.241$) based on 10,000 bootstrap samples was entirely above zero (0.004 to 0.529). There was no evidence that article location influenced intention to buy sugar independent of its effect on presumed media influence ($c' = 0.254, p = .322$).

Notice how much more interesting and understandable the second description is. Unlike the first, the second paragraph focuses on the results in terms of the constructs measured rather than symbols, while still providing some of the descriptive and inferential statistics for the reader. However, those statistics are primarily used as punctuation for substantive claims rather than as the focus of the text itself. And by avoiding explicit discussion of hypotheses supported or not, attention is kept off the investigator and his or her clairvoyance or lack thereof. Most readers will not care whether an investigator correctly forecasted his or her results, nor is the reader likely to remember what hypotheses 1, 2, and 3 were at this point in a scientific article.

Second, I recommend reporting the model coefficients, direct, indirect, and total effects in unstandardized form. Throughout this book, I emphasize estimation and interpretation of effects in their unstandardized metric, and I report unstandardized effects when I report the results of a mediation analysis in my own research. There is a widespread belief that standardized effects are best reported, because the measurement scales used in most sciences are arbitrary and not inherently meaningful, or that standardized effects are more comparable across studies or investigators using different methods. But standardization simply changes one arbitrary measurement scale into another arbitrary scale, and because standardized effects are scaled in terms of variability in the sample, they are not comparable across studies conducted by different investigators regardless of whether the same measurement scales are used. By keeping the results in an unstandardized metric, the analytical results (equations, regression coefficients, etc.) map directly onto the measurement scales used in the study, and they can be directly compared across studies conducted using the same measurement system. If you provide information about the variability of each variable in the model, a reader interested in standardized effects can generate them for him- or herself.

For reasons discussed in sections 2.2, 3.1, and 6.3, I strongly discourage reporting standardized effects involving a dichotomous X. Standardized regression coefficients (and therefore direct, indirect, and total effects) for a dichotomous X are not meaningful, as they are influenced by the distribution of the cases between the two groups as well as differences between the group means. Furthermore, standardization of X destroys the interpretation of the effects in terms of differences between the means of the two groups on M and Y. If you feel compelled to report some kind of standardized metric for the effects in a mediation analysis involving a dichotomous X, use the partially standardized effect size measure discussed in section 6.3. For good discussions of the pros and cons of the reporting of standardized versus unstandardized effects in regression and causal modeling, see Kim and Ferree (1976) or Kim and Mueller (1981). If an editor or reviewer questions the legitimacy of reporting unstandardized coefficients, refer him or her to various published examples such as Giner-Sorolla and Espinosa (2011), Hart (2011), Guendelman et al. (2011), or Nevicka, Ten Velden, De Hoogh, and Van Vianen (2011). Other examples are in abundance.

Ultimately the choice to report standardized or unstandardized effects is yours to make. Report both if you desire. Regardless of your choice, make sure you tell the reader somewhere (in table notes or the text itself) whether the effects are expressed in a standardized or unstandardized metric. Don't assume that symbolic representations or text such as β or "beta coefficient" will be understood by all, as these mean different things to different people depending on where they were trained, what books they learned from, and various conventions in different disciplines.

Third, although there is no harm in reporting hypothesis tests or confidence intervals for the paths that define the indirect effect (a and b), whether those effects are statistically significant need not be a part of the argument supporting evidence of the existence of an indirect effect. Notice that the second preceding description does not provide p-values for a or b (though p-values are provided in the table), because whether a and/or b is statistically significant is not pertinent to whether the indirect effect is different from zero. An indirect effect is quantified as the product of paths. Provide your point estimate of the indirect effect, as well as an inferential test supporting your claim that it is not zero. Whether or not a and b are statistically different from zero can be useful supplementary information for the reader, but it need not be part of your claim that an indirect effect exists. As discussed in section 4.2, it is only their sign that matters, for the signs of a and b determine the sign of ab and therefore its interpretation in terms of the process at work being modeled.

Fourth, be precise in your language when talking about direct and indirect effects. In a simple mediation analysis, X exerts an effect on Y directly and/or indirectly through M. It is not correct to talk about the "indirect effect of M" unless there is another variable causally between M and Y. Although M affects Y in a mediation process, it does not do so indirectly except in serial multiple mediator models. It is X that affects Y indirectly *through* M. I also find the term "mediated effect," which some use as a synonym for indirect effect, to be an awkward label. To call the indirect effect the mediated effect suggests that ab or M is the causal agent of interest, but in fact it is X that is cause of Y, which exerts its effect indirectly through M, not ab or M itself.

Fifth, as should be apparent from the last few chapters, you should report both the direct and the indirect effect(s) in a mediation analysis as well as an inferential test for each. I cannot encourage the use of normal theory approaches like the Sobel test. Rather, I strongly recommend the use of bootstrap confidence intervals when conducting inferential tests of indirect effects, for they tend to perform best and respect the irregularity of the sampling distribution of the indirect effect. However, merely stating that bootstrapping was used is not sufficient. Make sure your description includes both the number of bootstrap samples and the method used for constructing confidence intervals (i.e., percentile, bias-corrected, or bias-corrected and accelerated).

Finally, I often see mediation analyses overreported, with a description of multiple methods used that seems to track the evolution of mediation analysis. A report might include a discussion as to whether the causal steps criteria for mediation are met, followed by a Sobel test, and perhaps (if the investigator has been keeping up with the literature in mediation analysis) end with a more appropriate and modern test of the indirect effect using a bootstrap confidence interval or the distribution of the product approach. My guess is that investigators who do this realize that publishing is partly a political process and by describing multiple approaches and tests, one's bases are covered against any potential critics. I understand this, yet it also seems like analytical overkill to me. There is value to establishing converging evidence through multiple analytical strategies, but pick a method, defend it if need be, and focus your description of the analysis on the one you have chosen. If you feel a need to satisfy potential critics by describing alternative methods and the results they yield, do so in footnotes.

6.6 Chapter Summary

This chapter ends the second part of this book dedicated to mediation analysis. Statistical mediation analysis has changed substantially since the publication of Baron and Kenny (1986). The heyday of the causal steps "criteria to establish mediation" approach is over, where mediation is established by a set of hypotheses tests on each path in a causal model. Also disappearing in the 21st century is a concern about whether a process can be labeled as complete or partial mediation. Modern mediation analysis emphasizes an explicit estimation of the indirect effect, inferential tests of the indirect effect that don't make unnecessary assumptions, and an acknowledgment that evidence of a statistically significant association between X and Y is not necessary to talk about and model intervening variable processes (in which case the concepts of complete and partial mediation simply don't make sense).

What has not changed over the years are limitations to the causal claims one can make when one's data do not lend themselves to unequivocal causal inference. Confounding and epiphenomenal association can induce noncausal associations between variables in a mediation model, and it behooves researchers to consider such possibilities and at least account for them mathematically in the model with the judicious inclusion of various statistical controls when available. Even if one is comfortable that such alternative explanations are unlikely to account for one's findings, statistical mediation analysis by itself does not substantiate a proposed causal ordering of variables in the causal system. There has been some progress made in the development of various measures of effect size in mediation analysis, but there is no "silver bullet" effect size index that can be unconditionally recommended. With the changes that have occurred in the last 10 or so years in the advice methodologists offer researchers, writing about mediation analysis can be a challenge because many readers and reviewers of scientific work are not yet aware that things have changed since the turn of the century. I have offered some advice in this chapter for navigating the writing and publishing waters. Most important, in my opinion, is that you not let strict rules and conventions handcuff your creativity when describing data analysis.

Part III

MODERATION
ANALYSIS

7

Fundamentals of Moderation Analysis

Most effects that scientists study are contingent on one thing or another. An effect may be large for women and small for men, or positive among certain types of people and negative among other types, or zero for one category of stimuli but not zero for another category. When an investigator seeks to determine whether a certain variable influences or is related to the size of one variable's effect on another, a moderation analysis is the proper analytical strategy. This chapter introduces the fundamentals of estimation and inference about moderation (also known as *interaction*) using linear regression analysis. In addition to basic principles, this chapter covers some of the subtle details about interpretation of model coefficients, how to visualize moderated effects, and how to probe an interaction in a regression model through the estimation of conditional effects.

Although I consider myself primarily a statistical methodologist, now and then I dabble in substantive research in a variety of different areas, such as public opinion, political communication, and various applied domains such as health psychology. A few years ago, the U.S. war with Iraq prompted me to conduct a number of studies related to war, the media, and public opinion (Hayes & Reineke, 2007; Hayes & Myers, 2009; Myers & Hayes, 2010). One of these studies was conducted with a graduate student of mine (Jason Reineke) in an attempt to replicate a classic finding from 1970s experimental social psychology on reactions to censorship (Worchel & Arnold, 1973). During the first and second invasion of Iraq, the two George Bush administrations (George H. W. and George W.) instituted a policy restricting the access of journalists to locations where they could photograph images of the caskets of U.S. soldiers who had died returning to the United States for repatriation at Dover Air Force base in Delaware. Though not a literal censorship policy as the term is generally understood and used, this policy clearly had the effect of reducing public exposure to images of the human costs of warfare in terms of U.S. lives lost. We wondered whether people who knew about this policy would, in accordance with reactance theory (Wicklund, 1974), express greater interest in viewing such images than people who didn't know about it. We conducted an experiment to answer this question. In a telephone survey administered prior to the 2004 federal election, we told half of the respondents about this policy, and the other half (randomly determined) we did not. We then asked them how interested they would be in seeing such images or video if a local newspaper or television station published them.

Reactance theory predicts that participants told about this policy would perceive it as a threat to their freedom (in this case, their freedom to access information of their choosing) and, as a result, would express greater interest in recovering the lost freedom by seeking out the information they were being prohibited from accessing. But this is not at all what we found. On average, there was no statistically significant difference in interest in viewing the images between those told and not told about the policy. But a closer examination of the data revealed that this lack of effect was contingent on party identification. Republican participants told about the policy actually expressed *less* interest in viewing the images on average than Republicans not told about it, whereas among Democrats, there was no difference in interest caused by exposure to the policy information.

The result of this study nicely illustrates the concept of *moderation*, the topic of this and the next two chapters. The effect of X on some variable Y is moderated by M if its size, sign, or strength depends on or can be predicted by M. In that case, M is said to be a *moderator* of X's effect on Y, or that M and X *interact* in their influence on Y. Identifying a moderator of an effect helps to establish the boundary conditions of an effect or the circumstances, stimuli, or type of people for which the effect is large versus small, present versus absent, positive versus negative, and so forth. In this study, party identification was a moderator of the effect of knowledge of the policy on interest in viewing the images. That is, giving participants information about the Bush administration policy had different effects on interest in viewing the images for people of different political leanings.

Moderation is depicted in the form of a conceptual diagram in Figure 7.1. This diagram represents a process in which the effect of some variable of interest X (sometimes called the *focal predictor*) on Y is influenced or dependent on M, as reflected by the arrow pointing from M to the line from X to Y. Readers familiar with structural equation modeling programs such as AMOS or EQS that allow the analyst to draw the model to tell the program what to do should not attempt to estimate a moderation model by constructing such a diagram in their program, for this will not work. Nor should one assume that because there is no arrow pointing from M to Y that

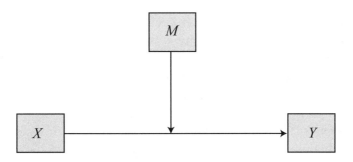

FIGURE 7.1. A simple moderation model depicted as a conceptual diagram.

M is not a predictor variable in a moderation model. Unlike in mediation analysis, the conceptual model in a moderation model is very different in form from its corresponding statistical diagram, which represents how such a model is set up in the form of an equation. As will be described in section 7.1, the statistical diagram corresponding to this conceptual model will require not two but three antecedent variables, and M will be one of those antecedents.

Moderation plays an important role in many social science theories. Consider *The Elaboration Likelihood Model of Persuasion* (Petty & Cacioppo, 1986), which attempts to explain the conditions under which messages designed with the intent to persuade are likely to result in short-term, long-term, or no attitude change. Research supporting the elaboration likelihood model almost exclusively is based on evidence of moderation. For instance, in conditions in which participants are motivated to deeply process message content because the message pertains to some issue or policy that will directly affect them, strong arguments result in greater attitude change than do weak ones relative to when participants are less inclined to engage in such message elaboration, such as when the topic or issue has no direct impact on their lives. And high motivation to elaborate on message content reduces the impact of peripheral cues, such as the number of arguments, relative to when motivation is lower. Thus, personal involvement in the topic (M) moderates the effect of argument strength (X) or source characteristics (X) on attitude change (Y).

Cultivation theory (see, e.g., Shanahan & Morgan, 1999) is another explanatory model in which moderation is pivotal. Our understanding about the world outside of our immediate experience comes primarily through television and other media forms. Although the advent of cable and the Internet has changed the media landscape considerably, television remains an important window through which the world is perceived. According to cultivation theory, frequent exposure to the televised world cultivates a perception of the world consistent with that depiction. For example, some argue that the world as portrayed by the televised news and popular dramas is a hostile and dangerous place. Thus, according to cultivation theory, the more exposure to the televised world as depicted as hostile and dangerous, the more a person will see the world as mean and hostile. Such cultivation is so theoretically powerful that frequent television viewers will in time become more homogeneous than less frequent viewers in their attitudes and beliefs. In other words, variables such as sex, education, and ethnicity that predict attitudes and beliefs among less frequent viewers are less predictive of such beliefs among frequent television viewers. This homogenization of the frequently viewing public is referred to in cultivation theory as *mainstreaming*, and it is a moderation phenomenon. Television viewing frequency (M) moderates the effect of certain individual differences (X) such as sex and ethnicity on various attitudes and beliefs (Y), such as how violent and dangerous the world is perceived as being.

As a third example, it has been well established by research in public health, communication, and political science that people who differ in education frequently differ in their knowledge of numerous public affairs topics (e.g., various community issues and controversies, the positions held by politicians, etc.), science and health-related information (e.g., cancer prevention) and a variety of other topics (Gaziano, 1983; Hwang & Jeong, 2009). Many have speculated about and there is much research on the potential causes of these *knowledge gaps* and how they can be reduced or eliminated (see, e.g., Tichenor, Donohue, & Olien, 1970). The most obvious means of reducing such gaps in knowledge, it would seem, is some kind of an information campaign targeting the public in the hope that the less educated will become more knowledgeable following exposure to the relevant information. However, it turns out that this does not always work and can even backfire. People who are more educated are more likely to have the cognitive skills and resources to benefit from exposure to information. As a result, information campaigns can sometimes increase rather than narrow knowledge gaps, as the more educated who are exposed to the information (relative to those not exposed) are more likely to acquire the relevant knowledge than those who are less educated. In other words, research has established that sometimes education (M) moderates the effect of exposure to information (X) on knowledge in such a manner that knowledge gaps are increased rather than decreased.

Although mediation analysis is popular throughout the social and behavioral sciences, it is less commonly covered in statistics classes than is moderation. Moderation is very widely covered, although not always in the way I present here. Most burgeoning researchers are exposed to moderation analysis when they take a course that covers analysis of variance, which is a form of regression analysis restricted to categorical predictors. In a *factorial* research design, a researcher has two (or more) categorical variables that are crossed, yielding a cross-classification of some kind, such as in a 2 (experimental condition: control versus treatment) $\times$ 2 (sex: male versus female) design. Factorial analysis of variance is used to ascertain whether the effect of one variable on a dependent variable of interest differs across levels of the second variable. If so, then it is said that the two variables *interact* in their influence on the dependent variable. *Statistical interaction* is just another term for moderation, and I use the terms interchangeably in this chapter. So if you know something about testing interactions in analysis of variance, you already know something about moderation analysis.

Mathematically, factorial analysis of variance is identical to the regression-based procedure I emphasize here for moderation analysis, but the regression procedure is more general and flexible. Factorial analysis of variance assumes categorical predictors (although continuous variables are sometimes used as covariates in analysis of *covariance*). The regression-based procedure I describe beginning in the next section makes no such restriction on the nature of the variables being analyzed. It can be used for categorical predictors, continuous predictors, or any combination thereof.

7.1 Conditional and Unconditional Effects

Consider a multiple regression model of the form $Y = i_1 + b_1X + b_2M + e_Y$, which estimates Y from two predictors X and M. More specifically, suppose $i_1 = 4$, $b_1 = 1$, and $b_2 = 2$ and therefore

$$\hat{Y} = 4.000 + 1.000X + 2.000M$$

Table 7.1 provides values of $\hat{Y}$ from this model for various combinations of X and M, and the model is depicted in visual form in Figure 7.2, panel A.

Try choosing *any* value of M in Table 7.1 and observe that as X increases by one unit (e.g., from -1 to 0, 0 to 1, and so forth) but M is held constant at that value chosen, $\hat{Y}$ changes by 1.00 unit. For example, suppose you choose $M = 1$. When $X = 0$ and $M = 1$, $\hat{Y} = 6$, but when $X = 1$ and $M = 1$, $\hat{Y} = 7$. If you were to choose a different value, say $M = 2$, the same would be true. For example, when $X = -1$ and $M = 2$, $\hat{Y} = 7$, and when $X = 0$ and $M = 2$, $\hat{Y} = 8$. It is no coincidence that this difference in $\hat{Y}$ as X changes by one unit with M held fixed is b_1. Most generally, for any value $M = m$ and $X = x$,

$$b_1 = [\hat{Y} \mid (X = x, M = m)] - [\hat{Y} \mid (X = x - 1, M = m)]$$

TABLE 7.1. Fitted Values of Y Generated from Two Models Using X and M as Predictor Variables

X	M	$\hat{Y} = 4 + 1X + 2M$	$\hat{Y} = 4 + 1X + 2M + 1.5XM$
−1	0	3	3
−1	1	5	3
−1	2	7	4
0	0	4	4
0	1	6	6
0	2	8	8
1	0	5	5
1	1	7	8
1	2	9	12
2	0	6	6
2	1	8	11
2	2	10	16

In other words, the effect of a one unit increase in X on $\hat{Y}$ is not dependent on M. Regardless of the value of M, a change of one unit in X translates into a change of b_1 units in $\hat{Y}$. The effect of a one unit change in X on $\hat{Y}$ is *unconditional* on M, in the sense that it does not depend on M.

The same can be said for b_2. Choose any value of X, and when M increases by one unit, $\hat{Y}$ increases by $b_2 = 2$ units. For instance, when $X = 1$ and $M = 0$, $\hat{Y} = 5$, and when $X = 2$ and $M = 1$, $\hat{Y} = 7$. Most generally, for any value $M = m$ and $X = x$,

$$b_2 = [\hat{Y} \mid (M = m, X = x)] - [\hat{Y} \mid (M = m - 1, X = x)]$$

So the effect of a one unit change in M on $\hat{Y}$ is unconditional on X, in that it is not dependent on X.

A regression model in this form is not well-suited to testing questions about moderation. In fact, such a model is the very opposite of what the concept of moderation embodies. If X's effect on Y is moderated by another variable in the model, that means its effect depends on that other variable. But this model constrains X's effect to be unconditional on M, meaning that it is invariant across all values of M.

A

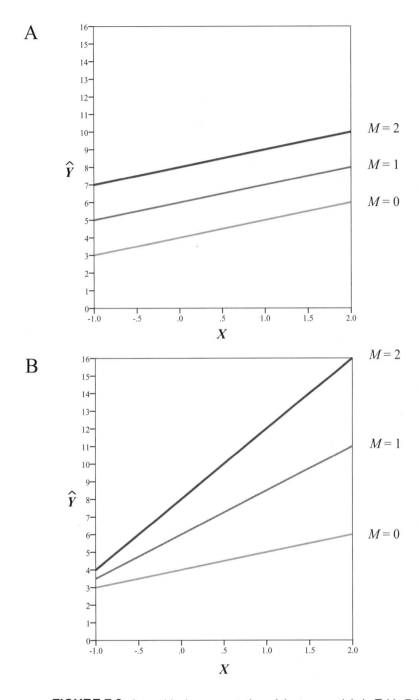

FIGURE 7.2. A graphical representation of the two models in Table 7.1.

Eliminating the Constraint of Unconditionality

We want to get around this constraint in the model such that X's effect can be dependent on M, meaning that for different values of M, X's effect on Y is different. In generic terms, such a model can be written as

$$Y = i_1 + f(M)X + b_2M + e_Y \tag{7.1}$$

where $f(M)$ is any function of M. Consider a simple function of the form $f(M) = b_1 + b_3M$. This function of M looks like a simple linear regression model where b_1 is the intercept and b_3 is the slope or regression coefficient for M, except that rather than estimating some outcome variable from M, it is a model of the effect of X on Y. Substituting $b_1 + b_3M$ for $f(M)$ in equation 7.1 yields

$$Y = i_1 + (b_1 + b_3M)X + b_2M + e_Y$$

which can be expanded by distributing X across the two terms defining the function of M, resulting in

$$Y = i_1 + b_1X + b_2M + b_3XM + e_Y \tag{7.2}$$

or, in terms of estimated values of Y,

$$\hat{Y} = i_1 + b_1X + b_2M + b_3XM$$

where XM is a variable constructed as the product of X and M. The resulting equation is the *simple linear moderation model*, depicted conceptually in Figure 7.1 and in the form of a statistical diagram in Figure 7.3. It is a very valuable model, for it provides a simple means of modeling data in which X's effect on Y is dependent on M or *conditional*, as well as an approach to testing hypotheses about moderation.

To see what effects adding the product of X and M as a predictor has, consider a specific example where $i_1 = 4$, $b_1 = 1$, $b_2 = 2$, and $b_3 = 1.5$; thus,

$$\hat{Y} = 4.000 + 1.000X + 2.000M + 1.500XM$$

This model is identical to the prior example, except it now includes the term $1.500XM$. Values of $\hat{Y}$ this model generates for different combinations of X and M can be found in Table 7.1, and the model is depicted visually in Figure 7.2, panel B.

Observe what has happened as a result of the addition of b_3XM to the model that constrained X's effect on Y to be unconditional on M. Now a one-unit change in X results in a change in $\hat{Y}$ that depends on M. For instance, when $M = 0$, changing X by one unit changes $\hat{Y}$ by one unit, but when $M = 1$, changing X by one unit changes $\hat{Y}$ by 2.5 units, and when

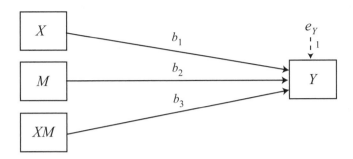

FIGURE 7.3. A simple moderation model depicted as a statistical diagram.

$M = 2$, changing X by one unit changes $\hat{Y}$ by four units. More generally, in a model of the form in equation 7.2, the effect of a one-unit change in X on $\hat{Y}$ is expressed by the function

$$\theta_{X \to Y} = b_1 + b_3 M \qquad (7.3)$$

where $\theta_{X \to Y}$ is the *conditional effect of X on Y*, defined as the amount by which two cases that differ by one unit on X are estimated to differ on Y. It should not come as a surprise that this is exactly the same function plugged into equation 7.1 to generate the simple linear moderation model expressed as equation 7.2. In this example, $\theta_{X \to Y} = 1.000 + 1.500M$. Plugging values of M into this equation yields an estimate of how much a one-unit change in X changes Y given that value of M. Various values of $\theta_{X \to Y}$ for different values of M can be found in Table 7.2. As can be seen, as M increases by one unit, the difference in $\hat{Y}$ between two cases that differ by one unit on X changes by b_3 units.

Figure 7.2 most dramatically illustrates the difference between the model that constrains X's effect to be unconditional and the one that allows Xs effect on Y to depend on M. In panel A, X's effect on $\hat{Y}$ is constrained to be independent of M. As a result, the slopes of each line linking X to $\hat{Y}$ are identical and the lines are therefore parallel. However, in panel B, X's effect on $\hat{Y}$ depends on M. Visually, this manifests itself in slopes for each line linking X to Y that differ for different values of M. As a result, the lines are not parallel. The degree of nonparallelism that will exist in a visual representation of moderation will depend on b_3, where b_3 in graphical terms is the change in the slope of the line linking X to $\hat{Y}$ as M increases by one unit. The larger b_3 in absolute value, the more divergent from parallel are the slopes.

TABLE 7.2. The Conditional Effect of X for Values of M and the Conditional Effect of M for Values of X for the Model $\hat{Y} = 4.000 + 1.000X + 2.000M + 1.500XM$

	$\theta_{X \to Y} = b_1 + b_3 M$			$\theta_{M \to Y} = b_2 + b_3 X$	
M	$b_1 + b_3 M$	$\theta_{(X \to Y)\mid M}$	X	$b_2 + b_3 X$	$\theta_{(M \to Y)\mid X}$
0	b_1	1.000	-1	$b_2 - b_3$	0.500
1	$b_1 + b_3$	2.500	0	b_2	2.000
2	$b_1 + 2b_3$	4.000	1	$b_2 + b_3$	3.500
3	$b_1 + 3b_3$	5.500	2	$b_3 + 2b_3$	5.000

Symmetry in Moderation

It was illustrated earlier that the simple moderation model described by equation 7.2 can be expressed as

$$Y = i_1 + (b_1 + b_3 M)X + b_2 M + e_Y \tag{7.4}$$

or, alternatively, as

$$Y = i_1 + \theta_{X \to Y} X + b_2 M + e_Y \tag{7.5}$$

where $\theta_{X \to Y} = b_1 + b_3 M$. Equations 7.4 and 7.5 make it most clear how X's effect on Y is dependent on M. But the simple moderation model can also be written in another mathematically equivalent form which expresses M's effect as moderated by X:

$$Y = i_1 + b_1 X + (b_2 + b_3 X)M + e_Y \tag{7.6}$$

or, alternatively,

$$Y = i_1 + b_1 X + \theta_{M \to Y} M + e_Y \tag{7.7}$$

where $\theta_{M \to Y}$ is the conditional effect of M on $Y = b_2 + b_3 X$. Expressed in this form, it is apparent that in the simple moderation model, M's effect on Y is dependent on X, with that dependency expressed as $b_2 + b_3 X$. Indeed, observe in Table 7.1 that the amount by which two cases that differ by one unit on M differ on $\hat{Y}$ depends on X. For instance, when $X = 0$, two cases differing by one unit on M differ by two units on $\hat{Y}$, but when $X = 1$, two cases differing by one unit on M differ by 3.5 units on $\hat{Y}$. Various values of the conditional effect of M on Y for different values of X can be found in Table 7.2. Observe that as X increases by one unit, the conditional effect of M on Y changes by b_3 units.

Thus, b_3 has two interpretations, depending on whether X or M is construed as the moderator. When M is conceptualized as the moderator of X's effect on Y, then b_3 estimates how much the difference in Y between two cases that differ by a unit on X changes as M changes by one unit. But if X is conceptualized as the moderator of M's effect on Y, then b_3 estimates how much the difference in Y between two cases that differ by a unit on M changes as X changes by one unit. Of course, the mathematics underlying the simple moderation model don't know or care which variable you are conceptualizing as the moderator in your analysis. Both interpretations are correct.

Interpretation of the Regression Coefficients

The interpretation of b_3 in the simple moderation model was described above. Most generally, for any value $X = x$ and $M = m$,

$$b_3 = \frac{\left([\hat{Y} \mid (X = x, M = m)] - [\hat{Y} \mid (X = x - 1, M = m)]\right)}{- \left([\hat{Y} \mid (X = x, M = m - 1)] - [\hat{Y} \mid (X = x - 1, M = m - 1)]\right)} \tag{7.8}$$

But how are b_1 and b_2 interpreted? The interpretation of b_1 is made clear by an examination of equation 7.3. Observe that if M is set to 0, then equation 7.3 reduces to $\theta_{X \to Y} = b_1$. So b_1 is the conditional effect of X on Y when $M = 0$. That is, b_1 quantifies how much two cases that differ by one unit on X but with $M = 0$ are estimated to differ on Y. For any value $X = x$,

$$b_1 = [\hat{Y} \mid (X = x, M = 0)] - [\hat{Y} \mid (X = x - 1, M = 0)] \tag{7.9}$$

Thus, it is neither appropriate to interpret b_1 as relationship between X and Y controlling for M "on average" or "controlling for M and XM," nor is it the "main effect of X" (to use a term from analysis of variance lingo). Rather, it represents the association between X and Y conditioned on $M = 0$. As depicted in Figure 7.4, b_1 is the slope of the line linking X to Y when $M = 0$. In analysis of variance terms, b_1 is akin to a *simple effect*—the simple effect of X when $M = 0$.

Similarly, examining equations 7.6 and 7.7, notice that when X is set to 0, $\theta_{M \to Y} = b_2$. Thus, b_2 is the conditional effect of M on Y when $X = 0$. For any value $M = m$,

$$b_2 = [\hat{Y} \mid (M = m, X = 0)] - [\hat{Y} \mid (M = m - 1, X = 0)] \tag{7.10}$$

Like b_1, it too is a conditional effect, in that it quantifies how much two cases that differ by one unit on M are estimated to differ on Y conditioned on $X = 0$. It should not be interpreted as M's effect controlling for X and XM or as M's average effect on Y or M's main effect. It describes the association

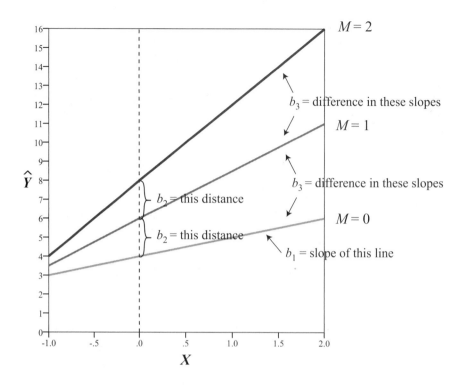

FIGURE 7.4. A visual representation of b_1, b_2, and b_3 in a model of the form $\hat{Y} = i_1 + b_1X + b_2M + b_3XM$. In this figure, $b_1 = 1.00$, $b_2 = 2.00$, and $b_3 = 1.50$.

between M and Y when $X = 0$. See Figure 7.4 for a visual representation of b_2.

Notice that these interpretations of b_1 and b_2 are very different from their interpretation when XM is not included as a predictor. When XM is a predictor along with X and M in the model of Y, b_1 and b_2 are conditional effects. But for a model of the form $\hat{Y} = i_1 + b_1X + b_2M$, without XM as a predictor, b_1 and b_2 are *partial effects* and *unconditional*. In the unconditional model, b_1 quantifies how much two cases that differ by one unit on X are estimated to differ on Y *holding M constant*, and b_2 quantifies how much two cases that differ by one unit on M are estimated to differ on Y *holding X constant*. These are completely different in meaning, and their substantive interpretation typically is dramatically different as well. Do not confuse these interpretations, as some have (see, e.g., Hayes, Glynn, & Huge, 2012). When XM is in a model with X and M, the coefficients for X and M are conditional effects—conditioned on the other variable being zero. When XM is not in the model, these are partial effects.

The Importance of b_3 When Asking about Moderation

The simple moderation model allows X's effect on Y to be a linear function of M. Of course, allowing that effect to depend on M doesn't mean that it actually does in reality. In most any sample of data, b_3 will be different from zero even when X's effect on Y is independent of M. Of interest when testing a moderation hypothesis is not just allowing X's effect to be contingent on M, but also determining whether b_3 deviates too far from zero than would be expected given that b_3, like any statistic, is subject to sampling variance. In other words, an inferential test about $_Tb_3$ ultimately determines whether X's effect really depends on M or whether the obtained b_3 is within the realm of what would be expected to occur just by chance given the assumption that M does not moderate X's effect.

Most scientists would agree that evidence that $_Tb_3$ is different from zero (as determined by a hypothesis test or a confidence interval) is needed in order to claim that M functions as a moderator of X's effect. If the evidence is not consistent with such a claim, a more parsimonious model would fix X's effect on Y to be unconditional on M. In other words, given that b_1 and b_2 are conditional effects when XM is in the model, absent evidence the X's effect is moderated by M, it is best to estimate a model without the product of X and M, which thereby renders b_1 and b_2 as estimates of partial rather than conditional effects.

Such a model cleansing strategy does not apply to b_1 and b_2 whenever XM is in the model. If you choose to retain XM in the model, X and M must be included as well, even if b_1 and b_2 are not statistically significant. Excluding X or M will bias the estimate of the moderation of X's effect by M. There are almost no circumstances in which you would want to estimate a model including XM as a predictor without also including X and M. So when XM is in the model, keep X and M in the model as well, *regardless of the outcome of an inferential test of b_1 and/or b_2*. It is simply not appropriate to exclude them except in circumstances you typically do not encounter in day-to-day research.

7.2 An Example: Sex Discrimination in the Workplace

To illustrate how to test for and interpret moderation using this procedure, I rely on data from Garcia, Schmitt, Branscombe, and Ellemers (2010) published in the *European Journal of Social Psychology*. The data file is named PROTEST and can be downloaded from *www.afhayes.com*. In this study, 129 participants, all of whom were female, received a written account of the fate of a female attorney (Catherine) who lost a promotion to a less qualified male as a result of discriminatory actions of the senior partners. After reading this story, the participants were given a description of how Catherine responded to this act of sexual discrimination. Those randomly assigned to the *no protest* condition (coded PROTEST = 0 in the data file) learned that though very disappointed by the decision, Catherine decided not to take any action against this discrimination and continued working at the firm. The remainder of the participants, assigned to a *protest* condition (coded PROTEST = 1 in the data file), were told that Catherine approached the partners with the request that they reconsider the decision, while giving various explanations as to why the decision was unfair. Following this procedure, the participants were asked to respond to six questions evaluating Catherine (e.g., "Catherine has many positive traits," "Catherine is the type of person I would like to be friends with"). Their responses were aggregated into a measure of liking, such that participants with higher scores liked her relatively more (LIKING in the data file). In addition to this measure of liking, each participant was scored on the Modern Sexism Scale, used to measure how pervasive a person believes sex discrimination is in society. The higher a person's score, the more pervasive he or she believes sex discrimination is in society (SEXISM in the data file).

The focus of the study was to assess the extent to which the action of the lawyer affected perceptions of her—specifically how much they liked her—and whether the size of such effect depends on a person's beliefs about the pervasiveness of sex discrimination in society. The group means can be found in Table 7.3, which suggest that participants told that Catherine protested ($\overline{Y}$ = 5.789) liked her more than those told she did not protest ($\overline{Y}$ = 5.310). An inferential test of the difference with an independent groups t-test yields a rejection of the null hypothesis of no difference at the α = 0.05 level of significance, $t(127) = 2.458, p = .015$. This observed difference in liking cannot be attributed to chance.

A mathematically equivalent procedure that is more consistent with the modeling approach used in this book is to regress liking (Y) on protest condition (X), as such:

$$Y = i_1 + b_1 X + e_Y$$

As can be seen in Table 7.4 (model 1), $i_1 = 5.310$ and $b_1 = 0.479$. This simple linear model produces two estimates for Y, depending on whether $X = 0$ or 1. When $X = 0$, meaning those assigned to no protest condition,

$$\hat{Y} = 5.310 + 0.479(0) = 5.310$$

And when $X = 1$ (i.e., those assigned to the protest condition),

$$\hat{Y} = 5.310 + 0.479(1) = 5.789$$

TABLE 7.3. Descriptive Statistics for the Protest and Discrimination Study

		Y LIKING	M SEXISM
No-Protest Condition	Mean	5.310	5.071
($X = 0$)	SD	1.302	0.767
Protest Condition	Mean	5.789	5.138
($X = 1$)	SD	0.877	0.795
	Mean	5.637	5.117
	SD	1.050	0.784

These two values of $\hat{Y}$ correspond to the group mean evaluations (see Table 7.3).

The regression coefficient for protest condition (b_1) is positive and statistically different from zero, with the same t statistic and p-value as the independent group t-test produces. Because the two groups are coded such that they differ by a single unit (1 versus 0) on X, b_1 can be interpreted as the difference between group means. Two cases that differ by one unit on X are estimated to differ by 0.479 units on Y. That is,

$$b_1 = [\hat{Y} \mid (X = 1)] - [\hat{Y} \mid (X = 0)] = 5.790 - 5.313 = 0.479$$

The positive coefficient tells us that those with a higher value on X are estimated as higher on Y. In other words, participants told Catherine protested liked her more by 0.479 units than participants who were told she did not protest. And observe that the regression constant, $i_1 = 5.310$, is the estimated value of Y when $X = 0$. It estimates how much participants told Catherine did not protest (i.e., $X = 0$) liked Catherine on average, consistent with the value reported in Table 7.3.

This analysis only determines that, on average, those told Catherine protested liked her more than those told she did not protest. Garcia et al. (2010) expected that the effect of her decision to protest or not on her evaluation would depend on participants' perceptions of the pervasiveness of sex discrimination in society. This finding says nothing about whether her decision differentially affected people with different beliefs about how pervasive sexism is in society. *Regardless* of whether the groups differ

TABLE 7.4. Results from Various Regression Models Estimating Liking for the Attorney

		Coeff.	SE	t	p
Model 1					
$R^2 = 0.045, MSE = 1.060$					
Intercept	i_1	5.310	0.161	33.024	$< .001$
Condition (X)	b_1	0.479	0.195	2.458	.015
Model 2					
$R^2 = 0.052, MSE = 1.061$					
Intercept	i_1	4.747	0.611	7.768	$< .001$
Condition (X)	b_1	0.471	0.195	2.417	.017
Modern Sexism (M)	b_2	0.111	0.116	0.956	.341
Model 3					
$R^2 = 0.133, MSE = 0.978$					
Intercept	i_1	7.706	1.045	7.375	$< .001$
Condition (X)	b_1	−3.773	1.254	−3.008	.003
Modern Sexism (M)	b_2	−0.473	0.204	−2.319	.022
$X \times M$	b_3	0.834	0.244	3.422	.001
Model 4 (mean-centered M)					
$R^2 = 0.133, MSE = 0.978$					
Intercept	i_1	5.288	0.155	34.184	$< .001$
Condition (X)	b_1	0.493	0.187	2.631	.003
Modern Sexism (M')	b_2	−0.473	0.204	−2.318	.022
$X \times M'$	b_3	0.834	0.244	3.422	.001
Model 5 (mean-centered M, X coded −0.5 and 0.5)					
$R^2 = 0.133, MSE = 0.978$					
Intercept	i_1	5.535	0.094	59.125	$< .001$
Condition (X)	b_1	0.493	0.187	2.631	.010
Modern Sexism (M')	b_2	−0.056	0.122	−0.457	.648
$X \times M'$	b_3	0.834	0.244	3.422	.001

on average, in order to determine whether the effect depends on another variable, a formal test of moderation must be conducted.[1]

To test the moderation of X's effect by M, a term is included in the model of Y from X and M that allows X's effect to be a function of M. In this case, we estimate the coefficients of a regression model in which the effect of lawyer's decision to protest or not (X) on liking (Y) is allowed to vary linearly with beliefs in the pervasiveness of sex discrimination in society (M) by including the product of X and M as a predictor of Y along with X and M:

$$Y = i_1 + b_1X + b_2M + b_3XM + e_Y$$

Of key interest is the estimate of b_3 along with an inferential test. If b_3 is not statistically different from zero (via a hypothesis test or a confidence interval for $_Tb_3$ that straddles zero), this means that the effect of protesting is not dependent on (at least not linearly so) beliefs about the pervasiveness of sex discrimination. But if b_3 is statistically different from zero, we can conclude that the effect of the decision to protest or not on liking depends on sex discrimination beliefs.[2]

No special modeling software is needed to estimate the model. Simply construct the product of X and M and include it as a predictor of Y along with X and M using any OLS regression program. In SPSS, the commands that do the job are

```
compute proxsex=protest*sexism.
regression/dep=liking/method=enter protest sexism proxsex.
```

In SAS, try

```
data protest;set protest;proxsex=protest*sexism;run;
proc reg data=protest;model liking=protest sexism proxsex;run;
```

Table 7.4 (model 3) contains the OLS regression coefficients along with their standard errors, t and p-values, and 95% confidence intervals. As can be seen, the best fitting OLS regression model is

$$\hat{Y} = 7.706 - 3.773X - 0.473M + 0.834XM$$

[1]Evidence of an association between X and Y is not required in order for X's effect to be moderated. Thus, I strongly discourage the practice of avoiding a test of moderation just because there is no evidence of an association between X and Y.

[2]In practice, an investigator may want to include one or more covariates in the model in order to control for their effects in the estimation of X's effect on Y. Covariates can be included in a moderation model such as this, and the discussion that follows generalizes without modification. A concrete example of a moderation model with covariates is provided in Chapter 8.

In this model, $i_1 = 7.706$, $b_1 = -3.773$, $b_2 = -0.473$, $b_3 = 0.834$. Importantly, observe b_3 is statistically different from zero, $t(125) = 3.422, p < .001$ (though not generated by the commands above, a 95% confidence interval for $_Tb_3$ is 0.352 to 1.316). So we can conclude that the effect of Catherine's decision whether or not to protest on perceptions of her likability is moderated by participants' beliefs about the pervasiveness of sex discrimination in society. That is, the effect of the experimental manipulation of her decision to protest or not had different effects on different people, depending on their beliefs about sex discrimination.

Had there been no evidence of moderation (i.e., b_3 was not statistically different from zero), the most sensible approach would be to reestimate the model excluding the product, thereby allowing X's effect to be invariant across M. This could take the form of model 1 or model 2 in Table 7.4, depending on whether or not one desires to control for M when assessing X's effect on Y.

In this case, the effect of the decision to protest is clearly moderated. In fact, this moderation component of the model explains about 8.1% of the variance in liking of the attorney, as calculated from the difference in R^2 for the model that includes the product (model 3, $R^2 = 0.133$) compared to the model that excludes it (model 2, $R^2 = 0.052$). That is, $R^2_{model\,3} - R^2_{model\,2} = 0.081$. As discussed on page 74, this is equivalent to the squared semipartial correlation for XM in model 3.

By expressing the regression model in an equivalent form

$$\hat{Y} = 7.706 + \theta_{X \to Y}X - 0.473M$$

where

$$\theta_{X \to Y} = b_1 + b_3M = -3.773 + 0.834M \qquad (7.11)$$

and then plugging various values of M into equation 7.11, one gains insight into how the differences in liking between the two groups is a function of beliefs about the pervasiveness of sex discrimination. In the data, scores on the Modern Sexism Scale range between 2.87 and 7.00, with most between 4 and 6. Arbitrarily choosing 4, 5, and 6 as values of M, when $M = 4$, $\theta_{X \to Y} = -3.773 + 0.834(4) = -0.437$; when $M = 5$, $\theta_{X \to Y} = -3.773 + 0.834(5) = 0.397$; and when $M = 6$, $\theta_{X \to Y} = -3.773 + 0.834(6) = 1.231$. From these calculations, it appears that the difference in liking of Catherine between those told she did versus did not protest is negative among those on the lower end of the distribution of beliefs about sex discrimination, meaning that she was liked *less* when she protested relative to when she did not. However, the difference is positive among those scoring relatively higher on the Modern Sexism Scale, with liking higher among those told Catherine protested the decision relative to those told she did not. If this is not obvious (and it very well may not be until you become fluent interpreting models of this sort), a picture will help. How to visualize a model such as this is described in section 7.3.

Estimation Using PROCESS

PROCESS can estimate a moderation model, and it also provides a number of valuable output options for visualizing and probing an interaction described later. In SPSS, the PROCESS command for this analysis is

```
process vars=protest liking sexism/y=liking/x=protest/m=sexism/model=1
   /jn=1/quantile=1/plot=1.
```

In SAS, use

```
%process (data=protest,vars=protest liking sexism,y=liking,x=protest,
   m=sexism,model=1,jn=1,quantile=1,plot=1);
```

Output from the SPSS version of PROCESS can be found in Figure 7.5. In PROCESS, a simple moderation model with M moderating the effect of X on Y is estimated by requesting **model=1**. PROCESS saves you the trouble of having to calculate the product of X and M, for it does so automatically and generates a new variable for its own use corresponding to this product labeled "int_1" in the output.

PROCESS also produces the proportion of the variance in Y uniquely attributable to the moderation of X's effect by M in the section of output labeled "R-square increase due to interaction," calculated as described earlier. The p-value for this increase is the same as the p-value for b_3, as these procedures test the same null hypothesis, albeit framed in different ways. For a discussion of the test for the increase in R^2 when a variable is added to a model, see section 3.3. The **quantile** and **jn** options in the PROCESS command are described below and in sections 7.3 and 7.4.

Interpreting the Regression Coefficients

As discussed on page 217, in a regression model of the form $Y = i_1 + b_1 X + b_2 M + b_3 XM$, b_1 and b_2 are conditional effects. These regression coefficients estimate the effect of X when $M = 0$ and the effect of M when $X = 0$, respectively (see equations 7.9 and 7.10). As will be seen, these coefficients may or may not have any substantive interpretation, depending on the scaling of X and M.

```
process vars = protest liking sexism/y=liking/x=protest/m=sexism/model=1/
  jn=1/quantile=1/plot=1.

Model = 1
   Y = liking
   X = protest
   M = sexism

Sample size
     129

**************************************************************************
Outcome: liking

Model Summary
        R         R-sq         F         df1         df2          p
     .3654       .1335      6.4190     3.0000    125.0000       .0004

Model
                coeff         se          t          p        LLCI       ULCI
constant       7.7062      1.0449     7.3750      .0000      5.6382     9.7743
sexism         -.4725       .2038    -2.3184      .0220      -.8758     -.0692
protest       -3.7727      1.2541    -3.0084      .0032     -6.2546    -1.2907
int_1           .8336       .2436     3.4224      .0008       .3515     1.3156

Interactions:

 int_1    protest    X    sexism

R-square increase due to interaction(s):
         R2-chng         F         df1         df2          p
int_1      .0812      11.7126    1.0000    125.0000       .0008

**************************************************************************

Conditional effect of X on Y at values of the moderator(s)
     sexism      Effect        se          t          p        LLCI       ULCI
     4.1200      -.3384       .3016    -1.1220      .2640      -.9353      .2585
     4.5000      -.0217       .2361     -.0918      .9270      -.4890      .4456
     5.1200       .4951       .1872     2.6443      .0092       .1245      .8657
     5.6200       .9119       .2272     4.0144      .0001       .4623     1.3615
     6.1200      1.3287       .3127     4.2487      .0000       .7098     1.9476

Values for quantitative moderators are 10th, 25th, 50th, 75th, and 90th percentiles

******************** JOHNSON-NEYMAN TECHNIQUE **************************

Moderator value(s) defining Johnson-Neyman significance region(s)
     3.5087
     4.9753

Conditional effect of X on Y at values of the moderator (M)
     sexism      Effect        se          t          p        LLCI       ULCI
     2.8700     -1.3804       .5724    -2.4113      .0173     -2.5133     -.2474
     3.0765     -1.2082       .5252    -2.3007      .0231     -2.2476     -.1689
     3.2830     -1.0361       .4785    -2.1653      .0323     -1.9831     -.0891
     3.4895      -.8640       .4327    -1.9969      .0480     -1.7203     -.0077
     3.5087      -.8480       .4285    -1.9791      .0500     -1.6959      .0000
     3.6960      -.6918       .3879    -1.7834      .0769     -1.4596      .0759
     3.9025      -.5197       .3447    -1.5076      .1342     -1.2020      .1625
     4.1090      -.3476       .3037    -1.1445      .2546      -.9487      .2535
     4.3155      -.1755       .2659     -.6598      .5106      -.7017      .3508
     4.5220      -.0033       .2329     -.0143      .9886      -.4642      .4576
     4.7285       .1688       .2069      .8158      .4162      -.2407      .5783
     4.9350       .3409       .1909     1.7855      .0766      -.0370      .7188
     4.9753       .3745       .1892     1.9791      .0500       .0000      .7490
     5.1415       .5131       .1875     2.7360      .0071       .1419      .8842
     5.3480       .6852       .1973     3.4729      .0007       .2947     1.0757
```

(continued)

FIGURE 7.5. Output from the PROCESS procedure for SPSS for a simple moderation analysis of the protest and sex discrimination study.

```
        5.5545      .8573      .2185     3.9235      .0001      .4249    1.2898
        5.7610     1.0294      .2482     4.1468      .0001      .5381    1.5208
        5.9675     1.2016      .2838     4.2332      .0000      .6398    1.7633
        6.1740     1.3737      .3234     4.2481      .0000      .7337    2.0137
        6.3805     1.5458      .3655     4.2288      .0000      .8224    2.2693
        6.5870     1.7180      .4096     4.1946      .0001      .9074    2.5285
        6.7935     1.8901      .4549     4.1551      .0001      .9898    2.7904
        7.0000     2.0622      .5012     4.1149      .0001     1.0704    3.0541

****************************************************************************

Data for visualizing conditional effect of X of Y
     protest      sexism       yhat
      .0000       4.1200      5.7596
     1.0000       4.1200      5.4212
      .0000       4.5000      5.5800
     1.0000       4.5000      5.5584
      .0000       5.1200      5.2871
     1.0000       5.1200      5.7822
      .0000       5.6200      5.0508
     1.0000       5.6200      5.9627
      .0000       6.1200      4.8146
     1.0000       6.1200      6.1433

******************** ANALYSIS NOTES AND WARNINGS *************************

Level of confidence for all confidence intervals in output:
  95.00
```

FIGURE 7.5 continued.

Applied to this analysis, the regression coefficient for X is $b_1 = -3.773$. This is the estimated difference in liking between those told Catherine did versus did not protest *among those scoring zero on the Modern Sexism Scale* (i.e., $M = 0$). The coefficient is negative, meaning that among those scoring zero on their beliefs about the pervasiveness of sex discrimination in society, those told the lawyer protested ($X = 1$) liked her less than those told she did not ($X = 0$). Although this interpretation is mathematically correct, substantively it is nonsense. The Modern Sexism Scale as administered in this study is bound between 1 and 7. An estimate of the effect of the manipulation conditioned on a score of zero on the Modern Sexism Scale has no meaning because no such people could even exist. Disregard this estimate and its test of significance, for it is meaningless. Even if it were possible to score so low on the scale, in the data the lowest score is 2.87, so at best this would represent an interpolation of the results of the model well beyond the range of the available data. Such interpolation is generally inadvisable.

The same cannot be said about b_2. The regression coefficient for the Modern Sexism Scale is $b_2 = -0.473$ and statistically different from zero ($p = .022$). This is the estimated difference in liking of Catherine between two people who differ by one unit in their beliefs about the pervasiveness of sex discrimination in society *among those told she did not protest the discrimination*

$(X = 0)$. Thus, this is the conditional effect of beliefs on liking for the attorney among those assigned to the no protest condition. The sign is negative, meaning that among those told Catherine did not protest the decision, she was liked less among those who believe sex discrimination is more pervasive relative to those who perceive it as less pervasive. Unlike b_1, this is substantively meaningful.

The regression coefficient for the product of X and M is $b_3 = 0.834$. This coefficient quantifies how the effect of X on Y changes as M changes by one unit. Here, b_3 is statistically different from zero, meaning that the effect of the decision to protest or not on liking depends on beliefs about the pervasiveness of sex discrimination. More specifically, as beliefs about the pervasiveness of sexism in society increases by one unit, the difference in liking between those told Catherine did versus did not protest increases by 0.834 units. So b_3 quantifies a difference between differences (see equation 7.8).

Variable Scaling and the Interpretation of b_1 and b_2

As discussed already, b_1 and b_2 must be interpreted with care and considering the scaling of X and M, for depending on the scaling, these coefficients and their tests of significance may have no substantive interpretation. However, typically it is possible to rescale X and/or M prior to analysis in such a fashion that b_1 and b_2 are rendered interpretable.

One handy transformation is variable *centering*, which is accomplished by subtracting a constant from every value of a variable in the data. When X or M (or both) are centered prior to the construction of their product, b_1 and b_2 still represent conditional effects, but they are now conditioned on a value that renders the coefficient interpretable if it wasn't already.

For instance, suppose we *mean center* beliefs about the pervasiveness of sex discrimination around the sample mean. To do so, the mean of M is subtracted from each value of M in the data to produce a new variable M', as such:

$$M' = M - \overline{M}$$

In this case, we calculate $M' = M - 5.117$, as the sample mean for the Modern Sexism Scale is 5.117. This mean-centered version of M has a mean of zero and a standard deviation equal to the standard deviation of M. With this transformation accomplished, the simple moderation model is then estimated in the usual way but substituting M' for M, as such:

$$\hat{Y} = i_1 + b_1 X + b_2 M' + b_3 X M'$$

This model is mathematically equivalent to

$$\hat{Y} = i_1 + b_1 X + b_2(M - \overline{M}) + b_3 X(M - \overline{M}).$$

In SPSS, this regression analysis is accomplished using the code

```
compute sexismp=sexism-5.117.
compute proxsexp=protest*sexismp.
regression/dep=liking/method=enter protest sexismp proxsexp.
```

In SAS, use

```
data protest;set protest;sexismp=sexism-5.117;proxsexp=protest*sexismp;run;
proc reg data=protest;model liking=protest sexismp proxsexp;run;
```

The resulting model can be found in Table 7.4 as model 4. The model is

$$\hat{Y} = 5.288 + 0.493X - 0.473M' + 0.834XM'$$

Observe that relative to model 3 in Table 7.4, b_2 and b_3 are not changed by this transformation of M, and their interpretations are the same. Their standard errors are identical, as are confidence intervals and p-values. Furthermore, the fit of the model is the same as the model using M in its original form. Indeed, model 4 will produce exactly the same estimates of Y as will model 3, because mathematically they are identical models; one is just a reparameterization of the other.

But the reparameterization caused by centering M has affected b_1. Remember that b_1 is a conditional effect given that XM' is in the model. It estimates the effect of X on Y when $M' = 0$. So two cases that differ by one unit on X are estimated to differ by 0.493 units on Y when $M' = 0$. But notice that $M' = 0$ when $M = \overline{M} = 5.117$, so b_1 now estimates the difference in liking between those told the lawyer did versus did not protest among people *average* in their beliefs about the pervasiveness of sex discrimination. Among those average in such beliefs, those told the lawyer protested the discrimination liked her 0.493 units more on average than those told she did not protest. This difference between the conditions is statistically different from zero ($p = .010$). This is substantively meaningful, unlike when the model was estimated with M in its original metric.

In models 3 and 4 summarized in Table 7.4, b_2 estimates the effect of M on Y when $X = 0$. In this example, b_2 is substantively meaningful as the estimated difference in liking of Catherine between two people who differ by one unit in their beliefs about the pervasiveness of sex discrimination among those assigned to the no-protest condition. While meaningful, b_2 is determined by the arbitrary decision to code experimental conditions using $X = 0$ and $X = 1$. A different decision about how to code groups would most likely change b_2 and it could change b_1 and b_3 as well, depending on the choice made.

To illustrate, suppose the protest condition was coded $X = 0.5$ and the no-protest condition $X = -0.5$, but M was mean centered as in model 4. The coefficients for the resulting model after this recoding of X can be found in Table 7.4, model 5. This model is mathematically identical to models 3 and 4, fits exactly the same, and generates the same estimates of Y, but the rescaling of X has reparameterized the model. The coefficient for the interaction ($b_3 = 0.834$) is identical to models 3 and 4, as is its standard error and p-value. Rescaling X has not changed b_1 relative to model 4 because the two protest conditions still differ by a single unit on X. But b_2 has changed. This regression coefficient quantifies how much two people who differ by one unit in their beliefs about the pervasiveness of sex discrimination in society are estimated to differ in their liking of the attorney when $X = 0$. Although $X = 0$ seems senseless given that X is an arbitrary code for two groups, b_2 still has a meaningful interpretation. It is now the unweighted average effect of beliefs about sex discrimination on liking in the two conditions. This interpretation will become clearer in Chapter 8.

As should now be apparent, caution must be exercised when interpreting b_1 and b_2 in a model of the form $Y = i_1 + b_1 X + b_2 M + b_3 XM + e_Y$. Although their mathematical interpretations are the same regardless of how X and M are scaled, their substantive interpretations can be drastically affected by decisions about scaling, centering, and coding. Different transformations of X and M will change b_1 and b_2 and how they are interpreted. However, so long as the transformation changes only the mean of X or M, b_3 and inferences about $_T b_3$ will be unaffected.

There is a widespread belief that a transformation such as mean centering of X and M is mathematically necessary in order to properly estimate a model that includes the product of X and M as a predictor and therefore in order to test a moderation hypothesis correctly. Although there is some value to mean centering, it is *not* necessary. I will debunk the myth about the need to mean center in models of this sort in Chapter 9. In the meantime, should you choose to mean center X and M, PROCESS makes this easy. Simply add **center=1** to the PROCESS command, and all variables involved in the construction of a product will be mean centered and all output will be based on the mean-centered metrics of X and M.

7.3 Visualizing Moderation

A regression model with the product of two predictors is an abstract mathematical representation of one's data that can be harder to interpret than a model without such an interaction term. As described earlier, the coefficients for X and M are conditional effects that may not have any substantive interpretation at all, and the coefficient for XM is interpreted as a difference between differences that can be hard to make sense of without more information. Although the sign of b_3 carries unambiguous mathematical meaning, even if the sign is in the direction anticipated, this does not mean that the results are consistent with one's predictions. A picture of one's model can be an important interpretive aid when trying to understand a regression model with an interaction. To produce such a visual representation of the model, I recommend generating a set of estimates of Y from various combinations of X and M using the regression model and then plotting $\hat{Y}$ as a function of X and M. This can be done using any graphics program that you find handy.

In the sex discrimination study, the model of Y is $\hat{Y} = 7.706 - 3.773X - 0.473M + 0.834XM$ (i.e., using M rather than mean-centered M). To generate various values of $\hat{Y}$, select values of X and M that are within the range of the data, and then plug those values into the model to get estimates of Y. The choice of these values may be arbitrary, but it is important that they be within the range of the data and that they cover the distribution. If M is quantitative, one might use the mean and plus and minus one standard deviation, or various percentiles in the distribution. If M is dichotomous, there isn't much choice to make. Simply use the two values of M. For this example, I selected $M = 4.12$, 4.50, 5.12, 5.62, and 6.12, which correspond to the 10th, 25th, 50th, 75th, and 90th percentiles of the distribution of the Modern Sexism Scale in this sample. For X, I used 0 and 1, which are the codes for the no-protest and protest conditions, respectively. When these values are plugged into the regression model, the values of $\hat{Y}$ in Table 7.5 result.

Figure 7.6 is a visual representation of the model using the data in Table 7.5, generated in SAS using the following commands:

```
data;input protest sexism liking;
if (protest = 1) then condition = 'Protest (X=1) ';
if (protest = 0) then condition = 'No Protest (X=0)';
datalines;
0 4.12 5.76
1 4.12 5.42
```

TABLE 7.5. Values of $\hat{Y}$ Generated from the Protest and Sex Discrimination Model $\hat{Y} = 7.706 - 3.773X - 0.473M + 0.834XM$

X (PROTEST)	M (SEXISM)	$\hat{Y}$
0	4.12	5.76
1	4.12	5.42
0	4.50	5.58
1	4.50	5.56
0	5.12	5.28
1	5.12	5.78
0	5.62	5.05
1	5.62	5.96
0	6.12	4.81
1	6.12	6.14

```
0 4.50 5.58
1 4.50 5.56
0 5.12 5.28
1 5.12 5.78
0 5.62 5.05
1 5.62 5.96
0 6.12 4.81
1 6.12 6.14
run;
proc sgplot;reg x=sexism y=liking/group=condition
nomarkers lineattrs=(color=black);
xaxis label='Perceived Pervasiveness of Sex Discrimination (M)'
yaxis label='Liking of the Attorney (Y)';run;
```

A similar figure can be produced in SPSS with the commands below, although it will require some additional editing within SPSS to look as nice as the SAS version.

```
data list free/protest sexism liking.
begin data.
0 4.12 5.76
1 4.12 5.42
0 4.50 5.58
```

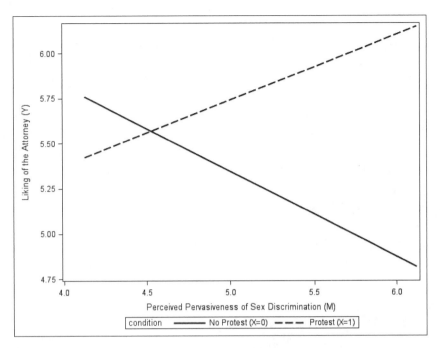

FIGURE 7.6. A visual representation (generated by SAS) of the moderation of the effect of the decision to protest (*X*) on liking (*Y*) by beliefs in the pervasiveness of sex discrimination in society (*M*).

```
1 4.50 5.56
0 5.12 5.28
1 5.12 5.78
0 5.62 5.05
1 5.62 5.96
0 6.12 4.81
1 6.12 6.14
end data.
graph/scatterplot=sexism with liking by protest.
```

Although PROCESS will not generate a plot of the interaction for you, it does have an option which will reduce some of the work needed to do so. Specifying the option **plot=1**, as in the example PROCESS command on page 225, produces a table of estimates of *Y* for various combinations of *X* and *M*. These can be found at the bottom of Figure 7.5. The data from this table can be given to the graphics program of your choosing. Alternatively, you could insert these data into the SPSS or SAS command on the previous page.

This picture of the model certainly makes it clearer what is happening in the data than the abstract numerical representation in the form of regression coefficients. There appears to be a much smaller difference in how Catherine is evaluated depending on her behavior among people relatively low in their beliefs about the pervasiveness of sex discrimination relative to those high in such beliefs. This is reflected in the distance between the solid and dashed lines that grows as M increases. Rephrased, the action chosen by Catherine seems to have had less effect on her evaluation among those who believe sex discrimination is relatively less pervasive than it did among those who see sex discrimination as highly pervasive. Most of the difference in liking seems to be on the upper end of the Modern Sexism Scale, where Catherine was liked more by participants told she protested than those told she did not. If anything, it seems the opposite may be happening among those who see sex discrimination as less pervasive in society.

7.4 Probing an Interaction

They say that a picture says a thousand words, but it takes more than a thousand words to convince some. The holistic interpretation of the pattern of results in the discrimination study I gave in the prior paragraph is not sufficient for the tastes of many. With evidence of moderation of X's effect on Y by M, this does not establish that, for instance, X has an effect on Y for people high on M but not for people low on M. All that b_3 and its test of significance (or a confidence interval) establishes is that the effect of X on Y depends on M. It says nothing more. Framed in terms of this example, neither the interaction itself as manifested by the estimate of b_3 nor the visual picture of that interaction depicted in Figure 7.6 establishes that people who believe sex discrimination is highly pervasive like someone who protests such discrimination more than someone who does not, or that people who believe sex discrimination is less pervasive like someone who accepts such discrimination more than someone who fights it. Descriptively, the results are consistent with that pattern to be sure. But the magnitude of the discrepancy in liking between the two conditions is subject to sampling error at each and every value of M. That is, there is a certain "chance" component to the estimate of X's effect on Y at any value of M one might choose.

To deal with the uncertainty, it is common to follow up a test of interaction with a set of additional inferential tests to establish where in the distribution of the moderator X has an effect on Y that is different from zero and where it does not. This exercise is commonly known as "probing" an interaction, like one might fondle an avocado or a mango in the produce section of the grocery store to assess its ripeness. The goal is to ascertain where in the distribution of the moderator X is related to Y and where it is not in an attempt to better discern the substantive interpretation of the interaction. In this section I describe two approaches to probing an interaction, one that is very commonly used, and the other less so but growing in popularity.

Pick-a-Point Approach

The pick-a-point approach (Rogosa, 1980; Bauer & Curran, 2005), sometimes called an analysis of *simple slopes* or a *spotlight analysis*, is the most popular approach to probing of interactions and is described in most discussions of multiple regression with interactions (e.g., Aiken & West, 1991; Cohen et al., 2003; Hayes, 2005; Jaccard & Turrisi, 2003; Spiller, Fitzsimons, Lynch, & McClelland, 2013). This procedure involves selecting a value or values of the moderator M, calculating the conditional effect of X on Y ($\theta_{X \to Y}$) at that value or values, and conducting an inferential test or generating a confidence interval. To do so, an estimate of the standard error of the conditional effect of X is required for values of M selected (see, e.g., Aiken & West, 1991; Cohen et al., 2003; Bauer & Curran, 2005):

$$se_{\theta_{X \to Y}} = \sqrt{se_{b_1}^2 + (2M)COV_{b_1 b_3} + M^2 se_{b_3}^2} \qquad (7.12)$$

where $se_{b_1}^2$ and $se_{b_3}^2$ are the squared standard errors of b_1 and b_3, M is any chosen value of the moderator, and $COV_{b_1 b_3}$ is the covariance of b_1 and b_3 across repeated sampling. All but the covariance between b_1 and b_3 is available as standard output in all OLS regression programs, and $COV_{b_1 b_3}$ is available as optional output.[3] The ratio of $\theta_{X \to Y}$ at a specific value of M to its standard error is distributed as $t(df_{residual})$ under the null hypothesis that $_T\theta_{X \to Y} = 0$ at that value of M. A p-value for the ratio can be obtained from any t table, or a confidence interval generated using equation 2.10 substituting for $\theta_{X \to Y}$ for b and $se_{\theta_{X \to Y}}$ for se_b.

I do not recommend doing these computations by hand, because the potential for error is very high unless you do them to many decimal places and really are comfortable with what you are doing. In addition, this approach can be implemented fairly easily to a high degree of accuracy by a computer using the regression-centering method described next. Furthermore, PROCESS generates output from the pick-a-point approach whether

---

[3] In SPSS, the covariance between regression coefficients can be obtained by adding bcov as an argument in a `statistics` subcommand following the `regression` command. In SAS, specify covb as an option following the `model` command in `proc reg`.

you want it or not, making even the regression-centering approach unnecessary if you have PROCESS handy. Example manual computations for the pick-a-point approach can be found in Aiken and West (1991) and Cohen et al. (2003).

The Pick-a-Point Approach Implemented by Regression Centering. A relatively easy way of implementing the pick-a-point approach is by centering M around the value or values at which you would like an estimate of the conditional effect X on Y and its standard error. Recall that in a model of the form $\hat{Y} = i_1 + b_1 X + b_2 M + b_3 XM$, b_1 estimates the effect of X on Y when $M = 0$. On page 228, I described the effects of scaling on the estimate and interpretation of b_1. By centering M around the mean prior to the computation of XM and estimation of the model, the regression analysis generated the effect of X on Y when M equals $\overline{M}$. In more general terms, defining $M' = M - m$, where m is any chosen value of the moderator, b_1 in

$$Y = i_1 + b_1 M' + b_2 X + b_3 XM'$$

quantifies $\theta_{(X \to Y)|M=m}$, the conditional effect of X on Y given $M = m$. The standard error of b_1 will be equivalent to the standard error generated by equation 7.12, and the t and p-value can be used to test the null hypothesis that $_T\theta_{(X \to Y)|M=m} = 0$.

When M is a quantitative variable, as in the sex discrimination study, a common strategy when probing an interaction is to estimate the conditional effect of X on Y when M is equal to the mean, a standard deviation below the mean, and a standard deviation above the mean (see, e.g., Aiken & West, 1991). This allows the investigator to ascertain whether X is related to Y among those "relatively low" ($\overline{M} - SD_M$), "moderate" ($\overline{M}$), and "relatively high" ($\overline{M} + SD_M$) on the moderator. Using the regression-centering strategy, the conditional effect of X on Y when M equals $\overline{M}$ was already derived on page 229 as $\theta_{(X \to Y)|M=5.117} = 0.493, t(125) = 2.631, p = .003$. In the data, $SD_M = 0.784$, so a standard deviation below and above the mean correspond to values of M equal to 4.333 and 5.901. The SPSS code below estimates the conditional effect of X on Y at those two values of M:

```
compute sexismp=sexism-4.333.
compute proxsexp=protest*sexismp.
regression/dep=liking/method=enter protest sexismp proxsexp.
compute sexismp=sexism-5.901.
compute proxsexp=protest*sexismp.
regression/dep=liking/method=enter protest sexismp proxsexp.
```

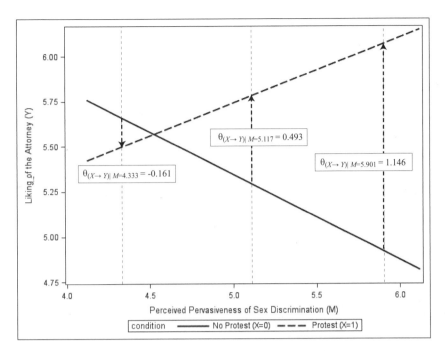

FIGURE 7.7. A visual representation of conditional effects of the decision to protest (X) on liking (Y) among those relatively low ($M = 4.333$), moderate ($M = 5.117$), and relatively high ($M = 5.901$) in their beliefs about the pervasiveness of sex discrimination in society.

In SAS, use

```
data protest;set protest;sexismp=sexism-4.333;proxsexp=protest*sexismp;run;
proc reg data=protest;model liking=protest sexismp proxsexp;run;
data protest;set protest;sexismp=sexism-5.901;proxsexp=protest*sexismp;run;
proc reg data=protest;model liking=protest sexismp proxsexp;run;
```

In both resulting models, the regression coefficient for protest condition is b_1. In this case, $\theta_{(X\rightarrow Y)|M=4.333} = -0.161$, $t(125) = -0.612, p = .542$, and $\theta_{(X\rightarrow Y)|M=5.901} = 1.146$, $t(125) = 4.216, p < .001$. These conditional effects correspond to the distance between the lines in Figure 7.6 at the corresponding values of M (see Figure 7.7). Combined with the estimate of X's effect on Y when $M = 5.117$, we can say that among those who see sex discrimination as relatively less pervasive, Catherine's choice to protest had no effect on how she was evaluated. But among those moderate or relatively high in how pervasive they believe sex discrimination is, she was liked more when she protested the discrimination than when she did not.

Implementation in PROCESS. PROCESS automatically produces output from the pick-a-point approach to probing interactions whenever a moderation model is specified with X's effect on Y moderated by another variable. By default, when M is dichotomous, PROCESS generates $\theta_{X \to Y}$ for the two groups defined by values of M, along with standard errors, p-values for a two-tailed test of the null hypothesis that $\theta_{X \to Y} = 0$, and confidence intervals for $_T\theta_{X \to Y}$. When M is a continuous variable, as it is in this case, PROCESS estimates $\theta_{X \to Y}$ for values of M equal to the sample mean as well as a standard deviation above and below the mean. When one standard deviation below or above the mean is beyond the range of the observed data, PROCESS will substitute the minimum or maximum value of the moderator for a standard deviation below or above the mean, respectively.

But this default in PROCESS can be overridden by specifying **quantile=1** in the command line, as in the PROCESS command on page 225 used to generate the output in Figure 7.5. When this quantile option is used, the conditional effect of X is estimated at values of the moderator corresponding to the 10th, 25th, 50th, 75th, and 90th percentiles in the sample distribution of M. One might label these as representative of "very low," "low," "moderate," "high," and "very high" in the sample (but not necessarily in an absolute sense). In this study, these percentiles correspond to measurements of 4.12, 4.50, 5.12, 5.62, and 6.12 on the Modern Sexism Scale. As can be seen in the PROCESS output, among participants "very low" [$\theta_{(X \to Y)|M=4.12} = -0.338, t(125) = -1.222, p = .265$] and "low" [$\theta_{(X \to Y)|M=4.50} = -0.022, t(125) = -0.092, p = .927$] in perceived pervasiveness of sex discrimination, Catherine's behavior had no statistically significant effect on how she was evaluated. But among those "moderate" [$\theta_{(X \to Y)|M=5.12} = 0.495, t(125) = 2.664, p = .009$], "high" [$\theta_{(X \to Y)|M=5.62} = 0.912, t(125) = 4.014, p < .001$] and "very high" [$\theta_{(X \to Y)|M=6.12} = 1.328, t(125) = 4.249, p < .001$], she was liked significantly more when she protested relative to when she did not.

PROCESS also has an option for estimating the conditional effect of X on Y for *any* chosen value of M. By specifying the option **mmodval=m**, where m is the chosen value of M, PROCESS will produce $\theta_{(X \to Y)|M=m}$ along with its standard error, t, and p-value, and a confidence interval. Only one value of M can be listed in the **mmodval=** argument.

The Johnson–Neyman Technique

The pick-a-point approach suffers from one major problem. This approach requires the selection of various values of M at which to estimate the conditional effect of X on Y. Different choices can lead to different claims, and the choice is often made arbitrarily. Absent any guidance from theory or application, investigators typically rely on conventions such as the mean, as well as plus and minus one standard deviation from the mean to represent "low," "moderate," and "high" on the moderator. Although such values of M are widely recommended in books and journal articles that discuss probing interactions (e.g., Aiken & West, 1991; Cohen et al., 2003) that does not make them any less arbitrary. Furthermore, such designations are, of course, sample specific. What is low in one sample may be moderate in another sample. If the moderator is highly skewed, the mean may be quite unrepresentative and actually quite low or high on whatever measurement scale is being used. In addition, one has to be careful when mindlessly following this convention that either "low" or "high" (or both) are not outside of the range of measurement, as can happen when M is highly skewed.

Some of these shortcomings of the use of $\overline{M}$ and $\overline{M} \pm 1SD$ are eliminated by the use of percentiles of the distribution. For instance, the 25th, 50th, and 75th percentiles will always be within the range of the data. As described earlier, PROCESS provides an option for the use of these percentiles (as well as the 10th and 90th percentiles) when probing an interaction using the pick-a-point approach. However, these are no less arbitrary than $\overline{M}$ and $\overline{M} \pm 1SD$. Though convenient in allowing the user to choose between these two strategies, PROCESS does not eliminate the arbitrariness of the selection when using the pick-a-point approach.

You can wash your hands of the arbitrariness of the choice of values of M by using the Johnson–Neyman (JN) technique, dubbed a *floodlight analysis* by Spiller et al. (2013). Originally conceived for dealing with tests of mean differences between two groups in analysis of covariance when the homogeneity of regression assumption is violated (Johnson & Neyman, 1936; Johnson & Fey, 1950; Rogosa, 1980), it was later extended by Bauer and Curran (2005) to regression models with interactions more generally. It is growing in popularity. Some recent examples of the application of the JN technique for probing interactions can be found in Beach et al. (2012), Bushman, Giancolo, Parrott, and Roth (2012), Prinzie et al. (2012), and Simons et al. (2012).

The JN technique, which can be applied only when M is a continuum, is essentially the pick-a-point approach conducted in reverse. Using the pick-a-point approach, one calculates the ratio of the conditional effect of X on Y given M to its standard error. Using the t distribution, a p-value for the obtained ratio is derived and an inference made based on the p-value. Rather than finding p for a given value of t, the JN technique derives the values of M such that the ratio of the conditional effect to its standard error is exactly equal to t_{crit}, the critical t value associated with $p = \alpha$, where α

is the level of significance chosen for the inference. Given the following equation

$$t_{crit} = \frac{\theta_{(X \to Y)|M}}{se_{\theta_{(X \to Y)|M}}}$$

or, in the case of a model of the form $\hat{Y} = i_1 + b_1 X + b_2 M + b_3 XM$,

$$t_{crit} = \frac{b_1 + b_3 M}{\sqrt{se_{b_1}^2 + (2M)COV_{b_1 b_3} + M^2 se_{b_3}^2}}$$

the JN technique derives the roots of the quadratic equation that results when M is isolated and set to zero. The roots of this equation will be the values of M for which the ratio of the conditional effect to its standard error is exactly t_{crit}, meaning $p = \alpha$. For computational details, see Bauer and Curran (2005) or Hayes and Matthes (2009).

A quadratic equation contains two roots, meaning that the JN technique will produce two solutions for M, which I refer to in my discussion below as JN_{M_1} and JN_{M_2} where $JN_{M_1} \leq JN_{M_2}$. These values of M demarcate the points along the continuum of M where the conditional effect of X on Y transitions between statistically significant and not significant at the α level of significance. As such, they identify the "region of significance" of the effect of X on Y. In practice, often one or both of these values will be outside of the range of the measurement scale of M or will be in the domain of imaginary numbers. Such values of JN_{M_1} or JN_{M_2} should be ignored as if they didn't exist. Given this caveat, there are three outcomes that are possible when the JN technique is used.

The first possible outcome is that the JN technique generates a single solution within the range of the measurement of the moderator. Call this value JN_{M_1}. When the JN technique produces a single value, this means that the conditional effect of X on Y is statistically significant at the α level when $M \geq JN_{M_1}$ or when $M \leq JN_{M_1}$ but *not* both. This defines either $M \geq JN_{M_1}$ or $M \leq JN_{M_1}$ as the region of significance of X's effect on Y.

The second possibility is that the JN technique generates two solutions within the range of the data. When this occurs, the region of significance of X's effect on Y is either $JN_{M_1} \leq M \leq JN_{M_2}$ or, alternatively, $M \leq JN_{M_1}$ *and* $M \geq JN_{M_2}$. The former means that the conditional effect of X on Y is statistically significant when M is between JN_{M_1} and JN_{M_2} but not beyond those two values. The latter means that the conditional effect of X on Y is statistically significant when M is less than or equal to JN_{M_1} and when M is greater than or equal to JN_{M_2} but not in between these two values.

A final possibility is no solutions within the range of the moderator. This can mean one of two things. One interpretation is that the conditional effect of X on Y is statistically significant across the entire range of the moderator, meaning that there are no points along the continuum of M where the conditional effect transitions between statistically significant and not. The second interpretation is that the conditional effect of X on Y is not statistically significant *anywhere* in the observed distribution of the moderator, again meaning no points of transition. In the former case, the region of significance of the effect X on Y is the entire range of M, whereas in the latter case, there is no region of significance.

Implementation in PROCESS. Derivation of regions of significance by hand using the JN technique would be vary tedious. Fortunately, this method is available in SPSS and SAS through the MODPROBE tool (Hayes & Matthes, 2009), and a Web-based calculator can be used that requires only regression output and an Internet connection (Preacher, Curran, & Bauer, 2006). PROCESS also implements this approach with the addition of **jn=1** to the PROCESS command, as on page 225 for the sex discrimination study.[4]

The resulting PROCESS output can be found in Figure 7.5. As can be seen, PROCESS identifies two values of perceived pervasiveness of sex discrimination as points which demarcate the regions of significance of the effect of Catherine's behavior on her evaluation: $M = 3.509$ and $M = 4.975$. But without more information, this is hard to interpret. To ease the interpretation, PROCESS slices the distribution of M into 21 arbitrary values, calculates $\theta_{X \to Y}$ at those values, along with their standard errors, p-values, and confidence interval endpoints, and then displays the results in a table. It also inserts the corresponding conditional effects when M equals the points identified by the JN technique. As can be seen, when $M \geq 4.975$, Catherine was liked more when she protested compared to when she did not (because the conditional effect of X is positive and statistically different from zero when $M \geq 4.975$). When $M \leq 3.509$, the decision to protest seemed to decrease her evaluation, as participants with $M \leq 3.509$ assigned to the protest condition liked Catherine less than those told she did not protest. Thus, the region of significance for the effect of the decision to protest or not on her evaluation is $M \leq 3.509$ and $M \geq 4.975$.[5]

---

[4]An earlier SPSS and SAS implementation of the JN technique for the special case where X is a dichotomous variable was published by Karpmann (1986).

[5]As described here, the JN technique affords a *nonsimultaneous* inference, meaning that one can claim that for any chosen value of M in the region of significance, the probability of incorrectly concluding the conditional effect of X on Y is different from zero when it is not is no greater than α. One cannot make a *simultaneous* inference and say that the conditional effects at all values of M in the region of significance are different from zero while keeping the Type I error rate for this simultaneous claim at α. The probability of a Type I error for this claim is higher than α. Potthoff (1964) describes a version of the JN technique that allows for simultaneous inference of this sort. The Potthoff correction is not implemented in PROCESS as of the publication of this book, but it is available in MODPROBE.

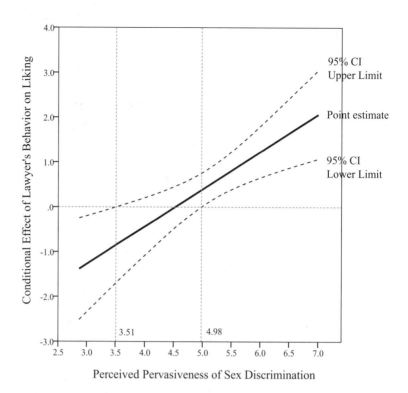

FIGURE 7.8. The conditional effect of the lawyer's behavior on liking ($\theta_{X \to Y}$) as a function of beliefs about the pervasiveness of sex discrimination in society.

A handy means of visualizing the region of significance derived from the JN technique is a plot of $\theta_{X \to Y}$ as a function of M along with confidence bands (see Bauer & Curran, 2005; Preacher et al., 2006; Rogosa, 1980). The region of significance is depicted as the values of M corresponding to points where a conditional effect of 0 is outside of the confidence band for $_T\theta_{X \to Y}$. Figure 7.8 displays the region of significance in this example. As can be seen, when $M \leq 3.509$ and $M \geq 4.975$, the confidence bands are entirely above or entirely below zero.

Figure 7.8 was produced using the SPSS code below, then doing considerable editing within SPSS and adding some final touches using a dedicated illustration program. The data between the **begin data** and **end data** commands in the code were generated by PROCESS, and the output from PROCESS simply cut and paste into the code prior to executing it.

```
data list free/sexism effect llci ulci.
begin data.
2.8700    -1.3804    -2.5133    -0.2474
```

```
3.0765    -1.2082    -2.2476    -0.1689
3.2830    -1.0361    -1.9831    -0.0891
  .
  .          (from PROCESS JN table) .
  .          .          .          .
6.5870     1.7180     0.9074     2.5285
6.7935     1.8901     0.9898     2.7904
7.0000     2.0622     1.0704     3.0541
end data.
graph/scatter(overlay)=sexism sexism sexism with llci ulci effect (pair).
```

The SAS code below produces a similar figure that requires no editing whatsoever.

```
data;input sexism effect llci ulci;
datalines;
2.8700    -1.3804    -2.5133    -0.2474
3.0765    -1.2082    -2.2476    -0.1689
3.2830    -1.0361    -1.9831    -0.0891
  .          .          .          .
  .          (from PROCESS JN table) .
  .          .          .          .
6.5870     1.7180     0.9074     2.5285
6.7935     1.8901     0.9898     2.7904
7.0000     2.0622     1.0704     3.0541
run;
proc sgplot;
series x=sexism y=ulci/curvelabel = '95% upper limit' lineattrs=(color=red
    pattern=ShortDash);
series x=sexism y=effect/curvelabel = 'point estimate' lineattrs=(color=
    black pattern=Solid);
series x=sexism y=llci/curvelabel = '95% lower limit' lineattrs=(color=red
    pattern=ShortDash);
xaxis label = 'Perceived pervasiveness of sex discrimination (M)';
yaxis label = 'Conditional effect of protest';
refline 0/axis=y transparency=0.5;refline 3.5 4.98/axis=x transparency=0.5;
run;
```

Although the JN technique eliminates the need to select arbitrary values of M when probing an interaction, it does not eliminate your need to keep your brain tuned into the task and thinking critically about the answer this method gives you. In this example, one interpretative caution is in order. The JN technique reveals that when $M \leq 3.509$, $\theta_{X \to Y}$ is negative and statistically different from zero, meaning Catherine was liked less. But recall from earlier discussion that the 10th percentile in the distribution of M in these data is 4.12. That is, roughly 10% of the participants in this study score less than 4.12 on the Modern Sexism Scale. A closer look at the data reveals that there are only two cases in the data with Modern Sexism scores smaller than 3.509. Given this, I would be very reluctant to make much out of this section of the region of significance. There simply is not enough data in this end of the distribution to be confident in the claim that the protesting lawyer is liked less than the protesting lawyer among those so low in perceived pervasiveness of sex discrimination.

7.5   Chapter Summary

When the question motivating a study asks *when* or *under what circumstances* X exerts an effect on Y, moderation analysis is an appropriate analytical strategy. This chapter introduced the principles of moderation analysis using OLS regression. If M is related to the magnitude of the effect of X on Y, we say that M moderates X's effect, or that X and M interact in their influence on Y. Hypotheses about moderation can be tested in several ways, the most common of which is to include the product of X and M in the model of Y along with X and M. This allows X's effect on Y to depend linearly on M. If such a dependency is established, it is no longer sensible to talk about X's effect on Y without conditioning that discussion on M.

A picture of a moderation model can go a long way toward better understanding the contingent nature of the association between X and Y. So too can a formal probing of the interaction by estimating the conditional effect of X on Y for various values of M. The pick-a-point approach is the most commonly implemented strategy for probing interactions, but the Johnson–Neyman technique is slowly gaining users and followers, and no doubt will in time be as popular or more so than the pick-a-point approach.

The next chapter extends the method introduced in this chapter by applying it to models in which M is categorical, as well as when both X and M are quantitative. As you will see, all the principles introduced in this chapter are easily generalized to such models, and once these principles are well understood, you will be in a strong position to tackle the integration of moderation and mediation analysis in the final few chapters of this book.

8

Extending Moderation Analysis Principles

Chapter 7 introduced the principles of moderation analysis applied to a study in which the focal predictor was a dichotomous experimental manipulation and the moderator was continuous. This chapter illustrates that these principles generalize and can be applied without modification to problems in which the moderator is dichotomous as well as when both focal predictor and moderator are continuous. The equivalence between moderation analysis using multiple regression and the 2×2 factorial analysis of variance is also demonstrated here, with the important caveat that this equivalence depends heavily on how the two dichotomous predictors or "factors" are coded. A failure to appreciate this important condition can lead to a misinterpretation of the results of a regression analysis when used as a substitute for factorial analysis of variance.

Chapter 7 introduced the principles of moderation analysis. In a model of the form $Y = i_1 + b_1X + b_2M + e_Y$, b_1 and b_2 quantify unconditional effects, in that X's effect on Y does not depend on M, and M's effect on Y does not depend on X. Adding the product of X and M to the model, thereby producing a model of the form $Y = i_i + b_1X + b_2M + b_3XM + e_Y$, relaxes this constraint and allows X's effect to depend on M and M's effect to depend on X. Thus, X's and M's effects on Y are conditional in such a model.

If I have done my job well writing Chapter 7, much of this chapter should be review to you to at least some extent, because everything discussed in that chapter applies without modification to the examples of moderation analysis presented here. In this chapter I show how these principles of moderation analysis are applied when the moderator is dichotomous (rather than a continuum, as in the previous chapter) as well as when both focal predictor and moderator are continuous. I also illustrate that one of the more common analytical techniques, the 2×2 factorial analysis of variance, is equivalent to multiple regression in which one dichotomous variable's effect on an outcome is moderated by a second dichotomous variable. However, as will be seen, this equivalence is dependent on how the two dichotomous predictor variables are coded. Happily, for all the examples presented in this chapter, PROCESS makes the estimation simple and it greatly eases the effort of probing and interpreting interactions regardless of whether the focal predictor and moderator are dichotomous, continuous, or any combination thereof.

8.1 Moderation Involving a Dichotomous Moderator

The method of moderation analysis introduced in Chapter 7 was illustrated using data from a study examining the extent to which a person's behavior (Catherine, who was sexually discriminated against and chose to protest or not) influenced how she was perceived (i.e., how much she was liked) differentially depending on what the perceiver brought to the process (i.e., a person's beliefs about how pervasive sex discrimination is in society). In that example, the focal predictor was a dichotomous variable coding experimental condition, and the moderator was a measured individual difference variable that located each person on a continuum of beliefs about the extent of sex discrimination in society. As described then, the effect of Catherine's decision to protest differentially affected how she was perceived as a function of the perceiver's belief about the pervasiveness of sex discrimination in society. Specifically, the effect was larger among those relatively higher in their beliefs about the pervasiveness of sex discrimination.

But what if our substantive focus was not on how people's behavior influences how they are perceived, but instead on how people's beliefs influence how they perceive others? Using the sex discrimination study, for example, we could ask whether there is a relationship between people's beliefs about the pervasiveness of sex discrimination and how Catherine was perceived. This question is easily answered with a simple regression analysis. The best fitting OLS regression model estimating liking of Catherine (Y) from beliefs about the pervasiveness of sex discrimination in society (X) is $\hat{Y} = 5.010 + 0.122X$. Thus, two people who differ by one unit in their perceptions of the pervasiveness of sex discrimination are estimated to differ by 0.122 units in how much they like Catherine. However, the regression coefficient for beliefs is not statistically significant, $t(127) = 1.034, p = .303$. Thus, there is no scientific basis for claiming that those beliefs influenced how Catherine was perceived.

Of course, this analysis completely ignores the fact that some of the participants were asked to evaluate a person who had just protested an act

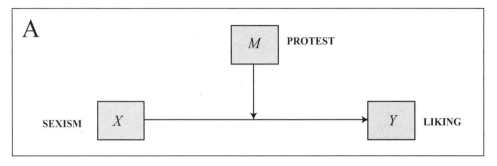

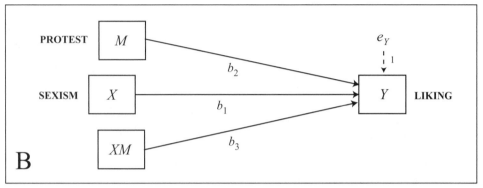

FIGURE 8.1. Moderation of the effect of beliefs about the pervasiveness of sex discrimination in society on evaluation of the attorney by her decision to protest or not, depicted as a conceptual diagram (panel A) and a statistical diagram (panel B).

of sex discrimination in her law firm, whereas others evaluated a person who ignored it in spite of the costs of that discrimination to her professional advancement. Certainly, the effects of our beliefs and world views on how we perceive others will depend in some part on how the behavior of those we are perceiving mesh with the beliefs we hold. Framed in this way, a more proper analysis would allow the effect of beliefs about the pervasiveness of sex discrimination on how Catherine is perceived to depend on whether or not she protested a recent act of sex discrimination. Calling her decision to protest or not M, we can estimate a simple moderation model just as in Chapter 7, which allows the effect of X to depend on M. Such a process is diagrammed in conceptual form in Figure 8.1, panel A, and translates into a statistical model with X, M, and XM as predictors of Y, as in the statistical diagram in Figure 8.1, panel B. In the form of an equation, the model is

$$Y = i_1 + b_1 X + b_2 M + b_3 XM \qquad (8.1)$$

where the focal predictor is a continuous individual difference variable (X) and the moderator is a dichotomous variable in form of an experimental manipulation (M). The SPSS and SAS code described on page 223 could

TABLE 8.1. Results from a Regression Analysis Examining the Moderation of the Effect of Beliefs about the Pervasiveness of Sex Discrimination in Society on Liking of the Attorney by Whether or Not She Chose to Protest an Act of Discrimination

		Coeff.	SE	t	p
Intercept	i_1	7.706	1.045	7.375	$< .001$
Modern Sexism Scale (X)	b_1	−0.473	0.204	−2.318	.022
Condition (M)	b_2	−3.773	1.254	−3.008	.003
Modern Sexism × Condition (XM)	b_3	0.834	0.244	3.422	.008

$$R^2 = 0.133, MSE = 0.978$$
$$F(3, 125) = 6.419, p < .001$$

be used to estimate the coefficients of the model in equation 8.1. I repeat it here for convenience sake. In SPSS, the commands are

```
compute proxsex=protest*sexism.
regression/dep=liking/method=enter sexism protest proxsex.
```

and in SAS, you can use use

```
data protest;set protest;proxsex=protest*sexism;run;
proc reg data=protest;model liking=sexism protest proxsex;run;
```

Even easier would be to use PROCESS. The PROCESS command would be the same as on page 225, except that the roles of experimental condition (PROTEST) and beliefs about sex discrimination (SEXISM) are reversed merely by assigning SEXISM to X and PROTEST to M. In SPSS, the command is

```
process vars=protest liking sexism/y=liking/x=sexism/m=protest/model=1
    /plot=1.
```

In SAS, use

```
%process (data=protest,vars=protest liking sexism,y=liking,x=sexism,
    m=protest,model=1,plot=1);
```

```
%process (data=protest,vars=protest liking sexism,y=liking,x=sexism,m=protest,model=1,plot=1);

                              Model =      1
                              Y      =     LIKING
                              X      =     SEXISM
                              M      =     PROTEST

                             Sample size:
                                 129

****************************************************************************

                             Outcome: LIKING

                             Model Summary
                R         R-sq        F          df1        df2          p
             0.3654     0.1335     6.4190     3.0000   125.0000     0.0004


                              Model
                     coeff        se          t          p         LLCI        ULCI
  constant         7.7062      1.0449      7.3750      0.0000      5.6382      9.7743
  PROTEST         -3.7727      1.2541     -3.0084      0.0032     -6.2546     -1.2907
  SEXISM          -0.4725      0.2038     -2.3184      0.0220     -0.8758     -0.0692
  INT_1            0.8336      0.2436      3.4224      0.0008      0.3515      1.3156

                             Interactions:


         INT_1    SEXISM    X     PROTEST

                R-square increase due to interactions(s):
                     R2-chng       F          df1        df2          p
         INT_1       0.0812    11.7126      1.0000   125.0000     0.0008

****************************************************************************

           Conditional effect of X on Y at values of the moderator(s)
      PROTEST    Effect        se          t          p         LLCI        ULCI

       0.0000   -0.4725      0.2038     -2.3184      0.0220     -0.8758     -0.0692
       1.0000    0.3611      0.1334      2.7071      0.0077      0.0971      0.6250

  Values for quantitative moderators are the mean and plus/minus one SD from mean

****************************************************************************

              Data for visualizing conditional effect of X on Y
                        SEXISM        PROTEST          yhat
                        4.3332        0.0000         5.6588
                        5.1170        0.0000         5.2885
                        5.9007        0.0000         4.9182
                        4.3332        1.0000         5.4981
                        5.1170        1.0000         5.7811
                        5.9007        1.0000         6.0641

*************************** ANALYSIS NOTES AND WARNINGS ***************************

          Level of confidence for all confidence intervals in output:
                                                   95.0000
```

FIGURE 8.2. Output from the PROCESS procedure for SAS for a simple moderation analysis of the protest and sex discrimination study.

The output from PROCESS for SAS can be found in Figure 8.2. A summary of the model can found in Table 8.1. The best fitting OLS regression model is

$$\hat{Y} = 7.706 - 0.473X - 3.773M + 0.834XM$$

The regression coefficient for XM is $b_3 = 0.834$ and is statistically different from zero, $t(125) = 3.422, p = .008$. Thus, the effect of beliefs about the pervasiveness of sex discrimination on evaluation of Catherine depends on whether or not she chose to protest the sex discrimination. Also provided by this analysis is the conditional effect of sexism beliefs on her evaluation among those assigned to the no-protest condition. This is b_1 and it is statistically different from zero. Finally, the analysis also yields the conditional effect of her decision to protest or not on liking among those scoring zero on the Modern Sexism Scale. This is b_2, but along with its test of significance, it is substantively meaningless because zero is outside of the range of measurement of X. Scores on the Modern Sexism Scale, as constructed in this study, cannot be less than one because that is the lower bounds of the measurement scale.

This model should look familiar to you because it is exactly the same model estimated in the analysis presented in Chapter 7 (see Table 7.4, model 3). The only difference between these two analyses and their corresponding models is how the question is framed, which variable is construed as the focal predictor and which is the moderator, and how these variables are symbolically labeled as X and M. In the analysis in Chapter 7, the focal predictor was a dichotomous variable coding whether Catherine protested or not (labeled X then, but M now), whereas in this analysis, the focal predictor is a continuous variable placing each person's beliefs about the pervasiveness of sex discrimination on a continuum (labeled M then, but X now), with the moderator being a dichotomous variable coding experimental condition.

So this example illustrates the symmetry property of interactions introduced in section 7.1. In a regression model of the form in equation 8.1, b_3 estimates both the moderation of X effect on Y by M and M's effect on Y by X. Rejection of the null hypothesis that $_Tb_3 = 0$ allows for either claim, with how the claim is made and the interaction substantively interpreted depending on which variable is construed as the focal predictor and which is the moderator.

Visualizing and Probing the Interaction

Because this is exactly the same model estimated in Chapter 7, the procedure described in section 7.3 can be used to generate a visual depiction of

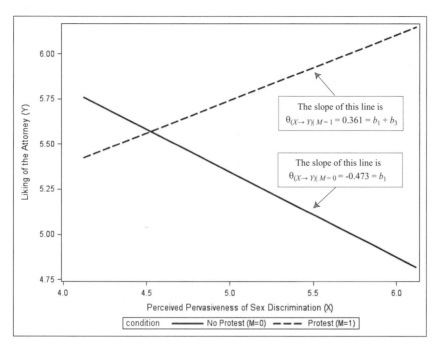

FIGURE 8.3. A visual representation of the moderation of the effect of the beliefs in the pervasiveness of sex discrimination in society (*X*) on liking (*Y*) by the lawyer's decision to protest or not (*M*).

the model. Naturally, because the model is the same, so too is its visual representation (see Figure 8.3).

Recall in Chapter 7 that interpretation of this model was based on the difference between points on the two lines at various values of sex discrimination beliefs. However, now that experimental condition is the moderator rather than the focal predictor, our interpretation of the model focuses on the slopes of the two lines. As can be seen, the slope linking beliefs in the pervasiveness of sex discrimination and liking of Catherine is positive among those told she protested, but negative among those told she did not. Among those told she protested, Catherine was liked more by those who believe sex discrimination is relatively more pervasive. But among those told she did not protest, Catherine was liked more by those who believe sex discrimination is relatively *less* pervasive.

The slopes of these lines can be quantified by formally probing the interaction. When the moderator is dichotomous, there is only one option. Using the pick-a-point approach, we can estimate the conditional effect of the focal predictor *X* on *Y* for the two values of moderator *M*. Using the same mathematics introduced in section 7.1, equation 8.1 can be rewritten as

$$Y = i_1 + \theta_{X \to Y} X + b_2 M + e_Y$$

where

$$\theta_{X \to Y} = b_1 + b_3 M \tag{8.2}$$

Plugging the two values of M representing each experimental condition into equation 8.2 yields the two conditional effects of X. That is, among those told Catherine did not protest ($M = 0$),

$$\theta_{(X \to Y)|M=0} = b_1 + b_3(0) = b_1 = -0.473$$

and among those told she protested,

$$\theta_{(X \to Y)|M=1} = b_1 + b_3(1) = b_1 + b_3 = -0.473 + 0.834 = 0.361$$

So between two people told she did not protest and who differ by one unit in their beliefs about sex discrimination, the person higher in those beliefs is estimated to like Catherine 0.473 units less on average. But among those told she did protest, the person one unit higher in such beliefs is estimated to like her 0.361 units more on average. These two conditional effects correspond to the slopes of the lines in Figure 8.3.

Probing an interaction typically involves more than merely quantifying the conditional effect of X as a function of M. In addition to estimating these conditional effects, an inferential test is usually conducted to determine whether the conditional effect of X for a given value of M is statistically different from zero. Equation 7.12 could be used to estimate the standard error of these two conditional effects, and then a p-value derived based on the $t(df_{residual})$ distribution. However, this is a lot of work and subject to error in hand computation.

A much easier approach is to recognize that the regression model already gives us an estimate of the conditional effect of X on Y when $M = 0$ as well as a test of the null hypothesis that $_T b_1 = 0$. Notice in the PROCESS output in Figure 8.2 that $b_1 = -0.473 = \theta_{(X \to Y)|M=0}$, $t(125) = -2.318, p = .022$, with a 95% confidence interval between -0.876 and -0.069. Because $M = 0$ corresponds to the group of participants told Catherine did not protest, we can conclude that among those told she did not protest, the relationship between beliefs in the pervasiveness of sex discrimination and how she was evaluated is not only negative but statistically different from zero.

So by coding one of the groups 0 when the moderator is dichotomous, the regression coefficient for X estimates the conditional effect of X on Y in the group coded 0, and a test of significance is available right in the regression output. But the regression model does not provide a test of significance of the conditional effect of X when $M = 1$, which is needed to complete the probing process in this analysis. We do know from these mathematics that this conditional effect is $b_1 + b_3 = 0.361$. But we don't have a test of significance or an interval estimate for this conditional effect. Fortunately, this is easy to generate by exploiting your understanding of the interpretation of the regression coefficients in a moderation model. In equation 8.1, b_1 estimates the effect of X on Y when $M = 0$, which corresponds to the conditional effect of beliefs among those told Catherine did not protest. But the decision to code the protest group $M = 1$ and the no-protest group $M = 0$ was totally arbitrary. By recoding the groups such that the protest group is coded 0 and the no-protest group coded 1, b_1 in equation 8.1 will then estimate the conditional effect of beliefs on evaluation among those told Catherine did protest. The SPSS code below accomplishes this.

```
compute protestp = 1-protest.
compute proxsex=protestp*sexism.
regression/dep=liking/method=enter sexism protestp proxsex.
```

The equivalent code in SAS is

```
data protest;set protest;protestp=1-protest;proxsex=protestp*sexism;run;
proc reg data=protest;model liking=sexism protestp proxsex;run;
```

The first thing this program does is reverse the coding of experimental condition, such that 0 becomes 1 and 1 becomes 0, held in a new variable named PROTESTP and denoted M' below. After this reverse coding, this new variable holding reverse-coded M is multiplied by X to produce the necessary product. Finally,

$$Y = i_1 + b_1 X + b_2 M' + b_3 XM' + e_Y$$

is estimated, which is equivalent to equation 8.1 but substituting M' for M, where $M' = 1 - M$. The resulting model is

$$\hat{Y} = 3.934 + 0.361X + 3.773M' - 0.834XM'$$

In this model, b_1 is the effect of X on Y when $M' = 0$, but this corresponds to the effect of X on Y when $M = 1$, because $M' = 0$ when $M = 1$. Notice that $b_1 = 0.361$, which is the conditional effect of X on Y when $M = 1$, just as calculated by hand earlier. That is, in this model, $b_1 = \theta_{(X \to Y)|M'=0} =$

$\theta_{(X \to Y)|M=1}$. A test of significance is also provided in the regression output [$t(125) = 2.707, p = .008$]. A confidence interval can be calculated in the usual way (see equation 2.10), or by requesting it in the SPSS Regression or SAS PROC REG command. Doing so yields a 95% confidence interval between 0.097 and 0.625. So we can claim that among those told Catherine protested, the relationship between beliefs about the pervasiveness of sex discrimination in society and how much she was liked is positive and statistically different from zero.

Albeit reasonably easy to do, not even this simple procedure is necessary when you use PROCESS, as PROCESS automatically implements the pick-a-point procedure whether you ask for it or not. It recognizes that M is a dichotomous moderator without having to be told, because when it scans the data, it finds only two values for the variable listed in **m=**. Thus, it estimates the conditional effect of X for the two values of the moderator coded in M. This implementation of the pick-a-point procedure can be found at the bottom of Figure 8.2 in the section of output labeled "Conditional effect of X on Y at values of the moderator(s)." By default, it provides the conditional effects of X when (in this case) $M = 0$ and $M = 1$, as well as standard errors, t-ratios, p-values, and confidence intervals.

8.2   Interaction between Two Quantitative Variables

Both examples of moderation analysis thus far have illustrated how to test a moderation hypothesis involving a dichotomous variable in the model. In the first example in section 7.2, the dichotomous variable was the focal predictor (whether the lawyer protested the discrimination or not) and the moderator was a quantitative dimension (participants' beliefs about the pervasiveness of sex discrimination in society). The roles of these two variables were reversed in section 8.1, with experimental condition being the moderator and sex discrimination beliefs as the focal predictor. The second example illustrated the generality of the mathematics of moderation analysis introduced at the beginning of Chapter 7. In this section I further demonstrate the generality of this procedure by showing how it is applied to testing moderation involving two quantitative variables. As you will see, no modifications to the procedure are required.

Recall the global climate change data used in the review of multiple regression in Chapters 2 and 3. In that study, participants were asked about their support for various policies and actions the federal government could implement to help mitigate climate change. The analysis described in Chapter 3 demonstrated that people who reported feeling more negative emotions about climate change were more supportive of government action, even after accounting for individual differences in positive emotions, political ideology, age, and sex. Though not discussed in these terms then, this model imposed the constraint that any effect of negative emotions was independent of all other variables in the model. Such a constraint may not be realistic. At a minimum, it is an assumption that can at least be tested. In this example of moderation analysis, we determine whether the effect of negative emotions on support for government action differs among people of different ages. Age is a quantitative variable ranging between 17 and 87 years in the data, and we will ask whether there is any linear association between age and the effect of negative emotions on support for government action. The answer to this question will be derived while controlling for political ideology, sex, and positive emotions.

A conceptual representation of the model can be found in Figure 8.4, panel A, which illustrates that negative emotions is the focal predictor X and age is the moderator M. In the form of a linear regression equation, the model is

$$Y = i_1 + b_1X + b_2M + b_3XM + b_4C_1 + b_5C_2 + b_6C_3 + e_Y \qquad (8.3)$$

where X is negative emotions about global climate change, M is age, and C_1, C_2, and C_3 are positive emotions, ideology, and sex, respectively. Evidence that b_3 is statistically different from zero would provide evidence that the effect of negative emotions on support for government action is moderated by age.

Although we could estimate this model in exactly this form, this is not exactly the model that will be estimated and interpreted in this example. In this model, b_3 does indeed estimate the moderation of X's effect by M, and the test of significance for b_3 will be a legitimate test of interaction. But this model will also generate two regression coefficients that have no meaningful interpretation. As parameterized here, recall that b_1 estimates the effect of X on Y when $M = 0$. In this example, M is age, meaning that b_1 quantifies how much two cases that differ by one unit in their negative emotions about global climate change but who are *0 years old* are estimated to differ in support for government action. This would be nonsensical, of course. Although in principle one could have an age of zero, no newborns participated in this study. The youngest person in the sample is 18 years old. By the same reasoning, b_2 quantifies how much two cases that differ by 1 year in age but measure zero in their negative emotions about climate change are estimated to differ in their support for government action. Zero is outside of the bounds of measurement of negative emotions, so b_2 and its test of significance will also be meaningless.

As discussed later in Chapter 9, what I do here is not at all necessary given that we are primarily interested in the interaction between X and M.

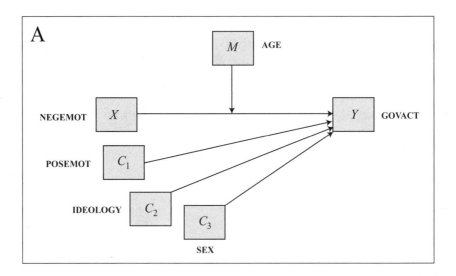

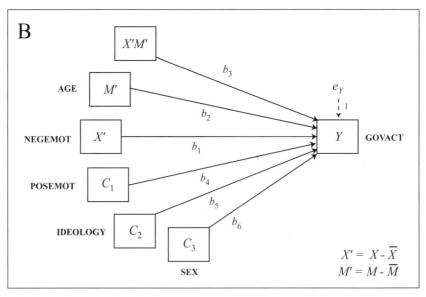

FIGURE 8.4. The moderation of negative emotions about climate change on support for government action by age with various covariates, depicted as a conceptual diagram (panel A) and a statistical diagram (panel B).

Nevertheless, I reparameterize the model by mean centering X and M so that b_1 and b_2 will estimate effects that are meaningful and interpretable, even though these coefficients are not the focus of this analysis. Thus, rather than using X and M in equation 8.3, I will put X' and M' in their place, where $X' = X - \overline{X}$ and $M' = M - \overline{M}$. As a result, b_1 will estimate the effect of X when $M = \overline{M}$ and b_2 will estimate the effect of M when $X = \overline{X}$. Thus, the model actually estimated and interpreted in this section is

$$Y = i_1 + b_1 X' + b_2 M' + b_3 X' M' + b_4 C_1 + b_5 C_2 + b_6 C_3 + e_Y$$

or, equivalently,

$$Y = i_1 + b_1(X - \overline{X}) + b_2(M - \overline{M}) + b_3(X - \overline{X})(M - \overline{M}) + b_4 C_1 + b_5 C_2 + b_6 C_3 + e_Y$$

and is represented in the form of a statistical diagram in Figure 8.4, panel B.

The SPSS code below estimates the model. The first line mean centers X by subtracting the sample mean negative emotions ($\overline{X} = 3.558$) from all measurements of negative emotions and stores the result in a new variable named NEGEMOTC. The second line mean centers M by subtracting the sample mean age ($\overline{M} = 49.536$) from the ages of all cases in the data and stores the result in a new variable named AGEC. The third line calculates the product of mean-centered X and M prior to execution of the regression command.

```
compute negemotc=negemot-3.558.
compute agec=age-49.536.
compute negage=negemotc*agec.
regression/dep=govact/method=enter negemotc agec negage posemot
    ideology sex.
```

Comparable code for SAS is

```
data glbwarm;set glbwarm;negemotc=negemot-3.558;
agec=age-49.536;negage=negemotc*agec;run;
proc reg data=glbwarm;model govact=negemotc agec negage posemot
    ideology sex;run;
```

The best fitting regression model along with standard errors and p-values for all coefficients can be found in Table 8.2. The model is

$$\hat{Y} = 5.532 + 0.433X' - 0.001M' + 0.006X'M' - 0.021C_1 - 0.212C_2 - 0.011C_3$$

TABLE 8.2. Results from a Regression Analysis Examining the Moderation of the Effect of Negative Emotional Responses to Global Climate Change on Support for Government Action by Age, Controlling for Positive Emotions, Political Ideology, and Sex

		Coeff.	SE	t	p
Intercept	i_1	5.532	0.146	37.906	< .001
Negative Emotions (X')	b_1	0.433	0.026	16.507	< .001
Age (M')	b_2	−0.001	0.002	−0.577	.564
Negative Emotions × Age ($X'M'$)	b_3	0.006	0.002	4.104	< .001
Positive Emotions (C_1)	b_4	−0.021	0.028	−0.768	.443
Political Ideology (C_2)	b_5	−0.212	0.027	−7.883	< .001
Sex (C_3)	b_6	−0.011	0.076	−0.147	.883

$$R^2 = 0.401, MSE = 1.117$$
$$F(6, 808) = 90.080, p < .001$$

Of interest is the regression coefficient for the product of age and negative emotions, which is positive and statistically significant, $b_3 = 0.006, t(808) = 4.104, p < .001$, and accounts for about 1.25% of the variance in support for government action (from the PROCESS output, discussed below). Thus, the effect of negative emotions on support for government action depends on age. Also statistically significant is the conditional effect of negative emotions. Among people average in age (because age was mean centered in this analysis) but equal in positive emotions, political ideology, and sex (because these are statistically being held constant) two people who differ by one unit in their negative emotional responses to global climate change are estimated to differ by $b_1 = 0.433$ units in their support for government action. Finally, holding age, positive emotions, negative emotions, and sex constant, people who are more politically conservative are less supportive of government action to mitigate global climate change ($b_5 = −0.212, p < .001$).

PROCESS provides a lot more information than SPSS or SAS's regression procedure. In addition to estimating the model and providing the coefficients, standard errors, and so forth, it also automatically estimates the conditional effects of negative emotions at various values of age, can generate data to help visualize the interaction, will implement the Johnson–Neyman technique for further probing the interaction, calculates the proportion of variance in the outcome attributable to the interaction, and can even center the focal predictor and moderator variables if you ask it to. The PROCESS command in SPSS that does all these things is

```
process vars=govact negemot age posemot ideology sex/y=govact/x=negemot/m=age/
   model=1/center=1/quantile=1/jn=1/plot=1.

Model = 1
   Y = govact
   X = negemot
   M = age

Statistical Controls:
CONTROL= posemot  ideology sex

Sample size
      815

**************************************************************************
Outcome: govact

Model Summary
          R       R-sq        F        df1       df2         p
      .6331      .4008    90.0798   6.0000  808.0000     .0000

Model
              coeff       se         t         p       LLCI      ULCI
constant     5.5322     .1459   37.9057     .0000     5.2458    5.8187
age          -.0014     .0023    -.5769     .5642     -.0060     .0033
negemot       .4332     .0262   16.5067     .0000      .3817     .4847
int_1         .0063     .0015    4.1035     .0000      .0033     .0094
posemot      -.0214     .0279    -.7676     .4430     -.0762     .0334
ideology     -.2115     .0268   -7.8827     .0000     -.2642    -.1588
sex          -.0112     .0760    -.1472     .8830     -.1604     .1380

Interactions:

 int_1    negemot     X      age

R-square increase due to interaction(s):
        R2-chng        F        df1       df2         p
int_1     .0125    16.8391    1.0000  808.0000     .0000

**************************************************************************

Conditional effect of X on Y at values of the moderator(s):
       age     Effect      se         t         p       LLCI      ULCI
  -22.5362      .2905     .0450    6.4539     .0000      .2022     .3789
  -13.5362      .3475     .0347   10.0223     .0000      .2794     .4155
    1.4638      .4425     .0262   16.8999     .0000      .3911     .4938
   13.4638      .5184     .0323   16.0506     .0000      .4550     .5818
   20.4638      .5627     .0396   14.2090     .0000      .4850     .6405

Values for quantitative moderators are 10th, 25th, 50th, 75th, and 90th percentiles

******************** JOHNSON-NEYMAN TECHNIQUE *************************

There are no statistical significance transition points within the observed
range of the moderator

**************************************************************************

Data for visualizing conditional effect of X of Y
   negemot        age       yhat
   -2.2280    -22.5362     3.9792
   -1.2280    -22.5362     4.2697
     .1120    -22.5362     4.6590
    1.4420    -22.5362     5.0454
    2.1120    -22.5362     5.2401
   -2.2280    -13.5362     3.8401
   -1.2280    -13.5362     4.1876
     .1120    -13.5362     4.6532
```

(continued)

FIGURE 8.5. Output from the PROCESS procedure for SPSS for a simple moderation analysis of the global climate change data.

```
          1.4420   -13.5362    5.1154
          2.1120   -13.5362    5.3482
         -2.2280     1.4638    3.6082
         -1.2280     1.4638    4.0507
           .1120     1.4638    4.6436
          1.4420     1.4638    5.2320
          2.1120     1.4638    5.5285
         -2.2280    13.4638    3.4227
         -1.2280    13.4638    3.9411
           .1120    13.4638    4.6358
          1.4420    13.4638    5.3253
          2.1120    13.4638    5.6726
         -2.2280    20.4638    3.3145
         -1.2280    20.4638    3.8772
           .1120    20.4638    4.6313
          1.4420    20.4638    5.3797
          2.1120    20.4638    5.7568

    Estimates in this table are based on setting covariates to their sample means

    ******************** ANALYSIS NOTES AND WARNINGS *************************

    Level of confidence for all confidence intervals in output:
      95.00

    NOTE: The following variables were mean centered prior to analysis:
      negemot  age

    ------ END MATRIX -----
```

FIGURE 8.5 continued.

```
process vars=govact negemot age posemot ideology sex/y=govact/x=negemot
   /m=age/model=1/center=1/quantile=1/jn=1/plot=1.
```

or in SAS,

```
%process (data=glbwarm,vars=govact negemot age posemot ideology sex,
   y=govact,x=negemot,m=age,model=1,center=1,quantile=1,jn=1,plot=1);
```

Output from the SPSS version can be found in Figure 8.5. The **center** option is the only thing new in this command not already seen in prior examples. Specifying **center=1** in the PROCESS command line tells PROCESS to mean center X and M. As discussed in greater detail in Chapter 9, centering is not required, but if you want to mean center the focal predictor and the moderator prior to estimating a model with an interaction, PROCESS will do it for you behind the scenes. For any model PROCESS estimates, use of this option will mean center *all* variables used in the construction of a product while leaving other variables in their original metric. All output should be interpreted in terms of the centered metric for effects involving variables that were centered, or in the original metric for variables that were not. Of course, you could mean center any subset of variables you want to outside of PROCESS if you preferred, and then enter the centered variables in the **vars=** list. Doing so would eliminate the need to use the **center** option.

Visualizing and Probing the Interaction

A visual representation of the interaction can be generated using the same procedure described in section 7.3, but because this model involves covariates, an additional step is required. First, select combinations of X and M to be included in the interaction plot. It doesn't matter too much which values you select so long as they are within the range of your data. You could choose various percentiles of the distribution, the minimum and maximum value, plus and minus one standard deviation from the sample mean, or whatever you want. If you plan on using the pick-a-point approach for probing the interaction, it makes most sense to choose values of M corresponding to those values at which you intend to formally estimate (or have already estimated) the conditional effect of X. Finally, remember that if you mean centered X and M, the values of X and M you choose should be based on the mean-centered metric rather than on the original metric of X and M.

Next, using the best fitting regression model, generate $\hat{Y}$ for the combinations of X and M that you have chosen. However, because the model contains three covariates, these need to be set to a value as well. Although you could choose any values you want to plug into the model along with X and M, convention is to use the means of the covariates. In this example, the means for C_1, C_2, and C_3 are 3.132, 4.083, and 0.488, respectively. Thus, the equation for generating $\hat{Y}$ for values of X and M when the covariates are set to their sample means is

$$\begin{aligned} \hat{Y} \;=\; & 5.532 + 0.433X' - 0.001M' + 0.006X'M' - 0.021(3.132) \\ & - 0.212(4.083) - 0.011(0.488) \end{aligned}$$

which simplifies to

$$\hat{Y} = 4.595 + 0.433X' - 0.001M' + 0.006X'M'$$

The values plugged into the model for the covariates end up merely adding or subtracting from the regression constant, depending on the signs of the regression coefficients for the covariates. This will have the effect of moving the plot up or down the Y-axis. Although it seems counterintuitive, you *can* use the sample mean for dichotomous covariates. If a dichotomous variable is coded zero and one, then the sample mean is the proportion of the cases in the group coded one. But using the mean works regardless of how the groups are coded, even if the mean is itself meaningless.

Finally, once you have values of $\hat{Y}$ generated for various values of X and M, then you will have a small dataset containing X, M, and $\hat{Y}$, which could be given to whatever graphing program you prefer in order to generate the interaction plot. In SPSS or SAS, the code in section 7.3 could be used. If you used mean centered predictors, then the plot will show X and M in their mean-centered metric, because these are the values you used to generate $\hat{Y}$. However, these are the same values of $\hat{Y}$ you would get had you not mean centered X and M, so you could at this point add $\overline{X}$ and $\overline{M}$ back into the values of X and M in the data you are using to generate the plot. Doing so will produce a plot in terms of the uncentered metric of X and M.

PROCESS takes much of the burden out of this procedure. When the **plot** option is used, PROCESS generates a table of estimates of Y for various combinations of the focal predictor and moderator while setting all covariates to their sample means. This table could then be used as input into any program you prefer to generate graphs. Alternatively, the table PROCESS generates can be cut and pasted into an SPSS or SAS program, which will generate the plot for you. In SPSS, the commands below can be used, with the data coming from the table generated by PROCESS (see the bottom of Figure 8.5 under the heading "Data for visualizing conditional effect of X on Y").

```
data list free/negemot age govact.
begin data.
 -2.2280    -22.5362    3.9792
 -1.2280    -22.5362    4.2697
  0.1120    -22.5362    4.6590
  1.4420    -22.5362    5.0454
  2.1120    -22.5362    5.2401
 -2.2280    -13.5362    3.8401
 -1.2280    -13.5362    4.1876

    .          .          .

   (from PROCESS PLOT table)

    .          .          .

  1.4420     13.4638    5.3253
  2.1120     13.4638    5.6726
 -2.2280     20.4638    3.3145
 -1.2280     20.4638    3.8772
  0.1120     20.4638    4.6313
```

```
     1.4420      20.4638     5.3797
     2.1120      20.4638     5.7568
end data.
compute age=age+49.536.
compute negemot=negemot+3.558.
graph/scatterplot=negemot with govact by age.
```

Notice that the **compute** statements in the last couple of lines add $\overline{X}$ and $\overline{M}$ back into the X and M data used to produce the plot, thereby resulting in a plot that shows X and M in their original, uncentered metric. I personally find doing so yields a plot that is somewhat easier to interpret because then I don't have to do the mental conversion of the centered M back into the original metric when staring at the figure and contemplating what it means.

The corresponding commands in SAS are

```
data;input negemot age govact;
age=age+49.536;
negemot=negemot+3.558;
datalines;
-2.2280     -22.5362     3.9792
-1.2280     -22.5362     4.2697
 0.1120     -22.5362     4.6590
 1.4420     -22.5362     5.0454
 2.1120     -22.5362     5.2401
-2.2280     -13.5362     3.8401
-1.2280     -13.5362     4.1876

   .            .           .
   (from PROCESS PLOT table)
   .            .           .

 1.4420      13.4638     5.3253
 2.1120      13.4638     5.6726
-2.2280      20.4638     3.3145
-1.2280      20.4638     3.8772
 0.1120      20.4638     4.6313
 1.4420      20.4638     5.3797
 2.1120      20.4638     5.7568
run;
proc sgplot;reg x=negemot y=govact/group=age
nomarkers lineattrs=(color=black);
```

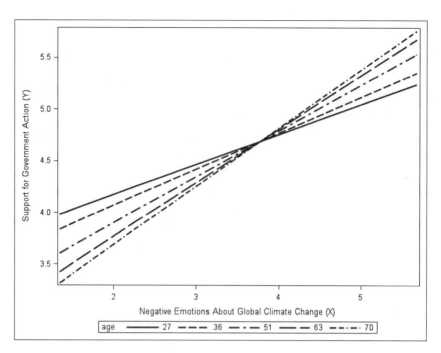

FIGURE 8.6. A visual representation of the moderation of the effect of negative emotions about global climate change (*X*) on support for government action (*Y*) by age (*M*).

```
xaxis label='Negative Emotions About Global Climate Change (X)';
yaxis label='Support for Government Action (Y)';run;
```

The interaction plot produced by the SAS code above is found in Figure 8.6. Because the **quantile** option was used in PROCESS when the data for this plot were generated, the slopes of the lines correspond to the conditional effects of negative emotions on support for government action for values of age corresponding to the 10th, 25th, 50th, 75th, and 90th percentiles of the distribution. As can be seen, the effect of negative emotions about global climate change on support for government action to mitigate climate change appears to be consistently positive, regardless of age. But the slope linking negative emotions to support for government action is more steep among those older in sample. That is, the effect of negative emotions appears to be larger among the relatively older than among the relatively younger.

The slopes of the lines in Figure 8.6 are $\theta_{X \rightarrow Y}$ for arbitrarily chosen values of *M*. These conditional effects of *X*, sometimes called "simple slopes," can be formally quantified and an inferential test conducted using the pick-a-point approach. As described in Chapter 7, the regression model

$$Y = i_1 + b_1 X' + b_2 M' + b_3 X' M' + b_4 C_1 + b_5 C_2 + b_6 C_3 + e_Y$$

can be written in equivalent form as

$$Y = i_1 + (b_1 + b_3 M') X' + b_2 M' + b_4 C_1 + b_5 C_2 + b_6 C_3 + e_Y$$

or

$$Y = i_1 + \theta_{X \to Y} X' + b_2 M' + b_4 C_1 + b_5 C_2 + b_6 C_3 + e_Y$$

where $\theta_{X \to Y} = b_1 + b_3 M'$. In terms of the regression coefficients from the model, $\theta_{X \to Y} = 0.433 + 0.006 M'$. Plugging in various values of M' produces the conditional effect of X at those values of M'. It also generates the conditional effects for values of M in its original metric corresponding to those mean-centered values because the conditional effect of X will not be dependent on whether the model is estimated based on mean-centered M or M in its original metric. However M' must be used in this function because the function was estimated using mean-centered M. You can use any values of M' you choose, such as the mean and plus and minus one standard deviation from the mean, various percentiles in the distribution, or anything else. Regardless of the choice, once $\theta_{X \to Y}$ is generated for those values, a standard error can be derived using equation 7.12 and a p-value calculated based on the $t(df_{residual})$ distribution.

PROCESS does all these tedious computations for you, the results of which are found in the section of output labeled "Conditional effect of X on Y at values of the moderator(s)." Because the **quantile** option was used, PROCESS implements the pick-a-point approach using values of mean centered age (because **center** option was used) which define the 10th, 25th, 50th, 75th, and 90th percentiles. As can be seen in Figure 8.5, these correspond to mean-centered values of age of −22.536, −13.536, 1.464, 13.464, and 20.464 or, in terms of uncentered ages, 27, 36, 51, 63, and 70 years old (calculated by adding $\overline{M} = 49.536$ to the centered ages). PROCESS calculates the conditional effects of negative emotions on support for government action at these values of age (from $0.433 + 0.006 M'$) for you. They are 0.291, 0.348, 0.443, 0.518, and 0.563, respectively, and as can be seen, all are statistically significant from zero with p-values less than .0001.

The Johnson–Neyman technique described in section 7.4 can be used here because the moderator variable is a quantitative dimension. Doing so eliminates the need to arbitrarily select values of the moderator at which to probe the interaction. But in these data, and according to PROCESS's implementation of the JN technique (requested with the **jn** option), there are

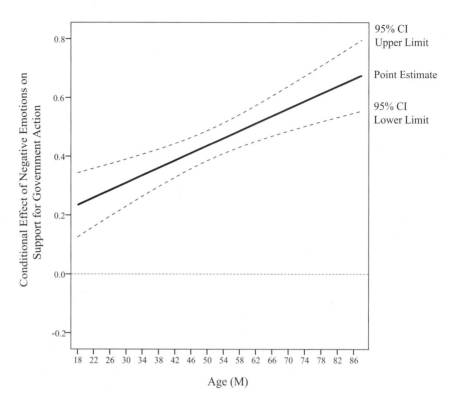

FIGURE 8.7. The conditional effect of the negative emotions about global climate change (X) on support for government action ($\theta_{X \to Y}$) as a function of age (M).

no points in the distribution of age where the conditional effect of negative emotions on support for government action transitions between statistically significant and not significant at the $\alpha = 0.05$ level of significance. This is because, as the pick-a-point section of the PROCESS output suggests, the effect of negative emotions is significantly positive for *any* value of age in the data.

If that isn't apparent to you, Figure 8.7 will make it clearer. In this figure, the solid black line is $\theta_{X \to Y}$, the conditional effect of X, defined by the function $b_1 + b_3 M'$, or $0.433 + 0.006M'$ based on this analysis.[1] The dotted lines are the upper and lower bounds of a 95% confidence interval for $_T\theta_{(X \to Y)|M}$ (approximately plus and minus two standard errors from $\theta_{X \to Y}$, using the standard error estimator in equation 7.12). Unlike in Figure 7.8, where the confidence interval straddled zero for some values of

[1] This function for $\theta_{X \to Y}$ requires the use of mean-centered M for generating $\theta_{(X \to Y)|M}$ because the model coefficients were estimated using mean-centered M. But the plot shows M in its original metric. This is acceptable because the conditional effect of X is same regardless of whether mean centered M or M in its original metric is used when the model is estimated.

the moderator but not others, in these data the confidence interval is always above zero. In other words, at any value of age you can choose, negative emotion's effect is significantly positive because the confidence interval is entirely above zero for all values of age. Thus, the region of significance for X is the entire distribution of M.

The visual depiction of the moderation as presented in Figure 8.7 can be a handy alternative relative to the more traditional plot in Figure 8.6. Figure 8.7 provides not only a point estimate of $\theta_{X \to Y}$ for any value of the moderator you can choose, but it also provides an inferential test at any chosen value in the form of a confidence interval and thus conveys much more information than does Figure 8.6.

Figure 8.7 was generated in SPSS using the code below, and then edited using SPSS's graphics editing features. This code could easily be tailored to your own data and model.

```
data list free/age.
begin data.
18 20 22 24 26 28 30 32 34 36 38 40 42 44 46 48 50 52
54 56 58 60 62 64 66 68 70 72 74 76 78 80 82 84 86 88
end data.
compute agemc=age-49.536.
compute b1=0.4332.
compute b3=0.0063.
compute seb1=0.0262.
compute seb3=0.0015.
compute covb1b3=-.0000029.
compute theta=b1+b3*agemc.
compute tcrit=1.963.
compute se=sqrt((seb1*seb1)+(2*agemc*covb1b3)+(agemc*agemc*seb3*seb3)).
compute llci=theta-tcrit*se.
compute ulci=theta+tcrit*se.
graph/scatter(overlay)=age age age WITH llci ulci theta (pair).
```

In SAS, the code below will produce a similar figure but will require much less editing.

```
data;input age @@;
agemc=age-49.536;b1=0.4332;b3=0.0063;
seb1=0.0262;seb3=0.0015;covb1b3=-.0000029;
theta=b1+b3*agemc;tcrit=1.963;
```

```
se=sqrt((seb1*seb1)+(2*agemc*covb1b3)+(agemc*agemc*seb3*seb3));
llci=theta-tcrit*se;
ulci=theta+tcrit*se;
datalines;
18 20 22 24 26 28 30 32 34 36 38 40 42 44 46 48 50 52
54 56 58 60 62 64 66 68 70 72 74 76 78 80 82 84 86 88
run;
proc sgplot;
series x=age y=ulci/curvelabel = '95% upper limit' lineattrs=(color=red
    pattern=ShortDash);
series x=age y=theta/curvelabel = 'point estimate' lineattrs=(color=black
    pattern=Solid);
series x=age y=llci/curvelabel = '95% lower limit' lineattrs=(color=red
    pattern=ShortDash);
xaxis label = 'Age';
yaxis label = 'Conditional effect of negative emotions';
refline 0/axis=y transparency=0.5;
run;
```

8.3 Hierarchical versus Simultaneous Entry

Many investigators test a moderation hypothesis in regression analysis using a method that on the surface seems different than the procedure described thus far. This alternative approach is to build a regression model by adding the product of X and M to a model already containing X and M. This procedure is sometimes called *hierarchical regression* or *hierarchical variable entry*. The goal using this method is to determine whether allowing X's effect to be contingent on M produces a better model than one in which the effect of X is constrained to be unconditional on M. According to the logic of hierarchical entry, if the contingent model accounts for more of the variation in Y than the model that forces X's effect to be independent of M, then the better model is one in which M is allowed to moderate X's effect. Although this approach works, it is a widely believed myth that it is *necessary* to use this approach in order to test a moderation hypothesis.

To test whether M moderates the effect of X on Y using hierarchical regression, the model for Y is built in steps. In the first step, Y is estimated from X and M and any additional variables other than XM of interest, such as various covariates and so forth. Call the resulting model "model 1" and its squared multiple correlation R_1^2. In the second stage, XM is added to model 1 to generate "model 2" and its squared multiple correlation, R_2^2.

Under the null hypothesis that M does not linearly moderate the effect of X on Y, model 2 should not fit better than model 1. That is, if the null hypothesis is true, adding the product term will not produce a model that provides any new information about individual differences in Y not already provided by model 1. The difference in the squared multiple correlations, $\Delta R^2 = R_2^2 - R_1^2$, is a descriptive measure of how much better model 2 fits relative to model 1. This is sometimes called the incremental increase in R^2, or simply "change in R^2."

Because R^2 cannot go down when a variable is added to a model, $\Delta R^2 \geq 0$. Even if the null hypothesis is true, expect model 2 to fit better than model 1 from a purely descriptive standpoint, even if only slightly so, just by chance. In science, we must rule out chance as a plausible explanation for a research finding before advancing other explanations, so the question is not whether model 2 fits better—it will—but whether it fits better than one would expect by chance if the null hypothesis is true. To answer this question, a p-value is needed. The mechanics of the test as to whether model 2 fits better than model 1 more than can be explained by chance has already been spelled out in section 3.3, where inference about a set of predictors in a regression model was introduced. The difference in R^2 is converted to an F-ratio using equation 3.7, where $R_2^2 - R_1^2 = \Delta R^2$ and $m = 1$, and a p-value derived from the F distribution with 1 and $df_{residual}$ degrees of freedom.

I illustrate this procedure using the protest and sex discrimination study. In section 8.1 we asked whether Catherine's decision to protest the sex discrimination or not (M) moderated the effect beliefs about perceived pervasiveness of sex discrimination (X) on how she was perceived (Y). The answer was yes, but this answer was derived using a different approach in which X, M, and XM were simultaneously included in the regression model. Using the hierarchical entry method, the fit of a model estimating Y from X and M is first calculated. Doing so yields, $R_1^2 = 0.045$. When XM is added to this model, $R_2^2 = 0.133$, which means $\Delta R^2 = 0.133 - 0.052 = 0.081$. The residual degrees of freedom for model 2 is 125. Using either equation 3.7 or calculated more precisely using the SPSS or SAS code on page 77, $F(1, 125) = 11.713, p = .001$. The null hypothesis can be rejected. The effect of Catherine's decision to protest or not on how she is evaluated depends on beliefs about the pervasiveness of sex discrimination.

Although this hierarchical entry procedure works, it is not necessary, as it will produce the same decision as the test that $_T b_3 = 0$ when estimating a model of the form $\hat{Y} = i_1 + b_1 X + b_2 M + b_3 XM$. The F-ratio for ΔR^2 is equal to the square of b_3/se_{b_3} (that is, $F = t_{b_3}^2$) and the F and t values will have the same p-value. Indeed, observe from Figure 8.2, the t statistic for b_3 is

3.4224, which when squared yields $F = 11.713$. Thus, there is no need to conduct or report both tests, as they are mathematically identical and will always give the same answer.

The hierarchical entry method does give ΔR^2—the proportion of variance in Y that is uniquely accounted for by the moderation of X's effect by M. One could argue that this gives the hiearchical entry method some advantage if one wants to report the incremental improvement in fit. However, ΔR^2 can be obtained from most regression outputs if you ask for it without using hierarchical entry, because ΔR^2 is equal to the squared semi-partial correlation for XM. Most regression programs have the ability to print the semipartial correlations for each variable in the model. If your preferred program does not, it can be calculated from information provided from the regression model with X, M, and XM as predictors:

$$\Delta R^2 = \frac{t_{b_3}^2 (1 - R^2)}{df_{residual}}$$

Of course, no one wants to do these computations by hand, and most programs don't automatically produce the semipartial correlation (which then has to be squared, introducing human-generated rounding error into the estimate of ΔR^2). Understanding this, PROCESS was programmed to automatically produce ΔR^2 for the interaction for the simple moderation model in a section of the output labeled "R-square increase due to interaction," but without you having to actually build the model hierarchically. As can be seen in Figure 8.2, $\Delta R^2 = 0.081$, just as computed by calculating the two R^2 for each model and manually calculating their difference. PROCESS also gives the F-ratio and p-value for this change in R^2, but as just described, this provides no information not already contained in the t and p-value for b_3.

All this said, there are two circumstances in which one might choose to use hierarchical entry. First, sometimes it is convenient from the perspective of describing research results to first talk about the effect of X in unconditional terms as estimated and tested before, if necessary, qualifying that claim after the results of model estimation in the second step are described. Putting X, M, and XM in the model simultaneously yields an estimate of X's effect that is necessarily conditional on M. Second, if more than one parameter estimate is needed to quantify moderation of X's effect on Y, such as when M is multicategorical with k levels (see, e.g., Aiken & West, 1991; Cohen et al., 2003; Hayes, 2005; West, Aiken, & Krull, 1996, for a discussion of interaction involving a multicategorical variable), hierarchical entry is an easy way to test the simultaneous null hypothesis that the regression coefficients for all $k - 1$ product terms are equal to zero. There are other ways, however, as in SAS with the use of the "test" option in PROC REG (see page 77 for example code).

8.4 The Equivalence between Moderated Regression Analysis and a 2 × 2 Factorial Analysis of Variance

Some believe mistakenly that the method of analysis one uses plays an important role in whether one can infer cause–effect. For this reason, the logic goes, the method of choice for experimentalists is analysis of variance (ANOVA), because multiple regression is used only for correlational studies in which cause–effect cannot be established. I think it has already been shown that multiple regression is a legitimate statistical tool for the analysis of experimental data. Even more than just legitimate, analysis of variance is just a special case of multiple regression, so the belief that ANOVA should be the method of choice when cause–effect inferences are desired and sought out through experimentation is misplaced. Remember that inferences are products of mind, not mathematics. Statistical methods do not produce causal inferences. Our inferences stem from the interpretation of the results a statistical model generates and the manner in which the data are collected.

In this section, I show the equivalence between regression analysis with the product of X and M in the model along with X and M and a 2 × 2 factorial ANOVA, which is one of the more common forms of ANOVA used when analyzing data from experimental research. But I also warn by way of example that this equivalence is dependent on how X and M are coded. A failure to appreciate this important caveat can result in a misinterpretation of the coefficients in a regression analysis and a misreporting and misrepresentation of your findings.

We return to the study by Hayes and Reineke (2007) that began Chapter 7. In this study, 541 residents of the state of Ohio in the United States responded to a telephone survey conducted just after the 2004 federal election. This survey included a couple of questions gauging respondents' interest (on a 1 to 5 scale, with higher values representing greater interest) in viewing images of caskets containing the bodies of U.S. servicemen and women killed in action in Iraq returning to the United States for burial. Prior to this question, half of the respondents (randomly assigned) were told about the Bush administration's policy, which restricted journalist access to locations where such images can be recorded, whereas the other half were given no such information. The participants were also classified based on questions they were asked about who they voted for in the 2004 presidential election as either supporters of George W. Bush or supporters of his opponent, Senator John Kerry of Massachusetts.

The data file corresponding to this study is CASKETS, and it can be found at *www.afhayes.com*. The dependent variable is INTEREST. The other two variables pertinent to this analysis are codes holding which of the two policy information conditions a respondent was assigned to (POLICY, with 0 = no information given and 1 = policy information given) as well as whether or not the respondent was a Kerry supporter (KERRY = 1) or a Bush supporter (KERRY = 0). Using these data, we will determine whether there is evidence that the effect of providing information about the Bush administration policy differentially affected Bush and Kerry supporters with respect to their interest in viewing the casket images. Thus, policy information is the focal predictor X, and the candidate the respondent supported in the election is the moderator M. So both X and M are dichotomous.

The typical approach to answering this question is covered in almost every introductory statistics course. When both X and M are dichotomous variables and interest is in the interaction between X and M, factorial ANOVA is most commonly used. Using a factorial ANOVA, it is possible to estimate the *main* and *interactive* effects of X and M on Y. This is a 2×2 *between-participants* factorial ANOVA because there are two levels of each variable or *factor*, and participants provide data to one and only one cell of the design, with a *cell* defined as the combination of the two factors.

I assume that you are familiar with the mechanics of factorial ANOVA and thus do not discuss its theory or computation here. For details or to review, see most any introductory statistics book or a good book on the design and analysis of experiments (e.g., Keppel & Wickens, 2004). A 2×2 factorial ANOVA can be conducted in most any statistics program, including SPSS and SAS. For instance, in SPSS, the commands below produce Table 8.3 and the ANOVA summary table found in Table 8.4:

```
unianova interest BY policy kerry/emmeans=tables(policy)/emmeans=tables
    (kerry)/emmeans=tables(policy*kerry).
```

In SAS, try

```
proc glm data=caskets;class policy kerry;
model interest = policy kerry policy*kerry;
lsmeans policy kerry policy*kerry;run;
```

TABLE 8.3. Interest in Viewing Casket Images from the Hayes & Reineke (2007) Study

| | Information about Policy (X) | | |
Candidate Supported (M)	No	Yes	Marginal Means
Bush	$\overline{Y}_1 = 1.784$	$\overline{Y}_2 = 1.397$	$\overline{Y}_{12} = 1.590$
Kerry	$\overline{Y}_3 = 2.384$	$\overline{Y}_4 = 2.357$	$\overline{Y}_{34} = 2.370$
Marginal Means	$\overline{Y}_{13} = 2.084$	$\overline{Y}_{24} = 1.877$	

TABLE 8.4. Summary Table for a 2 × 2 Between-Participant Factorial ANOVA of the Caskets Data

Source	SS	df	MS	F	p
Policy Information (X)	5.759	1	5.759	5.394	.021
Candidate Supported (M)	82.110	1	82.110	76.906	< .001
Interaction $(X \times M)$	4.372	1	4.372	4.095	.044
Error	573.338	537	1.068		

As can be seen in Table 8.4, the main effect of policy information (X) is statistically significant, $F(1, 537) = 5.394, p = .021$. The estimate of the main effect of X can be calculated from Table 8.3 in one of two ways. First, it is the unweighted average simple effect of X. A *simple effect* is a mean difference conditioned on a row or column in the table. So the simple effect of policy information among Kerry supporters is $\overline{Y}_4 - \overline{Y}_3 = 2.357 - 2.384 = -0.027$, and the simple effect of policy information among Bush supporters is $\overline{Y}_2 - \overline{Y}_1 = 1.397 - 1.784 = -0.387$. Thus,

$$\text{Main effect of } X = \frac{(\overline{Y}_4 - \overline{Y}_3) + (\overline{Y}_2 - \overline{Y}_1)}{2} = \frac{-0.027 - 0.387}{2} = -0.207$$

Simple algebra shows that this main effect can also be written as the difference in the marginal means for X, where a *marginal mean* is the unweighted mean of cell means in a given row or column in the 2 × 2 table. For instance, from Table 8.3 the marginal mean for the policy information condition is $\overline{Y}_{24} = (\overline{Y}_2 + \overline{Y}_4)/2 = (1.397 + 2.357)/2 = 1.877$, and the marginal mean for the no policy information condition is $\overline{Y}_{13} = (\overline{Y}_1 + \overline{Y}_3)/2 = (1.784 + 2.384)/2 = 2.084$. The difference between these means is

$$\text{Main effect of } X = \frac{\overline{Y}_{24} - \overline{Y}_{13}}{2} = 1.877 - 2.084 = -0.207$$

This statistically significant main effect of -0.207 is interpreted to mean that participants given information about the policy expressed 0.207 units less interest in viewing the images than participants not given this information.

The main effect of candidate support is also statistically significant, $F(1, 537) = 76.906, p < .001$. This main effect corresponds to the unweighted average simple effect of candidate supported on interest in the images, or the difference between the marginal means of candidate supported. The simple effect of candidate supported among those given information about the policy is $\overline{Y}_4 - \overline{Y}_2 = 2.357 - 1.397 = 0.960$ and the simple effect of candidate supported among participants not given information about the policy is $\overline{Y}_3 - \overline{Y}_1 = 2.384 - 1.784 = 0.600$. Thus,

$$\text{Main effect of } M = \frac{(\overline{Y}_4 - \overline{Y}_2) + (\overline{Y}_3 - \overline{Y}_1)}{2} = \frac{0.960 + 0.600}{2} = 0.780$$

This is equivalent to the difference between the marginal means for who the candidate supported:

$$\text{Main effect of } M = \frac{\overline{Y}_{34} - \overline{Y}_{12}}{2} = 2.370 - 1.590 = 0.780$$

In words, Kerry supporters expressed 0.780 more interest, on average, in viewing the casket images than did Bush supporters.

The interaction between policy information and candidate supported is also statistically significant, $F(1, 537) = 4.095, p = .044$, which addresses the central question of interest. The effect of providing information about the policy on interest in the images was indeed moderated by who the participant supported in the 2004 election. According to the symmetry property of interactions, this can also be interpreted as evidence that the difference in interest in viewing the casket images between Kerry and Bush supporters depended on whether information about the policy was provided or not.

In a 2×2 factorial ANOVA, interaction or moderation is quantified as a difference in the simple effect of one variable between levels of the second. When candidate supported is construed as the moderator, this means that the simple effect of policy information among Kerry supporters is different than the simple effect of policy information among Bush supporters. The former simple effect is $\overline{Y}_4 - \overline{Y}_3 = 2.357 - 2.384 = -0.027$ and the latter simple effect is $\overline{Y}_2 - \overline{Y}_1 = 1.397 - 1.784 = -0.387$. Thus,

$$X \times M \text{ interaction} = (\overline{Y}_4 - \overline{Y}_3) - (\overline{Y}_2 - \overline{Y}_1) = -0.027 - (-0.387) = 0.360$$

This interaction can also be conceptualized with policy information as the moderator of differences between Kerry and Bush supporters in interest in viewing the casket images. In that case, the interaction means that the simple effect of candidate supported among those given information about the policy $(\overline{Y}_4 - \overline{Y}_2) = 2.357 - 1.397 = 0.960$ is different than the simple effect of candidate supported among those not given information about the policy $(\overline{Y}_3 - \overline{Y}_1) = 2.384 - 1.784 = 0.600$. That is,

$$X \times M \text{ interaction} = (\overline{Y}_4 - \overline{Y}_2) - (\overline{Y}_3 - \overline{Y}_1) = 0.960 - 0.600 = 0.360$$

Simple Effects Parameterization

A 2×2 factorial analysis of variance is just a special case of multiple regression with dichotomous predictor variables. As such, the main and interactive effects of X and M can be expressed as a regression model of the form $Y = i_1 + b_1 X + b_2 M + b_3 XM + e_Y$. However, care must be exercised, because whether b_1 and b_2 can be interpreted as equivalent to the main effects from a factorial ANOVA will be highly dependent on the way that X and M are coded.

In the data, whether or not information about the policy was provided (POLICY) and who the respondent supported in the 2004 election (KERRY) are dummy-coded variables, meaning they are coded 0 and 1. If one were to regress Y on X, M, and XM using these dummy codes, the resulting regression coefficients, standard errors, t, and p-values can be found in Table 8.5 as model 1. In this model, b_1 and b_2 are *not* equivalent to the main effects of X and M in a 2×2 factorial ANOVA and should not be interpreted as such. Rather, when X and M are dummy codes and their product is included as a predictor in a regression model, the resulting model is a *simple effects parameterization* of the 2×2 design. In this model, b_1 estimates the simple effect of X for the level of M coded zero, and b_2 estimates the simple effect of M for the level of X coded zero. These are equivalent to what we've been calling *conditional effects* thus far. That is, b_1 estimates the effect of X (policy information) when $M = 0$ (Bush supporters), and b_2 estimates the effect of M (candidate supported) when $X = 0$ (no policy information given). Indeed, observe that b_1 and b_2 correspond to these simple effects in Table 8.3:

$$b_1 = \overline{Y}_2 - \overline{Y}_1 = 1.397 - 1.784 = -0.387$$

$$b_2 = \overline{Y}_3 - \overline{Y}_1 = 2.384 - 1.784 = 0.600$$

The t statistics and p-values for b_1 and b_2 can be used to test the null hypothesis that the population simple effects are equal to zero. So it is inappropriate

TABLE 8.5. Regression Analysis of the Caskets Study Using Simple Effect and Main Effect Parameterizations of the 2 ×2 Design

		Coeff.	SE	t	p
Model 1: Simple Effect Parameterization $R^2 = 0.138, MSE = 1.068$					
Intercept	i_1	1.784	0.089	19.952	< .001
Policy Information (X)	b_1	−0.387	0.127	−3.045	.002
Candidate Supported (M)	b_2	0.600	0.128	4.709	< .001
Information × Candidate Supported	b_3	0.360	0.178	2.204	.044
Model 2: Main Effect Parameterization $(R^2 = 0.138, MSE = 1.068$					
Intercept	i_1	1.980	0.045	44.521	< .001
Policy Information (X)	b_1	−0.207	0.089	−2.322	.021
Candidate Supported (M)	b_2	0.780	0.089	8.770	.001
Information × Candidate Supported	b_3	0.360	0.178	2.024	.044

to interpret b_1 and b_2 as tests of main effects when dummy coding of the two factors is used. These are simple effects or conditional effects and *not* main effects. However, b_3 in the simple effects parameterization does estimate the interaction between X and M in the ANOVA, defined as the difference between the simple effects of X at levels of M:

$$b_3 = (\overline{Y}_4 - \overline{Y}_3) - (\overline{Y}_2 - \overline{Y}_1) = (2.357 - 2.384) - (1.397 - 1.784) = 0.360$$

or the difference between the simple effects of M at levels of X:

$$b_3 = (\overline{Y}_4 - \overline{Y}_2) - (\overline{Y}_3 - \overline{Y}_1) = (2.357 - 1.397) - (2.384 - 1.784) = 0.360$$

The t statistic for b_3 in this model is the square root of the F-ratio for the interaction from the ANOVA, and they have the same p-value. These are mathematically identical tests.

Main Effects Parameterization

The main effects in a 2×2 ANOVA can be reproduced in a linear regression analysis through the use of a *main effects parameterization* rather than a simple effects parameterization. This is done by coding the two levels of both X and M with codes of -0.5 and 0.5 rather than dummy coding them 0 and 1. The resulting regression model estimating Y from X, M, and XM can be found in Table 8.5 as model 2. In this parameterization of the model, b_1 and b_2 now estimate the main effects of X and M, respectively. To verify, observe that indeed,

$$b_1 = \frac{(\overline{Y}_4 - \overline{Y}_3) + (\overline{Y}_2 - \overline{Y}_1)}{2} = \frac{(2.357 - 2.384) + (1.397 - 1.784)}{2} = -0.207$$

$$b_2 = \frac{(\overline{Y}_4 - \overline{Y}_2) + (\overline{Y}_3 - \overline{Y}_1)}{2} = \frac{(2.357 - 1.397) + (2.384 - 1.784)}{2} = 0.780$$

which are the same as the main effects of X and M, respectively, from the ANOVA. Furthermore, the t statistics for each of the regression coefficients are equal to the square root of the corresponding F-ratios for each effect in the 2×2 ANOVA, and the p-values for the regression coefficients are the same as the p-values from these effects in the ANOVA. Mathematically, these are identical analyses and they will produce exactly the same results.

Although coding X and M with -0.5 and 0.5 has dramatically changed b_1 and b_2 relative to when dummy codes are used, notice that b_3 is not at all affected by this change in the coding. b_3 still properly estimates the interaction between X and W, as can be seen in Table 8.5. Notice that b_3 as well as t and the p-value are the same as in the simple effects parameterization and in the 2×2 ANOVA.

In sum, there is nothing about ANOVA that makes it especially well-suited to the analysis of the 2×2 factorial design relative to multiple regression. Factorial ANOVA is just a special case of regression analysis with categorical predictor variables. However, care must be taken to parameterize the model correctly so that the coefficients for the variables that define the interaction can be interpreted as main effects rather than simple effects or something else.

Conducting a 2 × 2 Between-Participants Factorial ANOVA Using PROCESS

PROCESS can conduct a 2×2 factorial analysis while also simultaneously (and without special instruction) conducting follow-up analyses that probe the interaction through estimation and tests of the simple effects. As POLICY and KERRY are dummy coded in the data, these dummy codes first have to be converted to -0.5 and 0.5 simply by subtracting 0.5 from each code prior to execution of PROCESS. In SPSS, the commands which conduct the analysis are

```
compute kerryc=kerry-0.5.
compute policyc=policy-0.5.
process vars=interest policyc kerryc/y=interest/x=policyc/m=kerryc/plot=1/model=1.

Model = 1
    Y = interest
    X = policyc
    M = kerryc

Sample size
       541

*************************************************************************
Outcome: interest

Model Summary
          R         R-sq         F         df1         df2           p
       .3711        .1378     28.5965     3.0000     537.0000       .0000

Model
              coeff        se          t          p          LLCI        ULCI
constant     1.9803      .0445     44.5209      .0000      1.8930      2.0677
kerryc        .7802      .0890      8.7696      .0000       .6054       .9549
policyc      -.2066      .0890     -2.3224      .0206      -.3814      -.0318
int_1         .3601      .1779      2.0236      .0435       .0105       .7096

Interactions:

 int_1    policyc    X    kerryc

R-square increase due to interaction(s):
          R2-chng        F          df1         df2           p
int_1       .0066      4.0951     1.0000     537.0000       .0435

*************************************************************************

Conditional effect of X on Y at values of the moderator(s)
    kerryc     Effect        se          t          p          LLCI        ULCI
   -.5000     -.3866      .1270     -3.0454      .0024      -.6360      -.1372
    .5000     -.0266      .1247      -.2132      .8312      -.2715       .2183

*************************************************************************

Data for visualizing conditional effect of X of Y
    policyc     kerryc       yhat
   -.5000     -.5000       1.7836
    .5000     -.5000       1.3969
   -.5000      .5000       2.3837
    .5000      .5000       2.3571

******************** ANALYSIS NOTES AND WARNINGS *************************

Level of confidence for all confidence intervals in output:
   95.00
```

FIGURE 8.8. Output from the PROCESS procedure for a 2 × 2 ANOVA examining the main and interactive effects of candidate supported and policy information provided on interest in viewing images containing the caskets of U.S. servicemen and women killed in action.

```
compute kerryc=kerry-0.5.
compute policyc=policy-0.5.
process vars=interest policyc kerryc/y=interest/x=policyc/m=kerryc/
    plot=1/model=1.
```

In SAS, use

```
data caskets;set caskets;kerryc=kerry-0.5;policyc=policy-0.5;run;
%process (data=caskets,vars=interest policyc kerryc,y=interest,x=policyc,
    m=kerryc,plot=1,model=1);
```

The resulting PROCESS output from the SPSS version of this code can be found in Figure 8.8. As can be seen, because the two factors are coded −0.5 and 0.5, PROCESS generates a model equivalent to the main effects parameterization in Table 8.5. Had POLICY and KERRY been kept in their 0/1 form, PROCESS would produce output equivalent to the simple effects parameterization.

In addition to the main and interaction effects, PROCESS estimates the simple effects of X at each level of M using the pick-a-point approach, which is typically the next step when a significant interaction is found in a 2×2 ANOVA. The use of the **plot** option also generates the cell means. In the section of the PROCESS output labeled "Conditional effect of X on Y at values of the moderator(s)," the simple effect of policy information is statistically significant among Bush supporters, $\theta_{X \to Y|M=-0.5} = -0.387, t(537) = -3.045, p = .002$. Bush supporters told about the policy expressed less interest in viewing the images (Mean = 1.397) than those not told about the policy (Mean = 1.784). But among Kerry supporters, those told about the policy were no different in their interest in viewing the images (Mean = 2.357), on average, than Kerry supporters not told about the policy (Mean = 2.384), $\theta_{X \to Y|M=0.5} = -0.027, t(537) = -0.213, p = .831$. This simple effects analysis does not require splitting the file into groups and conducting separate t-tests among Bush and Kerry supporters, a strategy I discourage in part because it is lower in power than the approach implemented here. Rather, the regression-based procedure exploits information about mean differences contained in the entire model derived from estimates based on the complete sample rather than subgroups of the data.

The alternative simple effects analysis, with candidate supported as X and policy information condition as M, can also be conducted in PROCESS simply by reversing the roles of X and M in the PROCESS command. Covariates could also be added to the **vars=** list in order to produce a 2×2 factorial analysis of *co*variance (ANCOVA).

8.5 Chapter Summary

In a model of the form $Y = i_1 + b_1X + b_2M + b_3XM$, whether or not additional predictors are included in the model, b_3 estimates the extent to which X's relationship with Y depends on M, or M's relationship with Y depends on X. Evidence of such dependency supports a claim of moderation or interaction—that one variable's effect is contingent on another. It makes no difference whether X or M is dichotomous or continuous, both are dichotomous, or both are continuous, as the principles of moderation analysis described in Chapter 7 generalize without modification.

Many investigators who were introduced to ANOVA before multiple regression go away from their first exposure to the principles described in the last two chapters with the mistaken belief that the concept of a "main effect" in ANOVA generalizes to the interpretation of b_1 and b_2 in any regression model that includes an interaction. As demonstrated, b_1 and b_2 are conditional effects and not main effects. These are completely different concepts, and treating a conditional effect and a main effect as synonyms in meaning and interpretation will lead to misinterpretation and misreporting of your findings or worse. The exception is when X and M are dichotomous and coded such that the resulting model does in fact yield main effects as they are defined in ANOVA.

The belief that b_1 and b_2 are main effects is only one of several commonly held misconceptions about the proper estimation and interpretation of models of the sort described in the last two chapters. In the next chapter I debunk some of those additional myths before illustrating the application of the principles of moderation analysis to models with multiple interactions.

9

Miscellaneous Topics in Moderation Analysis

The central theme of this chapter is some of the pervasive misunderstandings about the role of variable scaling in model interpretation and how this has given rise to various myths about moderation analysis using regression, such as the need to mean center or standardize predictor variables prior to testing a moderation hypothesis. These myths and others are debunked in this chapter. Some of the problems associated with attempting to test moderation hypotheses by splitting the data file up and conducting separate analyses of subgroups of the data are also addressed here, as is a broad overview of the application of the principles of moderation to models with multiple and higher-order interactions. The chapter ends with some advice and recommendations about how to report a moderation analysis.

When I teach moderation analysis at my university or in various workshops I conduct on the topic of this book, at this point in the course I can tell that students are getting really excited but also a bit anxious. On the one hand, those following closely have begun to appreciate just how versatile multiple regression can be. On the other hand, they also begin to seriously question the legitimacy of some of the things they have done in the past, as well as the things they have read in books, journal articles, or even been told by their advisors and collaborators. Most notably, I believe their anxiety reflects their newfound appreciation that b_1 and b_2 in a regression model of the form $Y = i_1 + b_1 X + b_2 + b_3 XM$ are not "main effects" and may estimate something totally meaningless and uninterpretable. I am certain that many students go back to old data and papers they have written to see whether they have fallen victim to their prior misunderstandings and perhaps have inappropriately interpreted an analysis they have reported. Perhaps the thought has crossed your mind too.

The material described in this chapter is perhaps the most exciting to teach, and I hope you find it illuminating. This could be called the "myth-busting" chapter of the book, because it emphasizes various myths and misunderstandings about procedures that putatively one must, should, or could follow when testing a moderation hypothesis. These myths include that a moderation hypothesis can be tested by splitting one's data into subsets or groups and conducting separate analyses in each group, that one must center or standardize X and M prior to estimating an interaction between them in a regression model, or that standardized regression coefficients generated automatically by OLS regression programs are meaningful and should be reported in a moderation analysis. I address each of these myths and end with some advice about how to report a moderation analysis after talking about models with multiple and higher-order interactions, including "moderated moderation." Better known as three-way interaction, interpreting such a model can be quite complicated, but it doesn't take too much effort to extend the principles of simple moderation to more complex models, and PROCESS makes the estimation of models with multiple interactions as well as probing such interactions fairly easy.

9.1   Truths and Myths about Mean Centering

There is much ado in the literature about the need to mean center X and M in a model that includes their product. That is, rather than estimating a model of the form $Y = i_1 + b_1X + b_2M + b_3XM + e_Y$, one should instead estimate

$$Y = i_1 + b_1(X - \overline{X}) + b_2(M - \overline{M}) + b_3(X - \overline{X})(M - \overline{M}) + e_Y \qquad (9.1)$$

A simpler representation of equation 9.1 is

$$Y = i_1 + b_1X' + b_2M' + b_3X'M' + e_Y \qquad (9.2)$$

where $X' = X - \overline{X}$ and $M' = M - \overline{M}$. This makes it clearer that a regression model with mean-centered focal predictor and moderator can be thought of as an ordinary moderation model but after subtracting the sample means of X and M from X and M prior to the computation of the product of X and M.

Mean centering has been recommended in a few highly regarded books on regression analysis (e.g., Aiken & West, 1991; Cohen et al., 2003), and several explanations have been offered for why mean centering should be undertaken prior to computation of the product and model estimation. The explanation that seems to have resulted in the most misunderstanding is that X and M are likely to be highly correlated with XM and this will produce estimation problems caused by multicollinearity and result in poor or "strange" estimates of regression coefficients, large standard errors, and reduced power of the statistical test of the interaction. This is, in large part, simply a myth. As described later, there are some reasons that centering can be a beneficial thing to do, which is why it has been *recommended* by some. However, it is incorrect to claim that it is *necessary*, that a failure to do so will lead one to incorrect inferences about moderation, or that the resulting regression coefficients are somehow strange or uninterpretable.

One means of debunking this myth is to estimate a moderation model with and without mean centering of X and M and compare the results. Using the climate change study described in Chapters 2, 3, and 8, Table 9.1 provides the regression coefficients, standard errors, t, and p-values for a model estimating the moderating effect of age (M) on the relationship between negative emotional responses to global climate change (X) and support for government action (Y) to mitigate global climate change. Model 1 is based on the original data, without mean centering X and M, and model 2 comes from the same model but after first mean centering X and M and then calculating their product. The SPSS code to estimate model 2 is

```
compute negemotc=negemot-3.558.
compute agec=age-49.536.
compute negage=negemotc*agec.
regression/dep=govact/method=enter negemotc agec negage.
```

and in SAS, the code below accomplishes the analysis:

```
data glbwarm;set glbwarm;negemotc=negemot-3.558;
agec=age-49.536;negage=negemotc*agec;run;
proc reg data=glbwarm;model govact=negemotc agec negage;run;
```

Observe that there are some differences and some similarities between models 1 and 2 in Table 9.1. They have the same R^2 and $MS_{residual}$. Thus, they fit the data equally well. In fact, they generate exactly the same estimates of Y because these are mathematically equivalent models. Observe as well that although b_1, b_2, and their standard errors, t and p-values are different, this is not true for b_3. In both models 1 and 2, the regression coefficients for XM are identical, as are their standard errors, t, and p-values. Clearly, mean centering has done nothing to the test of the interaction. If your focus is on testing whether M moderates X's effect, you'll get the same results regardless of whether or not you mean center. The need to mean center predictor variables in order to test an interaction between those variables in a regression model is a myth.

The Effect of Mean Centering on Multicollinearity and the Standard Error of b_3

This misplaced concern about the potential damage to estimation and inference caused by the strong intercorrelation between X, M, and XM is entirely understandable given what we know about the determinants of the standard error of a regression coefficient. In a multiple regression model estimating some outcome variable Y, the standard error for predictor variable j in that model is

$$se_{b_j} = \sqrt{\frac{1}{1 - R_j^2}} \sqrt{\frac{MS_{residual}}{n(s_j^2)}} \tag{9.3}$$

where R_j^2 is the squared multiple correlation when estimating predictor j from the other predictor variables in the model, s_j^2 is the variance of predictor variable j, n is the sample size, and $MS_{residual}$ is the mean squared residual for the model of Y (see, e.g., Darlington, 1990, p. 126).

In equation 9.3, R_j^2 quantifies the proportion of the variance in predictor variable j that is explained by the other predictor variables in the model. Thus, $1 - R_j^2$ is the proportion of the variance in predictor variable j unexplained by the other predictor variables in the regression model. This proportion is known as predictor variable j's *tolerance*. The inverse of a variable's tolerance, $1/(1 - R_j^2)$, is its *variance inflation factor*, or VIF. It quantifies how much predictor variable j's standard error is influenced by its correlation with the other variables in the model. How a variable's tolerance, and therefore its VIF, enters into the standard error is more easily seen by reexpressing equation 9.3 in an equivalent form:

$$se_{b_j} = \sqrt{\frac{MS_{residual}VIF_j}{n(s_j^2)}} \tag{9.4}$$

An important insight to take away from equations 9.3 and 9.4 is that the more strongly correlated predictor variable j is with the other variables (i.e., the smaller its tolerance, and the larger its VIF), the larger is its standard error. That is, the more of the variance in predictor variable j that is explained by the other predictor variables in the model, the less stable b_j is over repeated sampling. All other things being equal, the larger a

TABLE 9.1. The Effects of Mean Centering and Three Variants of Standardization on Regression Coefficients in a Model with an Interaction

		Coeff.	SE	t	p
Model 1: Original Data $R^2 = 0.354, MSE = 1.200$					
Intercept	i_1	4.335	0.330	13.154	< .001
Negative Emotions (X)	b_1	0.147	0.085	1.729	.084
Age (M)	b_2	−0.031	0.006	−5.009	< .001
Negative Emotions × Age (XM)	b_3	0.007	0.002	4.476	< .001
Model 2: X and M Mean-Centered $R^2 = 0.354, MSE = 1.200$					
Intercept	i_1	4.597	0.038	119.596	< .001
Negative Emotions (X')	b_1	0.501	0.025	19.810	< .001
Age (M')	b_2	−0.005	0.002	−2.237	.026
Negative Emotions × Age ($X'M'$)	b_3	0.007	0.002	4.476	< .001
Model 3: Standardized Variant 1 $R^2 = 0.354, MSE = 1.200$					
Intercept	i_1	4.597	0.038	119.586	< .001
Negative Emotions (Z_X)	b_1	0.765	0.039	19.810	< .001
Age (Z_M)	b_2	−0.086	0.038	−2.237	.026
Negative Emotions × Age ($Z_X Z_M$)	b_3	0.178	0.040	4.476	< .001
Model 4: Standardized Variant 2 $R^2 = 0.354, MSE = 0.648$					
Intercept	i_1	0.007	0.028	0.263	.792
Negative Emotions (Z_X)	b_1	0.562	0.028	19.810	< .001
Age (Z_M)	b_2	−0.063	0.028	−2.237	.026
Negative Emotions × Age ($Z_X Z_M$)	b_3	0.131	0.029	4.476	< .001
Model 5: Standardized Variant 3 $R^2 = 0.354, MSE = 0.648$					
Intercept	i_1	0.000	0.028	0.000	1.000
Negative Emotions (Z_X)	b_1	0.165	0.096	1.927	.084
Age (Z_M)	b_2	−0.368	0.073	−5.009	< .001
Negative Emotions × Age (Z_{XM})	b_3	0.511	0.114	4.476	< .001

TABLE 9.2. Correlations, Tolerances (Tol.), and Variance Inflation Factors (VIF) before and after Mean Centering or Standardization in the Climate Change Moderation Analysis

Original Data	X	M	XM	Variance	Tol.	VIF
Negative Emotions (X)	1.000			2.336	0.087	11.473
Age (M)	−.057	1.000		266.694	0.148	6.776
Neg. Emot. × Age (XM)	.766	.549	1.000	9489.221	0.061	16.357

After Mean Centering	X'	M'	$X'M'$	Variance	Tol.	VIF
Negative Emotions (X')	1.000			2.336	0.988	1.012
Age (M')	−.057	1.000		266.694	0.997	1.003
Neg. Emot. × Age ($X'M'$)	.092	−.015	1.000	585.166	0.991	1.009

After Standardization	Z_X	Z_M	$Z_X Z_M$	Variance	Tol.	VIF
Negative Emotions (Z_X)	1.000			1.000	0.988	1.012
Age (Z_M)	−.057	1.000		1.000	0.997	1.003
Neg. Emot. × Age ($Z_X Z_M$)	.092	−.015	1.000	0.969	0.991	1.009

statistic's standard error, the lower the power of the hypothesis test of its corresponding parameter, and the wider an interval estimate for the parameter will be. Therefore, anything that can be done to reduce the correlation between predictor variable j and the other predictor variables in the model would seem to be a good thing.

As can be seen in Table 9.2, this concern about multicollinearity on the surface seems justified. The correlation between negative emotional responses (X) and age (M) is near zero, but observe the very strong correlation ($r = 0.766$) between the product of negative emotional responses and age (XM) and negative emotions (X). Furthermore, most of the variance in the product is accounted for by X and M, as its tolerance is very small (0.061) and its variance inflation factor is massive (16.357). According to equations 9.3 and 9.4, if this correlation between XM and X could be reduced in some way (which would thereby increase the tolerance of XM and decrease its variance inflation factor), then the standard error of b_3 would decrease.

It is not a myth that mean centering X and M prior to computing their product will reduce this correlation. Table 9.2 displays the correlations, tolerances, and variance inflation factors after mean centering X and M. Observe that this seems to have made the problem go away entirely. The correlation between XM and X has shrunk considerably ($r = 0.092$), and the tolerance and variance inflation factors are now near 1. Certainly, this must be good.

It turns out, however, that this does not matter one bit, for something else has changed as a result of mean centering that completely counteracts the effect of reduced multicollinearity. Observe that the variance for XM has also changed. The variance of a predictor variable figures into its standard error, and because the variance is in the denominator of the standard error formula, when it goes down, the standard error of its regression coefficient goes up. This counteracting effect of reduced variance relative to multicollinearity can be best seen by reexpressing equations 9.3 and 9.4 as

$$se_{b_j} = \sqrt{\frac{VIF_j}{s_j^2}} \sqrt{\frac{MS_{residual}}{n}}$$

Because mean centering does not change $MS_{residual}$ or n but it does change s_j^2 and VIF_j, any change in the standard error of a regression coefficient resulting from mean centering is determined by its effect on variances and tolerances (Sheih, 2011). By mean centering, the variance inflation factor for XM has been reduced by a factor of $16.357/1.009 = 16.21$. But the variance of XM has also been reduced by this same factor: $9489.221/585.166 = 16.21$. As a result, the standard error of XM is completely unaffected by mean centering X and M prior to computation of the product and estimation of the model. It is a myth that one must mean center X and M because of the problems produced by multicollinearity. This multicollinearity does not cause a problem in the test for the interaction, so there is no problem to solve by mean centering.

I stated earlier that the need to mean center is "for the most part" a myth. My condition on this claim stems from the fact that there can be some circumstances in which multicollinearity could appear to produce estimation problems or might actually do so. For example, if a model includes many predictor variables that are highly correlated and also includes a product involving several of those predictors (i.e., includes at least a couple of interactions), this can produce a tolerance that exceeds the minimum tolerance allowed by certain regression programs. For instance, SPSS is programmed to remove variables from a model automatically if the tolerance for any variable is smaller than some default preset (e.g., 0.000001). This default can easily be overriden simply by changing it in the regression command line. Whether doing so then results in problems with estimation will be specific to the data one is analyzing. If a model won't estimate, mean centering might make it estimable by your regression program. But in my experience, this situation is fairly rare. In most models you are likely to estimate involving one or two interactions, you will not find multicollinearity produces any concerns and you should trust whatever results your regression program gives you regardless of whether or not you mean center.

The Effect of Mean Centering on b_1, b_2, and Their Standard Errors

A second explanation given for why mean centering is preferred is that it makes b_1 and b_2, the regression coefficients for X and M, more meaningful. This is generally true and thus not a myth, although it is not necessarily true in all circumstances. Recall that in a model of the form $Y = i_1 + b_1X + b_2M + b_3XM$, b_1 estimates the difference in Y between two cases that differ by one unit on X when $M = 0$, and b_2 estimates the difference in Y between two cases that differ by one unit on M when $X = 0$. We saw in section 7.2 that b_1 and b_2 will be dependent on how X and M are scaled. If $M = 0$ is not meaningful in the measurement system for M, then b_1 and its test of significance are meaningless and have no substantive interpretation. But if $M = 0$ is meaningful, then so too is b_1 and its test of significance. The same is true for b_2.

Mean centering X and M prior to computation of the product and estimation of the model will produce b_1 and b_2 that are always meaningful, rather than meaningful only when X and/or M are meaningful when equal to zero. When X and M are mean centered and the coefficients in equations 9.1 or 9.2 estimated, b_1 estimates the difference in Y between two cases that differ by one unit on X among cases that are *average* on M. Similarly, b_2 estimates the difference in Y between two cases that differ by one unit on M among cases that are *average* on X. These will always estimate conditional effects of X on Y within the range of the data, and they can always be interpreted.

The difference between b_1 and b_2 and their standard errors in models 1 (original data) and 2 (mean-centered) has nothing whatsoever to do with the reduction in multicollinearity that results when X and M are mean centered. Rather, they differ because they estimate different effects—the effects of X and M among people who are average on the other variable rather than who are at zero on the other variable. Naturally, because these estimate different effects, their standard errors, t, and p-values are different.

Indeed, one need not mean center to estimate these conditional effects. One could use the coefficients from the model based on uncentered data to estimate the conditional effect of X when $M = \overline{M}$. Simply use b_1 and b_3 from the uncentered model and use $\overline{M}$ for M in equation 7.3. That is,

$$\theta_{(X \to Y)|M=\overline{M}} = b_1 + b_3\overline{M} = 0.147 + 0.007(49.536) = 0.501$$

which is exactly equal to b_1 from model 2 based on mean-centered X and M. Even the standard error for b_1 in the centered solution could be derived from the uncentered solution. Using equation 7.12, the estimated standard error for $\theta_{(X \to Y)|M=\overline{M}}$ in terms of parameter estimates and standard errors from the uncentered solution is

$$
\begin{aligned}
se_{\theta_{(X \to Y)|M=\overline{M}}} &= \sqrt{se_{b_1}^2 + (2M)COV_{b_1 b_3} + M^2 se_{b_3}^2} \\
&= \sqrt{0.085^2 + (2)(49.536)(0.000003) + (49.536)^2 0.002^2} \\
&= 0.025
\end{aligned}
$$

where 0.085 is the standard error for b_1, 0.002 is the standard error for b_3, 0.000003 is the covariance between b_1 and b_3, and $\overline{M} = 49.536$ is used for M. Thus, the standard errors that result after mean centering are no more or less accurate than those produced when estimating the model using the original, uncentered forms of X and M. The changes in b_1, b_2, and their standard errors have nothing to do with reduction in multicollinearity that results when mean centering is employed.[1]

In this section, I have debunked the myth that mean centering of X and M is necessary prior to the estimation of a model with an interaction between X and M. I cannot take credit for this, however, as this myth and its corollaries have been repeatedly debunked in the methodology literature yet doggedly persist in spite of that literature (see, e.g., Cronbach, 1987; Echambadi & Hess, 2007; Edwards, 2009; Friedrich, 1982; Hayes et al., 2012; Irwin & McClelland, 2001; Kam & Franzese, 2007; Kromrey & Foster-Johnson, 1998; Sheih, 2011; Whisman & McClelland, 2005). To be sure, there are interpretational advantages associated with mean centering, but the differences in model coefficients and standard errors have nothing to do with reduced multicollinearity that results from mean centering. If you are going to mean center, go ahead and do so, but don't say that you are doing so to reduce multicollinearity and its negative effects. Although mean centering does reduce multicollinearity, this has no consequence on the estimation accuracy, hypothesis tests, or standard errors of regression coefficients in most circumstances you are likely to encounter. Do so because it renders the tests of hypotheses and regression coefficients for X and M more meaningful and substantively interpretable and, as I discuss

---

[1] Because the mean of age is large and the regression coefficients and standard errors for b_1 and b_3 are small, substantial rounding error is produced in hand computations here unless they are done to a great degree of precision. Though not apparent from what is printed here, I did all these hand computations to many decimal places of resolution. You will get slightly different values if you attempt to verify these computations carrying them out to only three decimal places of accuracy.

in section 9.5, perhaps reduces errors in interpretation that your reader might otherwise make.

9.2 The Estimation and Interpretation of Standardized Regression Coefficients in a Moderation Analysis

Mean centering does nothing to change the scaling of regression parameters. Whether or not mean centering is used when estimating a model of the form $\hat{Y} = i_1 + b_1X + b_2M + b_3XM$, b_1, b_2, and b_3 are interpreted with respect to the measured metrics of X, M, and Y (i.e., in *unstandardized* form). Although I generally prefer to report and interpret regression analyses based on unstandardized coefficients, it is possible to generate regression coefficients that are analogous to standardized regression coefficients in regression models without a product term as a predictor. However, one must be careful when doing so. There are two variants of standardization one can use yielding b_1, b_2, and b_3 that could be interpreted as standardized regression coefficients, and another variant yielding regression coefficients that are widely reported but that should *never* be used or interpreted. In this section, I discuss these variants.

Throughout this section, I also debunk a version of the mean centering myth with respect to the need to standardize X and M prior to calculating their product when testing a moderation hypothesis. That is, some researchers mistakenly believe that such standardization is required for the same reasons X and M should be mean centered; that doing so reduces multicollinearity, produces more accurate estimates of the variables' effects, and yields a hypothesis test for the interaction that is higher in power. I have also heard people claim that they standardize prior to estimation of the model because it facilitates the interpretation or probing of the interaction. Like with mean centering, the need to standardize X and M is a myth, and doing so does next to nothing to facilitate the probing or interpretation of an interaction.

Variant 1

In the first variant of standardization, X and M are standardized to produce Z_X and Z_M. These standardized versions of X and M are then multiplied to produce Z_XZ_M. Then Y in its original, unstandardized metric is estimated in a multiple regression model from Z_X, Z_X, and Z_XZ_M:

$$Y = i_1 + b_1Z_X + b_2Z_M + b_3Z_XZ_M + e_Y \qquad (9.5)$$

The regression coefficients could be called *partially standardized* because Y is not standardized, and they express all effects relative to the original metric of the outcome. This could be useful if the outcome variable is measured on an inherently meaningful metric or if standardization of Y would otherwise obscure the applied value or apparent impact of the findings.

Using the global climate change study as an example, the SPSS code to estimate the moderating effect of age (M) on the relationship between negative emotional reactions to climate change (X) and support for government action (Y) is

```
descriptives variables = negemot age/save.
compute znegzage = znegemot*zage.
regression/dep=govact/method=enter znegemot zage znegzage.
```

In this code, the **save** option in the **descriptives** command generates two new variables in the dataset which are the standardized versions of X and M. The original variable names are retained by SPSS but with "Z" tacked onto the beginning. In SAS, the corresponding code is

```
proc stdize data=glbwarm out=glbwarmz;var negemot age;run;
data glbwarmz;set glbwarmz;znegzage=negemot*age;run;
proc reg data=glbwarmz;model govact = negemot age znegzage;run;
```

When looking at a regression output, i_1, b_1, b_2, and b_3 will be the coefficients listed wherever unstandardized regression coefficients are ordinarily provided (e.g., in SPSS, in the column labeled "Unstandardized Coefficients," or in the column labeled "Parameter Estimate" in SAS). Do not look for these coefficients in any section of the output labeled "Standardized regression coefficients" or something of the sort. That is not where to find them.

The model summary, partially standardized regression coefficients, and standard errors can be found in Table 9.1, model 3. In this model, b_1 is interpreted as the estimated amount by which two cases that differ by one standard deviation on X are estimated to differ on Y among those who are average on M. The regression coefficient for M, b_2, is interpreted similarly as the estimated amount by which two cases that differ by one standard deviation on M are estimated to differ on Y among those who are average on X. Finally, b_3 is the amount by which the difference in Y between two cases that differ by one standard deviation on X is estimated to change as M increases by one standard deviation. b_3 can also be interpreted as the amount by which the difference in Y between two cases that differ by one standard deviation on M is estimated to change as X increases by one standard deviation.

Observe that b_1 and b_2 are different, as are their t and p-values, relative to when X and M are mean centered (Table 9.1, model 2) or kept in their original metric (Table 9.1, model 1). This is because standardization has changed the metrics of X and M. b_1 and b_2 in models 2 and 3 both estimate the effect of X and M on Y when the other variable is set to the sample mean. However, after standardization, the metric of difference on X and M has changed from one unit to one *standard deviation*. So two cases that differ by one standard deviation in negative emotional responses to climate change but that are average in age (as defined by the sample mean in these data) are estimated to differ by $b_1 = 0.765$ units in support for government action. And two cases that differ by one standard deviation in age but are average in the negative emotions are estimated to differ by $b_2 = -0.086$ units in support for government action (with the negative sign meaning the older person expresses less support for government action).

Importantly, notice from Table 9.1 that although the regression coefficient for b_3 is different compared to when the original data or mean-centered data are used in the model, the t statistic and p-values for partially standardized b_3 are the same. So standardization of X and M has no effect on the test of the interaction, contrary to the myth that standardization is necessary to properly test a moderation hypothesis. As with b_1 and b_2, standardization has changed the metric of difference for X and M, which changes the interpretation of b_3 slightly. We can say that the estimated difference in support for government action between two cases that differ by one standard deviation in negative emotions increases by 0.178 units as age increases by one standard deviation.

To implement variant 1, I recommend the use of PROCESS rather than SPSS's regression routine or SAS PROC REG because of the options it provides for easily probing the interaction. Simply use the standardized versions of X and M in a properly formatted PROCESS command specifying model 1 rather than the unstandardized versions of X and M. PROCESS will generate $Z_X Z_M$ for you. The interaction can be probed using either the pick-a-point approach or the Johnson–Neyman technique. Conditional effects of X or regions of significance will be generated for various values of Z_M. If using the **mmodval** option in PROCESS, make sure you specify a value of M in the metric of Z_M rather than M.

These partially standardized regression coefficients can also be calculated by hand without much difficulty using the output from the mean-centered regression model (model 2). Simply multiply the regression coefficient for predictor variable j from the mean-centered model by the standard deviation of predictor variable j. The result will be the partially standardized regression coefficient for predictor j in equation 9.5. For example, from the mean-centered model (model 2), $b_1 = 0.501$, and the standard deviation of negative emotions is 1.529. Therefore, the partially standardized regression coefficient for negative emotions is $0.501(1.529) = 0.765$, which is b_1 from model 3.

Variant 2

Variant 2 is similar to variant 1 in that like variant 1, Z_X, Z_M, and $Z_X Z_M$ are used to estimate Y. But variant 2 requires the standardization of Y as well:

$$Z_Y = i_1 + b_1 Z_X + b_2 Z_M + b_3 Z_X Z_M + e_{Z_Y} \tag{9.6}$$

The resulting regression coefficients are *fully standardized* because the predictors and outcome are standardized. The regression coefficients from equation 9.6 are the closest analogue to standardized regression coefficients in a model that does not include a product of variables. The SPSS code used to generate this model is similar to the code for variant 1, except that a standardized version of Y is also created:

```
descriptives variables = negemot age govact/save.
compute znegzage = znegemot*zage.
regression/dep=zgovact/method=enter znegemot zage znegzage.
```

In SAS, use

```
proc stdize data=glbwarm out=glbwarmz;var negemot age govact;run;
data glbwarmz;set glbwarmz;znegzage=negemot*age;run;
proc reg data=glbwarmz;model govact = negemot age znegzage;run;
```

The model that results can be found in Table 9.1, model 4. The regression coefficients are interpreted identically to the partially standardized regression coefficients from variant 1, except that differences in Y should be framed in terms of standard deviation units rather than the original units of Y. So b_1 is interpreted as the estimated difference in *standard deviations* of Y between two cases that differ by one standard deviation on X but are average on M. b_2 is similarly interpreted as the estimated difference in *standard deviations* of Y between two cases that differ by one standard deviation on M but are average on X. Finally, b_3 quantifies how much the estimated difference in *standard deviations* of Y between two cases that differ by one standard deviation on X changes as M changes by one standard deviation.

Notice that just as was true for variant 1, the regression coefficient for b_3 for variant 2 is different compared to when the original data or mean-centered data were used in the model, but their t statistics and p-values are identical. So standardization of Y along with X and M prior to calculating the product has had no effect on the test of the interaction relative to the analysis of the original data, mean-centered data, or partially standardized data. Yet because standardization has changed the metric of Y relative to variant 1, the interpretation of b_3 changes slightly. We can now say that the estimated difference *in standard deviations* of support for government action between two cases that differ by one standard deviation in negative emotional responses decreases by 0.131 as age increases by one standard deviation.

Because they test the same hypothesis, the t and p-values for b_1 and b_2 are the same in variant 2 as they are in variant 1 and in the mean-centered model. In all these models, these are used to test the same null hypothesis that X's effect on Y is zero when $M = \overline{M}$ and M's effect on Y is zero when $X = \overline{X}$. But b_1 and b_2 for variant 2 differs because the change in scaling of Y resulting from standardization of Y has changed the scaling of these conditional effects. In this model, we can say that two cases that are average in age but differ by one standard deviation in negative emotions are estimated to differ by $b_1 = 0.562$ standard deviations in their support for government action. And two cases that are average in negative emotions but differ by one standard deviation in age are estimated to differ by $b_2 = -0.063$ standard deviations in support for government action, with the negative sign meaning that the older person expresses less support for government action.

PROCESS can be used to generate the standardized regression coefficients from variant 2. To do so, use the standardized versions of X, M, and Y in a properly formatted PROCESS command specifying model 1. PROCESS will generate $Z_X Z_M$ for you and will automatically probe the interaction and generate output in terms of the conditional effect of X for various values of Z_M. As with variant 2, specify a specific value of M in the metric of Z_M when using the **mmodval** option.

The completely standardized regression coefficients can also be calculated by hand without much difficulty using the output from the mean-centered regression model (model 2 in Table 9.1). Simply multiply the regression coefficient for predictor variable j from the mean-centered model by the standard deviation of predictor variable j and then divide the result by the standard deviation of Y. The result will be the completely standardized regression coefficient for predictor j in equation 9.6.

Variant 3

Variant 3 is like variant 2 except that the order of standardization and multiplication is reversed. Whereas in variant 2, where X and M are both standardized prior to calculating their product $Z_X Z_M$, in variant 3, X and M are first multiplied to produce XM which is then standardized to produce Z_{XM}. This standardized product is then included as a predictor of Z_Y along with Z_X and Z_M:

$$Z_Y = i_1 + b_1 Z_X + b_2 Z_M + b_3 Z_{XM} + e_{Z_Y} \tag{9.7}$$

Although one could implement variant 3 by standardizing Y, X, M, and XM and then estimating the model in the usual way, it turns out that this is not necessary. The regression coefficients for variant 3 are produced by any OLS regression program that provides standardized regression coefficients in the output. In SPSS, for instance, the regression coefficients in equation 9.7 are found in the regression coefficient summary when estimating $Y = i_1 + b_1 X + b_2 M + b_3 XM$ under the column labeled "Standardized Coefficients: Beta" and are printed whether you want them or not any time you conduct a regression analysis. They can be generated by SAS using the **/stb** option after the model command in PROC REG and will be found under the label "Standardized Estimate."

There is a major problem with this variant, which makes it impossible to ever recommend. Although this variant will give you a legitimate test of the interaction (notice in Table 9.1 that the t and p-values for b_3 are the same as they are for all other methods described in this chapter), this approach to standardization should not be used, because b_1, b_2, and b_3 are meaningless. I bring this variation to your attention only to make an important point. Because the regression coefficients in equation 9.7 are equivalent to the standardized regression coefficients generated by an OLS regression program automatically when estimating a model of the form $Y = i_1 + b_1 X + b_2 M + b_3 XM$, this means such standardized regression coefficients generated by your OLS regression program *should never be interpreted, they should never be reported, and you should never probe an interaction using these regression coefficients*. The only thing meaningful about these coefficients is their sign. You can substitute any nonsense symbol for the actual value of the regression coefficients (e.g., happy faces, suns and moons, kitty cats, stop signs) and these will convey just as much information to your reader about your model. So never interpret or report the standardized regression coefficients given to you automatically by an

OLS regression program such as SPSS or SAS when the model includes a product of predictors. This is true regardless of whether you have analyzed the original data, mean centered, or standardized the data manually on your own. Rather, always base your interpretation on the coefficients reported in your regression program as unstandardized, which actually will be standardized regression coefficients if you followed the procedure described for variants 1 or 2 earlier.

The problem with variant 3 can be illustrated by reconsidering the reason for including XM as a predictor in a regression model. In a model of the form $Y = i_1 + b_1 X + b_2 M$, X's effect on Y is constrained to be independent of M, which is the opposite of what is desired when interest is in testing the moderation of X's effect on Y by M. The model that allows X's effect to depend linearly on M was formed by adding XM as a predictor variable to this model, resulting in $Y = i_1 + b_1 X + b_2 M + b_3 XM$. This model can be rewritten in the mathematically identical form $Y = i_1 + (b_1 + b_3 M)X + b_2 M$, which clearly illustrates how X's effect is a function of M.

When X and M are standardized, the model for variant 1 (equation 9.5) can be rewritten as

$$Y = i_1 + (b_1 + b_3 Z_M)Z_X + b_2 Z_M + e_Y$$

and the model for variant 2 (equation 9.6) rewritten as

$$Z_Y = i_1 + (b_1 + b_3 Z_M)Z_X + b_2 Z_M + e_{Z_Y}$$

In both of these equivalent forms, it is clear that X's effect is conditional on M. That is,

$$\theta_{X \to Y} = b_1 + b_3 Z_M \tag{9.8}$$

Thus, all the rules for the computation of conditional effects and the methods for probing an interaction described in Chapter 7 generalize to models with standardized X and M.

However, the model for variant 3 (equation 9.7) *cannot* be rewritten in a form that allows X's effect to be rewritten as a linear function of M because $Z_{XM} \neq Z_X Z_M$. The implication is that b_1, b_2, and b_3 in equation 9.7 have none of the interpretational properties described in Chapters 7 and 8. The conditional effect of X cannot be estimated using equation 9.8, and an interaction cannot be probed or plotted using the regression coefficients from variant 3.

Whether you choose to report regression coefficients from a moderation model in unstandardized or standardized form is your choice to make. Standardization of X and M prior to estimation of their product yields estimates of each variable's effect on Y gauged in terms of differences between cases that differ by one standard deviation on X or M rather than simply "one unit" in the original metric of measurement. Although standardization does reduce multicollinearity (as demonstrated in Table 9.2), this has no effect on the test of interaction. The need to standardize X and M prior to computation of the product is a myth. Finally, never use variant 3, and never interpret or report the regression coefficients given to you automatically by your regression analysis program that are listed as standardized when including a product of predictors in the model. These are meaningless regardless of which variant you use.

Does Standardization Facilitate the Probing of an Interaction?

Two other reasons I have heard given for why standardization is a good idea is that it facilitates the interpretation of an interaction and makes it easier to probe. In my opinion, standardization does nothing to make an interaction easier to interpret. If you know what you are doing, an interaction is just as easy to interpret when X and M are left in their original metric as it is when standardized. This claim is, I believe, misguided.

If implementing the pick-a-point approach by hand, I suppose there is a grain of truth to the latter claim. There is always the potential for rounding error propagating through computations when doing computations by hand. The more noninteger numbers you can remove from the computation, the less of a problem rounding error will be, and the easier it is to do the computations with a calculator. When M is continuous and standardized and you are interested in estimating the conditional effect of X when $M = \overline{M} - 1SD$, $\overline{M}$, and $\overline{M} + 1SD$, the values of M at which the conditional effect of X is estimated become $Z_M = -1, 0,$ and 1. Thus, the conditional effects of X for values of M corresponding to "low," "moderate," and "high" are (from equations 7.3 or 9.8) $b_1 - b_3$, b_1, and $b_1 + b_3$, respectively. The elimination of noninteger values of the moderator makes these hand computations more accurate and easier to do.

But the biggest computational gains are produced through the simplification of the standard error for the conditional effect of X, as some of the terms in equation 7.12 disappear and fewer noninteger numbers or squares are required:

$$se_{\theta_{(X \to Y)|Z_{M=-1}}} = \sqrt{se_{b_1}^2 - 2COV_{b_1 b_3} + se_{b_3}^2}$$

$$se_{\theta_{(X \to Y)|Z_{M=0}}} = \sqrt{se_{b_1}^2}$$

$$se_{\theta_{(X \to Y)|Z_{M=1}}} = \sqrt{se_{b_1}^2 + 2COV_{b_1 b_3} + se_{b_3}^2}$$

Although these computations are indeed somewhat less tedious and susceptible to error when conducted by hand, this doesn't seem like a real advantage of standardization given that there is simply no reason to do these computations by hand these days in the first place. The regression centering method (see page 236) can be used to implement the pick-a-point approach by computer, and PROCESS can do all these computations for you without you having to even think much about the mathematics behind them. Thus, don't standardize X and M just because it makes it easier to probe the interaction. In this age of computers, it does not.

9.3   Artificial Categorization and Subgroups Analysis

Investigators without an understanding of how to test a moderation hypothesis involving a continuous moderator frequently attempt to simplify their analytical problem so that they can analyze their data using procedures they are familiar with. Most commonly, a mean or median split is used, where cases in the data below the mean or median of a continuous moderator are placed in a "low" group and everyone else is placed in a "high" group. The analysis then proceeds by examining whether X is related to Y in one group defined by a now dichotomous M but not the other group by conducting a 2×2 factorial ANOVA or, worse, two independent groups t-tests.

Returning to the protesting lawyer example, recall the question asked in section 7.2 was the extent to which Catherine's decision whether or not to protest the sex discrimination in her law firm influenced how she was evaluated differentially depending on the perceiver's beliefs about the pervasiveness of sex discrimination in society. An investigator unfamiliar with the principles introduced in Chapters 7 and 8 might use a mean split to classify participants as either "low" or "high" in those beliefs based on whether they score above or below the sample mean (5.117 in these data) on the Modern Sexism Scale. Once participants are categorized in this fashion, two independent groups t-tests might then be conducted in the low and high groups comparing mean liking of Catherine between those told she protested and those told she did not. In SPSS, the commands would be

```
temporary.
select if (sexism < 5.117).
ttest groups=protest(0,1)/variables=liking.
temporary.
```

```
select if (sexism >= 5.117).
ttest groups=protest(0,1)/variables=liking.
```

or in SAS, try

```
proc ttest data=protest;where sexism < 5.117;
class protest;var liking;run;
proc ttest data=protest;where sexism >= 5.117;
class protest;var liking;run;
```

This analysis shows that among those relatively low in their beliefs about the pervasiveness of sex discrimination in society, those told Catherine protested (Mean = 5.534, SD = 0.883) did not differ on average in how much they liked her compared to those told she did not protest (Mean = 5.649, SD = 0.882), $t(61) = 0.495, p = .622$. However, among those relatively high in such beliefs about sex discrimination in society, those told she protested liked her more on average (Mean = 6.012, SD = 0.817) than those told she did not (Mean = 4.918, SD = 1.598), $t(64) = -3.675, p < .001$.

There is a large literature admonishing researchers not to do this. Such artificial categorization of a continuum prior to analysis is almost always difficult to defend, for the split point usually is determined arbitrarily and thus produces groups that are not psychometrically meaningful (e.g., why the mean or the median as opposed to some other number?), it throws out information by treating people who are nearly indistinguishable (i.e., those close to the mean or median) as if they are maximally distinct on the dimension measured, it reduces statistical power of tests, and it can increase Type I error rate in some circumstances. Don't do this. For the many arguments against this practice, see Bissonnette, Ickes, Bernstein, and Knowles (1990), Cohen (1983), Hayes (2005), Humphreys and Fleishman (1974), Hunter and Schmidt (1990), Hutchinson (2003), Irwin and McClelland (2002), MacCallum, Zhang, Preacher, and Rucker (2002), Maxwell and Delaney (1993), Newsom, Prigerson, Schultz, and Reynolds (2003), Preacher, Rucker, MacCallum, and Nicewander (2005), Royston, Altman, and Sauerbrei (2006), Sedney (1981), Streiner (2002), and Vargha, Rudas, and Maxwell (2011).

Even if the resulting groups constructed arbitrarily in this fashion were psychometrically meaningful, or the groups did exist naturally and thus are inherently meaningful (e.g., men versus women), such a subgroup analysis does not actually test whether the effect of X on Y differs as a function of M. Suppose it is sensible to categorize people into either high or low in perceived pervasiveness of sex discrimination, thereby allowing us to quantify

$\theta_{(X \to Y)|M="high"}$ and $\theta_{(X \to Y)|M="low"}$. In terms of patterns of significance and not, there are four possible outcomes of the two t-tests ($\theta_{(X \to Y)|M="high"}$ statistically significant and $\theta_{(X \to Y)|M="low"}$ not significant, $\theta_{(X \to Y)|M="high"}$ and $\theta_{(X \to Y)|M="low"}$ also significant, and so forth). Not one of these patterns actually provides evidence as to whether $_T\theta_{(X \to Y)|M="high"} = {}_T\theta_{(X \to Y)|M="low"}$. Statistical significance in one group but not in the other does not imply a statistically significant difference between the two groups in the effect of X. Furthermore, statistical significance in both groups does not imply no statistically significant difference between them (cf, Gelman & Stern, 2006). If your question asks about moderation, you need to conduct a formal test of the difference between differences. Subgroups analysis does not accomplish this.

Of course, the differences between the conditional effects of X among those low and high could be tested with a factorial ANOVA if M is dichotomous, as it is in this example. A statistically significant interaction means that the simple of effect of X given $M =$ "high" is different from the simple effect of X given $M =$ "low." Applied to this example, after dichotomizing participants at the mean of perceived prevalence of sex discrimination, the interaction between perceived prevalence (low versus high) and whether Catherine protested is statistically significant, $F(1, 125) = 10.236, p = .002$. Although this solves the problem with subgroup analyses—that difference in significance does not imply significance of difference—it does not get around all the problems associated with artificial categorization. Testing for differences between conditional effects of X using a factorial ANOVA would be entirely appropriate if the levels of M were naturally existing categories (e.g., men and women) or experimentally created (e.g., conditions in an experiment). When they are not, respect the continuous nature of M and the differences between cases it quantifies and proceed as described in Chapters 7 and 8.

9.4   More Than One Moderator

Every example of moderation analysis thus far has been predicated on a single moderator of a single focal predictor's effect—the simple moderation model. Not infrequently, investigators propose or test hypotheses involving multiple moderators of a variable's effect. In this section, I describe a multiple moderation model in which two variables are estimated as moderating a single focal predictor's effect. I also touch upon *moderated moderation*, in which the moderation of one variable's effect by another is itself moderated. Also known as *three-way interaction*, moderated moderation hypotheses are advanced and tested quite regularly in the social sciences.

Although the principles of moderation analysis apply regardless of how many moderators are in a model, interpretation and probing of interactions can become complicated quite rapidly. I do not get quite as deep into the mechanics of visualizing, probing, and interpreting in this section as I have in previous sections, for space precludes such a treatment in an introductory level book such as this. A thorough exposition would require entire chapters. Greater detail than I provide here can be found in books dedicated exclusively to interactions in regression analysis (see, e.g., Aiken & West, 1991; Jaccard & Turrisi, 2003). Furthermore, PROCESS has the ability to estimate the two kinds of models described in this section, and it implements all the necessary computations for probing the interaction and generating data needed to visualize more complex models such as these without you having to think much at all about the mathematics behind them.

I also use the example here to make a point made in section 9.1 about mean centering. The models I will describe in this section involve multiple product terms that are highly correlated with each other and with the variables used to construct them. Such a situation is the very circumstance where mean centering is often described as being most important. Yet I do not mean center here, because doing so is not required and it has no effect on the interpretation of the results of the estimates of the effects of primary interest. To be sure, some of the regression coefficients are different than they would be without mean centering. But the parameterization does not affect the results obtained when the interaction is probed using the methods described below, nor will it change how a visual representation of the model appears. I leave it as an exercise to you to rerun the analyses described here in PROCESS but using the mean centering option. You will find that most everything that matters in terms of estimation and interpretation of the results is unaffected by the decision to center or not.

Multiple Additive Moderation

Consider a multiple linear regression model with three predictor variables X, M, and W:

$$Y = i_1 + b_1 X + b_2 M + b_3 W + e_Y \qquad (9.9)$$

While a very useful model for assessing the partial association between X and Y controlling for M and W, the limitation that the effect of X is constrained to be unconditional on both M and W should be acknowledged. That is, X's effect is quantified holding constant M and W, such that regardless of which values of M and W you choose, X's effect on Y is b_1.

For instance, suppose X is negative emotional responses to climate change, M and W are sex and age, respectively, and Y is support for government actions to mitigate climate change. In this model, the influence of negative emotions on support for government action is constrained to be the same for men and women and people of all ages. This constraint is simple enough to demonstrate for yourself using the same procedure described in section 7.1. Choose any arbitrary values of i_1, b_1, b_2, b_3, as well as M an W, and you will see that *regardless* of which values of M and W you substitute into equation 9.9, two hypothetical cases that differ by one unit on X are estimated to differ by b_1 units on Y.

Chapters 7 and 8 illustrated how this constraint can be relaxed by letting X's effect be a function of another variable in the model. But X's effect could also be estimated as function of more than one variable simultaneously, such as both M and W. Such a model is depicted in the form of a conceptual diagram in Figure 9.1, panel A. Recall from those prior chapters that to do so, b_1 was replaced with a linear function of M to produce the simple moderation model. Instead, we could replace it with a linear function of both M and W, as in

$$Y = i_1 + f(M, W)X + b_2M + b_3W + e_Y \tag{9.10}$$

For example, consider the additive linear function

$$f(M, W) = b_1 + b_4M + b_5W$$

which, when substituted into equation 9.10, yields

$$Y = i_1 + (b_1 + b_4M + b_5W)X + b_2M + b_3W + e_Y \tag{9.11}$$

Expanding equation 9.11 by distributing X among all terms in the parentheses yields

$$Y = i_1 + b_1X + b_2M + b_3W + b_4XM + b_5XW + e_Y \tag{9.12}$$

where XM and XW are two variables formed as the product of X and M and X and W, respectively. This model is represented in the form of a statistical diagram in Figure 9.1, panel B. In this model, X's effect on Y is estimated as an additive linear function of M and W. Thus, X's effect is conditional on both M and W. Expressed symbolically, equations 9.11 and 9.12 can be written in equivalent form as

$$Y = i_1 + \theta_{X \to Y}X + b_2M + b_3W + e_Y$$

where $\theta_{X \to Y}$ is the conditional effect of X on Y, defined as

$$\theta_{X \to Y} = b_1 + b_4M + b_5W \tag{9.13}$$

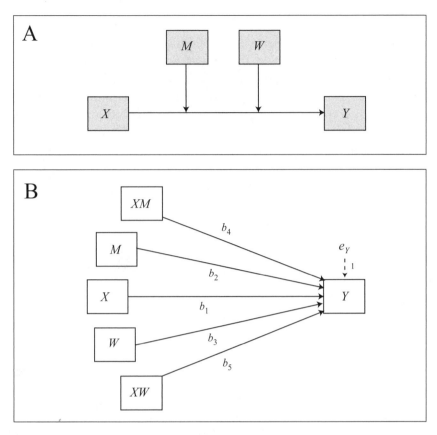

FIGURE 9.1. An additive moderation model depicted as a conceptual (panel A) and a statistical diagram (panel B).

Equation 9.13 makes it apparent that b_1 in equation 9.12 estimates the conditional effect of X on Y when both W and M are zero. Thus, b_1 is not a "main effect," in that it estimates X's effect only when both M and W are zero rather than X's effect "on average." Regression coefficients b_4 and b_5 determine how much X's effect is contingent on M and W, respectively. More specifically, b_4 quantifies how much the conditional effect of X on Y changes as M changes by one unit, holding W constant, and b_5 estimates how much the conditional effect of X on Y changes as W changes by one unit, holding M constant. Tests of significance or confidence intervals based on b_4 and b_5 answer the question as to whether M moderates X's effect and whether W moderates X's effect, respectively.

Although not obvious, b_2 and b_3 also estimate conditional effects just as does b_1. b_2 estimates the conditional effect of M on Y when X is zero while holding W constant, and b_3 estimates the conditional effect of W on

Y when X is zero while holding M constant. These are not equivalent to main effects in ANOVA and should not be interpreted as if they are.

I illustrate the estimation and interpretation of such a model using the climate change data by regressing support for government action (Y) on negative emotions about climate change (X), sex (M), age (W), two new variables constructed as the product of negative emotions and sex (XM), and negative emotions and age (XW). I also include positive emotions (C_1) and political ideology (C_2) as covariates. This is easy enough to do in SPSS or SAS's regression procedures merely by constructing the products prior to estimating. But if there are only two moderators of a single focal predictor's effect, as is the case here, PROCESS does all the necessary computations for you. The SPSS version of the command is

```
process vars=govact negemot sex age posemot ideology/y=govact/x=negemot/
    m=sex/w=age/model=2.
```

and in SAS, use

```
%process (data=glbwarm,vars=govact negemot sex age posemot ideology,
    y=govact,x=negemot,m=sex,w=age,model=2);
```

The resulting output can be found in Figure 9.2. Specifying **model=2** requests the estimation of a multiple moderator model with X as focal predictor and M and W as moderators of X's effect. PROCESS constructs the necessary products, estimates the model, and generates conditional effects of X on Y for various values of M and W. The best fitting OLS regression model is

$$\hat{Y} = 5.272+0.093X-0.741M-0.018W+0.205XM+0.005XW-0.024C_1-0.207C_2$$

Observe from the PROCESS output that $b_4 = 0.205, t(807) = 4.084, p < .001$ and $b_5 = 0.005, t(807) = 3.013, p = .021$. Both are statistically different from zero, meaning both sex and age function as moderators of the effect of negative emotions on support for government action. From the section of output titled "R-square increase due to interaction," the two interaction terms as a set account for 2.46% of the variance in support for government action, $F(2, 807) = 16.921, p < .001$. The moderation by sex uniquely accounts for 1.21% of the variance [$F(1, 807) = 16.676, p < .001$], whereas the moderation by age uniquely accounts for 0.66% of the variance, $F(1, 807) = 9.080, p = .003$.

```
process vars = govact negemot sex age posemot ideology/y=govact/x=negemot/m=sex
  /w=age/model=2.

Model = 2
    Y = govact
    X = negemot
    M = sex
    W = age

Statistical Controls:
CONTROL= posemot  ideology

Sample size
      815

***********************************************************************
Outcome: govact

Model Summary
         R        R-sq        F        df1        df2        p
      .6426      .4129    81.0915    7.0000    807.0000    .0000

Model
              coeff       se        t        p       LLCI      ULCI
constant     5.2716     .3361   15.6861    .0000    4.6119    5.9313
sex          -.7417     .1941   -3.8216    .0001   -1.1227    -.3607
negemot       .0931     .0820    1.1348    .2568    -.0679     .2540
int_1         .2045     .0501    4.0836    .0000     .1062     .3028
age          -.0182     .0061   -2.9974    .0028    -.0302    -.0063
int_2         .0047     .0016    3.0134    .0027     .0017     .0078
posemot      -.0235     .0276    -.8489    .3962    -.0777     .0308
ideology     -.2068     .0266   -7.7721    .0000    -.2590    -.1545

Interactions:

  int_1    negemot    X    sex
  int_2    negemot    X    age

R-square increase due to interaction(s):
         R2-chng       F        df1        df2        p
int_1      .0121    16.6759    1.0000    807.0000    .0000
int_2      .0066     9.0804    1.0000    807.0000    .0027
Both       .0246    16.9208    2.0000    807.0000    .0000

***********************************************************************

Conditional effect of X on Y at values of the moderator(s)
        age       sex     Effect      se        t         p       LLCI     ULCI
     33.2054    .0000     .2508     .0420    5.9707    .0000     .1683    .3332
     33.2054   1.0000     .4553     .0483    9.4241    .0000     .3604    .5501
     49.5362    .0000     .3284     .0365    8.9880    .0000     .2566    .4001
     49.5362   1.0000     .5328     .0357   14.9457    .0000     .4628    .6028
     65.8670    .0000     .4059     .0472    8.5953    .0000     .3132    .4986
     65.8670   1.0000     .6104     .0392   15.5868    .0000     .5335    .6873

Values for quantitative moderators are the mean and plus/minus one SD from mean

******************** ANALYSIS NOTES AND WARNINGS *************************

Level of confidence for all confidence intervals in output:
    95.00
```

FIGURE 9.2. Output from the PROCESS procedure examining the moderation of the effect of negative emotions about climate change on support for government action by sex and age.

PROCESS also estimates the conditional effect of X for various values of M and W, defined as

$$\theta_{X \to Y} = b_1 + b_4 M + b_5 W$$

which, in this example, is

$$\theta_{X \to Y} = 0.093 + 0.205M + 0.005W$$

Six such estimates can be found in the section titled "Conditional effect of X on Y at values of the moderator(s)." PROCESS sees that M is dichotomous so it uses the two values of M found in the data (0 and 1). Absent any other instruction otherwise, PROCESS selects the mean and plus and minus one standard deviation from the mean age, because it sees many values of W in the data and so assumes it is a continuum. This can be changed with the use of the **quantile** option. You could also select any value of values of M or W (or both) using the **mmodval** and **wmodval** options. See the PROCESS documentation in Appendix A for details.

PROCESS also calculates the standard errors of these conditional indirect effects, estimated as

$$se_{\theta_{X \to Y}} = \sqrt{ \begin{array}{c} se_{b_1}^2 + M^2 se_{b_4}^2 + W^2 se_{b_5}^2 + (2M)COV_{b_1 b_4} + \\ (2W)COV_{b_1 b_5} + (2MW)COV_{b_4 b_5} \end{array} }$$

where $COV_{b_i b_j}$ is the covariance between b_i and b_j. With this information, a t-ratio and p-value for testing the null hypothesis that $_T\theta_{X \to Y} = 0$ is provided, along with a 95% confidence interval.

As can be seen, the effect of negative emotions on support for government action is consistently positive and statistically significant for both males and females among the younger, moderate, and older in age. It is apparent both from the estimate of b_4 and the conditional effects produced by PROCESS that the effect of negative emotions on support for government action is larger for men than women. Notice that regardless of which value of age you choose, the difference in this effect between men and women is $b_4 = 0.2045$. For example, when age = 33.2054, the conditional effect for men is 0.4553 and for women it is 0.2508, a difference of $b_4 = 0.2045$. This difference is consistent for all values of age, a constraint inherent in this model.

In this model, b_5 estimates how the conditional effect of X on Y changes as W changes by one unit. Thus, among two hypothetical groups of people who differ by 1 year in age, the conditional effect of negative emotions on support for government action is $b_5 = 0.0047$ larger in the older group. For two groups 10 years apart, the difference in the effect is $10b_5 = 0.047$, and so forth. This difference is invariant to where you start on the distribution of age. But a constraint built into this model is that this difference in the conditional effect due to age is the same in both men and women, as can be seen in the PROCESS output. For example, the difference in the conditional effect of negative emotions among those moderate in age (49.536 years) compared to relatively young in age (33.205) is the same in both men and women. That is, $0.3284 - 0.2508 = 0.5328 - 0.4553$.

Moderated Moderation

Although the multiple moderation model is considerably more flexible than a multiple regression model that constrains X's effect to be unconditional (e.g., as does equation 9.9), it still has an important constraint. This constraint is best illustrated by considering the findings from the prior analysis. As discussed, in this model, X's effect is moderated by M and W, but M's moderation of X's effect is not dependent on W. That is, b_4 estimates how much X's effect on Y changes as M changes by one unit, but this is constrained to be the same regardless of W. In other words, as sex increases by one unit (i.e., the difference between women and men), the effect of negative emotions on support for government action increases by b_4 units *regardless* of age. But perhaps the sex differences in the link between negative emotions and support for government action is age dependent. Maybe the sex difference is smaller among younger people than among older people, for instance. The multiple moderation model cannot be used to determine this, because it constrains the interaction between X and M to be independent of W.

One means of overcoming this constraint is to estimate the regression coefficients not in equation 9.12 but, instead, the coefficients in equation 9.14:

$$Y = i_1 + b_1X + b_2M + b_3W + b_4XM + b_5XW + b_6MW + b_7XMW + e_Y \quad (9.14)$$

where XWM is the product of X, M, and W. This product, also known as a *three-way interaction* term, allows the moderation of X's effect on Y by M to depend on W. This model can be rewritten in equivalent form as

$$Y = i_1 + (b_1 + b_4M + b_5W + b_7MW)X + b_2M + b_3W + b_6MW + e_Y \quad (9.15)$$

which shows that X's effect on Y is a function of X, W, and their product and defined by $b_1 + b_4M + b_5W + b_7MW$. Another means of representing this model is

$$Y = i_1 + (b_1 + b_5W)X + [(b_4 + b_7W)M]X + b_2M + b_3W + b_6MW + e_Y$$

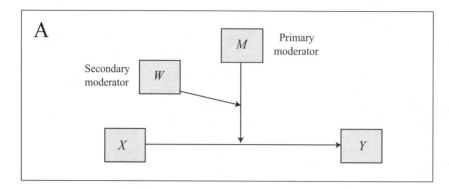

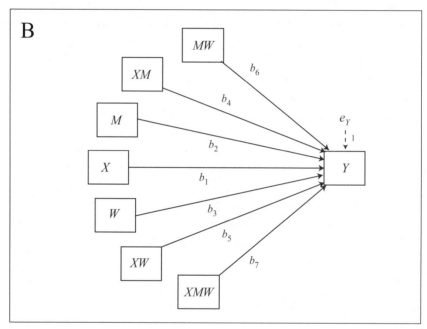

FIGURE 9.3. A moderated moderation model depicted in the form of a conceptual diagram (panel A) and a statistical diagram (panel B).

Expressed in this form, it is apparent that X's effect on Y has two components. One component is determined by W, expressed in functional form as $b_1 + b_5W$. The second component is determined by M, expressed in functional form as $b_4 + b_7W$. So M's influence on X's effect on Y is conditional on W. Thus, the moderation of X's effect on Y by M is itself moderated by W, a situation I refer to as *moderated moderation*. A conceptual representation of moderated moderation can be found in Figure 9.3, panel A. Panel B represents moderated moderation in the form of a statistical diagram.

In equations 9.14 and 9.15, most of the regression coefficients represent conditional effects and should not be interpreted as main effects and interactions as they are in a factorial ANOVA. The exception is b_7, which does estimate the three-way interaction between X, M, and W. But b_1, b_2, and b_3 are simple effects, not main effects. b_1 estimates the effect of X on Y when both M and W are zero, b_2 estimates the effect of M on Y when both X and W are equal to zero, and b_3 estimates the effect of W on Y when both X and M are equal to zero. By the same token, b_4 estimates the interaction between X and M when $W = 0$, b_5 quantifies the interaction between X and W when $M = 0$, and b_6 estimates the interaction between M and W when $X = 0$. Mean centering X, M, and W prior to computation of products and model estimation will make the interpretation of these coefficients closer to their counterparts in ANOVA, but usually not exactly the same. Whether or not mean centering is used, *all six of these terms should be included in a model that includes XMW, regardless of their statistical significance or lack thereof. A failure to do so will produce an invalid test of the three-way interaction between X, M, and W.*

PROCESS has a model built in that greatly simplifies the estimation of a moderated moderation model such as this. By specifying **model=3** along with outcome variables Y, focal predictor X, the primary and secondary moderators M and W, and any covariates of interest, PROCESS calculates all the necessary products, estimates the best-fitting OLS regression model, and probes the interaction for you. In the commands below, I also requested implementation of the Johnson–Neyman technique and estimates of Y for generating a plot of the model.

For instance, a PROCESS command that allows the moderation of the effect of negative emotions (X) on support for government action by sex (M) to depend on age (W) while controlling for positive emotions (C_1) and ideology (C_2) would be

```
process vars=govact negemot sex age posemot ideology/y=govact/x=negemot/
    m=sex/w=age/model=3/jn=1/plot=1.
```

whereas in SAS, try

```
%process (data=glbwarm,vars=govact negemot sex age posemot ideology,
    y=govact,x=negemot,m=sex,w=age,model=3,jn=1,plot=1);
```

The output generated by the SPSS version can be found in Figure 9.4. The best-fitting model is

$$\hat{Y} = 4.560 + 0.273X + 0.529M - 0.003W - 0.131XM + 0.001XW$$
$$-0.025MW + 0.007XMW - 0.021C_1 - 0.206C_2$$

```
process vars = govact negemot sex age posemot ideology/y=govact/x=negemot/m=sex
 /w=age/model=3/jn=1/plot=1.

Model = 3
    Y = govact
    X = negemot
    M = sex
    W = age

Statistical Controls:
CONTROL= posemot  ideology

Sample size
       815

**************************************************************************
Outcome: govact

Model Summary
          R         R-sq         F         df1         df2          p
       .6451        .4162    63.7645     9.0000    805.0000       .0000

Model
             coeff         se          t          p        LLCI       ULCI
constant     4.5595      .4850     9.4007      .0000      3.6075     5.5115
sex           .5294      .6465      .8188      .4131      -.7396     1.7984
negemot       .2728      .1181     2.3112      .0211       .0411      .5046
int_1        -.1308      .1675     -.7808      .4351      -.4595      .1980
age          -.0034      .0095     -.3562      .7218      -.0220      .0152
int_2         .0009      .0024      .3806      .7036      -.0038      .0056
int_3        -.0253      .0123    -2.0592      .0398      -.0494     -.0012
int_4         .0067      .0032     2.0961      .0364       .0004      .0129
posemot      -.0206      .0277     -.7453      .4563      -.0749      .0337
ideology     -.2055      .0266    -7.7265      .0000      -.2577     -.1533

Interactions:

 int_1    negemot     X    sex
 int_2    negemot     X    age
 int_3    sex         X    age
 int_4    negemot     X    sex       X    age

R-square increase due to three-way interaction:
          R2-chng    F(1,df2)        df2          p
 int_4     .0032      4.3934     805.0000       .0364

**************************************************************************

Conditional effect of X on Y at values of the moderator(s)
       age        sex     Effect         se          t          p        LLCI       ULCI
   33.2054      .0000      .3032      .0487     6.2259      .0000       .2076      .3988
   33.2054     1.0000      .3942      .0565     6.9713      .0000       .2832      .5052
   49.5362      .0000      .3181      .0368     8.6399      .0000       .2459      .3904
   49.5362     1.0000      .5182      .0363    14.2841      .0000       .4470      .5894
   65.8670      .0000      .3331      .0585     5.6954      .0000       .2183      .4479
   65.8670     1.0000      .6422      .0421    15.2609      .0000       .5596      .7248

Values for quantitative moderators are the mean and plus/minus one SD from mean

Conditional effect of X*M interaction at values of W
       age     Effect         se          t          p        LLCI       ULCI
   33.2054      .0910      .0736     1.2357      .2169      -.0535      .2355
   49.5362      .2000      .0500     3.9976      .0001       .1018      .2983
   65.8670      .3091      .0707     4.3707      .0000       .1703      .4479
```

(continued)

FIGURE 9.4. Output from the PROCESS procedure for a moderated moderation analysis examining the moderation by age of sex differences in the effect of negative emotions about climate change on support for government action.

```
********************** JOHNSON-NEYMAN TECHNIQUE *************************

Moderator value(s) defining Johnson-Neyman significance region(s)
    38.1138

Conditional effect of X*M on Y at values of the moderator (W)
       age     Effect        se         t         p       LLCI       ULCI
   17.0000    -.0172     .1169    -.1475     .8828    -.2467     .2122
   20.5000     .0061     .1069     .0573     .9543    -.2038     .2160
   24.0000     .0295     .0972     .3035     .7616    -.1613     .2203
   27.5000     .0529     .0878     .6019     .5474    -.1196     .2253
   31.0000     .0763     .0789     .9661     .3343    -.0787     .2312
   34.5000     .0996     .0707    1.4100     .1589    -.0391     .2383
   38.0000     .1230     .0633    1.9440     .0522    -.0012     .2472
   38.1138     .1238     .0630    1.9629     .0500     .0000     .2475
   41.5000     .1464     .0571    2.5625     .0106     .0343     .2585
   45.0000     .1697     .0526    3.2246     .0013     .0664     .2731
   48.5000     .1931     .0503    3.8408     .0001     .0944     .2918
   52.0000     .2165     .0503    4.3008     .0000     .1177     .3153
   55.5000     .2399     .0528    4.5425     .0000     .1362     .3435
   59.0000     .2632     .0574    4.5883     .0000     .1506     .3759
   62.5000     .2866     .0636    4.5073     .0000     .1618     .4114
   66.0000     .3100     .0710    4.3647     .0000     .1706     .4494
   69.5000     .3334     .0793    4.2022     .0000     .1776     .4891
   73.0000     .3567     .0883    4.0415     .0001     .1835     .5300
   76.5000     .3801     .0977    3.8920     .0001     .1884     .5718
   80.0000     .4035     .1074    3.7570     .0002     .1927     .6143
   83.5000     .4269     .1174    3.6366     .0003     .1965     .6573
   87.0000     .4502     .1276    3.5297     .0004     .1999     .7006

*************************************************************************

Data for visualizing conditional effect of X of Y
    negemot        age       sex      yhat
     2.0296    33.2054     .0000    4.1592
     3.5580    33.2054     .0000    4.6226
     5.0864    33.2054     .0000    5.0860
     2.0296    33.2054    1.0000    4.0326
     3.5580    33.2054    1.0000    4.6351
     5.0864    33.2054    1.0000    5.2376
     2.0296    49.5362     .0000    4.1343
     3.5580    49.5362     .0000    4.6206
     5.0864    49.5362     .0000    5.1068
     2.0296    49.5362    1.0000    3.8157
     3.5580    49.5362    1.0000    4.6077
     5.0864    49.5362    1.0000    5.3997
     2.0296    65.8670     .0000    4.1094
     3.5580    65.8670     .0000    4.6185
     5.0864    65.8670     .0000    5.1276
     2.0296    65.8670    1.0000    3.5988
     3.5580    65.8670    1.0000    4.5803
     5.0864    65.8670    1.0000    5.5619

Estimates in this table are based on setting covariates to their sample means

******************** ANALYSIS NOTES AND WARNINGS *************************

Level of confidence for all confidence intervals in output:
    95.00
```

FIGURE 9.4 continued.

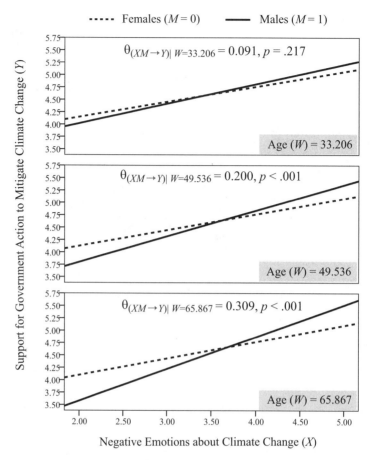

FIGURE 9.5. The conditional effect of negative emotions about climate change on support for government action as a function of sex and age. (The three panels for age correspond to values of age equal to a standard deviation below the mean, the sample mean, and a standard deviation above the mean.)

Notice that the regression coefficient for XMW is statistically significant, $b_7 = 0.007, t(805) = 2.096, p = .036$, meaning that there is evidence of a three-way interaction between negative emotions, sex, and age. That is, the magnitude of the moderation by sex of the effect of negative emotions on support for government action depends on age.

A visual representation of this model can be found in Figure 9.5, generated with the help of the estimated values of Y for various combinations of X, M, and W produced with **plot** option in PROCESS and found in the section of output labeled "Data for visualizing the conditional effect of X on Y." As can be seen, the effect of negative emotions on support for government action is consistently positive, but the difference in its effect between men and women is larger among those who are older. This moderation of the interaction between negative emotions and sex by age is not strong to be sure. Indeed, it accounts for only 0.32% of the variance in support for government action. But when represented visually in this fashion, it is clearly detectable by eye.

There are several options available for probing a three-way interaction in a moderated moderation model. One approach is a variant of the pick-a-point approach in which values of the secondary moderator W are chosen with the goal of ascertaining whether M moderates X's effect on Y conditioned on these various values of W. This requires estimation of the conditional effect of the XM interaction given W and conducting an inferential test for this interaction at that value of W. The conditional moderation of X by M is estimated as

$$\theta_{XM \to Y} = b_4 + b_7 W$$

with an estimated standard error of

$$se_{\theta_{(XM \to Y)}} = \sqrt{se_{b_4}^2 + (2W)COV_{b_4 b_7} + W^2 se_{b_7}^2}$$

Under the null hypothesis of no conditional interaction between X and M at a given value of W, the ratio of $\theta_{XM \to Y}$ to its standard error is distributed as $t(df_{residual})$.

PROCESS automatically implements this approach, the results of which can be seen in Figure 9.4 under the heading "Conditional effect of X*M interaction at values of W." Absent further instruction and with a continuous second moderator, PROCESS estimates $\theta_{XM \to Y}$ at values of W corresponding to the mean and plus and minus one standard deviation from the mean. Among those "relatively young" ($W = 33.205$), the effect of negative emotions on support for government action is not moderated by sex, $\theta_{XM \to Y} = 0.091, t(805) = 1.236, p = .217$. But among those "moderate" in age [$W = 49.536, \theta_{XM \to Y} = 0.200, t(805) = 3.998, p < .001$] and those "relatively old" [$W = 65.867, \theta_{XM \to Y} = 0.309, t(805) = 4.371, p < .001$], sex moderates the effect of negative emotions on support for government action. As discussed below, these three estimates of the conditional XM interaction are equal to the difference in the conditional effect of negative emotions in men compared to women at those three values of age.

An alternative approach when the secondary moderator is a continuum is to use the Johnson–Neyman technique to ascertain where the conditional interaction between X and M transitions between statistically significant and not along the distribution of W. The mathematics of the application of the Johnson–Neyman technique is the same as in simple moderation and equally complicated. Leave this to a computer program such as PROCESS. As can be seen in Figure 9.4, the interaction between negative emotions and sex transitions between statistically significant and nonsignificant at age = 38.114. Above this age, there is a significantly positive two-way interaction between negative emotions and sex. That is, there is a statistically significant difference in the effect of negative emotions between men and women among those at least 38.114 years of age. Below this age, sex does not moderate the effect of negative emotions on support for government action.

Another variant of the pick-a-point approach can be used in which the conditional effect of X is estimated for various values of M and W, followed by an inferential test for those combinations of X and W. This is not a formal probing of moderated moderation per se because it is not sensitive to how the conditional effect of X on Y given M is differentially related to W. However, it can be a handy and informative way of ascertaining how X is differentially related to Y as a function of both M and W in conjunction. The estimated conditional effect of X on Y given M and W is

$$\theta_{(X \to Y)} = b_1 + b_4 M + b_5 W + b_7 MW$$

with estimated standard error of

$$se_{\theta_{X \to Y}} = \sqrt{\begin{array}{l} se^2_{b_1} + M^2 se^2_{b_4} + W^2 se^2_{b_5} + W^2 M^2 se^2_{b_7} + \\ (2M)COV_{b_1 b_4} + (2W)COV_{b_1 b_5} + \\ (2MW)COV_{b_1 b_7} + (2MW)COV_{b_4 b_5} + \\ (2M^2 W)COV_{b_4 b_7} + (2MW^2)COV_{b_5 b_7} \end{array}}$$

(see Aiken & West, 1991, p. 54). Under the null hypothesis of no effect of X on Y at the chosen values of M and W, the ratio of $\theta_{X \to Y}$ to its standard error is distributed as $t(df_{residual})$. Obviously, this too you would never want to attempt to do by hand. Leave it up to a computer program such as PROCESS, which does it all for you. As can be seen in Figure 9.4, for both men and women, the relationship between negative emotions and support for government action is positive for those a standard deviation below the mean, at the mean, and a standard deviation above the mean age.

However, the pattern of differences in the effect of negative emotions between men and women is different here compared to in the prior model estimated on page 304. Whereas without the XMW term in the model, the sex difference in the conditional effect of negative emotions on support for government action was constrained to be the same regardless of age, in the moderated moderation model, the sex difference depends on age. Among those "relatively young" (age = 33.205), the difference in the effect of negative emotions between men and women is $0.394 - 0.303 = 0.091 = \theta_{(XM \to Y)|W=33.205}$, which we know is statistically different from zero from the implementation of the pick-a-point approach earlier. But among those "moderate" in age (49.536 years), the difference in the effect of negative emotions is no longer 0.091 but is, instead, $\theta_{(XM \to Y)|W=49.536} = 0.518 - 0.318 = 0.200$ and statistically different from zero ($p < .001$). Finally, among those "relatively older," (65.867 years) the sex difference in the effect of negative emotions is bigger still: $\theta_{(XM \to Y)|W=65.867} = 0.652 - 0.333 = 0.309, p < .0001$.

You are not stuck probing the moderation at the default values of the moderators that PROCESS chooses for you by default. When a moderator is a continuum, you can also use the **quantile** option. In addition, you could select any two values of M and W and have PROCESS estimate the conditional indirect of X at those two values. For instance, adding the options **mmodval=0** and **wmodval=50** to the PROCESS command line would generate and estimate and test of significance of the conditional effect of negative emotions on support for government action among 50-year-old women.

9.5 Reporting a Moderation Analysis

It takes time to develop a writing style that is your own and conveys your research findings in ways that are informative, interesting, and engaging to the reader. Science should be fun to communicate and fun to read, but it doesn't always seem that way given how many scientific articles are framed and written. Don't let your assumptions about science—that it should be cold, objective, and conveyed in third-person perspective— turn something that could and should be lively and fun into something dreadfully dull. Don't be afraid to say "I did" this or "We did" that, so long as you keep the focus on the science rather than the scientist.

Some of the more interesting studies you will find show that what is commonly assumed turns out to be true only sometimes, or that a well-known manipulation only works for some types of people. When writing about moderation, you have the opportunity to tell the scientific world that things aren't as simple as perhaps they have seemed or been assumed to be, and that there are conditions that must be placed on our understanding of the world. It is up to you how to tell your story about the contingencies of the effects you have found in your research. I offer only a few guidelines below for how you might think about articulating your results, how to con-template the reporting of findings that seem inconsistent or contradictory (as often happens when we analyze real data), and what you should try to always include in a description of an analysis so as to provide the reader what he or she needs to make sense of it.

First, at some point in your research career, you are going to come across one of three scenarios and wonder how to talk about your results under such circumstances. One scenario is a statistically significant interaction between focal predictor X and moderator M but no evidence of a statistically significant conditional effect of X at any value of M. The second scenario is a nonsignificant interaction but evidence that X is significantly related to Y for some but perhaps not all values of M. A third scenario is evidence of an interaction between X and M with additional evidence that X is related to Y at any value of M. Such results seem contradictory or paradoxical, but really they are not at all if you keep in mind that these are entirely different tests. A test of interaction is a test as to whether X's effect on Y depends linearly on M (or, in the case of a dichotomous M, whether X's effect on Y is different for the two groups defined by M). By contrast, a test of a conditional effect of X is a test as to whether X is significantly related to Y at a specific value of M chosen (or derived using the Johnson–Neyman technique). The outcome of one test implies nothing about the outcome of the other.

In the first scenario, you can claim that X's effect depends linearly on M but you won't be able to say specifically where on the continuum of M or for whom the effect of X on Y is different from zero. It may be that this doesn't bother you at all. Perhaps your primary focus is on whether X's effect depends on M and probing the interaction with the goal of making more specific claims is not important to you. But if the exercise and outcome of probing is important to you, this scenario requires some carefully chosen language, and though it may seem unsatisfying not to be able to provide a more specific claim, such is the nature of science at times. But remember if you are using the pick-a-point approach that whatever values of M you choose are entirely arbitrary. Just because X is not significantly related to Y among cases at, for example, the mean, one standard deviation below the mean, or one standard deviation above the mean, does not mean that X is unrelated to Y anywhere on the continuum of M. You are not wedded to the use of these three values as representations of "low," "moderate," and "high." Probe elsewhere if you choose. Alternatively, abandon the pick-a-point approach entirely and use the Johnson–Neyman technique instead, thereby eliminating the need to choose values of M when probing an interaction. If there is evidence that X is related to Y somewhere within the range of the data on M, the Johnson–Neyman technique will find where.

The second scenario can get you into trouble if you aren't careful when interpreting and writing, because a hypothesis about interaction is a hypothesis about the relationship between M and X's effect on Y. Establishing that X is significantly related to Y for one value of M but not for another does not establish that X's effect depends on M. Remember from section 9.3 that differences in degrees of significance or lack thereof does not imply significance of a difference. To say, for example, that X is significantly and positively related to Y in males but not in females does not mean that the relationship between X and Y is different between men and women. The claim that a conditional effect is not statistically different from zero does not mean that it actually is zero. Therefore, you can't claim that two things are different from each other just because one is not statistically different from zero when another is. A claim of difference between conditional effects should be based on an actual test as to whether X's effect on Y depends on M, that is, a test of interaction or moderation. Most critics of your work will take you to task if you imply interaction in your interpretation and discussion by talking about differences in significance if you can't establish convincingly with statistical evidence of interaction that X's effect on Y is actually related to M.

The third scenario is not nearly as difficult to deal with from a writing perspective as the first or second. Interaction between X and M does not mean that X's effect must zero for some values of M but not others. It may be that X is significantly related to Y at all values of M in the range of the data, or none of them. Just because you can't find some value of M where the conditional effect of X is not different from zero does not mean that M does not moderate X's effect on Y. M is a moderator of X's effect if X's effect depends on M. It may be that X is related to Y for both men and women, for example. If X is moderated by sex, that means that these conditional effects differ from each other. That does not preclude the possibility that X is related to Y in both groups. In this situation, you can claim both that X is related to Y wherever you look, and that X's effect also depends on M.

Second, as discussed in section 7.2 and throughout this chapter, the interpretation of the regression coefficients for X and M in a model that includes XM are highly dependent on the scaling of X and M. If you have centered a variable, say so. If you have standardized, say that too. If one or both of these variables is dichotomous, tell the reader what numerical codes were used to represent the two groups. Preferably, choose codes for the two groups that differ by one unit. The more information you give to the reader about how your variables are scaled or coded, the more the reader will be able to look at your results in the text, tables, or figures, discern their meaning, and interpret them correctly.

Third, as discussed in section 9.1, the decision to mean center or not has no effect on the estimate of the interaction between X and M. Whether to center or not is your choice to make. Personally, I think mean centering X or M, if not both, is a good idea in many circumstances, but my reasons have nothing to do with multicollinearity between X, M, and XM. As illustrated in section 7.2 and further discussed in section 9.1, b_1 and b_2 and their tests of significance in a model of the form $Y = i_1 + b_1 X + b_2 M + b_3 XM$ are heavily influenced by the scaling of X and M. b_1 estimates the effect of X on Y when $M = 0$ and b_2 estimates the effect of M on Y when $X = 0$. If X and M are kept in their original metric, one or both of these coefficients will be meaningless if zero is outside of the bounds of the metric of measurement. If you get in the habit of mean centering X and M, you know that b_1 and b_2 and their tests of significance will always be interpretable and meaningful because they estimate conditional effects of X and M when the other variable is at the sample mean. If M is dichotomous and mean-centered, b_1 estimates the weighted average effect of X between the two groups coded by M. If X is dichotomous and mean-centered, b_2 estimates the weighted average effect of M between the two groups coded by X.

With knowledge of the effects of scaling of X and M on the interpretation of the coefficients in a regression model with an interaction, you are less likely to fall victim to incorrect interpretation. However, don't assume that your reader will be equally informed, and so even if you know not to interpret a coefficient or hypothesis test that is meaningless, by mean centering you reduce the likelihood that your reader will do so. When X's effect is moderated by M, readers of your work unfamiliar with the interpretational principles described in this book are likely to misinterpret b_1 and b_2 as "main effects" when they are not. Mean centering X and M does not make these main effects, but they are closer to main effects than when X and M are uncentered. You can't stop people from misinterpreting a model, but you can reduce the severity of their mistakes through mean centering. So if this is something that concerns you, go ahead and mean center.

Fourth, as with mean centering, the decision to standardize X and M or to report standardized or unstandardized regression coefficients is your choice to make. But if you choose to do so, don't say you are doing so to reduce the effects of multicollinearity. Personally, I prefer to talk about regression results in unstandardized form. If you choose to report standardized regression coefficients, use either variant 1 or variant 2 described in section 9.2. When doing so, make sure that you are reporting and interpreting the coefficients corresponding to the *unstandardized* model in the output of your program and not the standardized model. Indeed, as a general rule, *never* report or interpret the coefficients listed in a standardized section of the output, and don't use these coefficients to probe an interaction. These regression coefficients do not have the interpretational properties described in the last few chapters. And don't standardize dichotomous variables or report standardized coefficients for a dichotomous predictor. For the most part, standardized regression coefficients for a dichotomous predictor are meaningless unless the cases are distributed evenly between the two groups. Keep standardized predictors in their original metric or, better still, use a 0/1 or $-0.5/0.5$ coding system (or any two values that differ by one unit) so that the regression coefficient for this predictor variable can be interpreted in a mean difference metric.

Fifth, I will repeat a point made at the end of Chapter 6 because it is important and applies here too. Avoid the use of terms such as "beta coefficient" or symbols such as b or β when talking about any regression analysis, including moderation analysis, without first telling your reader what these mean in table notes, footnotes, or the text itself. Many researchers throw such symbols around casually and without definition, believing that they are understood by all as conventions for talking about regression analysis.[2] Although there may be some such conventions in some disciplines, they are not universal, and I generally recommend assuming when you write that you are writing for an interdisciplinary audience. Different people trained in a different field than you or who learned regression from a different book or instructor may have learned to use different symbols or conventions. Using these terms or symbols undefined makes your writing seem somewhat parochial.

Sixth, the choice is up to you how much to focus your discussion of a model with an interaction between X and M on the regression coefficients for X and M. If you have evidence that M moderates X's effect, it typically is not particularly useful to spend too much time talking about the regression coefficients for X and M, because they will reflect a variable's association with Y conditioned on a single value of the other variable. Usually, the story to be told concerns the relationship between the moderator and the focal predictor's effect whenever you have evidence that X and M interact.

This would apply even if you choose to enter the XM product in a later step using hierarchical entry as described in section 8.3. It is common when using hierarchical regression to first enter X and M, substantively interpret the regression coefficients in that first stage with respect to one or more of the goals of the original study, and then enter the interaction to see if that earlier discussion needs to be qualified in light of evidence as to whether X's effect is contingent on M. Personally, I often don't see the value in spending lots of time telling your reader about relationships in step 1 of a hierarchical modeling procedure that ultimately must be qualified because

---

[2] A colleague of mine once asked a presenter at a talk we both attended whether he was reporting "bees or betas." Although I understood the question, it sounded bizarre and revealed his ignorance of variation within and between fields in how people are trained and talk about regression analysis.

those effects are contingent. In my opinion, often it makes more sense to go right step 2, describe the conditional nature of X's effect on Y, and probe the interaction. In other words, if you know X's effect is moderated by M, why hassle with hierarchical regression in the first place and describing a bunch of results from preliminary stages of the model-building process that ultimately aren't the complete story? Of course, it is your story to tell how you want, and if you feel that the results from preliminary stages of the model-building process are valuable, interesting, and/or of theoretical relevance, go ahead and include those results in your narrative.

In Chapter 12 I emphasize the importance of finding your own voice when writing about data analysis, but also note that having good models to follow as you are hunting for that voice can be helpful. The pick-a-point approach to probing interactions has been around a long time, and you should not have any difficulty finding models to assist you in choices about presentation. The Johnson–Neyman technique is less widely used, but its use is growing in frequency. Take a look at Barnhofer, Duggan, and Griffith (2011), Kochanska, Kim, Barry, and Philibert (2011), Kim and Kochanska (2012), Kim and Park (2011), Pakpour et al. (2011), and Taylor, Bomyea, and Amir (2011) for some examples of how others have described their application of both of these methods in the same analysis.

9.6 Chapter Summary

Absent the added flexibility that results when the product of two variables is included as a predictor in a linear model, multiple regression yields estimates of effects of one variable on another that are unconditional, meaning that they are not dependent on any variable in the model. A simple mathematical trick in which a focal predictor's effect is conceptualized as a linear function of a moderator produces an analytical tool with much greater utility that can be used to determine whether one variable's effect is contingent on another.

But this one fairly minor modification to a regression model introduces new complexities in interpretation that can easily trip up those without a good understanding of the principles introduced in this and the prior two chapters. Many myths have been perpetuated by a failure to appreciate how variable scaling, centering, and standardization influences the interpretation of regression coefficients in a regression model with an interaction. But when well understood, it is easy to see how multiple regression can be used to answer questions about how one variable's effect depends on another, and without splitting one's data file up into pieces and conducting subgroup analyses that skirt the central question a more rigorous moderation analysis answers.

With the fundamental principles and procedures of mediation and moderation analysis now well in your grasp, you are prepared to tackle the integration of mediation and moderation analysis into a single integrated analytical model. Conditional process modeling—the name I have given to this analytical integration—allows you to examine the extent to which a mechanism or set of mechanisms is contingent on a moderator or moderators. As you will see, lessons learned in the previous six chapters cannot just be forgotten as you turn to the next page, for most every concept introduced thus far reappears in this last section of the book dedicated to conditional process modeling.

Part IV

CONDITIONAL PROCESS ANALYSIS

10

Fundamentals of Conditional Process Analysis

Conditional process analysis is used when one's analytical goal is to describe and understand the conditional nature of the mechanism or mechanisms by which a variable transmits its effect on another. In this chapter, I describe a number of published examples that illustrate some of the many ways that moderation and mediation can be pieced together into a single integrated analytical model—a conditional process model. Following this, the fundamental principles, concepts, and procedures of conditional process analysis are then outlined, including the conditional direct and conditional indirect effect. I illustrate the application of these fundamentals by conducting a simple conditional process analysis using data from a study of team performance that illustrates how an indirect effect can be moderated and how to interpret such a phenomenon. After describing statistical inference, I show how PROCESS simplifies the work required to conduct a conditional process analysis.

Let's return to the example that started Chapter 4 on simple mediation analysis. Suppose we have established through a carefully designed experiment that gain frame messages are more effective than loss frame messages at influencing people to abandon their smoking habit. Furthermore, perhaps a mediation analysis reveals that this effect operates through counterarguing, in that loss frame messages invoke more counterarguing in the minds of the recipient, and this counterarguing reduces the persuasiveness of the message. However, even after accounting for individual differences in counterarguing, there is still evidence of a difference in smoking cessation between those exposed to the gain versus the loss frame.

The indirect effect of X (frame) on Y (smoking cessation intentions) through M (counterarguing) contains two components that, when multiplied together, yield an estimate of how much two cases that differ by one unit on X are estimated to differ on Y through the effect of X on M, which in turn affects Y. The first component is the effect of X on M, and the second is the effect of M on Y, holding X constant. In the notation of Chapter 4, these are paths a and b, respectively. Their product functions as a quantification of the mechanism by which gain frame messages influence behavior relative to loss frame messages.

In a mediation analysis, as in any analysis, we are losing some information when we reduce complex responses that no doubt differ from person to person or situation to situation down to a single number or estimate. For instance, when we say from the results of an experiment that people exposed to a loss frame message engage in more counterarguing on average than those exposed to the gain frame message, we are ignoring the very real possibility that for some types of people, or for some types of messages, or in some contexts or circumstances, or for some types of health-related issues, this may be less true or perhaps even false. Perhaps a loss frame message does not produce more counterarguing if the message includes a highly graphic visual image relative to when it does not. Or perhaps people who are less likely to engage in systematic processing of the message are less likely to counterargue regardless of how the message is framed. In short, no doubt there are moderators of the effect of framing on counterarguing. Just because we haven't explicitly modeled an effect as moderated doesn't mean that it isn't. In fact, it almost certainly is.

This same reasoning applies to the effect of M on Y. It certainly makes sense that engaging in counterarguing while processing a message could reduce its persuasive effectiveness. But maybe this is more true for open-minded people whose beliefs and behaviors are amenable to influence through reasoning than for people whose beliefs and behaviors are determined by ideology, religion, or who have deeply ingrained habits. A single estimate of the effect of counterarguing on intentions to quit smoking collapses across all individual differences and ignores the possibility that this effect may be and probably is moderated by *something*.

Finally, the direct effect in a mediation analysis is an effect too. Like all other causal paths in a mediation model, assuming that the direct effect is unmoderated by ignoring potential moderators and reducing the effect down to a single estimate may result in a description of a phenomenon that is incomplete, if not also wrong, if that effect is moderated.

It is safe to say that all effects are moderated by something. This is not to say that any analysis that fails to include moderation or that does not attempt to test for interaction between variables is bad, misguided, or should be avoided. Models are not intended to be complete mathematical representations of a process. Human behavior is too complicated to be reduced to a mathematical model, and no model we could ever imagine, much less estimate or test, would be complete and accurate (MacCallum,

2003). But an analysis that ignores the potential contingencies and boundary conditions of an effect is going to result in a greater oversimplification of complex processes relative to an analysis that acknowledges that complexity by formally modeling it, at least in part. With comfort in the principles of moderation analysis outlined in Chapters 7 to 9 you are now able to rigorously test a moderation hypothesis and examine or explore the potential contingencies that characterize most all phenomena that scientists study.

Thus far in this book, mediation and moderation have been treated as distinct, separate, and independent concepts with different analytical procedures and interpretations. Yet the earlier discussion clearly implies that processes modeled with mediation analysis likely are contingent and hence moderated, in that they operate differently for different people or in different contexts or circumstances. A more complete analysis, therefore, should attempt to model the mechanisms at work linking X to Y while simultaneously allowing those effects to be contingent on context, circumstance, or individual differences. This chapter begins the formal integration of mediation and moderation analysis by introducing an analytical method I have termed *conditional process modeling*. Conditional process modeling, or conditional process *analysis*, is used when one's research goal is to understand and describe the conditional nature of the mechanism or mechanisms by which a variable transmits its effect on another and testing hypotheses about such contingent effects.

The notion of combining moderation and mediation is not new. Authors of some of the seminal articles on mediation analysis discussed reasons investigators might want to entertain hypotheses that involve both moderation and mediation simultaneously. For instance, Judd and Kenny (1981) discuss the possibility that a causal antecedent variable X could moderate its own indirect effect on Y through M if the effect of M on Y depends on X. Some have gone so far as to say that *any* mediation analysis should as a matter of routine include a test of whether the effect of M on Y is moderated by X (Kraemer et al., 2002; Kraemer, Kiernan, Essex, & Kupfer, 2008). Similarly, James and Brett (1984) describe how the indirect effect of X on Y through M could be contingent on a fourth variable if that fourth variable W moderates one or more of the relationships in a three-variable causal system. Both of these are examples of what has come to be known as *moderated mediation*. Baron and Kenny (1986) also discuss moderated mediation when they make the point that an indirect effect could be contingent on a moderator variable, while also describing the possibility that an interaction between a moderator W and causal agent X on outcome Y could operate through a mediator M, a phenomenon that has been dubbed *mediated moderation*.

Not long after the turn of the 21st century, there was an explosion of articles in the methodology literature that more formally addressed moderated mediation and mediated moderation, and how moderation and mediation analysis can be analytically integrated. Muller et al. (2005) started the boom with their aptly titled article, "When Mediation is Moderated and Moderation is Mediated," in which they went beyond the causal-steps-like orientation of the past by addressing not only various criteria that one should meet to establish mediation of moderation or moderation of mediation but also how moderated indirect and direct effects can be quantified. However, their discussion focused entirely on only one specific form of moderated mediation in which a single variable moderated all three paths in a simple mediation model. Not long after, Morgan-Lopez and MacKinnon (2006) described a formal test of mediated moderation that researchers could use to establish that an interaction effect on some outcome is carried through a mediator.

Almost simultaneously, Edwards and Lambert (2007) and Preacher et al. (2007) published on the topic of moderated mediation but went far beyond the single model delineated by Muller et al. (2005). Edwards and Lambert (2007) described eight different models that could be constructed by allowing a single variable to moderate one or more of the causal paths in a mediation process and how the various direct and indirect effects can be estimated. While more limited in the number of models they discussed compared to Edwards and Lambert (2007), Preacher et al. (2007) introduced *conditional indirect effect* into the lexicon of statistical mediation analysis and showed how conditional indirect effects are calculated and hypotheses are tested through the construction of standard errors and bootstrap confidence intervals. They also illustrated how moderated mediation could be conceptualized in a model with two different moderators of different paths in the causal system. Various other papers have popped up since then in both the methodological and substantive literature addressing means of conceptualizing and quantifying the contingencies of a causal sequence of effects (e.g., Fairchild & MacKinnon, 2009).

Although all of these articles in some way contributed to the adoption of the methods and techniques discussed in this collective literature, Preacher et al. (2007) made it very easy for researchers to do so using software with which they were already familiar and using. This may in part account for the growth in publication of substantive research articles in many different fields that have included an analysis based on the principles of conditional process analysis I illustrate and discuss in the next few chapters. In the next section I provide a small sampling of the numerous ways that moderation and mediation can be combined in a single conceptual model. The section following formally defines the conditional indirect and conditional direct effect, concepts that are key in this kind of data analysis exercise. I then apply these ideas by stepping through a single and fairly simple exemplar of a conditional process analysis, ending with how PROCESS can be brought into service to simplify the estimation and inference of direct and indirect effects, both conditional and unconditional.

10.1 Examples of Conditional Process Models in the Literature

The mechanism linking X to Y can be said to be conditional if the indirect effect of X on Y through M is contingent on a moderator. There are many ways this could happen. For instance, the effect of X on M could be moderated by some variable W. The conceptual diagram in Figure 10.1, panel A, represents such a model. Alternatively, the effect of M on Y could be moderated by V, as in Figure 10.1, panel B.

An example of the former is found in Rees and Freeman (2009), who proposed and estimated such a process in a study of 197 male amateur golfers in the United Kingdom. They proposed that athletes with more task-related and emotional social resources available to them (*social support*, X) would perform better next time they played golf (*task performance*, Y) in part because of the boost in confidence such social support provides (*self-efficacy*, M), which in turn helps performance. However, they proposed that this social support → self-efficacy → task performance effect would be stronger among men experiencing more stress at home (*stressors*, W). Their reasoning was that social support would not be an important or salient source of confidence among people who were content and relaxed at home and so such support would do little to help task performance. But when that support occurred in the presence of a troubled, stressful home life, it would be a particularly effective confidence booster, and this would facilitate better play. Indeed, they found that more social support translated into greater self-efficacy and, in turn, a better golf score only among those experiencing relatively more stress at home. Among those experiencing relatively less stress, there was no indirect effect of social support on performance through self-efficacy. Additional examples of conditional processes in this form being proposed and modeled include Deng and Kahn (2009), Dittmar, Halliwell, and Stirling (2009), Goodin, McGuire, Stapleton, et al. (2009), van Dijke and De Cremer (2010), Wang, Stroebe, and Dovidio (2012), Wout, Murphy, and Steele (2010), and Zhou, Hirst, and Shipton (2012).

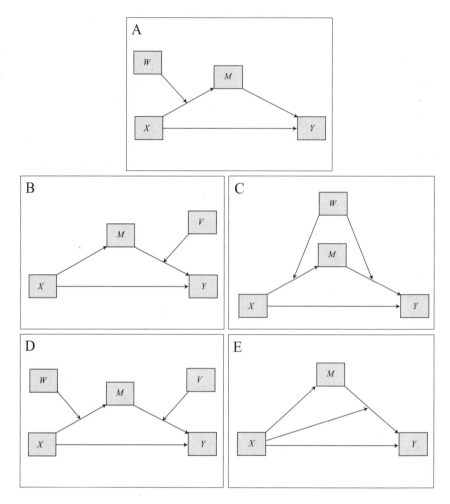

FIGURE 10.1. Some variants of a conditional process model found in published research.

Popan et al. (2010) offers an exemplar of a conditional process model with moderation of the effect of M on Y (panel B of Figure 10.1). Their study was designed to examine how the attributions made about the behavior of a member of an outgroup functions as a mechanism by which outgroup contact can influence attitudes held about the outgroup as a whole. Participants in this experiment were randomly assigned to recall up to 10 either positive or negative interactions with an outgroup member—someone with a different political orientation than their own—and provide detail about one of those interactions. They also reflected on the extent to which this person's behavior during the interaction seemed grounded in rational thought. Following this, their attitudes about the outgroup as a whole were assessed. Popan et al. found that participants who were asked to describe a positive interaction rather than negative interaction with a member of the outgroup (*valence of outgroup prime*, X) reported feeling more positive about the outgroup as a whole afterwards (*outgroup attitude*, Y) in part because the outgroup person's behavior was seen as relatively more rational (*rationality attribution*, M), which in turn was associated with a more positive attitude. However, this indirect effect was contingent upon how representative of the outgroup as a whole the outgroup member was perceived as being (*typicality of outgroup member*, V). The indirect effect of contact valence on outgroup attitudes through perceived rationality existed only among people who perceived the outgroup member as typical of the outgroup. Among those who thought the person was atypical, there was no indirect effect of contact valence on attitudes through perceived rationality. Many other examples of conditional process models involving moderation of the $M \rightarrow Y$ effect can be found, including Antheunis et al. (2010), Cole et al. (2008), Goodin, McGuire, Allshouse, et al. (2009), Luszczynska et al. (2010), Palomares (2008), and Warner, Schwarzer, Schüz, Wurm, and Tesch-Romer (2012).

A conditional process model can include moderation of more than one path in the causal sequence. For example, the effect of X on M and the effect of M on Y could be moderated by a common variable, as diagrammed in Figure 10.1, panel C. Though less commonly proposed and tested in the empirical literature than models with moderation of only a single path, examples do exist (e.g., Belogolovsky, Bamberger, & Bacharach, 2012; Huang, Zhang, & Broniarczyk, 2012; Kim & Labroo, 2011; Parade et al., 2010; Richter & Schmid, 2010; Silton et al., 2011). For instance, Parade et al. (2010) studied 172 females entering university with the goal of examining how feelings that one's parents are responsive the student's needs and are available for discussion and support (*parental attachment security*, X) influence satisfaction with relationships acquired in the first semester of college (*satisfaction with friends*, Y). They proposed that a more secure parental attachment style would result in less discomfort in social situations (*social anxiety*, M) during the transition to college life and this would translate into more positive experiences developing and relating to peers and friends in the university setting. However, this indirect effect was postulated to be moderated by race (*white* versus *minority*, W). They found that the relationship between secure attachment and social anxiety was stronger (i.e., more negative) among minority students than white students (i.e., moderation of $X \rightarrow M$ effect by W), as was the (negative) relationship between social anxiety and satisfaction with friends (i.e., moderation of the $M \rightarrow Y$ effect by W). Their conditional process analysis supported their claim of mediation of the effect of parental attachment security on friendship satisfaction by social anxiety only among minority students. In the white students, no such process appeared to be at work.

A variant of such a model involves the moderation of the effect of X on M by one variable W but moderation of the effect of M on Y by a different moderator V, as in Figure 10.1, panel D. For instance, Laran, Dalton, and Andrade (2011) examined the mechanism by which slogans, when present in an advertisement, can in some circumstances prompt behavior opposite of the intent of the ad. According to these investigators, slogans are generally seen as attempts at persuasion more so than are brand logos, and the more they are perceived as such by the consumer, the more likely the consumer will unconsciously react against the persuasion attempt by engaging in behavior contrary to the slogan. They exposed participants in the study to brand logos or brand logos combined with slogans (*advertising tactic*, X) that either did or did not emphasize saving money (*behavioral prime*, V). They also asked how much they felt that the logos and (for some participants) slogans they saw were designed to persuade (*persuasive intent*, M). Before answering the question about persuasive intent, some participants were asked to imagine they had run across the logo or slogan in a magazine filled with advertisements, whereas others were given no such instruction (*persuasion focus*, W). Participants were later presented with a hypothetical scenario in which they were to imagine a shopping trip where they could spend anywhere between $0 and $500, and they were asked how much they would spend (*willingness to spend*, Y). They found that logos combined with slogans were perceived as higher in persuasive intent than logos only, but only when participants were not primed to think in terms of the persuasive intent of advertising. This difference in perceived persuasive intent between logos and slogans resulted in an increased willingness to spend money, but only for slogans focused on *saving* money. Thus, they found an indirect effect of advertising tactic on willingness to spend through perceived persuasive intent only when participants were not primed to think in terms of the persuasive intent of advertisements and for slogans that focused on saving money.

An intriguing form of conditional process model is one in which X functions as a moderator of its own indirect effect on Y through M. It may be safe to call this the *original* conditional process model, as this kind of scenario was addressed by Judd and Kenny (1981) in their seminal *Evaluation Review* article published in 1981 on *process analysis*, what later became known as mediation analysis. A causal antecedent X can moderate its own indirect effect on Y through M if it moderates the effect of M on Y, as depicted in Figure 10.1, panel E. MacNeil et al. (2010) offer a good example of such a process in their study of 417 caregivers of elderly persons who suffer from some kind of mental or physical ailment (e.g., Alzheimer's or Parkinson's disease). According to their model, caregivers experiencing certain psychological maladies such as anxiety, depression, or resentment (*caregiver mental health*, X) are more likely to mistreat the person they are caring for (*potentially harmful behavior*, Y), because their own mental states enhance experiences of anger toward the recipient of their care (M), which in turn enhance the likelihood of harmful behavior. Their results were consistent with such a mediation process, but the association between anger and potentially harmful behavior was stronger among those feeling more depressed or resentful. Among the less resentful and depressed caregivers, anger was less likely to prompt maltreatment of the recipient of their care. Thus, the indirect effect of resentment and depression on mistreatment through anger was larger among those feeling more resentful or more depressed. For additional studies examining whether X moderates its own indirect effect, see D'Lima, Pearson, and Kelley (2012), Godin, Belanger-Gravel, and Nolin (2008), Moneta (2011), Oei et al. (2010), Pérez-Edgar et al. (2010), or Wiedemann, Schüz, Sniehotta, Scholz, and Schwarzer (2009).

As these five examples illustrate, moderation can be combined with mediation in a number of different ways. But these examples only scratch the surface of what is possible. Think about the number of possibilities when you increase the number of mediators, distinguish between moderation of paths in a parallel versus serial multiple mediator model, or allow for multiple moderators of different paths or the same path, and so forth. The possibilities are nearly endless. But regardless of the configuration of moderated paths or complexity of the model, conditional process analysis involves the estimation and interpretation of direct and indirect effects, just as in a simple mediation analysis. However, when causal effects in a mediation model are moderated, they will be conditional on those moderators. Thus, an understanding of the concepts of the *conditional direct effect* and the *conditional indirect effect* is required before one should attempt to undertake a conditional process analysis. The next section defines these terms and provides examples of their computation for a few models of increasing complexity.

10.2 Conditional Direct and Indirect Effects

Chapters 4 through 6 described the principles of statistical mediation analysis. In a mediation analysis, interest and effort focus on the estimation and interpretation of the direct and indirect effects of presumed causal agent X on putative outcome Y. The indirect effect in a mediation analysis is the product of a sequence of effects estimated using the available data that are assumed to be causal. For instance, in the simple mediation model, X's indirect effect on Y through M is quantified as the effect of X on M multiplied by the effect of M on Y controlling for X. In the notation of Chapter 4, the indirect effect is product of effects a and b estimated using equations 4.1 and 4.2.

But we've also seen in Chapters 7 through 9 that if a variable's effect is moderated, this means that the variable's effect cannot be quantified with a single number. For instance, suppose that the effect of X on M is moderated by W. In that case, there is no longer a single quantity that can be used to describe X's effect on M. Instead, X's effect on Y is now a function of W. Or perhaps M's effect on Y controlling for X is moderated by some variable V. Then M's effect on Y cannot be distilled down to a single number. Rather, M's effect on Y is a function of V. Indeed, it could be that both moderation processes are at work simultaneously, where X's effect on M is moderated by W and M's effect on Y is moderated by V.

The moderation of a path in a mediation model does not change the fact that the indirect effect of X on Y through M is still a product of paths of influence. But rather than being a product of two numbers, the indirect effect in such a circumstance becomes a product involving at least one function (depending on which path or paths are moderated), which makes the indirect effect a function of the moderator or moderators that influence the size of the effects in the causal system. In such a case, we can say that the "mediation is moderated," meaning that the indirect effect of X is conditional on a variable in the model rather than unconditional. That is, the $X \rightarrow M \rightarrow Y$ mechanism differs in size or strength as a function of a moderator variable or set of variables.

A direct effect can also be moderated. In a mediation model, the direct effect of X on Y quantifies the effect of X on Y independent of X's influence on Y through M. In a simple mediation model, it is estimated as c' in equation 4.2. But the direct effect of X on Y could be contingent on a moderator. For instance, if W moderates the effect of X on Y controlling for M, then the direct effect is no longer a single number such as c' but is instead a function of W. It is conditional on a variable in the model rather than unconditional.

When a direct or indirect effect is conditional, analysis and interpretation of the results of the modeling process should be based on a formal estimate of and inference about conditional direct and/or conditional indirect effects. In this section, I illustrate the computation of conditional direct and indirect effects for example models that combine moderation and mediation.

Example 1: Moderation of Only the Direct Effect

The simplest and arguably least interesting conditional process model is a model that combines simple mediation with moderation of the direct effect of X, as depicted in the conceptual diagram in Figure 10.2, panel A, on the left (or in statistical form, on the right). In this model, there is a single indirect effect of X on Y through M, as well as a direct effect that is a function of a fourth variable W. The statistical diagram represents two equations, one for consequent M and one for consequent Y. Assuming linear moderation of the direct effect of X by W, the two equations are

$$M = i_1 + aX + e_M \qquad (10.1)$$
$$Y = i_2 + c'_1 X + c'_2 W + c'_3 XW + bM + e_Y \qquad (10.2)$$

The indirect effect in this model is defined as the product of a and b, just as in any simple mediation model. Because neither the $X \rightarrow M$ nor the $M \rightarrow Y$ paths are moderated, this indirect effect is unconditional. However, the direct effect of X on Y is conditional, as it is a function of W. As in Chapter 7, this can be seen by rewriting equation 10.2 after grouping terms involving X and factoring out X:

$$Y = i_2 + (c'_1 + c'_3 W)X + c'_2 W + bM + e_Y$$

or, equivalently,

$$Y = i_2 + \theta_{X \rightarrow Y} X + c'_2 W + bM + e_Y$$

where $\theta_{X \rightarrow Y}$ is the *conditional direct effect* of X on Y, defined as

$$\theta_{X \rightarrow Y} = c'_1 + c'_3 W$$

So in this model, X exerts its effect on Y indirectly through M, independent of any other variable, but also directly, with the magnitude of the direct effect being dependent on W.

Example 2: Moderation of Only the Indirect Effect

A somewhat more interesting but still fairly simple conditional process model can be found in Figure 10.2, panel B. This conditional process model is nothing more than a simple mediation model with moderation of the indirect effect of X on Y through M. As depicted here, the indirect effect of X is conditional on V through moderation of the $M \rightarrow Y$ effect by V. When translated into a statistical model, the resulting equations representing such a process are

$$M = i_1 + aX + e_M \qquad (10.3)$$
$$Y = i_2 + c'X + b_1 M + b_2 V + b_3 MV + e_Y \qquad (10.4)$$

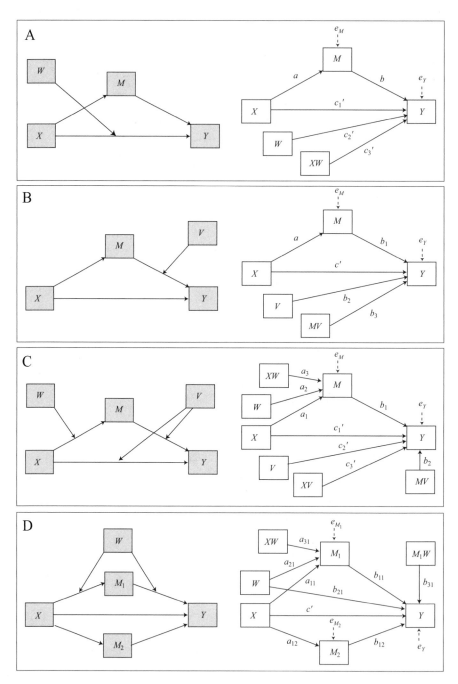

FIGURE 10.2. Some variants of a conditional process model in conceptual (left) and statistical (right) form.

As in any mediation model, X exerts its effect on Y through both direct and indirect pathways. The direct effect links X to Y independent of M and the effect of X on Y through M is, as always, the product of paths linking X to Y through M. The first of these components of the indirect effect is the path from X to M, estimated as a in equation 10.3, and the second component is the path from M to Y. However, as discussed in Chapter 7, the effect of M on Y (controlling for X) is *not* b_1 in equation 10.4. Rather, the effect of M on Y is a function of V in this model, as revealed by rewriting equation 10.4 in an equivalent form:

$$Y = i_2 + c'X + (b_1 + b_3 V)M + b_2 V + e_Y$$

Thus, the effect of M on Y is $\theta_{M \to Y} = b_1 + b_3 V$. It is a conditional effect that is a function of V. As a result, the indirect effect of X on Y through M is also a function of V, with the function formed as the product of effects linking X to Y through M. The result is the *conditional indirect effect* of X on Y through M:

$$a\theta_{M \to Y} = a(b_1 + b_3 V)$$

This conditional indirect effect quantifies how differences in X map onto differences in Y indirectly through M depending on the value of V. If the indirect effect of X differs systematically as a function of V, we can say that the mediation of X's effect on Y by M is moderated by V—*moderated mediation*.

The direct effect in this model is not moderated. Because the path from X to Y independent of M is not specified as moderated, it is estimated simply as c' in equation 10.4.

Example 3: Moderation of the Direct and Indirect Effects

Figure 10.2, panel C, represents a model with both the direct and indirect effects of X moderated, in this case by two moderators. As depicted, W moderates the indirect effect through its moderation of the effect of X on M, and V moderates the indirect effect through moderation of the effect of M on Y. At the same time, V moderates the direct effect of X. The equations corresponding to the model in statistical form are

$$M = i_1 + a_1 X + a_2 W + a_3 XW + e_M \tag{10.5}$$
$$Y = i_2 + c_1' X + c_2' V + c_3' XV + b_1 M + b_2 MV + e_Y \tag{10.6}$$

From equation 10.5, grouping terms involving X and factoring out X, the effect of X on M is not a_1 but, rather, $\theta_{X \to M} = a_1 + a_3 W$. Using the same procedure on equation 10.6, the effect of M on Y is $\theta_{M \to Y} = b_1 + b_2 V$. The indirect effect of X on Y through M is the product of these two conditional effects, meaning it is conditional—the conditional indirect effect—and defined as

$$\theta_{X \to M} \theta_{M \to Y} = (a_1 + a_3 W)(b_1 + b_2 V)$$

So the indirect effect of X is a function of both W and V. However, because the direct effect of X is moderated only by V, it is a function of only V:

$$\theta_{X \to Y} = c'_1 + c'_3 V$$

Example 4: Moderation of a Specific Indirect Effect in a Parallel Multiple Mediator Model

The model in Figure 10.2, panel D, is a more complex parallel multiple mediator model that includes moderation of effects to and from M_1 by a common moderator W, with all other pathways of influence from X to Y unmoderated. This model translates into the following three equations:

$$
\begin{align}
M_1 &= i_1 + a_{11}X + a_{21}W + a_{31}XW + e_{M_1} \tag{10.7} \\
M_2 &= i_2 + a_{12}X + e_{M_2} \tag{10.8} \\
Y &= i_3 + c'X + b_{11}M_1 + b_{12}M_2 + b_{21}W + b_{31}M_1W + e_Y \tag{10.9}
\end{align}
$$

The effect of X on M_1 is derived from equation 10.7 by grouping terms involving X and factoring out X, which results in $\theta_{X \to M} = a_{11} + a_{31}W$. Using the same procedure on equation 10.9, the effect of M_1 on Y is $\theta_{M \to Y} = b_{11} + b_{31}W$. The product of these conditional effects yields the conditional *specific* indirect effect of X on Y through M_1:

$$\theta_{X \to M_1} \theta_{M_1 \to Y} = (a_{11} + a_{31}W)(b_{11} + b_{31}W)$$

There is a second specific indirect effect of X in this model through M_2, but it is unconditional, because none of its constituent paths is specified as moderated. From equations 10.8 and 10.9, the specific indirect effect of X on Y through M_2 is $a_{12}b_{12}$. Finally, the direct effect of X on Y is also unmoderated and therefore unconditional. It is c' in equation 10.9.

10.3   Example: Hiding Your Feelings from Your Work Team

Popular music over the years has reinforced our intuitions as well as advice offered by close friends and extolled by talk show psychologists that little good can come from bottling up our feelings and hiding them from the view of others. We are told by the artists of the day that it is better that you

Express Yourself (Madonna), to beware that living by a *Code of Silence* (Billy Joel) means you'll never live down your past, and the longer your list of *Things I'll Never Say* (Avril Lavigne), the less likely you are to get the things you long for in life. So when others reach out with the request to *Talk to Me* (Anita Baker), it is important to let your guard down and *Communicate* (B-52s) what is on your mind.

Not necessarily so, at least in some work-related situations, according to research on teamwork by Cole et al. (2008). According to these researchers, sometimes it may be better to hide your feelings from others you work with about the things they do or say that bother you, lest those feelings become the focus of attention of the team and thereby distract the team from accomplishing a task in a timely and efficient manner. This study provides the data for this first example illustrating the mechanics of estimation and interpretation of a conditional process model, held in a data file named TEAMS, which can be found at *www.afhayes.com*.

The study involved 60 work teams employed by an automobile parts manufacturing firm and is based on responses to a survey from over 200 people at the company to a series of questions about their work team, as well as various perceptions of the team supervisor. Some of the variables in the study are measured at the level of the group and are derived from an aggregation of things that members of the same team said. Fortunately, there was much similarity in how team members responded to questions about the team, which justified this kind of aggregation. Other variables are based purely on reports from the team supervisor.

Four variables that are pertinent to this analysis were measured. Members of the team were asked a series of questions about the *dysfunctional behavior* of members of the team, such as how often members of the team did things to weaken the work of others or hinder change and innovation (DYSFUNC in the data file, such that higher scores reflect more dysfunctional behavior in the team). The *negative affective tone* of the group was also measured by asking members of the team how often they felt "angry," "disgusted," and so forth, at work (NEGTONE, with higher scores reflecting a more negative affective tone of the work environment). The team supervisor was asked to provide an assessment of *team performance* in general, such as how efficient and timely the team is, whether the team meets its manufacturing objectives, and so forth (PERFORM in the data, scaled with higher values reflecting better performance). In addition, the supervisor responded to a series of questions gauging how easy it is to read the nonverbal signals team members emoted about how they were feeling—their *nonverbal negative expressivity* (NEGEXP in the data file, with higher scores meaning the members of the team were more nonverbally expressive about their negative emotional states).

This goal of the study was to examine the mechanism by which the dysfunctional behavior of members of a work team can negatively affect the ability of a work team to perform well. They proposed a mediation model in which dysfunctional behavior (X) leads to a work environment filled with negative emotions (M) that supervisors and other employees confront and attempt to manage, which then distracts from work and interferes with task performance (Y). However, according to their model, when team members are able to regulate their display of negative emotions (V), essentially hiding how they are feeling from others, this allows the team to stay focused on the task at hand rather than having to shift focus toward managing the negative tone of the work environment and the feelings of others. That is, the effect of negative affective tone of the work environment on team performance is hypothesized in their model as contingent on the ability of the team members to hide their feelings from the team, with a stronger negative effect of negative affective tone on performance in teams that express their negativity rather than conceal it.

The conceptual diagram corresponding to this hypothesized process can be found in Figure 10.3, panel A. This is a conditional process model containing a mediation process ($X \rightarrow M \rightarrow Y$) combined with moderation of the $M \rightarrow Y$ effect by V. This conceptual diagram translates into a set of two equations because there are two consequent variables in the model (M and Y). The two equations representing this model, depicted in the form of a statistical diagram in Figure 10.3, panel B, are

$$M = i_1 + aX + e_M \tag{10.10}$$
$$Y = i_2 + c'X + b_1M + b_2V + b_3MV + e_Y \tag{10.11}$$

The regression coefficients can be estimated using two OLS regressions. In SPSS, the commands that accomplish the analysis are

```
compute toneexp=negexp*negtone.
regression/dep=negtone/method=enter dysfunc.
regression/dep=perform/method=enter dysfunc negtone negexp toneexp.
```

The corresponding commands in SAS are

```
data teams;set teams;toneexp=negtone*negexp;run;
proc reg data=teams;model negtone=dysfunc;run;
proc reg data=teams;model perform=dysfunc negtone negexp toneexp;run;
```

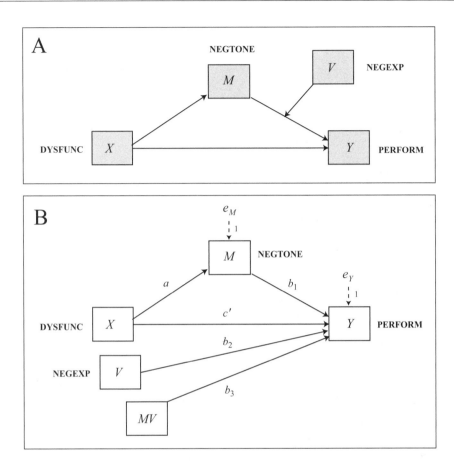

FIGURE 10.3. The conditional process model corresponding to the dysfunctional team behavior study in conceptual (panel A) and statistical (panel B) form.

The resulting coefficients and model summary information can be found in Table 10.1. As can be seen, the best fitting OLS regression models are

$$\hat{M} = 0.026 + 0.620X$$
$$\hat{Y} = -0.012 + 0.366X - 0.436M - 0.019V - 0.517MV$$

It appears that the more dysfunctional behavior displayed by team members, the more negative the affective tone of the work environment ($a = 0.620$), just as proposed by Cole et al. (2008). Furthermore, the effect of negative affective tone on work performance is indeed contingent on nonverbal negative expressivity, as evidenced by the statistically significant interaction between M and V in the model of Y ($b_3 = -0.517, p = .036$).

The regression coefficients for M and V are conditional effects with their product in the model. In this model, b_1 estimates the effect of negative affective tone on team performance in teams measuring zero in negative

TABLE 10.1. Model Coefficients for the Conditional Process Model in Figure 10.3

Antecedent		Consequent						
		M (NEGTONE)				Y (PERFORM)		
		Coeff.	SE	p		Coeff.	SE	p
X (DYSFUNC)	a	0.620	0.167	< .001	c'	0.366	0.178	.044
M (NEGTONE)		—	—	—	b_1	−0.436	0.131	.002
V (NEGEXP)		—	—	—	b_2	−0.019	0.117	.871
$M \times V$		—	—	—	b_3	−0.517	0.241	.036
Constant	i_1	0.026	0.062	.679	i_2	−0.012	0.059	.840
		$R^2 = 0.192$				$R^2 = 0.312$		
		$F(1, 58) = 13.800, p < .001$				$F(4, 55) = 6.235, p < .001$		

emotional expressivity but equal in dysfunctional behavior. This effect is negative and statistically different from zero, $b_1 = -0.436, p = 0.002$. This is substantively meaningful because zero is within the bounds of measurement in this study. A score of zero on nonverbal negative expressivity does not mean an absence of expressivity. Rather, zero is just barely above the sample mean ($\overline{V} = -0.008$). So holding constant dysfunctional behavior, among teams just slightly above average in expressivity, those functioning in a relatively more negative emotional climate are perceived by their supervisors as performing relatively less well.

The regression coefficient for nonverbal negative expressivity, b_2, estimates the effect of nonverbal negative expressivity on team performance among teams measuring zero in negative affective tone. Zero is within the bounds of measurement and is just below the sample mean ($\overline{M} = 0.047$). So among teams equal in dysfunctional behavior and slightly below the mean in negative affective tone, those teams whose members are more inclined to express their negative emotions perform less well. However, this effect is not statistically different from zero, $b_2 = -0.019, p = 0.871$.[1]

Evidence of moderation doesn't mean that pattern is as expected or hypothesized. To get a better handle on what the interaction between negative

[1]Mean centering or standardization is not required for the same reasons given in Chapter 9. Mean centering M and V prior to the estimation of the model would change the estimates of b_1, b_2, i_1, and i_2. But doing so would not change a or b_3. Ultimately, it is the direct and indirect effects that matter when it comes to interpretation of the results. Whether or not you mean center prior to analysis will not change the estimates of the direct and indirect effects in this model, inferential tests about those effects, or their interpretation.

affective tone and nonverbal negative expressivity means, we can generate the conditional effect of negative affective tone (M) on team performance (Y) for various values of nonverbal negative expressivity (V). Rewriting equation 10.11 in an equivalent form by grouping terms involving M and then factoring out M yields

$$\hat{Y} = -0.012 + 0.366X + (-0.436 - 0.517V)M - 0.019V$$

Thus, M's effect on Y is conditional on V and takes the form

$$\theta_{M \to Y} = b_1 + b_3 V = -0.436 - 0.517V \qquad (10.12)$$

Arbitrarily selecting values of V such as the 10th, 25th, 50th, 75th, and 90th percentiles and plugging these into equation 10.12 yields the effect of negative affective tone on team productivity among teams "very low," "low," "moderate," "high," and "very high" in emotional expressivity. If desired, hypothesis tests could be conducted to determine whether the conditional effect is different from zero at those values, or the Johnson–Neyman technique could be used to identify the region of significance.

   This could all be done the hard way using the equations and procedures described in Chapters 7 and 8, or PROCESS could be brought into service to take care of most of it. Observe that equation 10.11 is just a simple moderation model with M as focal predictor, V as moderator, Y as outcome, and X as a covariate. PROCESS model 1 estimates just such a model while also implementing the pick-a-point approach for probing the interaction. In SPSS, the command is

```
process vars=dysfunc negtone negexp perform/y=perform/x=negtone/m=negexp
    /model=1/quantile=1.
```

In SAS, use

```
%process (data=teams,vars=dysfunc negtone negexp perform,y=perform,
    x=negtone,m=negexp,model=1,quantile=1);
```

   The format of this PROCESS command might look peculiar, so some explanation is in order. In the conditional process model diagrammed in Figure 10.3, V is nonverbal negative expressivity and the moderator, yet there is nothing specified for V in this PROCESS command, and nonverbal negative expressivity is specified as M in this command. Furthermore, negative affective tone is M in the conditional process model, and X is

```
process vars=dysfunc negtone negexp perform/y=perform/x=negtone/m=negexp/
    /model=1/quantile=1.

Model = 1
    Y = perform
    X = negtone
    M = negexp

Statistical Controls:
CONTROL= dysfunc

Sample size
        60

**************************************************************************
Outcome: perform

Model Summary
        R          R-sq          F         df1         df2          p
     .5586        .3120      6.2350      4.0000     55.0000       .0003

Model
               coeff          se           t          p        LLCI        ULCI
constant      -.0119        .0585      -.2029      .8399      -.1292       .1054
negexp        -.0192        .1174      -.1634      .8708      -.2545       .2161
negtone       -.4357        .1306     -3.3377      .0015      -.6974      -.1741
int_1         -.5170        .2409     -2.1458      .0363      -.9998      -.0341
dysfunc        .3661        .1778      2.0585      .0443       .0097       .7224

Interactions:

 int_1    negtone     X     negexp

R-square increase due to interaction(s):
            R2-chng         F         df1         df2          p
int_1        .0576      4.6043      1.0000     55.0000       .0363

**************************************************************************

Conditional effect of X on Y at values of the moderator(s)
     negexp     Effect          se           t          p        LLCI        ULCI
     -.7300     -.0584        .2489      -.2344      .8155      -.5573       .4405
     -.4000     -.2290        .1844     -1.2417      .2196      -.5985       .1406
     -.0600     -.4047        .1357     -2.9834      .0042      -.6766      -.1329
      .5000     -.6942        .1482     -4.6841      .0000      -.9913      -.3972
      .8400     -.8700        .2047     -4.2506      .0001     -1.2802      -.4598

Values for quantitative moderators are 10th, 25th, 50th, 75th, and 90th percentiles

******************** ANALYSIS NOTES AND WARNINGS *************************

Level of confidence for all confidence intervals in output:
   95.00
```

FIGURE 10.4. SPSS PROCESS output for probing the interaction between negative affective tone and nonverbal negative expressivity.

dysfunctional behavior. Why is negative affective tone specified as X and dysfunctional behavior not assigned a role at all in this PROCESS command?

The explanation is that these symbols are arbitrary, so the symbols we use do not matter in principle. But in practice, PROCESS is programmed to expect certain symbols to be used in a simple moderation model (model 1) to denote which variable is the focal predictor and which is the moderator. Those are X and M, respectively. So that convention has to be followed in order for PROCESS to generate the model corresponding to equation 10.11. Dysfunctional behavior (X) in the conditional process model functions as a covariate in equation 10.11, so it is listed in the **vars=** list in the PROCESS command but not assigned a role elsewhere.

As can be seen in the PROCESS output in Figure 10.4 generated by this PROCESS command, it is estimating the correct model, and the regression coefficients, standard errors, p-values, and so forth are all the same as those produced by the SPSS regression command or PROC REG in SAS. But PROCESS also automatically calculates various conditional effects of negative affective tone on performance, along with hypothesis tests for those conditional effects (using the percentiles of the distribution for nonverbal negative expressivity by inclusion of **quantile=1** in the command line). Although formal hypotheses tests for these conditional effects of negative affective tone are not required (since ultimately we care about the conditional *indirect* effects to be discussed later and not the conditional effects we are generating here), it doesn't hurt to look at them, and PROCESS generates them whether we want them or not.

The section of output in Figure 10.4 titled "Conditional effect of X on Y at values of the moderator(s)" provides estimates of $\theta_{M\to Y}$ using equation 10.12, the conditional effect of negative affective tone (M in the conditional process model) on team performance (Y) for various values of nonverbal negative expressivity (V in the conditional process model). These values PROCESS used for V are -0.730, -0.400, -0.060, 0.500, and 0.840, which we can label as "very low," "low," "moderate," "high," and "very high" in nonverbal negative expressivity. As can be seen, regardless of the team's nonverbal negative expressivity, teams operating in an environment with a relatively more negative affective tone perform relatively less well, as the conditional effects at these five percentiles in the distribution of nonverbal negative expressivity are all negative. However, this negative association is larger in teams with greater nonverbal negative expressivity, and statistically significant only among teams moderate, high, or very high in their expressivity.

Combined, these results are consistent with the process as hypothe-sized by Cole et al. (2008). Teams whose members engage in relatively more dysfunctional behavior seem to produce a working environment that is relatively more negative in its tone, where team members are feeling irri-tated, angry, and so forth. And this negative tone is associated with lower team performance, but only among teams whose members fail to conceal how they are feeling. Among teams better versed at keeping their feel-ings to themselves, the negative affective tone produced by dysfunctional behavior does not seem to translate into reduced team performance.

Quantifying the Conditional Indirect and Direct Effects

The analysis just presented has been piecemeal, in that I have addressed how to estimate each of the coefficients in a conditional process model and how to interpret them using standard principles of regression analysis, moderation analysis, and so forth. But a complete analysis goes further by integrating the estimates of each of the effects in the model (i.e., $X \to M$, $\theta_{M \to Y}$) to yield the direct and indirect effects of X on Y. That is, the individual effects as quantified with the regression coefficients (conditional or otherwise) in equations 10.10 and 10.11 are not necessarily of immediate interest or relevance. Estimating them is a means to an end. What matters is the estimation of the direct and indirect effects, for they convey information about how X influences Y directly or through a mediator and how those effects are contingent on a moderator. Furthermore, once these effects are estimated, some kind of inferential technique should be applied for the purpose of generalization and ruling out "chance" as an explanation for the effects observed.

The Conditional Indirect Effect of X. As discussed throughout Chap-ters 4 through 6 as well as section 10.2, indirect effects are calculated as products of estimates of effects assumed to be causal, with those effects quantified with regression coefficients estimated through some kind of modeling method such as OLS regression. The analysis just described has resulted in an estimate of the effect of the proposed causal antecedent vari-able X, dysfunctional team behavior, on presumed causal consequent M, negative affective tone. The estimate of this $X \to M$ effect is a in equation 10.10. The analysis has also generated an estimate of the effect of negative affective tone on team performance, which is the final consequent Y. This $M \to Y$ effect was proposed by Cole et al. (2008) as moderated by nonverbal negative expressivity (V), and indeed it was. Thus, the effect of M on Y is conditional and estimated with the function $\theta_{M \to Y} = b_1 + b_3 V$. The indirect effect of dysfunctional behavior on team performance through negative af-fective tone is the product of these two effects, one unconditional (a), and

TABLE 10.2. Constructing the Conditional Indirect Effect of Dysfunctional Team Behavior on Team Performance through Negative Affective Tone for Various Values of Nonverbal Negative Expressivity

Nonverbal Negative Expressivity (V)	a	$\theta_{(M \to Y)} = b_1 + b_3 V$	$a\theta_{(M \to Y)} = a(b_1 + b_3 V)$
−0.730	0.620	−0.058	−0.036
−0.400	0.620	−0.229	−0.142
−0.060	0.620	−0.405	−0.251
0.500	0.620	−0.694	−0.430
0.840	0.620	−0.870	−0.539

one conditional $(\theta_{M \to Y}) = b_1 + b_3 V$. As one of these components of the indirect effect is conditional, then so too is the indirect effect itself (except in the case where the other component is zero), defined as

$$a\theta_{M \to Y} = a(b_1 + b_3 V) \qquad (10.13)$$

So there is no one numerical estimate of the indirect effect that can be used to characterize this process. Rather, in order to talk about the indirect effect of X on Y through M, one must condition that discussion on moderator V. This discussion is facilitated by actually calculating the conditional indirect effect for various values of V. Doing so proceeds much like the pick-a-point approach when probing interactions. Choose values of V where you desire an estimate of the conditional indirect effect and then do the computations. Earlier, we probed the interaction between M and V by estimating the conditional effect of M at values of V corresponding to the 10th, 25th, 50th, 75th, and 90th percentiles of the distribution, so we'll stick with those values here. These five values, representing very low, low, moderate, high, and very high on V are found in the first column of Table 10.2. The second and third columns provide the effects of X on M and the conditional effects of M on Y at those values of V, respectively. Notice that because the effect of X on M is not moderated, it is constant across all values of V. The last column is the product of the second and third columns and contains the conditional indirect effect of X on Y through M, conditioned on the value of V.

In generic terms, the conditional indirect effect of X on Y through M conditioned on V quantifies the amount by which two cases with a given value of V that differ by one unit on X are estimated to differ on Y indirectly through X's effect on M, which in turn influences Y. So consider two teams

0.500 units in nonverbal negative expressivity but that differ by one unit in dysfunctional behavior. According to this analysis (see Table 10.2), the team one unit higher in dysfunctional behavior is estimated to be 0.430 units lower in team performance as a result of the more negative affective tone produced by the more dysfunctional behavior (because a is positive), which lowers team performance (because $\theta_{M \to Y|(V=0.500)}$ is negative).

As can been in Table 10.2, the indirect effect of dysfunctional behavior on team performance through negative affective tone is consistently negative, but it is more negative among teams relatively higher in their nonverbal negative expressivity. So relatively more dysfunctional behavior seems to create a more negative affective tone in a work group (from path a), which translates into reduced team performance more so among teams with members who let their negative emotions be known to the team.

The Direct Effect. The direct effect of X on Y is neither hypothesized to be moderated nor is it estimated as such. Thus, there is only one direct effect of X in this model, estimated with c' in equation 10.11. This quantifies how much two teams that differ by one unit in their dysfunctional behavior are estimated to differ in performance when holding constant negative affective tone and nonverbal negative expressivity. The direct effect is positive, $c' = 0.366$. So two teams differing by one unit in dysfunctional behavior but equal in their negative affective tone and nonverbal negative expressivity are estimated to differ by 0.366 units in team performance, with the team displaying more dysfunctional behavior estimated to perform *better*.

10.4 Statistical Inference

My treatment of conditional process analysis thus far has been largely descriptive in nature. Description is important, but usually it is followed up with some kind of inferential technique in order to more rigorously substantiate the descriptive claims one is making. In this section, I discuss inference about the direct and conditional indirect effects quantified in the previous section.

In this model, the conditional direct effect of dysfunctional behavior on team performance is $c' = 0.366$. As this effect is not moderated, inference proceeds just as in ordinary mediation analysis by testing the null hypothesis that $_T c' = 0$ or constructing a confidence interval. This information is available from any OLS regression routine. As shown in the regression summary in Table 10.1, the null hypothesis of no direct effect can be rejected, as the p-value for the obtained estimate of 0.366 is less than 0.05. Naturally, therefore, a 95% confidence interval for $_T c'$ (using equation 2.10) is entirely above zero (0.010 to 0.732). The obtained estimate of 0.366 deviates too far from zero for "chance" to be a plausible alternative explanation. It seems that when holding constant the nonverbal negative expressivity of the team as well as the negative affective tone of the work environment, teams that manifest relatively more dysfunctional behavior perform relatively *better*, at least according to team supervisors.

As in simple mediation analysis, in conditional process modeling, evidence supporting the existence of a specific mechanism linking X to Y through M is not established by the outcome of a set of hypothesis tests on the constituent paths that define the indirect effect. Rather, inferences should be based on an estimate of the quantification of the mechanism—the indirect effect—defined as a product of the paths in the causal system. Complicating matters, however, is the fact that there is no single indirect effect one can quantify when the indirect effect is contingent on a moderator. Instead, one must settle for conditioning the inference on a specific value of the moderator and then conducting an inference on the conditional indirect effect at that value.

One of the contributions of Preacher et al. (2007) to the literature on moderated mediation analysis was their discussion of inference for conditional indirect effects. They suggested two approaches, one a normal theory-based approach that is an analogue of the Sobel test in unmoderated mediation analysis, and another based on bootstrapping. I discuss the normal theory approach first but do not recommend its use unless one has no other alternative. Instead, I advocate the use of bootstrap confidence intervals when one wishes to make a statistical inference about an indirect effect conditioned on a moderator.

Normal Theory Approach. The normal theory approach to inference about conditional indirect effects is based on the same philosophy as the normal theory-based Sobel test in unmoderated mediation models. Call ω the point estimate of the conditional indirect effect for a given value of V. For a conditional process model of this form, $\omega = a(b_1 + b_3 V)$. An estimate of the standard error of ω is then calculated, se_{ω}. The ratio $Z = \omega/se_{\omega}$ is then used as a test statistic for testing the null hypothesis that $_T\omega = 0$. A two-tailed p-value for Z is derived from the standard normal distribution in the usual way.

Preacher et al. (2007) provide first- and second-order standard error estimators for conditional indirect effects for a variety of different conditional process models. The formulas are complicated and not something you would want to implement by hand. For details on their derivation and the formulas themselves, see their Appendix.

To simplify life, Preacher et al. (2007) provide an SPSS tool (MODMED) that does the computations automatically. The second-order standard er-

TABLE 10.3. Inference for the Conditional Indirect Effect of Dysfunctional Behavior Using the Normal Theory Approach and Bootstrap Confidence Intervals (CI)

Nonverbal Negative Expressivity (V)	$\omega = a(b_1 + b_3 V)$	se_ω	Z	p	95% Bias-Corrected Bootstrap CI
−0.730	−0.036	0.160	−0.226	.821	−0.354 to 0.354
−0.400	−0.142	0.124	−1.141	.254	−0.459 to 0.094
−0.060	−0.251	0.110	−2.277	.023	−0.557 to −0.068
0.500	−0.430	0.150	−2.871	.004	−0.772 to −0.156
0.840	−0.539	0.196	−2.754	.006	−0.984 to −0.179

rors, Z, and p-values from MODMED can be found in Table 10.3. As can be seen, among teams moderate ($V = -0.060$), high ($V = 0.500$), and very high ($V = 0.840$) in nonverbal negative expressivity, the indirect effect of dysfunctional behavior on team performance through negative affective tone is statistically different from zero. But among team low ($V = -0.400$) or very low ($V = -0.730$) in nonverbal negative expressivity, the indirect effect is not statistically significant.

This approach suffers from the same limitation as the Sobel test described in Chapters 4 and 5 for indirect effects in simple and multiple mediator models. The conditional indirect effect is a product of normally distributed regression coefficients and thus its sampling distribution will not be normal. Yet the p-value for Z is derived in reference to the standard normal distribution—a reference distribution that is not appropriate. Furthermore, Preacher et al. (2007) show through simulation that this method is lower in power than bootstrap confidence intervals, which is the approach I do recommend. For these reasons, I don't recommend the normal theory approach except as a last resort.

Bootstrap Confidence Intervals. The rationale for using bootstrap confidence intervals for inference about conditional indirect effects is the same as the rationale for preferring this approach when the indirect effect is not estimated as moderated. The sampling distribution of ω is not likely to be normal and may be extremely non-normal. Bootstrap confidence intervals respect this non-normality because they are based on an empirically generated representation of the sampling distribution of ω rather than a (typically) inaccurate assumption about its shape.

A bootstrap confidence interval for $_T\omega$ is constructed in exactly the same way as described in Chapter 4. Many, many bootstrap samples of the data are taken and ω is calculated in each of these bootstrap samples.

The endpoints of a confidence interval for $_T\omega$ are then calculated using the percentiles of the distribution of ω over this repeated bootstrap sampling and estimation, with the addition of a bias correction to the percentile estimates if desired.

Ninety-five percent bias-corrected bootstrap confidence intervals for the conditional indirect effect of dysfunctional behavior on team performance through negative affective tone can be found in the last column of Table 10.3, generated in PROCESS (see section 10.5). As can be seen, in teams low and very low in nonverbal negative expressivity, the bootstrap confidence interval straddles zero, meaning a claim that it is different from zero is not justified. But in teams moderate, high, and very high in nonverbal negative expressivity, the confidence interval is entirely below zero. This supports the claim that the indirect effect when negative affective expressivity is at least moderate is indeed negative. Chance cannot credibly explain the discrepancy between the point estimates and zero.

In these data, it turns out that the choice between the normal theory approach and bootstrap confidence intervals is inconsequential in terms of the conclusions reached. Often this will be true, but sometimes they will produce different inferences. I would always trust bootstrap confidence intervals more than the normal theory approach when they disagree.

So the results of this conditional process analysis are consistent with the claim that when team members reveal their negative emotions in response to the negative working climate that dysfunctional behavior produces, team performance suffers. But if they are able to hide how they are bothered by such behavior, team performance is less affected. However, it may not be correct to conclude that dysfunctional behavior results in a net reduction in team performance, as the direct effect of dysfunctional behavior on performance was actually positive after accounting for differences between teams in negative affective tone and nonverbal negative expressivity. Not being an expert in organizational behavior, I am not in a position to explain this finding with any credibility, and Cole et al. (2008) do not address this in the discussion of their findings. I will speculate, however. Perhaps teams that engage in relatively more of the kind of dysfunctional behavior measured in this study are more likely to consist of members who are more competent, dedicated, and competitive. They backstab and undermine each other and are difficult to work with, but their competence and drive compels them to perform regardless. But if they let their negative affect show, this undermines what they could otherwise accomplish.

```
process vars=dysfunc negtone negexp perform/y=perform/x=dysfunc/m=negtone
 /v=negexp/model=14/quantile=1/boot=10000.

Model = 14
    Y = perform
    X = dysfunc
    M = negtone
    V = negexp

Sample size
       60

**************************************************************************
Outcome: negtone

Model Summary
         R       R-sq         F        df1        df2          p
     .4384      .1922   13.7999     1.0000    58.0000      .0005

Model
             coeff         se          t          p       LLCI       ULCI
constant     .0257      .0618      .4159      .6791     -.0979      .1493
dysfunc      .6198      .1668     3.7148      .0005      .2858      .9537

**************************************************************************
Outcome: perform

Model Summary
         R       R-sq         F        df1        df2          p
     .5586      .3120    6.2350     4.0000    55.0000      .0003

Model
             coeff         se          t          p       LLCI       ULCI
constant    -.0119      .0585     -.2029      .8399     -.1292      .1054
negtone     -.4357      .1306    -3.3377      .0015     -.6974     -.1741
dysfunc      .3661      .1778     2.0585      .0443      .0097      .7224
negexp      -.0192      .1174     -.1634      .8708     -.2545      .2161
int_1       -.5170      .2409    -2.1458      .0363     -.9998     -.0341

Interactions:

 int_1    negtone      X      negexp

******************* DIRECT AND INDIRECT EFFECTS *************************

Direct effect of X on Y
    Effect        SE          t          p       LLCI       ULCI
     .3661      .1778     2.0585      .0443      .0097      .7224

Conditional indirect effect(s) of X on Y at values of the moderator(s)

Mediator
            negexp     Effect    Boot SE   BootLLCI   BootULCI
negtone     -.7300     -.0362      .1733     -.3536      .3539
negtone     -.4000     -.1419      .1347     -.4592      .0939
negtone     -.0600     -.2508      .1179     -.5571     -.0678
negtone      .5000     -.4303      .1570     -.7715     -.1560
negtone      .8400     -.5392      .2049     -.9804     -.1786

Values for quantitative moderators are 10th, 25th, 50th, 75th, and 90th percentiles

******************* ANALYSIS NOTES AND WARNINGS *************************

Number of bootstrap samples for bias corrected bootstrap confidence intervals:
   10000

Level of confidence for all confidence intervals in output:
   95.00
```

FIGURE 10.5. Output from the PROCESS procedure for SPSS for a conditional process model (model 14) of the dysfunctional team behavior study.

10.5   Conditional Process Analysis in PROCESS

PROCESS has many models built into its programming that combine moderation and mediation in some fashion. In addition to doing all the required regression analyses for you, PROCESS will estimate both conditional and unconditional direct and indirect effects and provide all that is needed for inference. It knows which effects are conditional and which are not and produces output accordingly. When the direct or indirect effect is moderated, it produces a table containing the conditional effect for various values of the moderator or moderators. For inference, PROCESS generates standard errors, p-values, and confidence intervals for direct effects, and bootstrap confidence intervals for conditional indirect effects. Many of the models provide options for the inclusion of multiple moderators of the same path or of different paths, and it can combine moderation with parallel (but not serial) mediation. As in the analyses conducted in prior chapters, all PROCESS needs is a specification of the variables in the model, the model number being estimated (see the model templates beginning on page 442 and online at *www.afhayes.com*), the role each variable plays in the model (based on the conceptual diagram), and then any additional options you would like implemented.

Many but not all of the options for moderation and mediation analysis are available when estimating models that combine moderation and mediation. For instance, you can tell PROCESS to center variables that are used to form products, or request conditional effects for percentiles of the moderator, the mean and plus and minus one standard deviation from the mean, or a specific value of the moderator. For details on the various options available, a sampling of the models PROCESS can estimate, and instructions on its use, see Appendix A.

The model estimated in this chapter—a simple mediation model combined with moderation of the path from M to Y by a single variable V—is PROCESS model 14. Thus, the SPSS version of the PROCESS command which conducts the analysis described in this chapter is

```
process vars=dysfunc negtone negexp perform/y=perform/x=dysfunc/m=negtone
    /v=negexp/model=14/quantile=1/boot=10000.
```

In SAS, use

```
%process (data=teams,vars=dysfunc negtone negexp perform,y=perform,
    x=dysfunc,m=negtone,v=negexp,model=14,quantile=1,boot=10000);
```

As can be seen by comparing the PROCESS output in Figure 10.5 to the information in Table 10.1, the regression coefficients and their standard errors, the p-values, R^2, and so forth provided by PROCESS are the same as those generated by the separate OLS regression analyses conducted using SPSS Regression or SAS PROC REG. However, PROCESS also produces a lot more information needed for interpretation and inference that simply isn't available from SPSS or SAS otherwise. One of its most valuable features is the ease and speed with which it generates bootstrap confidence intervals for the conditional indirect effects. As requested by the **quantile** command, conditional indirect effects are produced at values of the moderator corresponding to the 10th, 25th, 50th, 75th, and 90th percentile of the distribution of negative affective expressivity. As specified in the **boot** command, bootstrap confidence intervals (bias-corrected) are based on 10,000 bootstrap samples. My description of the bootstrap confidence intervals described in the prior section were based on this PROCESS output. Outside of a structural equation modeling program that can bootstrap in this fashion, there is almost no other way of getting these confidence intervals without doing some tedious programming and work. PROCESS makes it easy.[2]

10.6   Chapter Summary

Knowledge of the mechanics, mathematics, and principles of conditional process modeling opens up analytical doors. This chapter has introduced the fundamentals of conditional process analysis using a relatively simple example that combines mediation of the effect of X on Y by M along with simple moderation of one of the paths in the causal sequence. Additional examples of a conditional process model in this form can be found in the literature with ease, but it is only one of the numerous ways that mediation and moderation can be and have been pieced together and combined into an integrated model. When a direct or indirect effect is moderated, it is conditioned on the variable that moderates it, meaning that there is not one single effect that characterizes how X influences Y directly or indirectly. Rather, the indirect or direct effect in such a circumstance is a function rather than a constant. Key to understanding the fundamentals of conditional process analysis is knowing how to estimate, make inferences about, and interpret conditional direct and indirect effects. The next chapter extends

[2]The MODMED macro for SPSS (Preacher et al., 2007) can generate bootstrap confidence intervals for conditional indirect effects for a model of this form, although doing so requires multiple runs of the macro, each run will be based on a different set of bootstrap samples, and the results must be compiled from multiple outputs.

the principles introduced here by applying them to a more complicated model involving moderation of both the direct and the indirect effect of X on Y.

11

Further Examples of Conditional Process Analysis

In this chapter, I provide an additional example of a conditional process analysis in which both the direct and indirect effects of X on Y are estimated as moderated by a common moderator. I also make the distinction here between moderated mediation and mediated moderation and show how a conditional process model in the form described in this chapter can be interpreted in terms of either moderated mediation or mediated moderation. I argue that mediated moderation rarely has a meaningful substantive interpretation and it is better to reframe a question about mediated moderation in terms of moderated mediation by focusing on the estimation and interpretation of conditional indirect effects rather than the indirect effect of a product of two variables through a mediator.

To someone learning about science, it may seem like scientists intentionally try to make things difficult. Our vocabulary is a case in point. Think about how many ways the word *validity* is used in science. No one wants his or her conclusions to be invalid. If we are worried about capitalizing on chance when exploring data, we are told to set aside half of our data so we can cross-validate our findings. People who conduct experiments are often criticized for producing results or laboratory conditions low in external or ecological validity, even when the internal validity of the design is pristine. We validate measurement instruments by considering criteria such as face validity, content validity, predictive validity, concurrent validity, and criterion-related validity. But even if we meet these tests of validation, our work can be panned if an instrument we have developed is low in discriminant validity. Scientists are great at making fine distinctions between related ideas, but not always so good at coming up with labels for those ideas that clearly distinguish them from each other.

Chapter 10 was dedicated to the fundamentals of conditional process analysis. In this chapter I build on the foundation laid by stepping through an analysis of a more complicated conditional process model that includes moderation of both the indirect and the direct effects in a simple mediation model. I do so by first using a piecemeal approach that focuses on each pathway in the model. With some understanding gained by this examination of the components of the process, I then bring the pieces together into an integrated conditional process analysis. I also describe a means of visualizing the conditional direct and indirect effects by plotting them as a function of a moderator of those effects.

When an indirect effect of X on Y through M is moderated, we call this phenomenon *moderated mediation*. In such a scenario, the mechanism represented by the $X \rightarrow M \rightarrow Y$ chain of events operates to varying degrees (or not at all) for certain people or in certain contexts. A similar-sounding phenomenon is *mediated moderation*, which refers to the scenario in which an interaction between X and some moderator W on Y is carried through a mediator M. I show in this chapter that a mediated moderation analysis is really nothing other than a mediation analysis with the product of two variables serving as the causal agent of focus. However, I argue that rarely can much meaningful come out of a mediated moderation analysis, because conceptualizing a process in terms of mediated moderation misdirects attention toward a variable in the model that actually doesn't measure anything.

So I will admit up front that parts of this chapter perhaps further contribute to the perception that scientists have a problem with their vernacular. But I hope my discussion of the difference between moderated mediation and mediated moderation toward the end clarifies rather than confuses the distinction.

11.1   Revisiting the Sexual Discrimination Study

In Chapter 7, I introduced a study by Garcia et al. (2010) in which participants evaluated an attorney (Catherine) subjected to sexual discrimination in her law firm. Recall that some of the participants in this study were told that following news that she lost a promotion to a less qualified male attorney at the firm, Catherine protested the decision by approaching the partners and making a case as to why it was unfair and that she should have been promoted. But some participants were told that she chose *not* to protest and, instead, accepted the decision, kept quiet, and went about her job at the firm. Of interest in that study was how Catherine would be perceived as a function of her decision to protest the discrimination rather than remaining silent. In turned out that different people perceived her differently, depending on their beliefs about the pervasiveness of sex discrimination in society.

In this section, I expand on these findings as well as the discussion of conditional process analysis in Chapter 10 by introducing a new variable to the model that Garcia et al. (2010) proposed as a potential mediator of the effect of Catherine's behavior on how she was evaluated. After reading the vignette describing Catherine's fate and how she responded, the participants were asked a series of questions, the responses to which were aggregated into a measure of *perceived appropriateness of the response* (RESPAPPR in the PROTEST data file, with higher scores reflecting a perception that her response was relatively more appropriate).

Garcia et al. (2010) argued that how Catherine is evaluated would depend on the extent to which her action was deemed appropriate for the circumstance. More specifically, insofar as protesting was perceived as an appropriate response to an apparent act of sex discrimination, she would be perceived more favorably. Of course, not everyone is expected to perceive her decision to protest as appropriate, but, on average, the expectation was that protesting would be seen as a more appropriate response than accepting the decision and remaining silent. This line of reasoning argues that perceived appropriateness of her response functions as mediator of the effect of her chosen course of action on how she was perceived.

The results of a simple mediation analysis using the procedure described in Chapter 4 is consistent with this proposal. Figure 11.1 contains PROCESS output from a simple mediation analysis using how much Catherine was liked as outcome variable Y, experimental condition as causal agent X (protest = 1, no protest = 0), and perceived appropriateness of her response as mediator M. As described in Chapter 4, such a model involves two equations, one estimating M from X and the other estimating Y from both X and M:

$$M = i_1 + aX + e_M$$
$$Y = i_2 + c'X + bM + e_Y$$

The SPSS PROCESS command which generates this output is

```
process vars=liking respappr protest/y=liking/x=protest/m=respappr
   /boot=10000/model=4.
```

whereas in SAS, the command is

```
%process (data=protest,vars=liking respappr protest,y=liking,x=protest,
    m=respappr,boot=10000,model=4);
```

As can be seen in Figure 11.1, the indirect effect of her decision to protest or not on how she was evaluated was 0.579 and different from zero by a bias-corrected bootstrap confidence interval (0.325 to 0.924) based on 10,000 bootstrap samples. This positive indirect effect reflects the fact that participants told that Catherine protested felt her response was more appropriate on average than did those told she accepted the decision ($a = \overline{M}_{protest} - \overline{M}_{no\,protest} = 1.440$), and the more appropriate her response was perceived as being, the more she was liked ($b = 0.402$). Accounting for the influence of perceived response appropriateness, there was no effect of her decision to protest on how she was evaluated ($c' = -0.100, p = .616$).

Although these findings are interesting perhaps, Garcia et al.'s (2010) reasoning about the process linking protest action to evaluation was a bit more sophisticated than this. Recall from the analysis presented in Chapter 7 that it was not the case that Catherine was uniformly more liked when she chose to protest relative to when she did not. Rather, how she was perceived depended on the perceiver's belief about the pervasiveness of sex discrimination in society. Her behavior influenced how she was perceived more so among those who regarded sex discrimination as relatively more pervasive (see Figures 7.6 and 7.7 for a visual representation, or the analysis in section 7.2 to refresh your memory). Participants who perceived the world differently, as one where sex discrimination is not so pervasive, perceived Catherine the same regardless of whether she protested the actions of the partners or accepted the decision.

Garcia et al. (2010) proposed that Catherine's decision to protest would be perceived as entirely justified and even necessary in a world unfair to women. Among those who see the world in this fashion, her decision to protest would be considered reasonable, even noble, and this would translate into a more positive evaluation because she acted appropriately and how she *should* have acted. But if she chose to remain silent and not defend herself against such unfairness when sticking up for herself was the more appropriate course of action, she'd be evaluated less positively because she didn't stand her ground. So the more a participant perceived sex discrimination to be rampant in society, the more protesting would be seen as appropriate relative to not protesting, and the more positively Catherine would be perceived as a result of her actions.

This reasoning predicts that the effect of the decision to protest or not on perceived response appropriateness should depend on perceived pervasiveness of sex discrimination. This prediction can be tested by examining

```
process vars=protest respappr liking/y=liking/x=protest/m=respappr
   /model=4/boot=10000.

Model = 4
   Y = liking
   X = protest
   M = respappr

Sample size
      129

**************************************************************************
Outcome: respappr

Model Summary
      R         R-sq        F         df1        df2         p
    .4992       .2492    42.1550    1.0000   127.0000      .0000

Model
             coeff         se          t          p        LLCI       ULCI
constant    3.8841       .1831    21.2078      .0000     3.5217     4.2466
protest     1.4397       .2217     6.4927      .0000     1.0009     1.8785

**************************************************************************
Outcome: liking

Model Summary
      R         R-sq        F         df1        df2         p
    .4959       .2459    20.5483    2.0000   126.0000      .0000

Model
             coeff         se          t          p        LLCI       ULCI
constant    3.7473       .3058    12.2553      .0000     3.1422     4.3524
respappr     .4024       .0695     5.7884      .0000      .2648      .5400
protest     -.1007       .2005     -.5023      .6163     -.4975      .2960

******************** DIRECT AND INDIRECT EFFECTS *************************

Direct effect of X on Y
    Effect        SE          t          p        LLCI       ULCI
    -.1007       .2005     -.5023      .6163     -.4975      .2960

Indirect effect of X on Y
             Effect     Boot SE    BootLLCI    BootULCI
respappr      .5793       .1520      .3253       .9240

******************** ANALYSIS NOTES AND WARNINGS ************************

Number of bootstrap samples for bias corrected bootstrap confidence intervals:
   10000

Level of confidence for all confidence intervals in output:
   95.00
```

FIGURE 11.1. SPSS PROCESS output from a simple mediation analysis examining the direct and indirect effects of the decision to protest on interpersonal evaluation.

```
process vars=sexism respappr protest/y=respappr/x=protest/m=sexism/quantile=1/model=1.


Model = 1
    Y = respappr
    X = protest
    M = sexism

Sample size
     129

**************************************************************************
Outcome: respappr

Model Summary
        R        R-sq         F        df1        df2          p
     .5442       .2962    17.5340     3.0000   125.0000       .0000

Model
               coeff         se         t          p        LLCI       ULCI
constant      6.5667     1.2095     5.4295      .0000     4.1730     8.9604
sexism        -.5290      .2359    -2.2426      .0267     -.9959     -.0622
protest      -2.6866     1.4515    -1.8509      .0665    -5.5594      .1861
int_1          .8100      .2819     2.8732      .0048      .2520     1.3679

Interactions:

 int_1     protest    X     sexism

R-square increase due to interaction(s):
            R2-chng         F        df1        df2          p
int_1         .0465     8.2551     1.0000   125.0000       .0048

**************************************************************************

Conditional effect of X on Y at values of the moderator(s)
      sexism      Effect        se         t          p        LLCI       ULCI
      4.1200       .6505      .3491     1.8633      .0648     -.0404     1.3414
      4.5000       .9583      .2733     3.5065      .0006      .4174     1.4992
      5.1200      1.4605      .2167     6.7386      .0000     1.0315     1.8894
      5.6200      1.8655      .2629     7.0950      .0000     1.3451     2.3858
      6.1200      2.2705      .3620     6.2724      .0000     1.5541     2.9869

Values for quantitative moderators are 10th, 25th, 50th, 75th, and 90th percentiles

******************** ANALYSIS NOTES AND WARNINGS *************************

Level of confidence for all confidence intervals in output:
  95.00
```

FIGURE 11.2. SPSS PROCESS output examining the moderation of the effect of the decision to protest on perceived response appropriateness by perceived pervasiveness of sex discrimination.

whether perceived pervasiveness of sex discrimination moderates the effect of the experimental manipulation of Catherine's behavior on how appropriate her behavior is perceived for the situation. As described in Chapter 7, this involves estimating the regression coefficients in a model of the form

$$Y = i_1 + b_1 X + b_2 M + b_3 XM + e_Y \tag{11.1}$$

where X is experimental condition, M is perceived pervasiveness of sex discrimination, and Y is perceived appropriateness of the response. Moderation exists if b_3 is statistically different from zero.

The PROCESS output in Figure 11.2 corresponding to the model delineated by equation 11.1 was generated with the following commands in SPSS:

```
process vars=sexism respappr protest/y=respappr/x=protest/m=sexism
   /quantile=1/model=1.
```

The corresponding PROCESS command in SAS is

```
%process (data=protest,vars=sexism respappr protest,y=respappr,x=protest,
   m=sexism,quantile=1,model=1);
```

Observe that $b_3 = 0.810$ and is statistically different from zero. Figure 11.3 depicts the interaction visually. It appears that protesting was seen as more appropriate than not protesting, but the difference in perceived response appropriateness was higher among those who reportedly felt sex discrimination is relatively more pervasive. Probing this interaction with the pick-a-point approach (using the 10th, 25th, 50th, 75th, and 90th percentiles of the distribution of the perceived pervasiveness of sex discrimination) reveals that protesting was seen as more appropriate than not protesting among all but those relatively low (SEXISM = 4.120, the 10th percentile) in perceived pervasiveness of sex discrimination. The Johnson–Neyman technique (not generated by the previous PROCESS command but easily implemented by adding jn=1 to the command line) identifies the region of significance for the effect of the decision to protest on perceived response appropriateness as scores on the Modern Sexism Scale of at least 4.153. Below this value, her decision to protest was perceived as no more or less appropriate than not protesting.

So the prior two analyses reveal that perceived appropriateness of the response may be one mechanism by which Catherine's action translates into an evaluation that is more or less positive. Protesting an act of sexual

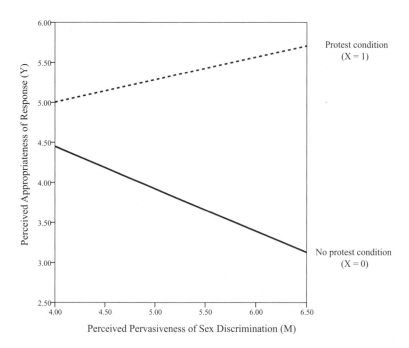

FIGURE 11.3. A visual representation of the moderation of the effect of the decision to protest (*X*) on perceived response appropriateness (*Y*) as a function of beliefs about the pervasiveness of sex discrimination in society (*M*).

discrimination was perceived as more appropriate than not protesting, and when Catherine acted in a manner that was perceived as more appropriate, she was more liked. But people differed in how appropriate they believed her decision to protest was. Among participants who believed more so than others that sex discrimination is highly pervasive, the more appropriate her decision to protest was perceived to be relative to not protesting. If anything, among such people, if Catherine did not protest, she was penalized in the form of a lower evaluation relative to how she was perceived among those believing sex discrimination is less pervasive.

Taken as a set, these results suggest that perceived appropriateness of the response may account for the moderation of the effect of her action on how she was evaluated by perceived pervasiveness of sex discrimination. One way of determining this would be to see if there is still evidence of this interaction between Catherine's behavior and perceived pervasiveness of sex discrimination in a model of how much she was liked after taking into account perceived appropriateness of the response. Doing so involves the estimation of the model in section 7.2 but including perceived response appropriateness as a covariate. The model that does this is

$$Y = i_1 + b_1 X + b_2 M + b_3 XM + b_4 C + e_Y$$

where Y is liking, X is experimental condition, M is perceived pervasiveness of sex discrimination, and C is perceived response appropriateness. In PROCESS, the command that executes this analysis is

```
process vars=sexism respappr protest liking/y=liking/x=protest/m=sexism
    /quantile=1/model=1.
```

In SAS, use

```
%process (data=protest,vars=sexism respappr protest liking,y=liking,
    x=protest,m=sexism,quantile=1,model=1);
```

The resulting PROCESS output can be found in Figure 11.4. As can be seen, evidence of moderation remains, as the regression coefficient for the product term is statistically significant, $b_3 = 0.543, p = .020$, albeit closer to zero compared to when perceived appropriateness of the response was not accounted for (recall that in the analysis in section 7.2, the regression coefficient for the corresponding interaction was $b_3 = 0.834, p < .001$).

A visual representation of this interaction can be found in Figure 11.5. Formally probing this interaction using the pick-a-point approach (see the bottom of the PROCESS output in Figure 11.4) reveals that when perceived appropriateness of Catherine's response is accounted for, her decision to protest or not seems to have had no effect on how she was perceived except among people very low (the 10th percentile of the distribution) in perceived pervasiveness of sex discrimination. Among such people, she was liked *less* when she chose to protest relative to when she did not. This is clearly a different pattern than the one depicted in Figures 7.6 and 7.7 and described in section 7.2, where her decision had an effect on how she was perceived *except* among people low in their beliefs about the pervasiveness of sex discrimination.

These three analyses, when qualitatively integrated into a story about the process at work linking Catherine's decision to how she was perceived, suggest that the pathways of influence in the simple mediation process modeled in the first analysis are contingent on the perceiver's beliefs about the prevalence of sex discrimination in society. This is a piecemeal approach to conditional process modeling, because there is no quantitative integration of the findings, and no formal inferential tests undertaken about some of the effects implied by these three analyses. The first analysis supports the claim that perceived appropriateness of the response is a mechanism carrying the effect of her decision to protest or not on how she was perceived. But

```
process vars=sexism respappr liking protest/y=liking/x=protest/m=sexism/
     quantile=1/model=1.

Model = 1
    Y = liking
    X = protest
    M = sexism

Statistical Controls:
CONTROL= respappr

Sample size
       129

**************************************************************************
Outcome: liking

Model Summary
         R        R-sq         F         df1         df2          p
      .5323       .2833    12.2551    4.0000    124.0000      .0000

Model
              coeff         se         t          p
constant     5.3471     1.0607     5.0412      .0000
sexism       -.2824      .1898    -1.4882      .1392
protest     -2.8075     1.1607    -2.4188      .0170
int_1         .5426      .2296     2.3628      .0197
respappr      .3593      .0706     5.0916      .0000

Interactions:

 int_1    protest    X     sexism

R-square increase due to interaction(s):
         R2-chng         F         df1         df2          p
int_1     .0323      5.5830     1.0000    124.0000      .0197

**************************************************************************

Conditional effect of X on Y at values of the moderator(s)
      sexism    Effect        se         t          p
      4.1200    -.5721      .2792    -2.0491      .0426
      4.5000    -.3659      .2259    -1.6196      .1079
      5.1200    -.0296      .1996     -.1480      .8826
      5.6200     .2417      .2457      .9840      .3270
      6.1200     .5130      .3274     1.5668      .1197

Values for quantitative moderators are 10th, 25th, 50th, 75th, and 90th percentiles

******************** ANALYSIS NOTES AND WARNINGS *************************

Level of confidence for all confidence intervals in output:
    95.00
```

FIGURE 11.4. SPSS PROCESS output examining the moderation of the effect of the decision to protest on liking by perceived pervasiveness of sex discrimination in society when controlling for perceived response appropriateness.

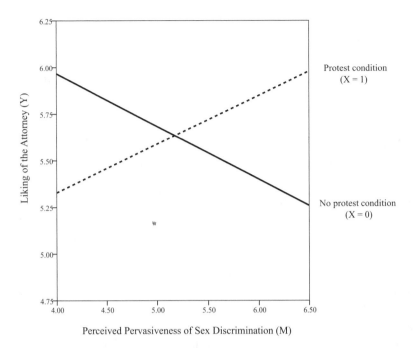

FIGURE 11.5. A visual representation of the moderation of the effect of the decision to protest (*X*) on liking (*Y*) by beliefs about the pervasiveness of sex discrimination in society (*M*) while controlling for perceived response appropriateness.

the second analysis shows that the extent to which her behavior was seen as appropriate for the circumstance is contingent on perceived pervasiveness of sex discrimination, suggesting that the indirect effect is moderated because the effect of the presumed causal antecedent on the proposed mediator is moderated. In the language of conditional process modeling, the indirect effect is conditional, but at no point thus far has the conditional indirect effect been quantified or have statistical inferences about its size been made as a function of the moderator. The third analysis shows that after accounting for the proposed mediator, the interaction between how Catherine acted and how she was perceived is smaller but still significantly significant.

In the following sections, I reconceptualize the analyses just undertaken by approaching them from two different interpretational perspectives, while simultaneously integrating them into a coherent conditional process model. The first approach formally estimates the conditional direct and indirect effects of Catherine's decision to protest or not on how she was perceived—*moderated mediation*. I then show how the identical model can be interpreted from the perspective of *mediated moderation* by estimating and attempting to substantively interpret the indirect effect of a product of variables. As will be seen, doing the latter is a bit of a challenge. To forecast where we are headed, I recommend that any question framed in terms of mediated moderation be reframed in terms of moderated mediation. Doing so will almost always produce results that are substantively more meaningful and interpretable.

11.2 Moderation of the Direct and Indirect Effects in a Conditional Process Model

The three analyses described in section 11.1 involve four variables measured or manipulated by Garcia et al. (2010). I label these variables Y, X, M, and W in this section. Participants' evaluation of Catherine (LIKING, Y) served as a consequent variable in two of those analyses and never an antecedent. Their study sought to explain variation in how much Catherine was liked, so this was the primary outcome variable of interest. Second, whether a participant was told that Catherine protested ($X = 1$) or did not protest ($X = 0$) an act of sexual discrimination by the senior partners (PROTEST) was experimentally manipulated and functioned as an antecedent variable in all three of those analyses. The effect of this manipulation served as the primary causal agent of interest in this study. The third variable was participants' scores on the Modern Sexism Scale, used as a measure of beliefs in the pervasiveness of sex discrimination in society (SEXISM, W). This variable always played the role of moderator in these analyses. Finally, participants were asked about how appropriate they believed Catherine's behavior was for the circumstance (RESPAPPR, M). This variable functioned as either antecedent, consequent, or mediator, depending on the analysis.

These three analyses, in the order they were introduced in section 11.1, are depicted in the form of conceptual diagrams in Figure 11.6. Panel A depicts the first analysis—the simple mediation analysis assessing the direct and indirect effects of Catherine's decision to protest or not on how she was evaluated through perceptions of response appropriateness. Panel B depicts the second analysis—a simple moderation analysis assessing participants' beliefs about how appropriate her chosen course of action was, moderated by participants' beliefs about the pervasiveness of sex discrimination. The third analysis is depicted in conceptual form in panel C. This analysis assessed the extent to which Catherine's behavior differentially influenced how she was perceived depending on the perceiver's belief about the prevalence of sex discrimination in society, but while holding constant or controlling for perceptions of the appropriateness of her response.

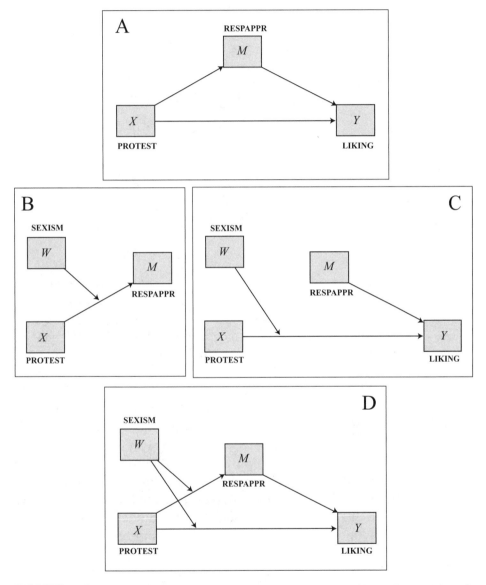

FIGURE 11.6. Conceptual diagrams of the three models estimated in section 11.1 (panels A, B, and C) and their integration in the form of a conditional process model (panel D).

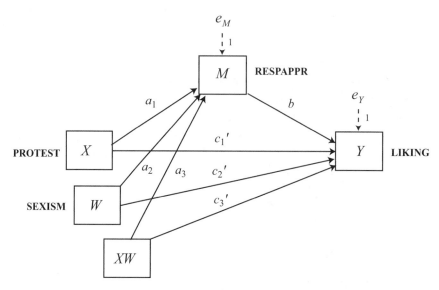

FIGURE 11.7. A statistical diagram of the conditional process model depicted in Figure 11.6, panel D.

Now imagine you could lift panels A, B, and C off the page and merge them into one diagram, such that the grey boxes labeled X, M, W, and Y in each panel completely overlap each other. The resulting diagram would appear as in Figure 11.6, panel D. This conceptual diagram represents an integration of these three analyses into a single coherent model—a conditional process model. This model depicts mediation of the effect of X on Y by M, with both the direct and indirect effects of X moderated by W. Moderation of the indirect effect is depicted in this model as resulting from moderation of the effect of X on M by W. This moderation renders the indirect effect conditional on W. The direct effect is also proposed as moderated by W, so the direct effect is also conditional on W. So there is no single direct or indirect effect of X on Y. Instead, the indirect and direct effects are functions of W. When the three analyses described in section 11.1 are conceptualized in this fashion as a single integrated model, analysis should focus on the estimation and interpretation of the conditional indirect and direct effects.

Figure 11.6, panel D, translates into the statistical diagram in Figure 11.7. This diagram represents two equations, one for M and one for Y:

$$M = i_1 + a_1 X + a_2 W + a_3 XW + e_M \qquad (11.2)$$
$$Y = i_2 + c_1' X + c_2' W + c_3' XW + bM + e_Y \qquad (11.3)$$

the parameters of which can be estimated using two OLS regression analyses. In SPSS, the commands that accomplish the analysis are

```
compute proxsex=protest*sexism.
regression/dep=respappr/method=enter protest sexism proxsex.
regression/dep=liking/method=enter protest sexism proxsex respappr.
```

whereas in SAS, the commands below do the job:

```
data protest;set protest;proxsex=protest*sexism;run;
proc reg data=protest;model respappr=protest sexism proxsex;run;
proc reg data=protest;model liking=protest sexism proxsex respappr;run;
```

The resulting model coefficients, standard errors, p-values, and model summary information can be found in Table 11.1. Expressed in the form of the two equations, the models for M and Y are

$$\hat{M} = 6.567 - 2.687X - 0.529W + 0.810XW$$
$$\hat{Y} = 5.347 - 2.808X - 0.282W + 0.543XW + 0.359M$$

Verify for yourself, if you wish, that the coefficients for the model of response appropriateness in Table 11.1 are identical to the PROCESS output in Figure 11.2 from the second analysis in the prior section, and the results for the model of how Catherine was evaluated are identical to the earlier PROCESS output in Figure 11.4 for the third analysis.

It is important to acknowledge and recognize that a few of the coefficients in Table 11.1 have no substantive interpretation because of the scaling of perceived pervasiveness of sex discrimination (SEXISM, W). The regression coefficients for the experimental manipulation (PROTEST, X) in both equations (a_1 and c_1') are conditioned on $W = 0$, which is beyond the scale of measurement. Had perceived pervasiveness of sex discrimination been mean centered prior to analysis, then a_1 and c_1' would estimate the effect of the manipulation among those average in perceived pervasiveness of sex discrimination. This would be substantively meaningful and interpretable.

However, this lack of interpretability does not generalize to a_2 and c_2'. Although they too estimate conditional effects (of W when $X = 0$), these are interpretable and substantively meaningful. They estimate the effect of perceived pervasiveness of sex discrimination on perceived appropriateness of the response and liking of Catherine, respectively, among those assigned to the no-protest condition ($X = 0$).

I argued in section 9.5 that it is probably a good idea to get into the habit of mean centering the variables that constitute a product if you are concerned about the possibility of others misinterpreting your results (due

TABLE 11.1. Model Coefficients for the Conditional Process Model in Figure 11.7

| | | Consequent | | | | | | |
| | | M (RESPAPPR) | | | | Y (LIKING) | | |
Antecedent		Coeff.	SE	p		Coeff.	SE	p
X (PROTEST)	a_1	−2.687	1.452	.067	c_1'	−2.808	1.161	.139
M (RESPAPPR)		—	—	—	b	0.359	0.071	< .001
W (SEXISM)	a_2	−0.529	0.236	.027	c_2'	−0.282	0.190	.139
X × W	a_3	0.810	0.282	.005	c_3'	0.543	0.230	.020
Constant	i_1	6.567	1.210	< .001	i_2	5.347	1.061	< .001
		$R^2 = 0.296$				$R^2 = 0.283$		
		$F(3, 125) = 17.534, p < .001$				$F(4, 124) = 12.255, p < .001$		

to the lack of familiarity of many with the subtleties of how variable scaling affects the interpretation of regression models with products of variables as predictors). I don't mean center in this analysis to continue to highlight that doing so is not necessary. And in this kind of analysis, where the focus is the estimation and interpretation of the conditional direct and indirect effects, it makes no difference whatsoever, because the conditional direct and indirect effects of X will be the same regardless of whether mean centering is done prior to model estimation.

Derivation of and Inference about the Direct and Indirect Effects

When this analysis is conceptualized in terms of *moderated mediation*, meaning moderation of the indirect (and, in this case, direct) effect of X, these effects must be estimated and then interpreted. Using the same logic described in Chapter 10, these effects can be derived by piecing together the coefficients from models of M and Y. An indirect effect in a model such as this one is the product of the effect of X on M and the effect of M on Y controlling for X, and the direct effect is the effect of X on Y controlling for M. But in this model, both of these effects are moderated and are functions of W, as described below.

We start first with the derivation of the indirect effect. Observe that the integrated model in statistical form (Figure 11.7 or equations 11.2 and 11.3) contains an interaction between X and W in the model of M, estimated by a_3. If a_3 is statistically different from zero, which it is here, this means that

X's effect on M is dependent on W. Thus, Catherine's decision to protest or not had different effects on how appropriate her behavior was seen to be, depending on how pervasive a person believes sex discrimination is in society (see Figure 11.3). So there is no single effect of her decision to protest or not on how appropriate that behavior is perceived. By grouping terms in equation 11.2 involving X and then factoring out X, it is revealed that X's effect depends on W and therefore is conditional. That is, the effect of X on M given W is not a_1 but instead is

$$\theta_{X \to M} = a_1 + a_3 W$$

This is the first component of the indirect effect of X on Y through M. The second component is the effect of M on Y controlling for X. This effect is not proposed or modeled as moderated, so this effect can be represented with a single estimate b from equation 11.3. Multiplying these two components yields the indirect effect of X on Y through M:

$$\theta_{X \to M} b = (a_1 + a_3 W)b = (-2.687 + 0.810W)(0.359) \qquad (11.4)$$

which is a function of W. So the indirect effect of Catherine's decision to protest or not on how she was perceived through perceptions of the appropriateness of her response depends on the perceiver's belief about the pervasiveness of sex discrimination in society.

    With evidence that the $X \to M$ path is moderated by W, the next step is the estimation of the conditional indirect effect for various values of W, along with an inferential test at those values. I have been using the percentiles of the distribution of perceived pervasiveness of sex discrimination throughout this example thus far, so I will stick with those percentiles defining very low (10th percentile = 4.120), low (25th percentile = 4.500), moderate (50th percentile = 5.120), high (75th percentile = 5.620), and very high (90th percentile = 6.120). Plugging these five values of W into equation 11.4 results in the conditional indirect effects in Table 11.2. Observe that the conditional indirect effect is consistently positive and increases with beliefs that sex discrimination is relatively more pervasive. But among those very low in such beliefs, the conditional indirect effect is not statistically different from zero based on a 95% bootstrap confidence interval (derived using PROCESS, as discussed below).[1] These results support (but by no means prove in any formal sense given the correlational nature of

---

[1]As noted throughout this book, I do not recommend the normal theory approach to hypothesis testing for indirect effects, conditional or otherwise. The formula for the standard error of the conditional indirect effect for a model of this form is provided by Preacher et al. (2007), and their MODMED macro for SPSS implements the normal theory approach described in Chapter 10.

the association between M and Y) the claim that except among those who believe sex discrimination is relatively less pervasive than others believe, Catherine's decision to protest is seen as more appropriate than not protesting in this circumstance (Figure 11.2 and the corresponding analysis), and the more appropriate the response was perceived to be, the more Catherine was liked (because b is positive). That is, the indirect effect of X on Y through M is positive except among those who don't see sex discrimination as particularly pervasive.

The direct effect of X on Y estimates how differences in X relate to differences in Y holding constant the proposed mediator or mediators. In this example, observe that the direct effect is proposed as moderated by W and is estimated as such by inclusion of the product of X and W in equation 11.3. Evidence of moderation is found in a statistically significant coefficient for this product term, c_3'. This coefficient is statistically significant, meaning that the direct effect of Catherine's decision to protest or not influences how she is evaluated *independent of* perceived response appropriateness but *depending on* the perceiver's belief about the prevalence of sex discrimination in society. Thus, the direct effect is conditional (see Figure 11.5).

The conditional direct effect is defined in terms of estimates of the coefficients in equation 11.3 by grouping terms involving X and then factoring out X. The resulting expression for the conditional direct effect is

$$\theta_{X \to Y} = c_1' + c_3'W = -2.808 + 0.543W \tag{11.5}$$

The conditional direct effects at values of perceived pervasiveness of sex discrimination at the 10th, 25th, 50th, 75th, and 90th percentiles of the distribution can be found in Table 11.2, along with standard errors and p-values when testing the null hypothesis that $_T\theta_{X \to Y|W} = 0$. The standard errors are derived from equation 7.12 (substituting W for M) introduced when the pick-a-point approach was described in Chapter 7. The p-values are derived from the t distribution with degrees of freedom equal to the degrees of freedom for the model of Y (equation 11.3).

Observe that although perceived pervasiveness of sex discrimination does moderate the direct effect of Catherine's decision to protest or not on how she was evaluated, this decision seemed to directly affect only those very low in their beliefs relative to others about the pervasiveness of sex discrimination in society. Among such people, Catherine was actually liked more when she did not protest than when she did, as the conditional direct effect is significantly negative when $W = 4.120$.

An interesting story can be told from the results in Table 11.2. It seems that the decision to protest rather than accept the discrimination translated into a more positive evaluation of Catherine among those who believe relatively more than others that sex discrimination is pervasive in society.

TABLE 11.2. Model Coefficients for the Conditional Process Model in Figure 11.7

	Indirect Effect		Direct Effect		
W	$\omega = (a_1 + a_3 W)b$	95% Bias-Corrected Bootstrap CI	$\theta_{X \to Y} = c'_1 + c'_3 W$	$se_{\theta_{X \to Y}}$	p
4.120	0.234	−0.007 to 0.564	−0.572	0.279	.043
4.500	0.344	0.147 to 0.634	−0.366	0.226	.108
5.120	0.525	0.308 to 0.828	−0.030	0.200	.883
5.620	0.670	0.378 to 1.059	0.242	0.246	.327
6.120	0.816	0.430 to 1.318	0.513	0.327	.120

This seems to be due, in part, to Catherine being perceived as having acted appropriately given her circumstance by these people who see sex discrimination as highly pervasive. Such people who were told she did not protest felt that such inaction was inappropriate and Catherine was penalized in the form of being thought of as less likable. But among those very low relative to others in their beliefs about the pervasiveness of sex discrimination, some other unidentified and unmodeled process is at work. Such people perceived Catherine as *less* likable when she protested, but perceived appropriateness of her response seems to have had nothing to do with it. There was no evidence of an indirect effect of Catherine's decision to protest on how she was perceived through perceived response appropriateness among such naysayers about sex discrimination, and when you account for perceived response appropriateness statistically, the conditional direct effect among such people is negative.

Estimation and Inference Using PROCESS

Any OLS regression program can be used to estimate the model coefficients, which in turn can be used to estimate the conditional direct and indirect effects as I have just done. Furthermore, using the procedures described in Chapters 7 and 8, probing the moderation of the direct effect is relatively straightforward. However, you need special software or code to get bootstrap confidence intervals for the conditional indirect effects in a conditional process analysis such as this. PROCESS will not only generate these confidence intervals, but it even does all of the model estimation, computation of conditional direct and indirect effects, and probing of the moderation of direct and indirect effects in one fell swoop, packaging it all for you in one tidy output.

In SPSS, the PROCESS command that conducts the analysis just described is

```
process vars=protest liking sexism respappr/y=liking/x=protest/w=sexism/
    m=respappr/model=8/quantile=1/boot=10000.
```

whereas in SAS, use

```
%process (data=protest,vars=protest liking sexism respappr,y=liking,
    x=protest,w=sexism,m=respappr,model=8,quantile=1,boot=10000);
```

By specifying **model=8** in the command line, PROCESS estimates the model depicted in Figure 11.7. It does all the hard work for you. All you have to do is tell PROCESS which variables in the data play the roles of X, M, W, and Y in the model, and request any options you would like PROCESS to carry out and produce in the output. In the PROCESS command I requested 10,000 bootstrap samples for the construction of bias-corrected bootstrap confidence intervals for the indirect effects, and the addition of **quantile=1** to the command requests conditional direct and indirect effects at values of the moderator which define the 10th, 25th, 50th, 75th, and 90th percentiles. Had I not used this option, PROCESS would have defaulted to the production of these direct and indirect effects at the mean and plus and minus one standard deviation from the mean. When the moderator is dichotomous, PROCESS estimates the conditional direct and indirect effect at the two values of the moderator.

The PROCESS output from SPSS that results from running the PROCESS command above can be found in Figure 11.8. PROCESS automatically estimates the coefficients in equations 11.2 and 11.3 using OLS regression. Estimates of a_1, a_2, and a_3 are found in the "Outcome: respappr" section of the output, along with tests of significance and confidence intervals. And in the output section labeled "Outcome: liking" can be found c'_1, c'_2, c'_3, and b.

The conditional direct and indirect effects found in Table 11.2 come from the PROCESS output under the heading "DIRECT AND INDIRECT EFFECTS." For the conditional direct effects, using the pick-a-point approach, PROCESS generates estimates along with standard errors, t, and p-values for the conditional direct effects. The conditional indirect effects

```
process vars=protest liking sexism respappr/y=liking/x=protest/w=sexism
   /m=respappr/quantile=1/model=8/boot=10000.

Model = 8
   Y = liking
   X = protest
   M = respappr
   W = sexism

Sample size
      129

*************************************************************************
Outcome: respappr

Model Summary
         R         R-sq        F          df1        df2          p
       .5442      .2962     17.5340     3.0000   125.0000       .0000

Model
              coeff        se          t          p        LLCI       ULCI
constant     6.5667     1.2095     5.4295      .0000     4.1730     8.9604
protest     -2.6866     1.4515    -1.8509      .0665    -5.5594      .1861
sexism       -.5290      .2359    -2.2426      .0267     -.9959     -.0622
int_1         .8100      .2819     2.8732      .0048      .2520     1.3679

Interactions:

 int_1    protest    X    sexism

*************************************************************************
Outcome: liking

Model Summary
         R         R-sq        F          df1        df2          p
       .5323      .2833     12.2551     4.0000   124.0000       .0000

Model
              coeff        se          t          p        LLCI       ULCI
constant     5.3471     1.0607     5.0412      .0000     3.2477     7.4465
respappr      .3593      .0706     5.0916      .0000      .2196      .4989
protest     -2.8075     1.1607    -2.4188      .0170    -5.1047     -.5102
sexism       -.2824      .1898    -1.4882      .1392     -.6581      .0932
int_2         .5426      .2296     2.3628      .0197      .0881      .9970

Interactions:

 int_2    protest    X    sexism

******************* DIRECT AND INDIRECT EFFECTS ************************

Conditional direct effect(s) of X on Y at values of the moderator(s)
     sexism      Effect        SE          t          p        LLCI       ULCI
     4.1200      -.5721      .2792    -2.0491      .0426    -1.1247     -.0195
     4.5000      -.3659      .2259    -1.6196      .1079     -.8131      .0813
     5.1200      -.0296      .1996     -.1480      .8826     -.4247      .3656
     5.6200       .2417      .2457      .9840      .3270     -.2445      .7280
     6.1200       .5130      .3274     1.5668      .1197     -.1351     1.1611
```

(*continued*)

FIGURE 11.8. Output from the PROCESS procedure for SPSS for a conditional process analysis of the protest and sex discrimination study.

```
Conditional indirect effect(s) of X on Y at values of the moderator(s)

Mediator
              sexism    Effect    Boot SE   BootLLCI   BootULCI
respappr      4.1200    .2337     .1428     -.0071     .5644
respappr      4.5000    .3443     .1216     .1473      .6355
respappr      5.1200    .5247     .1306     .3076      .8275
respappr      5.6200    .6702     .1708     .3783      1.0592
respappr      6.1200    .8157     .2247     .4298      1.3177

Values for quantitative moderators are 10th, 25th, 50th, 75th, and 90th percentiles

****************************************************************************

Indirect effect of highest order interaction

Mediator
              Effect   SE(Boot)   BootLLCI   BootULCI
respappr      .2910    .1357      .0566      .5894

******************** ANALYSIS NOTES AND WARNINGS *************************

Number of bootstrap samples for bias corrected bootstrap confidence intervals:
    10000

Level of confidence for all confidence intervals in output:
    95.00
```

FIGURE 11.8 continued.

for these same five values of perceived pervasiveness of sex discrimination follow in the output, along with 95% bias-corrected bootstrap confidence intervals for inference.

11.3   Visualizing the Direct and Indirect Effects

Direct and indirect effects that are moderated are functions of other variables in the model. Because there is no single number that characterizes the effect in such a case, and given that the function itself is just an abstract mathematical representation of the relationship between the moderator and the effect, a visual representation can aid both presentation and interpretation. To visualize conditional direct and/or indirect effects, produce a dataset that contains the estimated direct and indirect effects for various values of the moderator using the functions constructed from the coefficients in the model. Then graph the resulting data with the effect on the Y-axis, values of the moderator on the X-axis, and different lines for the direct and indirect effects.

An example for the results in the prior analysis can be found in Figure 11.9. Although your impulse might be to interpret the Y-axis as how much Catherine was liked, that is not the correct interpretation. The Y-axis corresponds to the estimated difference in liking between those told Catherine protested versus those told she did not. So a positive value means Catherine was liked more by those told she protested relative to those told she did not, whereas a negative value means she was liked more

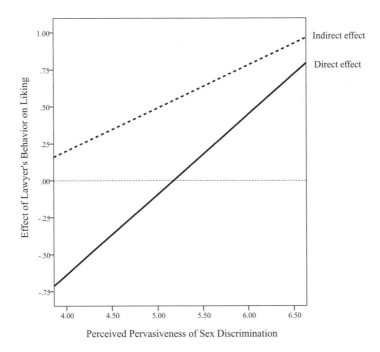

FIGURE 11.9. A visual representation of the conditional indirect and direct effects of the lawyer's behavior on liking as a function of beliefs about the pervasiveness of sex discrimination in society.

when she did not protest relative to when she did. Zero on the Y-axis corresponds to no difference between the two conditions. The slopes of the lines represent how much the effect of the lawyer's decision to protest or not on how she was perceived is influenced by individual differences in perceived pervasiveness of sex discrimination in society.

Figure 11.9 was generated in SPSS with the code below, with some additional editing in a dedicated graphics program:

```
data list free/sexism.
begin data.
4.120 4.500 5.120 5.620 6.120
end data.
compute direct = -2.808+0.543*sexism.
compute indirect = (-2.687+0.810*sexism)*0.359.
graph/scatter(overlay)=sexism sexism WITH direct indirect (pair).
```

In this code, the input to the functions are values of perceived pervasiveness of sex discrimination corresponding to the 10th, 25th, 50th, 75th, and 90th percentiles in the sample distribution. The first two **compute** commands then produce the direct and indirect effects using the functions in equations 11.4 and 11.5 based on the coefficients in the conditional process model.

A comparable figure can be generated in SAS with the following code. The resulting figure requires much less editing than the SPSS version.

```
data;input sexism @@;
direct = -2.808+0.543*sexism;
indirect = (-2.687+0.810*sexism)*0.359;
datalines;
4.120 4.500 5.120 5.620 6.120
run;
proc sgplot;
series x=sexism y=direct/curvelabel = 'Direct effect' lineattrs=(color=
    black pattern=Solid);
series x=sexism y=indirect/curvelabel = 'Indirect effect' lineattrs=(color=
    red pattern=ShortDash);
xaxis label = 'Perceived pervasiveness of sex discrimination';
yaxis label = 'Conditional effect of protest';
refline 0/axis=y transparency=0.5;
run;
```

The slopes of the lines in Figure 11.9 can be derived from equations 11.4 and 11.5. The slope of a line corresponds to how much the output of the function changes as the input to the function changes by one unit. From equation 11.5, the slope of the line for the direct effect is simply, c_3', as $\theta_{X \to M}$ increases by c_3' units as W increases by one unit. The slope of the line for the conditional indirect effect is not as obvious. From equation 11.4, the conditional indirect effect of X on Y through M is $(a_1 + a_3 W)b$. If W increases by one unit, then the conditional indirect effect of X on Y through M would be $[a_1 + a_3(W + 1)]b$. The slope of the line for the conditional indirect effect is the difference between these two values:

$$
\begin{aligned}
[a_1 + a_3(W + 1)]b - (a_1 + a_3 W)b &= a_1 b + a_3 bW + a_3 b - a_1 b - a_3 bW \\
&= (a_1 b - a_1 b) + (a_3 bW - a_3 bW) + a_3 b \\
&= a_3 b
\end{aligned}
$$

This result of this derivation has an important interpretation. Consider two groups of people that differ by one unit in their perceived pervasiveness of sex discrimination in society. According to this derivation, the indirect effect of the decision to protest on liking through perceived appropriateness of the response is a_3b units larger in the group that sees sex discrimination as more pervasive. That is, a_3b is the difference between the conditional indirect effects in these two groups. This will be relevant to my discussion and critique of mediated moderation in the following section. This product also provides a test statistic for a formal test of moderated mediation, as discussed in Chapter 12.

11.4 Mediated Moderation

Mediation is moderated if the indirect effect of X on Y through one or more mediators is contingent on a moderator. With evidence of moderated mediation, one can claim that the $X \rightarrow M \rightarrow Y$ chain of events functions differently or to varying degrees for different people, in different contexts or conditions, or whatever the moderator variable represents. Although similar in name and pronunciation to moderated mediation, the term *mediated moderation* refers to the phenomenon in which an interaction between X and a moderator W in a model of Y is carried through a mediator. As in any mediation phenomenon, the causal chain of events from XW to M to Y is interpreted as the mechanism by which X's moderated effect on Y is transmitted.

Mediation moderation hypotheses are regularly articulated and tested by scientists. For example, Clark, Wegener, Briñol, and Petty (2011) showed participants the cognitive test performance of a child who did either very well or very poorly and then asked them to list their thoughts about the child's performance. Following this, the participants were given information about the socioeconomic status of the child and his family that was either stereotypically consistent or inconsistent with the child's performance, after which they were asked to indicate how confident they were about the validity of their prior thoughts. They were also asked to make a recommendation as to whether the child should be placed in a program for gifted children or for children in need of remedial instruction.

Clark et al. (2011) found an interaction between performance and socioeconomic status in a model predicting placement recommendations, such that participants' recommendations were consistent with the child's performance only when the child's performance was consistent with the performance implied by the socioeconomic stereotype. According to their analysis, this interaction was mediated by thought confidence, in that participants were more confident about the thoughts they listed prior to being told about the child's socioeconomic status when those thoughts were consistent with performance implied by the stereotype, and accounting for thought confidence statistically reduced the size of the interaction in the model estimating placement recommendation. Additional examples of mediated moderation in the empirical literature include Ashton-James and Tracy (2012), Bugental, Beaulieu, and Silbert-Geiger (2010), Cohen, Sullivan, Solomon, Greenberg, and Ogilvie (2011), Ein-Gar, Shiv, and Tormala (2012), Grant, Gino, and Hofmann (2011), Jiang, Bazarova, and Hancock (2011), Morrison (2011), Rabinovich and Morton (2012), Rueggeberg, Wrosch, Miller, and McDade (2012), Terwel, Harinck, Ellemers, and Daamen (2010), and van Rompay, de Fries, and van Venrooij (2010).

Although there is an abundance of published examples of mediated moderation analysis, their frequency of occurrence in the literature should not be confused with meaningfulness of the procedure itself. I will argue toward the end of this section that rarely is the phenomenon of mediated moderation interesting when interpreted as such. It is almost always substantively more meaningful to conceptualize a mediated moderation process in terms of moderated mediation. But before doing this, I will describe how a mediated moderation analysis is undertaken.

Mediated Moderation as the Indirect Effect of a Product

Consider the simple moderation model, where X's effect on Y is moderated by a single variable, W:

$$Y = i_1 + c_1 X + c_2 W + c_3 XW + e_Y \qquad (11.6)$$

This equation is represented in the form of a statistical diagram in Figure 11.10. If c_3 is statistically different from zero, then one can claim that the effect of X on Y depends on W.

An investigator interested in testing a hypothesis about mediated moderation would attempt to ascertain whether the interaction between X and W in the model of Y operates through a mediator, M. Baron and Kenny (1986) describe the application of the causal steps approach for establishing mediated moderation. After first demonstrating that c_3 is statistically different from zero, one then tests whether W moderates X's effect in a model of the proposed mediator by estimating the coefficients in

$$M = i_2 + a_1 X + a_2 W + a_3 XW + e_M \qquad (11.7)$$

If a_3 is statistically different from zero, then one proceeds to the next stage of the analysis by testing whether M is related to Y in

$$Y = i_3 + c_1' X + c_2' W + c_3' XW + bM + e_Y \qquad (11.8)$$

If b is statistically significant from zero and c_3' is closer to zero than c_3, this establishes that the interaction between X and M in determining Y is

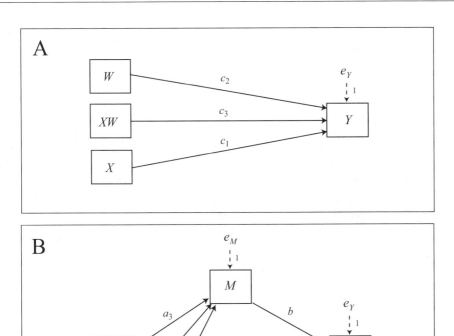

FIGURE 11.10. A statistical diagram representing mediated moderation, with the model of the total effect of *XW* (panel A) as well as the mediation of *XW*'s effect by *M* (panel B).

mediated by M. If c_3' is statistically significant, then it is said that M partially mediates the interaction, whereas if c_3' is not statistically significant, M is branded a complete mediator of the interaction.

Although the underlying mathematics of the modeling process just described are sound, the causal steps approach to mediation analysis suffers from the same limitations in this application as it does in any mediation analysis (see section 6.1) and so I cannot recommend testing mediated moderation in this fashion. The preferred procedure to test whether moderation is mediated is to estimate the indirect effect of XW on Y through proposed mediator M and then conduct an inferential test for this indirect effect (see, e.g., Fairchild & MacKinnon, 2009; Morgan-Lopez & MacKinnon, 2006).

A mediated moderation model is represented in the form of a statistical diagram in Figure 11.10, panel B, which translates into equations 11.7 and

11.8. The indirect effect of the product is, like any indirect effect, quantified as the product of paths linking the causal agent to the presumed outcome through the proposed mediator. In Figure 11.10, panel B and equations 11.7 and 11.8, the indirect effect of XW is therefore estimated as the product of a_3 and b.

A close examination of Figure 11.10, panel B, reveals that this statistical diagram could be construed as a representation of a simple mediation model with XW as the causal agent and X and W as covariates. Indeed, the same path analysis rules described in Chapter 4 and section 6.2 apply here. c_3' is the direct effect of XW, and the indirect effect of XW through M is $a_3 b$, as just derived. Together, these sum to yield the total effect of XW, estimated with c_3 in equation 11.6 and represented in Figure 11.10, panel A. That is,

$$c_3 = c_3' + a_3 b$$

Isolating the indirect effect reveals that the indirect effect of XW on Y through M is the difference between the total and direct effects of XW:

$$a_3 b = c_3 - c_3'$$

The outcome of an inferential test demonstrating that $_T a_3 _T b \neq 0$ establishes that XW influences Y indirectly through M. It would also establish that the direct effect of XW on Y is statistically different than the total effect of XW (i.e., $_T c_3 - _T c_3' \neq 0$). Any of the inferential methods discussed in Chapter 4 could be used. I recommend a bootstrap confidence interval.

To illustrate this procedure, I conduct a mediated moderation analysis using the data from the sex discrimination study by examining whether the moderation of the effect of Catherine's decision to protest or not on how she was evaluated by perceivers' beliefs about the pervasiveness of sex discrimination in society operates through perceptions of response appropriateness. That is, is perceived appropriateness of Catherine's response (M) the mechanism carrying this interaction between Catherine's behavior (X) and perceived pervasiveness of sex discrimination (W) in determining how much Catherine was liked (Y)?

The regression coefficients in equations 11.6, 11.7, and 11.8 could be estimated with any program capable of OLS regression, but you wouldn't get a proper inferential test of the indirect effect with most programs. PROCESS provides all that is needed. The statistical diagram of the model in Figure 11.10 can be construed as a simple mediation model with XW as the causal agent sending its effects on Y through M, with X and W as covariates. So PROCESS model 4 would be appropriate. The product of X and W first has to be created and this product is then used as X in the PROCESS command. In SPSS, the commands that conduct the analysis are

```
compute proxsex=protest*sexism.
process vars=protest liking respappr sexism proxsex/y=liking/x=proxsex/
   m=respappr/model=4/total=1/boot=10000.
```

In SAS, use

```
data protest;set protest;proxsex=protest*sexism;run;
%process (data=protest,vars=protest liking respappr sexism proxsex,
   y=liking,x=proxsex,m=respappr,model=4,total=1,boot=10000);
```

The resulting output can be found in Figure 11.11. The total, direct, and indirect effects of the interaction between protest decision and perceived pervasiveness of sex discrimination are found in the section of output labeled "TOTAL, DIRECT, AND INDIRECT EFFECTS."

The total effect of the product of protest decision and perceived pervasiveness of sex discrimination (XW, but listed as X in the PROCESS output) is $c_3 = 0.834, t(125) = 3.422, p < .001$. Of course, this is the same as the moderation reported in Chapter 7, because equation 11.6 represents the same simple moderation model (although the coefficient for the interaction is labeled c_3 here, as opposed to b_3 in Chapter 7). This total effect of the interaction between X and W partitions into indirect and direct components. The indirect effect of XW is 0.291, calculated as the product of the effect of XW in the model of perceived response appropriateness (M, $a_3 = 0.810$) and the effect of perceived response appropriateness in the model of liking (Y, $b = 0.359$). This indirect effect is statistically different from zero according to a 95% bias-corrected bootstrap confidence interval (0.057 to 0.589). Finally, the direct effect of XW is also statistically significant, $c_3' = 0.543, t(125) = 2.363, p = .020$. Even after accounting for perceived response appropriateness, perceived pervasiveness of sex discrimination moderates the effect of Catherine's chosen course of action on how she was perceived.

Notice that as promised, and just as in the mediation analyses presented in Chapters 4, 5, and 6, the total effect of XW is the sum of the direct and indirect effects of XW. That is,

$$c_3 = c_3' + a_3b = 0.834 = 0.543 + 0.291$$

Therefore, the indirect effect of XW on Y through M is the difference between the total effect of XW on Y and the direct effect of XW on Y:

$$a_3b = c_3 - c' = 0.291 = 0.834 - 0.543$$

```
compute proxsex=protest*sexism.
process vars=protest liking respappr sexism proxsex/y=liking/x=proxsex/
   m=respappr/model=4/total=1/boot=10000.

Model = 4
   Y = liking
   X = proxsex
   M = respappr

Statistical Controls:
CONTROL= protest  sexism

Sample size
      129

*************************************************************************
Outcome: respappr

Model Summary
         R       R-sq        F        df1       df2        p
      .5442      .2962    17.5340    3.0000   125.0000    .0000

Model
             coeff        se         t          p        LLCI       ULCI
constant    6.5667     1.2095     5.4295     .0000     4.1730     8.9604
proxsex      .8100      .2819     2.8732     .0048      .2520     1.3679
protest    -2.6866     1.4515    -1.8509     .0665    -5.5594      .1861
sexism      -.5290      .2359    -2.2426     .0267     -.9959     -.0622


*************************************************************************
Outcome: liking

Model Summary
         R       R-sq        F        df1       df2        p
      .5323      .2833    12.2551    4.0000   124.0000    .0000

Model
             coeff        se         t          p        LLCI       ULCI
constant    5.3471     1.0607     5.0412     .0000     3.2477     7.4465
respappr     .3593      .0706     5.0916     .0000      .2196      .4989
proxsex      .5426      .2296     2.3628     .0197      .0881      .9970
protest    -2.8075     1.1607    -2.4188     .0170    -5.1047     -.5102
sexism      -.2824      .1898    -1.4882     .1392     -.6581      .0932

************************* TOTAL EFFECT MODEL ***************************
Outcome: liking

Model Summary
         R       R-sq        F        df1       df2        p
      .3654      .1335     6.4190    3.0000   125.0000    .0004

Model
             coeff        se         t          p        LLCI       ULCI
constant    7.7062     1.0449     7.3750     .0000     5.6382     9.7743
proxsex      .8336      .2436     3.4224     .0008      .3515     1.3156
protest    -3.7727     1.2541    -3.0084     .0032    -6.2546    -1.2907
sexism      -.4725      .2038    -2.3184     .0220     -.8758     -.0692

**************** TOTAL, DIRECT, AND INDIRECT EFFECTS ****************

Total effect of X on Y
   Effect        SE         t          p        LLCI       ULCI
    .8336      .2436     3.4224     .0008      .3515     1.3156

Direct effect of X on Y
   Effect        SE         t          p        LLCI       ULCI
    .5426      .2296     2.3628     .0197      .0881      .9970

Indirect effect of X on Y
             Effect    Boot SE   BootLLCI   BootULCI
respappr      .2910      .1357      .0566      .5894

***************** ANALYSIS NOTES AND WARNINGS ************************

Number of bootstrap samples for bias corrected bootstrap confidence intervals:
   10000
```

FIGURE 11.11. PROCESS output from a mediated moderation analysis of the data from the sex discrimination study.

The results of this analysis are consistent with the claim that the moderation of Catherine's decision to protest on how she was evaluated by people's perceptions of the pervasiveness of sex discrimination is mediated by their perceptions of the appropriateness of her response to the discrimination. The coefficient for the interaction in the simple moderation model estimating how much Catherine was liked is reduced, albeit still statistically significant, when controlling for perceived response appropriateness. This difference between the total and indirect effect of the interaction is the indirect effect of the interaction through perceived response appropriateness, and it is statistically different from zero according to a bias-corrected bootstrap confidence interval.

Why Mediated Moderation Is Neither Interesting Nor Meaningful

If at this point you feel like you are experiencing déjà vu or wonder if you have been reading the same page repeatedly, then you are paying attention. Many of the numbers in the last couple of paragraphs should look familiar because you've seen them before. Compare the two statistical diagrams in Figures 11.7 and 11.10, panel B. Observe that they are the same. This is because the mediated moderation model just estimated is mathematically identical to the conditional process model estimated in section 11.2 when the analysis was framed in terms of moderated mediation. Indeed, notice that the two PROCESS outputs corresponding to these two analyses are identical as well, save differences in formatting (compare Figures 11.8 and 11.11). The models are the same, the equations of M and Y used to estimate the coefficients in the model are the same, and when they are each estimated on the same data, they will yield identical results. The only difference between them is how they are interpreted, and on what part of the model your attention is focused.

Moderated mediation focuses on the conditional nature of an indirect effect—how an indirect effect is moderated. If you think of the terms "mediation" and "indirect effect" as essentially synonymous conceptually, then moderated mediation means moderated indirect effects. Interpretive focus in a moderated mediation analysis is directed at estimating the indirect effect and how that effect varies as a function of a moderator. Mediated moderation, by contrast, asks about the mechanism through which an interaction between X and a moderator W operates, where the product of X and W is construed as the causal agent sending its effect to Y through M. Focus in mediated moderation is the estimation of the indirect effect of the product of X and W.

The problem I have with mediated moderation as a concept is that the product of X and W is meaningless. It is not a measure of anything.

Remember that the product of X and W in equations 11.6 and 11.7 originates from conceiving X's effect on Y as a linear function of the moderator W. When that linear function is conceived as X's effect rather than a single number represented by a single regression coefficient, the product pops out of the algebra as an additional variable included in the model estimating Y along with X and W (to refresh your memory, see the derivation beginning on page 214). So the product serves no function in the model other than to allow X's effect on Y to be contingent on W. Its presence in the model builds in flexibility, in that X's effect is not constrained to be invariant across values of W so long as XW is included as an additional predictor variable. Unlike X and W, both of which carry information about some construct measured or some variable manipulated, XW has no substantive grounding in the measurement or manipulation process. The product doesn't quantify anything. And if XW has no meaning and no substantive interpretation, then what does the indirect effect of a product mean? The answer, in my opinion, is that it means nothing. Therefore, so too is mediated moderation largely meaningless and substantively uninteresting. For a related discussion, see Edwards (2009, pp. 156–157).

It turns out that the indirect effect of the product of XW, a_3b, does have an interpretation, but it is an interpretation that makes sense only if you conceptualize the process being modeled in terms of moderated mediation rather than mediated moderation. Recall the derivation of the slope of the line for the conditional indirect effect of X on Y through M in the conditional process analysis described in section 11.2 (see page 380 and Figure 11.9). The slope of that line is a_3b. Thus, a_3b can be interpreted as how much the conditional indirect effect of X on Y through M changes as W changes by one unit. So an inference that the indirect effect of XW on Y through M is different from zero is really an inference about the difference between two conditional indirect effects. Of course, this means nothing if one is not thinking about the process in terms of the conditional nature of the mechanism linking X to Y through M. In order for a_3b to be substantively interpretable, one must reconceptualize the process being studied in moderated mediation terms rather than mediated moderation terms.[2]

I believe the elusiveness of the substantive interpretation of the indirect effect in mediated moderation is in part due to misdirecting one's analytical focus away from where it belongs, which is on X rather than XW. If one

---

[2]Notice that the PROCESS output in Figure 11.8 also includes a point estimate of the indirect effect of XW along with a bootstrap confidence interval, under the heading "Indirect Effect of the Highest Order Interaction." So it is not necessary to test mediated moderation in PROCESS using model 4. Model 8 accomplishes the job just as well, but it also generates the conditional direct and indirect effects of X, which model 4 does not provide.

phrased one's research question in statistical terms not as "Does XW carry its effect on Y through M?" but as "Does the indirect effect of X on Y through M depend on W?" then a_3b becomes meaningful as a measure of how the size of the indirect effect linking X to Y through M differs between groups differing by one unit on W. Furthermore, one ends up with a better understanding of the conditional nature of the process being investigated when one quantifies conditional indirect effects that are by their nature meaningful and substantively interpretable. So I recommend avoiding the articulation of hypotheses or research questions in terms of the mediation of the effect of a product, abandoning the term *mediated moderation* entirely, and instead reframing such hypotheses and research questions in terms of the contingencies of an indirect effect—moderated mediation.

11.5 Chapter Summary

The conditional indirect effect quantifies the indirect effect of some proposed causal agent X on a presumed outcome Y through a putative mediator M conditioned on the value of a moderator. By contrast, a conditional direct effect quantifies the effect of X on Y independent of the mediator but conditioned on a value of a moderator variable. Any path in a mediation model can be moderated, and which path is moderated determines the function that mathematically defines the conditional indirect effect. In Chapter 10, I illustrated conditional process analysis by estimating a simple mediation model that included moderation of the effect of M on Y. This chapter extended the principles introduced there to a model which included moderation of the effect of X on M along with moderation of the direct effect of X. By quantifying conditional indirect and direct effects in an integrated conditional process model, one is in a position to better numerically describe how the $X \to M \to Y$ mechanism is contingent compared to a piecemeal approach that focuses only on specific paths or steps in the process the model represents rather than the process as a whole.

If the indirect effect of X on Y through M is moderated by W, this means that mediation of the effect of X on Y is moderated, a phenomenon called *moderated mediation*. This is different from *mediated moderation*, which refers to the phenomenon in which the product of X and a moderator of X's effect (W) on Y carries its effect on Y through M. Although mediated moderation hypotheses are tested in abundance in the literature, the indirect effect of a product is substantively meaningless, because XW is not a measure of anything. However, in a conditional process model in the form estimated in this chapter, the indirect effect of the product can be interpreted as an estimated difference between conditional indirect effects in a moderated mediation process. Thus, I recommend that questions about mediated moderation be recast in terms of a moderated mediation process. This takes the focus off the meaningless XW as the causal agent and shifts it back where it belongs on X.

With the principles of conditional process modeling introduced in this book more or less mastered, you are in a good position to branch out beyond the examples presented in this and the prior chapter and try alternative models, potentially more complex than these. Let PROCESS help you by lifting some of the computational and programming burdens off your shoulders. In the final chapter of this book, I offer a strategy for approaching a conditional process analysis and address some interesting controversies and questions about processes characterized by both mediation and moderation.

12

Miscellaneous Topics in Conditional Process Analysis

This chapter touches on a variety of interesting controversies and introduces some additional procedures related to the integration of moderation and mediation analysis. I start by offering a strategy for approaching a conditional process analysis that acknowledges the need to balance hypothesis testing with data exploration. I address whether it is possible for a variable to simultaneously moderate and mediate one variable's effect on another. I provide a method for comparing conditional indirect effects and derive a formal test of moderated mediation that can be used for some types of conditional process models. I criticize a subgroups analysis approach to answering questions about moderated mediation and discuss two alternatives that can be used when the moderator of a mediation process is dichotomous. I close the book by offering some advice on writing about conditional process analysis.

The vast majority of scientists would probably argue that when push comes to shove, the theoretical horse should pull the statistical cart. Statistical methods are mathematical tools, some of them quite amazing in what they do, which can help us to discern order amid the apparent chaos in a batch of data. But ultimately, the stories that statistical methods help us tell are told by our brains, not by the mathematics, and our brains are good at making sense of things—of coming up with stories to explain what we perceive. The problem is that the same pattern of results can be interpreted in many different ways, especially if the pattern is found after an extensive round of exploratory data analysis. Without a theoretical orientation to guide our attempts at making sense of our data or, better still, to guide our research design and data collection efforts, our awesome storytelling ability can lead us astray by invoking explanations for findings that may sound good but that are mere conjecture even if we can find a theoretical hook on which to hang them post hoc.

I won't argue against this perspective, as I believe it is for the most part right on the money. But I also believe that statistical methods can play an important role in theory development as well—that the statistical cart need not always, should not always, and often does not follow the theoretical horse. When we learn something new analytically, this can change the way we think of things theoretically and how we then go about testing the ideas that our newfound awareness of an analytical method inspired (cf. Slater, Hayes, & Snyder, 2008, p. 2). Indeed, as Greenwald (2012) observed, many of the advancements in science over the last few decades or more resulted as much from innovations in method as from innovations in theory.

Although I may be a victim of selective exposure and memory, I believe things have changed since the publications of Edwards and Lambert (2007), Muller et al. (2005), and Preacher et al. (2007). I don't recall seeing investigators combining moderation and mediation analysis nearly as frequently prior to 2007 as I see it now. If I am right, it is likely that this is in part the result of the occasional reversal of the horse and cart that these three articles may have prompted in some. Knowing how to quantify and test the contingencies of mechanisms may have helped to stimulate investigators to think more about how their favored mechanisms might be contingent and why. Asking these questions is in part what theory refinement is, and this may be an example of what Greenwald (2012, p. 99) was talking about when he said that there is "nothing so theoretical as a good method." My hope is that Chapters 10 and 11 have stimulated you to think about your own research questions and theories in a different way.

In this final chapter, I touch upon a number of interesting questions, controversies, and procedures related to the principles and practice of conditional process modeling. I first address some basic issues in modeling, such as how to organize one's analysis and strike a balance between exploration and justification. I then ponder whether it is conceivable that a variable could simultaneously play the role of both moderator and mediator of one variable's effect on another. Following this, I describe a method for testing the difference between conditional indirect effects and show that for the model forms used as the examples in Chapters 10 and 11, this method translates into a formal test of moderated mediation. I make the case for why splitting one's data into subgroups and conducting separate mediation analysis in each group should be avoided as a means of testing hypotheses about the contingent nature of mechanisms. I then close this chapter and the book with some guidance on how to approach writing about conditional process modeling.

12.1   A Strategy for Approaching Your Analysis

People who write about methodology have an advantage over those who don't. I can pick and choose any study I want to illustrate certain principles and procedures. I don't even have to conduct the study myself or collect any data, as I can always call in a favor or get on my knees and ask for donations of data to my methodological causes. If I can't find a real study that works for this purpose, I can just make data up from a hypothetical study (and, of course, describe it as such). Naturally, when using real data I choose examples where the results are clean, all effects of interest are statistically significant, and the interpretation is obvious and elegant.

But everyone else has to cope with the realities of the messiness of science when they analyze their data. Things don't always turn out as we expected and articulated in hypotheses 1, 2, and 3. And sometimes after looking at the data, our thinking about the process at work changes and new hypotheses come to mind that are worth testing. Scientists routinely switch back and forth between the context of justification and the context of discovery, testing hypotheses conceived before the data were analyzed while also exploring one's data to see what else can be learned from patterns observed but not anticipated.

I say this in anticipation of criticism that could be lodged at some of the suggestions I offer below for how you can approach a conditional process analysis. I realize there is much room for differences in opinion here, and in no way am I saying the outline I provide below is how you *should* organize your analysis or that doing it differently than I outline here is ill advised. People have their own philosophies about how science should best proceed, and what I offer below may clash with that philosophy.

Step 1: Construct Your Conceptual Diagram of the Process

Throughout this book, I have used the conceptual diagram as a visual representation of a process. Decide what your "focal predictor" is for the analysis you are doing, for this is the variable whose effect you are most interested in estimating in the analysis. This will be X in your conceptual diagram. Then draw out the paths of influence from X to Y, your outcome of interest, through whatever intervening variables you think X influences and that in turn are thought to influence Y. Always include the direct effect in your conceptual (and statistical) model, for you should be open to the possibility that X influences Y through mechanisms other than those that you are explicitly modeling. When completed, you will have a diagram of the mediation component of the process.

Once you have the mediation component of your conditional process model depicted, then depict moderation of whatever paths you believe are contingent, and by what moderators. Moderation is denoted by connecting a variable to a path with an arrow, as in the examples throughout the last half of this book.

Keep things simple at this point. Don't worry about every conceivable path of influence from any variable to any other variable. Focus on X and its direct and indirect effects, moderated or not, for X is your primary interest—your focal predictor. Once you complete the second step, some of the things that seem missing in the conceptual diagram may end up in the statistical model anyway, such as paths linking moderators to consequent variables. Conditional process modeling as described in this book is not about finding the best fitting model of the data given the variables available, in the way that structural equation modeling is sometimes practiced. It is about estimating effects and interpreting them. Your focus should be on the various coefficients in the statistical model, and how they combine to quantify contingencies in the effect of X on Y through one or more mediators. Determining whether your model is the best fitting model you can justify is not the point. In fact, some models described in this book are saturated, meaning fit would be perfect when assessed quantitatively with various measures of fit used in structural equation modeling.

Step 2: Translate the Conceptual Model into a Statistical Model

We don't estimate the conceptual model. A conceptual model must be translated into a statistical model in the form of at least two equations, depending on the number of proposed mediators in the model. With an understanding of the principles of moderation and mediation analysis described in this book, you should be able to do this without too much difficulty. As a general rule, if variable A points an arrow at variable B in your conceptual diagram, then variable A should be a predictor variable in the equation for variable B. And if variable A's effect on variable B is proposed as moderated by variable C, then the equation for B will also include C and the product of A and C as predictors. Don't violate these rules, because a failure to follow them can result in a statistical model that does not correspond to the conceptual model you have diagrammed for the process of interest to you.

In complex models, this translation procedure can be tricky. Hayes and Preacher (2013) describe the steps required to accurately translate a complex conceptual model into a statistical model for a conditional process model involving moderated moderation and serial multiple mediation. These principles generalize to simple models. Fortunately, PROCESS is programmed to automatically translate the conceptual model you specify into a set of equations, so this step is not required if your desired model is already programmed into PROCESS. But PROCESS has no flexibility in this regard, in that if the statistical model PROCESS estimates does not correspond exactly to the model you want to estimate (probably but not necessarily because the conceptual model you specified does not exactly correspond to the model you most want to estimate), you are going to have to learn to translate the principles described in this book into code understood by a structural equation modeling program such as Mplus or LISREL. See Hayes and Preacher (2013) for some guidance if you want to deviate from what PROCESS does for you.

Step 3: Estimate the Statistical Model

Once the equations corresponding to the mediators and outcome are specified, then you estimate the coefficients of the statistical model. Throughout this book I have been assuming you believe OLS regression is appropriate for your data, so the coefficients would be estimated using any OLS regression program. PROCESS does all this for you once you specify the model desired and tell it which variables play which roles. Of course, this could also be done in a structural equation modeling program.

Step 4: Determine Whether Expected Moderation Exists

Here is where things get controversial. Suppose you have proposed, for instance, that X's effect on M is moderated by W, and that M's effect on Y is moderated by V. After estimating the coefficients in the statistical model, perhaps you find that the interaction between X and W in the model of M is statistically significant, but the interaction between M and V in the model of Y is not. Should you modify your model at this point based on this evidence, or should you forge ahead since your interest is on the conditional (or unconditional) direct and indirect effects of X and not on the individual components of the model? Your decision determines whether you move to step 4a or step 5. Of course, it may be that all paths you proposed as moderated actually are. In that case, proceed to step 5.

I can't tell you what to do, but I can offer you some thoughts about how you might think about proceeding. Your model proposes moderation of a path in the process that it turns out is not moderated as expected, at least according to the results of a hypothesis test. If you leave the interaction in the model, this will influence the estimate of the indirect effect of X on Y through M (which is necessarily conditional with this interaction in the model) along with all inferential tests thereof. But if you have no evidence that the path is actually moderated as you expected, wouldn't it be more sensible to constrain it to be unconditional rather than conditional on that moderator? If you believe so, you should remove it and start fresh, reconceptualizing your thinking in light of this evidence you now have based on the data. But remember that a null hypothesis can never be proven true. Just because an interaction is not significant, that doesn't mean your proposed moderator does not moderate the path you proposed it moderates. Parsimony might dictate that your model should be cleansed of this interaction, but null hypotheses tests are fallible, and sometimes real effects are so weak that we don't have the power to detect them given the limitations of our resources or other things out of our control.

Step 4A: If you have decided to remove nonsignificant interactions, then go back to step 1 and start fresh by redrawing your conceptual diagram in light of the evidence you now have and proceed through these steps again. A certain moral or ethical logic might dictate that you not pretend when describing your analysis that this is where you started in the first place. Yet Bem (1987) makes the argument that spending lots of time talking about ideas that turned out to be "wrongheaded" isn't going to produce a particularly interesting paper. You'll have to sort out for yourself where you stand on this continuum of scientific ethics.

It is worth pointing out that it is possible (even if perhaps somewhat uncommon) for an indirect effect to depend on a moderator absent evidence that a particular path is moderated by a formal test of significance. The rule of parsimony is a useful heuristic for deciding between models. Without evidence of moderation of a particular path in a model, it makes sense to assume the path is not moderated as expected and to reconfigure one's model in light of the evidence available. But statistically significant moderation of a path in a mediation model is not a necessary condition for an indirect effect to be moderated. In section 12.3 I propose a formal test as to whether an indirect effect is moderated for two different models that involves the coefficient for the interaction (irrespective of statistical significance) multiplied by something else, with that something else depending on the model. Furthermore, as Fairchild and MacKinnon (2009) discuss, it is possible for an indirect effect to be constant across all values of a moderator or moderators even when one has evidence that one or more of the constituent paths are moderated. Thus, use step 4 as a guide rather than a hard and fast rule.

Step 5: Probe and Interpret Interactions Involving Components of the Indirect Effect

At this stage, probe any interactions involving components of the indirect effect of X so that you will have some understanding as to the contingencies of the various effects that are the components of the larger conditional process model you are estimating. This exercise will help inform and clarify your interpretation of the conditional indirect effect(s) of X later on. This will require you to shift your thinking about the analysis toward pure moderation for the time being rather than condition process modeling. Any of the procedures described in Chapters 7 through 9 can be brought to the task, as can PROCESS models 1, 2, and 3, depending on the form of your larger model.

Step 6: Quantify and Test Conditional Indirect Effects (If Relevant)

Once you get to this step, you will have a model you either have accepted as is regardless of whether the data are consistent with every part of it, or one that has been cleansed of any moderation components that weren't consistent with the data. It could be that you have cleansed so thoroughly that you no longer have any moderation components left in your model, because none of them was statistically significant, and all that is left is a mediation model. In that case, you can stop what you are doing and consider my advice in section 6.5.

Assuming you have at least one significant interaction involving a component of an indirect effect or you have decided you don't want to rely on a hypothesis test for determining whether the indirect effect is moderated, you will now want to quantify the indirect effects as a function of the moderator(s) and conduct various inferential tests for those conditional indirect effects. Chapters 10 and 11 describe how this is done for a few specific and fairly simple models, but the principles apply to more complex models. Although it is not difficult to do these computations by hand, a computer program that does it for you is handy, and such a program will be necessary if you want to use bootstrap confidence intervals for inference as I recommend throughout this book. PROCESS both quantifies the indirect effects and generates bootstrap confidence intervals for you, without requiring any effort on your part. If you are doing your analysis with a structural equation modeling program with the ability to estimate functions of parameters, you'll need to hard-program the computation of those functions yourself. This requires a bit more effort than does the use of PROCESS. I provide example code for Mplus for a complex model in Hayes and Preacher (2013).

Step 7: Quantify and Test Conditional Direct Effects (If Relevant)

If your model includes moderation of the direct effect of X, you will want to probe this interaction by estimating the conditional direct effects. This is just moderation analysis, discussed in Chapters 7 to 9. PROCESS will also take the labor out of this, because it will automatically quantify the conditional direct effects for you and provide inferential tests at various values of the moderator, depending on the options for probing the interaction that you request.

Step 8: Tell Your Story

Once you have compiled the results from these various stages of the analysis, you are in a position to frame the story you now want to tell given what you know from the analysis just completed. The final section of this chapter ends the book with some thoughts on writing about conditional process modeling.

I realize that these steps may run contrary to the way that the business of science is typically described in research methods and statistics texts. We are taught to formulate hypotheses, design a study that will allow us to test those hypotheses, test those hypotheses with the data available, and then tell the world whether our hypotheses are supported or not. Yet my outline sounds a bit like data mining in places, as if the analyses are dictating the hypotheses rather than the other way around.

But real science does not proceed in the manner described in research methods and statistics textbooks. Rather, we routinely straddle the fence between the hypothetico-deductive approach and a more discovery-oriented or inquisitive mindset that is open to any story the data may inform. Sometimes the story we originally conceived prior to data analysis is simply wrong and we know it after analyzing the data. No one wants to read (as Daryl Bem once put it rather bluntly) "a personal history about your stillborn thoughts" (Bem, 1987, p. 173). Sometimes our data speak to us in ways that change the story we thought we were going to tell into something much more interesting, and hopefully more accurate.

Of course, there is always the danger of capitalizing on chance when you let your explorations of the data influence the story you tell. We are great at explaining patterns we see. Our brains are wired to do it. So replication is important, and it may be the only way of establishing the generality of our findings and claims in the end. If replication is not likely to happen by you in your lifetime but you have the luxury of lots of data (i.e., you have "power to burn"), randomly set aside half of your data before analyzing the other half. Explore all you want in one half, but don't report anything you find as real that doesn't replicate in the other half you have set aside for this validation purpose.

12.2 Can a Variable Simultaneously Mediate and Moderate Another Variable's Effect?

Can a variable both mediate and moderate another variable's effect on a third? In Chapter 1 I described a process in which internalization of the "thin-as-ideal" standard as portrayed in health and beauty magazines could be construed as either a mediator or moderator of the effect of exposure to the standard on various mental and physical health consequences. More frequent childhood exposure to the thin-as-ideal standard could prompt a greater internalization of the norm relative to those with less frequent exposure, with greater internalization leading to consequences such as negative body image and disordered eating at adolescence. More exposure during adolescence could then differentially affect subsequent body image and disordered eating, depending on the extent to which internalization of the standard had occurred in childhood.

So, in principle, it seems that a variable could play the roles of both moderator and mediator. However, it could be argued that exposure and health consequences measured at two different times really aren't the same variables, even if they are given the same name. Furthermore, this example does not by any means establish that it is sensible or even possible to construe a variable as *simultaneously* mediating and moderating one variable's effect on another.

To be sure, there are examples in the literature in which investigators used a variable as a mediator of X's effect on Y in one analysis but that same variable played the role of moderator of the *same X*'s effect on the *same Y* in a second analysis. For instance, D'Lima et al. (2012) conducted a study on college students examining the relationship between general self-regulation (e.g., goal planning, tracking progress toward goals) and problems experienced as a result of alcohol use. They found that protective behavioral strategies (e.g., eating before drinking, not playing drinking games) functioned as a mediator of this association, with self-regulators more likely to engage in protective behavioral strategies, which in turn was related to the likelihood of experiencing alcohol-related problems. Yet in a subsequent analysis, they found that the association between self-regulation and alcohol-related problems was more pronounced among students who did not use protective behavioral strategies relative to those who did. This is moderation.

Nir and Druckman (2008) offer another such example in a study of a local election in the Minneapolis area. They examined the extent to which regular voter exposure to balanced, two-sided news coverage of the candidates running for political office increased the length of time it took a voter to decide whom to vote for. They found that more of such exposure was associated with a more delayed time to decision relative to those with less exposure, but only among voters who expressed ambivalence about the candidates running for office. Thus, ambivalence moderated the association between exposure to balanced coverage and decision timing. They also examined whether ambivalence mediated the effect of exposure to balanced coverage on voting timing. That is, perhaps exposure to balanced coverage causes ambivalence, which in turn increases time to decision. But they found no evidence of such a process at work.

These two examples as well as others (e.g., Kapikiran, 2012; Peltonen, Quota, Sarraj, & Punamäki, 2010; Ning, 2012; Sirgy, Yu, Lee, Wei, & Huang, 2012; Somer, Ginzberg, & Kramer, 2012; Versey & Kaplan, 2012) suggest that investigators are comfortable with the idea that the same variable could both mediate and moderate the effect of X on Y. Yet according to the analytical logic of what has come to be known as the MacArthur approach to mediation and moderation analysis (Kraemer et al., 2002, 2008), it simply is not possible for a variable M that is construed as an effect of X to moderate X's effect. According to this school of thought, moderators must precede X and be uncorrelated with X, in which case M could not possibly transmit X's effect on Y.

The position that a moderator of X's effect must be uncorrelated with X is a rather unorthodox position. As an ideal, this may be a defensible position to take, but as a *requirement*, I am skeptical. Furthermore, the very model that Kraemer et al. (2002, 2008) recommend as being the best approach to testing for mediation of the effect of X on Y by M is one in which M simultaneously plays the role of both moderator and mediator, at least mathematically. According to their approach, to establish M as a mediator of X's effect on Y, X must precede M in time and also be related to M, as established by statistical significance of X in a model of M. In addition, in a model of Y that includes X, M, and their product XM, one must find evidence of either a "main effect" of M on Y or an interaction between X and M.

Their model is depicted in conceptual form in panel A of Figure 12.1 and in statistical form in panel B. This model translates into the following equations:

$$M = i_1 + aX + e_M \tag{12.1}$$

$$Y = i_2 + c_1'X + bM + c_2'XM + e_Y \tag{12.2}$$

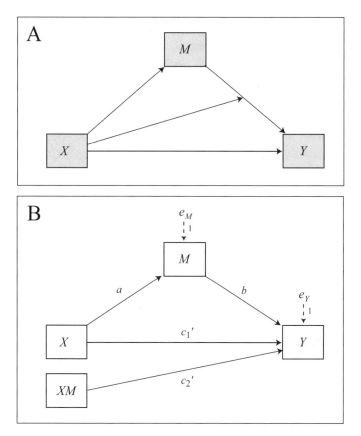

FIGURE 12.1. A conceptual (panel A) and statistical (panel B) diagram representing a conditional process model in which X moderates its own indirect effect.

After estimating the coefficients in equations 12.1 and 12.2,[1] the MacArthur approach deems M a mediator if a is statistically different from zero and either b or c'_2 is statistically different from zero. Kraemer et al. (2008) recommend centering M around a "central value" such as the median or zero, depending on the scaling of M, so that b estimates a "main effect" of M on Y. Whether b estimates a main effect as the concept is defined in ANOVA will depend on whether and how M is centered. They also recommend coding X with values of -0.5 and 0.5 if X is dichotomous (as it typically is in their treatment of this topic because they focus their discussion primarily on moderation and mediation in randomized clinical trials).

The MacArthur approach is essentially a modification to the causal steps approach described by Baron and Kenny (1986) and thus suffers from the same weakness, in that it uses a statistical significance criterion at each step

[1]This model can be estimated using PROCESS by specifying model 74.

in the causal model in order to claim M is a mediator. In addition, Kraemer et al. (2002, 2008) don't discuss formally quantifying the indirect effect. In this model, M's effect on Y is not b but, rather, $b + c_2'X$. Thus, the indirect effect of X on Y through M is $a(b + c_2'M)$, meaning it is a function of X (see, e.g., Preacher et al., 2007).

In the model they recommend using to test for mediation, X is estimated to affect Y indirectly through M, as well as directly independent of M. But the direct effect of X in this model is not c_1' as it might seem. Grouping terms in equation 12.2 involving X and then factoring out X yields the direct effect of X on Y:

$$\theta_{X \to Y} = c_1' + c_2'M$$

So the direct effect of X is conditioned on M. In other words, if c_2' in equation 12.2 is statistically different from zero, M moderates X's direct effect on Y. The MacArthur camp would reject this as a possibility, as a moderator can't be correlated with X. By their criteria, M *can* be deemed a mediator of X's effect if a and c_2' are both statistically different from zero, but that very circumstance implies that M is *not* uncorrelated with X. At the same time, a statistically significant c_2' means that X's direct effect on Y is moderated by M. Thus, in the model Kraemer et al. (2002, 2008) recommend as the best approach to testing mediation, meeting one subset of their criteria for establishing M as a mediator also means that M could be construed as a moderator of X's effect, at least statistically or mathematically so.

Just because something is mathematically possible doesn't mean that it is sensible theoretically or substantively interpretable when it happens (as it does, as evidenced in some of the example studies cited on page 332). I will not take a firm position on whether construing M as a simultaneous mediator and moderator of a variable's effect could ever make substantive or theoretical sense. I am uncomfortable categorically ruling out the possibility that M could be a moderator just because it is correlated with X. My guess is that there are many real-life processes in which things caused by X also influence the size of the effect of X on Y measured well after X. But M would have to be causally prior to Y in order for this to be possible, implying that M could also be construed as a mediator if M is caused in part by X but also influences Y in some fashion.

12.3   Comparing Conditional Indirect Effects and a Formal Test of Moderated Mediation

If the indirect effect of X on Y through M depends on a particular moderator, that means that the indirect effect is a function of that moderator. A sensible question to ask is whether the conditional indirect effect when the moderator equals one value is statistically different from the conditional indirect effect when the moderator equals some different value. For example, in the analysis presented in Chapter 10 we could ask whether the indirect effect of dysfunctional behavior on team performance through negative affective tone differs between teams moderate versus very high in nonverbal negative expressivity.

To answer this question, one must first estimate the difference between the conditional indirect effects at the two values of the moderator of interest. Once that difference is estimated, an inferential test of some kind can be undertaken to test whether the difference is equal to zero. For instance, in the dysfunctional team behavior study, the conditional indirect effect of dysfunctional team behavior (X) on team performance (Y) through negative affective tone (M) was a function of nonverbal negative expressivity (V). From the model in Figure 10.3, the logic beginning on page 346 and culminating in equation 10.13 results in the conditional indirect effect of X equal to $a(b_1 + b_3V)$. Thus, the difference between the conditional indirect effect of X on Y through M when $V = v_1$ versus $V = v_2$ is

$$
\begin{aligned}
a(b_1 + b_3v_1) - a(b_1 + b_3v_2) &= ab_1 + ab_3v_1 - ab_1 - ab_3v_2 \\
&= ab_3v_1 - ab_3v_2 \\
&= ab_3(v_1 - v_2)
\end{aligned}
$$

Because $ab_3(v_1 - v_2)$ involves a product of normally distributed regression coefficients, its sampling distribution is not likely to be normal. For this reason, a bootstrap confidence interval for $_Ta_Tb_3(v_1 - v_2)$ would be a reasonable inferential test. If a 95% confidence interval does not include zero, then the inference is that the conditional indirect effect of X on Y through M when $V = v_1$ is statistically different from the conditional indirect effect when $V = v_2$.

PROCESS has a feature built in that makes it simple to construct a bootstrap confidence interval for any function of the regression coefficients from any PROCESS model with a mediation component (models 4 and higher). This is accomplished through the use of the **save** option. In SPSS, the command

```
process vars=dysfunc negtone negexp perform/y=perform/x=dysfunc/m=negtone
    /v=negexp/boot=10000/model=14/save=1.
```

estimates the model described in section 10.3, defined by equation 10.10 and 10.11, and creates a new data file containing all 10,000 bootstrap estimates of every regression coefficient in the model. The regression coefficients will reside in the columns of this file, from left to right, corresponding to their order of appearance in the PROCESS output from top to bottom. In the PROCESS output in Figure 10.5, the regression coefficients appear in the order $i_1, a, i_2, b_1, c', b_2, b_3$ from top to bottom, and so they appear is this order of the columns in the data from left to right and are named COL1, COL2, and so forth, up to COL7. Each row of the data file will contain the regression coefficients from one bootstrap sample.

In the SAS version of PROCESS, a name for the resulting data file must be specified, as below:

```
%process (data=teams,vars=dysfunc negtone negexp perform,y=perform,
    x=dysfunc,m=negtone,v=negexp,model=14,boot=10000,save=mod14bt);
```

This produces a temporary work SAS data file named work.mod14bt containing the 10,000 bootstrap estimates of all the regression coefficients. If so desired, this file can then be saved permanently for use at a later point in time.

Once this file is constructed, a program can be written to read the file and produce a bootstrap confidence interval for whatever function of the regression coefficients is desired. For example, let's test the difference between the conditional indirect effect of dysfunctional team behavior on team performance through negative affective tone among teams that are moderate ($v_1 = -0.060$, the 50th percentile) versus very high ($v_2 = 0.840$, the 90th percentile) in nonverbal negative expressivity. The point estimate of the difference is $ab_3(v_1 - v_2)$. From Figure 10.5, $a = 0.620$ and $b_3 = -0.571$, resulting in a point estimate of $0.620(-0.571)(-0.060 - 0.840) = 0.319$. In the file of bootstrap estimates, a and b_3 can be found in column 2 and column 7, respectively, in variables named COL2 and COL7. The SPSS code below constructs a percentile-based 95% bootstrap confidence interval for the difference:

```
compute diff=col2*col7*(-0.060-0.840).
frequencies variables=diff/percentiles=2.5 97.5/format=notable.
```

In SAS, the comparable commands are

```
data mod14bt;set mod14bt;
diff=col2*col7*(-0.060-0.840);run;
proc univariate data=mod14bt noprint;var diff;
```

```
output out=percent pctlpts=2.5 97.5 pctlpre=P;run;
proc print data=percent;run;
```

Upon execution, this program displays a 95% confidence interval of 0.045 to 0.698 using the 10,000 bootstrap samples generated with the PRO-CESS command. This is a percentile bootstrap confidence interval. For a bias-corrected bootstrap confidence interval, use the **BCCI** command built into PROCESS, appending it to the end of the code above. In SPSS, the command would be

```
bcci var=diff/point=0.319/conf=95.
```

where the value in the **point** argument is the point estimate.[2] The corresponding command in SAS is

```
%bcci (data=mod14bt,var=diff,point=0.319,conf=95);
```

The resulting bias-corrected confidence interval is 0.079 to 0.804. Regardless of whether the percentile or bias corrected approach is used, the confidence interval does not contain zero. We can conclude that the conditional indirect effect for teams moderate in negative nonverbal expressivity is different than the conditional indirect effect for teams very high in negative nonverbal expressivity.

But notice that because $v_1 - v_2$ is a constant in all 10,000 bootstrap samples (i.e., it doesn't vary from sample to sample), the outcome of this test is entirely determined by ab_3. If a 95% confidence interval for $_Ta_Tb_3$ does not contain zero, then a 95% confidence interval for $_Ta_Tb_3(v_1 - v_2)$ also will not contain zero. Importantly, this is true for *any* two values of v_1 and v_2 you can choose (except v_1 and $v_2 = 0$). So col2*col7*(-0.060-0.840) could be replaced in the code above with just col2*col7. A 95% confidence interval for $_Ta_Tb_3$ that does not contain zero means that any two conditional indirect effects are significantly different from each other. This could be construed as a formal test of moderated mediation in the model depicted in Figure 10.3, as discussed at the end of this section.

The same procedure could be used to conduct a test of the difference between conditional indirect effects for the model estimated in section 11.2 (see Figure 11.6, panel D and Figure 11.7) defined by the equations 11.2 and

[2]The **bcci** command can also be used to generate a percentile confidence interval by leaving off the **point** argument.

11.3. Does the conditional indirect effect of Catherine's behavior (X) on how she was perceived (Y) through perceptions of response appropriateness (M) differ between two groups of people whose beliefs about the pervasiveness of sex discrimination in society (W) equal w_1 and w_2? The conditional indirect effect this model is estimated as $(a_1 + a_3 W)b$, and so the difference between conditional indirect effects for these two groups is

$$
\begin{aligned}
(a_1 + a_3 w_1)b - (a_1 + a_3 w_2)b &= a_1 b + a_3 w_1 b - a_1 b - a_3 w_2 b \\
&= a_3 w_1 b - a_3 w_2 b \\
&= a_3 b(w_1 - w_2)
\end{aligned}
$$

A bootstrap confidence interval for $_T a_{3T} b(w_1 - w_2)$ can be used as a test of significance of the difference. But as $w_1 - w_2$ is a constant across all bootstrap samples, if a confidence interval for $_T a_{3T} b$ does not contain zero, then a confidence interval for $_T a_{3T} b(w_1 - w_2)$ also will not contain zero *regardless* of the choice of values of w_1 and w_2. Thus, this procedure could be used as a formal test of moderated mediation in the model depicted in Figure 11.6, panel D and Figure 11.7. This SPSS or SAS code described above could be modified to construct this confidence interval. Adding the **save** option to the PROCESS command on page 376, a_3 and b will be in columns 4 and 6 of the resulting file (and named COL4 and COL6) because they appear 4th and 6th in descending order in the PROCESS output in Figure 11.8.

Recall from section 11.4, where this model was conceptualized as a model of *mediated moderation*, that the indirect effect of the product of X and W was estimated as $a_3 b$. A bootstrap confidence interval for the indirect effect of XW that does not include zero provided evidence of mediated moderation, meaning the indirect effect of XW on Y through M is not zero. The earlier derivation shows that a bootstrap confidence interval for $_T a_{3T} b$ provides a test of both mediated moderation *and* moderated mediation for this model. PROCESS automatically generates this confidence interval when specifying **model=8**, so when estimating model 8, no additional work is required.

This procedure will work for comparing any two conditional indirect effects in a model that includes moderation of the effect of X on M or the effect of M on Y (or both). If the function defining the conditional indirect effect is a straight line (as it is in these two examples), then whether the confidence interval for the difference between conditional indirect effects contains zero will not depend on the two values of the moderator selected. In that case, a test of moderated mediation boils down to testing whether the slope of the line linking the conditional indirect effect to values of the moderator is equal to zero. But if the function is not a straight line, then whether the confidence interval for the difference between conditional indirect effects includes zero will depend on the two values of the moderator chosen. In that case, identifying at least two values of the moderator for which the difference in conditional indirect effects is statistically different from zero implies moderated mediation. If the function that defines the conditional indirect effect is not a straight line, mediation may still be moderated even though a particular comparison between two conditional indirect effects results in a claim that they are not statistically different.

12.4 The Pitfalls of Subgroups Analysis

There are numerous examples in the literature in which investigators attempted to test a moderated mediation hypothesis through the use of a *subgroups analysis*. When the proposed moderator is categorical, this approach involves conducting separate mediation analyses in each of the groups defined by levels of the moderator. Most typically, the moderator is dichotomous, such as two experimental conditions (Martinez, Piff, Mendoza-Denton, & Hinshaw, 2011; Tsai & Thomas, 2011), biological sex (e.g., Carvalho & Hopko, 2011; Dockray, Susman, & Dorn, 2009; Goldstein, Flett, & Wekerle, 2010; Hasan, Begue, & Bushman, 2012; Magee, Caputi, & Iverson, 2011; Molloy, Dixon, Hamer, & Sniehotta, 2010), children versus adolescents (Grøntved et al., 2011), or some other distinction such as school attended (Oldmeadow & Fiske, 2010). In some instances, the causal steps approach has been used in each group and claims of moderated mediation based on whether the criteria for mediation are met in one group but not another. Other researchers have based their claims of differential mediation across groups on formal tests of the indirect effect using more defensible inferential approaches such as bootstrap confidence intervals. However, the mediation analyses are conducted separately in the groups and claims of moderated mediation are based on the pattern of significance or nonsignificance of the indirect effects in the two groups.

For example, in a study of 111 children and adolescents, Dockray et al. (2009) examined whether the direct and indirect effects of depression on body mass, with cortisol reactivity as a possible mediator, differed between boys and girls. Using the causal steps approach along with a Sobel test for the indirect effect in separate analyses of the 56 boys and the 55 girls in the study, they found evidence of mediation only in girls. In girls, the estimated indirect effect of depression on Body Mass Index through cortisol reactivity was four times larger than the indirect effect in boys, but statistically significant only in girls. They also report evidence of a statistically significant association between depression and cortisol reactivity only in girls.

The goal of such an analysis is the same as the goal in conditional process analysis described in the last two chapters. Of interest is establishing whether the direct and/or indirect effects of X on Y vary systematically as a function of a moderator. But there are several problems associated with this subgroups approach to answering questions about the contingencies of mechanisms. These problems are severe enough that I cannot recommend using this approach.

First, the subgroups approach may not accurately reflect the process purportedly at work. For instance, if it is hypothesized that the indirect effect of X on Y through M is moderated due to the moderation of M's effect on Y by W, a subgroups analysis does not respect the implied equality of the other paths in the mediation model. A subgroups analysis, in the lingo of structural equation modeling, *freely* estimates *all* paths in the mediation model, thereby allowing them all to differ across groups. If one's moderated mediation hypothesis is not specific about which path is moderated, this is not a problem, but for more precise hypotheses about how the mechanism linking X to Y through M differs between groups, subgroups analysis is not a good choice.

Second, a direct or indirect effect may be descriptively different in the two groups but may not actually be different when subjected to a formal statistical test of differences. Alternatively, when the causal steps approach is used for assessing mediation in each group separately, the criteria for mediation may be met in one group but not in another, but that doesn't mean there is an indirect effect in one group but not another. A subgroups analysis provides no formal test of moderation of any of the paths in the model, nor does it provide a test of difference between direct or indirect effects across groups.

Third, the subgroups approach conflates statistical significance with sample size. If the groups differ in sample size, power to detect direct or indirect effects in the groups will differ. For instance, it may be that the indirect effect of X on Y through M is actually the same in the groups, but if one group is smaller than another, power to detect the indirect effect in the smaller group will be less than power in the larger group. The probability of a Type II error is inversely related to sample size, so Type II errors are more likely in the analysis of the smaller subgroups in the set. Thus, it can appear that the effects differ between groups when in fact the difference in results is due to differences in statistical power between the separate analyses.

Finally, this approach requires that the proposed moderator be categorical. Although it may be by design or measurement, this approach cannot be used when the moderator is a continuous variable. That in itself is not a problem, but the temptation to artificially categorize a continuous proposed moderator so that the subgroups analysis approach can be used may be too strong for some to resist, thereby resulting in two problems (artificial categorization and subgroups analysis) instead of none. As discussed in section 9.3, rarely is artificial categorization of a continuum a good idea.

Two alternative approaches mitigate these problems to varying degrees. One is multiple-group structural equation modeling. This approach involves the simultaneous estimation of the paths in separate mediation models, but the fit of models that impose various equality constraints across groups on one or more paths is compared to the fit of models that freely estimate the paths across groups. For examples of this technique in action, see Dittmar et al. (2009) and Lehmann, Burkert, Daig, Glaesmer, and Brähler (2011).

Multiple-group structural equation modeling provides a more formal test of moderation of various paths in the model, but it does not provide a formal test of difference between indirect effects unless additional steps are taken. For instance, if a model that constrains the paths from X to M and from M to Y to be the same across groups does not fit any worse than a model that freely estimates those paths across groups, this suggests that the indirect effect of X on Y through M is the same in the groups. Alternatively, a program such as Mplus could be used to impose an equality constraint on the product of paths across groups to see if such a model fits no worse than one that allows the product to differ across groups.

The second alternative is the kind of regression-based conditional process analysis that has been the focus of the last two chapters. The form of the conceptual and corresponding statistical model will depend on which paths in the causal system are believed to be moderated and which are not. For the sake of illustration, consider a model that allows all three of the paths to be moderated by W. Such a model is represented in conceptual form in Figure 12.2, panel A. This model in the form of a statistical diagram appears as in Figure 12.2, panel B, which represents two equations:

$$M = i_1 + a_1X + a_2W + a_3XW + e_M \tag{12.3}$$
$$Y = i_2 + c_1'X + c_2'W + c_3'XW + b_1M + b_2MW + e_Y \tag{12.4}$$

The indirect effect of X on Y through M is defined as the product of the $X \rightarrow M$ and $M \rightarrow Y$ effects, each of which is moderated. The effect of X on

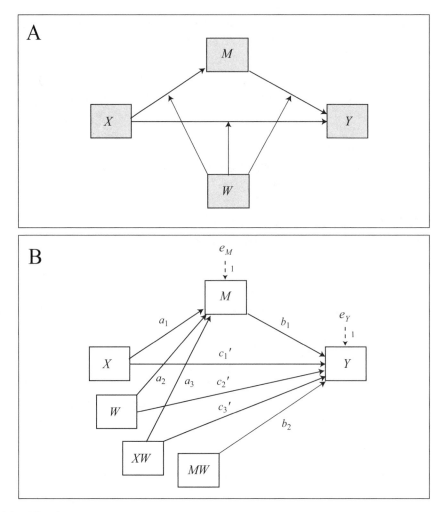

FIGURE 12.2. A conceptual (panel A) and statistical (panel B) diagram representing a simple mediation model with all three paths moderated by a common moderator.

M is derived from equation 12.3 by grouping terms involving X and then factoring out X, resulting in

$$\theta_{X \to M} = a_1 + a_3 W$$

which is a function of W. Likewise, the effect of M on Y comes from equation 12.4 and is constructed in the same fashion, grouping terms involving M and factoring out M:

$$\theta_{M \to Y} = b_1 + b_2 W$$

So the effect of M on Y is also a function of W. The indirect effect of X on Y through M is the product of these two conditional effects:

$$\theta_{X \to M}\theta_{M \to Y} = (a_1 + a_3 W)(b_1 + b_2 W) \tag{12.5}$$

which is itself a conditional effect—a conditional indirect effect and a function of W.

The direct effect of X on Y is also a conditional effect. From equation 12.4, grouping terms involving X and then factoring out X yields

$$\theta_{X \to Y} = c'_1 + c'_3 W \tag{12.6}$$

So the direct effect is conditional because it is a function of W.

When W is a dichotomous moderator variable, estimation of this model faithfully represents the spirit of a subgroups analysis approach in that it allows all three paths to differ between the two groups, but the paths are estimated using the entire dataset rather than two separate analyses, each based on a subset of the data. A test of moderation for each path in the model is available in the form of the regression coefficients for the products along with their tests of significance. For instance, c'_3 estimates the difference in the direct effect between the two groups, and an inferential test that $_Tc'_3 = 0$ can be used to rule out "chance" as the explanation for the observed difference. Equation 12.5 can be used to derive estimates of the indirect effect for different values of W, and the direct effect conditioned on a value of the moderator can be derived from equation 12.6.

This model can be estimated using PROCESS by specifying model 59 as well as which variables in the data play the roles of X, Y, M, and W. In addition to the regression coefficients, PROCESS will provide tests of significance and confidence intervals for the conditional direct and indirect effects, the latter based on a bootstrap confidence interval. The only thing that PROCESS does not provide automatically is a test of the difference between the conditional indirect effects. But this can be derived using the same logic described in section 12.3. In generic terms, the difference between the conditional indirect effect of X on Y through M when $W = w_1$ and when $W = w_2$ is

$$(a_1 + a_3 w_1)(b_1 + b_2 w_1) - (a_1 + a_3 w_2)(b_1 + b_2 w_2)$$

which reduces to

$$a_1 b_2 (w_1 - w_2) + a_3 b_1 (w_1 - w_2) + a_3 b_2 (w_1^2 - w_2^2)$$

In the special case where W is dichotomous and coded 0 and 1, so $w_1 = 1$ and $w_2 = 0$, this expression further reduces to

$$a_1 b_2 + a_3 b_1 + a_3 b_2$$

Use of the **save** option in PROCESS as described in section 12.3 would save all the bootstrap estimates of the regression coefficients to a file. The program offered in the prior section could then be modified to read the file and produce a bootstrap confidence interval for $_T a_{1T} b_2 + _T a_{3T} b_1 + _T a_{3T} b_2$. If a 95% confidence interval does not contain zero, this means that the indirect effect of X on Y through M differs between the two groups coded with W.

12.5 Writing about Conditional Process Modeling

Until recently, I sat on my local graduate studies committee, charged yearly with the responsibility of sorting through stacks of applications for graduate school and trying to figure out who is likely to succeed in a rigorous and quantitatively driven social science Ph.D. program. For some time, I put much more emphasis on quantitative Graduate Record Examination scores and grades in quantitative courses (such as statistics, mathematics, and economics) than other committee members. As I have taught nothing but data analysis for the last decade, I have repeatedly seen firsthand the struggles of students who aren't prepared to think abstractly and quantitatively. But after a few years I began to realize that the students who were comfortable with the mathematics weren't necessarily the ones getting the best jobs after graduate school. Although there are many determinants of success no doubt, I have become convinced that the ability to communicate in writing is at least as if not more important than the ability to manipulate numbers and think in abstractions. You don't have to be a good data analyst to be a good scientist, but your future on the front lines of science is limited if you can't write effectively.

In my experience, respectable writing comes in spurts with long delays between, and what comes out between periods of inspiration often is drivel that ends up getting cut. It took me a couple of days to write the first draft of this section, most of it spent procrastinating because I wasn't sure how I wanted it to start, I couldn't immediately think of anything I wanted to say that I hadn't already said, and I had other things I wanted to do. But with time running out to deliver this manuscript, I had no choice but to force myself to sit and do it. Once I started typing, the first few pages came out in about an hour.

My point is that you should give yourself plenty of time to write. Your first draft is not what you want others to read, and if you don't give yourself the opportunity to think about what you want to say, choose your words carefully, and then reflect on what you have written, you are not going to be communicating as effectively as you probably can and must. As an editor of a journal, I know how poor writing is perceived by other scholars. Most reviewers don't have the patience or time to read the work of others that wasn't ready to be submitted. They will simply reject and move on to the next thing in their busy schedules, and they will do so without feeling the least bit guilty about it.

It never hurts to have a good model to follow when writing about anything. Although I encourage all scientific writers to find their own voice rather than rely on conventions and the expectations of others, sometimes following the lead of a good writer whose work you admire can go a long way toward improving your own scientific communication and developing your own style. For instance, I have always been a big fan of the prose of Daniel T. Gilbert, a social psychologist currently at Harvard University. His writing has a degree of levity not found in most journal articles, and I find his playfulness with words and the stories he tells when framing his work keeps me interested in reading more. After all, who begins a scientific article with stories about bubble-gum-chewing robots (Gilbert & Osborne, 1989) or aliens descending from space to peek in on the work of psychologists (Gilbert & Krull, 1988), and who dares describe the goal of social psychology as figuring out how Aunt Sofia reasons about the behavior of her nephews (Gilbert & Malone, 1995)? I don't know whether his influence on my own writing is apparent to those who know him, but I believe my writing is better in part because of my early exposure to his.

A model need not be someone whose work you have historically admired. It could also be a particular analysis presented in a way that you felt was clear, easy to read, and seemed to convey just what you needed to know. The problem is that unlike the case with ANOVA or multiple regression, conditional process analysis is a relatively new analytical strategy, so the number of models to follow is small and they are scattered about, although that is likely to change quickly. You will also find citation databases such as Thomson Reuters *Web of Knowledge* to be helpful in this regard. People doing conditional process analysis are probably citing some of the seminal papers in this area, such as Edwards and Lambert (2007), Muller et al. (2005), and Preacher et al. (2007), so looking for papers that cite one of these articles can help identify models to follow.

I am frequently asked by others to refer them to specific examples of conditional process analysis in the literature that I feel could serve as good models. No doubt there are many out there. Of course, I believe that some of my own research articles do a reasonably good job of presenting the results of a conditional process analysis in a manner that I would endorse (see Berndt et al., in press; Parker, Hossein, & Hayes, 2011; Pollack et al., 2012). For alternative approaches to communicating such an analysis, see

Bolton, Harvey, Grawitch, and Barber (2012) or Stiglbauer, Selenko, Batinic, and Jodlbauer (2012), for example.

One of the challenges you are likely to face when writing about a conditional process analysis is staying within the page allowance that most journal editors provide. A well-written analysis will usually contain multiple tables, perhaps a figure or two to depict the conceptual model and perhaps an interaction or two, and enough text to describe what was found in substantive terms while also providing sufficient detail about the analysis for the reader to understand what was done. Many reviewers, editors, and readers will not be familiar with this approach and may need to be educated within the text, further lengthening the manuscript. Yet I am also amazed how much I am able to cut from my own writing with sufficient editing, so don't be wedded to every word you write, and don't be afraid to delete that sentence or two you spent much time pondering, crafting, and fine-tuning but that upon third or fourth reading really isn't necessary to convey what needs to be conveyed.

That said, I would err on the side of presenting more information rather than less whenever space allows it. Conditional direct and indirect effects are functions of the parameter estimates of regression models. I recommend providing these functions for the reader in the text itself, or in a text box in figures if you are graphically depicting your results, in order to better help your readers understand how the conditional effects you present and interpret map on to the regression coefficients you might be presenting in a table or elsewhere. Cole et al. (2011) provides a good example of this (also see Berndt et al., in press). Tables can also be an effective way of presenting how a conditional effect (direct or indirect) varies systematically as a function of a moderator or moderators. With a bit of creativity, you pack a lot of information pertinent to the moderation of mediation into a table, including bootstrap confidence intervals or p-values for conditional effects, as in Table 11.2.

The first section of Chapter 11 contained three analyses which I described as a "piecemeal" approach to conditional process modeling. I commented that this approach fails to integrate the three analyses into a coherent conditional process analysis, and then I proceeded to do so in section 11.2. This might suggest that this piecemeal approach is to be avoided because it is somehow wrong or misguided. Not so. Although this piecemeal approach is incomplete, there is nothing inherently wrong about describing and analyzing the components of a larger model first in order to better understand what your data are telling you. In fact, starting with a piecemeal approach and then following through with an integrated conditional process analysis is exactly what I have done in my own work (such as in Pollack et al., 2012). An alternative is to reverse the order of these two sets of analyses, first starting with the integrated model and presenting the findings, and then breaking it into its components and doing a more fine-grained analysis of different parts of the model to better understand what the integrated model is telling you. Neither of these two ways of telling the story is any better or worse than the other. How you tell your story is up to you.

Other than this advice, all of the recommendations and guidelines I offer for describing mediation and moderation analysis in sections 6.5 and 9.5 apply to conditional process analysis as well. Don't leave certain details unstated, such as whether you centered variables used to construct products, whether your regression coefficients are unstandardized (my preferred metric) or standardized, and how dichotomous variables are coded. Try not to use symbols without defining them for your reader. Avoid reporting standardized coefficients for dichotomous predictors. Never report regression coefficients listed as "standardized" in a model that includes a product of predictors. Specify how many bootstrap samples were generated, and whether confidence intervals are percentile based or bias corrected, and so forth.

12.6   Chapter Summary

Conditional process modeling is the integration of moderation and mediation analysis into a unified analytical model. We often approach the study design phase with clear ideas about what we will find when the study is conducted and the kind of paper we will write after the data are in and analyzed. But things can go wrong along the way. Reality sometimes intervenes and shows us something we didn't expect. Sometimes our a priori conceptions about the processes we are trying to study turn out to be incorrect. Conditional process modeling involves making decisions about how to proceed when various stages of the analysis reveal things unexpected. What to do isn't always obvious, and the course of action you take will depend on your own philosophy about science and the modeling enterprise as a whole.

There are many interesting controversies and debates in the mediation and moderation analysis literature, only a small fraction of which I even attempt to address in this book. One controversy I do address pertains to whether mediation and moderation are mutually exclusive. Can a variable function as both a mediator and a moderator in the same analysis? Can a variable both mediate and moderate another variable's effect? Although I do not take a stand on this controversy, I do illustrate in this chapter that mathematically it seems like it is possible, even if it turns out it could never make sense substantively or theoretically.

I do take a stand on the practice of subgroups analysis when attempting to answer questions about whether mediation is moderated. Conditional process modeling allows you to model the conditional nature of mechanisms without having to slice the data up and conduct separate mediation analyses on subsets of the data. There are various arguments for avoiding this method of analysis, and I recommend you do so. With an understanding of the principles described in Chapters 10 and 11, there are very few legitimate excuses for employing this procedure.

I also tackle the question as to how to compare conditional indirect effects. I illustrate that for some models, an inference about a product of regression coefficients in a conditional process model can lead to the claim that any two conditional indirect effects one can quantify from that model are statistically different from each other. I also show that a test of mediated moderation can also be construed as a test of moderated mediation.

I said in the preface to my first book that a book is never finished, you simply run out of time. I am out of time and out of space, having now only scratched the surface of how the ideas described in this book can be applied and extended. Furthermore, I imagine that there are many new questions you may now have about mediation and moderation analysis, whether epistemological or practical, that perhaps a future edition will better address. I know that if you have been following along, you have certainly developed some skills that will help you to answer some of these questions on your own. I hope that you have found some of the principles and procedures I have described here useful in advancing your own research agenda and that PROCESS makes your analytical life a little bit easier.

APPENDICES

Appendix A
Using PROCESS

This appendix describes how to install and execute PROCESS, how to set up a PROCESS command, and it documents its many features, some of which are not described elsewhere in this book. As PROCESS is modified and features are added, supplementary documentation will be released at *www.afhayes.com*. Check this web page regularly for updates. Also available at this page is a complete set of model templates identifying each model that PROCESS can estimate.

This documentation focuses on the SPSS version of PROCESS. All features and functions described below are available in the SAS version as well and work as described here, with minor modifications to the syntax. At the end of this documentation (see page 438), a special section devoted to SAS describes some of the differences in syntax structure for the SAS version compared to what is described below.

Overview

PROCESS is a computational tool for path analysis–based moderation and mediation analysis as well as their integration in the form of a conditional process model. In addition to estimating unstandardized model coefficients, standard errors, t and p-values, and confidence intervals using either OLS regression (for continuous outcomes) or maximum likelihood logistic regression (for dichotomous outcomes), PROCESS generates direct and indirect effects in mediation models, conditional effects (i.e., "simple slopes") in moderation models, and conditional indirect effects in conditional process models with a single or multiple mediators. PROCESS offers various methods for probing two- and three-way interactions and can construct percentile bootstrap, bias-corrected bootstrap, and Monte Carlo confidence intervals for indirect effects. In mediation models, multiple mediator variables can be specified to operate in parallel or in serial. Heteroscedasticity-consistent standard errors are available for inference about model coefficients, in the Sobel test for indirect effects, and when probing interactions in moderation analysis. Various measures of effect size for indirect effects are generated in simple and parallel multiple mediation models, along with bootstrap confidence intervals for effect size inference. An option is available for partialing out contextual-level variation when individual data are nested under a higher-level organizational structure. Individual paths in moderated mediation models can be estimated as moderated by one or two variables either additively or multiplicatively. Some models estimated by PROCESS allow up to four moderators simultaneously.

Preparing for Use

PROCESS can be used as either a command-driven macro or installed as a custom dialog for setting up the model using SPSS's point-and-click user interface. When executed as a macro, the PROCESS.sps file (available from *www.afhayes.com*) should first be opened as a syntax file. Once it has been opened, execute the entire file exactly as is. *Do not modify the code at all.* Once the PROCESS.sps program has been executed, it can be closed and the PROCESS command is available for use in any SPSS program. Running PROCESS.sps activates the macro, and it will remain active so long as SPSS remains open. The PROCESS file must be loaded and reexecuted each time SPSS is opened in order to use the features of the PROCESS command. See the "Examples" section starting on page 422 for how to set up a PROCESS command in a syntax window. Please also read "Model Designation and Estimation" (page 426) and the "Notes" section (page 439) for important details pertinent to execution, including calling PROCESS with the SPSS INSERT command.

To install PROCESS as a custom dialog into the SPSS menus, execute PROCESS.spd (available from *www.afhayes.com*) by double-clicking it on the desktop or opening and installing it from within SPSS under the Utilities menu. Administrative access to the machine on which PROCESS is being installed is required when using a Windows operating system, and you must execute SPSS as an administrator. Once successfully installed, PROCESS will appear as a new menu item in SPSS nested under Analyze → Regression. If you do not have administrative access, contact your local information technology specialist for assistance in setting up administrative access to the machine on which you wish to install PROCESS.

Although the dialog box offers a "Paste" button, its use is not recommended. Users interested in embedding PROCESS commands in their own syntax should use the syntax-driven macro (PROCESS.sps) rather than the custom dialog. Execution of PROCESS.sps as described earlier is not necessary when the model is set up using a dialog box. Some options available in the macro cannot be accessed through the dialog box.

Syntax Structure

The first line of syntax below is required for all PROCESS commands. The remaining commands in brackets are optional or model dependent. Brackets, parentheses, and asterisks should not be included in the PROCESS command. "**" Denotes the default argument when the option is omitted.

```
process vars=varlist/y=yvar/x=xvar/m=mvlist/model=num
                              [/w=wvar] [/z=zvar]
                              [/v=vvar] [/q=qvar]
                              [/wmodval=wval]
                              [/zmodval=zval]
                              [/vmodval=vval]
                              [/qmodval=qval]
                              [/mmodval=mval]
                              [/xmodval=xval]
                              [/cluster=clvar]
                              [/contrast=(0**)(1)]
                              [/boot=z(1000**)]
                              [/mc=g(0**)]
                              [/conf=ci(95**)]
                              [/effsize=(0**)(1)]
                              [/normal=(0**)(1)]
                              [/jn=(0**)(1)]
                              [/coeffci=(0)(1**)]
                              [/varorder=vord(2**)]
                              [/hc3=(0**)(1)]
                              [/covmy=cov(0**)]
                              [/total=(0**)(1)]
                              [/center=(0**)(1)]
                              [/quantile=(0**)(1)]
                              [/detail=(0)(1**)]
                              [/plot=(0**)(1)]
                              [/seed=sd]
                              [/percent=(0**)(1)]
                              [/iterate=it(10000**)]
                              [/converge=cvg(.00000001)]
                              [/save=(0**)(1)].
```

Examples

(1) Simple Moderation

```
process vars=newlaws alcohol concerns use age/y=newlaws/x=alcohol
    /m=concerns/model=1/quantile=1/center=1/plot=1/jn=1.
```

- Estimates a simple moderation model with the effect of alcohol on newlaws moderated by concerns.

- use and age are included in the model as covariates.

- alcohol and concerns are mean centered prior to analysis.

- Generates the conditional effects of alcohol on newlaws at values of concerns equal to the 10th , 25th, 50th, 75th, and 90th percentiles of the distribution in the sample.

- Produces a table of estimated values of newlaws for various values of alcohol and concerns.

- Implements the Johnson–Neyman technique to identify the values on the continuum of concerns at which point the effect of alcohol on newlaws transitions between statistically significant and nonsignificant at the .05 level.

(2) Moderated Moderation

```
process vars=mathprob gender explms treat/y=mathrpob/x=treat/m=explms
    /w=gender/model=3/mmodval=4.
```

- Estimates a moderated moderation model predicting mathprob from treat while including a three-way interaction between treat, explms, and gender in the model along with all required two-way interactions.

- Generates the conditional effect of treat on mathprob for both males and females when explms = 4.

(3) Simple Mediation

```
process vars=donate winner votes/y=votes/x=donate/m=winner/model=4
    /total=1/effsize=1/boot=10000.
```

- Estimates the total and direct effect of donate on votes, as well as the indirect effect of donate on votes through winner.

- Generates a bias-corrected 95% bootstrap confidence interval for the indirect effect using 10,000 bootstrap samples.

- Produces point estimates and bias-corrected 95% bootstrap confidence interval estimates of various indices of effect size for the indirect effect.

(4) Parallel Multiple Mediation

```
process vars=know educ attn elab sex age/y=know/x=educ/m=attn elab/model=4/
    /contrast=1/normal=1/conf=90/save=1.
```

- Estimates the direct effect of educ on know, as well as the total and specific indirect effects of educ on know through attn and elab, with attn and elab functioning as parallel mediators.

- sex and age are included in the model as covariates.

- Produces the Sobel test for the specific indirect effects.

- Generates 90% bias-corrected bootstrap confidence intervals for the indirect effects using 1,000 bootstrap samples.

- Calculates the difference between the two specific indirect effects and produces a bias-corrected bootstrap confidence interval for the difference.

- Creates a new data window containing the 1,000 bootstrap estimates of each of the regression coefficients.

(5) Serial Multiple Mediation

```
process vars=commit close desire happy nbhrhood/y=happy/x=commit
   /m=close desire/model=6/hc3=1/effsize=1/boot=10000/cluster=nbhrhood.
```

- Estimates the direct effect of commit on happy, as well as the total and all possible specific indirect effects of commit on happy through close and desire.

- close and desire function as mediators in serial, with close affecting desire.

- Standard errors for model coefficients are based on the HC3 heteroscedasticity-consistent standard error estimator.

- Generates 95% bias-corrected bootstrap confidence intervals for the indirect effects using 10,000 bootstrap samples.

- Produces point estimates and bias-corrected 95% bootstrap confidence intervals for various indices of effect size for the indirect effects.

- With cases nested within neighborhoods (coded with a variable named nbhrhood), partials out neighborhood-level effects from all estimates.

(6) Conditional Process Model Example 1

```
process vars=frame euskept peffic risk turnout/y=turnout/x=frame/m=risk
   /w=euskept/z=peffic/model=68/boot=20000/wmodval=2/center=1.
```

- Estimates the direct effect of frame on turnout, as well as the conditional indirect effects of frame on turnout through risk. The effect of frame on risk is modeled as multiplicatively moderated by both peffic and euskept, and the effect of risk on turnout is modeled as moderated by euskept.

- euskept, peffic, and frame are mean centered prior to analysis.

- Calculates the conditional indirect effects of frame on turnout through risk among cases 2 units above the sample mean on euskept and with values of peffic at the sample means, as well as with peffic one standard deviation above and below the sample mean.

- Generates bias-corrected 95% bootstrap confidence intervals for the conditional indirect effects using 20,000 bootstrap samples.

(7) Conditional Process Model Example 2

```
process vars=calling livecall carcomm workmean jobsat/y=jobsat/m=carcomm
    workmean/x=calling/w=livecall/model=7/boot=5000/seed=34421.
```

- Estimates the direct effect of `calling` on `jobsat`, as well as the conditional indirect effects of `calling` on `jobsat` through both `carcomm` and `workmean` operating in parallel. The effects of calling on both `carcomm` and `workmean` are modeled as moderated by `livecall`.

- Produces the conditional indirect effects of `calling` when `livecall` is equal to the sample mean as well as plus and minus one standard deviation from the mean.

- Generates bias-corrected 95% bootstrap confidence intervals for the conditional indirect effects using 5,000 bootstrap samples.

- Seeds the random number generator for bootstrap sampling with the value 34421.

(8) Conditional Process Model Example 3

```
process vars=protest sexism respappr anger liking age sex/y=liking
    /x=protest/m=respappr anger/w=sexism/model=8/boot=5000/quantile=1
    /percent=1.
```

- Estimates the effect of `protest` on `liking` directly as well as indirectly through `respappr` and `anger`, with both direct and indirect effects moderated by `sexism`. The effect of `protest` on `respappr` as well as the effect `protest` on `anger` is modeled as moderated by `sexism`.

- `age` and `sex` are included in the model as covariates.

- Generates 95% percentile-based bootstrap confidence intervals based on 5,000 bootstrap samples for the conditional indirect effect of `protest` at the 10th, 25th, 50th, 75th, and 90th percentile values of `sexism`.

- Produces the indirect effects of the product of `protest` and `sexism` on `liking` through `respappr` as well as through `anger`, along with a percentile-based 95% bootstrap confidence interval.

Model Designation and Estimation

PROCESS can estimate many different models, and which model is estimated is determined by the *num* argument in the required **model** specification. The more popular and frequently used models that PROCESS can estimate are depicted conceptually and in the form of a path diagram beginning on page 442, along with their corresponding model number as recognized by PROCESS in the **model** specification. PROCESS can estimate over 70 models. Additional templates containing the conceptual and statistical diagrams corresponding to models PROCESS can estimate can be found at *www.afhayes.com*.

Each model has certain minimum requirements as to which variables must be designated and provided in the PROCESS command. Any variable in the dataset that appears in the model must be listed in the *varlist* argument of the PROCESS command (e.g., **vars**=*xvar yvar mvlist wvar*). Furthermore, all models require

- a single outcome variable *yvar* listed in the **y** specification (i.e., **y**=*yvar*), where *yvar* is the name of the variable in your data functioning as Y in the model

- a single antecedent causal agent *xvar* listed in the **x** specification (i.e., **x**=*xvar*), where *xvar* is the name of the variable in your data functioning as X in the model

- either a single moderator (models 1, 2, and 3) or at least one mediator (models 4 and higher) specified in the *mvlist* in the **m** specification (i.e, **m**=*mvlist*), where *mvlist* is the name of the variable or variables in the data functioning as moderator (models 1, 2, and 3) or mediator(s) (models 4 and higher).

Other than **x**, **y**, **m**, **model**, and **vars**, the remaining required inputs to PROCESS will be model dependent. In general, any variable that is a part of the conceptual model in the model template must be provided as an input to PROCESS, and any variable that is not a part of the conceptual model must be left out unless such variables are to be treated as covariates by inclusion in *varlist*. For instance, observe in the model templates section (see page 442) that model 21 has, in addition to X, M, and Y, two moderators W and V. Thus, PROCESS must also be told which two variables in the dataset correspond to *W* and *V* in the diagram. This would be done with the use of the **w** and **v** specifications (e.g., **w**=*wvar* and **v**=*vvar*), where *wvar* and *vvar* are the names of the variables in the data file corresponding to *W* and *V*.

The **y**, **x**, **w**, **z**, **v**, and **q** specfications each allow only one variable, and a variable can be listed in one and only one of the *yvar*, *xvar*, *mvlist*, *wvar*, *zvar*, *vvar*, and *qvar* arguments. For instance, a variable cannot be listed as both **w** in *wvar* and **m** in *mvlist*. However, both would have to appear in *varlist*.

In the SPSS version of PROCESS, the variable names listed in the *varlist*, *yvar*, *xvar*, *mvlist*, *wvar*, *zvar*, *vvar*, and *qvar* arguments must match the case (i.e., uppercase, lowercase, or combinations thereof) of the variables in the dataset. So ATTITUDE, Attitude, and AttiTuDe are different variables according to PROCESS. Thus, **y=ATTITUDE** will produce an error even if Attitude exists in your data file. In addition, the potential for errors at execution is increased when variable names are more than eight characters in length. Thus, the user is advised to *reduce all long variable names in the dataset and that are to be used in a PROCESS command down to eight characters at maximum.*

Although PROCESS has a number of error-trapping routines built in, it will not catch all errors produced by improper formatting of a PROCESS command, improper listing of variables and variable names, and so forth. Any errors it has trapped will be displayed in an errors section of the PROCESS output. Errors it has not successfully trapped will appear as a long list of SPSS execution errors that will be largely unintelligible.

Multiple Mediators

All mediation models (models 4 and higher) can have up to 10 mediators operating in parallel, with the exception of model 6, which is restricted to between two and four and models the mediators as operating in serial. Mediators operating in parallel are all modeled as affected by *xvar* and, in turn, affect *yvar*, but they are not modeled to transmit their effects to any other mediators in the model (see section 5.1). Mediators operating in serial are linked in a causal chain, with the first mediator affecting the second, the second the third, and so forth (see section 5.4). The order of the mediators in *mvlist* is not conquential to the estimation of the model except in model 6. In model 6, the first variable in *mvlist* is assumed to be causally prior to the second variable in *mvlist*, which is causally prior to the third, and so forth.

Pairwise comparisons between specific indirect effects can be requested for models 4, 5, and 6 by setting the argument in the **contrast** option to 1 (i.e., **contrast=1**). These comparisons will appear in the output in the indirect effects section with labels (C1), (C2), and so forth. A table that maps the label to the specific indirect effects being compared is provided at the bottom of the output. Bootstrap or Monte Carlo confidence intervals are provided for inference for these pairwise comparisons when the contrast option is used in conjunction with bootstrapping or the Monte Carlo option. See section 5.3 for a discussion of contrasts between indirect effects.

Models 7 and higher include the moderation of an effect either to or from a mediator. The model templates toward the end of this appendix and at *www.afhayes.com* illustrate which path is moderated for a given model. In models with multiple mediators, the moderation applies to all correspond- ing paths for each mediator. For example, if model 7 is specified with two mediators, med1 and med2, then both the effect from *xvar* to med1 and the effect from *xvar* to med2 will be estimated as moderated by *wvar*. There is no way of restricting the estimation of the moderation to only one of the paths using the PROCESS procedure. Doing so requires the use of a structural equation modeling program.

Covariates

Any variable that appears in *varlist* but that does not appear anywhere else in the PROCESS command will be treated as a covariate. By default, covariates are included as predictor variables in the models of all mediators (i.e., all models of the variables in *mvlist*) as well as in the model of *yvar*. This can be changed through the use of the **covmy** option. Setting the *cov* argument to 1 (i.e., **covmy=1**) includes the covariates in the model of all mediators in *mvlist* but not outcome variable *yvar*. Using an argument of 2 (i.e., **covmy=2**) specifies estimation of a model that includes all covariates in the model of outcome *yvar* but not the mediator variables in *mvlist*. It is not possible to specify some covariates only in the model of *yvar* and other covariates only in the model(s) of *mvlist*.

Probing Interactions and Generating Conditional Effects

In any model that involves a moderated effect, PROCESS will produce estimates of conditional effects (direct and/or indirect) at various values of the moderator based on the equations at the bottom of each of the model templates beginning on page 442. By default, when a moderator is dichotomous, conditional effects at the two values of the moderator are generated. But when a moderator is quantitative, conditional effects are estimated by default at the sample mean of the moderator, as well as plus and minus one standard deviation from the moderator mean.

Three alternatives for probing interactions are available in PROCESS. For quantitative moderators, the **quantile** option generates conditional effects at the 10th, 25th, 50th, 75th, and 90th percentiles of the distribution of the moderator. This option is available by setting the argument in the **quantile** option to 1 (i.e., **quantile=1**). Unlike when the mean and ± one standard deviation from the mean is used, these quantile values are guaranteed to be within the range of the observed data. For a discrete quantitative moderator (i.e., a quantitative moderator with relatively few observed values), some of the quantile values of the moderator may be identical. For example, the 10th and 25th percentile of the moderator may be the same value. This will produce some redundancy in the output.

The second alternative is to request the conditional effect of interest at a specific value of the moderator or moderators. This is accomplished through the use of the **wmodval, zmodval, vmodval, mmodval, qmodval**, and **xmodval** options, setting the corresponding argument (*wval, zval, vval, mval, wval*, and/or *xval*) to the value of the moderator at which you'd like the estimate of the conditional effect. For example, model 22 includes two moderators, W and V. To generate an estimate of the conditional indirect effect of *xvar* on *yvar* through the variables in *mvlist* when $W = 1$ and $V = 2$, append **wmodval=1** and **vmodval=2** to the PROCESS command. This will also generate an estimate of the conditional direct effect of X when $W = 1$. When used in conjunction with the **center** option, values of the moderator provided should be based on the mean-centered metric rather than the original metric of measurement. This option for probing an interaction is not available in the custom dialog version of PROCESS.

The third alternative is the Johnson–Neyman technique, requested by setting the argument in the **jn** option to 1 (i.e., **jn=1**). This is available for models 1 and 3. For model 1, this approach identifies the value(s) on the moderator variable (*mvlist*) continuum at which point (or points) the effect of *xvar* on *yvar* transitions between statistically significant and not, using the α-level of significance as the criterion. By default, $\alpha = 0.05$. This can be changed using the **conf** option, setting the desired confidence to $100(1 - \alpha)$. For example, for $\alpha = 0.01$, specify **conf=99**. For model 3, PROCESS computes the point or points along the continuum of moderator *wvar* at which the two-way interaction between *xvar* and *mvlist* transitions between statistically significant and not. In addition to identifying these points, PROCESS produces a table to aid in the identification of the regions of significance. See section 7.4 for a discussion of the Johnson–Neyman technique.

When a model includes more than one moderator, a table of conditional effects is generated for all combinations of the moderators based on the options or defaults used and described earlier. For example, in model 21, if **wmodval=1** is specified but the **vmodval** option is not used and V is a quantitative moderator, PROCESS will generate a table of conditional indirect effects when $W = 1$ and V is equal to the mean, as well as plus and minus one standard deviation from the mean.

Statistical Inference for Indirect Effects

PROCESS offers a normal theory approach (i.e., the Sobel test), bootstrap confidence intervals, and Monte Carlo confidence intervals for inference about the indirect effect in models with a mediation component.

By setting the argument in the **normal** option to 1 (i.e., **normal=1**), PRO-CESS generates the normal theory-based Sobel test for the indirect effects in simple and parallel multiple mediator models (models 4, 5). A p-value is derived using the standard normal distribution. This test is not available for the total indirect effect or conditional indirect effects in mediation models with moderated paths. The standard error estimator for an indirect effect used in the normal theory test is determined by the *vord* argument in the **varorder** option. When set to 1 (i.e., **varorder=1**), the first-order standard error estimator is used, whereas when is set to 2 (i.e., **varorder=2**, the default), the second-order standard error is used.

Bootstrap confidence intervals are the default and preferred over the normal theory-based Sobel test for inference about indirect effects because of the unrealistic assumption the Sobel tests makes about the shape of the sampling distribution of the indirect effect. By default, PROCESS generates 95% bias-corrected bootstrap confidence intervals for all indirect effects in any model that involves a mediation component (models 4 and higher). Percentile-based bootstrap confidence intervals will be generated rather than bias-corrected confidence intervals by setting the argument in the **percent** option to 1 (i.e., **percent=1**). The number of bootstrap samples can be set with the z argument in the **boot** option to any desired number (e.g., **boot=5000**; the default number of bootstrap samples is 1,000, but at least 5,000 is recommended for scientific publications). Set z to 0 to turn off bootstrapping. The level of confidence for confidence intervals can be changed by setting *ci* to the desired number anywhere between 50 and 99.9999 (90, 99, etc.) in the **conf** option (e.g., **conf=99**). If the number of bootstrap samples requested is too small given the requested level of confidence desired, PROCESS will automatically increase the number of bootstrap samples as required. A note will be produced at the bottom of the output to this effect when it occurs.

Monte Carlo confidence intervals can be requested instead of bootstrap confidence intervals for simple and multiple mediator models (models 4 and 5) through the use of the **mc** option, setting the g argument to the number of samples desired. For example, **mc=5000** requests Monte Carlo confidence intervals for the indirect effect based on 5,000 samples. The Monte Carlo option takes precedence over the bootstrapping option, so if **mc** is used in conjunction with **boot**, Monte Carlo confidence intervals will result. The **mc** option is ignored by PROCESS when estimating models 7 and above. In that case, bootstrap confidence intervals are generated and the number of bootstrap samples will default to 1,000 unless a larger number is requested.

In addition to the point estimate of the indirect effect and the endpoints of a confidence interval, PROCESS will also generate a bootstrap or Monte Carlo estimate of the standard error of the indirect effect. The standard error of the indirect effect is defined as the standard deviation of the z bootstrap or g Monte Carlo estimates.

Because bootstrapping and Monte Carlo methods are based on random sampling from the data (for bootstrapping) or from theoretical distributions (for Monte Carlo confidence intervals), confidence intervals and standard errors will differ slightly each time PROCESS is run as a result of the random sampling process. The more bootstrap or Monte Carlo samples that are requested, the less this variation between runs. It is possible to replicate a set of random samples by seeding the random number generator, setting sd in the **seed** option to any integer between 1 and 2,000,000,000 prior to running PROCESS (e.g., **seed=23543**). By default, the random number generator is seeded with a random number.

Saving Bootstrap Estimates

When estimating models 4 and above in conjunction with bootstrap confidence intervals for indirect effects, the bootstrap estimates of all regression coefficients can be saved for examination or additional analysis by setting the argument in the **save** option to 1 (i.e., **save=1**). This will produce a new data file in the SPSS session with as many rows as bootstrap samples requested, and as many columns as parameter estimates in the model being estimated. The columns of the data file containing the bootstrap samples will be in the order the parameter estimates first appear in PROCESS output from top to bottom. Parameter estimates for the total effect of X will not be included in this file when the **save** option is used in conjunction with the **total** option in models 4, 5, and 6.

The resulting data file must be saved in order to store it permanently, as subsequent runs of the PROCESS command with the **save=1** option will overwrite the prior file if it is not first saved permanently.

Confidence Intervals for Model Coefficients

By default, PROCESS generates ordinary least squares (for continuous *mvlist* or *yvar*) or maximum-likelihood-based (for dichotomous *yvar*) confidence intervals for all regression coefficients, as well as direct, total, and conditional effects. To suppress their printing, set the argument in the **coeffci** option to 0 (i.e., **coeffci=0**). The confidence level is set using the **conf** option (e.g., **conf=90** for 90% confidence intervals. The default is 95%).

Effect Size Indices for Indirect Effects

When estimating an unmoderated mediation model (models 4, 5, or 6) setting the argument in the **effsize** option to 1 (i.e., **effsize=1**) generates various estimates of the size of the indirect effect. Effect sizes available include the partially and completely standardized indirect effect, κ^2 (Preacher & Kelley, 2011), R^2 (Fairchild et al., 2009), the ratio of the indirect to total effect, and the ratio of the indirect to the direct effect. When used in conjunction with the bootstrapping option, bootstrap confidence intervals for these effect size measures are generated. The R^2 and κ^2 measures are available only in models with a single mediator, no covariates, and no clustering. Effect size measures are not generated for models with a dichotomous *yvar* or models with covariates.

The Total Effect in Unmoderated Mediation Models

In mediation models with no moderated effects (models 4, 5, and 6), PROCESS generates the direct and indirect effects of *xvar* on *yvar* by default, along with corresponding linear models used to estimate these effects. In models 4, 5, and 6 with continuous mediator(s) and outcome, the total effect of *xvar* on *yvar* is the sum of the direct and indirect effects of *xvar*. By setting the argument in the **total** option to 1 (i.e., **total=1**), PROCESS will produce the total effect of *xvar* on *yvar* with a test of significance, along with the corresponding model of *yvar* without the proposed mediators in the model. Use of the **total** option with a dichotomous outcome will generate similar output, but the total effect will not be equal to the sum of the direct and indirect effects due to the arbitrary scaling of the error in estimation in the logistic regression model. Thus, the difference between the total and direct effects is not equivalent to the indirect effect.

Missing Data

PROCESS assumes complete data and will exclude cases from the analysis that are missing on any of the variables in *varlist*. Any missing data substitution or imputation desired by the user should be conducted prior to the execution of PROCESS.

Mean Centering in Models with Interactions

In models that include parameters for estimating interaction effects (i.e., all models PROCESS estimates except 4 and 6), moderation is assumed to be linear, with products of variables serving to represent the moderation. The user has the option of requesting PROCESS to mean center all variables used in the construction of products of predictors prior to model estimation by setting the argument in the *center* option to 1 (i.e., **center=1**). All output for conditional effects will be based on moderator values using the mean-centered metric (e.g., the conditional effect of *xvar* on *yvar* at values of *wvar* will be based on values of *wvar* after mean centering).

By default, variables used to form products are not mean centered. When mean centering is requested, arguments of options used for estimating conditional effects at specific values of the moderator(s) should be values based on a mean-centered metric. For example, the SPSS command

```
PROCESS vars=smoking surgery anxiety addict/y=smoking/x=surgery/
    m=anxiety/w=addict/model=7/wmodval=1.5.
```

will produce the conditional indirect effect of surgery on smoking through anxiety when addict = 1.5, whereas the SPSS command

```
PROCESS vars=smoking surgery anxiety addict/y=smoking/x=surgery/
    m=anxiety/w=addict/model=7/center=1/wmodval=1.5.
```

produces the conditional indirect effect of surgery on smoking through anxiety when addict is 1.5 measurement units above the sample mean of addict.

Visualizing Interactions in Moderation-Only Models

To help visualize and interpret the nature of the moderation of *xvar*'s effect on *yvar* in models 1, 2, and 3, the **plot** option generates a table of predicted values of *yvar* from the model using various values of *xvar* and the moderator or moderators. This table is generated by setting the argument in the **plot** option to 1 (i.e., **plot=1**). Any covariates in the model are set to their sample mean when deriving the predicted values in the table generated.

In the table, the estimated value of *yvar* is listed as "yhat." For OLS regression, this is simply the estimate of *yvar* from the regression model for various values of *xvar* and the moderator(s), with covariates (if any) set to their sample means. For logistic regression, "yhat" is the estimated log odds of the event coded with *yvar* (with the higher code arbitrarily treated as the event modeled). The **plot** option for logistic regression models will also produce a column labeled "prob," which is the estimated log odds converted to a probability using the formula

$$\text{prob} = \frac{e^{yhat}}{1 + e^{yhat}}$$

Nonindependence and Spuriousness Due to Cluster Effects

Subsets of cases in an analysis sometimes are nested under a common organizational unit or "cluster," such as patients in hospitals, kids in schools, or households within neighborhoods. When cases are derived from several organizational units, some of the relationships observed may be attributable to unmodeled effects of organizational units or clusters. When there are many cases in many organizational units, multilevel modeling is the best strategy for dealing with the nonindependence such clustering can produce. An alternative approach when the number of cluster units is small and one is willing to assume fixed effects of the variables in the model is to remove any effect due to organizational unit or cluster by using dummy variables to partial out effects due to cluster from estimates of the coefficients and standard errors in the model.

PROCESS has an option that implements the latter procedure, sometimes called the "fixed effects approach to clustering" (see, e.g., Cohen et al., 2003, pp. 539–544). By specifying the variable that codes organizational unit as the *clvar* argument in the **cluster** option, PROCESS automatically produces $k - 1$ dummy variables coding which of the k clusters a case is nested under. These $k - 1$ dummy variables are then included as additional predictors in all linear models generated as part of the analysis. PROCESS allows a maximum of 20 cluster units when this option is requested. This option is not available in the custom dialog interface.

For example, the SPSS command

```
PROCESS vars=smoking surgery anxiety hsptl/y=smoking/x=surgery/m=anxiety
    /model=4/cluster=hsptl.
```

estimates the direct effect of surgery on smoking, as well as the indirect effect of surgery through anxiety while partialing out differences between cases in anxiety, surgery, and smoking due to which hospital a person attended, with hospital coded in a variable in the data file named hsptl. Notice that the clustering variable must also be provided in *varlist*.

The model coefficients for the dummy variables are not displayed in the output, nor are they added to the data file. However, model summary information (e.g., R^2) will include the effects of cluster as well as the other variables in the model.

An important limitation of the cluster option is that no variables in the model can be measured at the level of the cluster (i.e., in multilevel terms, none of the variables can be measured at level-2). That is, there must be variation in each of the variables in the model (including the covariates) within cluster. When this condition is not satisfied, a matrix inversion error will result and PROCESS will terminate.

Heteroscedasticity-Consistent Standard Errors

By default, PROCESS uses an estimator for the standard errors of the regression coefficients that assumes homoscedasticity of the errors in estimation of the outcome variable. PROCESS can also generate standard errors using the HC3 estimator, described in Long and Ervin (2000) and Hayes and Cai (2007). This heteroscedasticity-consistent standard error estimator is requested by setting the argument in the **hc3** option to 1 (i.e., **hc3=1**). Any computation that uses the standard error of a regression coefficient will automatically employ the HC3 estimator when this option is requested, including the Sobel test, Monte Carlo confidence intervals for indirect effects, the Johnson–Neyman method, tests of conditional effects in moderation analysis, and the test of the significance of R^2 for models of *yvar*, as well as *mvlist* in mediation analysis.

When heteroscedasticity-consistent standard errors are requested for models 1, 2, and 3, neither the change in R^2 due to interaction(s) nor a test of significance for the change is provided in the output.

Abbreviated Output

By default, PROCESS produces all regression coefficients, standard errors, *t* and *p*-values, and model summary information for the models of *yvar* and, in all but models 1, 2, and 3, the proposed mediators in *mvlist*. In complex models this output can be quite lengthy. If desired, the user can suppress the printing of model information with use of the **detail** option, setting the argument to 0 (i.e., **detail=0**).

Binary Outcome Variables

PROCESS can estimate models with either a continuous or a binary *yvar* and will automatically detect whether or not *yvar* is binary and estimate accordingly. If PROCESS detects only two distinct values on the outcome variable, the direct and indirect effects, as well as the path(s) from the proposed mediator(s) to the outcome, are estimated using logistic regression; otherwise OLS is used. Confidence intervals for indirect effects are estimated in the usual way as the product of the path from the independent variable to the proposed mediator and the path from the proposed mediator to the outcome. Measures of effect size are not available for models with a binary outcome. Note that with binary outcomes the indirect and total effects of *xvar* are scaled differently, and so the total effect will not typically be equal to the sum of the direct and indirect effects. Thus, the difference between the total and the direct effect of *xvar* on *yvar* cannot be used as a substitute for the indirect effect, nor can one use this difference in a metric of effect size, such as the proportion of the effect that is mediated.

Logistic regression coefficients are estimated using a Newton–Raphson iteration algorithm. The number of iterations and convergence criterion can be set using the **iterate** and **converge** options in the command syntax, which default to 10,000 and 0.00000001, respectively.

Indirect Effects in Mediated Moderation

Mediated moderation is a term sometimes used to describe the phenomenon in which the moderation of an effect is carried to an outcome variable through a mediator. Of interest when testing a mediated moderation hypothesis is the estimation of the indirect effect of the product of *xvar* and the moderator(s). Along with estimates of the conditional indirect effect of *xvar* on *yvar* at values of the moderator, output from models 8 and 12 includes the indirect effect of the highest-order interaction in the model. In model 8, the highest-order interaction is the two-way interaction between *xvar* and *wvar*, and in model 12, the highest-order interaction is the three-way interaction between *xvar*, *wvar*, and *zvar*. A bootstrap confidence interval for the indirect effect of the highest-order product term can be used for inference as to whether "moderation is mediated." As described in section 12.3, an inference about the indirect effect of this highest-order interaction can also be interpreted as a test of whether the indirect effect of *xvar* on *yvar* through the variable(s) in *mvlist* is moderated by *wvar*. See section 11.4 for a discussion of the meaningfulness and substantive interpretability of mediated moderation relative to moderated mediation.

Multiple Independent and Dependent Variables

In some cases the user might like to estimate a model that includes multiple independent variables, each linked to the same mediator or set of mediators. PROCESS does not allow more than one variable to be listed in *xvar*. Nevertheless, as described in section 6.4, PROCESS can be used to estimate the coefficients in such a model. By default, covariates are mathematically treated exactly like independent variables in the estimation, with paths to all mediators and the outcome, so if the desired model has k independent variables, PROCESS can be run k times, each time listing one variable as the independent variable in *xvar* and treating remaining $k - 1$ independent variables as covariates. Each run of PROCESS will generate the effects for the variable currently listed in *xvar*. It is recommended that a common random number seed be used for each run of PROCESS when bootstrapping or using the Monte Carlo option, so that the same set of samples will be used when confidence intervals for indirect effects are estimated for different independent variables.

Even though only a single variable can be provided in *yvar*, PROCESS can be used to estimate the direct and indirect effects of X on k dependent variables (Y) when the indirect effect passes through the same mediator or set of mediators and no causal path between the k Y variables is assumed. This is accomplished by running PROCESS k times, once for each dependent variable. By setting the random number seed to the same value for each run, the bootstrap or Monte Carlo samples will be the same at each run, and the results obtained will be as if all the paths were estimated in one model with k dependent variables. See section 6.4 for a discussion.

Mapping PROCESS Models onto MODMED and Edwards and Lambert (2007) Models

PROCESS can estimate conditional indirect effects for all models described in Preacher et al. (2007) and implemented in MODMED for SPSS. However, the model numbers are different. Edwards and Lambert (2007) describe various models that combine moderation and mediation using names rather than numbers, all of which can also be estimated by PROCESS. The table below maps model numbers in MODMED to corresponding model numbers in PROCESS and the model names used by Edwards and Lambert (2007).

MODMED	Edwards and Lambert (2007)	PROCESS
1	—	74
2	Direct effect and first-stage moderation	8
3	Second-stage moderation	14
4	—	22
5	Total effect moderation	59
—	First-stage moderation	7
—	First- and second-stage moderation	58
—	Direct effect moderation	5
—	Direct effect and second-stage moderation	15

Installation, Execution, and Syntax Modifications for SAS Users

The SAS version of PROCESS functions similarly to the SPSS version, and most of the instructions described in this appendix apply to the SAS version, with only the minor modifications described below. Like the SPSS version, the SAS version is a program file (PROCESS.sas), which when executed creates a new command that SAS understands called **%process**. Once PROCESS.sas is executed (without changing the file whatsoever), then the **%process** command is available for use and the program can be closed. Once you close SAS, you have to define the **%process** command by executing PROCESS.sas again. **PROCESS for SAS requires the PROC IML module**. To determine whether you have the PROC IML module installed, run the following commands in SAS:

```
proc iml;
print "PROC IML is installed";
quit;
```

When this code is executed, check the log for any errors, as well as your output window for the text "PROC IML is installed." Any errors in the log or a failure to see this text suggests that PROC IML is not installed on your version of SAS.

The syntax structure for PROCESS for SAS is almost identical to the SPSS version, with five important exceptions:

- The command name is **%process** rather than **process**.

- All parts of the command between **%process** and the ending semicolon (;) must be in parentheses.

- The data file being analyzed must be specified in the command as **data=***file* where *file* is the name of a SAS data file.

- Options and specifications must be delimited with a comma (,) rather than a slash (/). For example, suppose the data corresponding to example 7 on page 425 were stored in a SAS work file named "jobs." The SAS version of the PROCESS command corresponding to example 7 would be

```
%process (data=jobs,vars=calling livecall carcomm workmean jobsat,y=jobsat,
    m=carcomm workmean,x=calling,w=livecall,model=7,boot=5000,seed=34421);
```

- The **save** option requires a file name for the resulting file of bootstrap estimates. For example, **save=mod14bt** tells SAS to save the bootstrap estimates of the regression coefficients to a temporary work file named mod14bt.

Notes

- In the SPSS version of PROCESS variable names are case sensitive and must match the case in the SPSS data file.

- "xxx" is a reserved variable name. Do not include any variable in your data set named "xxx" in the PROCESS procedure.

- PROCESS does not recognize variable names beyond the eighth character. Longer variable names will sometimes confuse PROCESS and are best avoided unless precautions are taken to rename variables that have the same first eight characters, thereby making them distinct to PROCESS.

- For all models, *xvar*, *yvar*, *wvar*, *zvar*, *qvar*, and *vvar* can be either dichotomous or quantitative with at least interval-level properties. The SPSS version of PROCESS ignores the properties of the data specified in the "Measure" column of the Variable View section of the data file.

- For models 4 and higher, variables in *mvlist* must be quantitative variables and are assumed to have at least interval-level measurement properties. In models 1, 2, and 3, the variable in *mvlist* can be either quantitative or dichotomous.

- A case will be deleted from the analysis if user- or system-missing on any of the variables in *varlist*.

- Do not use STRING formatted variables in any of your models. Doing so will produce errors. All variables should be NUMERIC format.

- All covariates in the *vars* list are always assigned to the model of *yvar*, *mvlist*, or both (the default). It is not possible to assign some covariates to the model of *yvar* and others to the model(s) of *mvlist*.

- The *yvar*, *xvar*, *wvar*, *zvar*, *qvar*, *vvar*, and *clvar* arguments are limited to one variable each. Up to 10 variables can be listed in *mvlist*, except when estimating model 6, in which case *mvlist* is limited to four variables. Each variable should be specified in only one of these arguments.

- PROCESS does not offer any models that combine moderation with serial multiple mediation.

- All regression coefficients in the output are unstandardized. For continuous mediators or outcomes, all paths are estimated using OLS regression. For a dichotomous outcome, the path coefficients are maximum-likelihood-based logistic regression coefficients. PROCESS does not have an option for generating standardized regression coefficients. Users interested in standardized coefficients should standardize the variables in the model prior to execution of PROCESS. In mediation models based on standardized variables as input, a bootstrap confidence interval for an indirect effect produced by PROCESS should not be interpreted as a confidence interval for the standardized indirect effect. Standardization of dichotomous predictor variables or reporting of standardized effects for dichotomous predictors generally are not meaningful and should be avoided.

- In PROCESS, the bootstrapping routine is used only for the construction of bootstrap confidence intervals and bootstrap standard errors of indirect effects (conditional or unconditional) in models with a mediation component. Neither model coefficients, their standard errors, nor any other inferential tests are based on bootstrap methods.

- Bootstrapping takes time. The larger the sample, and the more complex the model, the longer the computations take. If you see the message "Running matrix" in the bottom right-hand corner of one of the SPSS windows, this means PROCESS is working on your data. Please be patient. Logistic regression with a large dataset combined with bootstrapping can take a very long time.

- The custom dialog version of PROCESS will construct a few variable names in your data file as it is working, and then delete these variables when it completes the computations. As a result, SPSS will ask you if you want to save your data when you quit SPSS. If you have made no modifications to the data file yourself and the data were already saved before executing, there is no need to save the data file again.

- The PROCESS procedure code cannot be imbedded in a syntax file with an INCLUDE command in SPSS, but it can be called with an INSERT command. This eliminates the need to manually load and run PROCESS.sps prior to execution of a set of commands which call the PROCESS macro. See the *Command Syntax Reference* available through the Help menu in SPSS for details on the use of the INSERT command.

PROCESS MODEL TEMPLATES

Additional templates are available at *www.afhayes.com.*

Model 1

Conceptual Diagram

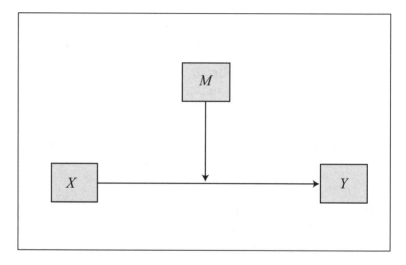

Statistical Diagram

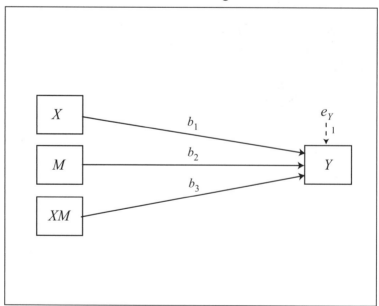

Conditional effect of X on $Y = b_1 + b_3 M$

Model 2

Conceptual Diagram

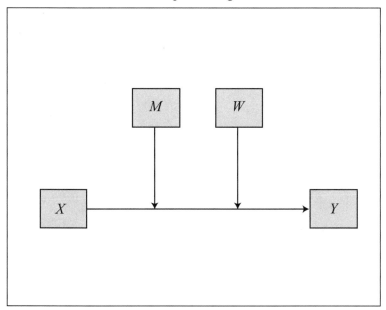

Statistical Diagram

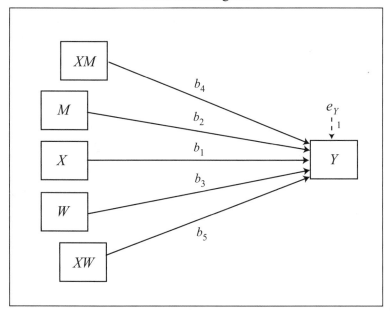

Conditional effect of X on $Y = b_1 + b_4M + b_5W$

Model 3

Conceptual Diagram

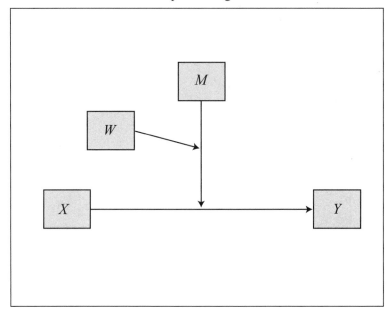

Statistical Diagram

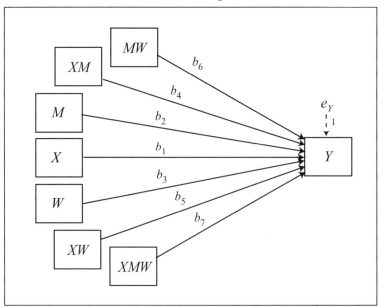

Conditional effect of X on $Y = b_1 + b_4M + b_5W + b_7MW$

Model 4

Conceptual Diagram

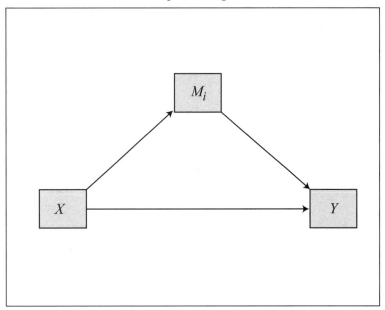

Statistical Diagram

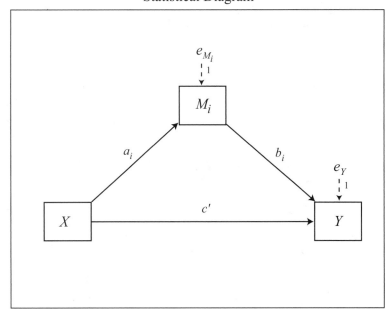

Indirect effect of X on Y through $M_i = a_i b_i$

Direct effect of X on $Y = c'$

Note: Model 4 allows up to 10 mediators operating in parallel.

Model 6
(2 mediators)

Conceptual Diagram

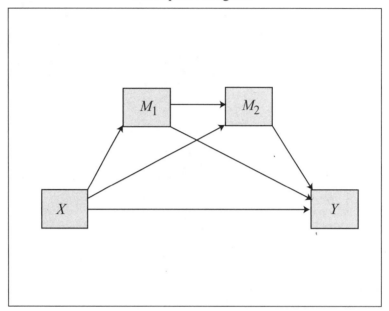

Statistical Diagram

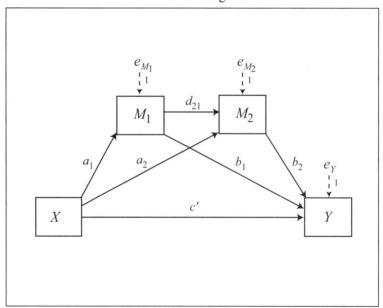

Indirect effect of X on Y through M_i only $= a_i b_i$
Indirect effect of X on Y through M_1 and M_2 in serial $= a_1 d_{21} b_2$
Direct effect of X on $Y = c'$

Note: Model 6 allows up to four mediators operating in serial.

Model 7

Conceptual Diagram

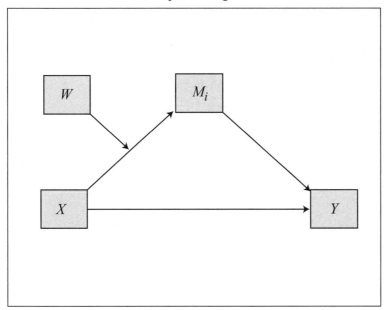

Statistical Diagram

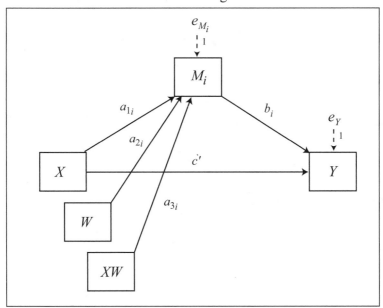

Conditional indirect effect of X on Y through $M_i = (a_{1i} + a_{3i}W)b_i$

Direct effect of X on $Y = c'$

Note: Model 7 allows up to 10 mediators operating in parallel.

Model 8

Conceptual Diagram

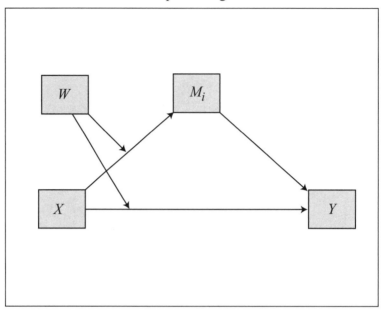

Statistical Diagram

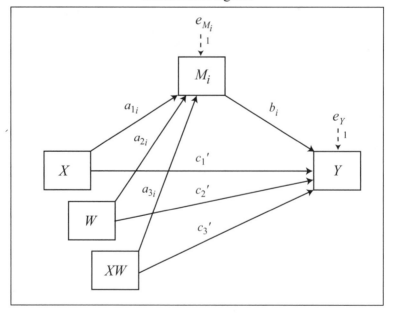

Conditional indirect effect of X on Y through $M_i = (a_{1i} + a_{3i}W)b_i$

Conditional direct effect of X on $Y = c_1' + c_3'W$

Note: Model 8 allows up to 10 mediators operating in parallel.

Model 12

Conceptual Diagram

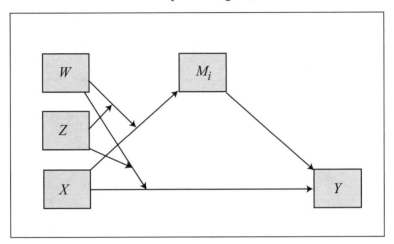

Statistical Diagram

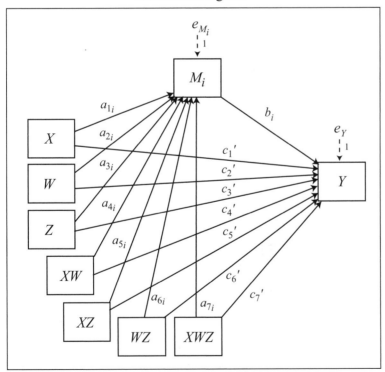

Conditional indirect effect of X on Y through $M_i = (a_{1i} + a_{4i}W + a_{5i}Z + a_{7i}WZ)\, b_i$

Conditional direct effect of X on $Y = c_1{}' + c_4{}'W + c_5{}'Z + c_7{}'WZ$

Note: Model 12 allows up to 10 mediators operating in parallel.

Model 14

Conceptual Diagram

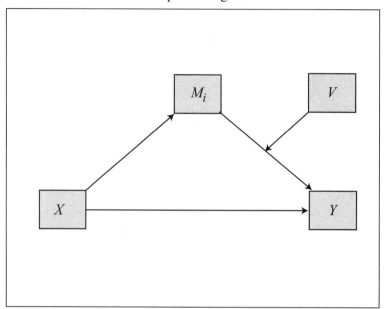

Statistical Diagram

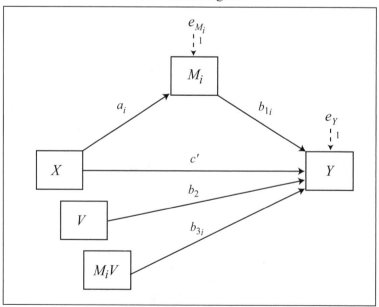

Conditional indirect effect of X on Y through $M_i = a_i (b_{1i} + b_{3i}V)$

Direct effect of X on $Y = c'$

Note: Model 14 allows up to 10 mediators operating in parallel.

Model 15

Conceptual Diagram

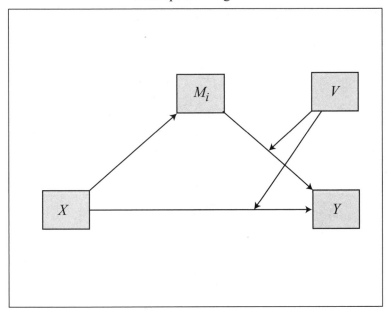

Statistical Diagram

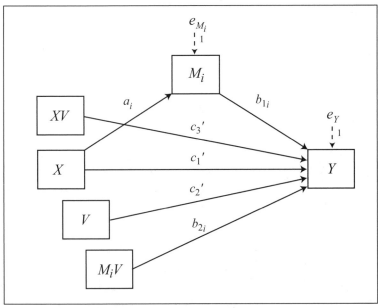

Conditional indirect effect of X on Y through $M_i = a_i(b_{1i} + b_{2i}V)$
Conditional direct effect of X on $Y = c_1' + c_3'V$

Note: Model 15 allows up to 10 mediators operating in parallel.

Model 21

Conceptual Diagram

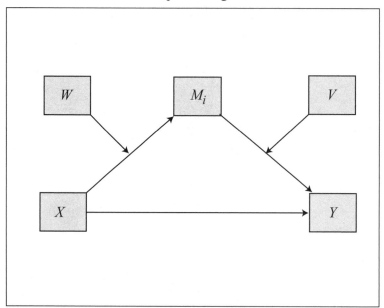

Statistical Diagram

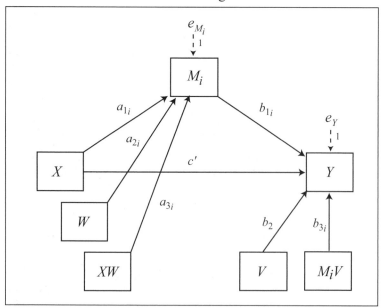

Conditional indirect effect of X on Y through $M_i = (a_{1i} + a_{3i}W)(b_{1i} + b_{3i}V)$

Direct effect of X on $Y = c'$

Note: Model 21 allows up to 10 mediators operating in parallel.

Model 22

Conceptual Diagram

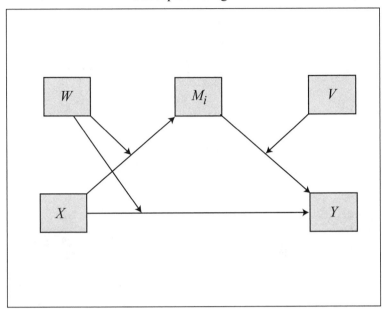

Statistical Diagram

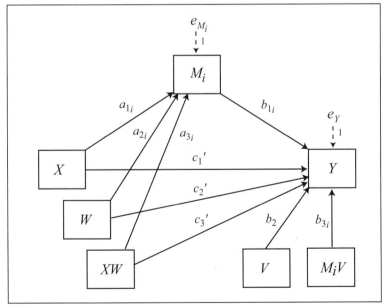

Conditional indirect effect of X on Y through $M_i = (a_{1i} + a_{3i}W)(b_{1i} + b_{3i}V)$

Conditional direct effect of X on $Y = c_1' + c_3'W$

Note: Model 22 allows up to 10 mediators operating in parallel.

Model 58

Conceptual Diagram

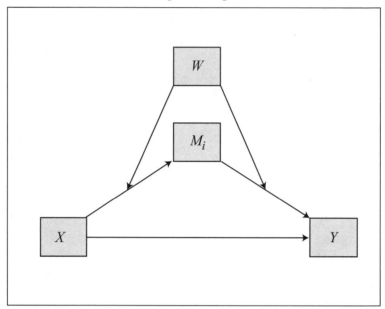

Statistical Diagram

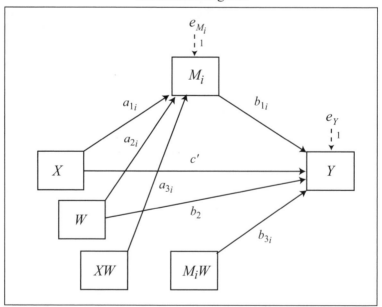

Conditional indirect effect of X on Y through $M_i = (a_{1i} + a_{3i}W)(b_{1i} + b_{3i}W)$
Direct effect of X on $Y = c'$

Note: Model 58 allows up to 10 mediators operating in parallel.

Model 59

Conceptual Diagram

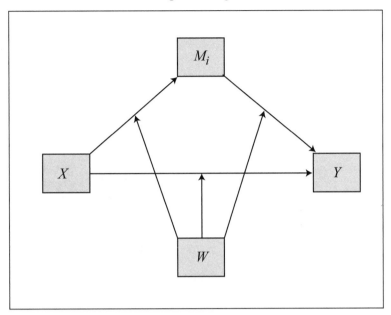

Statistical Diagram

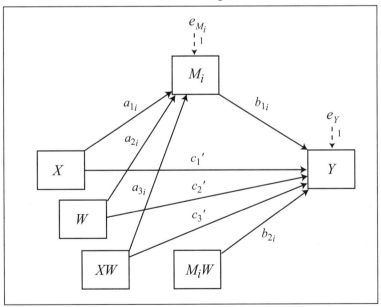

Conditional indirect effect of X on Y through $M_i = (a_{1i} + a_{3i}W)(b_{1i} + b_{2i}W)$

Conditional direct effect of X on $Y = c_1' + c_3'W$

Note: Model 59 allows up to 10 mediators operating in parallel.

Model 74

Conceptual Diagram

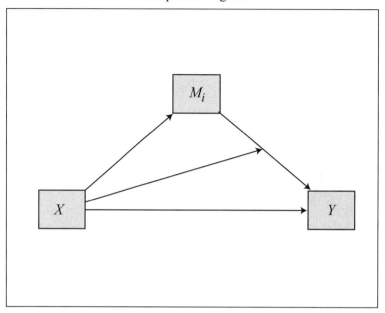

Statistical Diagram

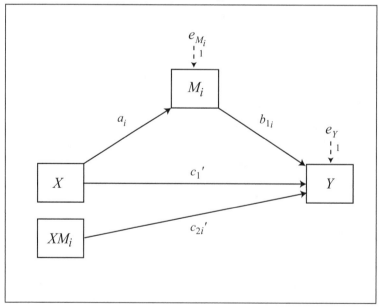

Conditional indirect effect of X on Y through $M_i = a_i(b_{1i} + c_{2i}'X)$
Conditional direct effect of $X = c_1' + c_{2i}'M$

Note: Model 74 allows up to 10 mediators operating in parallel. PROCESS does not produce a table of conditional direct effects for model 74. With only one mediator, use model 1 to generate the conditional direct effects, specifying M as *moderator*.

Appendix B
Monte Carlo Confidence Intervals in SPSS and SAS

The code in this Appendix defines a macro for the generation of a Monte Carlo confidence interval for the indirect effect of X on Y through M in a mediation analysis. The code can be typed into SPSS or SAS or downloaded from *www.afhayes.com*, saved for later use if desired, and then executed. Running this code defines a new command called MCMED. The main arguments for the macro are the a and b coefficients (**a=** and **b=**) corresponding to the $X \rightarrow M$ and $M \rightarrow Y$ paths, respectively, and their standard errors (**sea=** and **seb=**, both default to 1 if omitted). In addition, the number of Monte Carlo samples can be set (**samples=**, defaults to 10,000 if omitted), as can the covariance of a and b (**covab=**, defaults to zero if omitted) and the desired confidence (**conf=**, defaults to 95 if omitted).

The SPSS version of MCMED will construct a new data file containing the Monte Carlo samples of a, b, and ab. This file can be used to produce a visual representation of the sampling distribution of ab. The SAS version constructs a temporary work data file named MCVALS and automatically produces a histogram of the estimates of ab.

Lines in the code below with a "print" command must be entered as one continuous line. Do not break print commands up into multiple lines of code, as this will produce errors.

SPSS version:

```
define mcmed (a=!charend ('/') !default(0)/b=!charend ('/') !default(0)
   /sea=!charend('/') !default(1)/seb=!charend('/') !default(1)
   /samples=!charend ('/') !default(10000)/covab=!charend ('/')
   !default(0)/conf=!charend ('/') !default(95)).
preserve.
```

```
set printback=off.
matrix.
compute r={(!sea)*(!sea),!covab;!covab,(!seb)*(!seb)}.
compute errchk=0.
do if (det(r) <= 0).
compute errchk=2.
end if.
do if (!seb <= 0 or !sea <=0).
compute errchk=1.
end if.
compute cilow=((100-!conf)/200).
compute cihigh=1-cilow.
compute cilow=trunc(!samples*cilow).
compute cihigh=trunc((!samples*cihigh)+.999)+1.
do if (cilow < 1 or cihigh > !samples).
compute errchk=3.
end if.
compute pars={!a;!sea;!b;!seb;!covab;!samples;!conf}.
print pars/title="*** Input Data ***"/rlabels="a:", "SE(a):", "b:",
   "SE(b):", "COV(ab):", "Samples:", "Conf:"/format = F8.4.
do if (errchk=0).
compute mns=make(!samples,1,!a),make(!samples, 1, !b).
compute x1=sqrt(-2*ln(uniform(!samples,2)))&*cos((2*3.14159265358979)*
   uniform(!samples,2)).
compute x1=(x1*chol(r))+mns.
compute ab=x1(:,1)&*x1(:,2).
compute x1={x1,ab}.
compute abtmp=ab.
compute abtmp(GRADE(ab))=ab.
compute ab=abtmp.
save x1/outfile=*/variables=a b ab.
compute mc={(!a*!b), ab(cilow,1), ab(cihigh,1)}.
print mc/title="**** Monte Carlo Confidence Interval ****"/clabels=
   "ab", "LLCI", "ULCI"/format = F8.4.
end if.
do if (errchk=1).
print/title="ERROR: Standard errors must be positive".
else if (errchk=2).
print/title="ERROR: Entered covariance is not compatible with the
   standard errors of a and b".
```

```
else if (errchk=3).
print/title="ERROR: Number of samples is too small for this level of
    confidence".
end if.
end matrix.
restore.
!enddefine.
```

SAS version:

```
%macro mcmed (a=0,sea=1,b=0,seb=1,samples=10000,conf=95,covab=0);
proc iml;
r=((&sea*&sea)||(&covab))//((&covab)||(&seb*&seb));
errchk=0;
if (det(r)<=0) then;do;errchk=2;end;
tmp=det(r);
if ((&sea<=0) | (&seb<=0)) then;do;errchk=1;end;
cilow=((100-&conf)/200);cihigh=1-cilow;
cilow=floor(&samples*cilow);cihigh=floor((&samples*cihigh)+0.999)+1;
if ((cilow < 1) | (cihigh > &samples)) then;do;errchk=3;end;
pars=&a//&sea//&b//&seb//&covab//&samples//&conf;
rwnm="a:"//"SE(a):"//"b:"//"SE(b):"//"COV(ab):"//"Samples:"//"Conf:";
print pars [label="*** Input Data ***" rowname=rwnm];
create mcvals from pars;append from pars;close mcvals;
if (errchk=0) then;do;
mns=j(&samples,1,&a)||j(&samples,1,&b);
x1=rannor(j(&samples,2,0));x1=(x1*root(r))+mns;
ab=x1[,1]#x1[,2];x1=x1||ab;
create mcvals from x1[colname='a' 'b' 'ab'];append from x1;
abtmp=ab;abtmp[rank(abtmp)]=ab;ab=abtmp;
mc=(&a*&b)||ab[cilow,1]||ab[cihigh,1];
clnm="ab"||"LLCI"||"ULCI";
print mc [label="*** Monte Carlo Confidence Interval ***" colname=clnm
    format=12.4];
end;
if (errchk=1) then;do;print "ERROR: Standard errors must be positive";end;
if (errchk=2) then;do;print "ERROR: Entered covariance is not compatible
    with the standard errors of a and b";end;
if (errchk=3) then;do;print "ERROR: Number of samples is too small for this
```

```
    level of confidence";end;
quit;
proc univariate data=mcvals noprint;var ab;histogram;run;
%mend;
```

Once the macro is defined by running the code, a properly formatted MCMED command can be executed. For example, the SPSS code below produces a 95% Monte Carlo confidence interval for the indirect effect in the analysis reported in section 4.5, based on 10,000 Monte Carlo samples:

```
mcmed a=0.173/b=0.769/sea=0.030/seb=0.103.
```

In SAS, the corresponding command is

```
%mcmed (a=0.173,b=0.769,sea=0.030,seb=0.103);
```

In some applications of mediation analysis, the covariance between a and b is not zero. When an estimate of this covariance is available, it can be included in the MCMED command. The confidence width can also be modified, or the number of Monte Carlo samples set at some value larger than 10,000. For example, the SPSS code below generates a 99% Monte Carlo confidence interval for the indirect effect based on 100,000 samples, given estimates of a, b, their covariance, and their standard errors:

```
mcmed a=0.5/b=1.2/sea=0.35/seb=0.65/covab=0.08/samples=100000/conf=99.
```

In SAS, the corresponding command is

```
%mcmed (a=0.5,b=1.2,sea=0.35,seb=0.65,covab=0.08,samples=100000,conf=99);
```

References

Aiken, L. S., & West, S. G. (1991). *Multiple regression: Testing and interpreting interactions*. Thousand Oaks, CA: Sage Publications.

Alter, A. L., & Balcetis, E. (2011). Fondness makes the distance grow shorter: Desired locations seem closer because they seem more vivid. *Journal of Experimental Social Psychology, 47*, 16–21.

Alvarez, A. N., & Juang, J. P. (2010). Filipino-Americans and racism: A multiple mediation model of coping. *Journal of Counseling Psychology, 38*, 545–556.

Alwin, D. F., & Hauser, R. M. (1975). The decomposition of effects in path analysis. *American Sociological Review, 40*, 33–47.

Amato, P. R. (2001). Children of divorce in the 1990s: An update of the Amato and Keith (1991) meta-analysis. *Journal of Family Psychology, 15*, 355–370.

Amato, P. R., & Keith, B. (1991). Parental divorce and the well-being of children: A meta-analysis. *Psychological Bulletin, 110*, 26–46.

Anagnostopoulos, F., Slater, J., & Fitzsimmons, D. (2010). Intrusive thoughts and psychological adjustment to breast cancer: Exploring the moderating and mediating role of global meaning and emotional expressivity. *Journal of Clinical Psychology in Medical Settings, 17*, 137–149.

Anderson, C. A., & Bushman, B. J. (2001). Effects of violent video games on aggressive behavior, aggressive cognition, aggressive affect, physiological arousal, and prosocial behavior: A review of the scientific literature. *Psychological Science, 12*, 353–359.

Anderson, C. A., Shibuya, A., Ibori, N., Swing, E. L., Bushman, B. J., Sakamoto, A., et al. (2010). Violent video game effects on aggression, empathy, and prosocial behavior in Eastern and Western countries: A meta-analytic review. *Psychological Bulletin, 136*, 151–173.

Andreeva, V. A., Yaroch, A. L., Unger, J. B., Cockburn, M. G., Rueda, R., & Reynolds, K. D. (2010). Moderated mediation regarding the sun-safe behavior of U.S. Latinos: Advancing the theory and evidence for acculturation-focused research and interventions. *Journal of Immigrant Minority Health, 12*, 691–698.

Antheunis, M. L., Valkenburg, P. M., & Peter, J. (2010). Getting acquainted through social network sites: Testing a model of online uncertainty reduction and social attraction. *Computers in Human Behavior, 26*, 100–109.

Aroian, L. A. (1947). The probability function of the product of two normally distributed variables. *Annals of Mathematical Statistics, 18*, 265–271.

Ashton-James, C. E., & Tracy, J. L. (2012). Pride and prejudice: How feelings about the self influence judgments of others. *Personality and Social Psychology Bulletin, 38,* 466–476.

Bamberger, P., & Belogolovsky, E. (2011). The impact of pay secrecy on individual task performance. *Personnel Psychology, 79,* 965–996.

Barnhofer, T., & Chittka, T. (2010). Cognitive reactivity mediates the relationship between neuroticism and depression. *Behaviour Research and Therapy, 48,* 275–281.

Barnhofer, T., Duggan, D. S., & Griffith, J. W. (2011). Dispositional mindfulness moderates the relation between neuroticism and depressive symptoms. *Personality and Individual Differences, 51,* 958–962.

Baron, R. M., & Kenny, D. A. (1986). The moderator–mediator variable distinction in social psychological research: Conceptual, strategic, and statistical considerations. *Journal of Personality and Social Psychology, 51,* 1173–1182.

Bauer, D. J., & Curran, P. J. (2005). Probing interactions in fixed and multilevel regression: Inferential and graphical techniques. *Multivariate Behavioral Research, 40,* 373–400.

Bauer, D. J., Preacher, K. J., & Gil, K. M. (2006). Conceptualizing and testing random indirect effects in moderated mediation in multilevel models: New procedures and recommendations. *Psychological Methods, 29,* 142–163.

Baumgartner, J., & Morris, J. S. (2006). *The Daily Show* effect: Candidate evaluations, efficacy, and American youth. *American Politics Research, 34,* 341–367.

Beach, S. R. H., Lei, M. K., Brody, G. H., Simons, R. L., Cutrona, C., & Philibert, R. A. (2012). Genetic moderation of contextual effects on negative arousal and parenting in African-American parents. *Journal of Family Psychology, 26,* 46–55.

Bear, G. (1995). Computationally intensive methods warrant reconsideration of pedagogy in statistics. *Behavior Research Methods, Instruments, and Computers, 27,* 144–147.

Belogolovsky, E., Bamberger, P. A., & Bacharach, S. B. (2012). Workforce disengagement stressors and retiree alcohol misuse: The mediating effects of sleep problems and the moderating effects of gender. *Human Relations, 65,* 705–728.

Bem, D. (1987). Writing the empirical journal article. In M. P. Zanna & J. M. Darley (Eds.), *The complete academic: A practical guide for the beginning social scientist* (pp. 171–201). Mahwah, NJ: Lawrence Erlbaum Associates.

Berger, V. W. (2000). Pros and cons of permutation tests in clinical trials. *Statistics in Medcine, 19,* 1319–1328.

Berndt, N. C., Hayes, A. F., Verboon, P., Lechner, L., Bolman, C., & De Vries, H. (in press). Self-efficacy mediates the impact of craving on smoking abstinence in low to moderately anxious patients: Results of a moderated mediation approach. *Psychology of Addictive Behaviors.*

Berry, W. D. (1993). *Understanding regression assumptions.* Thousand Oaks, CA: Sage Publications.

Biesanz, J. C., Falk, C. F., & Savalei, V. (2010). Assessing mediational models: Testing and interval estimation for indirect effects. *Multivariate Behavioral Research, 45,* 661–701.

Bissonnette, V., Ickes, W., Bernstein, I., & Knowles, E. (1990). Personality moderating variables: A warning about statistical artifact and a comparison of analytic techniques. *Journal of Personality, 58,* 567–587.

Bizer, G. Y., Hart, J., & Jekogian, A. M. (2012). Belief in a just world and social dominance orientation: Evidence for a mediational pathway predicting negative attitudes and discrimination against individuals with mental illness. *Peronality and Individual Differences, 52,* 661–701.

Blashill, A. J., & Wal, J. S. V. (2010). The role of body image dissatisfaction and depression on HAART adherence in HIV positive men: Tests of mediation models. *AIDS and Behavior, 14,* 280–288.

Bollen, K. A. (1989). *Structural equations with latent variables.* New York, NY: John Wiley and Sons.

Bollen, K. A., & Stine, R. (1990). Direct and indirect effects: Classical and bootstrap estimates of variability. *Sociological Methodology, 20,* 115–140.

Bolton, L. R., Harvey, R. D., Grawitch, M. J., & Barber, L. K. (2012). Counterproductive work behaviours in response to emotional exhaustion: A moderated mediational approach. *Stress and Health, 28,* 222–233.

Brandt, M. J., & Reyna, C. (2010). The role of prejudice and the need for closure in religious fundamentalism. *Personality and Social Psychology Bulletin, 36,* 715–725.

Breitborde, N. J. K., Srihari, V. H., Pollard, J. M., Addington, D. N., & Woods, S. W. (2010). Mediators and moderators in early intervention research. *Early Intervention in Psychiatry, 4,* 143–152.

Breusch, T. S., & Pagan, A. R. (1979). A simple test for heteroscedasticity and random coefficient variation. *Econometrica, 47,* 1287–1294.

Broeren, S., Muris, P., Bouwmeester, S., van der Heijden, K. B., & Abee, A. (2011). The role of repetitive negative thoughts in the vulnerability for emotional problems in non-clinical children. *Journal of Child and Family Studies, 20,* 135–148.

Brown, G., & Baer, M. (2011). Location in negotiation: Is there a home field advantage? *Organizational Behavior and Human Decision Processes, 114,* 190–200.

Brown, J. E., Nicholson, J. M., Broom, D. H., & Bittman, M. (2011). Television viewing by school-age children; associations with physical activity, snack food consumption, and unhealthy weight. *Social Indicators Research, 101,* 221–225.

Bryan, A., Schmiege, S. J., & Broaddus, M. R. (2007). Mediational analysis in HIV/AIDS research: Estimating multivariate path analytic models in a structural equation modeling framework. *AIDS and Behavior, 11,* 365–383.

Buckland, S. T. (1984). Monte Carlo confidence intervals. *Biometrics, 40,* 811–817.

Bugental, D. B., Beaulieu, D. A., & Silbert-Geiger, A. (2010). Increases in parental investment and child health as a result of early intervention. *Journal of Experimental Child Psychology, 106,* 30–40.

Bushman, B. J., Giancolo, P. R., Parrott, D. J., & Roth, R. M. (2012). Failure to consider future consequences increases the effects of alcohol on aggression. *Journal of Experimental Social Psychology, 48,* 591–595.

Cafri, G., Yamamiya, Y., Brannick, M., & Thompson, J. K. (2005). The influence of sociocultural factors on body image: A meta-analysis. *Clinical Psychology:*

Science and Practice, 12, 421–433.

Calogero, R. M., & Jot, J. T. (2011). Self-subjugation among women: Exposure to sexist ideology, self objectification, and the protective function of the need to avoid closure. *Journal of Personality and Social Psychology, 110,* 211–228.

Carvalho, J. P., & Hopko, D. R. (2011). Behavioral theory of depression: Reinforcement as a mediating variable between avoidance and depression. *Journal of Behavior Therapy and Experimental Psychiatry, 42,* 154–162.

Casciano, R., & Massey, D. S. (2012). Neighborhood disorder and anxiety symptoms: New evidence from a quasi-experimental study. *Health and Place, 18,* 180–190.

Cerin, E., & MacKinnon, D. P. (2009). A commentary on current practice in mediating variable analyses in behavioural nutrition and physical activity. *Public Health Nutrition, 12,* 1182–1188.

Chang, C. (2008). Chronological age versus cognitive age for younger consumers: Implications for advertising persuasion. *Journal of Advertising, 37,* 19–32.

Chang, C. (2010). Message framing and interpersonal orientation at cultural and individual levels: Involvement as a moderator. *International Journal of Advertising, 29,* 765–794.

Chen, C., Green, P. G., & Crick, A. (1998). Does entrepreneurial self-efficacy distinguish entrepreneurs from managers? *Journal of Business Venturing, 13,* 295–316.

Cheong, J., MacKinnon, D. P., & Khoo, S. T. (2003). Investigation of mediational processes using parallel process latent growth curve modeling. *Structural Equation Modeling, 10,* 238–262.

Cheung, G. W., & Lau, R. S. (2008). Testing mediation and suppression effects of latent variables. *Organizational Research Methods, 11,* 296–325.

Cheung, M. W. (2009). Comparison of methods for constructing confidence intervals for standardized indirect effects. *Behavior Research Methods, 41,* 425–438.

Clark, J. K., Wegener, D. T., Briñol, P., & Petty, R. E. (2011). Discovering the shoe that fits: The self-validating role of stereotypes. *Psychological Science, 20,* 846–852.

Cohen, F., Sullivan, D., Solomon, S., Greenberg, J., & Ogilvie, D. M. (2011). Finding everland: Flight fantasies and the desire to transcend mortality. *Journal of Experimental Social Psychology, 47,* 88–102.

Cohen, J., Cohen, P., West, S. G., & Aiken, L. S. (2003). *Applied multiple regression and correlation for the behavioral sciences* (3rd ed.). Mahwah, NJ: Lawrence Erlbaum Associates.

Cohen, J. B. (1968). Multiple regression as a general data analytic system. *Psychological Bulletin, 70,* 426–443.

Cohen, J. B. (1983). The cost of dichotomization. *Applied Psychological Measurement, 7,* 240–253.

Cole, D. A., & Maxwell, S. E. (2003). Testing mediational models with longitudinal data: Questions and tips in the use of structural equation modeling. *Journal of Abnormal Psychology, 112,* 558–577.

Cole, M. S., Bedeian, A. G., & Bruch, H. (2011). Linking leader behavior and leadership consensus to team performance: Integrating direct consensus and dispersion models of group composition. *Leadership Quarterly, 22,* 383–398.

Cole, M. S., Walter, F., & Bruch, H. (2008). Affective mechanisms linking dysfunctional behavior to performance in work teams: A moderated mediation study. *Journal of Applied Psychology, 93,* 945–958.

Cook, R. D., & Weisberg, S. (1983). Diagnostics for heteroscedasticity in regression. *Biometrika, 70,* 1–10.

Cortina, J. M., & Dunlap, W. P. (1997). On the logic and purpose of significance testing. *Psychological Methods, 2,* 161–172.

Costa, J., & Pinto-Gouveia, J. (2011). The mediation effect of experiential avoidance between coping and psychopathology in chronic pain. *Clinical Psychology and Psychotherapy, 18,* 34–37.

Coyle, T. R., Pillow, D. R., Snyder, A. C., & Kochunov, P. (2011). Processing speed mediates the development of general intelligence (g) in adolescence. *Psychological Science, 22,* 1265–1269.

Craig, C. C. (1936). On the frequency function of xy. *The Annals of Mathematical Statistics, 7,* 1–15.

Cronbach, L. J. (1987). Statistical tests for moderator variables: Flaws in analyses recently proposed. *Psychological Bulletin, 102,* 414–417.

Cuijpers, P., van Straten, A., Warmeredam, L., & Andersson, G. (2009). Psychotherapy versus the combination of psychotherapy and pharmcotherapy in the treatment of depression: A meta-analysis. *Depression and Anxiety, 26,* 279–288.

Cukor, J., Wyka, K., Jayasinghe, N., Weathers, F., Giosan, C., Leck, P., et al. (2011). Prevalence and predictors of posttraumatic stress symptoms in utility workers deployed to the World Trade Center following the attacks of September 11, 2001. *Depression and Anxiety, 28,* 210–217.

Darlington, R. B. (1990). *Regression and linear models.* New York, NY: McGraw-Hill.

Davis, J. A. (1985). *The logic of causal order.* Newbury Park, CA: Sage Publications.

Davydov, D. M., Shapiro, D., & Goldstein, I. B. (2010). Relationship of resting baroflex activity to 24-hour blood pressure and mood in healthy people. *Journal of Psychophysiology, 24,* 149–160.

de Zavala, A. G., & Cichocka, A. (2011). Collective narcissism and anti-Semitism in Poland. *Group Processes and Intergroup Relations, 15,* 213–229.

Dearing, E., & Hamilton, L. C. (2006). Contemporary advances and classic advice for analyzing mediating and moderating variables. In K. McCartney, M. R. Burchinal, & K. L. Bub (Eds.), *Best practices in quantitative methods for developmentalists* (pp. 88–104). Boston, MA: Blackwell.

Debeer, E., Hermans, D., & Raes, F. (2009). Associations between components of rumination and autobiographical memory specificity as measured by a minimal instructions autobiographical memory test. *Memory, 17,* 892–903.

Deng, X., & Kahn, B. E. (2009). Is your product on the right side?: The location effect on perceived product heaviness and package evaluation. *Journal of Marketing Research, 46,* 724–738.

DiGrande, L., Perrin, M. A., Thorpe, L. E., Thalji, L., Murphy, J., Wu, D., et al. (2008). Posttraumatic stress symptoms, PTSD, and risk factors among lower

Manhattan residents 2–3 years after the September 11, 2001 terrorist attacks. *Journal of Traumatic Stress, 21,* 264–273.

Dittmar, H., Halliwell, E., & Stirling, E. (2009). Understanding the impact of thin media models on women's body-focused affect: The roles of thin-ideal internalization and weight-related self-discrepancy activation in experimental exposure effects. *Journal of Social and Clinical Psychology, 28,* 43–72.

D'Lima, G. M., Pearson, M. R., & Kelley, M. L. (2012). Protective behavioral strategies as a mediator and moderator of the relationship between self-regulation and alcohol-related consequences in first-year college students. *Psychology of Addictive Behaviors, 26,* 330–337.

Dockray, S., Susman, E., & Dorn, L. D. (2009). Depression, cortisol reactivity, and obesity in childhood and adolescence. *Journal of Adolescent Health, 45,* 344–350.

Downs, G. W., & Rocke, D. M. (1979). Interpreting heteroscedasticity. *American Journal of Political Science, 23,* 816–828.

Druckman, D., & Albin, C. (2011). Distributive justice and the durability of peace agreements. *Review of International Studies, 37,* 1137–1168.

Duffy, R. D., Allen, B. A., & Dik, B. J. (2011). The presence of a calling and academic satisfaction: Examining potential mediators. *Journal of Vocational Behavior, 79,* 74–80.

Duncan, G. T., & Layard, M. W. (1973). A Monte-Carlo study of asymptotically robust tests for correlation coefficients. *Biometrika, 60,* 551–558.

Duncan, L. E., & Stewart, A. J. (2007). Personal political salience: The role of personality in collective identity and action. *Political Psychology, 28,* 143–164.

Echambadi, R., & Hess, J. D. (2007). Mean-centering does not alleviate collinearity problems in moderated regression models. *Marketing Science, 26,* 438–445.

Edgell, S. E., & Noon, S. M. (1984). Effect of violation of normality on the *t* test of the correlation coefficient. *Psychological Bulletin, 95,* 576–583.

Edgington, E. S. (1964). Randomization tests. *Journal of Psychology, 57,* 445–449.

Edgington, E. S. (1978). Firmly rooted in tradition. *Contemporary Psychology, 23,* 20–22.

Edgington, E. S. (1995). *Randomization tests.* New York, NY: Dekker.

Edwards, J. R. (2009). Seven deadly myths of testing moderation in organizational research. In C. E. Lance & R. J. Vanderberg (Eds.), *Statistical and methodological myths and urban legends* (pp. 143–164). New York, NY: Routledge.

Edwards, J. R., & Lambert, L. S. (2007). Methods for integrating moderation and mediation: A general analytical framework using moderated path analysis. *Psychological Methods, 12,* 1–22.

Efron, B. (1987). Better bootstrap confidence intervals. *Journal of the American Statistical Association, 82,* 171–185.

Efron, B., & Tibshirani, R. J. (1993). *An introduction to the bootstrap.* Boca Raton, FL: Chapman & Hall.

Ein-Gar, D., Shiv, B., & Tormala, Z. L. (2012). When blemishing leads to blossoming: The positive effect of negative information. *Journal of Consumer Research, 38,* 846–859.

Eveland, W. P. (1997). Interactions and nonlinearity in mass communication: Connecting theory and methodology. *Journalism and Mass Communication Quarterly, 74*, 400–416.

Fairchild, A. J., & MacKinnon, D. P. (2009). A general model for testing mediation and moderation effects. *Prevention Science, 10*, 87–99.

Fairchild, A. J., MacKinnon, D. P., Toborga, M. P., & Taylor, A. B. (2009). *R*-squared effect-size measures for mediation analysis. *Behavior Research Methods, 41*, 486–498.

Fairchild, A. J., & McQuillin, S. D. (2010). Evaluating mediation and moderation effects in school psychology: A presentation of methods and review of current practice. *Journal of School Psychology, 48*, 53–84.

Feldman, L. (2011). The effects of journalist opinionation on learning from the news. *Journal of Communication, 61*, 1183–1201.

Finkel, S. E. (1995). *Causal analysis with panel data.* Thousand Oaks, CA: Sage Publications.

Fonner, K. L., & Roloff, M. E. (2010). Why teleworkers are more satisfied with their jobs than are office-based workers: When less contact is beneficial. *Journal of Applied Communication Research, 38*, 336–361.

Fox, J. (1991). *Regression diagnostics.* Thousand Oaks, CA: Sage Publications.

Frazier, P. A., Tix, A. P., & Barron, K. E. (2004). Testing moderator and mediator effects in counseling psychology research. *Journal of Counseling Psychology, 51*, 115–134.

Frick, R. W. (1998). Interpreting statistical testing: Process and propensity, not population and random sampling. *Behavior Research Methods, Instruments, and Computers, 30*, 527–535.

Friedrich, R. J. (1982). In defense of multiplicative terms in multiple regression equations. *American Journal of Political Science, 26*, 797–833.

Fritz, M. S., & MacKinnon, D. P. (2007). Required sample size to detect the mediated effect. *Psychological Science, 18*, 233–239.

Fritz, M. S., Taylor, A. B., & MacKinnon, D. P. (2012). Explanation of two anomolous results in statistical mediation analysis. *Multivariate Behavioral Research, 47*, 61–87.

Garcia, D. M., Schmitt, M. T., Branscombe, N. R., & Ellemers, N. (2010). Women's reactions to ingroup members who protest discriminatory treatment: The importance of beliefs about inequality and response appropriateness. *European Journal of Social Psychology, 40*, 733–745.

Gaudiano, B. A., Herbert, J. D., & Hayes, S. C. (2010). Is it the symptom or the relation to it?: Investigating potential mediators of change in acceptance and commitment therapy for psychosis. *Behavior Therapy, 41*, 543–554.

Gaziano, C. (1983). The knowledge gap: An analytical review of media effects. *Communication Research, 19*, 447–486.

Gelman, A., & Stern, H. (2006). The difference between "significant" and "not significant" is not itself statistically significant. *The American Statistician, 60*, 328–331.

Gibbs, J. L., Ellison, N. B., & Lai, C. H. (2011). First comes love, then comes Google: An investigation of uncertainty reduction strategies and self-disclosure in online dating. *Communication Research, 38*, 70–100.

Gilbert, D. T., & Krull, D. S. (1988). Seeing less and knowing more: The benefits of perceptual ignorance. *Journal of Personality and Social Psychology, 54*, 193–202.

Gilbert, D. T., & Malone, P. S. (1995). The correspondence bias. *Psychological Bulletin, 117*, 21–38.

Gilbert, D. T., & Osborne, R. E. (1989). Thinking backward: Some curable and incurable consequences of cognitive business. *Journal of Personality and Social Psychology, 57*, 940–949.

Giner-Sorolla, R., & Espinosa, P. (2011). Social cuing of guilt by anger and of shame by disgust. *Psychological Science, 22*, 49–53.

Godin, G., Belanger-Gravel, A., & Nolin, B. (2008). Mechanism by which BMI influences leisure-time physical activity behavior. *Obesity, 16*, 1314–1317.

Gogineni, A., Alsup, R., & Gillespie, D. F. (1995). Mediation and moderation in social work research. *Social Work Research, 19*, 57–63.

Goldfeld, S. M., & Quandt, R. E. (1965). Some tests for homoscedasticity. *Journal of the American Statistical Association, 60*, 539–547.

Goldstein, A., Flett, G. I., & Wekerle, C. (2010). Child maltreatment, alcohol use, and drinking consequences among male and female college students: An examination of drinking motives as mediators. *Addictive Behaviors, 35*, 636–639.

Gong, T. Y., Shenkar, O., Luo, Y., & Nyaw, M.-K. (2007). Do multiple partners help or hinder international joint venture performance?: The mediating roles of contract completeness and partner cooperation. *Strategic Management Journal, 28*, 1021–1034.

Gonzales, V. M., Reynolds, B., & Skewes, M. C. (2011). Role of impulsivity in the relationship between depression and alcohol problems among emerging college drinkers. *Experimental and Clinical Psychopharmacology, 19*, 303–313.

Good, P. I. (2001). *Resampling methods: A practical guide to data analysis* (2nd ed.). Boston, MA: Birkhauser.

Goodall, C. E., & Slater, M. D. (2010). Automatically activated attitudes as mechanisms for message effects: The case of alcohol advertisements. *Communication Research, 37*, 620–643.

Goodin, B. R., McGuire, L., Allshouse, M., Stapleton, L., Haythornewaite, J. A., Burns, N., et al. (2009). Associations between catastrophizing and endogeneous pain-inhibitory processes: Sex differences. *Journal of Pain, 10*, 180–190.

Goodin, B. R., McGuire, L. M., Stapleton, L. M., Quinn, N. B., Fabian, L. A., Haythornthwaite, J. A., et al. (2009). Pain catastrophizing mediates the relationship between self-reported strenuous exercise involvement and pain ratings: Moderating role of anxiety sensitivity. *Psychosomatic Medicine, 71*, 1018–1025.

Goodman, L. A. (1960). On the exact variance of products. *Journal of the American Statistical Association, 55*, 708–713.

Grabe, S., Ward, L. M., & Hyde, J. S. (2008). The role of the media in body image concerns among women: A meta-analysis of experimental and correlational studies. *Psychological Bulletin, 134*, 460–476.

Grant, A. M., Gino, F., & Hofmann, D. A. (2011). Reversing the extraverted leadership advantage: The role of employee proactivity. *Academy of Management Journal, 54*, 528–550.

Grawitch, M. J., & Munz, D. C. (2004). Are your data nonindependent?: A practical guide to evaluating nonindependence and within-group agreement. *Understanding Statistics, 3*, 231–257.

Greenwald, A. G. (2012). There is nothing so theoretical as a good method. *Psychological Science, 7*, 99–108.

Greitemeyer, T., & McLatchie, N. (2011). Denying humanness to others: A newly discovered mechanism by which violent video games increase aggressive behavior. *Psychological Science, 22*, 659–665.

Griffin, D., & Gonzales, R. (1995). Correlational analysis of dyad-level data in the exchangeable case. *Psychological Bulletin, 118*, 430–439.

Groetz, L. M., Levine, M. P., & Murnen, S. K. (2002). The effect of experimental presentation of thin media images on body satisfaction: A meta-analytic review. *International Journal of Eating Disorders, 31*, 1–16.

Grøntved, A., Steene-Johannessen, J., Kynde, I., Franks, P. W., Helge, J. W., Froberg, K., et al. (2011). Association between plasma leptin and blood pressure in two population-based samples of children and adolescents. *Journal of Hypertension, 29*, 1093–1100.

Guendelman, M. D., Cheryan, S., & Monin, B. (2011). Fitting in but getting fat: Identity threat and dietary choices among U.S. immigrant groups. *Psychological Science, 22*, 959–967.

Hart, P. S. (2011). One or many?: The influence of episodic and thematic climate change frames on policy preferences and individual change behavior. *Science Communication, 33*, 28–51.

Hasan, Y., Begue, L., & Bushman, B. J. (2012). Viewing the world through blood-red tinted glasses: The hostile expectation bias mediates the link between violent video game exposure and aggression. *Journal of Experimental Social Psychology, 48*, 953–956.

Havlicek, L. L., & Peterson, N. L. (1977). Effect of violation of assumptions upon significance levels of the Pearson *r*. *Psychological Bulletin, 84*, 373–377.

Hayes, A. F. (1996). The permutation test is not distribution-free: Testing $H_0 : \rho = 0$. *Psychological Methods, 1*, 184–198.

Hayes, A. F. (2005). *Statistical methods for communication science*. New York: Routledge.

Hayes, A. F. (2009). Beyond Baron and Kenny: Statistical mediation analysis in the new millennium. *Communication Monographs, 76*, 408–420.

Hayes, A. F., & Cai, L. (2007). Using heteroscedasticity-consistent standard error estimators in OLS regression: An introduction and software implementation. *Behavior Research Methods, 39*, 709–722.

Hayes, A. F., Glynn, C. J., & Huge, M. E. (2012). Cautions regarding the interpretation of regression coefficients and hypothesis tests in linear models with interactions. *Communication Methods and Measures, 6*, 1–11.

Hayes, A. F., & Matthes, J. (2009). Computational procedures for probing interactions in OLS and logistic regression: SPSS and SAS implementations. *Behavior Research Methods, 41*, 924–936.

Hayes, A. F., & Myers, T. A. (2009). Testing the proximate casualties hypothesis: Local troop loss, attention to war news, and support for military intervention. *Mass Communication and Society, 12*, 379–402.

Hayes, A. F., & Preacher, K. J. (2013). Conditional process modeling: Using structural equation modeling to examine contingent causal processes. In G. R. Hancock & R. O. Mueller (Eds.), *A second course in structural equation modeling* (2nd ed., pp. 219–266). Greenwich, CT: Information Age Publishing.

Hayes, A. F., Preacher, K. J., & Myers, T. A. (2011). Mediation and the estimation of indirect effects in political communication research. In E. Bucy & R. L. Holbert (Eds.), *Sourcebook for political communication research: Methods, measures, and analytical techniques* (pp. 434–465). New York: Routledge.

Hayes, A. F., & Reineke, J. (2007). The effects of government censorship of war-related news coverage on interest in the censored coverage. *Mass Communication and Society, 10,* 423–438.

Hayes, A. F., & Scharkow, M. (2013). The relative trustworthiness of inferential tests of the indirect effect in statistical mediation analysis: Does method really matter? *Psychological Science.*

Hofmann, S. G., & Smits, J. A. J. (2008). Cognitive-behavioral therapy for adult anxiety disorders: A meta-analysis of randomized placebo-controlled trials. *Journal of Clinical Psychiatry, 69,* 621–632.

Holbert, R. L., & Stephenson, M. T. (2003). The importance of indirect effects in media effects research: Testing for mediation in structural equation modeling. *Journal of Broadcasting and Electronic Media, 47,* 556–572.

Holland, P. W. (1986). Statistics and causal inference. *Journal of the American Statistical Association, 81,* 945–960.

Hsu, L., Woody, S. R., Lee, H. J., Peng, Y., Zhou, X., & Ryder, A. G. (2012). Social anxiety among East Asians in North America: East Asian socialization or the challenge of acculturation? *Cultural Diversity and Ethnic Minority Psychology, 18,* 181–191.

Huang, J. Y., Sedlovskaya, A., Ackerman, J. M., & Bargh, J. A. (2011). Immunizing against prejudice: Effects of disease protection on attitudes toward outgroups. *Psychological Science, 22,* 1550–1556.

Huang, S., Zhang, Y., & Broniarczyk, S. M. (2012). So near and yet so far: The mental presentation of goal progress. *Journal of Personality and Social Psychology, 103,* 225–241.

Huang-Pollock, C. L., Mikami, A. Y., Pfiffner, L., & McBurnette, K. (2009). Can executive functions explain the relationship between attention deficit hyperactivity disorder and social adjustment? *Journal of Abnormal Child Psychology, 37,* 679–691.

Hughes, K., & Coplan, R. J. (2010). Exploring processes linking shyness and academic achievement in childhood. *School Psychology Quarterly, 25,* 213–222.

Humphreys, L. G., & Fleishman, A. (1974). Pseudo-orthogonal and other analysis of variance designs involving individual-differences variables. *Journal of Educational Psychology, 66,* 464–472.

Hunter, J. E., & Schmidt, F. L. (1990). Dichotomization of continuous variables: The implications for meta-analysis. *Journal of Applied Psychology, 75,* 334–349.

Hutchinson, P. T. (2003). Dichotomization and manipulation of numbers. *Canadian Journal of Psychiatry, 48,* 429–430.

Hwang, Y., & Jeong, S.-H. (2009). Revising the knowledge gap hypothesis: A meta-analysis of thirty five years of research. *Journalism and Mass Communication Quarterly*, *86*, 513–532.

Iacobucci, D., Saldanha, N., & Deng, X. (2007). A mediation on mediation: Evidence that structural equations models perform better than regressions. *Journal of Consumer Psychology*, *17*, 140–154.

Irwin, J. R., & McClelland, G. H. (2001). Misleading heuristics and moderated multiple regression models. *Journal of Marketing Research*, *38*, 100–109.

Irwin, J. R., & McClelland, G. H. (2002). Negative consequences of dichotomizing continuous predictor variables. *Journal of Marketing Research*, *40*, 366–371.

Jaccard, J., & Turrisi, R. (2003). *Interaction effects in multiple regression* (2nd ed.). Thousand Oaks, CA: Sage Publications.

Jackson, J. (2011). Intragroup cooperation as a functon of group performance and group identity. *Group dynamics: Theory, Research, and Practice*, *15*, 343–356.

James, L. R., & Brett, J. M. (1984). Mediators, moderators, and tests for mediation. *Journal of Applied Psychology*, *69*, 307–321.

Jensen, J. D. (2008). Scientific uncertainty in news coverage of cancer research: Effects of hedging on scientists' and journalists' credibility. *Human Communication Research*, *34*, 347–369.

Jensen, J. D. (2011). Knowledge acquisition following exposure to cancer news articles: A test of the cognitive mediation model. *Journal of Communication*, *61*, 514–534.

Jensen, J. D., King, A. J., & Guntzviller, L. M. (2010). Utilization of internet technology by low-income adults: The role of health literacy, health numeracy, and computer assistance. *Journal of Aging and Health*, *22*, 804–826.

Jiang, L. C., Bazarova, N. N., & Hancock, J. T. (2011). The disclosure–intimacy link in computer-mediated communication: An attributional extension of the hyperpersonal model. *Human Communication Research*, *37*, 58–77.

Johnson, P. O., & Fey, L. C. (1950). The Johnson–Neyman technique, its theory and application. *Psychometrika*, *15*, 349–367.

Johnson, P. O., & Neyman, J. (1936). Tests of certain linear hypotheses and their application to some educational problems. *Statistical Research Memoirs*, *1*, 57–93.

Jordan, A. B. (2010). Children's television viewing and childhood obesity. *Pediatric Annals*, *39*, 569–573.

Judd, C. M., & Kenny, D. A. (1981). Process analysis: Estimating mediation in treatment evaluations. *Evaluation Review*, *5*, 602–619.

Judge, T. A., Piccolo, R. F., Podsakoff, N. P., Shaw, J. C., & Rich, B. L. (2010). The relationship between play and job satisfaction: A meta-analysis of the literature. *Journal of Vocational Behavior*, *77*, 157–167.

Kalyanaraman, S., & Sundar, S. S. (2006). The psychological appeal of personalized content in web portals: Does customization affect attitudes and behavior? *Journal of Communication*, *31*, 254–270.

Kam, C. D., & Franzese, R. J. (2007). *Modeling and interpreting interactive hypotheses in regression analysis*. Ann Arbor, MI: University of Michigan.

Kapikiran, N. A. (2012). Positive and negative affectivity as mediator and moderator of the relationship between optimism and life satisfaction in Turkish university students. *Social Indicators Research, 106,* 333–345.

Karpmann, M. B. (1986). Comparing two non-parallel regression lines with the parametric alternative to the analysis of covariance using SPSS-X or SAS—the Johnson–Neyman technique. *Educational and Psychological Measurement, 46,* 639–644.

Kelley, K. (2007). Methods for the behavioral, educational, and social sciences: An R package. *Behavior Research Methods, 39,* 979–984.

Kennedy, P. E. (1995). Randomization tests in econometrics. *Journal of Business and Economic Statistics, 13,* 85–94.

Kenny, D. A., & Judd, C. M. (1986). Consequences of violating the independence assumption in analysis of variance. *Psychological Bulletin, 99,* 422–431.

Kenny, D. A., Mannetti, L., Pierro, A., Livi, S., & Kashy, D. A. (2002). The statistical analysis of data from small groups. *Journal of Personality and Social Psychology, 83,* 126–137.

Keppel, G., & Wickens, T. D. (2004). *Design and analysis: A researcher's handbook* (4th ed.). Upper Saddle River, NJ: Prentice Hall.

Kim, J. O., & Ferree, G. D. (1976). Standardization in causal analysis. *Sociological Methods and Research, 10,* 187–210.

Kim, J. O., & Mueller, C. W. (1981). Standardized and unstandardized coefficients in causal analysis: An expository note. *Sociological Methods and Research, 4,* 428–438.

Kim, M., & Park, I. J. K. (2011). Testing the moderating effect of parent–adolescent communication on the acculturation gap-distress relation in Korean-American families. *Journal of Youth and Adolescence, 40,* 1661–1673.

Kim, S., & Kochanska, G. (2012). Child temperament moderates effects of parent–child mutuality on self-regulation: A relationship-based path for emotionally negative infants. *Child Development, 83,* 1275–1289.

Kim, S., & Labroo, A. A. (2011). From inherent value to incentive value: When and why pointless effort enhances consumer preference. *Journal of Consumer Research, 38,* 712–742.

Kimki, S., Eshel, Y., Zysberg, L., & Hantman, S. (2009). Getting a life: Gender differences in postwar recovery. *Sex Roles, 61,* 554–565.

Kley, H., Tuschen-Caffier, B., & Heinrichs, N. (2012). Safety behaviors, self-focused attention and negative thinking in children with social anxiety disorder, socially anxious, and nonanxious children. *Journal of Behavior Theory and Experimental Psychiatry, 43,* 548–555.

Knobloch-Westerwick, S., & Hoplamazian, G. J. (2012). Gendering the self: Selective magazine reading and reinforcement of gender conformity. *Communication Research, 39,* 358–384.

Kochanska, G., Kim, S., Barry, R. A., & Philibert, R. A. (2011). Children's genotypes interact with maternal responsive care in predicting children's competence: Diathesis–stress or differential susceptibility? *Development and Psychopathology, 23,* 605–616.

Kraemer, H. C., Kiernan, M., Essex, M., & Kupfer, D. J. (2008). How and why criteria defining moderators and mediators differ between the Baron and Kenny & MacArthur approaches. *Health Psychology, 27,* S101–S108.

Kraemer, H. C., Wilson, G. T., Fairburn, C. G., & Agras, W. S. (2002). Mediators and moderators of treatment effects in randomized clinical trials. *Archives of General Psychiatry, 59*, 877–883.

Krause, M. R., Serlin, R. C., Ward, S. E., & Rony, Y. Z. (2010). Testing mediation in nursing research: Beyond Baron and Kenny. *Nursing Research, 59*, 288–294.

Krieger, J. L., & Sarge, M. A. (2013). A serial mediation model of message framing on intentions to receive the human papillomavirus (HPV) vaccine: Revising the role of threat and efficacy perceptions. *Health Communication, 28*, 5–19.

Kromrey, J. D., & Foster-Johnson, L. (1998). Mean centering in moderated multiple regression: Much ado about nothing. *Educational and Psychological Measurement, 58*, 42–68.

Lachman, M. E., & Agrigoroaei, S. (2012). Low perceived control as a risk factor for episodic memory: The mediational role of anxiety and task interference. *Memory and Cognition, 40*, 287–296.

Landreville, K. D., Holbert, R. L., & LaMarre, H. L. (2010). The influence of late-night TV comedy viewing on political talk: A moderated-mediation model. *International Journal of Press-Politics, 15*, 482–498.

Laran, J., Dalton, A. N., & Andrade, E. B. (2011). The curious case of behavioral backlash: Why brands produce priming effects and slogans produce reverse priming effects. *Journal of Consumer Research, 37*, 999–1014.

Lau, R., & Cheung, G. W. (2012). Estimating and comparing specific mediation effects in complex latent variable models. *Organizational Research Methods, 15*, 3–16.

Lau, R. R., Silegman, L., Heldman, C., & Babbit, P. (1999). The effects of negative political advertisements: A meta-analytic assessment. *The American Political Science Review, 93*, 851–875.

LeBreton, J. M., Wu, J., & Bing, M. N. (2009). The truth(s) on testing for mediation in the social and organizational sciences. In C. E. Lance & R. J. Vanderberg (Eds.), *Statistical and methodological myths and urban legends* (pp. 107–141). New York: Routledge.

Lecheler, S., de Vreese, C., & Slouthuus, R. (2011). Issue importance as a moderator of framing effects. *Communication Research, 79*, 400–425.

Lehmann, A., Burkert, S., Daig, I., Glaesmer, H., & Brähler, E. (2011). Subjective underchallenge at work and its impact on mental health. *International Archives of Occupational and Environmental Health, 84*, 655–664.

Leonard, S. A., & Rasmussen, K. M. (2011). Larger infant size at birth reduces the negative associations between maternal prepregnancy body mass and breastfeeding duration. *Journal of Nutrition, 141*, 645–653.

Leone, L., & Chirumbolo, A. (2008). Conservatism as motivated avoidance of affect: Need for affect scales predict conservativism measures. *Journal of Research in Personality, 42*, 755–762.

Levine, M. P., & Murnen, S. K. (2009). "Everybody knows that mass media are/are not [pick one] a cause of eating disorders": A criticial review of evidence for a causal link between media, negative body image, and disordered eating in females. *Journal of Social and Clinical Psychology, 28*, 9–42.

Li, N. P., Patel, L., Balliet, D., Tov, W., & Scollon, C. N. (2011). The incompatibility of materialism and the desire for children: Psychological insights into the fertility discrepancy among modern countries. *Social Indicators Research, 101,* 391–404.

Liu, W., & Gal, D. (2011). Bringing us together or driving us apart: The effect of soliciting consumer input on consumers' propensity to transact with an organization. *Journal of Consumer Research, 38,* 242–259.

Lockhart, G., MacKinnon, D. P., & Ohlrich, V. (2011). Mediation analysis in psychosomatic medicine research. *Psychosomatic Medicine, 73,* 29–43.

Long, J. S. (1997). *Regression models for categorical and limited dependent variables.* Thousand Oaks, CA: Sage Publications.

Long, J. S., & Ervin, L. H. (2000). Using heteroscedasticity-consistent standard errors in the linear regression model. *The American Statistician, 54,* 217–224.

Lopez-Guimera, G., Levine, M. P., Sanchez-Cerracedo, D., & Fauquet, J. (2010). Influence of mass media on body image and eating disordered attitudes and behaviors in females: A review of effects and processes. *Media Psychology, 13,* 387–416.

Ludbrook, J., & Dudley, H. (1998). Why permutation tests are superior to *t* and *F* tests in biomedical research. *The American Statistician, 52,* 127–132.

Luke, D. A. (2004). *Multilevel modeling.* Thousand Oaks, CA: Sage Publications.

Luksyte, A., & Avery, D. R. (2010). The effects of citizenship dissimilarity and national pride on attitudes toward immigrants: Investigating mediators and moderators of intergroup contact. *International Journal of Intercultural Relations, 34,* 629–641.

Lunneborg, C. E. (2000). *Data analysis by resampling.* Pacific Grove, CA: Duxbury.

Luszczynska, A., Cao, D. S., Mallach, N., Petron, K., Mazurkiewicz, M., & Schwarzer, R. (2010). Intentions, planning, and self-efficacy predict physical activity in Chinese and Polish adolescents: Two moderated mediation analyses. *International Journal of Clinical and Health Psychology, 10,* 265–278.

MacCallum, R. C. (2003). Working with imperfect models. *Multivariate Behavioral Research, 38,* 113–139.

MacCallum, R. C., Zhang, S., Preacher, K. J., & Rucker, D. D. (2002). On the practice of dichotomization of quantitative variables. *Psychological Methods, 7,* 19–40.

MacKinnon, D. P. (2000). Contrasts in multiple mediator models. In J. Rose, L. Chassin, C. C. Presson, & S. J. Sherman (Eds.), *Multivariate applications in substance use and research: New methods for new questions* (pp. 141–160). Mahwah, NJ: Lawrence Erlbaum Associates.

MacKinnon, D. P. (2008). *An introduction to statistical mediation analysis.* New York: Routledge.

MacKinnon, D. P., Fairchild, A. J., & Fritz, M. S. (2007). Mediation analysis. *Annual Review of Psychology, 58,* 593–614.

MacKinnon, D. P., Fritz, M. S., Williams, J., & Lockwood, C. M. (2007). Distribution of the product confidence limits for the indirect effect: Program PRODCLIN. *Behavior Research Methods, 39,* 384–389.

MacKinnon, D. P., Krull, J. L., & Lockwood, C. M. (2000). Equivalence of the mediation, confounding, and suppression effect. *Prevention Science, 1,* 173–181.

MacKinnon, D. P., Lockwood, C. M., Hoffman, J. M., & West, S. G. (2002). A comparison of methods to test the significance of the mediated effect. *Psychological Methods, 7,* 83–104.

MacKinnon, D. P., Lockwood, C. M., & Williams, J. (2004). Confidence limits for the indirect effect: Distribution of the product and resampling methods. *Multivariate Behavioral Research, 39,* 99–128.

MacKinnon, D. P., Warsi, G., & Dwyer, J. H. (1995). A simulation study of mediated effect measures. *Multivariate Behavioral Research, 30,* 41–62.

MacNeil, G., Kosberg, J. I., Durkin, D. W., Dooley, W. K., DeCoster, J., & Williamson, G. M. (2010). Caregiver mental health and potentially caregiving behavior: The central role of caregiver anger. *The Gerontologist, 50,* 76–86.

Magee, C. A., Caputi, P., & Iverson, D. C. (2011). Short sleep mediates the association between long work hours and increased Body Mass Index. *Journal of Behavioral Medicine, 34,* 83–91.

Magill, M. (2011). Moderators and mediators in social work research: Toward a more ecologically valid evidence base for practice. *Journal of Social Work, 11,* 387–401.

Maguen, S., Luxton, D. D., Skopp, N. A., Gahm, G. A., Reger, M. A., Metzler, T. J., & Marmar, C. R. (2011). Killing in combat, mental health symptoms, and suicidal ideation in Iraq war veterans. *Journal of Anxiety Disorders, 25,* 563–567.

Maric, M., Wiers, R. W., & Prins, P. J. M. (2012). Ten ways to improve the use of statistical mediation analysis in the practice of child and adolescent treatment research. *Clinical Child and Family Psychological Review, 15,* 177–191.

Martinez, A. G., Piff, P. K., Mendoza-Denton, R., & Hinshaw, S. P. (2011). The power of a label: Mental illness diagnoses, ascribed humanity, and social rejection. *Journal of Social and Clinical Psychology, 30,* 1–23.

Maxwell, S. E., & Delaney, H. D. (1993). Bivariate median splits and spurious statistical significance. *Psychological Bulletin, 113,* 181–190.

May, R. B., & Hunter, M. A. (1993). Some advantages of permutation tests. *Canadian Psychology, 34,* 401–407.

May, R. B., Masson, M. E. J., & Hunter, M. A. (1989). Randomization tests: Viable alternatives to normal curve tests. *Behavior Research Methods, Instruments, and Computers, 21,* 482–483.

Meade, C. S., Conn, N. A., Skalski, L. M., & Safren, S. A. (2011). Neurocognitive impairment and medication adherence in HIV patients with and without cocaine dependence. *Journal of Behavioral Medicine, 34,* 128–138.

Mesango, C., Harvey, J. T., & Janelle, C. M. (2012). Choking under pressure: The role of fear of negative evaluation. *Psychology of Sport and Exercise, 13,* 60–68.

Micceri, T. (1989). The unicorn, the normal curve, and other improbable creatures. *Psychological Bulletin, 105,* 156–166.

Mijanovich, T., & Weitzman, B. C. (2010). Disaster in context: The effects of 9/11 on youth distant from the attacks. *Community Mental Health Journal, 46,* 601–611.

Miller, T. L., del Carmen, T. M., Reutzel, C. R., & Certo, S. T. (2007). Mediation in strategic management research: Conceptual beginning, current application, and future recommendation. In D. Ketchen & D. D. Bergh (Eds.), *Research methods in strategy and management* (pp. 295–318). London: Elsevier.

Molloy, G. J., Dixon, D., Hamer, M., & Sniehotta, F. F. (2010). Social support and regular physical activity: Does planning mediate this link? *British Journal of Health Psychology, 15,* 859–870.

Moneta, G. B. (2011). Metacognition, emotion, and alcohol dependence in college students: A moderated mediation model. *Addictive Behaviors, 36,* 781–784.

Mook, D. G. (1987). In defense of external invalidity. *American Psychologist, 38,* 379–387.

Mooney, C. Z., & Duval, R. D. (1993). *Bootstrapping: A nonparametric approach to statistical inference.* Newbury Park, CA: Sage Publications.

Morano, M., Colella, D., Robazza, C., Bortoli, L., & Capranica, L. (2011). Physical self-perception and motor performance in normal-weight, overweight, and obese children. *Scandanavian Journal of Medicine and Science in Sports, 21,* 465–473.

Morgan, S. L., & Winship, C. (2007). *Counterfactuals and causal inference: Methods and principles for social research.* Cambridge, UK: Cambridge University Press.

Morgan-Lopez, A., & MacKinnon, D. P. (2006). Demonstration and evaluation of a method for assessing mediated moderation. *Behavior Research Methods, 38,* 77–89.

Morrison, K. R. (2011). A license to speak up: Outgroup minorities and opinion expression. *Journal of Experimental Social Psychology, 47,* 756–766.

Muller, D., Judd, C. M., & Yzerbyt, V. Y. (2005). When mediation is moderated and moderation is mediated. *Journal of Personality and Social Psychology, 89,* 852–863.

Myers, T. A., & Hayes, A. F. (2010). Reframing the casualties hypothesis: (Mis)perception of troop casualties and public opinion about military intervention. *International Journal of Public Opinion Research, 22,* 256–275.

Napier, J. L., & Jost, J. T. (2008). Why are conservatives happier than liberals? *Psychological Science, 19,* 565–572.

Naumann, J., Richter, T., Christmann, U., & Groeben, N. (2008). Working memory capacity and reading skill moderate the effectiveness of strategy training in learning from hypertext. *Learning and Individual Differences, 18,* 197–213.

Nevicka, B., Ten Velden, F. S., De Hoogh, A. H. B., & Van Vianen, A. E. M. (2011). Reality at odds with perceptions: Narcissistic leaders and group performance. *Psychological Science, 22,* 1259–1264.

Newsom, J. T., Prigerson, H. G., Schultz, R., & Reynolds, C. F. (2003). Investigating moderator hypotheses in aging research: Statistical, methodological, and conceptual difficulties with comparing separate regressions. *International Journal of Aging and Human Development, 57,* 119–150.

Ning, H. K. (2012). Influence of student learning experience on academic performance: The mediator and moderator effects of self-regulation and motivation. *British Educational Research Journal, 38,* 219–237.

Nir, L., & Druckman, J. N. (2008). Campaign mixed-message flows and timing of vote decision. *International Journal of Public Opinion Research, 20,* 326–346.

O'Connor, B. P. (2004). SPSS and SAS programs for addressing interdependence and basic levels-of-analysis issues in psychological data. *Behavior Research*

Methods, Instruments, and Computers, 36, 17–28.

Oei, N. Y. L., Tollenaar, M. S., Elzinga, B. M., & Spinhoven, P. (2010). Propranolol reduces emotional distraction in working memory: A partial mediating role of propranolol-induced cortisol increases? *Neurobiology of Learning and Memory, 93,* 388–395.

Oishi, S., Seol, K. O., Koo, M., & Miao, F. F. (2011). Was he happy?: Cultural difference in conceptions of Jesus. *Journal of Research in Personality, 45,* 94–91.

Oja, H. (1987). On permutation tests in multiple regression and analysis of variance problems. *Australian Journal of Statistics, 29,* 91–100.

O'Keefe, D. J. (2011). The asymmetry of predictive and descriptive capabilities in quantitative communication research: Implications for hypothesis development and testing. *Communication Methods and Measures, 5,* 113–125.

O'Keefe, D. J., & Jensen, J. D. (1997). The relative persuasiveness of gain-framed and loss-framed messages for encouraging disease prevention behaviors: A meta-analysis. *Journal of Health Communication, 12,* 623–644.

Oldmeadow, J. A., & Fiske, S. T. (2010). Social status and the pursuit of positive social identity: Systematic domains of intergroup differentiation and discrimination for high- and low- status groups. *Group Processes and Intergroup Relations, 13,* 425–444.

Orom, H., Penner, L. A., West, B. T., Downs, T. M., Rayfords, W., & Underwood, W. (2009). Personality predicts prostate cancer treatment decision making. *Psycho-Oncology, 18,* 290–299.

Ostrander, R., & Herman, K. C. (2006). Potential cognitive, parenting, and developmental mediators of the relationship between ADHD and depression. *Journal of Consulting and Clinical Psychology, 74,* 89–98.

Pakpour, A. H., Zeidi, I. M., Chatzisarantis, N., Molsted, S., Harrison, A. P., & Plotnikoff, R. C. (2011). Effects of action planning and coping planning within the theory of planned behaviour: A physical activity study of patients undergoing haemodialysis. *Psychology of Sport and Exercise, 12,* 609–614.

Palomares, N. A. (2008). Explaining gender-based language use: Effects of gender identity salence on references to emotion and tentative language in intra- and intergroup contexts. *Human Communication Research, 34,* 263–286.

Parade, S. H., Leerkes, E. M., & Blankson, A. N. (2010). Attachment to parents, social anxiety, and close relationships of female students over the transition to college. *Journal of Youth and Adolescence, 39,* 127–137.

Parker, R., Hossein, N., & Hayes, A. F. (2011). Distributive justice, promotion instrumentality, and turnover intentions in public accounting firms. *Behavioral Research in Accounting, 23,* 169–186.

Patrick, V. M., & Hagtvedt, H. (2011). Aesthetic incongruity resolution. *Journal of Marketing Research, 48,* 393–402.

Pearl, J. (2009). *Causality: Models, reasoning, and inference* (2nd ed.). Cambridge, UK: Cambridge University Press.

Peltonen, K., Quota, S., Sarraj, E. E., & Punamäki, R. (2010). Military trauma and social development: The moderating and mediating role of peer and sibling relations in mental health. *International Journal of Behavioral Development, 34,* 554–563.

Peréz, L. G., Abrams, M. P., López-Martínez, A. E., & Asmundson, G. J. G. (2012). Trauma exposure and health: The role of depressive and hyperarousal symptoms. *Journal of Traumatic Stress, 25,* 641–648.

Pérez-Edgar, K., Bar-Haim, Y., McDermott, J. M., Chronis-Tuscano, A., Pine, D. S., & Fox, N. A. (2010). Attention biases to threat and behavioral inhibition in early childhood shape adolescent social withdrawal. *Emotion, 10,* 349–357.

Petty, R. E., & Cacioppo, J. T. (1986). The elaboration likelihood model of persuasion. In L. Berkowitz (Ed.), *Advances in experimental social psychology* (Vol. 19, pp. 123–205). San Diego, CA: Academic Press.

Pollack, J. M., VanEpps, E. M., & Hayes, A. F. (2012). The moderating effect of social ties on entrepreneurs' depressed affective and withdrawal intentions in response to economic stress. *Journal of Organizational Behavior, 33,* 789–810.

Popan, J. R., Kenworthy, J. B., Frame, M. C., Lyons, P. A., & Snuggs, S. J. (2010). Political groups in contact: The role of attributions for outgroup attitudes in reducing antipathy. *European Journal of Social Psychology, 40,* 86–104.

Potthoff, R. F. (1964). On the Johnson–Neyman technique and some extensions thereof. *Psychometrika, 29,* 241–256.

Preacher, K. J., Curran, P. J., & Bauer, D. J. (2006). Computational tools for probing interactions in multiple linear regression, multilevel modeling, and latent curve analysis. *Journal of Educational and Behavioral Statistics, 31,* 437–448.

Preacher, K. J., & Hayes, A. F. (2004). SPSS and SAS procedures for estimating indirect effects in simple mediation models. *Behavior Research Methods, Instruments, and Computers, 36,* 717–731.

Preacher, K. J., & Hayes, A. F. (2008a). Asymptotic and resampling strategies for assessing and comparing indirect effects in multiple mediator models. *Behavior Research Methods, 40,* 879–891.

Preacher, K. J., & Hayes, A. F. (2008b). Contemporary approaches to assessing mediation in communication research. In A. F. Hayes, M. D. Slater, & L. B. Snyder (Eds.), *The Sage sourcebook of advanced data analysis methods for communication research* (pp. 13–54). Thousand Oaks, CA: Sage Publications.

Preacher, K. J., & Kelley, K. (2011). Effect size measures for mediation models: Quantitative strategies for communicating indirect effects. *Psychological Methods, 16,* 93–115.

Preacher, K. J., Rucker, D. D., & Hayes, A. F. (2007). Assessing moderated mediation hypotheses: Theory, methods, and prescriptions. *Multivariate Behavioral Research, 42,* 185–227.

Preacher, K. J., Rucker, D. D., MacCallum, R. C., & Nicewander, W. A. (2005). Use of the extreme groups approach: A critical reexamination and new recommendations. *Psychological Methods, 10,* 178–192.

Preacher, K. J., & Selig, J. P. (2012). Advantages of Monte Carlo confidence intervals for indirect effects. *Communication Methods and Measures, 6,* 77–98.

Prinzie, P., Dekovic, M., van den Akker, A. L., de Haan, A. D., Stoltz, S. E. M. J., & Hendriks, A. A. J. (2012). Fathers' personality and its interaction with children's personality as predictors of perceived parenting six years later. *Personality and Individual Differences, 52,* 183–189.

Rabinovich, A., & Morton, T. A. (2012). Ghosts of the past and dreams of the future: The impact of temporal focus on responses to contextual ingroup devaluation. *Personality and Social Psychology Bulletin, 38,* 397–410.

Raudenbush, S. W., & Bryk, A. S. (2002). *Hierarchical linear models: Applications and data analysis methods* (2nd ed.). Thousand Oaks, CA: Sage Publications.

Rees, T., & Freeman, P. (2009). Social support moderates the relationship between stressors and task performance through self-efficacy. *Journal of Social and Clinical Psychology, 28,* 244–263.

Richman, J. A., Shannon, C. A., Rospenda, K. M., Flaherty, J. A., & Fendrich, M. (2009). The relationship between terrorism and distress and drinking: Two years after September 11, 2001. *Substance Use and Abuse, 44,* 1665–1680.

Richter, T., & Schmid, S. (2010). Epistemological beliefs and epistemic strategies in self-regulated learning. *Metacognition and Learning, 5,* 47–65.

Righetti, F., & Finkenauer, C. (2011). If you are able to control yourself, I will trust you: The role of perceived self-control in interpersonal trust. *Journal of Personality and Social Psychology, 100,* 874–886.

Ro, H. (2012). Moderator and mediator effects in hospitality research. *International Journal of Hospitality Management, 31,* 952–961.

Rodgers, J. L. (1999). The bootstrap, the jackknife, and the randomization test: A sampling taxonomy. *Multivariate Behavioral Research, 34,* 441–456.

Rogosa, D. (1980). Comparing nonparallel regression lines. *Psychological Bulletin, 88,* 307–321.

Royston, P., Altman, D. G., & Sauerbrei, W. (2006). Dichotomizing continuous predictors in multiple regression: A bad idea. *Statistics in Medicine, 25,* 127–141.

Ruby, M. B., Perrino, E. W., Gillis, R., & Viel, S. (2011). The invisible benefits of exercise. *Health Psychology, 30,* 67–74.

Rucker, D. D., Preacher, K. J., Tormala, Z. L., & Petty, R. E. (2011). Mediation analysis in social psychology: Current practice and new recommendations. *Personality and Social Psychology Compass, 5/6,* 359–371.

Rueggeberg, R., Wrosch, C., Miller, G. E., & McDade, T. W. (2012). Associations between health-related self-protection, dirunal cortisol, and C-reactive protein in lonely older adults. *Psychosomatic Medicine, 74,* 937–944.

Schumann, K., & Ross, M. (2011). Why women apologize more than men: Gender differences in thresholds for perceiving offensive behavior. *Psychological Science, 21,* 1649–1655.

Sedney, M. A. (1981). Comments on median split procedures for scoring androgyny measures. *Sex Roles, 7,* 217–222.

Selig, J. P., & Preacher, K. J. (2009). Mediation models for longitudinal data in developmental research. *Research in Human Development, 6,* 144–164.

Shanahan, J. E., & Morgan, M. (1999). *Television and its viewers: Cultivation theory and research.* London, UK: Cambridge University Press.

Sheih, G. (2011). Clarifying the role of mean centering in multicollinearity of interaction effects. *British Journal of Mathematical and Statistical Psychology, 64,* 462–477.

Shenk, C. E., Noll, J. G., & Cassarly, J. A. (2010). A multiple meditational test of the relationship between childhood maltreatment and non-suicidal self-injury. *Journal of Youth and Adolescence, 39,* 335–342.

Shrout, P. E., & Bolger, N. (2002). Mediation in experimental and nonexperimental studies: New procedures and recommendations. *Psychological Methods, 7,* 422–445.

Shrum, L. J., Lee, J., Burroughs, J. E., & Rindfleisch, A. (2011). An online process model of second-order cultivation effects: How television cultivates materialism and its consequences. *Human Communication Research, 37,* 34–57.

Sibley, C. G., & Perry, R. (2010). An opposing process model of benevolent sexism. *Sex Roles, 62,* 438–452.

Silton, R. L., Heller, W., Engels, A. S., Towers, D. N., Spielberg, J. M., Edgar, C. J., et al. (2011). Depression and anxious apprehension distinguish frontocingulate cortical activity during top-down attentional control. *Journal of Abnormal Psychology, 120,* 272–285.

Simons, R. L., Lei, M. K., Stewart, E. A., Beach, S. R. H., Brody, G. H., Philibert, R. A., et al. (2012). Social adversity, genetic variation, street code, and aggression: A genetically informed model of violent behavior. *Youth Violence and Juvenile Justice, 10,* 3–24.

Simpson, H. B., Maher, M. J., Wang, Y., Bao, Y., Foa, E. B., & Franklin, M. (2011). Patient adherence predicts outcome from cognitive behavioral therapy in obsessive–compulsive disorder. *Journal of Consulting and Clinical Psychology, 79,* 247–252.

Sirgy, M. J., Yu, G. B., Lee, D. J., Wei, S., & Huang, M. W. (2012). Does marketing activity contribute to a society's well-being?: The role of economic efficiency. *Journal of Business Ethics, 107,* 91–102.

Slater, M. D., Hayes, A. F., & Snyder, L. B. (2008). Overview. In A. F. Hayes, M. D. Slater, & L. B. Snyder (Eds.), *The Sage sourcebook of advanced data analysis methods for communication research* (pp. 1–12). Thousand Oaks, CA: Sage Publications.

Sobel, M. E. (1982). Asymptotic confidence intervals for indirect effects in structural equation models. In S. Leinhart (Ed.), *Sociological methodology* (pp. 290–312). San Francisco, CA: Jossey-Bass.

Somer, E., Ginzberg, K., & Kramer, L. (2012). The role of impulsivity in the association between childhood trauma and dissociative psychopathology: Mediation versus moderation. *Psychiatry Research, 196,* 133–137.

Spencer, S. J., Zanna, M. P., & Fong, G. T. (2005). Establishing a causal chain: Why experiments are often more effective than mediational analyses in examining psychological processes. *Journal of Personality and Social Psychology, 89,* 845–851.

Spiller, S. A., Fitzsimons, G. J., Lynch, J. G., & McClelland, G. H. (2013). Spotlights, floodlights, and the magic number zero: Simple effects tests in moderated regression. *Journal of Marketing Research, 50,* 277–288.

Stiglbauer, B., Selenko, E., Batinic, B., & Jodlbauer, S. (2012). On the link between job insecurity and turnover intentions: Moderated mediation by work involvement and well-being. *Journal of Occupational Health Psychology, 17,* 354–364.

Still, A. W., & White, A. P. (1981). The approximate randomization test as an alternative to the F test in analysis of variance. *British Journal of Mathematical and Statistical Psychology, 34,* 243–252.

Stone, C. A., & Sobel, M. E. (1990). The robustness of total indirect effects in covariance structure models estimated with maximum likelihood. *Psychometrika, 55,* 337–352.

Stone-Romero, E. F., & Raposa, P. J. (2010). Research design options for testing mediation models and their implications for facets of validity. *Journal of Managerial Psychology, 25,* 697–712.

Streiner, D. L. (2002). Breaking up is hard to do: The heartbreak of dichotomizing continuous data. *Canadian Journal of Psychiatry, 47,* 262–266.

Takeuchi, R., Yun, S., & Wong, K. F. E. (2011). Social influence of a coworker: A test of the effect of employee and coworker exchange ideologies on employees' exchange qualities. *Organizational Behavior and Human Decision Processes, 115,* 226–237.

Tal-Or, N., Cohen, J., Tsfati, Y., & Gunther, A. C. (2010). Testing causal direction in the influence of presumed media influence. *Communication Research, 37,* 801–824.

Taylor, A. B., MacKinnon, D. P., & Tein, J.-Y. (2008). Tests of the three-path mediated effect. *Organizational Research Methods, 11,* 241–269.

Taylor, C. T., Bomyea, J., & Amir, N. (2011). Malleability of attentional bias for positive emotional information and anxiety vulnerability. *Emotion, 11,* 127–138.

Teixeira, P. J., Silva, M. N., Coutinho, S. R., Palmeira, A. L., Mata, J., Vieira, P. N., et al. (2010). Mediators of weight loss and weight loss maintenance in middle-aged women. *Obesity, 18,* 725–735.

ter Braak, C. J. F. (1992). Permutation versus bootstrap significance tests in multiple regression and ANOVA. In K. J. Jöckel, G. Rothe, & W. Sendler (Eds.), *Bootstrapping and related techniques* (pp. 79–85). Berlin, Germany: Springer-Verlag.

Terwel, B. W., Harinck, F., Ellemers, N., & Daamen, D. D. L. (2010). Voice in political decision making: The effect of group voice on perceived trustworthiness of decision makers and subsequent acceptance of decisions. *Journal of Experimental Psychology: Applied, 16,* 173–186.

Tichenor, P. A., Donohue, G. A., & Olien, C. N. (1970). Mass media flow and differential growth in knowledge. *Public Opinion Quarterly, 34,* 159–170.

Tofighi, D., & MacKinnon, D. P. (2011). Rmediation: An R package for mediation analysis confidence intervals. *Behavior Research Methods, 43,* 692–700.

Tsai, C. I., & Thomas, M. (2011). When does feeling of fluency matter?: How abstract and concrete thinking influences fluency effects. *Psychological Science, 22,* 348–354.

Usborne, E., & Taylor, D. M. (2010). The role of cultural identity clarity for self-concept clarity, self-esteem, and subjective well-being. *Personality and Social Psychology Bulletin, 36,* 883–897.

van Dijke, M., & De Cremer, D. (2010). Procedural fairness and endorsement of prototypical leaders: Leader benevolence or follower control? *Journal of Experimental Social Psychology, 46,* 85–96.

Van Jaarsveld, D. D., Walker, D. D., & Skarlicki, D. P. (2010). The role of job demands and emotional exhaustion in the relationship between customer and employee incivility. *Journal of Management, 36,* 1486–1504.

van Rompay, T. J. L., de Fries, P. W., & van Venrooij, X. G. (2010). More than words: On the importance of picture–text congruence. *Journal of Interactive Marketing, 24,* 22–30.

Vargha, A., Rudas, T., & Maxwell, S. E. (2011). Dichotomization, partial correlation, and conditional independence. *Journal of Educational and Behavioral Statistics, 58,* 264–282.

Versey, H. S., & Kaplan, G. A. (2012). Mediation and moderation of the association between cynical hostility and systolic blood pressure in low-income women. *Health Education and Behavior, 39,* 219–238.

Vigil, J. M. (2010). Political leanings vary with facial expression processing and psychosocial functioning. *Group Processes and Intergroup Relations, 13,* 547–558.

Von Hippel, C., Issa, M., Ma, R., & Stokes, A. (2011). Stereotype threat: Antecedents and consequences for working women. *European Journal of Social Psychology, 41,* 151–161.

Wagner, J. A., Tennen, H., & Osborn, C. Y. (2010). Lifetime depression and diabetes self-management in women with type 2 diabetes: A case control study. *Diabetic Medicine, 27,* 713–717.

Wang, K., Stroebe, K., & Dovidio, J. F. (2012). Stigma consciousness and prejudice ambiguity: Can it be adaptive to perceive the world as biased? *Personality and Individual Differences, 53,* 241–245.

Warner, L. M., Schwarzer, R., Schüz, B., Wurm, S., & Tesch-Romer, C. (2012). Health-specific optimism mediates between objective and perceived physical functioning in older adults. *Journal of Behavioral Medicine, 35,* 400–406.

Webster, R. J., & Saucier, D. A. (2011). The effects of death reminders on sex differences in prejudice towards gay men and women. *Journal of Homosexuality, 58,* 402–426.

West, S. G., Aiken, L. S., & Krull, J. L. (1996). Experimental personality designs: Analyzing categorical by continuous variable interactions. *Journal of Personality, 61,* 1–48.

Whisman, M. A., & McClelland, G. H. (2005). Designing, testing, and interpreting interactions and moderator effects in family research. *Journal of Family Psychology, 19,* 111–120.

White, H. (1980). A heteroskedasticity-consistent covariance matrix estimator and a direct test for heteroskedasticity. *Econometrica, 48,* 817–838.

Wicklund, R. A. (1974). *Freedom and reactance.* Potomac, MD: Lawrence Erlbaum Associates.

Wiedemann, A. U., Lippke, S., Reuter, T., Ziegelmann, J. P., & Ralf, S. (2011). How planning facilitates behaviour change: Additive and interactive effects of a randomized controlled trial. *European Journal of Social Psychology, 41,* 42–51.

Wiedemann, A. U., Schüz, B., Sniehotta, F., Scholz, U., & Schwarzer, R. (2009). Disentangling the relation between intentions, planning, and behaviour: A moderated mediation analysis. *Psychology and Health, 24,* 67–79.

Williams, J., & MacKinnon, D. P. (2008). Resampling and distribution of the product methods for testing indirect effect in complex models. *Structural Equation Modeling, 15,* 23–51.

Wohl, M. J. A., & Branscombe, N. R. (2009). Group threat, collective angst, and ingroup forgiveness for the war in Iraq. *Political Psychology, 30*, 193–217.

Woo, J. S. T., Brotto, L. A., & Gorzalka, B. B. (2011). The role of sex guilt in the relationship between culture and women's sexual desire. *Archives of Sexual Behavior, 40*, 385–394.

Wood, M. (2005). Bootstrapped confidence intervals as an approach to statistical inference. *Organizational Research Methods, 8*, 454–470.

Worchel, S., & Arnold, S. E. (1973). The effects of censorship and attractiveness of the censor on attitude change. *Journal of Experimental Social Psychology, 9*, 365–377.

Wout, D. A., Murphy, M. C., & Steele, C. M. (2010). When your friends matter: The effect of White students' racial friendship networks on meta-perceptions and perceived identity contingencies. *Journal of Experimental Social Psychology, 46*, 1035–1041.

Xenos, M., & Becker, A. (2009). Moments of Zen: Effects of *The Daily Show* on information seeking and political learning. *Political Communication, 26*, 317–332.

Zadeh, Z. Y., Farnia, F., & Ungerleider, C. (2010). How home enrichment mediates the relationship between maternal education and children's achievements in reading and math. *Early Education and Development, 21*, 568–594.

Zeller, M. H., Reiter-Purtill, J., & Ramey, C. (2008). Negative peer perceptions of obese children in the classroom environment. *Obesity, 16*, 755–762.

Zhao, X., Lynch, J. G., & Chen, Q. (2010). Reconsidering Baron and Kenny: Myths and truths about mediation analysis. *Journal of Consumer Research, 37*, 197–206.

Zhou, Q., Hirst, G., & Shipton, H. (2012). Promoting creativity at work: The role of problem-solving demand. *Applied Psychology: An International Review, 61*, 56–80.

Author Index

Subject Index

About the Author

Andrew F. Hayes, PhD, is Professor of Quantitative Psychology and Professor of Communication at The Ohio State University. He is the author of *Statistical Methods for Communication Science* and coeditor of the *Sage Sourcebook on Advanced Data Analysis Methods for Communication Research*, and has published many journal articles and book chapters in the areas of research methods, data analysis, public opinion, political communication, social psychology, and numerous other topics. Dr. Hayes is one of the founding editors of *Communication Methods and Measures*, for which he serves as Editor-in-Chief through 2015. He teaches research design and data analysis at the undergraduate and graduate levels and frequently conducts workshops on moderation and mediation analysis throughout the world. His website is *www.afhayes.com*.